The Medieval *Gospel of Nicodemus*

Texts, Intertexts, and Contexts
in Western Europe

MEDIEVAL & RENAISSANCE

TEXTS & STUDIES

VOLUME 158

The Medieval *Gospel of Nicodemus*

Texts, Intertexts, and Contexts
in Western Europe

edited by

Zbigniew Izydorczyk

MEDIEVAL & RENAISSANCE TEXTS & STUDIES
Tempe, Arizona
1997

Library of Congress Cataloging-in-Publication Data

The Medieval Gospel of Nicodemus : texts, intertexts, and
contexts in Western Europe / edited by Zbigniew Izydorczyk.
    p. cm. — (Medieval & Renaissance Texts & Studies ; v. 158)
Includes bibliographical references and index.
ISBN 0–86698–198–5 (alk. paper)
    1. Gospel of Nicodemus — Versions. I. Izydorczyk, Zbigniew
S., 1956–   . II. Series
BS2860.N6M43 1997
229'.8—dc21   96–40460

                                                              CIP

∞
This book is made to last.
It is set in Palatino,
smythe-sewn and printed on acid-free paper
to library specifications.

Printed in the United States of America

Table of Contents

List of Abbreviations

Bibliographic abbreviations

AP	*Acta Pilati*, Acts of Pilate
BHL	Socii Bollandiani, *Bibliotheca hagiographica Latina antiquae et mediae aetatis* (Brussels, 1898–99)
CC SL	Corpus Christianorum, Series Latina
CC CM	Corpus Christianorum, Continuatio Medievalis
CSEL	Corpus Scriptorum Ecclesiasticorum Latinorum
Cura	*Cura sanitatis Tiberii*
DI	*Descensus Christi ad inferos*
EETS OS	Early English Text Society, Original Series
EETS ES	Early English Text Society, Extra Series
EETS SS	Early English Text Society, Special Series
EN	*Evangelium Nicodemi*
EP	*Epistola Pilati ad Claudium*
GCS	Die griechischen christlichen Schriftsteller der ersten drei Jahrhunderte
GN	*Gospel of Nicodemus*
IMEV	Carleton Brown and Rossell Hope Robbins, *The Index of Middle English Verse* (New York: Columbia University Press, 1943)
IPMEP	R. E. Lewis, N. F. Blake, and A. S. G. Edwards, *Index of Printed Middle English Prose* (New York: Garland, 1985)
LALMA	Angus McIntosh, M. L. Samuels, and Michael Benskin, *A Linguistic Atlas of Late Medieval English*, 4 vols. (Aberdeen: Aberdeen University Press, 1986)
Lyden	*Dat Lyden ende die Passie Ons Heren Jhesu Christi*
MGH	Monumenta Germaniae Historica
PG	Jacques Paul Migne, ed., *Patrologiae cursus completus . . . Series Graeca . . .* , 167 vols. (Paris: Jacques Paul Migne, 1857–76)
PL	Jacques Paul Migne, ed., *Patrologiae cursus completus . . . Series Latina . . .* , 221 vols. (Paris: Jacques Paul Migne, 1844–64)
PMLA	*Publications of the Modern Language Association of America*
Ruh, *Verfasserlexikon*	Kurt Ruh, ed., *Die deutsche Literatur des Mittelalters. Verfasserlexikon* (Berlin: W. de Gruyter, 1978–)
SN	*Somnium Neronis*

STC   A. W. Pollard and G. R. Redgrave, *A Short-Title Catalogue of Books Printed in England, Scotland, and Ireland and of English Books Printed Abroad 1475–1640*, 2d ed., revised and enlarged by W. A. Jackson, F. S. Ferguson, and K. F. Pantzer, 3 vols. (London: The Bibliographical Society, 1976–91)

Libraries

AM	Det Arnamagnæanske Institut (Arnamagnæan Institute), Copenhagen
Bibl. Apost. Vat.	Bibliotheca Apostolica Vaticana, Vatican City
Bibl. mun.	Bibliothèque municipale
BL	British Library, London
BN	Bibliothèque nationale, Paris
Bodl. Lib.	Bodleian Library, Oxford
BRU	Bibliotheek der Rijksuniversiteit, Leiden
BSB	Bayerische Staatsbibliothek, Munich
CCCC	Corpus Christi College, Cambridge
CUL	Cambridge University Library
HAB	Herzog-August-Bibliothek, Wolfenbüttel
ÍB	Hid Íslenzka bókmenntafélag (Icelandic Literary Society), Reykjavík
JS	Jón Sigurðsson Collection, Reykjavík
Lbs.	Landsbóksafn Íslands (National Library), Reykjavík
ÖNB	Österreichische Nationalbibliothek, Vienna
SBPK	Staatsbibliothek Preussischer Kulturbesitz, Berlin
Sinaï	Mount Sinaï, St. Catherine Monastery
SKB	Kungliga Biblioteket (Royal Library), Stockholm
SRA	Riksarkivet (Royal Archive), Stockholm
Upps.	Universitetsbiblioteket (University Library), Uppsala

Preface

At least twice in its fifteen hundred years of history the apocryphal *Gospel of Nicodemus* (*GN*) has been a victim of its own success. First, at the close of the Middle Ages, its popularity and prestige attracted the censure of church reformers striving to rid Christian religion of fancy and superstition. Then, half a millennium later, the daunting multiplicity of its medieval versions and manuscripts, extant in most European languages, discouraged comprehensive, cross-linguistic studies of its literary career in Western Europe. Although the past century has shed much light on individual vernacular strands of the apocryphon's tradition, it has produced no broadly based overview of the *GN* in all its textual, literary, and linguistic forms. The only generally available survey of its Western vernacular translations, adaptations, and influence remains Richard Wülcker's 1872 essay *Das Evangelium Nicodemi in der abendländischen Literatur*. Although it has served well generations of scholars, this essay is by now sadly out of date: its factual information is fragmentary, its bibliographical references are outdated and unreliable, and its treatment of various intertextual relationships rarely goes beyond the superficial. Based on second- and third-hand information, it often frustrates modern expectations of thoroughness and exactitude. That it continues to be used, however, demonstrates a clear need for a guide to the apocryphon's textual forms, intertextual relationships, and contextual variety in Western Europe.

In response to that need, the present volume brings together a series of essays documenting and exploring the presence of the *GN* in Western literary traditions of the Middle Ages. The essays cover a vast territory, both thematically and linguistically, for networks of the apocryphon's translations, adaptations, thematic borrowings, and allusions extended to most Romance, Germanic, and Celtic vernaculars. Accordingly, the medieval languages surveyed here include Latin, French, Catalan, Occitan, and Italian; English, High German, Dutch, Low German, and Norse; and Irish, Welsh, and Cornish.[1]

The polyglot nature and vast scope of this undertaking have

---

[1] The *GN* was also known in Spanish and Portuguese, but for want of contributors these two vernaculars are not covered in the present volume.

dictated its collaborative format. The essays collected here, all but two commissioned for this volume, have been written by scholars specializing in different linguistic and literary traditions. Some have been actively involved in the editing of medieval recensions of the apocryphon, others have pursued textual or critical issues arising from it, still others have been attracted to it through the study of works it inspired or influenced. This diversity of scholarly backgrounds and critical interests of the contributors accounts for the diversity of theoretical perspectives on and practical approaches to the apocryphon in the present volume. However, the substance and character of each essay are determined not solely by the author's critical ideology but also, and perhaps more fundamentally, by the extent of the *GN*'s presence in a particular linguistic tradition and the current state of scholarship on it.

The volume opens with an introduction which summarizes the *GN*, situates it in the context of Pilate apocrypha, and indicates the range and character of its Western vernacular traditions. The first essay, which I co-wrote with Jean-Daniel Dubois, focuses on the early Christian backgrounds of the apocryphon. In it, we survey the witnesses to its knowledge in Christian antiquity and list all its ancient and non-Western medieval textual traditions. In this context, we also suggest a possible milieu for the *GN*'s origin and report what is known about its early development; we do not, however, offer any definitive conclusions, given the inconclusive state of research on the subject.

My remarks on the Latin *GN*, usually referred to as the *Evangelium Nicodemi*, provide a backdrop for subsequent discussions of vernacular traditions, all directly or ultimately derived from it. In this essay, I describe, in a necessarily summary fashion, the main textual types of the Latin apocryphon and, emphasizing its open-ended character, identify the various appendices which coalesced with it in its medieval redactions. Moreover, I explore medieval attitudes towards the apocryphal character of the *GN* and sketch the extent of its influence on Latin theological, devotional, and liturgical discourses of the Middle Ages.

Discussions of vernacular traditions of the *GN* begin with Richard O'Gorman's essay on the *GN* in Old French literature, which reveals a wealth of material, much of it still unstudied and unedited. In the first part of the essay, the author presents an overview of direct translations and adaptations of the Latin text: he introduces the three poetic renditions of the *GN*, updates the information on the texts and manuscripts of its "short" and "long" prose versions, and signals the presence of its adaptations in several composite works on the Passion. The second part focuses on thematic influence of the *GN* on romance literature (the story of Joseph of Arimathea) and on Passion narratives and plays (the Harrowing of Hell). O'Gorman's broad outline of the apocryphon's translations and influence urges further research on the Old French traditions and identifies several convenient points of departure for future investigations.

In contrast to O'Gorman's wide-angle, panoramic perspective on the *GN* in medieval France, Josep Izquierdo's essay on Catalan and Occitan traditions takes a close-up view of two verse and two prose works which contain translations of the pseudo-gospel. In his study of the Occitan *Sens e razos d'una escriptura* and the Catalan *E la mira car tot era ensems*, Izquierdo identifies the poems' relationships to the Latin apocryphon and to other sources, and argues that each poem is compositionally unified. The presentation of the two prose adaptations of the *GN*, *Lo Gènesi* (extant in Catalan, Occitan, and Italian) and *Gamaliel* (extant in French, Occitan, and Catalan) highlights the complexity of intertextual relations which bind the two and which extend to *Sens e razos* and to the Latin text that stands behind them all.

At least a dozen manuscripts with Italian translations of the *GN* are extant but, unfortunately, only two have been printed so far. Given this sorry state of research on the primary sources, Amilcare A. Iannucci concentrates on thematic influence, direct and indirect, of the *GN* on the literature of medieval Italy. In particular, he compares the different treatments and transformations of the *Descensus Christi ad inferos* in a variety of *laude*, *devozioni*, Passion plays, *cantare*, and sermons. The essay culminates in an account of Dante's subtle use of the apocryphon as an underlying pattern in portions of the *Divine Comedy*.

Unlike many of their Romance counterparts, most Germanic translations of the *GN* have been both extensively studied and edited in the twentieth century. C. W. Marx's exposition of the rich Old and Middle English traditions is organized around the notion of use as an indicator of status and influence. Marx investigates the apocryphon's use by examining the nature of manuscripts that contain the various translations of the *GN*, the character of materials compiled in those manuscripts, and the genres of writing most receptive of the *GN*'s influence. The changes in Middle English treatments of the pseudo-gospel he relates to the changes in doctrinal, literary, and linguistic climates of late medieval England.

Kirsten Wolf's overview of the *GN*'s influence on Norse literature, based on published and manuscript sources, presents the material from three linguistic areas: Old Norse-Icelandic, Old Danish, and Old Swedish. The author focuses on the extant translations of the apocryphon into vernacular prose and verse, but she also notes thematic indebtedness to the *GN* of various religious and secular works. Her exposition of the translations concentrates on the character of their textual transmission, on the translators' treatment of the apocryphon's contents, and on their stylistic practices vis-à-vis the Latin source.

Although the presence of the *GN* in High German literature has been discussed in a number of recent publications, Werner Hoffmann's essay proves that the subject has by no means been exhausted. In his survey of the numerous verse and prose renditions of the apocryphon, Hoffmann pays particular attention to the textual practices of translators and vernacular compilers, and, whenever possible, identifies the exact Latin and vernacular versions of the *GN* which served as their sources. In its attention to factual detail, the essay provides numerous corrections and additions to a recent comprehensive edition of the High German translations. An overview of the *GN*'s diffusion in and thematic influence on other works, focusing on the ways in which portions of the apocryphon or its motifs have been adapted to new contexts, mostly prose and dramatic passions, completes the exposition.

A similar approach, with its emphasis on translation and adaptation techniques and its attention to sources and contexts, informs Hoffmann's study of the *GN* in Dutch and Low German. Besides presenting the extant prose and verse renditions of the pseudo-gospel, this essay explores the diffusion of the apocryphal material through devotional texts on the Passion, and especially through *Dat Lyden ende die Passie Ons Heren Jhesu Christi*, based on a Middle Dutch *GN*.

Although Ann Dooley's search of pre-eleventh-century Irish texts has yielded no positive evidence of the *GN*'s influence, and a survey of later literature suggests a certain restraint in the use of themes derived from the pseudo-gospel, a strong presence of the *GN* in the Irish tradition cannot be denied, given that it was translated into Irish at an early date. The extant versions of that translation have been edited and translated into English in recent years. Dooley's investigation takes that recent work as a point of departure and supplements it with a discussion of an insufficiently appreciated textual witness. It also highlights certain features of the Irish texts of the *GN* by examining and comparing their beginnings, endings, and proper names; reviewing additions to the texts; and considering variation among the Irish manuscripts.

The Welsh traditions of the *GN*, including three translations and an important thematic legacy, are surveyed here by David N. Klausner. His opening comments on problems with identifying Irish texts of Nicodemus's narrative and an exposition of the extant versions provide a background for a discussion of the apocryphon's reception in Wales. Since textual evidence for direct knowledge of the apocryphon—beyond the three translations—is limited, that discussion concentrates on the dissemination in Welsh literature of the Harrowing of Hell, a motif highly indebted to the *GN* and of considerable currency in medieval Wales. In an appendix, Klausner signals faint and probably indirect reflexes of the *GN* in the Cornish *Ordinalia*.

Varied as these essays are in format and approach, they all share a common subject and common goals. They all identify the surviving vernacular versions of the *GN*, comment on their place in broader literary or cultural contexts, and imply areas in need of further research. Through ample and detailed bibliographic notes, they also provide summaries of research done to date on individual strands of the apocryphon's tradition and convenient starting points for future investigations.

The thematic bibliography that concludes the volume is based partly on the independent research Rémi Gounelle and I have done over the years and partly on the lists of works cited as provided by the contributors. It is intended as a guide to research on the *GN* in all its linguistic versions, including those mentioned but not discussed in detail in this volume. Consequently, its scope is larger than the collective scope of the essays presented here. The bibliography is arranged primarily according to linguistic traditions; brief expository annotations that accompany individual items indicate their nature and focus.

Acknowledgements

Putting together this volume and seeing it through the publication has been a lengthy and arduous process. The project was conceived in 1989, and the bulk of the essays was completed by 1992. Forging those essays into a book would not have been possible without the contributors' continued support and patience. I should also like to express my gratitude to all those who, over the years, took an active interest in this project and assisted me at various stages of its execution. My special thanks are owed to Mirosław Bielewicz, Robert Byrnes, Linwood DeLong, Murray Evans, Rémi Gounelle, Carol Harvey, Patty Hawkins, Brian Morgan, John Parry, Brian Turner, and, above all, to Marta. This book would have taken much longer to prepare if it had not been for the scholarly, institutional, and financial assistance of the Association pour l'étude de la littérature apocryphe chrétienne and the University of Winnipeg.

Introduction

ZBIGNIEW IZYDORCZYK

he Passion of Jesus—his trial before Pilate, death, Descent into Hell, and Resurrection—has arrested and inspired Christian imagination since apostolic times. Before it came to life on medieval pageants and stages, the Passion was a frequent subject of pious narratives. Some of them simply retold the story as found in the four gospels, but others, more daring, revised it and embellished it with imaginative details.

1. The *Gospel of Nicodemus*

One of the most successful and culturally pregnant among the daring narratives was the apocryphon commonly known as the *Gospel of Nicodemus*. In its typical medieval form, this work contained three thematic sections: an account of the Passion, Resurrection, and Ascension; the story of Joseph of Arimathea; and a report on Christ's Descent into Hell. This does not mean, however, that the apocryphon had a fixed, clearly delimited, or stable scope; on the contrary, throughout its long history, it thrived as a living, dynamic text, ever evolving and changing in content and style.

1.1. Titles

Perhaps as a reflex of that dynamic textuality or, maybe, of its changing scholarly perceptions, modern appellations for the apocryphon also lack stability and consistency. The title *Gospel of Nicodemus* and its late medieval Latin source, *Evangelium Nicodemi*, usually refer to the full version of the work (the accounts of the Passion, Joseph of Arimathea, and the Descent). However, some scholars use this title for the first two sections of the apocryphon only.[1] This practice stems ultimately

---

[1] Cf. Marek Starowieyski, ed., *Apokryfy Nowego Testamentu*, vol. 1, *Ewangelie*

from Constantinus de Tischendorf's edition, which presented the work in two discrete parts, one comprising the Passion and Joseph's story (chaps. 1–16) and the other the Descent (chaps. 17–27).[2] Tischendorf himself called the first part *Gesta Pilati*, and the second *Descensus Christi ad inferos*. The division of the work into the *Gesta* and the *Descensus* gained much currency and is frequently observed today. The early medieval title for both parts, *Gesta Salvatoris*, occurring in a number of codices and medieval book lists, is evoked today only rarely.[3] Much more common is the title *Acts of Pilate* (or *Acta Pilati*), derived from patristic sources which refer in Latin to "acta" and in Greek to "hypomnēmata" of Pilate.[4] The Greek term, which occurs also in manuscript titles of the oldest Greek version of the apocryphon, translates into Latin as "commentarii" or "acta" and corresponds to English "reports," "memorials," or "commentaries." The title *Acta Pilati* is used primarily with reference to the earliest forms of the work as well as to the Greek and Eastern versions of what Tischendorf called *Gesta Pilati* (Eastern versions do not transmit the story of the Descent); however, it is also used to designate the only Greek recension that does include the *Descensus*.

These inconsistent titling practices are potentially misleading. To avoid confusion and yet to remain within the bounds of scholarly tradition, this book adopts, whenever feasible, the following usage: the title *Gospel of Nicodemus* (abbreviated *GN*) refers to the apocryphon generically or to the European vernacular translations; *Evangelium Nicodemi* (*EN*) refers to the Latin texts; *Acta Pilati* (*AP*) refers to the earliest forms and to Greek and Oriental versions; *Gesta Pilati* (*GP*) refers to the first two thematic sections of the Latin apocryphon; and *Descensus Christi ad inferos* (*DI*) refers to the last thematic section of the apocryphon.

1.2. Scope of the apocryphal tradition

The majority of essays in this volume focus on the reading and writing

---

apokryficzne, pt. 2 (Lublin: Towarzystwo Naukowe Katolickiego Uniwersytetu Lubelskiego, 1986), 420. [All bibliographical references are cited in full on their first appearance in a particular essay; subsequently, they are cited in abbreviated form.]

[2] Constantinus de Tischendorf, ed., *Evangelia apocrypha*, 2d rev. ed. (Leipzig: H. Mendelssohn, 1876), 333–432.

[3] Cf. the subtitle of H. C. Kim's edition of the apocryphon, *The Gospel of Nicodemus: Gesta Salvatoris*, Toronto Medieval Latin Texts, vol. 2 (Toronto: Pontifical Institute of Mediaeval Studies, 1973).

[4] For the former, see the comments on Justin Martyr in the following essay, sect. 1.1. The latter is used, for instance, by Eusebius of Caesarea; see ibid., sect. 1.3.

of the *GN* in Western Europe during the Middle Ages. In spite of their linguistic range, the essays cover only a portion of the apocryphon's entire textual tradition and cultural legacy.

As the first chapter explains, themes that eventually converged in the apocryphon began to coalesce as early as the second century (cf. Pilate's correspondence with Rome). The original Greek composition may have acquired shape or, perhaps, currency during the controversies between Christianity and the Roman Empire in the early fourth; by the end of that century, its existence is attested in patristic writings. The apocryphon began to spread from its Greek font to other Eastern languages already in late antiquity or the early Middle Ages, that is, before the period of its translations into Western vernaculars. That expansion continued throughout and, in some cases, beyond medieval times. As a result, textual vestiges of the *GN* can also be found in Greek, Coptic, Arabic, Ethiopic, Syriac, Palestinian Aramaic, Armenian, Georgian, and Slavonic. With its focus on the medieval West, this book thus deals with a vibrant yet relatively late and geographically limited branch of the overall apocryphal tradition.

1.3. Texts of the *Evangelium Nicodemi*

All West European vernacular versions of the *GN* ultimately derive not from the original Greek text but from its Latin translation, which can be traced back to the fifth century. During the Middle Ages that translation evolved at least three major textual forms, traditionally designated as A, B, and C. To judge by the number of extant manuscripts, the most widely diffused was A; B and C had a more limited circulation. Hybrid redactions mixing features of the major forms were also common, and at least one of them, with features of A and C (the Troyes redaction, best preserved in Troyes, Bibliothèque municipale MS. 1636), left a considerable vernacular legacy.

Typical late medieval Latin versions of the *EN* included both the *Gesta* and the *Descensus*. To the latter was often appended the *Epistola Pilati ad Claudium*, which in turn could be followed by the *Cura sanitatis Tiberii*, *Vindicta Salvatoris*, *Somnium Neronis*, or some other thematically related texts. These additional texts were subsumed by the *EN* and tended to lose their separate identities. Other intertextual practices led to the inclusion of the *EN*, in full or in part, into various compilatory compositions, such as the *Legenda aurea* or the *Speculum historiale*, and to countless minor borrowings from and allusions to it in a wide spectrum of religious literature. Before its credibility was seriously challenged and eventually destroyed by the Reformation, the Latin apocryphon managed to penetrate into a variety of literary, theological, devotional, and liturgical discourses.

1.4. Summary of the *Evangelium Nicodemi*

Since the Latin type A of the *EN* was most common throughout the
Middle Ages and since it is often used as a point of reference in discussions of the apocryphon, it may be useful to summarize it briefly
here. The following summary is based on the text preserved in the
celebrated tenth-century Einsiedeln, Stiftsbibliothek MS. 326, fols. 11r–
29v (saec. IX–X), as edited by Kim.

The apocryphal narrative begins with the arrival before Pilate of
high priests and scribes of the Jews, who accuse Jesus of calling himself king, of violating the Sabbath, and of trying to dissolve their law.
At their request, Pilate summons Jesus through a messenger, who, to
their chagrin, reveres Jesus and spreads his own kerchief for him to
walk upon. When Jesus finally enters the judgement hall, the imperial
standards miraculously bow before him, causing another consternation.
Pilate too grows uneasy, especially after his wife, Procula, sends him
a message urging him to let Jesus go because she suffered a vision at
night on his account. But the accusers insist that Jesus must be condemned, claiming, among other things, that he was born of fornication.
This charge is categorically denied by twelve righteous Jews who were
present at the espousals of Joseph and Mary. There follow a conversation between Pilate and Jesus (based largely on Jn. 18:30–38), and, after
Pilate's failed attempts to exculpate Jesus, further accusations.

Now the Jews charge Jesus with blasphemy, punishable by death,
yet some among them seem distressed by this course of events. First
Nicodemus speaks out in Jesus' defense, and then others—including
the woman with the issue of blood, named Veronica—relate Jesus'
miracles. Pilate's sympathy is clearly with Jesus, and he offers to
release him on account of the feast of unleavened bread. The Jews
choose to free Barabbas instead. Angered by their stubbornness, Pilate
harangues them, ceremonially washes his hands of guilt, and pro-
nounces his sentence against Jesus. The account of the Crucifixion
follows essentially Luke 23. Stripped of his garments, Jesus is crucified
between two thieves, Dismas and Gestas; his side is pierced with a
spear by Longinus; and after the conversion of Dismas, Jesus dies amid
supernatural signs. He is buried by Joseph of Arimathea, who has
requested his body from the distraught Pilate, wrapped it in clean
linen, and laid it in his own sepulcher.

Then the Jews seize Joseph for defending Jesus and throw him into
prison, thinking to deal with him after the Sabbath; but when they
reopen his cell, they find it empty. They are still wondering at Joseph's
disappearance when the guards of the sepulcher arrive and declare
that they saw an angel announce to some women Jesus' Resurrection;
the Jews buy their silence with money. However, more witnesses come

forth: three rabbis arriving from Galilee claim to have seen Jesus teaching his apostles on the Mount of Olives and then ascending into heaven. The Jewish council bribes them, too, and sends them back to their home regions. Nevertheless, the Jews remain concerned and, at Nicodemus's advice, send out scouts to search for Jesus in the mountains; the scouts fail to find him but locate Joseph in his home town of Arimathea. The leaders of the Jews ask Joseph to come to Jerusalem; having complied, Joseph tells them how he was released from prison by the risen Christ. The Jews are stupefied and deeply shaken by his revelations. One of the Levites suddenly remembers the prophecy of Simeon, and they decide to recall the three rabbis who came from Galilee. After the three have confirmed the truthfulness of their earlier statements, Annas and Caiaphas ponder the assumptions of Enoch, Elijah, and Moses and the Ascension of Christ. In response, Joseph tells them that not only did Christ rise from the dead but he also raised many others, among them the two sons of Simeon, Leucius and Carinus, who still remain in Arimathea. Finding their graves indeed empty, the Jews send for them and behind closed doors adjure them to relate the manner of their resurrection. The two brothers ask for paper and write down the story of the Harrowing of Hell.

According to their account, they sat enveloped in the darkness of hell, when suddenly bright light pierced the shadows and made the patriarchs and prophets rejoice. They began to rehearse their messianic prophecies, first Isaiah, then Simeon, and finally John the Baptist. Seth recalled what Michael, the angel of the Lord, foretold him about the coming of the Savior, when he had gone to paradise to ask for the oil of mercy for the dying Adam. While the saints were thus rejoicing, Satan called out to Hell to prepare for the reception of Jesus Christ, who had boasted that he was the Son of God and whose death he, Satan, contrived. But when Hell learned that it was the same Jesus who had raised Lazarus from the dead, and when he heard a powerful voice demanding entry for the king of glory (Ps. 23:7), he cast Satan out of his dwelling and ordered the denizens of hell to bar the gates. Amid jubilation, Isaiah and David recited more prophecies; then the great voice called out again, and the king of glory came in. Hell, Death, and their servants panicked and filled the underworld with a welter of terrified questions. Treading on Death, the king of glory seized Satan and handed him to Hell, who reproached Satan for causing Christ's death and their own destruction. Then Jesus extended his hand to Adam and made a sign of the cross over him and over all the saints, who praised and glorified their Savior. He then led them all out of hell and entrusted them to the Archangel Michael, who brought them into the glory of the terrestrial paradise. There they met with Enoch and Elijah, awaiting the advent of the Antichrist, and with the

Good Thief, carrying the sign of the cross. Later the two sons of Simeon returned to life with a multitude of others, who celebrated the Pasch in Jerusalem and were baptized in the river Jordan.

Having finished, Leucius and Carinus hand their separate accounts to the Jews and, transfigured, disappear from sight. Their versions are found to be identical to the letter. The Jews leave the synagogue with great agitation and fear, and Joseph and Nicodemus bring the news about these events to Pilate, who writes everything down and deposits his report in the judgement hall.

Although at first glance the apocryphon may appear purely narrative, it is in fact profoundly dramatic. Its dominant mode of discourse is direct speech, dialogical and polylogical, with narration being reserved for brief introductions of speakers and, especially in the accounts of the Crucifixion and Joseph's imprisonment, for concise summaries of events, so compressed at times as to obscure temporal dimensions of events.[5] The trial scene in particular shows much theatrical potential, both in its use of direct speech and in its unity of time, place, and action. The *DI*, in spite of being presented as a written report, is marked by similar theatricality, fully exploited by medieval playwrights. It is not inconceivable that already in its infancy the original Greek *Acts* was connected with theater or dramatic liturgy, perhaps inspiring, perhaps being inspired by them,[6] and that the inherent dramatic potential of the *Acts* was subsequently enhanced in the process of its linguistic transformations and growth.

2. The cycle of Pilate

Given the absence of concern for textual integrity and definitive textual boundaries in manuscript culture, it is hardly surprising that the *Gospel of Nicodemus* provided both a source and a point of gravity for a host

---

[5] Is it possible that the apocryphon's compression of the forty days before Christ's Ascension, remarked on by Felix Scheidweiler, "Nikodemusevangelium. Pilatusakten und Höllenfahrt Christi," in *Neutestamentliche Apokryphen in deutscher Übersetzung*, vol. 1, *Evangelien*, 5th ed., ed. Wilhelm Schneemelcher (Tübingen: J. C. B. Mohr [Paul Siebeck]), 396–97, has resulted from this dramatic mode of presentation rather than from deliberate theological reflection?

[6] Jean-Daniel Dubois, "L'Affaire des étendards de Pilate dans le premier chapitre des *Actes de Pilate*," in *Papers Presented to the Tenth International Conference on Patristic Studies, Oxford 24–29 August 1987*, ed. E. A. Livingstone, Studia Patristica, vol. 19 (Louvain: Peeters Press, 1989), 351–58; and Rémi Gounelle, "Recherches sur les *Actes* apocryphes *de Pilate* grecs, recension B," 2 vols. (Mémoire présenté pour l'obtention du Diplôme d'Études Approfondies, Université Paris X-Nanterre, 1991), 1:75–81.

of minor, often derivative compositions. Known collectively as the cycle of Pilate, those texts are quite diverse in form and content, and include private and official letters, reports, narratives, and legal pronouncements. What links them all is the emphasis on the person of Pilate, textual and thematic links to the *GN*, and frequent co-occurrence with the *GN* in manuscripts (in fact, they are sometimes fully integrated with it). Most of them were originally written in crude Greek or Latin and later translated into various Eastern and Western languages.

The notion of the cycle of Pilate is rather loose and has never been unambiguously defined. There is no absolute agreement as to which texts should be included in it and which should not, but there is a general consensus that the cycle constitutes the immediate textual milieu for the *AP*. Since the Pilate cycle will occasionally enter the discussions of the apocryphon in this book, it may be worthwhile to mention its main texts here. The following list does not, however, aim to be either definitive or exhaustive, given the fuzziness of the notion and the incomplete state of research:[7]

Epistola Pilati ad Claudium: Pilate briefly reports on Christ's miracles, death, and Resurrection, blaming the Jews and portraying himself as sympathetic to Christianity. It is extant in Greek, Latin, and Syriac as well as in medieval vernaculars.[8]

Anaphora Pilati: Pilate writes to the emperor concerning the deeds and death of Christ and mentions the miracles that attended his Crucifixion and Resurrection. Composed in Greek possibly in the fifth century, it survives in two Greek versions, A and B; version A was translated into Syriac, Arabic, Armenian, and Old Slavonic.[9]

Paradosis Pilati: a continuation of *Anaphora* A, also of the fifth century, containing an account of the arrest and martyrdom of Pilate, presented here as a follower of Christ.[10]

Tiberii rescriptum: Tiberius replies angrily to Pilate's letter and condemns him. The work was written in Greek, probably in the fifth century; it is also extant in Old Slavonic.[11]

---

[7] For additional texts that might be considered candidates for the Pilate cycle, see my essay on the Latin *EN*, sects. 1.3.4–1.3.7.

[8] Mauritius Geerard, *Clavis apocryphorum Novi Testamenti,* Corpus Christianorum, Series Apocryphorum (Turnhout: Brepols, 1992), no. 64; Geerard gives full bibliographic references, not repeated here. I discuss this apocryphal letter in my essay on the Latin *EN*, sect. 1.3.1.

[9] Geerard, *Clavis,* nos. 65, 66; Starowieyski, *Apokryfy,* 463.

[10] Geerard, *Clavis,* no. 66; Starowieyski, *Apokryfy,* 466.

[11] Geerard, *Clavis,* no. 65; Starowieyski, *Apokryfy,* 468. Slavonic versions are mentioned by Francis J. Thomson, "Apocrypha Slavica: II," *Slavonic and East European Review* 63, no. 1 (1985): 81.

Epistolae Pilati et Herodis: Pilate confides in Herod that he has been justified by Christ, and Herod confesses to Pilate all the misfortunes that befell him. This correspondence belongs to the tradition that blames the Jews and exculpates Pilate. It was composed in Greek, possibly in the fifth century, and survives also in Syriac.[12]

Epistola Pilati ad Tiberium: Pilate reveals that he sentenced Christ partly through his own weakness but partly through his loyalty to the emperor. This letter, which again presents Pilate in a positive light, was written in Renaissance Latin, probably in the sixteenth century.[13]

Cura sanitatis Tiberii: Tiberius is miraculously healed by an image of Christ, Peter confirms the truth of Pilate's report on Jesus, and Nero exiles Pilate, who commits suicide. The work was composed in Latin, possibly in northern Italy, between the fifth and the eighth centuries.[14]

Vindicta Salvatoris: a sequence of two narratives, one about the healing of Titus and his destruction of Jerusalem, and the other about the condemnation of Pilate and the healing of Tiberius. It was composed in Latin, possibly around the beginning of the eighth century in southern Gaul.[15]

Mors Pilati: a late medieval retelling, in Latin, of the healing of Tiberius and of Pilate's suicide, with additions about Christ's tunic and troubles caused by Pilate's corpse.[16]

Vita Mariae Magdalenae: Mary Magdalene travels to Rome to denounce Pilate before the emperor. This is probably a medieval Greek composition.[17]

Encomium in Mariam Magdalenam: a story of Mary Magdalene; the extant text deals with her childhood, her part in the paschal and post-Resurrection events, and the revelations she received from the Archangel Gabriel. This work survives only in Coptic.[18]

Homilia de lamentis Mariae (Evangelium Gamalielis): Jesus was crucified through the conspiracy of Herod and the Jews, and Pilate was a true believer in Christ, destined to suffer martyrdom for his faith. The apocryphon includes dialogues between Virgin Mary and Jesus at the tomb

---

[12] Geerard, *Clavis,* no. 67; Starowieyski, *Apokryfy,* 473.

[13] Geerard, *Clavis,* no. 68; Starowieyski, *Apokryfy,* 476.

[14] Geerard, *Clavis,* no. 69; for fuller dicussion, see my essay on the Latin *EN,* sect. 1.3.2.

[15] Geerard, *Clavis,* no. 70; for fuller discussion, see my essay on the Latin *EN,* sect. 1.3.3.

[16] Geerard, *Clavis,* no. 71; Aurelio de Santos Otero, ed., *Los evangelios apócrifos,* 3d ed., Biblioteca de autores cristianos, vol. 148 (Madrid: La Editorial Catolica, 1975), 495–96.

[17] Geerard, *Clavis,* no. 72.

[18] Ibid., no. 73.

and between Pilate and the resurrected Good Thief. This work is extant in Arabic, Ethiopic, and Coptic.[19]

Homilia de morte Pilati (*Martyrium Pilati*): for his faith in Jesus, Pilate was crucified twice, once by the Jews and then by Tiberius, and, together with his wife and two children, he was buried near the sepulcher of Jesus. This was composed in Coptic but survives in Arabic and Ethiopic.[20]

Narratio Iosephi de Arimathea: Joseph's account of the Passion, of the Good Thief, and of his own miraculous release from prison mentioned in the *Gospel of Nicodemus*. Originally a Greek composition, it is extant also in Old Slavonic.[21] A Georgian version of the *Narratio* includes an account, surviving also in Greek and Latin, of the foundation of the church in Lydda and its protection by an image of Mary, Mother of God.[22]

De bono latrone: a story of the Good Thief's first encounter with Jesus during the flight to Egypt and of his subsequent exile from the house of his father, in Latin.[23]

Not listed in the "Cyclus Pilati" section of Geerard's *Clavis apocryphorum* but included by some in the cycle of Pilate are:

Narratio de Martha: probably an original Slav compilation based on the *Anaphora, Paradosis,* and *Tiberii rescriptum,* on the theme of Pilate's death.[24]

Sententia Pilati: a post-medieval, sixteenth- or seventeenth-century work of Italian origin, containing many curious chronological and historical details pertaining to Christ's Passion.[25]

3. Western vernacular traditions

The first harbinger of the awakening vernacular interest in the *GN* was the Old English prose translation made in the early or mid-eleventh century. It antedates by well over a century the second oldest version, in medieval Irish prose, dated to the twelfth or early thirteenth century. Although the beginnings of the *GN*'s vernacular career were thus connected with prose, it was the medium of poetry that sustained the initial

---

[19] Ibid., no. 74.

[20] Ibid., no. 75.

[21] Ibid., no. 76; Starowieyski, *Apokryfy,* 487–88.

[22] Geerard, *Clavis,* no. 77.

[23] Ibid., no. 78.

[24] Thomson, "Apocrypha Slavica," 81.

[25] Santos Otero, *Los evangelios,* 532–35.

surge of its popularity in the thirteenth century. To that period belong the Old French translations by André de Coutances, by one Chrétien, and by an anonymous poet; the Occitan *Sens e razos d'una escriptura;* the Old Norse *Niðrstigningarsaga;* the High German *Urstende* by Konrad von Heimesfurt and the *Christi Hort* by Gundacker von Judenburg. In the fourteenth century, new poetic adaptations of the *GN* continued to be produced (the Catalan *E la mira car tot era ensems,* the Middle English *Cursor mundi* and *Stanzaic Gospel of Nicodemus,* the Old Danish poetic *GN,* the High German translation by Heinrich von Hesler), but the emphasis shifted to prose, which soon became the primary medium for vernacular translations. As a result of that shift, the extant prose versions of the fourteenth and fifteenth centuries far outnumber the poetic ones. In medieval French, for example, we have at least three "short" prose translations, an expanded "long" version, and one partial text; in Occitan, we have *Gamaliel;* in Catalan, *Lo Gènesi;* in Italian, apparently several versions, only two of which have been printed; in Middle English, at least six; one in Old Swedish; twelve in High German; one in Low German; four in Dutch; three in Irish; and three in Welsh.

3.1. Immediate sources

The immediate sources of these verse and prose translations of the *GN* were twofold, Latin and vernacular. Most frequently exploited was Latin text-type A, which was rendered—in full or in part—into practically every Western vernacular. Adaptations of *EN* B are much less common and seem to have been diffused primarily in Romance languages. The Occitan *Sens e razos d'una escriptura* translates the entire B version and is itself the source of *Gamaliel,* through which version B spread to French and Catalan. The Catalan *Lo Gènesi,* which translates chapters 12–27 of *EN* B, was made available also in Occitan and Italian. Irish, Welsh, Old Norse, Middle Dutch, and Middle English translators did not use this Latin version. In Middle High German, a mixed redaction combining *Gesta* B and *Descensus* A was used by Konrad von Heimesfurt, and a similar Latin text stands behind a prose translation from Bavaria (translation G). Another prose version (translation K), from Eastern Central Germany, although based principally on A, shows a number of interpolations from B. However, the two High German prose texts (i.e., G and K) survive in unique manuscripts and left no important legacy; thus only Konrad's poetic rendition spread B variants outside the Romance vernaculars. The third Latin version to produce vernacular adaptations was the Troyes redaction, a mixture of *EN* A and C. It lies behind one "short" French version (to which two English texts, MS. Harley 149 and the first printed edition, are indebted), the Middle English *Stanzaic Gospel of Nicodemus,* Dutch and Low German prose versions (translations D and

L), the High German *editio princeps*, and possibly the Catalan *E la mira car tot era ensems*. Such wide diffusion of translations of the Troyes redaction is rather unexpected, given that it survives in fewer manuscripts than *EN* B.

Not all vernacular reflexes of the apocryphon were derived directly from the Latin *Evangelium Nicodemi*. Some originated in Latin digests or summaries of the apocryphon, especially those in the *Speculum historiale* or the *Legenda aurea*. The French text in Paris, Bibliothèque nationale MS. f. fr. 15219, for example, is based on the former, while the English *Stanzaic Life of Christ* is derived from the latter. Since the *Speculum* and the *Legenda* were also available in many medieval translations (not fully discussed in this volume), they must have played an important role in the diffusion of the Nicodemean material.

Vernacular versions of the *GN* could themselves serve as sources for translations and adaptations, for the apocryphon traveled easily across vernacular boundaries. The so-called French "long" version of the *GN* was rendered from Occitan, as was the corresponding Catalan version; the Catalan *Lo Gènesi* gave rise to the Occitan and Italian renditions; several English texts, including two prose versions and the sequence of the *Complaint of Our Lady* and the *GN*, are indebted to French; and there was some movement from Dutch (translation D) to High German (Rhenish Franconian), from Low German (translation L) to Dutch (Limburg, Ripuarian), and from High German (translation E) to Low.

Finally, some versions originated not through translation but through quarrying and recycling earlier versions in the same vernacular. This process can be seen at work in the Occitan *Gamaliel*, which exploits *Sens e razos d'una escriptura*; in Heinrich von München's *Weltchronik*, which draws on three earlier High German verse translations; and in a High German prose translation (E), which borrows from the *Urstende*.

3.2. Translators

The translators/authors of these vernacular *Gospels of Nicodemus* are for the most part unknown. Poetic versions are more likely than prose texts to be associated with a particular name (even if we know nothing about the person who went by it). André de Coutances, one Chrétien, Konrad von Heimesfurt, Gundacker von Judenburg, Heinrich von Hesler, Heinrich von München, Jan van Boendale—all are connected with verse renditions of the apocryphon. In contrast, only two of some three dozen prose translations are associated with specific translators, the Middle English version ascribed to John Trevisa and the Welsh version B translated by Dafydd Fychan.

3.3. Attitudes towards the *Gospel of Nicodemus*

Latin scribes and redactors of the *Evangelium Nicodemi* were well aware that it was not a true gospel, and occasionally they even appended to it notes labeling it as an apocryphon. That awareness did not prevent them, however, from adapting and using it in a variety of religious discourses. The respect for it is evident in the occasional comments about its trustworthiness and value as a witness to the events not recorded in the gospels. In some cases, its appreciation seems to have verged on veneration, as, for instance, when it was copied in the midst of the New Testament as if it belonged to it. Yet in spite of such manifestations of high esteem for it, the *EN* was not generally considered a divinely inspired text and did not rival the spiritual authority of the canonical writings.

Vernacular translators and authors display a similar range of attitudes. The Occitan author of *Sens e razos d'una escriptura* relies on John 21:25 to account for the fact that the *GN* reports events not mentioned in John or Matthew; a similar comment occurs in the High German version incorporated into the *Klosterneuburger Evangelienwerk.* The Old Norse translator of the *Niðrstigningarsaga* explains at the beginning of his work that his source, the *GN*, contains nothing dubious, even though it is not as prominent as other holy texts. Others appeal to the *GN*'s value as a historical record. They point out that Nicodemus, well acquainted both with Jewish leaders and with Jesus, was present at the trial; his report is trustworthy because he personally witnessed the events he describes. Remarks to this effect occur also in Gundacker von Judenburg and in Heinrich von Hesler.

Several vernacular versions are closely associated with the canonical texts in some of their manuscripts. The Old English translation in Cambridge University Library MS. Ii. 2. 11 follows the Old English version of the four gospels and might, perhaps, be considered as a fifth gospel, were it not for its more subdued manner of presentation; more likely, it was intended as a supplement rather than a counterpart to the canonical texts. Another version to appear in the context of biblical translations is the High German translation A (*Augsburger Bibelhandschrift*), extant in nine manuscripts. The translator apparently treated the apocryphon like other biblical texts, to be changed as little as possible, the practice which prompted at least one copyist to add an emphatic note that the *GN* does not belong to the Bible.[26] Although Irish writers did not compile the apocryphon with canonical material, the fact that

---

[26] For versions mixed with or embedded in canonical narratives, see also below, sect. 3.5.

they put it to exegetical uses, as, for example, in the Leabhar Breac commentary on the Passion narrative of Matthew, reflects the high regard for it in the Irish church.

3.4. Translation practices

Although some translators, like the one responsible for the High German text A, or like Jan van Boendale, who rendered the *GN* into Dutch verse, followed Latin originals very closely, others took varying degrees of license with their sources. They engaged in selectively omitting, adding to, rearranging, or altering the text, in order to tailor the apocryphon to various contexts and uses.

The most drastic form of omission resulted from the decision to translate only some sections of the apocryphon. The sections usually chosen covered the episodes of Joseph of Arimathea and of the Descent into Hell (e.g., André de Coutances, High German versions F, K) or only of the Descent (e.g., *Niðrstigningarsaga*, Dutch version C). Less frequently the focus of the translation was on the Resurrection and the story of Joseph (e.g., the Anglo-Norman and Middle English sequences of the *Complaint* and the *GN*); the account of the trial does not seem to have been translated independently of the other sections, probably because of its similarity to the gospel accounts.

On a smaller scale, passages or phrases could be omitted to abridge, to eliminate repetition or redundancy, to streamline the plot, or to simplify doctrine or style. The redactor of the second version of the *GN* in the Leabhar Breac, for example, considerably condenses the apocryphon; the author of the Dutch translation B omits chapter 2, probably on dogmatic grounds; the author of the *Niðrstigningarsaga* deletes doctrinal elements as well as details that are not essential to the movement of the story; and a similar desire for clarity and economy motivates Konrad von Heimsefurt's extensive tightening of the narrative.

Amplifications could range from glosses added to clarify sometimes murky Latin phrasing to factual or exegetical details to longer interpolations reflecting specific preoccupations of the redactors. Simple additions of the first type, explicating parts of the text and ensuring its clarity (through double translations, for example), were almost a habit of mind for most redactors and occur even in those versions which follow the Latin closely, such as the Swedish prose *GN*. Additions of exegetical and factual character were likewise common, and we find them frequently in the Irish, Low German, High German, and Old Norse texts. More extensive interpolations could serve a variety of purposes: some were used to illustrate specific points of doctrine (cf. the two passages on divine duplicity in the *Niðrstigningarsaga*), others to enhance the didactic value of the *GN* (cf. the creed in the Middle English version in MS.

Harley 149; comments on the greed of the soldiers guarding the sepulcher in the *Cursor mundi*), still others to bring it in line with current
devotional trends (cf. the scenes of flagellation, crowning with thorns,
and Crucifixion in the Dutch version B) and to increase its dramatic
effect (cf. the *planctus* in the Occitan *Sens e razos d'una escriptura* and
another in the Catalan *E la mira car tot era ensems*).

Other changes that accompanied the apocryphon's movement from
Latin to vernaculars involved transpositions and rearrangements of episodes, altering motives for actions, even remodeling entire scenes on the
basis of external sources. All of them can be found, for instance, in
Konrad von Heimesfurt's *Urstende*, which treats the apocryphon with
much freedom, rearranging its structure, increasing the amount of dialogue, and borrowing details from courtly literature. Such extensive
revisions place certain redactions of the *GN* at a considerable distance
from the Latin work and make it difficult to determine whether a
particular rendition of the Nicodemean material should in fact be considered a version of the apocryphon or an independent imaginative
elaboration of its motifs.

3.5. Interactions with other texts

Some medieval redactors made an effort to contextualize the story of the
GN and to relate it explicitly to the overall pattern and meaning of
events in which it participated, to the whole economy of salvation. They
accomplished this by framing or extending the apocryphon with additional material which projected the *GN* episodes against the background
of salvation history as it had unfolded or as it was to unfold in time.
Thus in the Middle English *Cursor mundi*, the apocryphon is preceded
and followed by comments on the significance and nature of the Redemption. The Occitan *Sens e razos d'una escriptura* creates for the *GN* an
anagogical context: the apocryphal narrative is followed by the legend of
the Antichrist, the signs before Doomsday, and an account of the Last
Judgement. Similar additions occur also in the Catalan *E la mira car tot
era ensems*, whose rendering of the *Descensus* is preceded by sections on
the trial, Passion, death, and burial of Christ, incorporates the story of
the Antichrist, and concludes with the signs of the Last Judgement. The
motive behind such adaptations was usually didactic.

Like their Latin counterparts, vernacular redactions of the *GN* combined with other texts rather easily. Many of the appendices which in
Latin manuscripts frequently appear fused with the core text occur also
in the translated versions, suggesting that the Latin redactors' perception
of the *GN* as a quasi-historical record, as an independent confirmation of
and supplement to the four gospels, was also shared by some vernacular
readers. Since the various appendices were not evenly distributed across

vernaculars, their presence may be a reflection of the popularity of specific Latin redactions in certain parts of Western Europe. We find the largest number of additions in German versions: the *Epistola Pilati ad Claudium*, the Pilate-Veronica legend from the *Cura sanitatis Tiberii* or *Historia apocrypha of the Legenda aurea*, the *Somnium Neronis*, and the *De horis canonicis*. In contrast, Dutch translations limit themselves to Pilate's letter. Other vernacular texts append the *Epistola* (French, English, Welsh), the *Cura* (French, English), the *Vindicta Salvatoris* (English), an excerpt from Gregory of Tours (English), and a "run" on the joys of heaven (Irish).

Another common intertextual practice involved mixing the apocryphal text with the canonical narratives. In several High German versions, both in verse and in prose, either the canonical text is embedded in the apocryphal or the apocryphal in the canonical. Konrad von Heimesfurt, for example, draws on the New Testament to provide a framework for the apocryphal narrative; the High German translation E both introduces and augments the story of the *GN* with canonical passages (it includes also other additions, such as the stories of Mary and Joseph's marriage and of the Antichrist, reported by Enoch); Gundacker von Judenburg and the Catalan author of *Lo Gènesi* base their accounts of the trial before Pilate partly on the *GN* and partly on the gospels; Heinrich von Hesler explicitly compares the canonical accounts with the *GN*; and the *Klosterneuburger Evangelienwerk* (translation H), which also contains observations about the differences between the gospels and the *GN*, uses the apocryphon in a piecemeal fashion, its portions embedded at various points in the canonical narrative. That such close association of the *GN* with the canonical material occurs more frequently in the German-speaking areas than elsewhere may be related to the fact that it was in the same areas that manuscripts placing the *GN* in the company of biblical texts were most common.

While its close association with the New Testament confirms that the *GN* was perceived as almost equal to the evangelical narratives in its historical authority, its ties to Passion texts, especially those of affective piety, reveal that it was also recognized as a potentially powerful stimulus to devotion. Passion tracts—narrative, contemplative, exegetical—were the most frequent manuscript environments for the vernacular apocryphon. But their relationship with the *GN* went beyond co-occurrence. One of the English prose versions typically follows the English translation of pseudo-Bonaventure's *Meditationes vitae Christi*. Although the apocryphon begins here at chapter 12.1, portions of the earlier chapters are embedded into the *Meditationes*. Similarly, in the Anglo-Norman sequence of the *Complaint of Our Lady* and the *Gospel of Nicodemus* and in its Middle English translation, the imprisonment and release of Joseph is incorporated into Mary's narrative, and the text of the *GN* begins where the imprisonment finishes. Finally, in one of the manuscripts of the High German translation E, the apocryphon is placed in the midst of a massive compilation of texts on the Passion, based primarily on Ludolph of Saxony's *Vita Christi*.

Although the Latin *EN* does not frequently occur in legendaries, several versions adapted the apocryphal material to hagiographic contexts. For example, the Occitan *Gamaliel* merged the traditions of Nicodemus, Gamaliel, and St. Stephen and effectively refocused the apocryphon, which nonetheless served as its backbone. This extensively remodeled *GN* circulated widely not only in Occitania but also in the Kingdom of Aragon and in France (the "long" version of the *GN*).

3.6. Diffusion of influence

The impact of the *GN* on vernacular literatures extends beyond the translations: its fragments are scattered across a variety of works, from devotional tracts to didactic narratives to chronicles to drama; its narrative structures and themes spread even to secular compositions; and many of its apocryphal details became part of commonplace Christian knowledge, of the medieval Christian lore.

Vernacular redactions of the *GN* left an important literary legacy. In Middle English, for example, the *Stanzaic Gospel of Nicodemus* and the *Stanzaic Life of Christ* are known to have directly influenced later texts, namely, the drama cycles. In Italian, the *devozione* from L'Aquila is sustained by an abridged Italian translation of *EN* B. In High German, Heinrich von München's compilation of the earlier verse translations was the source of *Die Neue Eue*, a devotional tract extant in over thirty manuscripts, which was in turn excerpted by other authors, such as Heinrich von St. Gallen in his treatise *Extendit manum;* Konrad von Heimesfurt's *Urstende* was used by the author of the *Befreiung der Altväter* and by Hawich der Kellner in his *Stephanslegende*, while Heinrich von Hesler's *Evangelium Nicodemi* influenced the *Weihenstephaner Chronik* and the *Tiroler Passion*. And one of the Dutch translations (designated as D) was freely adapted in the Passion treatise *Dat Lyden ende die Passie Ons Heren Jhesu Christi*, extensively diffused in both manuscripts and printed editions.

The apocryphon spread its influence not only through vernacular translations but also through the more widely distributed Latin versions; and not only through Latin summaries and excerpts in the *Speculum historiale*, *Legenda aurea*, *Meditationes vitae Christi*, and *Vita beate Marie rhythmica* but also through their vernacular translations. Distinguishing between the immediate sources of influence is often difficult and at times impossible, especially if the allusions to the apocryphon are brief or general or subtle. For example, little can be ascertained about the form in which the apocryphon was known to Langland or Dante. Occasionally, however, specific textual details allow us to identify the exact source: the High German *Passional*, merging pseudo-Augustinian "Sermo 160" with a summary of the Descent, is almost certainly indebted to the *Legenda aurea*.

Certain details disseminated by the *GN* were so commonplace in most vernacular literatures that their discussion would entail listing hundreds of texts. The names and stories of Longinus, Veronica, Dismas, and Gestas—all introduced and popularized by the pseudo-gospel—were known even to those who did not read the *GN* because, by the late Middle Ages, they were part of the general religious milieu. Even certain episodes, such as Joseph of Arimathea's Christophany, acquired the same commonplace status.

The story of the Descent into Hell, too, was a *locus communis* but, since it was also alluded to in the Apostles' Creed, it was elaborated in a number of sources besides the *GN*. Medieval writers could, therefore, use several models for their accounts of the event, and not all references to and accounts of the Harrowing of Hell are necessarily indebted to it. For example, pre-eleventh-century English and Irish and pre-thirteenth-century High German texts on the Harrowing are not on the whole inspired by the apocryphon. On the other hand, the *GN* was definitely the most vibrant and most widely diffused model for the episode in the later Middle Ages, a model whose influence was spread through a variety of intermediaries. If not the only, it was, perhaps, the most likely source, directly or indirectly, for late medieval writers on the Harrowing.

The influence of the *Descensus* frequently manifested itself—and can be recognized—through the presence of its typical narrative patterns, characters, sequences and types of speeches, or episodes. The Old French *Passion des jongleurs*, for instance, retells, in vividly dramatic language, most of the *Descensus* story, including the discussions among the infernal powers and the encounter with Enoch and Elijah. But when the apocryphon was filtered through the prevailing devotional attitudes or aesthetic sensibilities, its influence appears less as an overt imitation and more as a subtle allusion to certain of its motifs. In the Middle English *Devils' Parliament* and, perhaps, in its Irish counterpart as well—both reflexes of fifteenth-century popular piety—the echoes of the *GN* grow faint, yet remain audible; similarly, the *Divine Comedy* suggests rather than displays Dante's familiarity with the *Descensus*, used as a subtext or as a patterning device. Sometimes, however, even though the author evokes the title of the *GN*, his composition seems to bear little or no relationship to the apocryphon. This is the case with the Old Norse *Niðurstigningsvísur*, which seems to be using the *GN* as an authority validating its popular conception of the Harrowing rather than as a source.

The influence of the story of Joseph of Arimathea is notable espe-cially in the genre of romance. The events described in the *GN* provided a starting point for the development of a rich body of legend, most fully elaborated in Robert de Boron's *Joseph d'Arimathie*. Robert himself did not rely directly on the *GN*, and at least one of his translators blamed him for it: Jacob van Maerlant complained in the prologue to his *Historie van den grale* that his source contains many factual errors. Maerlant corrected them by drawing on the *GN*. Although common in romances, retellings of Joseph's involvement in the sacred events were not confined to them. Joseph's story was also dramatized in several vernaculars, including French (the *Mystère de la Passion Nostre Seigneur*), Italian (the *devozione* from L'Aquila), and High German (the *Heidelberger Passions-spiel*, the *Tiroler Passion*).

The influence of the *Gesta* is perhaps the most difficult to document because of its similarity to the canonical narratives. The fact that the *Gesta* was sometimes omitted in vernacular translations suggests that it was perceived as less attractive or, perhaps, useful than the two later sections. Nevertheless, it too was widely known and quarried, especially for such details as the episode of the imperial standards bowing before Jesus, Procula's dream, or the dialogues between Jesus and Pilate. Not infrequently, this part of the apocryphon was interspersed with the canonical text, as mentioned above (sect. 3.5).

4. State of research

Although all ancient and Eastern versions of the *Acta Pilati* are available in some form in print, those editions are being currently re-evaluated in the light of new manuscript evidence and new knowledge about the dissemination of Christian writings in late antiquity and the early Middle Ages. This work is being done under the auspices of the Asso-ciation pour l'étude de la littérature apocryphe chrétienne in preparation for a comprehensive edition of the apocryphon in the Corpus Chris-tianorum, Series Apocryphorum. It is hoped that the results of current research will shed new light on the problem of origin and early trans-mission of the *AP*.

As part of the same project, the study of the Latin *Evangelium Nicodemi* has now entered a crucial stage of classifying extant texts in over four hundred manuscripts. This classification will provide the basis for subsequent editorial work. At the same time, external evidence is being gathered for a detailed study of the *EN*'s dissemination in medi-eval libraries and of the circumstances of its transmission during the Middle Ages.

Not all Western vernacular traditions of the *GN* have been researched to the same extent. The pseudo-gospel has been studied most intensely in the Germanic languages: English, German, Dutch, Icelandic, Swedish, and Danish. Although some work still remains to be done, especially in exploring the relationship between the apocryphon and various Passion tracts, publishing some of the unedited versions, and relating the extant texts to the Latin traditions, the impact of the *GN* on those literatures has been fairly well elucidated. The groundwork for research on Celtic traditions has also been already laid, and future research on the relationships among the various Irish and Welsh versions and on their Latin sources will no doubt enhance the finer details of the picture. Less advanced, it seems, is research on the *GN* in Romance languages, although much work is now in progress. In French, for example, more work is needed on the manuscripts of the *GN* and of various works that incorporate it in part or in full; in Catalan and Occitan, new editions to replace the sometimes unreliable nineteenth-century texts might further the study of the apocryphon; and in Italian, editions of the unstudied manuscripts of the *GN* are desiderata for assessing its place in and impact on Italian literature.

Nicodemus's Gospel before and beyond the Medieval West[1]

ZBIGNIEW IZYDORCZYK

JEAN-DANIEL DUBOIS

*T*extual richness and complex intertextual affinities of the *Gospel of Nicodemus* (GN) in the late Middle Ages are products of a centuries-long process of development. If the final stages of that process marked a wide trail in extant religious and literary documents, the earliest ones left hardly a trace.

1. The *Acts of Pilate* in patristic tradition

Manuscript evidence for the formative period of the GN's history is lacking, as most manuscripts of late antiquity did not withstand the ravages of time. It is, therefore, only through fleeting references in the writings of church fathers that we can witness the birth and infancy of the apocryphon. Patristic testimony, often brief and oblique, may not allow the same clarity of understanding or the same degree of certainty as material evidence, yet so far it alone can offer us some glimpses of the nascent cycle of Pilate and the GN.

---

[1] We wish to acknowledge the scholarly assistance of the Association pour l'étude de la littérature apocryphe chrétienne and to express our gratitude to the members of the team in charge of a new, comprehensive edition of the *Acts of Pilate* (*AP*) for the Corpus Christianorum, Series Apocryphorum: Brigitte Tambrun-Krasker, Centre national de la recherche scientifique (C. N. R. S.), Paris, Christiane Furrer, Faculté de théologie, Université de Lausanne, and Rémi Gounelle, Faculté de théologie, Université de Lausanne (Greek versions); Albert Frey, Institut des sciences bibliques, Université de Lausanne, and Alain Desreumaux, C. N. R. S., Paris (Syriac and Aramaic); Bernard Outtier, C. N. R. S., Paris (Armenian and Georgian); Gérard Roquet, École pratique des hautes études, Sciences historiques et philologiques, Paris (Coptic); and Robert Beylot, C. N. R. S., Paris-Lyon (Ethiopic).

1.1. Justin Martyr

The earliest mentions of some "Acts" of Pilate occur in the apologetic writings of Justin Martyr, dated shortly after the middle of the second century AD. In his first *Apology*, chapter 35.9, Justin takes it for granted that his adversaries can consult the minutes of the trial of Jesus if they wish to verify the truthfulness of his statements about Jesus' death.[2] However, a few pages earlier (chap. 34.2), Justin makes a similar appeal to another non-Christian source, maintaining with equal certitude that the registers of the census under governor Quirinus bear witness to Jesus' birth in Bethlehem,[3] although there is no evidence that such registers had ever existed. Consequently, his mention of the "Acts" does not necessarily guarantee their actual existence.[4] This conclusion is further corroborated by the fact that Justin refers to the "Acts" in the context of prophetic "proofs" concerning Jesus' destiny. He actually transliterates into Greek the official Latin term "acta," as if to endow that source with the nondisputable appearance and authority enjoyed by scriptural prophecies. The historicity or authenticity of the document may thus have been of little or no importance to him.

Later in his *Apology*, chapter 48.3, Justin alludes to the same "Acts" to prove that Jesus really performed the various miracles attributed to him.[5] Here, again, the allusion seems to serve Christian apologetics, in that the "Acts" are evoked to confirm the fulfilment of the Old Testament prophecies.

Given Justin's willingness to assume the existence of certain imperial documents and the prophetic and apologetic contexts of his allusions to the "Acts," one may wonder whether he really knew the work we call *Acts of Pilate*. It seems more likely that he either thought that such "Acts of Pilate"—like the registers of Quirinus—must have existed somewhere,[6] or had in mind a series of "proof-texts" about Jesus' Passion, such as those known to the apologists of the early church.

---

[2] Justin Martyr, *Apologies. Texte grec, traduction française, introduction et index*, ed. Louis Pautigny (Paris: A. Picard, 1904), 72.

[3] Ibid., 70.

[4] For a different interpretation of this textual evidence, see R. Cameron, ed., *The Other Gospels: Non-canonical Gospel Texts* (Guildford [Surrey]: Lutterworth Press, 1982), 163.

[5] Justin, *Apologies*, 98.

[6] Cf. Felix Scheidweiler, "Nikodemusevangelium. Pilatusakten und Höllenfahrt Christi," in *Neutestamentliche Apokryphen in deutscher Übersetzung*, vol. 1, *Evangelien*, 5th ed., ed. Wilhelm Schneemelcher (Tübingen: J. C. B. Mohr [Paul Siebeck], 1987), 395.

1.2. Tertullian

Toward the end of the second century, Tertullian uses similar pro-Christian arguments in his *Apologeticum*. In chapter 5, he attempts to convince his adversaries that they should abandon their persecution of Christians and rescind their unjust laws. In such general context, he makes a specific reference (chap. 5.2) to a report concerning the divinity of Jesus, allegedly received by emperor Tiberius from Palestine and debated by the Roman senate.[7] Shortly afterward, Tertullian —like Justin—urges his opponents to consult their annals ("consulite commentarios vestros," chap. 5.3).[8] Tertullian's mention of the dispatch from Palestine is the first reflex of the tradition—closely associated with the *Gospel of Nicodemus* in the Middle Ages—of Pilate's correspondence with Rome; that he refers to the extant *AP* here, however, is doubtful.

Tertullian appeals to the same tradition in chapter 21.24 of the *Apologeticum*,[9] after an account of a series of miracles accompanying Jesus' Passion and confirming what the prophets had announced long before. "Ea omnia super Christo Pilatus," writes Tertullian, "et ipse iam pro sua conscientia christianus, Caesari tunc Tiberio nuntiavit. Sed et Caesares credidissent super Christo, si aut Caesares non essent necessarii saeculo, aut si et christiani potuissent esse Caesares" ("All these facts about Christ were reported to Tiberius, the reigning emperor, by Pilate, who was by now a Christian himself, as far as his conscience was concerned. And the Caesars, too, would have believed about Christ, had Caesars not been necessary for the world, or if Christians could have been Caesars"[10]). Thus, that Tertullian was familiar with the tradition of epistolary exchange between Pilate and the emperor seems very likely. It is not clear, however, in view of the brevity of Tertullian's references, whether that correspondence was indeed identical with the texts of the Pilate cycle extant today and whether at the time that correspondence was in any way connected with the *AP*, whose existence in the second century cannot be verified.

---

[7] Tertullian, Q. S. Fl. *Tertulliani Apologeticum*, ed. E. Dekkers, in *Quinti Septimi Florentis Tertulliani Opera*, pt. 1, *Opera catholica. Adversus Marcionem*, CC SL, vol. 1 (Turnhout: Brepols, 1954), 94–95.

[8] Ibid., 95.

[9] Ibid., 127.

[10] Tertullian, *Apology*, trans. Sister Emily Joseph Daly, in *The Fathers of the Church: A New Translation*, vol. 10 (Washington, D.C.: The Catholic University of America Press, 1962), 66.

1.3. Eusebius of Caesarea

Tertullian's comments were apparently echoed in the fourth century by Eusebius of Caesarea. In chapter 2.2.1 of his *Ecclesiastical History*, Eusebius mentions that "Pilate communicated to the Emperor Tiberius the story of the resurrection from the dead of our Saviour Jesus as already famous among all throughout all Palestine, together with the information he had gained of his other wonders and how he was already believed by many to be a God, in that after death he had risen from the dead."[11] This description of Pilate's report to Tiberius might reflect knowledge of a text from the cycle of Pilate, such as the *Anaphora Pilati*. But since shortly thereafter Eusebius cites a passage from Tertullian which refers to reports from Palestine, it seems more likely that Eusebius derived his knowledge of the correspondence between Pilate and Tiberius from Tertullian.

And yet Eusebius is the first patristic writer to provide possible clues to the context and circumstances of the emergence of the *AP*.[12] In his *Ecclesiastical History*, chapters 1.9 and 9.5–7,[13] he repeatedly refers to "hypomnēmata" ("memorials," "reports") of Pilate, forged as part of fierce anti-Christian propaganda; with the approval of Maximin Daïa, they were posted throughout towns and villages and taught to school children.[14] Given their audience—the populace at large and children—they must have been rather rudimentary in language and style and unsophisticated in concepts (possibly a list of charges against Jesus and some account of the trial). Eusebius makes no explicit reference to the Christian counterparts to those "hypomnēmata," but one suspects, admittedly on circumstantial evidence, that the *AP* known to us remain in some relation to those circulated under Maximin. Possibly, they were a Christian response to the polemics against Christianity evoked by Eusebius, and especially to the attacks against the divinity of Christ. If the pagan forgery indeed provoked the Christian text into

---

[11] Eusebius of Caesarea, *The Ecclesiastical History*, trans. Kirsopp Lake, 2 vols., The Loeb Classical Library (Cambridge, Mass.: Harvard University Press, 1964–65), 1:110–11.

[12] See Jean-Daniel Dubois, "Les *Actes de Pilate* au quatrième siècle," *Apocrypha – Le Champ des apocryphes 2, La Fable apocryphe 2* (1991): 85–98.

[13] Eusebius, *Ecclesiastical History*, 1:72–75, 2:338–51.

[14] Eusebius, *Ecclesiastical History*, chap. 9.5 (2:339; cf. chap. 9.7 [2:343]): "Having forged, to be sure, Memoirs of Pilate and our Saviour, full of every kind of blasphemy against Christ, with the approval of their chief they sent them round to every part of his dominions, with edicts that they should be exhibited openly for everyone to see in every place, both town and country, and that the primary teachers should give them to the children, instead of lessons, for study and committal to memory."

existence, then the birth of the apocryphon could be connected with a specific climate of social and religious controversies in the fourth century.

1.4. Epiphanius

A tangible proof of the existence of the Christian *Acts of Pilate* in the fourth century comes from the writings pertaining to the controversies about the fixation of the date of Easter. One of the participants in those debates, Epiphanius, testifies in his *Panarion*, chapters 50.1.5 and 50.1.8,[15] that the sect of Quartodecimans in Asia Minor, and especially in Cappadocia, using the *AP* («'απο τῶν ᾿Ακτων δῆθεν Πιλάτου»), determines the date of Easter on the eighth day before the calends of April (25 March). Epiphanius rejects that date not because the work on which it is based is apocryphal but because, he says, he knows other versions ("antigrapha") of the *AP* which give a different date for the Passion. Thus by the end of the fourth century, the text of the *AP* appears to have already diversified, reflecting the diversity and even controversy among early Christian communities.

1.5. Pseudo-Chrysostom

About a decade after Epiphanius's *Panarion*, a pseudo-Chrysostomian homily, dating from 387, confirms Epiphanius's report that the Quartodecimans fixed the date of Easter on the 25th day of March on the basis of the *AP*:

> Mais nous gardons, nous autres, la vertu du mystère dans son intégrité. En effet, le temps où le Sauveur a souffert n'est pas inconnu; car les *Actes faits sous Pilate* contiennent aussi la date de la Pâque. Il y est rapporté que le Sauveur a souffert le 8 des calendes d'avril: cette date tombe après l'équinoxe et est acceptée par les gens exacts. Tiens-toi à cette règle; ainsi tu te rendras compte que le Christ a souffert à cette date-là; le sachant, tu veilleras à faire toujours la Pâque après l'équinoxe, à l'imitation du Christ, tu fuiras d'une part la faute des hérétiques, et tu rechercheras d'autre part, la raison des temps.[16]

---

[15] Epiphanius, *Panarion*, ed. Karl Holl, rev. J. Dummer, GCS, vol. 31 (Berlin: Akademie Verlag, 1980), 245–46.

[16] F. Floëri and P. Nautin, *Homélies pascales*, vol. 3, Sources chrétiennes, vol. 48 (Paris: Cerf, 1957), 127, par. 17.

(But it is we who preserve the mystery's force in its entirety. Indeed, the time of the Savior's suffering is not unknown since the *Acts done under Pilate* also contains the date for Easter. It is reported in it that the Savior suffered on the 8th of the calends of April: this date falls after the equinox and is accepted by those who are scrupulous. Respect this rule; in this way you will realize that Christ suffered on that day. Knowing this, you will always be sure to celebrate Easter after the equinox, following Christ's example. You will, on the one hand, flee the mistake of heretics, and, on the other, you will search for the reason of time.)

The author of this homily, apparently a member of the sect, urges the adoption of the date given in the *AP*, which he refers to by the ancient title attested in the manuscripts of the oldest Greek version of the apocryphon, "Memorials [Gk. hypomnēmata, Lat. acta] of what happened to our Lord Jesus Christ under Pontius Pilate, governor over Judea." The pseudo-Chrisostomian homily provides, therefore, further proof of the apocryphon's circulation in the late fourth century and of its value to some Christian communities.

1.6. The liturgy of Jerusalem

Fifth-century writers, both Eastern and Western, are silent about the *AP*, but the apocryphon's active presence in the Christian milieu may, perhaps, be inferred from certain aspects of paschal liturgy of Jerusalem. One of the stations visited by pilgrims during the celebration of Good Friday was Pilate's praetorium, venerated as a place of Jesus' trial. That veneration was probably associated with the transformation of the portrait of Pilate: from a Roman governor responsible for Christ's death, he became a Christian figure, a Roman governor supporting the spread of Christianity. It seems that the *AP*, which emphasizes Pilate's pro-Christian stance, must have played a role in that transformation.[17]

1.7. Gregory of Tours

When in the sixth century Gregory of Tours evoked "Gesta Pilati ad Tiberium imperatorem missa" in his *Decem libris historiarum,* chapter

---

[17] Jean-Daniel Dubois, "La Représentation de la Passion dans la liturgie du Vendredi Saint: les *Actes de Pilate* et la liturgie ancienne de Jérusalem," in *Liturgie et anthropologie. Conférences St-Serge, XXVIᵉ semaine d'études liturgiques,* ed. A. M. Triacca and A. Pistoia (Rome: C. L. V.-Edizioni Liturgiche, 1990), 77–89.

1.21,[18] he gave an impression that the text consisted primarily of a miraculous narrative concerning Joseph of Arimathea combined with the story of the Passion. These two narratives indeed correspond to the first thirteen chapters of the extant *Acts of Pilate*. Gregory knew also the story of Pilate's suicide, often included in the cycle of Pilate apocrypha, but he seemed unaware of the narrative of the Descent into Hell, apparently not yet part of the *AP*. It is possible that he knew a version of the apocryphal text corresponding to Tischendorf's Greek recension A.

1.8. Photius

That the apocryphon continued to be used in the Latin West towards the end of the first millennium is evident from numerous extant Latin manuscripts. Greek manuscripts, however, are much later, and it is significant that the *Library* of Photius,[19] the ninth-century bishop of Constantinopole, does not mention any text that might be identified with the *Acts of Pilate*. This suggests that the *AP* was not generally known in the Greek-speaking world at that time. In the *Library*, Codex 171, Photius refers to a book of Eustratios addressed to Chrysippos, a priest in Jerusalem (fifth century), which only alludes to Gamaliel and Nicodemus.[20] The same Chrysippos is the supposed redactor of the *Encomium* of Theodor the Martyr,[21] which also alludes to Gamaliel and Nicodemus and to the discovery of their relics on the occasion of the invention of the relics of Stephen the Protomartyr. None of these texts, however, appears to be directly linked with the *AP*.

2. Manuscript and textual traditions

While the earliest stages in the life of the *GN* can be gleaned only from the scant remarks of church fathers, its subsequent medieval history emerges primarily from extant manuscript sources. Both the codices and the texts they preserve provide a flood of information—most of it still to be interpreted—on the apocryphon's evolution and dissemination throughout medieval Christendom.

---

[18] Gregory of Tours, *Gregorii episcopi Turonensis Libri historiarum X*, 2d ed., ed. Bruno Krusch and Wilhelmus Levison, MGH, Script. rer. Mer., vol. 1, pt. 1 (1951; repr., Hannover: Impensis Bibliopolii Hahniani, 1965), 17–18.

[19] Photius, *Bibliothèque*, ed. René Henry, indexed by J. Schamp, 9 vols. (Paris: Les Belles Lettres, 1957–91).

[20] Ibid. 2:165–67.

[21] Chrysippos, "Encomium of Theodor the Martyr," ed. A. Sigalas, *Byzantinisches Archiv* 7 (1921): 1–16.

2.1. Greek

Although the earliest manuscript of the *GN* preserves fragments of a Latin text, it has been traditionally assumed—and current research supports that assumption—that the apocryphon was originally composed in Greek. Extant Greek manuscripts preserve two major recensions of the *AP*, first distinguished by Constantinus de Tischendorf in his critical edition of the apocryphon.[22] Recension A has now been identified in some fifteen manuscripts, the oldest of which dates back to the twelfth century (Munich, Bayerische Staatsbibliothek [BSB] Cod. graec. 276).[23] It is usually designated in the title as "hypomnēmata," begins with a prologue dating the Passion, and covers the Passion of Jesus, the reports of his Ascension, and the story of Joseph of Arimathea (chaps. 1–16 of Tischendorf's edition). Only two manuscripts, Paris, Bibliothèque nationale (BN) MSS. gr. 770 (an. 1315) and gr. 947 (an. 1574), open with an additional prologue narrating the discovery by a certain Ananias of a work written by Nicodemus; this prologue occurs also, in full or in part, in the earliest Latin version, in Coptic, and in Syriac. None of the manuscripts of this Greek recension includes the *Descensus Christi ad inferos* (*DI*), which is absent from all Eastern translations and most likely did not belong to the original apocryphon. It is from this form A of the Greek *AP* that all translations into Latin and Eastern languages were carried out.

The Greek recension B of the *AP* survives in about 30 codices, the oldest of which has been assigned to the fourteenth century (Ann Arbor, Mich., University Library MS. 58).[24] It is typically designated in manuscript titles as "diēgēsis," a detailed or explicative narrative. The prologue which opens it represents a (con)fusion of the two prologues found in recension A and maintains that the work was written in Hebrew by Ananias and translated by Nicodemus. The bulk of recension B covers much the same ground as A but differs from it in the

---

[22] Constantinus de Tischendorf, ed., *Evangelia apocrypha*, 2d rev. ed. (Leipzig: H. Mendelssohn, 1876), 210–332. Tischendorf's edition overshadowed and replaced those by Andreas Birch, ed., *Auctarium Codicis apocryphi N. T. Fabriciani . . .*, vol. 1 (Copenhagen: Arntzen et Hartier, 1804), and by Johann Carl Thilo, ed., *Codex apocryphus Novi Testamenti*, vol. 1 (Leipzig: F. C. G. Vogel, 1832).

[23] Most manuscripts have been identified by Brigitte Tambrun-Krasker, whose research is now continued by Rémi Gounelle and Christiane Furrer.

[24] The best and most detailed studies of this Greek recension are those by Rémi Gounelle, "Recherches sur les *Actes* apocryphes *de Pilate* grecs, Recension B," 2 vols., Mémoire présenté pour l'obtention du Diplôme d'Études Approfondies, Université Paris X-Nanterre (1991), and idem, "*Acta Pilati* grecs B (*BHG* 779u–w), traditions textuelles," *Recherches augustiniennes* 26 (1992): 273–94. The following remarks are greatly indebted to these studies.

distribution of emphases. For example, B strives, to a greater extent than A, to portray Pilate as a Christian; it expands the account of the Crucifixion, death, and entombment at the expense of the proceedings before Pilate; and it endows the figure of Virgin Mary with special significance. Furthermore, recension B incorporates the story of the Descent into Hell, quite similar to that of the so-called Latin version A (see below). It appears, therefore, that Greek B is a result of a careful revision of the original Greek text, perhaps with the aid of a Latin translation. Since chapters 1–12.2 of recension B occur in homiliaries among readings for Good Friday and chapters 12.3–17 among those for Easter Sunday, such revision might have been motivated liturgically.[25] In contrast to Greek A, Greek B was never translated into other languages.

In many manuscripts, the Greek *AP* is accompanied by various annexes, usually other texts of the cycle of Pilate, such as the *Paradosis Pilati*, the *Anaphora Pilati*, and the correspondence between Pilate and Tiberius, Herod, or Claudius. This association may have influenced the way the *AP* was perceived and used over the centuries, although Brigitte Tambrun-Krasker's research indicates that Pilate apocrypha were not confined to the manuscripts of the *AP*.

2.2. Latin

Although the Latin *Evangelium Nicodemi* is clearly translated from Greek, several Latin codices attest to the history of the apocryphon before the period of the earliest known Greek manuscripts.[26] The most important among them, a palimpsest from Vienna, Österreichische Nationalbibliothek MS. 563, may go as far back as the fifth century.[27] Its fragmentary text preserves the two prologues and parts of

---

[25] Gounelle, "Recherches sur les *Actes* apocryphes *de Pilate* grecs," 2:72. It is noteworthy that Greek B was still printed in Athens at the end of the nineteenth century and at the beginning of the twentieth to stimulate orthodox piety; for a list of those editions, see bibliography, sect. 1.1.1.1.

[26] For a list of Latin manuscripts antedating the twelfth century, see Zbigniew Izydorczyk, "The Unfamiliar *Evangelium Nicodemi*," *Manuscripta* 33 (1989): 178. All known Latin manuscripts of the *EN* are listed by idem, *Manuscripts of the "Evangelium Nicodemi": A Census*, Subsidia Mediaevalia, vol. 21 (Toronto: Pontifical Institute of Mediaeval Studies, 1993).

[27] The manuscript has been described by Guy Philippart, "Fragments palimpsestes latins du Vindobonensis 563 (Vᵉ siècle?). Évangile selon S. Matthieu. Évangile de l'enfance selon Thomas. Évangile de Nicodème," *Analecta Bollandiana* 90 (1972): 391–411, and by Myriam Despineux, "Une Version latine palimpseste du Vᵉ siècle de l'Évangile de Nicodème (*Vienne, ÖNB MS 563*)," *Scriptorium* 42 (1988): 176–83; the text of the *EN* has been edited by Guy Philippart, "Les Fragments palimpsestes de l'Évangile de Nicodème dans le *Vindobonensis 563* (Vᵉ s.?)," *Analecta Bollandiana* 107 (1989): 171–88.

chapters 1–16 but no *DI*. Later manuscripts support at least three distinct recensions of the Latin apocryphon (referred to as *EN* A, B, and C, respectively), whose exact mutual relationships have not yet been determined. Most numerous are texts of type A, the least of type C. The recensions differ, at times considerably, in terms of language, style, and, to some extent, contents, even though they all include an account of the Passion, Resurrection, and Ascension of Jesus, the narrative of Joseph of Arimathea, and the story of Christ's Harrowing of Hell. The differences confirm that the *EN* was subject to considerable editorial activity since the early Middle Ages. Each of the three major recensions provided a basis for later vernacular translations.

Other Pilate apocrypha also abound in Latin. However, in contrast to many Eastern works on Pilate which showed Pilate as Christian or at least as sympathetic to Christianity, such as the *Paradosis Pilati*, the Latin texts tend to portray him as a villain responsible for Christ's death and deserving of his inglorious end.[28]

2.3. Coptic

The *Acts of Pilate* did not remain confined to the Greco-Roman world but were translated and adapted by various Southern and Eastern Christian communities. The perfectly preserved Papyrus no. 1 of the Museo Egizio di Torino proves that the apocryphon was known in the Coptic church.[29] Written probably in the tenth century, the Turin papyrus preserves a complete Coptic translation of the *AP*, which on linguistic grounds might, perhaps, be placed in the fifth century.[30]

---

[28] The Latin traditions of the *Evangelium Nicodemi* and of the associated Pilate apocrypha are explored more fully later in this volume.

[29] Before the meticulous edition by Francesco Rossi, *Trascrizione di un codice copto del Museo Egizio di Torino con illustrazione e note*, Memorie della Reale accademia delle scienze di Torino, 2d ser., vol. 35 (Turin: Stamperia reale, 1883), over a hundred years ago, the Coptic text was known to scholars only through its Latin translation prepared by A. Peyron for Tischendorf, who included it in the critical apparatus to his edition of the apocryphon. The papyrus was subsequently edited and translated into French by E. Révillout, *Les Apocryphes coptes, II. Acta Pilati et supplément à l'Évangile des douze apôtres*, Patrologia Orientalis, vol. 9, pt. 2 (Paris: F. Didot, 1907). Recently, M. Vandoni and T. Orlandi, *Vangelo di Nicodemo*, pt. 1, *Testo copto dai papiri di Torino*, pt. 2, *Traduzione dal copto e commentario*, Testi e documenti per lo studio dell'antichità, vols. 15 and 15a (Milan: Instituto Editoriale Cisalpino, 1966), produced yet another edition, accompanied by an Italian translation and commentary. For the dating of the Turin papyrus, see Vandoni and Orlandi, *Vangelo di Nicodemo*, 1:9.

[30] Vandoni and Orlandi, *Vangelo di Nicodemo*, 2:76–77. G. C. O'Ceallaigh, "Dating the Commentaries of Nicodemus," *Harvard Theological Review* 56 (1963): 30, argues that "the original Coptic translation [is] no earlier than the tenth [century]."

The Coptic version corresponds by and large to Tischendorf's Greek recension A. It has two prologues but, like the Greek, does not contain the narrative of the Descent into Hell, although the theme of catabasis is well attested in such Coptic works as *Pistis Sophia*, two Nag Hammadi tractates *Silvanos* and *Trimorphic Protennoia* (NHC 7 and 13, respectively), and two fragments on Christ's victory over hell from *The Book of the Resurrection of Christ by Bartholomew* in London, British Library (BL) MS. Or. 6954, fols. 44–45.[31] Unlike the Greek text, the Coptic translation shows considerable precision in the use of terminology for administrative, judiciary, and religious concepts, which betrays its decidedly Egyptian background.

Independent of the Turin papyrus are the two Coptic fragments of the *AP* published soon after the appearance of Rossi's edition by P. Lacau from Paris, BN MSS. copt. 129[17], fol. 50, and copt. 129[18], fol. 140.[32] The first fragment, a folio paginated 27–28, reflects for the most part Tischendorf's Greek *AP* A, chapter 9.1.3–9.3.2;[33] the second fragment, paginated 31–32, compares with *AP* A, chapters 10.1.6–11.1.[34] These two folios clearly come from the same manuscript, and their pagination indicates that the manuscript originally contained a complete version of the *AP*.[35] A careful comparison of the fragments and the Turin papyrus against the Greek material reveals that most of the readings unique to the fragments can be found in Greek manuscripts unknown to Tischendorf. Furthermore, whereas the biblical quotations and allusions in the Turin papyrus seem in harmony with the canonical form of the Bible, those in the two fragments preserve a divergent text. This evidence strongly suggests that the Greek text underlying the fragments must have been different from that which lies behind the

---

[31] B. Layton, *Catalogue of Coptic Literary Manuscripts in the British Library Acquired since the Year 1906* (London: The British Library, 1987), 110–11, no. 99.

[32] P. Lacau, ed., "Acta Pilati," in *Fragments d'apocryphes coptes*, Mémoires publiés par les Membres de l'Institut français d'archéologie orientale du Caire, vol. 9 (Cairo: Institut français d'archélogie orientale, 1904). Lacau's work was improved upon by O. von Lemm, "Kleine koptische Studien. XLII. Eine neutestamentliche apokryphe Geschichte" and "XLIV. Eine neue Bartholomeus-Apokalypse," *Izvestiia Imperatorskoj Akademii Nauk* (St. Petersburg), 5th series, vol. 21, no. 3 (1904): 76–89, 151–61 (reprinted in O. von Lemm, *Kleine koptische Studien I–LVIII*, ed. P. Nagel, Subsidia Byzantina, vol. 10 [Leipzig: Zentralantiquariat der DDR, 1972], with the same pagination). These fragments were also reprinted in Révillout, *Les Apocryphes coptes*, II, 127 [153]–129 [155] and 129 [155]–132 [158].

[33] Tischendorf, *Evangelia apocrypha*, 240–42; cf. the Latin *Gesta Pilati*, chaps. 9.1.3–9.3.2 (Tischendorf, *Evangelia apocrypha*, 358–59).

[34] Tischendorf, *Evangelia apocrypha*, 246–48; cf. *Gesta Pilati*, chaps. 10.1.8–11.1 (Tischendorf, *Evangelia apocrypha*, 361–63).

[35] Lacau, *Fragments*, 1 n. 3.

papyrus and that the *AP* must have been translated into Coptic twice, each time from a different Greek exemplar.

If we believe the testimony of Johannes de Hildesheim, writing in the second half of the fourteenth century, the medieval Coptic church put the *GN* to liturgical use. In his *Liber de gestis ac trina beatissimorum trium regum translatione,* Johannes remarks, without citing his source, that in Coptic churches the apocryphon is read during mass.[36] Unfortunately, he offers no details or explanations of this practice, so it is impossible to know which version might have enjoyed such popularity. Modern scholarship has not yet been able to verify this tantalizing comment.

The Coptic tradition has also preserved several pieces from the Pilate cycle, such as the *Encomium in Mariam Magdalenam* and *Homilia de lamentis Mariae,*[37] but their exact relation to the Coptic *Acts* still needs to be investigated. The *Homilia de morte Pilati* was originally composed in Coptic although it is now extant only in Arabic and Ethiopic.[38]

2.4. Arabic

The widespread circulation of Pilate apocrypha in the southern and eastern Mediterranean basin is further confirmed by their translations into Arabic. Although no texts of the *Acts of Pilate* have yet been found, several pieces from the Pilate cycle have. Two of them, the *Homilia de morte Pilati* and the *Homilia de lamentis Mariae,*[39] are preserved in

---

[36] See Ugo Monneret de Villard, *Le leggende orientali sui magi evangelici,* Studi e testi, vol. 163 (Vatican City: Biblioteca Apostolica Vaticana, 1952), 192.

[37] Geerard, *Clavis,* nos. 73, 74. For the former, see R. G. Coquin and G. Godron, "Un Encomion copte sur Marie-Madeleine attribué à Cyrille de Jérusalem," *Bulletin de l'Institut français d'archéologie orientale* 90 (1990): 169–212; for the latter, Lacau, *Fragments,* 15–18, and E. Révillout, *Les Apocryphes coptes, I,* Patrologia Orientalis, vol. 2, pt. 2 (Paris: F. Didot, 1907), 170–74.

[38] Geerard, *Clavis,* no. 75. Related to the *AP* are also the Sa'îdic fragments in the Bodleian Library, published by John W. B. Barns, "Bodleian Fragments of a Sa'îdic Version of the *Acta Pilati,*" in *Coptic Studies in Honor of Walter Ewing Crum,* ed. M. Malinine, Bulletin of the Byzantine Institute of America, vol. 2 (Boston, Mass.: Byzantine Institute, 1950), 245–50.

[39] Three manuscripts of the *Homilia de morte Pilati* were known already to Thilo, *Codex apocryphus,* clvii–clix: Paris, BN MSS. karshuni 273 (saec. XVI), and ar. 152 (saec. XVI), and Vatican City, Biblioteca Apostolica Vaticana (Bibl. Apost. Vat.) MS. ar. 55. The second of these was edited early in the twentieth century by E. Galtier, "Le Martyre de Pilate," in *Mémoires et fragments inédits,* ed. E. Chassinat (Cairo: Institut français d'archélogie orientale, 1912), 31–103, and again, with an English translation, by A. Mingana, "Timothy's Apology for Christianity, the Lament of the Virgin, the Martyrdom of Pilate," in *Woodbrooke Studies: Christian Documents in Syriac, Arabic and Garshuni,* ed. and trans. Alphonse Mingana (Cam-

several mostly post-medieval manuscripts but are descended from much earlier traditions as both are also extant in homilies attributed to Cyriacus of Behensā, a Coptic author and bishop of Oxyrhynchos. Moreover, these two texts provided sources for Ethiopic translations. Even more symptomatic of the *AP*'s diffusion and influence are the Arabic redactions of the *Anaphora* and *Paradosis* of Pilate, two common satellites of the Greek *AP* which frequently accompany the apocryphon in its other linguistic versions.[40]

The catabasis myth was also treated in Arabic: a text comprising an extensive dialogue between Death and the Devil as well as a brief account of the Descent was first edited and translated into Russian from a ninth-century manuscript by I. Krachkovskij.[41] This dialogic piece is reminiscent of the *DI* but apparently not directly related to it, being based on the hymns of Ephraem the Syrian.[42]

2.5. Ethiopic

Dependent on the Arabic are the Ethiopic traditions concerning Pilate. The *Homilia de lamentis Mariae* and the *Homilia de morte Pilati* were both translated from Arabic through the efforts of Abbā Salāmā (1348–1387/ 88); the former survives in numerous codices, the latter in four.[43] The

---

bridge: W. Heffer and Sons, 1928), 2:241–333, who used several additional codices (Birmingham, Selly Oak Colleges MSS. Mingana Syr. [Karshuni] 127 [an. 1683]; Mingana Syr. 355 [ca. 1800]; and Vatican City, Bibl. Apost. Vat. MS. Vat. sir. [Karshuni] 199 [an. 1545]). The same text is preserved also in Paris, BN MS. ar. 4874[2] (saec. XIX). The *Homilia de lamentis Mariae* has been edited by Mingana, "Timothy's Apology," 163–240, from Mingana Syr. [Karshuni] 87 (saec. XV) and Mingana Syr. 127. Cf. Georg Graf, *Geschichte der christlichen arabischen Literatur,* vol. 1, *Die Übersetzungen,* Studi e testi, vol. 118 (Vatican City: Biblioteca Apostolica Vaticana, 1944), 238–40.

[40] The Arabic *Anaphora Pilati* and *Paradosis Pilati* have been edited, together with the Syriac recensions, by Margaret Dunlop Gibson, *Apocrypha Sinaitica,* Studia Sinaitica, vol. 5 (London: C. J. Clay and Sons, 1896), 1–14 [translation] and 16–26 [edition], from Mount Sinaï, St. Catherine Monastery MSS. Ar. 445 [saec. XII; copied from a codex dated 799] and Ar. 508 [saec. IX–X]). Since the late nineteenth century, several other manuscripts of these two texts have been identified: Paris, BN MS. ar. 4896[2] (saec. XVI); Sinaï MSS. Ar. 35 (saec. IX–X) and Ar. 9 (an. 965); Strasbourg, Bibliothèque nationale et universitaire MS. ar. 150 (an. 905); Milan, Biblioteca Ambrosiana MS. X. 198 Sup. (saec. XI); Cambridge, University Library MSS. Addit. 2281 (Karshuni; an. 1484) and Addit. 2885 (Karshuni; an. 1771); Cairo, Coptic Museum MS. Ar. 32 (Liturgical no. 15; an. 1634); and Oxford, Bodl. Lib. MS. Syr. 140 (Karshuni).

[41] I. Krachkovskij, "Novozavetnyj apokrif v arabskoj rukopisi 885–886 goda po R. Khr.," *Vizantijskij vremennik* 14 (1907): 246–75.

[42] See G. Garitte, "Homelie d'Éphrem 'Sur la mort et le diable.' Version géorgienne et version arabe," *Le Muséon* 82 (1969), 123–63.

[43] Both works were edited (the *Homilia de morte Pilati* from only one manuscript), with German translations, by M.-A. van den Oudenrijn, *Gamaliel. Aethio-*

Homilia de morte Pilati is extant in two versions: in one Pilate suffers martyrdom through crucifixion, and in the other through decapitation.[44] As far as we know, no Ethiopic version of the *Acts of Pilate* survives, but given the interest in and veneration for the figure of Pilate south of the Nile Valley,[45] it is possible that such a text once existed.

2.6. Syriac

More tangible than for the Arabic and Ethiopic traditions is the evidence for the knowledge of the *Acts of Pilate* in Syriac and Palestinian Christian communities. In 1908 I. E. Rahmani published a Syriac recension of the *AP* from two acephalous manuscripts, a fourteenth-century codex from Mossoul (siglum A) and a parchment from St. Samona in Mediad near Mardin (siglum B).[46] Two folios from a third manuscript—Birmingham, Selly Oak Colleges MS. Syr. 639—written around 1200 in a "West Syrian hand," have been published by Mingana.[47]

In general, the Syriac text resembles the Greek A and Coptic ver-

---

pische Texte zur Pilatusliteratur (Fribourg: Universitätsverlag, 1959); for the dating of the *Homilia de lamentis Mariae*, see pp. xviii–xxi, and for its manuscripts, pp. xlix–liv. A new edition of the *Homilia de morte Pilati* (from all four codices), accompanied by a French translation, has been recently published by Robert Beylot, *Le Martyre de Pilate éthiopien*, Patrologia Orientalis, vol. 45, fasc. 4, no. 204 (Turnhout: Brepols, 1993).

[44] The second version was first edited and translated into Italian by E. Cerulli, "L'Oriente Cristiano nell'unità delle sue tradizioni," in *Atti del Convegno Internazionale sul tema: L'Oriente Cristiano nella storia della civiltà (Roma 31 marzo–3 aprile 1963, Firenze 4 aprile 1963)*, Problemi attuali di scienza e di cultura, quaderno, no. 62 (Rome: Accademia Nazionale dei Lincei, 1964), 9–43 (reprinted in E. Cerulli, *La letteratura etiopica con un saggio sull'Oriente Cristiano*, 3d enl. ed. [Florence: G. C. Sansoni, 1968], 193–229).

[45] Cf. E. Cerulli, "Tiberius and Pontius Pilate in Ethiopian Tradition and Poetry," *Proceedings of the British Academy* 59 (1973): 141–58; idem, "Un Hymne éthiopien à Pilate sanctifié," *Mélanges de l'Université Saint-Joseph* 49 (1975–76): 591–94; and Robert Beylot, "Bref Aperçu des principaux textes éthiopiens dérivés des Acta Pilati," *Langues orientales anciennes. Philologie et linguistique* 1 (1988): 181–95.

[46] I. E. Rahmani, ed. and trans., *Hypomnemata Domini nostri seu Acta Pilati antiqua versio Syriaca*, Studia Syriaca, vol. 2 (Typis Patriarchalibus in Seminario Scharfensi in Monte Libano, 1908). Rahmani dated MS. B to the eighth century, but O'Ceallaigh, "Dating the Commentaries," 42–49, contests that dating.

[47] Alphonse Mingana, *Catalogue of the Mingana Collection of Manuscripts Now in the Possession of the Trustees of the Woodbrooke Settlement, Birmingham*, vol. 3, *Additional Christian Arabic and Syriac Manuscripts* (Cambridge: W. Heffer and Sons, 1939), 79–81 (text) and 81–85 (translation). Four additional manuscripts of the Syriac *AP* are currently being studied by A. Frey: Sinaï, MS. Syr. 82 (saec. XIII ?); Sharfah MS. Patr. 79 (today in Dar'Un-Harissa, Lebanon; this is a copy of Rahmani's manuscript A from Mossoul); Birmingham, Selly Oak Colleges MS. Mingana Syr. 4; and Cambridge, Mass., Harvard University, Houghton Library MS. Syr. 91 (possibly a copy of the Mingana Syr. 4).

sions. It contains the first prologue of Ananias, although placed at the end of the apocryphon; the second prologue may have been lost together with the beginning of the text. Like other Eastern versions, it lacks an account of Christ's Descent into Hell. Among its idiosyncrasies may be counted the names of the two thieves, given here as Titus (good) and Dymachos (evil); these particular names occur in other Eastern traditions (Arabic and Ethiopic) but are unknown in Greek or Latin.[48] In spite of Rahmani's claim of great antiquity for the Syriac *AP*—he believed it reflects a fourth-century Greek prototype—its numerous abridgements and alterations resemble late revisions in other languages and place the translation, according to O'Ceallaigh, in the tenth century or later.[49]

In the two manuscripts used by Rahmani, additional Pilate apocrypha are annexed to the *AP*. They include the correspondence between Pilate and Herod and fragments of an exchange between Pilate and one Theodorus concerning the legality of Pilate's sentence against Jesus. One of the codices contains also a note by one Ursinus or Orsinus, apparently Jesus' contemporary, which confirms that Pilate sent a letter to Tiberius reporting the death of Jesus crucified by the Jews. This might represent a confirmation of Tertullian's report on the dispatches from Palestine to Tiberius, except that Orsinus is not otherwise known and hence this testimony appears suspect. The Syriac translations of the *Anaphora Pilati* and *Paradosis Pilati*, published from Sinaï MS. Syr. 82, by Gibson, circulated independently of the extant *AP*.[50]

2.7. Palestinian Aramaic

Though concrete, the evidence for the presence of the *Acts of Pilate* in Palestine is unfortunately rather limited. It consists of a few scraps of text in Palestinian Aramaic, corresponding to the Greek recension A, chapters 1.6–2.5, recovered from the lower script of two ninth-century palimpsest fragments.[51] The Palestinian Aramaic translation of which

---

[48] For the thieves' other names, see Bruce M. Metzger, "Names for the Nameless in the New Testament: A Study in the Growth of Christian Tradition," in his *New Testament Studies: Philological, Versional, and Patristic*, New Testament Tools and Studies, vol. 10 (Leiden: E. J. Brill, 1980), 33–39.

[49] O'Ceallaigh, "Dating the Commentaries," 47; cf. similar comments by Vandoni and Orlandi, *Vangelo di Nicodemo*, 2:40 n. 13, and by Scheidweiler, "Nikodemusevangelium," 397 n. 3.

[50] Gibson, *Apocrypha Sinaitica*; cf. Sebastian Brock, "A Fragment of the *Acta Pilati* in Christian Palestinian Aramaic," *Journal of Theological Studies*, n.s., 22 (1971): 158–59 n. 4.

[51] The text has been printed by F. Schulthess, ed., *Christlich-palästinische Fragmente aus der Omajjaden-Moschee zu Damaskus*, Abhandlungen der königlichen

the extant passages are remnants was made from a Greek rather than from a Syriac source; the date of that translation is still uncertain.[52]

2.8. Armenian

The *Acts of Pilate* were also known to the Armenians, Georgians, and Slavs. The Armenian manuscript tradition of the *AP*, comprising at least nine codices, goes back to the twelfth century or earlier and reflects two forms of the translation.[53] Four manuscripts—Paris, BN MSS. arm. 110 (an. 1194) and arm. 178 (saec. XII), Jerusalem, St. James Monastery MS. Arm. 1a (an. 1417), and Venice, San Lazzaro MS. 104 (saec. XV–XVI)—preserve what appears to be the older text; the remaining manuscripts—Erevan, Matenadaran MSS. 993 (an. 1456), 1521 (an. 1404), and 4670 (an. 1401); and Jerusalem, St. James Monastery MSS. Arm. 9 (saec. XVI) and Arm. 173 (an. 1512)[54]—represent later redactions. The original translation was done, according to Conybeare, "most likely before 600 A.D." from Greek.[55] The later recensions are characterized by a number of peculiar readings and additional borrowings from the canonical gospels. Since many of their variants have counterparts in Greek or other recensions, Conybeare argued that they "must be the result of a fresh comparison with Greek text of the original Armenian version."[56] These revised texts often fluctuate, with most extensive and, perhaps, telling alterations affecting the charges of the Jews against Jesus. None of the Armenian texts includes the *DI*.

Gesellschaft der Wissenschaften zu Göttingen, philologisch-historische Klasse, N.F., vol. 8, no. 3 (Berlin: Weidmannsche Buchhandlung, 1905), 134–36, and identified by Brock, "A Fragment," 157–58.

[52] With his current research on these fragments, A. Desreumaux hopes to shed some light on the transmission context of the manuscript to which they once belonged.

[53] The Armenian translation of the *AP* has been known in the West mainly through F. C. Conybeare, ed., "Acta Pilati," in *Studia biblica et ecclesiastica: Essays Chiefly in Biblical and Patristic Criticism*, vol. 4 (Oxford: Clarendon Press, 1896), 59–132. Without printing the originals, Conybeare retranslated two Armenian versions into Greek and Latin. The Armenian text has been published by H. E. Tayets'i, *T'angaran haykakan hin ew nor dprut'eants'*, vol. 2, *Ankanon girk' nor ktakaranats'* (Venice: San Lazzaro, 1898), 313–45; although based on five manuscripts, Tayets'i's text conflates two distinct recensions of the apocryphon. A completely new edition of the Armenian versions is being prepared by B. Outtier, who is studying several manuscripts unknown to Conybeare and Tayets'i.

[54] Related to the *AP* may be an unedited homiletic fragment in Kipchak (Old Turkish in Armenian script), preserved in Paris, BN MS. arm. 194.

[55] Conybeare, "Acta Pilati," 65. This dating is contested by O'Ceallaigh, who places it in the early twelfth century ("Dating the Commentaries," 41).

[56] Conybeare, "Acta Pilati," 62.

In one of the later branches of the Armenian textual tradition, comprising several manuscripts, the authorship of the *AP* is attributed to James of Jerusalem (son of Zebedee, the traditional apostle of the Armenians). This redaction, printed apparently in 1710,[57] also links the *AP* with the *Paradosis Pilati* and the text called *Mystery of the Passion*. In other branches, copies of the *AP* are transmitted jointly with various other pieces of the cycle of Pilate, such as an account of the dream of Pilate's wife and the letters of Pilate, or with certain thematically related texts, such as the letter of James to Quadratus and a homily for Good Friday.

2.9. Georgian

According to C'. K'urc'ikiże, the recent editor of the Georgian *Acts of Pilate*, the Georgian translation survives in about twenty manuscripts, ranging from the eleventh (Sinaï MS. Georg. 78, an. 1031) to the nineteenth century.[58] Of the eight codices she used for the edition, three contain sixteen chapters, while the remaining five end in chapter 13. This frequent abridgement is apparently indicative of the desire to suppress the account of the three rabbis concerning the Ascension and to confine the narrative to the events known from the canonical texts. K'urc'ikiże's text is relatively close to Tischendorf's Greek recension A, although with some modifications. For example, the beginning of the apocryphon is altered, and the accusation that Christ was born of fornication is omitted. Like Greek A, the Georgian version does not contain the *DI*. To judge from the textual and linguistic features, the Georgian translation was done in the eighth century at the latest.

Although K'urc'ikiże's edition constructs a single, uniform text, B. Outtier's independent research indicates that the Georgian tradition comprises two sorts of texts which may involve—like their Coptic counterparts—two different Greek sources. The more recent Georgian redaction, preserved in nineteenth-century manuscripts, uses a Greek text different from the one that underlies the early Georgian translation.

---

[57] Cf. Raymond H. Ke'vorkian, *Catalogue des "incunables" arméniens* (Geneva: P. Cramer, 1986), no. 128.

[58] C'. K'urc'ikiże, ed., *Nik'odimosis apok'rip'uli c'ignis k'art'uli versia* (Tbilisi: Mecniereba, 1985). The first Georgian text of the *AP* was published in 1907 by A. Khakhanov in the Proceedings of the Oriental Section of the Russian Archaeological Society in Moscow ("Evangelie Nikodima," in *Drevnosti vostochnyia: Trudy Vostochnoj kommissii Imperatorskogo moskovskogo arkheologicheskogo obshchestva* [Moscow], vol. 3, no. 1 (1907): 1–20). Somewhat earlier, I. A. Džavachišvili had copied the apocryphon from Sinaï MS. Georg. 78; his transcript, however, did not appear in print until 1947 (*Sinis mt'is k'art'ul helnacert'a ağceriloba* [Tbilisi: Academy of Sciences, 1947]).

Apart from the *AP*, the Georgians knew also other Pilate apocrypha. Perhaps the most important among them is the *Narratio Iosephi de Arimathaea*, which in the Georgian version includes an account of the foundation of the church in Lydda (that account is extant also in Greek and Latin but as an independent text).[59]

2.10. Slavonic

Slavonic versions of the *Acts of Pilate*, although known since the nineteenth century, remain relatively unexplored. Of well over sixty manuscripts in various Slavonic languages listed by Aurelio de Santos Otero,[60] fewer than a quarter have been closely studied or edited. Most recently, A. Vaillant published the so-called "long version" of the apocryphon from three manuscripts.[61] This "long" redaction is based on a full Latin text and includes a translation of the *DI*. It survives in some eighteen manuscripts, including two Glagolithic fragments (which, according to Biserka Grabar, stand closer to the original translation than the Cyrillic copies)[62] and is excerpted in four others. Linguistic evidence suggests that it was translated in the eleventh or twelfth century in Croatia or Dalmatia;[63] it is not impossible, however, that the apocryphon was translated more than once and that not all manuscripts of the "long version" contain the same translation.

---

[59] See Geerard, *Clavis*, no. 77, and the literature listed there. Most recently, the text has been discussed by Michel van Esbroeck, "L'Histoire de l'Église de Lydda dans deux textes géorgiens," *Bedi Kartlisa* 35 (1977): 108–31.

[60] Aurelio de Santos Otero, *Die handschriftliche Überlieferung der altslavischen Apokryphen*, vol. 2 (Berlin: W. de Gruyter, 1981), 61–98. Santos Otero's list of manuscripts containing the *Acts* in Slavonic translations is, however, neither exhaustive nor accurate; for numerous corrections and additions, see Francis J. Thomson, "Apocrypha Slavica: II," *The Slavonic and East European Review* 63, no. 1 (1985): 79–83.

[61] André Vaillant, ed., *L'Évangile de Nicodème: Texte slave et texte latin*, Centre de recherches d'histoire et de philologie de la IVème section de l'E. P. H. E, vol. 2, Hautes études orientales, vol. 1 (Geneva: Droz, 1968). This version was previously edited by Ljubomir Stojanović, "Nekoliko rukopisa iz bečke Carske Biblioteke," *Glasnik Srpskog učenog društva* (Belgrade) 63 (1885): 89–120, and by Ivan Franko, *Apokryfy i lehendy z ukraïns'kykh rukopysiv*, Pamiatnyky ukraïn'sko-rus'koï movy i literatury, edited by Stepan Komarevs'kyi, vol. 2 (Lvov: Naukove Tovarystvo im. Shevchenka, 1899), 252–72 and 293–304.

[62] Biserka Grabar, "Über das Problem der längeren Fassung des Nikodemusevangeliums in der älteren slavischen Literatur," in *Byzance et les Slaves: Études de civilisation. Mélanges Ivan Dujčev* (Paris: Association des amis des études archéologiques des mondes byzantino-slaves et du christianisme oriental, 1979), 201–6.

[63] Thomson, "Apocrypha Slavica," 80. Vaillant, *L'Évangile de Nicodème*, ix, dates it to the tenth century.

The "short version" of the Slavonic *AP*—without the *DI*—represents two translations, both made in Bulgaria and both derived from the Greek recension A. One of them, extant in two manuscripts, probably belongs to the twelfth century; the other, attested by nineteen codices, may be some two centuries later.[64] The latter translation is usually combined with the *Anaphora Pilati* and the *Paradosis Pilati*.[65]

At least nine manuscripts (and perhaps as many as twenty-five) contain a sixteenth-century Russian redaction of the *AP*, combining the "short version" with the *DI* of the "long" one.[66] The *AP* was also translated into Old Czech, jointly with the *Cura sanitatis Tiberii* (several manuscripts besides the one mentioned by de Santos Otero), and into Old Polish (not listed by de Santos Otero).[67] Other apocrypha relating to Pilate, such as *Anaphora, Paradosis, Tiberii rescriptum, Narratio Iosephi de Arimathea*, and *Narratio de Martha*, often circulated independently of the *AP* and survive in numerous manuscripts.[68]

Badly in need of systematic study, the Slavonic translations may prove important for reconstructing the transmission history of the *AP*. Since the Slavonic tradition absorbed both Western and Eastern

---

[64] Thomson, "Apocrypha Slavica," 80.

[65] The "short version" was printed in full or in part by A. N. Pypin, *Lozhnyia i otrechennyia knigi russkoj stariny*, Pamiatniki starinnoj russkoj literatury izdavaemye grafom Grigoriem Kushelevym-Bezborodko, vol. 3, Slavistic Printings and Reprintings, vol. 97, no. 2 (1862; repr., The Hague: Mouton, 1970), 91–108; G. Daničić, "Dva apokrifna jevangjelja," *Starine* (Jugoslovenska Akademija Znanosti i Umiejetnosti, Zagreb) 4 (1872): 130–46; I. Ia. Porfir'ev, *Apokrificheskiia skazaniia o novozavetnykh litsakh i sobytiiakh, po rukopisiam Solovetskoj biblioteki*, Sbornik Otdeleniia russkogo iazyka i slovesnosti Imperatorskoj Akademii Nauk, vol. 52, no. 4 (St. Petersburg: Tipografiia Imperatorskoj Akademii Nauk, 1890), 164–97; M. N. Speranskij, "Slavianskiia apokrificheskiia evangeliia," in *Trudy vos'mogo arkheologicheskogo s'ezda v Moskve, 1890* (Moscow: Tovarishchestvo tip. A. I. Mamotova, 1895), 2:92–133, 144–55; and I. Iagich, "Kriticheskia zametki k slavianskomu perevodu dvukh apokrificheskikh skazanij," *Izvestiia Otdeleniia russkogo iazyka i sloves-nosti Imperatorskoj Akademii Nauk* (St. Petersburg), vol. 3, no. 3 (1898): 793–822.

[66] Thomson, "Apocrypha Slavica," 81.

[67] Cf. ibid., 82. For the Czech versions, see also Jiří Pražák, *Katalog rukopisů křižovnické knihovny, nyní deponovaných ve Státní knihovně České socialistické republiky v Praze* (Prague: Státní knihovna České socialistické republiky, 1980), 107, and Josef Truhlář, *Katalog Českých rukopisů C. K. Veřejné a Universitní knihovny Pražské* (Prague: Nákladem České Akademie Císaře Františka Josefa pro Vědy, Slovesnost a Umění, 1906), 24; for the Polish version, see Roman Pollak, ed., *Piśmiennictwo staropolskie* (Państwowy Instytut Wydawniczy, 1963), 229.

[68] The text published by Josip Hamm in *Acta Pilati i Cvitje*, Stari Pisci Hrvatski, vol. 40 (Zagreb: Jugoslavenska Akademija Znanosti i Umjetnosti, 1987), under the title *Acta Pilati* is a story of Pilate, not the *Gospel of Nicodemus* proper; similarly, G. Il'inskij, "Apokrif 'Acta Pilati' v spiske Orbel'skoj Triodi XIII veka," *Russkij filologicheskij vestnik* 56 (1906): 213–17, prints a text combining the *Anaphora* and the *Paradosis Pilati*.

models, it may not only illuminate the points of contact and the nature of interactions between Latin and Greek texts, but also bring to light some archaic features not attested in the extant versions of either source tradition.

3. Conclusion

Although patristic testimonies concerning the *Acts of Pilate* are scarce, what there is suggests that some Pilate apocrypha, and especially Pilate's correspondence with Rome, may have been known since Tertullian. In the fourth century, Eusebius describes a social and religious milieu from which the *AP* might have emerged: the anti-Christian climate under Maximin Daïa, intensified by the publication of the false "Memorials of Pilate." The *AP* may have originated in the ensuing controversies between Christianity and the Roman Empire, when philosophers and thinkers revived and adapted the arguments of earlier controversies between the Jews and the Christians concerning Jesus' divine origin and miracles. The evidence from the latter half of the fourth century (Epiphanius, pseudo-Chrysostom) indicates that the *AP* must already have been in circulation for some time since its texts have already diversified; moreover, that evidence suggests that it was used during the disputes about the fixation of the date for Easter. The fifth-century paschal liturgy of Jerusalem may also show traces of its influence. By the sixth century, the *AP* is apparently known in the Latin West (Gregory of Tours), although still without the *DI*. The interest in the apocryphon did not, of course, continue steady throughout its early history. For example, to judge by the apparent silence of the written sources, the *AP* seems to have stayed dormant in Latin Christendom during the seventh and eighth centuries; and while in the ninth its popularity began to waken in the West, in the Greek-speaking world it remained dormant (cf. Photius) until the later Middle Ages.

Valuable evidence for the early history of the *AP* and its dissemination throughout Christendom emerges also from its extant textual traditions. Emanating from the ancestor of the extant Greek version A, early translations spread its influence throughout the Greco-Roman world and beyond. The earliest among them is, perhaps, the Latin translation preserved in the Vienna palimpsest; it was probably executed before or during the fifth century, the putative date of the palimpsest's lower writing. At that stage, the *AP* did not yet include the *DI*, which makes its earliest appearance in the ninth-century Latin manuscripts and is absent from all Eastern versions (with the exception of Greek B). Contemporary with the Latin may be the two Coptic translations, one of which has been tentatively placed, on linguistic grounds, in the fifth century. Perhaps a century later the apocryphon reached Armenian communities; probably by AD 600, it was translated into Armenian. Copies of the first Georgian translation may have appeared in the eighth century and of the Syriac in the tenth. The manuscript containing the Palestinian Aramaic fragments is dated to the ninth, but the translation itself may be older. Finally, the apocryphon was read and translated from Latin into Slavonic in Croatia or Dalmatia since the eleventh or twelfth century; other Slavonic translations, from the Greek *AP* A, were made in Bulgaria in the twelfth and again in the fourteenth. There is also some evidence that the *AP*, if not actually translated into Arabic and Ethiopic, exerted considerable influence in both languages through the texts derived from or related to it.

The process of translation often involved more than finding equivalents for the Greek lexicon and grammar. Many translators engaged in ideologically motivated revisions, ranging from simple substitutions of better known names (as in the case of the Syriac names of the two thieves crucified with Christ) to ideologically motivated deletions of portions of the text (as the omission of the charge that Christ was born of fornication in the Georgian text) to large-scale suppression of non-canonical matter (as in the Armenian versions ending in chap. 13). Common among them was also the practice of appending other Pilate apocrypha to the *AP*.

The picture of the apocryphon's past as it emerges from the above survey of patristic and textual traditions is still only fragmentary. Gaps in the available data and in our understanding of what is extant are too large to permit a confident reconstruction of a coherent pattern of the apocryphon's evolution through Christian antiquity and the medieval past. It is hoped, however, that current research of the international team of scholars working under the auspices of the Association pour l'étude de la littérature apocryphe chrétienne will eventually disperse some of the shadows still concealing the apocryphon's path through early Christian history.

The *Evangelium Nicodemi* in the Latin Middle Ages[1]

ZBIGNIEW IZYDORCZYK

*T*he Latin *Evangelium Nicodemi* (*EN*) has been the object of scholarly attention and critical inquiry ever since the Renaissance.
What attracted and continued to intrigue scholars over the centuries was the mystery of its origin in Christian antiquity; its subsequent transmission and vicissitudes during the Middle Ages seem to
have stirred relatively little interest. The present essay attempts to
reverse this trend: it shifts the focus onto the Middle Ages and onto
the *EN*'s prominence in the medieval religious landscape. It argues
that, although born in late antiquity, the *EN* matured, flourished, and
helped shape the European cultural heritage during the medieval period. Drawing on heretofore untapped manuscript resources, it sheds
light on the textual richness and complexity of the Latin apocryphon,
explores medieval attitudes towards it, and surveys textual pathways
of its influence on the religious culture of the medieval West.[2]

1. Textual traditions

Throughout its long history in Latin Christendom, the *EN* developed
a variety of textual forms, which we have only begun to disentangle.[3]

---

[1] I should like to thank Prof. Mark Golden, Prof. John Magee, Prof. A. G.
Rigg, and especially Rémi Gounelle for their advice and help in the preparation
of this essay. I should also like to acknowledge the assistance of the staff at the
Interlending and Document Supply Services, University of Winnipeg.

[2] Since this essay focuses primarily on textual traditions, it does not discuss
the iconographic legacy of the *EN*. A list of major studies on the subject is, however, included in Part 3 of the thematic bibliography at the end of this volume.

[3] All manuscripts of the *EN* mentioned in this essay are listed and briefly
described in Zbigniew Izydorczyk, *Manuscripts of the "Evangelium Nicodemi": A
Census*, Subsidia Mediaevalia, vol. 21 (Toronto: Pontifical Institute of Mediaeval
Studies, 1993). The work of assessing and classifying the manuscripts is still in

In some of them, the *EN* acquired idiosyncratic language and factual details; in others, it absorbed additional texts, which altered it in scope and focus; and in still others, it became adapted to poetic, hagiographic, or encyclopedic contexts. The apocryphon's fecundity is hardly surprising. If the canonical gospels, transmitted with considerable concern for fidelity under the watchful eye of the church, developed a wide range of variant readings, it is no wonder that Latin apocrypha, such as the *EN*, copied under much less stringent conditions, tended to change and evolve rather easily. Scribes often felt it necessary to polish their style, grammar, or diction; to add what they considered overlooked or suppress what struck them as inappropriate; or to change the narrative or its theological underpinnings.[4] In this process of successive, gradual revisions, the underlying, original apocryphal texts tended to recede into the scribal past and, in a sense, into the abstract. What remained were only their allo-texts, transformed and sometimes on the verge of losing their original identity.

1.1. The Vienna palimpsest

Our earliest unambiguous evidence for the existence of a Latin translation of the Greek *Acts of Pilate*, known in the late medieval and modern West as the *Evangelium Nicodemi*, comes from a fifth-century manuscript, Vienna, Österreichische Nationalbibliothek MS. 563.[5] The manuscript is a palimpsest: it preserves, below an eighth-century layer of excerpts from the fathers, a fifth-century stratum comprising—besides a handful of passages from the canonical Gospel according to Matthew and the apocryphal *Infancy Gospel of Thomas*—extensive fragments of the *EN*. No explicit reference to the *EN* in the Latin writings of the fathers antedates the lower script of the palimpsest, and no Latin father quotes from or unambiguously describes a text that might be identified as the *EN*.

Two Latin writers may have alluded to Pilate's correspondence with the emperor, which was frequently appended to the *EN* in medi-

---

progress and will likely take several years to complete. The ensuing essay presents, therefore, only a preliminary overview of the material.

[4] Marek Starowieyski, "Ewangelie apokryficzne," *Znak* 29 (1977): 527.

[5] The manuscript has been discussed by Guy Philippart, "Fragments palimpsestes latins du Vindobonensis 563 (Ve siècle?). Évangile selon S. Matthieu. Évangile de l'enfance selon Thomas. Évangile de Nicodème," *Analecta Bollandiana* 90 (1972): 391–411, and Myriam Despineux, "Une Version latine palimpseste du Ve siècle de l'Évangile de Nicodème (Vienne, ÖNB MS 563)," *Scriptorium* 42 (1988): 176–83. The text of the *EN* has been edited from this manuscript by Guy Philippart, "Les Fragments palimpsestes de l'Évangile de Nicodème dans le *Vindobonensis 563* (Ve s.?)," *Analecta Bollandiana* 107 (1989): 171–88.

eval manuscripts. In his *Apologeticum* 5.2, Tertullian (b. ca. 160, d. after 220) maintains that Tiberius received news "ex Syria Palaestina" confirming Christ's divinity, and elsewhere (21.24) he specifies that it was Pilate who sent the news.[6] Two centuries later, Augustine's contemporary, Paulus Orosius, alludes to a similar dispatch from Pilate to Tiberius in the *Historiarum adversum paganos libri VII*, chapter 7.4.[7] His information was, however, second hand, derived most likely from Rufinus's translation of Eusebius of Caesarea's *Ecclesiastical History* 2.2.1–2.[8] Tertullian's and Orosius's remarks suggest considerable antiquity for the tradition of Pilate's letters but are silent about the *EN* itself. Orosius's ultimate Greek source, Eusebius, does make several scattered allusions to some "hypomnēmata" of Pilate (1.9.3, 1.11.9, 9.5.1, and 9.7.1),[9] and Rufinus not only translates them all but even inserts an independent allusion in the apologetic speech of Lucian of Antioch (added to 9.6.3).[10] Unfortunately, just as it is not possible, on the basis of Eusebius's references, to affirm that he indeed knew the text now extant in Greek manuscripts,[11] so it is impossible, on the basis of Rufinus's translation, to draw any conclusion about knowledge of the *Acts*, in any linguistic version, in the West.

It is not until the late sixth century that the *EN* leaves its first recognizable imprint on Latin literature. Gregory of Tours (b. 538, d. 594), a bishop-historian, relates in his *Decem libris historiarum* 1.21 the story of the incarceration and deliverance of Joseph of Arimathea, "ut Gesta Pilati ad Tiberium imperatorem missa referunt" ("as the Acts of Pilate sent to emperor Tiberius report");[12] the same "gesta," he claims, "apud nos hodie retenentur scripta" (1.24; "are preserved, written down, among us today").[13] Thus, in the absence of any patristic attes-

---

[6] Tertullian, *Q. S. Fl. Tertulliani Apologeticum*, ed. E. Dekkers, in *Quinti Septimi Florentis Tertulliani Opera*, pt. 1, *Opera catholica. Adversus Marcionem*, CC SL, vol. 1 (Turnhout: Brepols, 1954), 94–95 and 127, respectively.

[7] Paulus Orosius, *Pauli Orosii Historiarum adversum paganos libri VII*, ed. Carolus Zangemeister, CSEL, vol. 5 (Vienna: apud C. Geroldi Filium Bibliopolam Academiae, 1882), 441.

[8] Eusebius of Caesarea, *Die Kirchengeschichte. Die lateinische Übersetzung des Rufinus*, ed. Eduard Schwarz and Theodor Mommsen, 3 pts., *Eusebius Werke*, vol. 2, GCS, vol. 9 (Leipzig: J. C. Hinrichs, 1903–9), 1:111.

[9] Ibid. 1:72, 80; 2:810, 814.

[10] Ibid. 2:813.

[11] Jean-Daniel Dubois, "Les *Actes de Pilate* au quatrième siècle," *Apocrypha – Le Champ des apocryphes 2, La Fable apocryphe 2* (1991): 88–93.

[12] Gregory of Tours, *Gregorii episcopi Turonensis Libri historiarum X*, 2d ed., ed. Bruno Krusch and Wilhelmus Levison, MGH, Script. rer. Mer., vol. 1, pt. 1 (1951; repr., Hannover: Impensis Bibliopolii Hahniani, 1965), 17–18. This passage on Joseph was copied as a preface to the *EN* in one of the manuscript traditions; see below, sect. 1.3.7.

[13] Gregory of Tours, *Libri historiarum X*, 19. The authenticity of this passage,

tation of the *EN* before the sixth century, the Vienna palimpsest remains the sole reliable witness to the emergence and early shape of the Latin *EN*.

The palimpsest *EN* begins with a prologue in which Aeneas[14] introduces himself as discoverer and Greek translator of the original Hebrew document concerning Christ and dates his discovery to AD 425 or 440.[15] A second prologue dates Christ's Passion and names Nicodemus as author of the work. The text proper comprises only the first part of the *EN*, called by Constantinus de Tischendorf *Gesta Pilati* and coextensive with the extant Greek *Acts* A;[16] it is preserved here in a fragmentary state. The *Gesta* consists of two major thematic sections: the trial before Pilate, culminating in the Crucifixion, and the imprisonment and miraculous release of Joseph of Arimathea, with the subsequent testimonies proving Christ's Ascension. The account of the Harrowing of Hell, or the *Descensus Christi ad inferos* (*DI*)—the third major section of later Latin versions—is absent from the palimpsest. The palimpsest may have lost some of its folios through accidental damage, or, more likely, the *DI* may have been absent from its Greek source; the *DI* is attested neither in the early Greek version A of the apocryphon nor in the Oriental recensions translated from it.

This earliest Latin version of the *EN* shows, in its linguistic features, strong dependence on the Greek text. The translator followed the original slavishly, at times hellenizing his lexicon and reproducing Greek syntax at the expense of meaning.[17] Yet, in spite of its flaws, that translation had become the seed from which a rich Latin tradition subsequently emerged.

1.2. Later Latin versions

The process of revising the Latin *EN* must have begun shortly after its translation from Greek, for texts preserved in the ninth-century codices

---

clearly inspired by the *EN*, has been called into question by G. C. O'Ceallaigh, "Dating the Commentaries of Nicodemus," *Harvard Theological Review* 56 (1963): 23 n. 11, who maintains that it is a later interpolation. However, the passage is preserved in the earliest codices of the *Historiae*, representing different lines of the work's textual transmission (Gregory of Tours, *Libri historiarum X*, pp. xxiii–xxxv). If the story of Joseph is an interpolation, it must have been inserted very early, before the text began to diversify.

[14] The name is not clearly legible in the manuscript; cf. Philippart, "Les Fragments," 175 n. 13.

[15] O'Ceallaigh, "Dating the Commentaries," 49–50.

[16] Constantinus de Tischendorf, ed., *Evangelia apocrypha*, 2d rev. ed. (Leipzig: H. Mendelssohn, 1876), 333–88.

[17] Despineux, "Une Version latine," 180.

—the earliest surviving, besides the palimpsest—differ not only from the Vienna version but from each other as well. Textual diversification continued, perhaps even intensified, in the first few centuries of the second millennium, producing a plethora of interrelated yet discrete medieval forms and versions. So far three major textual types have been tentatively distinguished on the basis of their common lexical and thematic characteristics: A, B, and C.[18] The distinction between A and B was drawn already by Ernst von Dobschütz, who pointed out that the manuscripts used by Tischendorf for his critical edition of the *EN* represented two distinct recensions.[19] Out of the two versions of chapters 1–16, Tischendorf constructed a single, eclectic text of the *Gesta Pilati;* the two versions of chapters 17–27, he printed separately as *DI* A and B. Tischendorf also used one manuscript of *EN* C,[20] but neither he nor Dobschütz recognized it as a separate text-type.

1.2.1. Evangelium Nicodemi A

Perhaps the most popular, because attested in the greatest number of manuscripts, were versions of type A.[21] A standard text of this type begins with the second prologue of the original translation (as reflected in the Vienna palimpsest), giving the date of Christ's Passion. In the account of the trial before Pilate and Crucifixion, the lexicon and syntax correspond to the palimpsest closely. This close relationship is relaxed in the second thematic section, the story of Joseph of Arimathea (beginning in chap. 12), which diverges noticeably, abridging and summarizing various incidents.

Early texts of type A differ among themselves in various details. Most of them belong to one of two subgroups: some date the Passion to the consulate "Rufini et Rubellionis," while others to the consulate

[18] Zbigniew Izydorczyk, "The Unfamiliar *Evangelium Nicodemi,*" *Manuscripta* 33 (1989): 169–91.

[19] Ernst von Dobschütz, "Nicodemus, Gospel of," in *A Dictionary of the Bible,* ed. James Hastings (New York: C. Scribner's Sons, 1919), 3:545. Tischendorf's sources D^b (Einsiedeln, Stiftsbibliothek MS. 326, saec. IX–X) and D^c (Rome, Biblioteca dell'Accademia Nazionale dei Lincei e Corsiniana MS. 1146, saec. XIV) represent recension A; his A (Vatican City, Biblioteca Apostolica Vaticana [Bibl. Apost. Vat.] MS. Vat. lat. 4578, saec. XIV), B (Vatican City, Bibl. Apost. Vat. MS. Vat. lat. 4363, saec. XII), and C (Venice, Biblioteca Nazionale Marciana MS. 4326 [Lat. XIV, 43], saec. XIV–XV) recension B.

[20] His witness "Ambr.," i.e., Milan, Biblioteca Ambrosiana MS. O. 35 Sup. (saec. XIV).

[21] For a summary of this version, based on H. C. Kim, *The Gospel of Nicodemus: Gesta Salvatoris,* Toronto Medieval Latin Texts, vol. 2 (Toronto: Pontifical Institute of Mediaeval Studies, 1973), see the Introduction. I will cite the *EN* by chapter and paragraph numbers.

"Bassi et Tarquillionis." The differences between the two groups extend beyond the prologue, manifesting themselves most starkly in chapters 1.6 to 3.1, in the form of omissions, additions, and independent lexical and stylistic choices.[22]

However, what constitutes the most significant departure from the Vienna text is the inclusion and integration of the catabasis theme, the *Descensus Christi ad inferos*. Like the *Gesta Pilati* which it continues, the plot of the *DI* may have originated in the Greek-speaking world. Similar narratives found, for instance, in the fifth- or sixth-century homilies of pseudo-Eusebius of Alexandria and pseudo-Epiphanius are often assumed to have been derived from the Greek archetype of the *DI*.[23] If such an archetypal narrative indeed existed, it must have circulated independently of the Greek *Acts*, for neither the oldest Greek versions nor the oldest Latin and Oriental translations contain any trace of it.[24] It is quite possible that the *DI* was first attached to the *Gesta Pilati* in Latin some time between the fifth and the ninth centuries. Whether it was translated from Greek specifically for this purpose, or whether it

---

[22] For a more detailed discussion of the two subgroups and lists of early manuscripts that support them, see Izydorczyk, "The Unfamiliar *Evangelium Nicodemi*," 178–80.

[23] Cf. Johann Carl Thilo, ed., *Codex apocryphus Novi Testamenti*, vol. 1 (Leipzig: F. C. G. Vogel, 1832), cxix–cxx; Tischendorf, *Evangelia apocrypha*, lxviii; Richard Adalbert Lipsius, *Die Pilatus-Akten kritisch untersucht* (Kiel: Schwers'sche Buchhandlung, 1871), 7; Dobschütz, "Nicodemus, Gospel of," 545; J. A. MacCulloch, *The Harrowing of Hell. A Comparative Study of an Early Christian Doctrine* (Edinburgh: T. & T. Clark, 1930), 196. The pseudo-Eusebian homilies in question are "In Diabolum et Orcum" (in PG 86:383–404), "Oratio de adventu et annuntiatione Joannis (Baptistæ) apud Inferos" (in PG 86:509–26), and "In sancta et magna parasceve, et in sanctam passionem Domini" (in PG 62:721–24). Pseudo-Epiphanius's homily is entitled "Sacti Patris nostri Epiphanii episcopi Cypri oratio in divini corporis sepulturam Domini et Servatoris nostri Jesu Christi, et in Josephum qui fuit ab Arimathæa, et in Domini in infernum descensum, post salutarem passionem admirabiliter factum" (in PG 43:439A–64D). These homilies are described by MacCulloch, *The Harrowing of Hell*, 174–98. They were translated from Greek into Latin, Old Slavonic, Arabic, and Armenian. See Edward Kennard Rand, "Sermo de confusione diaboli," *Modern Philology* 2 (1904): 261–78; Sirarpie Der Nersessian, "An Armenian Version of the Homilies on the Harrowing of Hell," *Dumbarton Oaks Papers* 8 (1954): 203–24; idem, "A Homily on the Raising of Lazarus and the Harrowing of Hell," in *Biblical and Patristic Studies in Memory of Robert Pierce Casey*, ed. J. Neville Birdsall and Robert W. Thomson (Freiburg i. Br.: Herder, 1963), 219–34; Zbigniew Izydorczyk, "Two Newly Identified Manuscripts of the *Sermo de confusione diaboli*," *Scriptorium* 43 (1989): 253–55; and G. Lafontaine, "La Version arménienne du sermon d'Eusèbe d'Alexandrie 'sur la venue de Jean aux Enfers,'" *Le Muséon* 91 (1978): 87–104.

[24] The Greek recension of the *DI* occurs only in late, revised versions of the *Acts*, apparently influenced by the Latin text; see Dobschütz, "Nicodemus, Gospel of," 545; Rémi Gounelle, "Recherches sur les *Actes* apocryphes de Pilate grecs, recension B," 2 vols. (Mémoire présenté pour l'obtention du Diplôme d'Études Approfondies, Université Paris X-Nanterre, 1991) 2:93–96.

had existed in Latin before coalescing with the apocryphon of the Passion, remains a matter of speculation.

There is, however, some evidence to suggest that the surmised translation of the "descensus" narrative did not merge with the Latin *Gesta* without some prior interaction with other Latin texts. The story of Seth's journey to paradise in search of the oil of mercy for his ailing father—absent from the pseudo-Eusebian and pseudo-Epiphanian accounts but present in the Latin *DI*—is taken directly from the Latin translation of the Greek *Life of Adam and Eve*. In particular, the Archangel Michael's prophecy of the coming of the Messiah (*EN* 19.1, "nullo modo poteris ex eo accipere . . . ad arborem misericordiae") corresponds almost verbatim to that which occurs in the Latin *Vita Adae et Evae*.[25] It is unlikely that the prophecy was incorporated already into the Greek narrative of Christ's Descent because the correspondences between the Latin *Vita* and the Latin *DI* are so close that they cannot be explained by parallel translations from their respective Greek sources.[26] The *DI* must, therefore, have been amplified with the Seth story and Michael's prophecy only after both were made available in Latin.[27]

The relationship between the *EN* and another Latin text, the so-called pseudo-Augustinian "Sermo 160: De pascha II," has not yet been satisfactorily explained.[28] In one of its earliest manuscripts,

---

[25] Wilhelm Meyer, "Vita Adae et Evae," *Abhandlungen der philosophisch-philologischen Classe der königlich bayerischen Akademie der Wissenschaften*, vol. 14 (Munich: Verlag der K. Akademie, in Commission bei G. Franz, 1878), 187–250. Although the known Greek texts of the *Life* do not contain this prophecy, its occurrence in a Georgian translation, apparently based on the same Greek recension as the Latin one, suggests that it must have been present in an early Greek version.

[26] The prophecy in the Greek version of the *DI*, part of *Acts of Pilate* B, is later than its Latin counterpart and apparently derivative; see Marcel Nagel, "La Vie greque d'Adam et d'Ève. Apocalypse de Moïse," Thèse présenté devant l'Université de Strasbourg II (Université de Lille III: Service du reproduction des thèses, 1974), 1:165.

[27] For a detailed discussion of the relationships among the various versions of the *EN* and the *Vita Adae et Evae*, see Nagel, "La vie greque," 1:159–75. Nagel offers a convincing critique of an earlier opinion, first expressed by Meyer and echoed by many later scholars, that Michael's prophecy was interpolated into the Seth passage after the latter had become part of the *DI* and that it was subsequently transplanted back into the *Vita*. I am indebted to Rémi Gounelle for bringing Nagel's dissertation to my attention.

[28] The "Sermo" has been edited by D. Ozimic, *Der pseudo-augustinische Sermo CLX . . .* Dissertationen der Universität Graz, no. 47 (Graz, 1979), 17–36; and by J. P. Migne with the works of Augustine (PL 39:2059–61) and Martin of Laon (PL 208:925–32). The bulk of section two of the "Sermo," as given by Migne, is absent from the Chicago, Newberry Library MS. 1, fols. 90r–91v (saec. IX), discussed below, but occurs in three homilies of Eusebius "Gallicanus": "De pascha, I" (Eusebius "Gallicanus," *Collectio homiliarum, de qua critice disseruit Ioh. Leroy*, ed. Fr. Glorie, 2 vols., CC SL, vols. 101 and 101A [Turnhout: Brepols, 1970–1], 1:141–

Chicago, Newberry Library MS. 1, fols. 90r–91v (saec. IX), the "Sermo" begins with a fragment of a homily by Gregory the Great; this is followed by a series of rhetorical questions and apostrophes conveying the infernal legions' astonishment and confusion at Christ's appearance in hell and their chastisement of Satan for causing Christ's death. The text ends with a long prayer of the patriarchs and prophets for deliverance and with an account of the Resurrection. Portions of the "Sermo" correspond to the *DI* not only by virtue of common motifs (terrified questioning, rebuke of Satan, plea for deliverance) but in actual phrasing as well. The pseudo-Augustinian text shows close verbal parallels to parts of three chapters of the *EN*: 22.1.22–34 ("Unde es tu, Iesu, tam fortis . . . totius mundi potestatem accepturus esses."), 23.1.7–36 ("Ecce iam iste Iesus diuinitatis suae fulgore . . . impios et iniustos perdidisti."), and 24.1.19–20 ("Aduenisti redemptor mundi . . . factis adimplesti."). Even if the *DI* was translated from Greek into Latin, it could have acquired these passages at either its Greek or Latin stage, for rhetorically and thematically similar texts were available in both linguistic areas.[29] If the passages were part of the original Greek *DI*, then the Latin translation of the *DI* was most probably the source of the "Sermo." Assuming that D. N. Dumville's dating of the liturgical drama from the Book of Cerne, based on the "Sermo," to the early eighth century is correct,[30] it would be reasonable to expect that the Latin *DI* was in circulation in the seventh. However, the absence of the corresponding passages from the homilies of pseudo-Eusebius of Alexandria and pseudo-Epiphanius, allegedly the earliest witnesses to the Greek *DI*,[31] might suggest that the questions, the rebuke, and the plea are of immediate Latin origin. If so, the "Sermo" or, more likely, some earlier texts from which it was culled may have also inspired parts of the *DI*; both the "Sermo" and the *DI* could, under this hypothesis, be reflexes of an earlier Latin tradition.

---

43); "De pascha, IA" (ibid. 1:145–50); and "De resurrectione Domini" (ibid. 2:881–86). For earlier editions of these sermons, see ibid. 1:138–39 and 2:878–79.

[29] For the Greek sources, see MacCulloch, *The Harrowing of Hell*, 77–80, and J. Kroll, *Gott und Hölle. Der Mythos vom Descensuskampfe* (Leipzig: B. G. Teubner, 1932), 50–57. In Latin, the already noted sermons of Eusebius "Gallicanus" bear a strong resemblance to both the "Sermo" (into which they were interpolated from at least the tenth century) and the corresponding sections of the *EN*.

[30] D. N. Dumville, "Liturgical Drama and Panegyric Responsory from the Eighth Century? A Re-examination of the Origin and Contents of the Ninth-Century Section of the Book of Cerne," *Journal of Theological Studies* 23 (1972): 374–406.

[31] The pseudo-Epiphanian sermon includes a series of rhetorical questions, but they differ from those in the "Sermo" and the *DI*.

1.2.2. Evangelium Nicodemi *B*

The second textual type of the *EN*, known as *EN* B, emerges from several manuscripts of the twelfth to the fifteenth centuries.[32] In contrast to *EN* A, it has retained not the second but the first prologue of the textual form represented by the Vienna palimpsest, sometimes preceded by a homiletic preface, "Audistis, fratres karissimi, quae acta sunt..." ("You have heard, most beloved brothers, what took place..."). It reproduces—at times verbatim, at times paraphrasing—not only the trial and Crucifixion scenes of the palimpsest, as does type A, but also the accounts of Joseph of Arimathea and of the three rabbis, both considerably abridged in A. However, the majority of B manuscripts show two apparently deliberate omissions in the text of the *Gesta:* one excising portions of the proceedings before Pilate (chaps. 2.3–4.5) and replacing them with the sentence, "Quid multa? iam omnia nota sunt uobis a sancto euuangelio" ("What more needs to be said? All these things are already known to you from the holy gospel"),[33] and the other deleting the accounts of the release of Barabbas, the Crucifixion, and Christ's death (chaps. 9–11). The redactor of this expurgated version was evidently interested in additional, extra-canonical details concerning the Passion and death of Christ.

In the *DI*, the distance between types A and B increases even further; in comparison with A, B expands the discovery of Leucius and Carinus, condenses and rearranges elements of their report, adds such details as the arrival of the Good Thief in hell, and expunges Hell's lament and the meeting with Enoch and Elijah in paradise.

1.2.3. Evangelium Nicodemi *C*

The third of the tentatively identified types of the *EN*, type C, appears to be related to A, although this relationship rests primarily on the coincidence of narrative contours, with lexicon, style, and minor factual details showing wide variance. This type occurs in seven codices, the

---

[32] Seventeen manuscripts are listed in Izydorczyk, "The Unfamiliar *Evangelium Nicodemi*," 181. To that list should be added Prague, Státní knihovna MS. IX. F. 4 (saec. XII–XIV). A text of type B has been edited from Cambridge, Corpus Christi College (CCCC) MS. 288, fols. 39r–54r (saec. XIII), by Katherine Anne Smith Collett, "The Gospel of Nicodemus in Anglo-Saxon England" (Ph.D. diss., University of Pennsylvania, 1981), and, with extensive discussion of the manuscript and text, by Rémi Gounelle, "Recherches sur le manuscrit CCCC 288 des *Acta Pilati*" (Mémoire présenté pour l'obtention ès la maîtrise de lettres classiques, Université de Paris X-Nanterre, 1989); I cite from the latter.

[33] Gounelle, "Recherches sur le manuscrit," 44–45.

earliest two with connections to Spain.[34] The same connection is also suggested by the form of the name given to the Good Thief in C, Limas. This name is exceedingly rare: apart from the *EN* C, it occurs, as far as I know, only in a Spanish illustration of the Crucifixion in the Gerona codex (an. 975) of the commentary on the Apocalypse by an Asturian monk, Beatus of Liébana. In that illustration, possibly the work of En or Ende, a devout woman who collaborated with presbyter Emeterius on decoration of the codex, the name "Limas" identifies the Bad Thief (the Good Thief is called Gestas here).[35] Although the Gerona codex reverses the Thieves' names, it is so far the only other witness to the name "Limas" and, therefore, a further link between *EN* C and the Iberian peninsula.

Recension C opens in the middle of the second prologue with the characteristic incipit "Quod inventum est in publicis codicibus praetorii Pontii Pilati ..." ("That which has been found in public codices of Pontius Pilate's council-chamber ..."). For the most part, it retains the episodes of A and recounts them in the same order but adds many details absent from both A and B. It reports, for instance, that Pilate's messenger was called Romanus, that the standards which bowed before Jesus were crowned with imperial images, that Christ dined with Lazarus after raising him from the dead, and so on.[36] After chapter 12, the text is frequently abridged and occasionally rearranged. For example, chapters 13.2, 15, 16.1, 16.3, 19.1, and 20.3 are foreshortened, while chapters 14.3, 16.2, 18.1–3, 21.3, and 25–26 (meeting with Enoch, Elijah, and the Good Thief) are entirely omitted. Considerable rearrangement of material occurs in chapters 2.4, 14.2, 22, 23, and 27.

C's most significant narrative departure from A consists in an additional chapter reporting Pilate's consultations with the Jews in the synagogue (chap. 28 in Tischendorf's edition). At his command, the high priests consult the holy books and discover that their "bible" points to Christ as the long-awaited Messiah. They admit their guilt but adjure Pilate not to reveal to anybody Christ's divine nature. The chapter usually concludes with a chronology from Adam to Christ,

---

[34] The manuscripts are given by Izydorczyk, "The Unfamiliar *Evangelium Nicodemi*," 183; to that list should be added Lisbon, Biblioteca Nacional MS. Alcobaça CCLXXXV/419 (saec. XII/2). Barcelona, Archivo de la Corona de Aragón MS. Ripoll 106 (saec. X), once belonged to the Benedictines at Ripoll, dioc. Vich; Paris, Bibliothèque nationale (BN) MS. n. a. lat. 2171 (saec. XI), written in Visigothic script, was at the Benedictine monastery at Silos, dioc. Burgos.

[35] The illustration is reproduced in John Williams, *Early Spanish Manuscript Illumination* (New York: G. Braziller, 1977), plate 29; the Gerona codex and illuminations are discussed in Beatus of Liébana, *Beati in Apocalypsin libri duodecim. Codex Gerundensis* (Madrid: Edilan, 1975).

[36] Idiosyncratic passages occur also in chaps. 5.1, 11.2, and 19.1.

showing that Christ came indeed at the precise juncture in time specified by the holy books. The entire episode demonstrates that the
pharisees recognized Christ's divinity yet for political reasons ma-
liciously concealed the truth. The motif of the Jews' wickedness, so
strongly emphasized in the trial scene, is here enhanced and focused
on the priestly cast. This chapter agrees so well with the preceding sections that, although it occurs only in relatively few manuscripts, it has
been considered an integral part of the apocryphon by most of its editors, from Melchior Lotter (d. 1549) to Tischendorf.

1.2.4. Other versions

Each of the three major textual traditions was in the process of continual change, under constant pressure from scribes and compilers. Not
infrequently, texts representative of the major types were fused together, resulting in hybrid versions. One such mixed version, preserved in
fourteen manuscripts, shows features of recensions A and C; its oldest
known manuscript is Troyes, Bibliothèque municipale (Bibl. mun.) MS.
1636 (saec. XII), and I refer to it as the Troyes redaction.[37] Unlike the
other versions, it concludes the second prologue with a statement that
the Latin translation was made at the instance of emperor Theodosius.
Through much of the *Gesta*, it reads with C, albeit not consistently,
retaining many of C's idiosyncratic passages; when it draws on A, it is
often (but not always) to supply the passages excised from C. The *DI*,
highly abridged in C, is restored on the basis of A; however, it ends
with perhaps the most characteristic passage of C, namely, the discussions between Pilate and the high priests in the temple.

Any text type could become the basis for abridged, amplified, or
restructured versions, and a number of such revised versions survive.
Some, like the text edited by David J. G. Lewis,[38] begin only with the
story of Joseph of Arimathea and often compress parts of the text.
Others add new characters and entire episodes to the story, as does
Oxford, Bodleian Library (Bodl. Lib.) MS. Addit. A 367, fols. 2r–25v
(saec. XII ex.), which expands the list of witnesses testifying about
Christ's miracles,[39] or Paris, BN MS. lat. 5559, fols. 2r–50v (saec. XV
ex.), which interpolates discussions between Judas and the priests as
well as the arrest of Christ. Still others abridge or rearrange portions of

---

[37] This redaction of the *EN* has not been edited. For a list of its manuscripts,
see Zbigniew Izydorczyk, "The Latin Source of an Old French *Gospel of Nicodemus*," *Revue d'histoire des textes* 25 (1995): 265–79.

[38] David J. G. Lewis, ed., "A Short Latin *Gospel of Nicodemus* Written in
Ireland," *Peritia* 5 (1986): 262–75.

[39] Izydorczyk, "The Unfamiliar *Evangelium Nicodemi*," 171–72.

the text or, as do some manuscripts of B type, delete the episodes recounted in the canonical gospels.

There is some evidence that at various times critically minded Latin scribes may have compared and revised their copies of the *EN* against Greek exemplars. Some of the earliest Latin manuscripts, for instance, include in chapters 1.2 and 4.2 readings consonant with the Greek but not present in the palimpsest. Therefore either the palimpsest represents an already revised, pruned Latin version of an earlier, fuller text, or those additional readings were inserted as a result of subsequent comparisons with Greek versions.[40] More evidence of such comparative activity may be provided by three fifteenth-century manuscripts from central Europe which include a full translation of the Greek conclusion to the *Acts of Pilate*, chapter 16.7–8. This conclusion was part of the original Latin translation, and its small fragments are preserved in the palimpsest. It seems to have disappeared, however, from later Latin versions, with only a few sentences surviving in texts of type B. And yet in Prague, Státní knihovna MS. XX. A. 7, fol. 139rb–va (saec. XIV–XV), and Cracow, Biblioteka Jagiellońska MS. 2724, fol. 301v (saec. XV/1), the complete Latin text of that conclusion resurfaces immediately after the *Epistola Pilati ad Claudium* (*EP*), which follows a complete text of the *EN*; in Cracow, Biblioteka Jagiellońska MS. 1509, fol. 94r (saec. XV ex.), a somewhat abridged version of the passage in question actually concludes chapter 16. While it is possible that the three manuscripts reflect the original Latin text, suppressed in the main lines of transmission but still available in the fourteenth century, it is perhaps more likely that the conclusion was translated anew and appended to the Latin text at a later date.

In spite of their differences, all Latin versions seem to share common Latin ancestry. Their genetic relatedness is admittedly more pronounced in the *Gesta* than in the *DI*, for through the *Gesta* they all inherit some features of the original translation as preserved in the Vienna palimpsest. The accounts of the Descent into Hell are less congruent but not dissimilar; individual episodes may be rearranged, but they add up to essentially the same story told in often similar terms. Some redactions may have been corrected against Greek texts, but at present there is no evidence that the apocryphon in its entirety was translated from Greek into Latin more than once during the Middle Ages.

---

[40] Ibid., 179–81.

1.3. Appendices to the *Evangelium Nicodemi*

Published editions of the *EN*, with their clearly delimited text, might convey an impression that throughout its long history the apocryphon remained constant and stable. Yet even a cursory look at its extant manuscripts reveals the contrary. If medieval texts in general thrived in variance and plurality, then those related to, but not absorbed by, the scriptural canon flourished in a state of continual metamorphosis. The medieval *EN* was, in fact, fluid, flexible, and adaptable. During the period of its early growth, the apocryphon focused on the Passion and Resurrection of Jesus, presented in a highly dramatic, dialogic manner. But as the text continued to expand beyond the *DI*, successive additions began to refocus the entire composition by shifting attention to the historical context and consequences of the Easter drama. Those additions replaced histrionic discourse of the core apocryphon with narration, exposition, or scriptural argument, whichever seemed most expedient. In spite of these thematic and rhetorical differences between the ancient text and its later appendices, medieval writers and readers perceived them all as somehow belonging together, as parts of one and the same, rather loosely defined, work.

1.3.1. Epistola Pilati ad Claudium

The most common extension of, or appendix to, the *EN*, found in all but three pre-eleventh-century manuscripts with more or less complete text, is the *Epistola Pilati ad Claudium*.[41] The presence of the *EP* in the majority of early copies indicates that this spurious letter became associated with the apocryphon at an early date, perhaps at the same time the apocryphon acquired the title identifying it as an official imperial document found in Pilate's archives, "In nomine sanctae Trinitatis incipit gesta Saluatoris Domini nostri Ihesu Christi quae inuenit Theodosius magnus imperator in pretorio Pontii Pilati in codicibus publicis" (Laon, Bibl. mun. MS. 265, fol. 2r [saec. IX]; "In the name of the Holy Trinity here begins the Acts of our Lord Savior Jesus Christ,

---

[41] Mauritius Geerard, *Clavis apocryphorum Novi Testamenti*, Corpus Christianorum, Series Apocryphorum (Turnhout: Brepols, 1992), no. 64. This letter has been published as part of the *EN* by Thilo, *Codex apocryphus*, 796–800, Tischendorf, *Evangelia apocrypha*, 413–16 (as chap. 13 of the *DI* A or 29 of the *EN*), and Kim, *The Gospel of Nicodemus*, 49–50 (as chap. 28). For a list of pre-eleventh-century manuscripts, see Izydorczyk, "The Unfamiliar *Evangelium Nicodemi*," 178. Early manuscripts with the complete text which do not include the *EP* are London, British Library (BL) MS. Royal 5 E. XIII, fols. 82r–100r (saec. IX ex.), and Paris, BN MS. n. a. lat. 1605, fols. 4r–16v (saec. IX ex.); the conclusion of Orléans, Bibl. mun. MS. 341 (289), pp. 415–44 (saec. IX–X), illegible on microfilm, may also lack it.

which Theodosius, the great emperor, found in public codices in Pilate's council-chamber"). Both the title and the *EP* are standard features of the *EN* as early as the ninth century. Pilate's letter is addressed to Claudius (in some late manuscripts to Tiberius) and briefly reports the events that took place in Jerusalem. It also alludes to the prophecies of the coming of the Messiah, lays the blame for the death of Christ on the Jews, and expresses Pilate's conviction that Christ was indeed sent by God and truly arose from the dead. The *EP* marks the end of the dialogic, dramatic apocryphon, introducing narrative and expository modes of discourse. Thematically, however, it still coheres well with the pseudo-gospel. Its indictment of the Jews echoes and reinforces their negative portrayal in the trial scenes (and in chap. 28 of *EN* C). Furthermore, the enormity of their actions is brought into sharp relief by the contrast with the positive, pro-Christian self-portrait of Pilate, which resonates in concert with that suggested by the *EN*.

Throughout the Middle Ages, the *EP* enjoyed wide circulation also independently of the *EN*. With its credibility supported by Tertullian's and Orosius's allusions to Pilate's dispatch to Rome, it was viewed as a historical document, as a pagan, non-partisan confirmation of the historicity of the central events of the Redemption. It makes an appearance in the Latin and Greek versions of the apocryphal *Passio sanctorum apostolorum Petri et Pauli* (the so-called Marcellus text), chapters 19–21, of an early but uncertain date.[42] Later it was frequently incorporated into medieval chronicles, such as those of Ivo of Chartres, Martinus Polonus,[43] and Matthew of Paris,[44] and during the Renaissance it became a common feature of epistolary collections, together with the letters of Lentulus and Abgarus. However, this independence did not prevent medieval scribes from perceiving and treating the *EP* as an integral part of the *EN*. Their attitude is reflected in manuscript layouts. The transition from the *EN* to the *EP* is usually accomplished by means of a connecting sentence, such as "Et post haec ipse Pilatus scripsit epistolam ad urbem Romam Claudio dicens . . ." (Laon, Bibl. mun. MS. 265, fol. 34r; "And thereafter Pilate himself wrote a letter to the city of Rome, saying to Claudius . . ."), or "Et post uolens caesari omnia renunciare, ipse Pilatus scripsit epistolam ad urbem Romam Claudio imperatori dicens . . ." (Paris, BN MS. lat. 3784, fol. 112v, saec. XI; "And afterwards, wishing to announce everything to the emperor,

[42] Richard Adalbert Lipsius and Maximilian Bonnet, *Acta apostolorum apocrypha*, pt. 1 (1891; repr., Darmstadt: Wissenschaftliche Buchgesellschaft, 1959), 134–39.
[43] Cf. Thilo, *Codex apocryphus*, 796–97.
[44] Matthew of Paris, *Matthæi Parisiensis, monachi Sancti Albani, Chronica majora*, vol. 1, *The Creation to A.D. 1066*, ed. Henry Richards Luard, Rer. Brit. M. A. Script., vol. 57 (London: Longman, 1872), 95–96.

Pilate himself wrote a letter to the city of Rome, saying to emperor Claudius ...'"). Occasionally, the *EP* is marked with a separate rubric or title in the margin,[45] but more typically it is not visibly set off from the rest of the text. Colophons or closing statements for the *EN*, if present, usually follow the *EP*, making it into an integral part of the apocryphon.[46]

1.3.2. Cura sanitatis Tiberii

The *EN* was often expanded beyond the *EP* with the so-called *Cura sanitatis Tiberii*, a rapid, uneven narrative, with a few drawn-out but nondramatic speeches.[47] Its stylistic distance from the main body of the apocryphon is matched by its thematic divergence—it is no longer concerned with the Passion of Jesus but with its effects: the temporal rewards for those who believed in Christ and temporal punishments for those who opposed him. It narrates the Roman mission of Volusianus to find the healer Jesus Christ, who might cure emperor Tiberius of his illness. Having learned about Christ's death, Volusianus condemns and imprisons Pilate and returns to Tiberius with Veronica and her image of Christ. Tiberius honors the image and is instantly healed; he becomes a champion of Christianity and executes all its detractors. Soon afterward he himself dies "credens in Christo" ("believing in

---

[45] For instance, in Berlin, Staatsbibliothek Preussischer Kulturbesitz (SBPK) MS. Theol. lat. fol. 241, fol. 136ra (saec. XV); Bordeaux, Bibl. mun. MS. 111, fol. 284ra (saec. XIV); or Brussels, Bibliothèque royale Albert Iᵉʳ MS. 1079–84, fol. 115rb (saec. XIII).

[46] The comment in the *codex Halensis*, now Halle/Saale, Archiv der Francke-'schen Stiftungen MS. P 7 (saec. XV), about the independence of the *EP* from the *EN*, quoted by Thilo, *Codex apocryphus*, 796, is rather atypical for the medieval period.

[47] Geerard, *Clavis*, no. 69. The *Cura* has been studied and edited by Ernst von Dobschütz, *Christusbilder. Untersuchungen zur christlichen Legende*, Texte und Untersuchungen zur Geschichte der altchristlicher Literatur, vol. 18, N.F., vol. 3 (Leipzig: J. C. Hinrichs, 1899), 209–14, 157**–203**. It was also printed by Pietro Francisco Foggini, *De Romano Divi Petri itinere* (Florence: Typ. Manniano, 1741), 37–46; J. D. Mansi, ed., *Stephani Baluzii Tutelensis Miscellanea novo ordine digesta* ... (Lucca: V. Junctinius, 1764), 4:55–60; Anton Schönbach, review of *Evangelia apocrypha*, edited by Constantinus de Tischendorf, *Anzeiger für deutsches Altertum und deutsche Litteratur* 2 (1876): 173–80; and Etienne Darley, *Les Acta Salvatoris. Un Évangile de la passion & de la résurrection et une mission apostolique en Aquitaine* (Paris: A. Picard & Fils, 1913), 47–51.

In two apparently related manuscripts—Prague, Státní knihovna MS. XIV. E. 10, fols. 59ra–61rb (saec. XIV/1), and Vatican City, Bibl. Apost. Vat. MS. Reg. lat. 648, fols. 48r ff. (saec. XII)—a further text, *De Nerone et Domitiano* (inc. "Nero fecit primam persecutionem," expl. "qui erat in exilium missus"), is added after the *Cura*, probably attracted to it by the subject matter.

Christ"). The work ends with a rather poorly integrated episode in
which Peter confirms before Nero the truth of Pilate's letter (in most
manuscripts quoted in full at this point) and refutes the mendacious
claims of Simon Magus. Nero again exiles Pilate, who dies wretchedly,
and then Nero himself meets an inglorious end.

The *Cura* undermines the sympathetic, pro-Christian conception of
Pilate that emerges from the *EN* and the *EP*. In contrast to Eastern
churches, medieval Latin Christianity considered Pilate guilty of com-
plicity in the death of Jesus and viewed him not as a saint but as a villain. This negative perception is reflected in the *Cura*, which shows
Pilate condemned, imprisoned, exiled, and eventually committing suicide. It is, therefore, a corrective for what Western Christianity saw as
an unduly charitable portrayal of Pilate. The resulting loss of an
important pagan witness and convert to Christianity is more than compensated for by the introduction of Tiberius as an imperial defender of
Christ. On the one hand, the conversion of Tiberius, of which his healing is a visible sign, demonstrates the power of Christ to bend the
minds and hearts of supreme rulers of this world; on the other hand,
his earthly status and authority enhance the temporal credibility and
respectability of the relatively new Christian faith and foreshadow the
conversion of the empire as a whole.

The *Cura* is probably later than the *EP*. It may have been composed in northern Italy between the fifth and the eighth centuries, the
former being the approximate date of the Latin translation of the *EN*,
the latter the date of the earliest manuscript of the *Cura* (Lucca, Biblioteca Capitolare MS. 490).[48] A composite piece, the *Cura* is textually
indebted to the *EN*, the Marcellus *Passio sanctorum apostolorum Petri et
Pauli*, and perhaps other sources as well.[49] Its indebtedness to the *EN*
consists partly in the presence of the same characters and partly in the
echoes of the events treated at length in the apocryphon. The figures
common to the *EN* and the *Cura* include Veronica—a witness to
Christ's miracles in the former and the owner of Christ's image in the
latter—and the rabbis who bring the news about Christ's Ascension in
the *EN* and testify before Volusianus in the *Cura*.[50] A major episode
borrowed by the *Cura* from the pseudo-gospel is the story of Joseph of
Arimathea. In his report to Volusianus, Joseph speaks of Christ's
entombment and the subsequent Christophanies, conflating in the

---

[48] In this manuscript, as in some later ones, the *Cura* stands as an independent work, unconnected with the *EN*; it was printed by Mansi. On the dating and
localization of the *Cura*, see Dobschütz, *Christusbilder*, 213–14.

[49] Dobschütz, *Christusbilder*, 200–203.

[50] Their number in the *Cura* is increased through confusion with the twelve
righteous Jews who spoke before Pilate.

process his own Christophany in prison with that of the three rabbis who saw him on Mount Malec. Although the *Cura* is not entirely accurate in its rendition of details from the *EN*, it was doubtlessly inspired by it. To the *Passio sanctorum apostolorum Petri et Pauli*, chapters 15–21,[51] the *Cura* owes the closing episode with Nero and Simon Magus and, possibly, the letter of Pilate to Claudius.

In numerous manuscripts, the *Cura* and the *EN* are more than contiguous—they are merged into a single text. Their integration came about gradually. In two of the earliest manuscripts in which the two occur together—Barcelona, Archivo de la Corona de Aragón MS. Ripoll 106, fols. 136r–39r (saec. X), and Einsiedeln, Stiftsbibliothek MS. 326, fols. 29v–34v (saec. IX or X)—they are adjacent but still discrete: both the end of Pilate's letter, which continues the *EN* without a break, and the beginning of the *Cura* are clearly marked. From the eleventh century onward, however, the *Cura* appears completely fused with the preceding *EP* by means of a transitional sentence deictically anchored in the latter: "Hanc Pilatus Claudio direxit adhuc uiuente Tiberio imperatore licet grauissimo laborante morbo . . ." (Berkeley, University of California, Bancroft Library MS. UCB 20, fol. 48r, saec. XII; "Pilate sent this to Claudius while Tiberius was still alive although suffering from a most severe illness . . ."). This connecting sentence, in the absence of a separate title, suppresses the independent identity of the *Cura* and subordinates it to the *EN*. Their fusion is often confirmed by colophons and closing statements that follow the *Cura*: more often than not those statements announce the conclusion of the *EN*, as for instance in Bologna, Biblioteca Universitaria MS. 2601, fol. 127v (saec. XV), "Explicit libellus passionis salvatoris et Domini nostri Yesu Christi" ("Here ends the book of Passion of our Savior and Lord Jesus Christ"); Cambridge, University Library MS. Dd. 3. 16, fol. 31rb (saec. XIV), "Explicit ewangelium Nichodemi . . ." ("Here ends the Gospel of Nicodemus . . ."); and London, Lincoln Inn Library MS. Hale 73 (saec. XIV), "Epistola Nichodemi finit" ("The letter of Nicodemus ends here"). Such an inclusive perception of the *EN*, *EP*, and *Cura* is also reflected in the *editio princeps* of the *EN*: in 1473 an Augsburg printer, Günther Zainer, published the three under the single title *Euangelium Nichodemi*. Although he broke the entire text into three large paragraphs (beginning in the second prologue, in chapter 11.3, and in chapter 27.1, respectively), there is no indication that he perceived them as discrete, independent works.[52]

---

[51] Lipsius and Bonnet, *Acta apostolorum apocrypha*, 133–39.

[52] The *editio princeps* has been reprinted with modern division into paragraphs by Achim Masser and Max Siller, eds., *Das Evangelium Nicodemi in*

1.3.3. Vindicta Salvatoris

The *Cura sanitatis Tiberii* was one of the sources of another text on conversion and vengeance which hovered on the fringes of the *EN*. Composed possibly ca. AD 700 in southern Gaul, the *Vindicta Salvatoris* consists of two superficially connected narratives.[53] One tells of the healing of Titus, king of Aquitaine, who believes in Christ after hearing about him from Nathan, a Jewish emissary to Rome. Thankful for the miracle, Titus besieges and destroys Jerusalem, the site of the Lord's Passion. The other narrative relates the condemnation of Pilate by Velosianus and the healing of Tiberius by the image of Christ. In Joseph of Arimathea's testimony before Velosianus concerning the Resurrection of Jesus (chap. 21), the *Vindicta* is much closer to the *EN* than to the *Cura*; in fact, it quotes verbatim parts of Joseph's account of his Christophany and release from prison (*EN* 15.6).

Two of the earliest manuscripts of the *Vindicta*—Saint-Omer, Bibl. mun. MS. 202, fols. 20v–25v (saec. IX), and Paris, BN MS. lat. 5327, fols. 55r–61v (saec. X)—contain also copies of the *EN*. In the Saint-Omer manuscript, the *Vindicta* is separated from the *EN* by the interposed *Passio s. Margaritae*; in the Paris codex, it is adjacent to the closing statement of the *EN*, "Explicit gesta Domini Salvatoris" ("Here ends the Acts of Lord Savior") and begins with a rubric, "Incipit sermo de vindicta Domini" ("Here begins a sermon on the vengeance of the Lord"). The two texts occur together in over twenty later manuscripts, and their joint transmission suggests that they were perceived as having some bearing on each other, although, with few exceptions, the *Vindicta* does not develop the sort of attachment to the *EN* that was characteristic of the *Cura*.[54] It may be contiguous with the *EN*, but textually and graphically it was usually marked off as a distinct, independent work.

---

spätmittelalterlicher deutscher Prosa. Texte, Germanische Bibliothek, 4th Series, Texte und Kommentar (Heidelberg: C. Winter, 1987), 448–67. This re-edition detaches the *Cura* from the *EP*, supplies a heading for the former, and discontinues paragraph numbering, thus obscuring textual cohesion between the *EN* and the *Cura*.

[53] Geerard, *Clavis*, no. 70. This text has been edited by Tischendorf, *Evangelia apocrypha*, 471–86; its beginning has been printed from different manuscripts by E. Kölbing and Mabel Day, eds., *The Siege of Jerusalem*, EETS OS, vol. 188 (London: Oxford University Press, 1932), 83–85. For its dating and localization, see Dobschütz, *Christusbilder*, 216, 276.

[54] In at least one manuscript, Paris, BN MS. lat. 18201 (saec. XII–XIII), the *Vindicta* is presented as *Liber secundus* (fol. 122rb) of the *EN*.

1.3.4. Somnium Neronis

More closely associated with the *EN* was the text now called *Somnium Neronis*, which sometimes takes the place of the *Cura* as an adjunct to the *EP*. The title of this thematically and stylistically heterogeneous text reflects accurately the contents of only the first of its several loosely related sections.[55] The *Somnium* proper is based on the *Passio sanctorum apostolorum Petri et Pauli*, chapter 22,[56] and contains an exchange between Nero and Peter (in a different form present also in the *Cura*), in which Peter confirms the truth of Pilate's account of the Crucifixion, Nero's palace collapses after the "gesta Salvatoris" (i.e., the *EN*) have been read, and Nero has a vision of the bleeding Christ, who mentions Pilate's letter and instructs the emperor to avenge his death through Vespasian. This appendix to the *EN* seems to have been motivated by the desire to reiterate the veracity of Pilate's letter, which it always follows, and to demonstrate the potency of divine truth inherent in the *EN*, the center of gravity for both the *EP* and the *Somnium*. Christ's charging Nero with exacting vengeance shows an enemy of Christianity turned into an instrument of God's wrath against the Jews, whose culpability is a prominent theme in the *EN* and the *EP*.

Individual thematic strands present in the first section of the *Somnium* proper not only look back to the main apocryphon but also anticipate the remaining portions of this appendix. Nero's vision serves as a transition to a list of signs that preceded the destruction of Jerusalem (the appearance of a burning star over Jerusalem, a sudden illumination of the temple in the middle of the night, unnatural births of various kinds, and the opening of the heavy temple gates at night). These are drawn from Rufinus's Latin translation of Eusebius's adaptation (*Ecclesiastical History* 3.8.1–9) of Josephus's *Jewish Wars* 6.5.3.[57] The ensuing detailed description of the destruction of Jerusalem is likewise based ultimately on Josephus, as mediated by Eusebius and

---

[55] This appendix to the *EN* has been titled and edited by Ernst von Dobschütz, "A Collection of Old Latin Bible Quotations: *Somnium Neronis*," *Journal of Theological Studies* 16 (1915): 1–27. Its first section has also been printed by Thilo, *Codex apocryphus*, cxl n. 139, and, more recently, by Wolfgang Speyer, "Neue Pilatus-Apokryphen," *Vigiliae Christianae* 32 (1978): 53–59 (without knowledge of Dobschütz's edition). The two earliest manuscripts of this appendix are Einsiedeln, Stiftsbibliothek MS. 169, pp. 102–12, and Paris, BN MS. lat. 5327, fols. 54v–55r, both saec. X.

[56] Lipsius and Bonnet, *Acta apostolorum apocrypha*, 139.

[57] Eusebius of Caesarea, *Die Kirchengeschichte*, 1:214–21; Flavius Josephus, *The Jewish Wars*, ed. H. St. J. Thackeray, 2 vols., The Loeb Classical Library (Cambridge, Mass.: Harvard University Press, 1967–68), 2:459–67.

Rufinus.[58] The rest consists of a long discursive treatise made up in large part of scriptural quotations derived from the Old Latin translation of the Bible. The treatise demonstrates, first, that the destruction of Jerusalem was long foretold by the prophets (Moses, Joshua, Isaiah, Jeremiah, Ezekiel, Hosea, Esdras, and others) and, second, that Christ is indeed the "lapis angularis" ("corner stone") mentioned by Isaiah and that the time of carnal observations of the synagogue has ceased. Not all manuscripts preserve the full text of the *Somnium:* some include only Nero's vision, others add the destruction of Jerusalem, and still others end at various points in the anti-Jewish treatise.

The exact date and provenance of the *Somnium Neronis* have not yet been established. Dobschütz offers no thoughts on the subject, while Speyer remarks with regard to Nero's vision only that late antiquity as time of its origin is not improbable.[59] What seems fairly certain is that the *Somnium* was composed only after the addition of the *EP* to the *EN*. First, its opening sentence, "Cumque haec Claudius suscepisset et Neroni imperatori legisset . . ." ("And when Claudius received these and read to emperor Nero . . .") points directly to the *EP* as its antecedent, and the references to Pilate's letter and to the "gesta Salvatoris" suggest that from its inception the *Somnium* was related to the two. Second, the *Somnium*, in contrast to the *EP*, the *Cura*, and the *Vindicta*, never occurs independently in manuscripts but is always an appendix of the *EN*.[60] As far as I know, it had no autonomous existence in the Middle Ages but was always subsumed by the *EN*, whose colophons often mark its closure.[61]

1.3.5. De Veronilla *and* De Persecutoribus Christi

The *EP*, *Cura*, *Vindicta*, and *Somnium* were the earliest appendices to the *EN*. They were also most common at the height of the *EN*'s popularity: the first is present in approximately 65 percent of over 420 known manuscripts of the apocryphon, the second in 23 percent, and

[58] Dobschütz, "A Collection," 8.

[59] Speyer, "Neue Pilatus-Apokryphen," 57.

[60] In three manuscripts, Cambridge, St. John's College MS. K. 23 (229), fol. 76v (saec. XII), CCCC MS. 320, fol. 113v (saec. XII), and London, BL MS. Royal 10 A. VIII, fol. 149v (saec. XIII), the *Somnium* occurs in conjunction with the *EP* only.

[61] Cf. Aachen, Stadtarchiv MS. KK Regulierherren Nr. 9 (saec. XV), fol. 91ra, "Explicit passio Domini" ("Here ends the Passion of the Lord"); Munich, Bayerische Staatsbibliothek (BSB) Clm 642 (saec. XI), fol. 26r, "Explicivnt gesta Domini Saluatoris" ("Here end the acts of Lord Savior"); Paris, BN MS. lat. 5327 (saec. X), fol. 55r, "Explicit gesta Domini Salvatoris" ("Here ends the Acts of Lord Savior"); Poznań, Miejska Biblioteka Publiczna Rkp. 188 (saec. XV), fol. 87v, "Explicit ewangelium Nicodemii etc." ("Here ends the Gospel of Nicodemus, etc.").

the third and fourth in 6 percent each. Later medieval scribes continued the practice of grafting texts onto the *EN*, but their amplifications
had a more limited circulation. One such later addition, *De Veronilla*,
was a short version of the healing of Tiberius akin to the *Cura*, composed perhaps as early as the tenth century.[62] This text is known
from only four manuscripts, in all of which it is adjacent to or fused
with the *EN*. In the earliest one, Stuttgart, Württembergische Landesbibliothek MS. Theol. phil. 8° 57 (saec. XII), it follows the closing statement of the *EN*, "Finiunt gesta nostri Saluatoris" (fol. 82v; "Here end
the acts of Our Savior") and bears its own title, "Incipit de Veronilla et
de imagine Domini in sindone depicta" ("Here begins [the story] of
Veronilla and of the image of the Lord depicted on muslin").[63] In two
others, Graz, Universitätsbibliothek MS. 628, fol. 122rb–vb (saec. XV/1),
and Prague, Státní knihovna MS. III. D. 13, fols. 24vb–25ra (saec. XIV),
De Veronilla is attached directly, without any graphic signal or intervening white space, to an account of the deaths of the two Herods,
De persecutoribus Christi (beginning, "Paulisper quod de persecutoribus
Christi actum sit videamus. Primus Herodes sub quo passi sunt
infantes . . ."; "Let us briefly consider what was done concerning the
persecutors of Christ. First Herod, under whom the children suffered
death . . ."), which is in turn joined in the same manner to the *EP*.[64]
Except in the Stuttgart copy, the *De Veronilla* concludes with a closing
statement for the *EN*: "Explicit ewangelium Nicodemi etc." ("Here
ends the Gospel of Nicodemus, etc.") in the Berlin manuscript, fol.
45va; "Explicit ewangelium Nicodemi quod est apocrofim et ab eclesia
sancta non tenetur etc. Deo gracias. Alleluya" ("Here ends the Gospel
of Nicodemus, which is apocryphal and not recognized by the Holy
Church. Thanks be to God. Alleluia") in Graz, fol. 122vb; and "Expli-
ciunt gesta Nycodemi de passione Domini. Amen" ("Here end the acts
of Nicodemus concerning the Passion of the Lord. Amen") in Prague,
fol. 25rb.

---

[62] Schönbach, review of *Evangelia apocrypha*, 181–82.

[63] The text from this manuscript has been edited by Hans Ferd. Massmann,
*Der keiser und der kunige buoch oder die sogenannte Kaiserchronik, Gedicht des zwölften
Jahrhunderts*, pt. 3 (Quedlinburg: G. Basse), 579–80, 605–6; cf. also Dobschütz,
Christusbilder, 278*.

[64] The same may be the case in the fourth manuscript, Berlin, SBPK MS.
Theol. lat. fol. 533 (saec. XV in.), which I have not had an opportunity to consult.

1.3.6. Epilogue, De imperatoribus, De destructione ierusalem, De arbore crucis Domini

Several thirteenth- to fifteenth-century manuscripts, mostly of French and British origin, attach to the *EN* an epilogue addressing a monastic audience and restating the title of the apocryphon:

> Nunc ergo, dilectissimi fratres, hanc lectionem quam audistis Nichodemus hebraicis commendauit litteris. Et postea multis succedentibus annis uenit ad Ierusalem magnus imperator Theodosius ibique inuenit illas in pretorio Pilati presidis in publicis descriptas codicibus sicque per illum imperatorem ad nostram deuenerunt notitiam. (Cambridge, St. John's College MS. E. 24, fol. 93r, saec. XV)

> (And so, most beloved brothers, Nicodemus committed this lesson which you have heard into Hebrew letters. And afterwards, many years having passed, the great emperor Theodosius came to Jerusalem and found them there in Pilate's council-chamber, written in public codices; and thus through that emperor they came to our knowledge.)

Although it may appear to be concluding the *EN*, this epilogue is in fact used as a link to further texts on the topics already exploited in other appendices—those of Roman emperors and the destruction of the Jews. These texts are elaborated most fully in the above-quoted Cambridge manuscript, in which the epilogue, ending in the middle of the line, is immediately continued in this manner:

> In illis ergo diebus in quibus crucifixus est Dominus noster Ihesus Christus, Tyberius cesar in urbe Roma quietus manebat quia leprosus erat effectus nichilque adhuc de misterio Christi passionis et resurrectionis audiebat....

> (In those days, therefore, when our Lord Jesus Christ was crucified, emperor Tiberius remained resting in the city of Rome because he was affected by leprosy and had not yet heard about the mystery of Christ's Passion and Resurrection....)

This as yet unpublished text, which I have tentatively called *De imperatoribus*, begins with a somewhat modified theme of Tiberius's conversion, derived ultimately from the *Cura*. The suffering emperor hears about Christ from Pilate, believes the report, and attempts—unsuccessfully—to establish Christianity as the official religion of the empire. After he accepts baptism and is healed, he brings about the deaths of many enemies of Christ. Without any explicit transition, there follow brief notes on several emperors, with their names (Julius Caesar,

Octavian, Herod, Gaius, Claudius) flushed in the margins, and a more extensive account of the ugly life of Nero. The composition ends with a comment on Nero's successors and on the ascension of Vespasian (in other manuscripts Tiberius) to the imperial dignity.

On fol. 96v in the Cambridge manuscript, a rubric, *De Tyto et Uaspasiano,* and a large initial in the margin may indicate the beginning of a new text, also unedited, which in another manuscript—Rouen, Bibl. mun. MS. U. 65, fol. 243rb (saec. XIV)—is perhaps more aptly entitled *De destructione Ierusalem.* This piece was probably intended as a continuation of the *De imperatoribus,* for it begins with the deictic phrase "Iste igitur Uaspasianus . . ." ("Therefore that Vespasianus . . .") effecting a certain degree of textual cohesion between the two. The *De destructione* is a narrative, fashioned after the *Vindicta* (chaps. 1–17), about the conversion and healing of Titus and about his siege and destruction of Jerusalem. It does not, however, continue the story of the miraculous image of Christ but turns instead to Josephus's account (*Jewish Wars* 6.4.6–6.5.2),[65] possibly in Hegesippus's Latin rendition (*Historiae* 5.43),[66] of the burning of the temple and Titus's attempts to save it. In connection with this conflagration, the supernatural signs that heralded the destruction of Jerusalem are rehearsed (cf. *Historiae* 5.44).[67] The *De destructione* ends with the acclamation of Titus as emperor and his condemnation of the Jewish leaders who came to him asking for cessation of persecution (cf. *Jewish Wars* 6.6.1–3; and *Historiae* 5.45–46).[68]

Finally, the *De destructione* is followed by two short, separately titled texts, which seem to belong—although more loosely—to the larger compilatory whole. One of them, introduced on fol. 103r with a rubric "Nota bene de miraculis arboris sancti sic" ("Mark well concerning the miracles of the holy tree as follows") is a version of the legend of the cross; the other, beginning on fol. 103v with the rubric "Nota de Iuda proditore" ("Note concerning Judas the traitor") is a story of Judas. Both of them, edited under the single title *De arbore crucis Domini* by E. M. Thompson,[69] recur in various configurations in other manuscripts of this compilation.[70]

---

[65] Josephus, *The Jewish Wars,* 2:448–59.

[66] Hegesippus, *Hegesippi qui dicitur Historiae libri V,* ed. Vincentius Ussani, CSEL, vol. 66 (Vienna: Hoelder-Pichler-Tempsky, 1932), 390–91.

[67] Hegesippus, *Historiae libri V,* 391–95.

[68] Josephus, *The Jewish Wars,* 2:469–79; Hegesippus, *Historiae libri V,* 395–401.

[69] E. M. Thompson, "Apocryphal Legends," *Journal of the British Archaeological Association* 37 (1881): 241–43.

[70] I owe information on several of those manuscripts to Robert Miller, Brasenose College, Oxford.

The Cambridge collection is not unique. The already mentioned manuscript Rouen, Bibl. mun. MS. U. 65, has the same sequence—*EN* (beginning only in 24.1), *EP*, epilogue, *De imperatoribus*, and *De destructione*—while two others, Oxford, Bodl. Lib. MS. Bodl. 556, fols. 1r–13v (saec. XIII in.), and London, BL MS. Cotton Vesp. E. I, fols. 182v–96v (saec. XV), lack only the *De destructione*. Several codices rearrange the pieces more radically. They reduce the prominence of the *EN* by excising its first section, the account of the trial before Pilate, and begin only in *EN* 11.3, with the words of Matthew 27:57, "Cum sero factum esset, uenit quidam homo . . ." ("When evening fell, there came a man . . ."). The *EN* is embedded in the midst of other texts, so that it no longer dominates or sets the tone for the whole sequence. In Cambridge, Magdalene College MS. F. 4. 15, fols. 87v–91r (saec. XIII), the compilation begins with excerpts from the rood-tree legend on the building of Solomon's temple,[71] followed by a large chunk of the *De destructione* (without the burning of the temple or the subsequent episodes). Then excerpts from the *De arbore* begin abruptly, only to merge with the *EN* (opening with Joseph of Arimathea), extended in turn with the *EP*, the epilogue, and the *De imperatoribus* (on Tiberius only). This arrangement of texts suggests a deliberate design: the construction of the temple is juxtaposed with the annihilation of the holy city, and the story of the cross, culminating in the redemptive Crucifixion and Resurrection, is bound up with both.[72] At least four manuscripts begin the compilation with the *De arbore* and continue with the *EN*, *EP*, epilogue, and *De imperatoribus*.[73] Although transitions between individual texts in these compilations are rough, manuscript layouts (lack of titles, chapters of the *EN* signaled in the same manner as other constituent texts) suggest that they were supposed to form loosely organized yet integral collections of legendary-historical accounts supplementing the gospels.

---

[71] "Post egressionem . . . ," edited by J. R. Mozley, "A New Text of the Story of the Cross," *Journal of Theological Studies* 31 (1930): 117–27. The text used in the compilation extends from chap. 14, "Dauid autem regnauit super Israel . . ." (ibid., 122.20), to chap. 16, ". . . que fecerat dominus Dauid seruo suo et Israel populo suo" (123.32); it ends with the first sentence of chap. 17, "Regnauit autem Salomon xl annis . . ." (124.12–15).

[72] The same pattern of texts occurs in Paris, BN MS. lat. 6755 (saec. XIII/2), and, without the *De imperatoribus*, in Oxford, Bodl. Lib. MS. Rawl. D. 1236 (saec. XIII).

[73] They are London, BL MS. Harley 4725 (saec. XIV); Paris, BN MSS. lat. 1722 (saec. XII–XIII) and lat. 3338 (saec. XIII–XIV; this manuscript inserts the *Cura* between the *EP* and the *De imperatoribus* and adds the *De destructione* at the end); Winchester, Cathedral Library MS. 7 (saec. XIII).

The epilogue, usually a transition to the *De imperatoribus*, could also serve as a link to the complete text of the *De arbore*, followed by a version of the *Cura;* this sequence is found in some fifteenth-century manuscripts from central Europe. In one of them, Schlägl, Stiftsbibliothek MS. 156 Cpl. 145 (saec. XV/2), the legend of the cross begins, just like the other subdivisions of the *EN* in that manuscript, with a larger initial. It is not separated from the apocryphon with extra space, and the running title in the top margin continues to identify it as the *EN*.[74] In other manuscripts, layout features do not suggest such a tight connection between the texts, yet even there their co-occurrence seems to be deliberate rather than accidental.[75]

1.3.7. Gregory of Tours and pseudo-Augustine

The last pair of satellite texts that attach themselves to the *EN* in several British codices of the twelfth century or later differs from the appendices discussed above in that they usually precede rather than follow the apocryphon and are concerned with the stories of Joseph of Arimathea and Christ's Descent into Hell rather than with Rome and Jerusalem. The first of these texts is an excerpt beginning "Gregorius Turonensis in gestis Francorum de passione et resurrectione Domini refert hec. Apprehensus autem et Ioseph qui cum aromatibus corpus Christi conditum in suo monumento recondidit ..." (CCCC MS. 441, p. 392a, saec. XIII; "Gregory of Tours in his *Historia Francorum* relates the following concerning the Passion and Resurrection of the Lord: Moreover, Joseph, who laid in his sepulcher the body of Christ anointed with aromatic oils, also having been arrested ..."), attributed to Gregory of Tours. It corresponds to the passage mentioned above from the *Decem libris historiarum*, chapter 1.21, which alludes to the *Gesta Pilati* and is the earliest echo of the *EN* in Latin literature.[76]

The second excerpt opens, "Augustinus quoque sanctus in sermonibus de sabbato pasche refert hec. Attonite mentes obstupuere tortorum ..." ("Also St. Augustine in his sermons on the sabbat of the

---

[74] The running title changes to "Conversio Tiberii" on fol. 389v, where the *Cura* begins.

[75] The other manuscripts are České Budějovice, Státní vědecká knihovna MSS. 1 VB 28 (saec. XV/2; the *Cura* ends on fol. 93v, "Explicit ewangelium Nycodemi cum aliis narracionibus ..."; "Here ends the Gospel of Nicodemus with other stories ...") and 1 VB 58 (saec. XV); Klosterneuburg, Stiftsbibliothek MS. 495 (saec. XV in.); and the manuscript used by Thompson, "Apocryphal Legends."

[76] In the form in which it usually accompanies the apocryphon, this passage has been printed from Oxford, Bodl. Lib. MS. Bodl. 556, fol. 1r (saec. XIII in.), by David C. Fowler, "The Middle English Gospel of Nicodemus in Winchester MS. 33," *Leeds Studies in English*, n.s., 19 (1988): 79–81.

Pasch relates the following: The dazed minds of the torturers became stupefied . . ."), and is lifted from the sermons of Eusebius "Gallicanus" "De pascha I" and "De pascha IA,"[77] which were often combined with the pseudo-Augustinian "Sermo 160." It relates the terror of the infernal troops at Christ's Descent and is reminiscent of, though not identical with, chapter 22 of the *EN*. Placed before the title of the *EN*, the two extracts usually serve as an introduction to the apocryphon;[78] they were probably viewed as patristic recommendations of the *EN*, raising its prestige and guaranteeing its doctrinal correctness.

1.4. Verse adaptation of the *Evangelium Nicodemi*

Besides the prose versions, there survives one Latin verse adaptation of the *EN*, entitled *Palestra de victoria Christi*.[79] This as yet unedited epic poem is the only known Latin counterpart to vernacular poetic translations and paraphrases of the apocryphon. Its exact origin remains unknown. Karl Langosch suggests that it may have been composed in the thirteenth century in southeastern Germany, while Willi Beine argues that the late dates of extant manuscripts indicate a much later date of composition, possibly the beginning of the fifteenth century, and associates the poem with the Prague-Wrocław-Cracow triangle.[80] Walther lists ten manuscripts, one of which, Gdansk, Bib-

---

[77] Eusebius "Gallicanus," *Collectio homiliarum*, 1:141–50; cf. 2:881–86.

[78] Both texts precede the title in CCCC MSS. 288, fol. 38r–v (saec. XIII), and 441, pp. 392–93 (saec. XIII); Edinburgh, National Library of Scotland MS. Adv. 18. 5. 18, 204r–5r (saec. XIII); London, BL MSS. Addit. 17003, fols. 66v–68r (saec. XV), and Royal 7 C. XII, fol. 219ra–rb (saec. XII). Only in Oxford, Bodl. Lib. MS. Bodl. 556, fol. 1r–v (saec. XII ex.), do they follow the title. In London, BL MS. Arundel 52, fols. 47r (saec. XIII–XIV), the two passages follow the *EN*. Two manuscripts, Cambridge, Pembroke College MS. 256, fol. 58r (saec. XII ex.), and Oxford, Bodl. Lib. MS. Addit. A. 44, fol. 105r–v (saec. XIII in.), include only the excerpt from Gregory of Tours.

[79] Beg. "Sceptritenentis arat sollers mea Clyo palestram . . ."; Hans Walther, *Carmina medii aevi posterioris Latina*, vol. 1, *Initia carminum ac versuum medii aevi posterioris Latinorum* . . . (Göttingen: Vandenhoeck & Ruprecht, 1959), nos. 5449, 5450, 17323; idem, *Carmina medii aevi posterioris Latina*, vol. 1, pt. 1, *Initia carminum ac versuum medii aevi posterioris Latinorum* . . . *Ergänzungen und Berichtigungen zur 1. Auflage von 1959* (Göttingen: Vandenhoeck & Ruprecht, 1969), no. 17323.

[80] Karl Langosch, "Überlieferungsgeschichte der mittellateinischen Literatur," in *Geschichte der Textüberlieferung der antiken und mittelalterlichen Literatur*, ed. Karl Langosch et al., vol. 2 (Zürich: Atlantis, 1964), 80; Willi Beine, "Palestra," in *Die deutsche Literatur des Mittelalters: Verfasserlexikon*, 2d rev. ed., ed. Kurt Ruh, vol. 7 (Berlin: Walter de Gruyter, 1989), 275–76.

lioteka Polskiej Akademii Nauk MS. Mar. Q. 24, was lost during World War II.[81] Three additional manuscripts, all of Polish origin but kept until the 1920s in the Imperatorskaia Publichnaia Biblioteka in St. Petersburg, were described in detail by Aleksander Brückner in his studies of medieval Latin poetry in Poland.[82] It appears, therefore, that the poem circulated widely in Poland and throughout central Europe in the fifteenth century. Brückner identifies some borrowings from it in a poem by Martinus of Słupca, the teacher of Johannes who owned a copy of the *Palestra*, and finds excerpts from it in a manuscript made in 1447 in Cracow by Nicolaus of Lublin.[83]

The *Palestra* begins with thirty-seven hexameters of proposition and invocation; the narrative proper is rendered in over seven hundred leonine distichs. In most manuscripts the poem is preceded by a prose prologue summarizing its contents. I shall quote it here from Cracow, Biblioteka Jagiellońska MS. 2195, fol. 142r–v, written in 1466 by Martin of Łęczyca,[84] to give an indication of the poem's scope:[85]

Primo auctor breuiter tractat de creacione mundi et de creacione Ade et de lapsu eiusdem ac quomodo filius Dei, ne totum genus hvmanum periret, de gloriosa virgine Maria natus, se

---

[81] Personal communication from Prof. Dr. hab. Zbigniew Nowak, director of the library. Not listed by Walther but noticed by Beine, "Palestra," 275, is Wrocław, Biblioteka Uniwersytecka MS. I O 23, fols. 72v–91r (saec. XV/1), from the Cistercian library at Rudy, near Racibórz, Poland; cf. Stanisław Rybandt, *Katalog ksiąg zachowanych z średniowiecznej biblioteki Cystersów w Rudach* (Warsaw: Instytut Wydawniczy Pax, 1979), 60–62.

[82] They were Lat. XVII, Fol. 29, fols. 103v–24r, written in 1451 by Maternus, a Cistercian monk from Koprzywnica, Poland (Aleksander Brückner, "Średniowieczna poezya łacińska w Polsce. Część druga," *Rozprawy Akademii Umiejętności w Krakowie. Wydział Filologiczny* 22 [1893]: 39–40); Lat. XVII, Qu. 18, fols. 1–44 (saec. XV), belonging to "Iohannes de Slupcza Clericus Gneznensis diocesis publicus," who wrote parts of this manuscript but not the *Palestra*, copied in an older hand (idem, "Średniowieczna poezya łacińska w Polsce," *Rozprawy Akademii Umiejętności w Krakowie. Wydział Filologiczny* 16 [1892]: 312–53); and Lat. XVII, Qu. 140, fols. 137–79, from the Benedictine monastery at Łysiec (Holy Cross) in the Świętokrzyskie Mountains, parts of which, including the *Palestra*, were copied in 1451 by Stanislaus of Cracow (idem, "Średniowieczna poezya . . . Część druga," 40–42). Between 1922 and 1924, the Imperial Library in St. Petersburg returned all three manuscripts to the Biblioteka Narodowa in Warsaw, where they unfortunately perished during World War II (personal communication from Dr. Andrzej Piber, Director of the Department of Manuscripts).

[83] Aleksander Brückner, "Średniowieczna poezya," 325–26; idem, "Średniowieczna poezya . . . Część druga," 49.

[84] Brückner, "Średniowieczna poezya . . . Część druga," 6–28.

[85] I have normalized punctuation and capitalization but preserved orthographic and grammatical idiosyncrasies. I should like to thank Biblioteka Jagiellońska for permission to print this text and Mr. Ryszard Tatarzyński for his help with its transcription.

crucifigii pro nostra redempcione voluit. Quem crucifixum Ioseph ab Arimatia honorifice sepeliuit, propter quod Iudei ipsum incarceraverunt, signantes hostium carceris sigillis propriis et sepulcrum Cristi muniuerunt custodibus. Tercia autem die carcerem apperuerunt vt Ioseph occiderent sed inclusum in carcere non invenerunt. Tunc mirantibus Iudeis supervenerunt custodes sepulcri Cristi, qui Iudeis dixerunt se angelum ad sepulcrum Cristi vidisse qui Cristum dixit ex mortuis resurexisse. Sed Iudei custodes corrumperunt pecunia vt dicerent corpus Cristi per discipulos suos sublatum esse. Et postea facit exclamacionem contra munera. Interea insonuit Iudeis[86] quomodo Ioseph esset inventus in Arimathia, quem Iudei pacifice vocauerunt per litteras in Ierusalem vt narraret eis quis eum de carceribus liberasset. Ioseph autem veniens narrauit quod Cristus resurgens a mortuis ipso orante sibi ante diem in carcere apparuit et osculans eum de carcere eduxerit, carcerem ad alta aeris eleuans, et quod non solum Cristus resurrexisset sed multos secum excitauit ab inferis. De numero quorum duos filios Simeonis dixit esse in Arimathia nihil loquentes sed tamen Deum laudantes. Ad quos Iudei perientes dvxerunt eos in Ierusalem cum honore, adiurantes eos per Deum vt dicerent qualiter ab inferis essent liberati. Illi autem poposcerunt cartas et scripserunt gesta Cristi in inferis, dicentes quod diu ante passionem Cristi spiritualis lux resplenduit apud inferos, vnde gauisi sunt sancti quia Cristum sperabant cito venturum et eos liberatorum. Cum autem tempus appropinquauit passionis Cristi, Sathan veniens ad infernum clamabat ad demones inferiores vt prepararent tormenta quia Ihesus venturus esset in infernum, qui sibi multa mala in mundo intulerat et hoc quod esset timens mortem narrauit. Cum autem demones respondent quod iste Ihesus esset qui Lazarum suscitauerat, diswaserunt sibi ne eum invaderet eo quod nimis potentem senserant vocem dicentis "Lazare, veni foras." Sathan autem de hac diswasione reprehendit demones. Cum ergo sic litigarent, venit vox angelorum dicentium "Tollite portas, principes, vestras." Deinde Ihesus venit et demones expugnans sanctos patres liberauit [fol. 124v] et eductos de inferno Michaeli comisit, qui eos ad terrestrem paradisum perduxit, vbi cum Elya, Enoch et latrone tripudium habuerunt, quos Cristus die quadragesima ad celos perduxit. Cuius ascensionem demones cognoscentes in aera fugerunt et angeli de

---

[86] Graz, Universitätsbibliothek MS. 1259, fol. 32r, reads "fama insonuit."

inferioribus choris mirabantur. Deinde sedet in solio patris, vbi requiescunt septem columne, id est, septem dona Spiritus sancti et angeli astantes cum sanctis coram throno colaudant eum. Librum eciam vite in manu tenent, in quo scripti sunt omnes sancti cum meritis suis, primo gloriosa virgo Maria, deinde angeli et martires ex post. Qui quia sunt sine numero et merita ipsorum nullus artifex potest describere neque gloriam ipsorum meditari, ideo propter breuitatem imponens finem libello carmen cecinerit metricum.

(First the author briefly discusses the Creation of the world, and the creation of Adam, and his Fall, and how the Son of God, born of the glorious Virgin Mary, wished to be crucified for our Redemption, lest the entire humankind perished. After he was crucified, Joseph of Arimathea buried him with honor; because of that, the Jews imprisoned him, marking the door of the prison with their seals, and they set guards at Christ's sepulcher. However, on the third day they opened the prison to kill Joseph but did not find the prisoner in the prison. While the Jews were marveling, there came the guards of Christ's sepulcher, who told the Jews that they had seen an angel at Christ's sepulcher who said that Christ had risen from the dead. But the Jews enticed the guards with money to say that the body of Christ had been taken away by his disciples. And afterwards he [the author] makes an exclamation against gifts. Meanwhile the Jews heard how Joseph had been found in Arimathea; they peaceably invited him by letters to Jerusalem so that he might tell them who had freed him from prison. And indeed when he came, Joseph related that while he was praying, Christ, rising from the dead, appeared to him in prison before dawn and, kissing him, led him out of prison, lifting the prison high into air, and that not only Christ himself had risen but he had roused up many from hell. He said that two sons of Simeon, who were among them, were in Arimathea, saying nothing but yet praising God. Approaching them, the Jews led them to Jerusalem with honor, adjuring them in the name of God to say how they had been freed from hell. But they requested paper and wrote the deeds of Christ in hell, saying that long before Christ's Passion, spiritual light shone brightly in the underworld, whereat the saints rejoiced because they expected that Christ would soon come and free them. And when the time of Christ's Passion approached, Satan, coming to hell, kept calling out to lesser devils to prepare torments because Jesus was coming to hell, who had caused him much grief in the world, and reported that he feared death. But when the demons respond that he was the Jesus who had resuscitated Lazarus, they advised against his assailing him because they had sensed immense power in the voice of him who said, "Come forth, Lazarus." But Satan chided the demons for that advice. So when they argued thus, there came a voice of angels saying, "Lift up your gates, princes." Thereupon came Jesus and subduing the demons liberated holy fathers and, having led them out, he entrusted them to Michael, who led them to the terrestrial paradise, where they solemnly rejoiced together with Elijah, Enoch and the Thief; on the fortieth day Christ led them into heavens. Recognizing his Ascension, demons fled in the air, and angels of the lower choirs marveled. He then sits on the throne of the Father, where the seven columns rest, i.e., the seven gifts of the Holy Spirit, and the angels and saints attending before his throne praise him together. They also hold in their hands the Book of Life, in which are entered all the saints with their merits, and in the first place the glorious Virgin Mary, and then angels, and martyrs thereafter. Because they are innumerable and because no artist could either describe or meditate on their glory, therefore for the sake of brevity, bringing the book to an end, he will have sung his metrical poem.)

Most of the poem is taken up with a poetic paraphrase of the imprisonment and release of Joseph and of the Harrowing of Hell—the middle sections of this summary read like an epitome of the *EN*. Its beginning and end, however, provide a frame that extends beyond the narrative and doctrinal bounds of the apocryphon. It opens with an account of the Fall of humanity, which explains the need for Christ's Incarnation and painful death on the cross. A vision of the glorified Christ, enthroned and surrounded by angels and saints, and of the prominently displayed Book of Life, in which are inscribed the names of all the saints, forms the poem's conclusion. The *Palestra* thus presents a complete story of the Redemption, from the events that necessitated it to its fruition in the restoration of humankind to its heavenly inheritance.

In shaping his material, the poet took some liberties with his apocryphal source. He did not slavishly follow the original but freely explored its poetic potential. He interpolated, altered, and abridged with little hesitation, following the storyline rather than the wording of the *EN*. He described, for instance, the illumination of hell at the moment of Christ's birth and associated the prophets' speeches with that occasion. Throughout the *Palestra*, the language is deliberately, at times

studiously, poetic, saturated with classical echoes, often far removed
from the simple idiom of the apocryphon.

1.5. *Speculum historiale* and *Legenda aurea*

Large portions of the Latin *EN* were also disseminated through the
medium of two extremely popular compilations, Vincent of Beauvais's
Speculum historiale and Jacobus a Voragine's *Legenda aurea*.[87] The former, completed and revised probably before 1260 as part of the *Speculum maius*, an encyclopedic compendium of excerpts and quotations,
contains a history of humanity from Creation until 1254, constructed
from scriptural, apocryphal, and legendary materials. In this context,
it includes an exposition of Christ's Passion, Descent into Hell, and
Resurrection, an exposition highly indebted to the *EN*. In chapter 40,
"De discussione causæ eius coram Pilato" ("On the examination of his
case before Pilate"), Christ's exchange with Pilate concerning truth and
the reports of Christ's miracles are partly quoted and partly paraphrased from *EN* 3.2, 4.5, 5.1, and 6.1 to 8. The following chapter, "De
illusione Herodis, & iudicio Pilati" (chap. 41; "On Herod's mockery
and Pilate's judgement"), briefly recounts Pilate's wife's dream in
terms borrowed from the *EN* (2.1), and chapter 48, "De sepultura
Domini" ("On the entombment of the Lord"), relates the imprisonment
of Joseph of Arimathea on the basis of *EN* 12.1. In the accounts of
Joseph's Christophany and Christ's Descent into Hell (chaps. 56–63),
short excerpts give way to large-scale adaptation, as Vincent incorporates, for the most part verbatim, much of the second and third sections of the *EN* (chaps. 12.2 to 27), with only occasional omissions
designed to speed up the flow of the narrative.[88]

The *Legenda aurea*, the other compilation to include large portions
of the *EN*, was written before 1267 and became perhaps the most influential hagiographical collection of the Middle Ages. Like Vincent,
Jacobus makes liberal use of apocryphal narratives; he evokes the *EN*
repeatedly: in chapter 53, quoting Pilate's and Christ's exchange concerning truth (*EN* 3.2); in chapters 54 and 67, alluding to Joseph's
imprisonment (*EN* 12); and in chapter 68, reporting Seth's journey to
paradise (*EN* 19.1). Most important for popularization of the *EN* is,
however, chapter 54, "De resurrectione Domini" ("On the Resurrection

---

[87] Vincent of Beauvais, *Speculum historiale* (1624; repr., Graz: Akademische
Druck- u. Verlagsanstalt, 1965); Jacobus a Voragine, *Jacobi a Voragine Legenda aurea
vulgo Historia Lombardica dicta*, ed. Th. Graesse (1890; repr., Osnabrück: O. Zeller,
1969).

[88] Vincent of Beauvais, *Speculum historiale*, 236, 238, 242–44.

of the Lord")." Here Jacobus first summarizes pseudo-Augustine's
"Sermo 160" and then reproduces the entire *DI* (*EN* 18–27), albeit with
cuts and abridgements. On the whole, the *Legenda* gives less of the *EN*
than the *Speculum*, but it may have played a more central role in the
apocryphon's dissemination, for its abbreviated version of the *DI*
acquired a quasi-independent status and was often transmitted as a
separate text.[90]

Both the *Speculum* and the *Legenda* circulated in hundreds, if not
thousands, of manuscripts.[91] In fact, it is likely that more people
knew the *EN* or about the *EN* indirectly from these secondary sources
than directly from the manuscripts of the apocryphon itself. Diffusing
the apocryphal narrative, the two may have also contributed to the
wide adoption of its current title, *Evangelium Nicodemi*, which both of
them employ repeatedly, although not exclusively.

The *EN*, in the form in which it was available to medieval readers (and
in which it is still preserved in over four hundred manuscripts), was
hardly a uniform, well-defined, discrete text. Its form and scope fluc-
tuated on par with its title. The old Passion-Resurrection narrative continued to evolve linguistically and stylistically throughout its history,
its apocryphal character and self-acknowledged status as translation
inviting scribal intervention. Thematically, it tended to expand beyond
its original boundaries by attracting and absorbing other texts: medieval scribes showed little hesitation in supplying thematic correction or
completion whenever they thought these were called for. Thus they
reworked the portrait of Pilate, recasting him as a villain justly condemned; completed the story of the Redemption with the conversion
of a Roman emperor, foreshadowing the ultimate triumph of Christianity; and appended accounts of divine vengeance against the Jews, emphatically severing the umbilical tie between Christianity and Judaism.
Receptive of various extensions, the *EN* remained highly pliable. It was
easily transformed into homilies, adapted to historiographic contexts,
fitted into poetic form, cut and pasted into hagiographic and encyclo-

[89] Jacobus a Voragine, *Legenda aurea*, 226, 241–44, 302–3.
[90] Cf. Augsburg, Universitätsbibliothek Cod. II. 1. 2°. 163, fols. 241v–42v (saec.
XV); Berlin, SBPK MS. Theol. lat. qu. 57, fols. 92vb–93va (saec. XV); and Oxford,
Bodl. Lib. MS. Ashm. 1289, fol. 72rb–vb (saec. XIV in.).
[91] M.-C. Duchenne, Gregory G. Guzman, and J. B. Voorbij, "Une Liste des
manuscrits du *Speculum historiale* de Vincent de Beauvais," *Scriptorium* 41 (1987):
286–94; Barbara Fleith, "Le Classement des quelque 1000 manuscrits de la *Legenda
aurea* latine en vue de l'établissement d'une histoire de la tradition," in *Legenda
aurea: Sept siècles de diffusion. Actes du colloque international sur la Legenda aurea:
Texte latin et branches vernaculaires*, ed. Brenda Dunn-Lardeau (Montréal: Éditions
Bellarmin, 1986), 19–24.

pedic compilations. Throughout the Middle Ages, it was a vibrant, living work: growing and mutating, teaching and delighting generations of readers.

2. The *Evangelium Nicodemi* and the canonical Scriptures

The *EN* enjoyed a somewhat ambiguous status among religious texts of the Middle Ages: it was generally recognized as extracanonical, yet the influence it exerted and the respect it commanded situate it among the period's most prestigious, culturally most significant texts. Since the ninth century, when its dissemination first began to gain momentum, until it finally succumbed to the censures of the Reformation, the *EN* nourished pious imagination and satiated pious curiosity practically unrestrained by ecclesiastical authority.

That the *EN* was generally known and treated as an apocryphon during the later Middle Ages is clear from its immediate manuscript contexts as well as from occasional inscriptions that unambiguously identify it as such. Assuming that many medieval manuscripts were not random assemblages but rather purposeful and deliberate collections of texts, the frequency with which the *EN* occurs alongside other scripturally marginal, noncanonical works suggests that it was viewed as sharing their essential nature. Several of its manuscripts are *par excellence* apocryphal collections, containing nothing or little besides apocryphal texts; such are, for instance, Berkeley, University of California, Bancroft Library MS. UCB 20 (saec. XII); Paris, BN MSS. lat. 1652 (saec. XV), lat. 5556 (saec. XIV), and lat. 5559A (saec. XIV/1); and Vatican City, Bibl. Apost. Vatic. MS. Vat. lat. 5094 (saec. XII). In others, the *EN* occurs among authored works, but even then frequently in the company of such texts as *Pseudo-Matthew* and other infancy narratives, *Liber Methodii*, *Transitus Mariae*, *Visio Pauli*, *Vita Adae et Evae*, or the correspondence of pseudo-Jesus and pseudo-Lentulus.

Since the ninth century, occasional explicit comments about the *EN's* apocryphal character corroborate the evidence of apocryphal contexts. We do not know whether before the ninth century the *EN* was at all viewed through the prism of the Scriptures, and hence as apocryphal. It is not mentioned by title in any of the early lists of apocrypha, not even in the extensive and important *Decretum pseudo-Gelasianum*, compiled in the fourth and sixth centuries.[92] The only medieval list-

---

[92] Ernst von Dobschütz, ed., *Das Decretum Gelasianum de libris recipiendis et non recipiendis*, Texte und Untersuchungen, vol. 38, no. 3 (Leipzig: J. C. Hinrichs, 1912), 320.

ing of apocryphal books to include the *EN*, the twelfth-century Samaritan *Elenchus* which refers to it as "sefer be sôrêĕt," or "a book of gospel," was unknown to the Europeans.[93]

Nevertheless, from at least the ninth century, some scribes began emphatically to dissociate the *EN* from the canonical writings. An important manuscript from that period, Laon, Bibl. mun. MS. 265, contains a note intended to dispel any doubt about the *EN*'s spuriousness: "Hunc librum qui uocatur gesta saluatoris nullatenus recipimus quia nullum habet pondus auctoritatis, quia sanctus papa Gelasius cum lxx episcopis, uiris erudissimis, inter apocriphas deputauit scripturas" (fol. 2r; "We by no means accept this book which is called Acts of the Savior because it has no weight of authority as holy pope Gelasius, together with seventy bishops, most learned men, classed it among apocryphal scriptures"). Since, as observed above, the surviving manuscripts of the *Decretum pseudo-Gelasianum* make no mention of the *EN* under any recognizable title, the comment is rather puzzling. Several explanations are possible. The scribe may have associated the condemnation of one Leucius, "discipulus diaboli" ("the devil's disciple") and the supposed author of the apocryphal *Acts of John*, with the names of the two sons of Simeon, Leucius and Carinus, raised from the dead, according to the *DI*;[94] or he may have used an amplified, no longer extant copy of the *Decretum*; or, finally, he may have just assumed that such a condemnation existed, without consulting the *Decretum*. In any case, his note is the earliest indication of the concern about the possibility of mistaking the Latin *EN* for a canonical text and the earliest acknowledgement of its apocryphal character.

The connection between the *EN* and the New Testament canon was not brought to the fore until the twelfth century, after the term "evangelium" became attached to the apocryphon.[95] The title *Evange-*

---

[93] Marek Starowieyski, ed., *Apokryfy Nowego Testamentu*, vol. 1, *Ewangelie apokryficzne*, pt. 1 (Lublin: Towarzystwo Naukowe Katolickiego Uniwersytetu Lubelskiego, 1986), 63.

[94] Dobschütz, *Das Decretum Gelasianum*, 298.

[95] In later manuscripts, inscriptions indicative of the scribes' or the readers' awareness of the work's apocryphal status are relatively common. We find them, for instance, in Geneva-Cologny, Bibliothèque Bodmer MS. Bodmer 127 (saec. XII), fol. 2r, "hec inter apocrypha [esse ?] putatur" ("this is considered [to be ?] among apocrypha"); in Paris, BN MS. lat. 4999A (saec. XII ex.), fol. 76r, "Euangelium Nichodemi quod apocrifum reputatur" ("the Gospel of Nicodemus which is deemed apocryphal"); in Brussels, Bibliothèque royale Albert Ier MS. II 937 (saec. XIII), fol. 6v, "apocrifim" ("apocryphal") written in the margin opposite the opening of the *DI*; in Graz, Universitätsbibliothek MS. 628 (saec. XV/1), fol. 122vb, "Explicit ewangelium Nicodemi quod est apocrofim et ab eclesia sancta non tenetur etc." ("Here ends the Gospel of Nicodemus, which is apocryphal and not accepted by the Holy Church, etc."); and in Wolfenbüttel, Herzog-August-Biblio-

lium Nicodemi made one of its early Latin appearances in the list of Hugh Pudsey's (d. 1195) benefactions to the library of Durham Cathedral.[96] It became widespread only in the fourteenth and fifteenth centuries, at least partly due to its use by Vincent of Beauvais and Jacobus a Voragine. The earliest copies of the *EN*, dating from between the ninth and twelfth centuries, overwhelmingly favor the title that does not draw attention to the scriptural canon, *Gesta Salvatoris;* this appellation remained common in later manuscripts as well.

Even during the high Middle Ages, titles other than *Evangelium Nicodemi* abound. Some, like *Acta Christi Domini* (Paris, BN MS. lat. 3454, saec. XII)—but not *Acta Pilati,* a common modern title for the Greek version—*Parlipomenon de gestis D. N. J. C.* (Paris, BN MS. lat. 14864, saec. XII ex.), or *Explanatio dominicae passionis* (Paris, BN MS. lat. 1933, saec. XII–XIII), highlight the main theme of the work, that is, the events of the Passion of Jesus Christ. Others exploit the authority of Nicodemus (mentioned in Jn. 3:1, 7:50, and 19:39) but do not refer to the work as "evangelium"; such are, for example, *Passio Domini secundum Nicodemum* (Cambridge, Peterhouse MS. 242, saec. XIII), *Tractatus secundum Nicodemum* (London, BL MS. Royal 8 B. XV, saec. XIV), *Historia Nicodemi* (Oxford, Bodl. Lib. MS. Digby 16, saec. XIV), and *Epistola Beati Nichodemi* (Basel, Universitätsbibliothek MS. A X 102, saec. XV/2).

Still others use the word "evangelium" but do not associate it with Nicodemus. In several manuscripts, the apocryphon is entitled *Evangelium Nazaraeorum,*[97] and some influential writers were clearly familiar with this designation; we find it, for example, in Ludolph of Saxony's *Vita Christi* (pt. 2, chap. 75), Thomas of Chobham's *Summa de arte praedicandi,* and Vincent of Beauvais's *Speculum naturale.*[98] The authentic *Evangelium Nazaraeorum* was apparently familiar to Jerome, who repeatedly quoted from the Hebrew gospel used by the Nazaraeans and even claimed to have translated it. It was known in the Middle Ages only through a handful of fragments, quoted by Sedulius Scotus and Haimo of Auxerre in the ninth century, by Peter Comestor

---

thek Cod. Guelf. 83.2 Aug. fol. (saec. XV), fol. 246ra, "Et sic est finis euangelii Nichodemi et apocrifum . . ." ("And thus ends the Gospel of Nicodemus and an apocryphon . . .").

[96] Durham Cathedral, *Catalogues of the Library of Durham Cathedral,* Publications of the Surtees Society, vol. 7 (London: J. B. Nichols and Son, 1838), 119.

[97] The manuscripts in question are CCCC MS. 288 (saec. XIII); Oxford, Merton College MS. 13 (saec. XIV ex.–XV); Paris, BN MS. lat. 3338 (saec. XIII ex.–XIV in.); and Vatican City, Bibl. Apost. Vatic. MS. Vat. lat. 4578 (saec. XIV).

[98] Ludolph of Saxony, *Vita Jesu Christi,* ed. L. M. Rigollot (Paris: Victor Palmé, 1878), 4:205; Thomas of Chobham, *Summa de arte praedicandi,* ed. Franco Morenzoni, CC CM, vol. 82 (Turnhout: Brepols, 1988), 110.696; Vincent of Beauvais, *Speculum naturale* (1624; repr., Graz: Akademische Druck- u. Verlagsanstalt, 1964), 8.

in *Historia scholastica* (chap. 178) in the twelfth, by a redactor of Peter of Riga's *Aurora* in the thirteenth, and by a few anonymous writers.[99] The brevity of the extant fragments makes it difficult to determine the exact contents of that spurious gospel; according to Jerome, many considered it the Hebrew original of the Gospel according to Matthew, but this view is not generally accepted today. If not a result of genuine confusion, the appropriation of the title *Evangelium Nazaraeorum* for the apocryphon of the Passion allegedly written by Nicodemus may have been, like the addition of excerpts from pseudo-Augustine and Gregory of Tours, an attempt to find a respectable patron for the *EN* and thereby bring it into the mainstream of religious culture. The same motive may have prompted an English redactor to ascribe the Latin translation to St. Ambrose of Milan,[100] and another anonymous scribe to mention emperor Constantine in the prologue.[101]

Recognition of the *EN*'s apocryphal nature did not automatically necessitate its rejection or condemnation. Medieval attitudes to apocrypha were as varied as the term "apocryphon" was polysemous. Since Christian antiquity the term was used to refer to several categories of texts: to secret books intended only for the initiated, such as certain gnostic writings; to books containing teachings deemed false, untrue, or heretical; to books outside the canon, whose liturgical, public use was forbidden but which could be used in private devotions; and to books that remained in some relation to the Bible but whose authorship was uncertain or unknown. Patristic views on apocrypha ranged accordingly from openly hostile to tolerant, depending on the nature of the texts designated as apocryphal.[102] For the Middle Ages, it was

---

[99] Geerard, *Clavis*, no. 10. Erich Klostermann, *Apocrypha*, vol. 2, *Evangelien*, 3rd ed., Kleine Texte für Vorlesungen und Übungen, vol. 8 (Berlin: W. de Gruyter, 1929), 4–12; P. Vielhauer, "Jewish-Christian Gospels," in *New Testament Apocrypha*, vol. 1, *Gospels and Related Writings*, ed. Edgar Hennecke, rev. W. Schneemelcher, English trans. ed. R. McL. Wilson (Philadelphia: Westminster Press, 1963), 137–39; Starowieyski, *Apokryfy Nowego Testamentu*, 76; Peter Comestor, *Historia scholastica*, PL 198:1633.

[100] That ascription occurs in four manuscripts, all connected with the British Isles: Rome, Biblioteca Alessandrina MS. 120 (saec. XIV); Cambridge, St. John's College MS. B. 20 (saec. XII); Cambridge, Trinity College MS. B. 5. 19 (saec. XIII in.); and Oxford, Bodl. Lib. MS. Bodl. 428 (saec. XIII/1). It also occurs in a medieval book list from Peterborough Abbey; see M. R. James, *Lists of Manuscripts Formerly in Peterborough Abbey Library* (London: Oxford University Press, 1926), 67.

[101] Paris, Bibliothèque Mazarine MS. 1730 (saec. XIV).

[102] The literature on the subject is very rich; for a useful survey of patristic views, with quotations from relevant authors, see Stephanus Székely, *Bibliotheca apocrypha. Introductio historico-critica in libros apocryphos utriusque testamenti cum explicatione argumenti et doctrinae* (Freiburg i. Br.: B. Herder, 1913), 1–9; Marek Starowieyski, "Les Apocryphes chez les écrivans du IVe siècle," in *Miscellanea historiae ecclesiasticae VI, Congrès de Varsovie* (Brussels: Editions Nauwelaerts, 1983),

the obscurity of origin rather than heretical, damnable content that constituted the primary determinant of apocryphal character. Medieval definitions emphasize unknown provenance but admit that, although apocrypha lack authority, they may contain seeds of truth scattered among falsehoods. "Apocrifa autem dici ecclesiastici doctores tradunt; non quia omnia mentiantur, sed quia dubiae et suspectae auctoritatis esse videantur" ("The doctors of the Church report that apocrypha are so called not because they are mendacious, but because their authority may seem dubious or suspect"), explains Bernaldus Presbyter Constantiensis (b. ca. 1054, d. 1100) in his treatise *De excommunicatis vitandis, de reconciliatione lapsorum et de fontibus iuris ecclesiastici*.[103] He adds, "Nam sepissime multa canonica suis neniis interserunt, quae nequaquam catholici cum eisdem neniis refutare debebunt" ("For very often they intersperse among their trifles canonical matter, which those who are orthodox should by no means refute together with those trifles"). A similar definition occurs in Johannes Balbus's *Catholicon* (1286):[104] "Apocrifa proprie dicuntur illa scripta quorum origo et autor ignoratur et quamuis sint ibi multa uera tamen non habentur in autoritate propter plura falsa que ibi continentur" ("'Apocrypha' are properly called those writings whose origin and author are unknown, and although they may contain much truth, they are not considered authoritative on account of more falsehoods which they contain").[105]

While accepting and popularizing apocrypha as a potential source of truth, medieval writers often felt compelled to explain and justify their inclusion. Thus, refusing to exclude from her *Legendae* allegedly apocryphal sources, Hrotsvitha of Gandersheim (b. ca. 935, d. after 972), points out the limitations of human interpretive faculties, which may be deceived by surface appearances; it is better to err on the side of caution, since, she says, "quod videtur falsitas, / forsan probabitur esse veritas" ("what appears to be falsehood will, perhaps, be shown

---

132–41; and idem, "Izydor z Sewilli i Apokryfy," *Acta Universitatis Nicolai Copernici*, Historia 27, Nauki Humanistyczno-Społeczne, Zeszyt 254 (1992): 151–57.

[103] Bernaldus Presbyter Constantiensis, *De excommunicatis vitandis, de reconciliatione lapsorum et de fontibus iuris ecclesiastici*, ed. Fridericus Thaner, in *Libelli de lite imperatorum et pontificum saeculis XI. et XII. conscripti*, vol. 2, MGH (Hannover: Impensis Bibliopoli Hahniani, 1892), 124.

[104] Johannes Balbus, *Catholicon* (1460; repr., Farnborough, Hunts.: Gregg International Publishers, 1971), s.v. "apocrifus."

[105] Carolus Du Fresne Du Cange, *Glossarium mediæ et infimæ latinitatis*, ed. Léopold Favre, vol. 1 (1883–87; repr. [10 vols. in 5], Graz: Akademische Druck- u. Verlagsanstalt, 1954), s.v. "apocrypha," attributes this definition to Johannes de Janua.

to be truth").[106] Hrotsvitha does not presume to distinguish between truth and falsehood where pious matter blurs the distinction, lest in doing so she condemn some grains of truth. A similar sentiment is expressed three centuries later by the anonymous author of the *Vita beate virginis Marie et Salvatoris rhythmica*. In the prologue to book 1, he warns against hasty condemnation of apocryphal sources: "Si quis ut apocrifum hoc velit reprobare / Caveat, ne veritatem presumat condempnare" (vv. 33–34; "Should someone wish to reprove this as apocryphal, let him beware lest he presume to condemn the truth").[107] Other writers appeal to genuine scriptural texts which allude to the fact that many events in Christ's life have not been recorded in the canonical gospels, implying that they may have been described elsewhere. Thus they argue, on the strength of John 20:30–31, John 21:25, and Luke 1:1–2, that many early Christian writers wrote gospels but that for the confirmation of our faith only four are necessary.[108] One such defense of the *EN*, based on John 21:25, is inserted into the first prologue of at least one Latin manuscript of the *EN*, Paris, BN MS. n. a. lat. 1154, fol. 11r, and this was also part of the argument used by John Wyclif to defend the apocryphon in the fourteenth century.[109]

This enthusiasm for noncanonical writings was, however, usually held in check by other biblical passages, such as Proverbs 30:6, Deuteronomy 4:2 and Revelation 22:18–19, which acted as restraints on

---

[106] Hrotsvitha of Gandersheim, *Hrotsvithae Opera*, ed. H. Homeyer (Munich: F. Schöningh, 1970), 37.

[107] A. Vögtlin, ed., *Vita beate virginis Marie et Salvatoris rhythmica*, Bibliothek des Litterarischen Vereins, vol. 180 (Tübingen: Gedruckt für den Litterarischen Verein in Stuttgart, 1888); Walther, *Carmina medii aevi*, nos. 10692, 17018, 17250. Cf. a gloss to the *Vita rhythmica* which states, "Apocrifum est, cuius auctor ignoratur; unde eius scriptura nec pro vero recipitur nec pro falso reprobatur" ("An apocryphon is [a work] whose author is unknown; hence its text is neither accepted as true nor rejected as false"); see Max Päpke, *Das Marienleben des Schweizers Wernher. Mit Nachträgen zu Vögtlin's Ausgabe der Vita Marie rhythmica*, Palaestra, vol. 81 (Berlin: Mayer & Müller, 1913), 123.

[108] A gloss to the *Vita rhythmica* reads: "Beatus Jeronimus testatur quod multi scripserunt ewangelia, sicut est Ewangelium Nazareorum, Ewangelium Thome, Ewangelium Mathei, Ewangelium Bartholomei, Ewangelium Nichodemi, Ewangelium Hebreorum, sicut ipse beatus Jeronimus transtulit, Ewangelium Petri, quod scribitur secundum Marcum. Tamen ad confirmacionem fidei sufficiunt quatuor ewangelia, que tenet ecclesia" ("Blessed Jerome testifies that many wrote gospels, such as the Gospel according to the Nazareans, Gospel of Thomas, Gospel of Matthew, Gospel of Bartholomew, Gospel of Nicodemus, Gospel according to the Hebrews which blessed Jerome himself translated, Gospel of Peter which is written according to Mark. But for the confirmation of faith the four gospels which are accepted by the church are sufficient"); see Päpke, *Das Marienleben*, 137–38.

[109] John Wyclif, *De veritate Sacrae Scripturae*, ed. Rudolf Buddensieg, Wyclif Society (London: Trübner, 1905), 1:237.

excessive credulity and fantastic imagination. The caution advised by
these texts and exercised by those who wrote apologies for the use of
apocrypha sometimes took the shape of explicit admonitions to readers
to exercise their own discretion in reading and believing works of
uncertain authorship. Jacobus a Voragine (or his source), for instance,
usually alerts his readers to the spuriousness of his sources, whose
credibility, he advises, they should judge for themselves.[110] He does
not, however, attach a similar warning to his summary of the DI. The
legendary Harrowing of Hell, attested also in what he considered to be
the writings of St. Augustine (i.e., the pseudo-Augustinian "Sermo
160," which he quotes in extenso), apparently raised no doubts in his
mind and required no such precaution.

One reason why the EN was often felt to be in little need of justification or defense was that it was regarded as a historical record of
events, fortified as it was by alleged patristic authority and rooted in
Christian tradition. Its common title (Gesta Salvatoris ...), the second
prologue, and the appendices relating to the emperors of Rome all
implied a historical document (which does not mean, however, that it
could not be used to support an exegetical or theological argument; see
below). As an independent record of Christ's Passion, "triduum
mortis," and Resurrection, the EN was appreciated by medieval historians, such as Adémar de Chabannes (989–1034), who made his own
copy of the apocryphon (Paris, BN MS. lat. 3784, fols. 108v–14r),[111]
and often exploited by chroniclers who incorporated it into their
works. A fourteenth-century English author of the Eulogium (historiarum sive temporis) includes the entire EN, followed by the EP and a
version of the Cura.[112] He introduces them with a single title, Chronica
Domini Nostri Jesu Christi, and a statement of intention, "Cum de
Regibus et Principibus et de eorum gestis in bellis, in victoriis, in
pugna, et fuga pluries tractavimus, de Rege Regum jam intendimus
aliquid enarrare" ("Since we have frequently spoken of kings and
princes and of their deeds in wars, in victories, in battle, and in flight,
we now intend to relate something about the King of Kings"), indicat-

---

[110] "Hucusque in praedicta hystoria apocrypha legitur, quae utrum recitanda
sit, lectoris arbitrio relinquatur" (chap. 45; "That much is found in the aforesaid
apocryphal history; it may be left to the reader's judgement whether to read it
out"); cf. chaps. 53 and 67 (Jacobus a Voragine, Legenda aurea, 185, 234, 301).

[111] Richard Landes, "A Libellus from St. Martial of Limoges Written in the
Time of Ademar of Chabannes (998–1034)," Scriptorium 37 (1983): 190 n. 48, and
204.

[112] Frank Scott Haydon, ed., Eulogium (historiarum sive temporis): Chronicon ab
orbe condito usque ad annum Domini M. CCC. LXVI a monacho quodam Malmesburiensi exaratum, vol. 1, Rer. Brit. M. A. Script., vol. 9 (London: Longman, Brown,
Green, Longmans, and Roberts, 1858).

ing an essentially historical interest in the narrative. John of Glastonbury's attitude to the *EN* is similar, although he uses the text more
selectively. Aiming to demonstrate the antiquity of the Glastonbury
foundation and its connection with Joseph of Arimathea, the chronicler
abridges and adapts chapters 12–15 of the *EN* under the heading
"Incipit tractatus de sancto Ioseph ab Arimathia, extractus de libro
quodam quem invenit Theodosius imperator in Ierusalem in pretorio
Pilati" ("Here begins the treatise of St. Joseph of Arimathea, taken
from a book which emperor Theodosius found in Pilate's council-
chamber in Jerusalem").[113] The sentence introducing the narrative explains that what follows are undisputed facts extracted from "antiquis
historiagraphorum dictis" ("ancient sayings of historiographers").[114]

In the intense religious atmosphere of the later Middle Ages and
pre-Reformation, this acceptance of the *EN* at times grew so enthusias-
tic that some scribes began to perceive it as quasi-canonical, their
respect for it verging on veneration. Not only is it sometimes placed
among exegetical works, but in several manuscripts it is directly connected with the canonical gospels. In a late fourteenth-century manuscript of the Bible executed possibly for Richard II of England (London,
BL MS. Royal 1 E. IX), the *EN* is treated as if it were a fifth gospel: it
follows the Old Testament and the four gospels but precedes the
Epistles, Acts, and Apocalypse. It is here endowed with an almost
canonical status, and only the lesser extent of its decoration betrays
that those responsible for production of the manuscript did in fact
distinguish, however hesitantly, between canonical and apocryphal
texts. In three additional manuscripts from the same period, the *EN* is
adjacent to the canonical Scriptures, its own status bordering on theirs
(Brno, Státní vědecká knihovna MS. Mk 79, saec. XV in.; Munich, BSB
Clm 11403, saec. XV/2, and Clm 28168, saec. XIV); in several others, it
is separated from them with empty folios or minor intervening texts
(Gdańsk, Biblioteka Polskiej Akademii Nauk MS. 1956, saec. XV;
Klosterneuburg, Stiftsbibliothek MS. 151, saec. XV in.; Munich, BSB

---

[113] John of Glastonbury, *The Chronicle of Glastonbury Abbey: An Edition, Translation and Study of John of Glastonbury's "Cronica sive Antiquitates Glastoniensis
Ecclesie,"* ed. James P. Carley, trans. David Townsend (Bury St. Edmunds, Suffolk:
Boydell Press, 1985), 46; cf. Carl Horstman, ed., *Nova legenda Angliae: As Collected
by John of Tynemouth, John Capgrave, and Others, and First Printed, with New Lives,
by Wynkyn de Worde* . . . (Oxford: Clarendon Press, 1901), 2:78–80.

[114] It is also noteworthy that in six manuscripts the *EN* co-occurs with Geof-
frey of Monmouth's *Historia regum Britanniae*; see Julia C. Crick, *Dissemination and
Reception in the Later Middle Ages*, The Historia Regum Britanniae of Geoffrey of
Monmouth, vol. 4 (Cambridge: D. S. Brewer, 1991), 45–46, and idem, *A Summary
Catalogue of Manuscripts*, The Historia Regum Britanniae of Geoffrey of Mon-
mouth, vol. 3 (Cambridge: D. S. Brewer, 1989), 272.

Clm 22353, saec. XV; and Trier, Bibliothek des Bischöflichen Priester-seminars MS. 114, saec. XVI in.).[115] Nevertheless, it would be an exaggeration to claim that late medieval users of the *EN* generally considered its authority as equal to that of the canonical gospels. For the majority of late medieval readers, the *EN* probably remained a humanly pious rather than divinely inspired text. The manuscripts mentioned above reflect a rather extreme tendency which eventually provoked a strong reaction from both Protestant and Catholic circles and which may be responsible for the *EN*'s ultimate downfall.

3. The influence of the *Evangelium Nicodemi*

To judge by the number of extant manuscripts of the *EN* and its para-phrases, the apocryphon enjoyed wide readership in the Middle Ages, especially from the twelfth century onwards. Not surprisingly, its influence spread to many domains of religious life: its vivid traces can be found in the writings of ecclesiastical thinkers and educators, in works aiding private piety, and in certain texts and practices of com-munal devotion. At least until the fifteenth century, the *EN* was read with enthusiasm and quoted without qualms about its apocryphal character, its imagination and antiquity compensating, it seems, for its lack of canonical authority.

3.1. Theological and didactic discourses

Although it was the pious, historical-legendary content rather than theological underpinnings of the *EN* that captivated medieval audi-ences, the pervasive presence of the apocryphon in the cultural milieu was bound to affect at least the peripheries of religious belief. It could be found in the libraries of many scholars and teachers who helped shape medieval theological discourse. Martin Hibernensis (b. 819, d. 875), the first master of the school of Laon and a colleague of John Scotus Eriugena, owned a copy of the *EN*, which later passed to his successors, Bernard (b. 847, d. 903) and Adelelm (b. ca. 865, d. 930) of Laon (it now survives as Laon, Bibl. mun. MS. 265). Jan Kanty (Johan-nes Cantius; b. 1390, d. 1473; canonized 1767), a doctor of theology at the Jagiellonian University in Cracow, copied the *EN* for his own use (now Cracow, Biblioteka Jagiellońska MS. 2724). And Gabriel Biel (b. ca. 1410, d. 1495), the last scholastic of the Middle Ages, inserted an

---

[115] Several manuscripts of vernacular translations of the *EN*, especially from the German-speaking regions, follow suit; see below, pp. 305–9.

ownership note in the manuscript that belonged to the Brothers of the Common Life in Butzbach (now Giessen, Universitätsbibliothek MS. 729). Through readers like these, the *EN* could have influenced, if only in a minor way, theological reflection of the Middle Ages.

Besides reinforcing in obvious ways the belief in and speculation about Christ's Descent into Hell, the *EN* may have helped shape late medieval notions about infernal topography, although such influence was not, as far as I know, explicitly acknowledged by medieval writers. In some of its forms, the *EN* implied that the infernal space was not uniform: there was one location where the ancient patriarchs and prophets awaited Christ's coming, the limbo of the fathers, and there was the abyss. Texts of the B type introduce a sharp contrast between the "profundum abyssi" into which Satan is cast and the place of the patriarchs (chap. 25). By specifying that Christ "partem deiecit in tartarum, partem secum reduxit ad superos" (chap. 25.2; "cast part into Tartarus, part he brought again with him on high"),[116] B texts may have contributed, however indirectly, to the evolution of the notion of purgatory, for they demonstrate that "the fate of certain men is suscep-tible to amelioration after death, if only in exceptional circumstances" and that "the souls cast into Tartarus, the hell of the damned, are excluded from the possibility of improvement in their condition."[117] If *EN* B antedates the eleventh century, as Jacques Le Goff assumes, then it might indeed have exerted some of that pressure under which new ideas about the underworld crystallized in the first centuries of the second millennium; if it is later, as the relatively late dates of its manuscripts suggest,[118] it may be a symptom of that conceptual change, albeit one that could easily stimulate further evolution.

Not infrequently, the *EN* entered medieval reflection on eschatolo-gical matters, especially in relation to the question of bodily resurrec-tion. It figures prominently in the writings of Albert the Great (b. ca. 1200, d. 1280), who repeatedly appeals to its authority in his *De resur-rectione*. Commenting on Matthew 27:52–53 and the implied partial resurrection of the dead "quorum quidam nominantur in EVANGELIO NICODEMI" (Tract. 2, Q. 4.2; "some of whom are named in the GOSPEL OF NICODEMUS"), he explains that "ideo necessarium fuit aliquos

---

[116] In *EN* A, Inferus seems to be reproaching Satan for causing the universal deliverance from hell, "et totius mundi noxios, impios et iniustos perdidisti" (chap. 23.2; "and you lost the guilty, the ungodly, and the unrighteous"). In the very next paragraph, however, Christ addresses only "sanctes mei omnes" (chap. 26.1; "all my saints").

[117] Jacques Le Goff, *The Birth of Purgatory*, trans. Arthur Goldhammer (Chic-ago: University of Chicago Press, 1984), 44–45.

[118] Izydorczyk, "The Unfamiliar *Evangelium Nicodemi*," 181.

resurgere statim in morte Christi, ut aliqua praesumptio resurrectionis remaneret in electis" (Tract. 2, Q. 4, ad 2; "it was, therefore, necessary to resurrect some immediately after Christ's death so that some confidence in the Resurrection should remain in the elect").[119] By naming those who rose before Christ to testify to the mystery of his Resurrection, the EN confirms that they were known in Jerusalem; "si enim fuissent ignoti, non fuisset eis creditum" (Tract. 2, Q. 5, ad 5; "if they had been unknown, they would not have been believed").[120] The EN thus provides supplementary information necessary for proper understanding of a difficult passage in Matthew. In his discussion of the whereabouts, during the forty days after Christ's Resurrection, of those who rose at the moment of his death, Albert quotes a portion of EN 17.1, and concludes:

> solvendum est per dictam auctoritatem [i.e., the EN], quia ultra Iordanem in paradiso fuerunt in plena fruitione divinitatis Iesu. Unde etiam narratur IBI, qualiter Elias et Enoch tripudium habuerunt cum ipsis et latro. (Tract. 2, Q. 7, Art. 7)[121]

> (it should be resolved by the said authority [i.e., the EN] that they were beyond Jordan in paradise in full enjoyment of Jesus' divinity. Hence it is also narrated THERE how Elijah and Enoch rejoiced with them and the Thief.)

For Albert, the EN is apparently as authoritative as the patristic tradition and, therefore, a legitimate source of knowledge concerning matters of faith.

Similarly, Thomas of Chobham, an early thirteenth-century writer, in his Summa de arte praedicandi adduces the EN as an independent witness to the partial bodily resurrection at the time of Christ's rising from the grave. He considers that event as foreshadowing future general resurrection:

> Patet etiam per doctrinam euuangelicam, quod corpora nostra resurgent, quia Dominus post resurrectionem corpus suum ostendit palpabile, et multa corpora sanctorum que dormierant resurrexerunt cum Domino. Et in Euuangelio Nazareorum [i.e., EN][122] legitur qui illi fuerint et quomodo cum Iudeis disputauerint.[123]

---

[119] Albert the Great, De resurrectione, ed. Wilhelmus Kübel, in Sancti doctoris ecclesiae Alberti Magni . . . Opera omnia, vol. 26 (Münster in Westfalen: Aschendorff, 1958), 262.

[120] Ibid., 263.

[121] Ibid., 270.

[122] On the use of the title Evangelium Nazaraeorum, see above, p. 77.

[123] Thomas of Chobham, Summa, 110.

(The teaching of the gospels makes it also clear that our bodies will rise because the Lord showed his tangible body after the Resurrection, and many bodies of saints who had slept rose up with the Lord. And it is read in the Gospel according to the Nazaraeans [i.e., *EN*] who they were and how they contended with the Jews.)

Thomas's use of the *EN* to strengthen his eschatological argument in the essentially pastoral context of the *Summa* is characteristic of the ease with which the apocryphon entered popular theological instruction. Besides reaffirming bodily resurrection, one of the most pervasive influences of the *EN* on medieval catechesis consisted in popularization of the idea of Joseph of Arimathea's Christophany, which in common belief became Christ's first (or second, after his similarly apocryphal visit to his mother) appearance. The widely used and respected *Elucidarium* disseminated that belief, appealing directly to the *EN*:

D.—Quotiens apparuit?
M.—Duodecies. Primo die octies: primo Joseph ab Arimathia in carcere in quo positus erat eo quod eum sepelierat, ut scripta Nicodemi declarant.[124]

(D.—How many times did he appear?
M.—Twelve. On the first day eight times: first to Joseph of Arimathea in prison, where he was placed because he had buried him, as the writings of Nicodemus declare.)

Joseph's Christophany, mentioned on the strength of the same apocryphal authority already by Gregory of Tours, was frequently cited throughout the Middle Ages, although some theologians, such as Hugh of St. Cher, had strong reservations regarding its authenticity.[125]

3.2. Devotional literature

The establishment of Christ's life as the basis for the liturgical year and the growing theological interest in Christ's humanity in the eleventh

---

[124] Yves Lefèvre, ed., *L'Elucidarium et les lucidaires* (Paris: E. de Boccard, 1954), 391. Cf. Werner of St. Blasius, "Sermo de resurrectione Domini," PL 157:927D.

[125] See, for instance, his commentary on Lk. 23:50, "Unde tradunt quidam, sed non est autenticum, Dominum primo apparuisse Joseph incarcerato, quia solus de discipulis erat incarceratus pro eo, licet hoc in Evangelio non legatur" ("Hence some report—although this is not authentic—that the Lord first appeared to the imprisoned Joseph, because he alone among the disciples was imprisoned for him, although this may not be read in the gospel"), *Hugonis de Sancto Charo S. Romanæ Ecclesiæ tituli S. Sabinæ primi cardinalis Ordinis Prædicatorum, tomus sextus in Evangelia secundum Matthæum, Lucam, Marcum, & Joannem ...* (Venice: N. Pezzana, 1732), fol. 271va.

and twelfth centuries turned the events of Christ's earthly existence into focal points of devotion. From the twelfth century onward, terse gospel harmonies began to absorb extrabiblical—legendary and apocryphal—elements, expanding in scope and altering the nature of the genre.[126] In their search for emotive details, authors of the lives of Christ, and especially of Passion narratives, frequently turned to the *EN*. The pseudo-gospel had much to offer: it enhanced—by naming them—the reality of certain characters mentioned in the canonical gospels, embellished the gospel accounts with additional miracles, and elaborated what was merely hinted at in the canonical texts. Its venerable age, combined with the patronage of Nicodemus and, occasionally, of other church authorities made it, in spite of its noncanonical status, an attractive and trustworthy source.

In the fourteenth and fifteenth centuries, the *EN* became—directly or through one of its summaries—a standard source for accounts of the Passion. It was frequently quoted, paraphrased, or just mentioned to satisfy the need for authority. For instance, the prose *Tractatus de gestis Domini Salvatoris*, preserved in a fifteenth-century manuscript, London, BL MS. Royal 7 B. XII, but compiled probably earlier by an English author,[127] draws on the apocryphon freely. It deals with the life of Christ and various related matters, incorporating portions of the *Disputatio Judaei cum Christiano* of Gilbert Crispin (bk. 11) and materials on the cross (bk. 12) and on the body and blood of Christ (bks. 13, 14). The seventh book, fols. 98r–118r, described in the list of contents on fol. 11r as treating "de descensione Domini ad inferos, de nobili eius triumpho illic exacto" ("on the Descent of the Lord into Hell, on his noble triumph accomplished there") contains substantial excerpts from the *DI*. They were culled probably from a version of the *EN* which included the legitimizing passages from Gregory of Tours and pseudo-Augustine on Joseph and on the Harrowing, respectively; the author opens his treatise with these very passages, followed by a spirited defense of the *EN*'s credibility and respectability:

Nemo vituperandum censeat quod hic in subsequenti volumine verba Nichodemi euangelistarii dictis interserantur licet a quibusdam iniuste inter apocriphancium noncupentur con-

---

[126] Elizabeth Salter, *Nicholas Love's "Myrrour of the Blessed Lyf of Jesu Christ,"* Analecta Cartusiana, vol. 10 (Salzburg: Institut für englische Sprache und Literatur, Universität Salzburg, 1974), 59–60.

[127] George F. Warner and Julius P. Gilson, *British Museum. Catalogue of Western Manuscripts in the Old Royal and King's Collections*, vol. 1 (London: Printed for the Trustees, 1921), 170, suggest that "A story of the wars of Baldwin [IV?], King of Jerusalem, told on the authority of an eyewitness (lib. xii, cap. 46) seems to fix the date of composition as about the end of the twelfth century."

sorcia, cum symbolum et alia autentica scripta sanctorum patrum alicubi verbo ad verbum ipsius consonent tractatui; nec scripta eius in decretis vel alibi prohibita legantur. (Fol. 10r)

(No one should consider blameworthy that here in the ensuing volume the words of Nicodemus the evangelist are interspersed among the sayings, even if some may unjustly consign them to the company of apocrypha, since the creed and other authentic writings of the holy fathers agree in some places word for word with his treatise; nor may his writings be found prohibited in decretals or anywhere else.)

While the compiler of the above treatise worked directly from a manuscript of the *EN*, other writers relied on intermediary sources which filtered and colored the substance of the apocryphal gospel. Although he appeals to the authority of Nicodemus, the author of the early thirteenth-century *Vita beate virginis Marie et Salvatoris rhythmica*, a long narrative poem important for its legacy in central European vernaculars, certainly did not use the *EN* itself. The four books of the *Vita rhythmica* give a detailed account of the lives of the Virgin and her son, drawn from a variety of sources, many of which are identified in the prologues to individual books and in marginal glosses. The poet, aware that some of his sources are apocryphal, defends their credibility (vv. 1478–1505; 3632–53; 6062–71), yet—since his declared intention is to praise the Virgin and Christ, not to judge the truth or falsehood of his sources (vv. 43–46; 8002–7)—he pleads with his readers to correct his errors as they see fit (vv. 39–46; 1514–17; 3654–61; 6080–87; 7994–8001; 8008–13).

The poem alludes to the *EN* several times in the sections on the Passion and Resurrection, but the apocryphon plays a rather minor role in the overall design of the narrative. The poet disregards it in the accounts of the trial before Pilate and the Crucifixion and does not mention the names of Veronica, Longinus, Dismas, or Gestas; he turns to it only in the section entitled "De signis que fiebant in passione Domini" (vv. 5808–911; "On the signs that accompanied the Passion of the Lord"), a sort of afterthought on the extraordinary portents associated with the Passion, drawn in part from Peter Comestor's *Historia scholastica*.[128] In that chapter, he first alludes to the imminent Harrowing of Hell and the patriarchs' jubilant expectation of deliverance (vv. 5838–45), and then recounts, in a curiously distorted manner, the episode of the standards bowing before Christ (vv. 5848–67), based ultimately on *EN* 1.5. He

---

[128] Achim Masser, *Bibel, Apokryphen und Legenden. Geburt und Kindheit Jesu in der religiösen Epik des deutschen Mittelalters* (Berlin: E. Schmidt, 1969), 52–53.

explains that the standards had been made by the Jews and on festive occasions were carried by them around Solomon's temple. It is under such circumstances that the standards bowed before Christ:

> Sed cum circa templum hec portantur, cum ligatus
> Jesus coram preside stabat flagellatus,
> Tunc versus locum in quo Jesus stetit simul illa
> Inclinabant baiulis invitis se vexilla. (Vv. 5854–57)

(But as these were being carried around the temple when Jesus was standing bound and scourged before the governor, the standards simultaneously inclined, against the will of the bearers, towards the place where Jesus was standing.)

This explanation of the standards' origin and this account of the episode contrast with the *EN*, in which the standards, implied to be imperial ensigns, are held by "uiri pagani" ("pagan men"; *EN* A and C) or "uiri gentili" ("gentile men"; *EN* B). A separate account of the Harrowing of Hell, entitled "De gaudio sanctorum quum Jesus venit ad infernum" ("On the joy of the saints when Jesus came into hell"), compressed into twenty lines (vv. 6042–61), gives little more than a sketch of the episode. In later sections, the *Vita rhythmica* mentions Pilate's letter to Rome concerning the events in Jerusalem (vv. 6126–29) and Joseph of Arimathea's Christophany (vv. 6142–45). All these thematic echoes of the pseudo-gospel, except for Pilate's letter, are accompanied in the manuscripts of the *Vita* by marginal glosses (at vv. 5838, 5848, 6042, 6142), explicitly identifying the *EN* as their source. Although the evidence is not always compelling, the implied genetic relationships are not impossible, and the *EN* may in fact lie behind the poem, even if only at several removes from it. In a few instances, however, similar glosses pointing to the *EN* as the underlying text are attached to passages narrating events with no obvious counterparts in the known versions of the apocryphon. One such gloss occurs at v. 4774, at the head of the section describing how the Jews bribed Pilate to condemn Jesus; another at v. 5114, beside a passage contrasting the derisive laughter of the executioners and the sorrow of Christ's followers; and yet another at v. 6430, beginning an account of the angelic powers' jubilation at Christ's Ascension.[129] The vagueness

---

[129] Such inaccurate references to the *EN* are not unusual in Passion tracts. The unedited prose treatise *Historia passionis Iesu Christi* in Freiburg im Breisgau, Universitätsbibliothek MS. 178b (saec. XV), mentions the *EN* twice: once incorrectly, suggesting that the *EN* contains a conversation between Herod and Christ (fol. 6r, "In ewangelio Nycodemi dicitur quod Herodes quesiuit a Christo, 'Es tu ne puer iste. . . .'" ["It is said in the Gospel of Nicodemus that Herod asked Christ, 'Are you not that boy. . . .'"]), the second time more accurately in the context of Pilate's argument with the Jews about Christ's innocence (fol. 7v).

and distortions in the genuine echoes of the *EN*, the absence of the personal names popularized by it, and the misplaced and inaccurate glosses all suggest that the author (or the glossator, if different from the author) was not intimately familiar with the apocryphon and that the apocryphal echoes in the *Vita rhythmica* originated not directly in the *EN* but either in an intermediate compilation or in imperfect recollection.

Particularly interesting is the connection of the *EN* with the tradition of affective meditation of Christ's suffering manhood, which first acquired prominence in religious life and literature in the eleventh century. Devotional practice of reflection on and compassion with Christ and his mother was spread during the later Middle Ages through such brief but emotionally charged texts as the *Planctus Mariae* (beg. "Quis dabit . . ."), usually ascribed to Bernard of Clairvaux but probably by Olgerius of Tridino, and the *Dialogus beatae Mariae et Anselmi de passione Domini*,[130] as well as through the more extensive *Meditationes vitae Christi* of pseudo-Bonaventure[131] and the equally comprehensive *Vita Jesu Christi* of Ludolph of Saxony. Different as these texts are in their approaches to affective devotion, they all betray the presence of the *EN* in medieval literature of affective piety.

Both the *Planctus* and the *Dialogus* present, in response to the pious request of a medieval speaker, the Virgin's account of Christ's Passion and of her own compassion with his suffering. Both are rendered in direct speech and create an effect of dramatic immediacy, the intense words of the Virgin reaching the reader with their full emotive force, unmitigated by a reporting voice. This dramatic mode of presentation is similar to the drama of the *EN*, which enables the reader to create a similar effect of presence at and experience of the reported events. Perhaps this formal similarity and a wealth of detail useful for meditation on Christ's Passion, death, and Resurrection attracted the *EN* to collections of meditative texts. From the thirteenth century on, the *EN* not only occurs in the same manuscripts as the *Planctus* and the *Dialogus* but is frequently contiguous with them. The frequency of its appearance in the company of the two texts suggests deliberate arrangement rather than coincidence: the *EN* accompanies the *Planctus* in at least

---

[130] Most recently, the *Planctus* has been edited by C. W. Marx, "The *Quis dabit* of Oglerius of Tridino, Monk and Abbot of Locedio," *Journal of Medieval Latin* 4 (1994): 118–29; for the *Dialogus*, see Oskar Schade, *Interrogatio sancti Anshelmi de passione Domini* (Königsberg: Typis academicis Dalkowskianis, 1870), and PL 159: 271–90.

[131] Pseudo-Bonaventure, *Meditationes vitae Christi*, in *S. R. E. Cardinalis S. Bonaventurae . . . Opera omnia*, ed. A. C. Peltier vol. 12 (Paris: L. Vivès, 1868), 509–630.

eighteen manuscripts, in fourteen directly preceding or following it; it is adjacent to the *Dialogus* in ten, and in another five separated from it by intervening texts.[132] Moreover, in a number of manuscripts the *EN* is not merely placed next to a single meditative text but inserted in the middle of meditative collections. In London, BL MS. Cotton Vesp. E. I, for example, it follows the meditation on the Passion ascribed to St. Bernard and is in turn followed by the *Planctus* and further meditations.[133]

The *Meditationes vitae Christi* and the *Vita Jesu Christi*, two of the most influential late medieval affective treatises on the life of Christ, show which details from the *EN* were used in meditations and how they were integrated into meditative texts. The author of the *Meditationes* explains in his prologue that since not everything about Christ worthy of meditation has been written down, he narrates—according to devout imagination—what could be believed to have happened.[134] This explanation is in effect an apology for the use in meditations of apocryphal, extra-canonical material. Although the author does not quote it extensively, he derives several details directly or indirectly from the *EN*. He knows, for instance, the name of Longinus (chap. 80), makes Christ convey the patriarchs to the terrestrial paradise and meet there with Enoch and Elijah (chap. 85), and briefly relates Joseph's Christophany (chap. 89), admittedly on the authority of the *EN* (chap. 96, "Quomodo autem apparuit Joseph, dicitur in Evangelio Nicodemi"; "But how Christ appeared to Joseph is related in the Gospel of Nicodemus").[135]

In his *Vita*, Ludolph of Saxony often relies on the *Meditationes*, excerpting from it liberally. His passages on the Harrowing of Hell (pt. 2, chap. 68),[136] with echoes of the *EN*, are copied directly from pseudo-Bonaventure's work. However, at least three times he refers independently to the *EN*, which he knew probably from some intermediate text, such as the *Legenda aurea*. In fact, the earliest allusion to the apocryphon, in pt. 2, chapter 61.11,[137] which reports Christ's answers

---

[132] For the manuscripts of the *Planctus*, see Izydorczyk, *Manuscripts*, nos. 18, 24, 53, 61, 63, 65, 109, 167, 181, 209, 227, 239, 250, 279, 294, 313, 380, and 404 (cf. 41, 151); for those of the *Dialogus*, see nos. 2, 86, 114, 116, 123, 138, 186, 236, 244, 262, 308, 339, 350, 403, and 421.

[133] Other manuscripts with the *EN* embedded in meditative contexts include Paris, BN MS. lat. 3628 (saec. XV); Hannover, Niedersächsische Landesbibliothek MS. I 247 (saec. XIV); and Oxford, Bodl. Lib. MS. Bodl. 555 (saec. XV in.).

[134] Pseudo-Bonaventure, *Meditationes*, 511.

[135] Ibid., 608, 613, 619, 623.

[136] Ludolph of Saxony, *Vita Jesu Christi*, 169–70.

[137] Ibid., 58.

to Pilate about truth (*EN* 3.2), may have been excerpted from the *Legenda*, chapter 53,[138] with only a change of the title to *Evangelium Nazaraeorum*. The second allusion, this time to the *Evangelium Nicodemi*, in pt. 2, chapter 62.27,[139] gives Pilate's sentence against Christ (*EN* 9.5). Finally, the story of Joseph's Christophany and deliverance from prison is related again "ut legitur in Evangelio Nazaræorum" (pt. 2, chap. 75; "as can be read in the Gospel according to the Nazaraeans");[140] it is introduced in the same way as in the *Meditationes* but gives more details concerning Joseph's incarceration.

3.3. Liturgical practices and texts

The extent of the *EN*'s influence on communal worship is difficult to establish. That the apocryphon interacted in some ways with liturgical practices and observances is almost certain, but the precise nature of those interactions escapes definition, since unequivocal textual proof for them is elusive, especially for the first millennium. The *EN* would not be the first or the only apocryphon to interact with liturgical texts and practices; other apocrypha too inspired or reinforced various forms of worship and ritual. Thus, for example, liturgical celebration of the life of the Virgin Mary (Immaculate Conception, Nativity, Presentation in the Temple) is greatly indebted to the *Protoevangelium Iacobi*, as are the cults of Mary's parents, Anne and Joachim; celebration of the Assumption of the Virgin was influenced by the *Transitus Mariae;* and strict observance of Sunday rest may owe something to the letter on the subject received from heaven.[141] Moreover, apocryphal texts were occasionally adapted to liturgical contexts and actually used in public worship, as illustrated by an apocryphal gospel of infancy preserved in a thirteenth-century Hereford manuscript,[142] which was incorporated into the Office of the Feast of the Conception (December 10). Even more frequently, apocrypha were adapted as homilies, such as those based on *Pseudo-Matthew* and the *Transitus Mariae* in the Carolingian homiliary from Saint-Père, Chartres.[143] Liturgical affiliations of the *EN* would, therefore, be neither unique nor, indeed, unexpected.

---

[138] Jacobus a Voragine, *Legenda aurea*, 226.

[139] Ludolph of Saxony, *Vita Jesu Christi*, 84.

[140] Ibid., 205.

[141] Edina Bozóky, "Les Apocryphes bibliques," in *Le Moyen âge et la Bible*, ed. Pierre Riché and Guy Lobrichon (Paris: Beauchesne, 1984), 433–34.

[142] M. R. James, ed., *Latin Infancy Gospels: A New Text, with a Parallel Version from Irish* (Cambridge: At the University Press, 1927).

[143] Henri Barré, *Les Homéliaires carolingiens de l'école d'Auxerre*, Studi e testi, vol. 225 (Vatican City: Biblioteca Apostolica Vaticana, 1962), 22, 24.

The relationship between the *EN* and liturgy may extend as far back as the apocryphon's formative period. Its dramatic character and its abundant use of direct speech are reminiscent of liturgical commemorations of Christ's Passion and Resurrection.[144] The *DI* especially seems to be rooted, thematically and rhetorically, in dramatic liturgy. Not only does it elaborate the popular theme of catabasis, but its antithetical questions echo Christological hymns,[145] and its reiterative recitation of Ps. 23 resembles early celebrations of the Passion and the Ascension.[146] The evidence for the liturgical background of the *EN* is thus suggestive yet, admittedly, circumstantial; so is, with the exception of homiletic literature, the evidence for the *EN*'s subsequent reciprocal influence, at least until the height of the Middle Ages.

It is tempting, but perhaps too convenient, to relate all medieval liturgical evocations of Christ's Descent into Hell to the *EN*. It should be remembered that the Christian theme of catabasis, with its many legendary accretions, probably antedates the Latin text of the *DI* and certainly circulated apart and beyond the apocryphon.[147] Thus, for instance, when a letter attributed to Germanus (d. 516) interprets portions of the mass as commemorating Christ's victory over the underworld and the release of the saints, its links to the *EN* are tenuous. The "Aius" before the reading of the gospel, the author of the letter explains, is sung "in specie angelorum ante faciem Christi ad portas inferi clamantium: Tollite portas principes vestras . . ." ("in the image of angels before the countenance of Christ, exclaiming towards the gates of hell: Lift up your gates, princes . . .") and the "Sanctus" is intoned "in specie sanctorum, qui redeunte Domino Jesu Christo de inferis canticum laudis Dominum sequent[e]s cantaverunt" ("in the image of the saints, who, following Lord Jesus Christ on his return from hell, sang a song of praise").[148] Despite the allusion to Ps. 23,

---

[144] Jean-Daniel Dubois, "La Représentation de la Passion dans la liturgie du Vendredi Saint: Les *Actes de Pilate* et la liturgie ancienne de Jérusalem," in *Liturgie et anthropologie. Conférences St-Serge, XXVIᵉ semaine d'études liturgiques*, ed. A. M. Triacca and A. Pistoia (Rome: C. L. V.-Edizioni Liturgiche, 1990), 77–89.

[145] Kroll, *Gott und Hölle*, 24–28.

[146] Allen Cabaniss, "The Harrowing of Hell, Psalm 24, and Pliny the Younger: A Note," *Vigiliae Christianae* 7 (1953): 71; A. Cooper, "Ps 24:7–10: Mythology and Exegesis," *Journal of Biblical Literature* 102 (1983): 56; A. Rose, " 'Attolite portas, principes, vestras . . .' Aperçus sur la lecture chrétienne du Ps. 24 (23) B," in *Miscellanea liturgica in onore di Sua Eminenza il cardinale Giacomo Lercaro, acivescovo di Bologna* (Rome: Desclée, 1966), 1:453–78.

[147] Cf. Kroll, *Gott und Hölle*; MacCulloch, *The Harrowing of Hell*; J. Monnier, *La Descente aux enfers, étude de pensée religieuse, d'art et de littérature* (Paris: Fischbacher, 1904).

[148] PL 72:91B–C.

specific textual evidence for the influence of the *EN* is here lacking, and while it is not impossible that the author knew the *EN*, the letter does not compellingly demonstrate that knowledge.

However, some liturgical practices which may have arisen independently of the *EN* appear to have developed an almost symbiotic relationship with it in the later Middle Ages. The entrance ceremony of the ritual for the dedication of the church, composed ca. 750,[149] may or may not have been indebted to the *EN* for its origin, but its subsequent elaborations and vitality are likely due to the pseudo-gospel. That ceremony involved knocking on the church door, as if on the gates of hell, accompanied by the antiphonal recitation of Ps. 23; in its later medieval forms, the ritual included a triple procession around the church, with the psalm recited by the bishop outside and by the deacon inside every time the procession reached the door. The same ritual pattern evoking Christ's Descent into Hell, his victory over the devil, and the deliverance of the saints was adopted for other liturgies as well. In his *Ecclesiale*, Alexander of Villa Dei (b. ca. 1170, d. 1250) describes the Palm Sunday procession involving triple knocking on the church door and the antiphonal performance of Ps. 23.[150] More important, the same ceremonial elements, with the addition of the antiphon "Cum rex gloriae," formed the basis of some elaborate paschal celebrations, such as the Latin Easter play from Klosterneuburg or the dramatic *Elevatio crucis* from Barking and Bamberg.[151] These late medieval paschal liturgies may owe, if not their origin, at least their enduring popularity to the suggestive, imaginative vision of the Descent in the *EN*. At the same time, these forms of communal, ecclesiastically approved worship may have helped sanction and legitimize the text whose vision of the Descent they enacted.

A similar, mutually beneficial relationship may have obtained between the *EN* and veneration of certain New Testament saints. Chapter 7 of the apocryphon may have spurred the cult of St. Veronica by giving a name—and therefore an identity—to the woman with the issue of blood (mentioned in Mt. 9:20–22; Mk. 5:25–29; and Lk. 8:43–

---

[149] Michel Andrieu, *Les "Ordines Romani" du haut moyen âge*, vol. 4, *Les Textes (suite) ("Ordines" XXXV–XLIX)* (Louvain: "Specilegium Sacrum Lovaniense," 1956), 339–49.

[150] Alexander of Villa Dei, *Ecclesiale*, ed. L. R. Lind (Lawrence: University of Kansas Press, 1958), vv. 603–22.

[151] Karl Young, *The Drama of the Medieval Church* (1933; repr., Oxford: Clarendon Press, 1967), 1:164–66, 172–75, 425; Karl W. Ch. Schmidt, *Die Darstellung von Christi Höllenfahrt in den deutschen und der ihnen verwandten Spielen des Mittelalters* (Marburg: H. Bauer, 1915), 24–25.

44).[152] The naming of Longinus,[153] the soldier who pierced Christ's side (*EN* 10.1; Jn.19:34), and his conflation with the centurion who acknowledged Christ's divinity (Mt. 27:54; Mk. 15:39; Lk. 23:47) may have enhanced his veneration. The Good Thief, Dismas, may owe to the *EN* his place in medieval devotion[154] and, together with his evil counterpart, Gestas, in medieval superstition.[155] That the *EN* was one of the principal sources for Dismas the Confessor's legend is clear from its account in the *Catalogus sanctorum*, bk. 3, chapter 288, a popular fifteenth-century collection of hagiographical lore compiled by Petrus de Natalibus, which briefly summarizes chapter 26 of the *EN* on the meeting between the saints and the Good Thief in paradise.[156] Once the traditions of these characters' sainthood (or, in Gestas's case, wickedness) had grown strong, they probably began to promote the apocryphon to which they were indebted.

---

[152] *BHL* 8549.

[153] *BHL* 4965; on the name of Longinus, see Konrad Burdach, *Der Gral. Forschungen über seinen Ursprung und seinen Zusammenhang mit der Longinuslegende* (1938; repr., Darmstadt: Wissenschaftliche Buchgesellschaft, 1974), 224–32.

[154] See the *Oratio de sancto Disma bona* in London, BL MS. Addit. 34069, fol. 303 (saec. XV), from Hildesheim. The cult of St. Dismas flourished in Spain; see B. de Gaiffier, review of *Gesammelte Aufsätze zur Kulturgeschichte Spaniens*, vols. 9 and 10 (Münster in Westfalen: Aschendorff, 1954 and 1955), *Analecta Bollandiana* 74 (1956): 274.

[155] The names of the two thieves were used on amulets and in charms; the following verses were supposed to protect against theft:

Imparibus meritis pendent tria corpora ramis,
Dismas & Gesmas, medio Divina potestas.
Alta petit Dismas, infelix infima Gesmas,
Nos & res nostras conservet summa Potestas,
Hos versus dicas ne tu furto tua perdas.

(With unequal merits, three bodies hang suspended from branches: Dismas and Gesmas, and the divine power in the middle. Dismas seeks the heights, unhappy Gesmas the depths, may the highest power preserve us and our property; say these verses lest you lose your property to theft.)

Quoted after Johannes Albertus Fabricius, ed., *Codici apocryphi Novi Testamenti, pars tertia nunc primum edita*, 2d rev. ed. (Hamburg: C. Herold, 1743), 472; see also Walther, *Carmina medii aevi*, nos. 4582 and 8774, and Jürgen Stohlman, "Nachträge zu Hans Walther, *Initia carminum ac versuum medii aevi (IV)*," *Mittellateinische Jahrbuch* 12 (1977): 301, no. 4582. A version of these verses accompanies an English charm in Oxford, Bodl. Lib. MS. Ashm. 1378, pp. 61–62 (saec. XV). Short verses on Dismas and Gestas occur also in Oxford, Bodl. Lib. MS. Rawl. C. 485, fol. 124; Oxford, Balliol College MS. 288, fol. 278v; and London, BL MS. Arundel 346, fol. 24v (saec. XV).

[156] Petrus de Natalibus, *Catalogus sanctorum et gestorum eorum ex diuersis voluminibus collectus* (Lyons: J. Sacon, 1519), fol. 65rb. Petrus remembers the *EN* also in the legend of St. Adam, in which he reports Seth's visit to paradise (bk. 3, chap. 2 [fol. 35rb]).

The precise nature of the *EN*'s influence, difficult to establish with respect to liturgical observances, is likewise elusive vis-à-vis celebratory paschal poetry. Although such poetry frequently exploits the theme of Christ's Descent, the poetic frame of reference, motifs, and idiom are usually biblical, patristic, and classical rather than apocryphal. The allusions to the Harrowing of Hell are often too brief and too general to allow for identification of specific textual sources or models; such is the case not only in the hymns of Prudentius, Sidonius Apollinaris, Sedulius, and Venantius Fortunatus but in many later sequences as well.[157] I am aware of only one short abecedarius (18 lines), the eighth-century anonymous "Versum de contentione Zabuli cum Averno," which appears to have been inspired by the *EN*.[158] The poem contains a verbal exchange between Infer and Satanas, strongly reminiscent of their altercation in chapter 20 of the *EN*.[159] The contention begins with Satanas boasting that the powerful of the world have no power to escape Hell's dominion ("Potentes quos seculi / Ad te, Infer, iam adduxi, te non valent effugere"). But Infer reminds him that one mighty and strong in war ("potens et fortis in bello") released Lazarus from the infernal abode ("Abstractus de sede mea Lazarus, quem adduxisti"). Infer fears that warrior, but Satanas claims to know his name, Jesus ("Ego scio, quis est ille, Iesus enim dicitur"), and declares his intention to bring Jesus into hell. Terrified, Infer forewarns Satanas that Jesus will overcome him and chain him in torments. Because of its brevity, the poem gives only a gist of the quarrel as developed in *EN* 20, but it includes at least one significant detail: a reference to the raising of Lazarus, which in both versions leads to the identification of Jesus' name and to Infer's final warning to Satan.

More typically, however, even longer poems devoted to Christ's paschal triumph in the underworld exhibit only superficial similarity to the *EN*. The "Triumphus Christi heroicus," printed with the works

---

[157] Ruth Ellis Messenger, "The Descent Theme in Medieval Latin Hymns," *Transactions and Proceedings of the American Philological Association* 67 (1936): 126–47.

[158] Edited by Paulus von Winterfeld, *Poëtae Latini aevi Carolini*, vol. 4, pt. 1, MGH (Berlin: apud Weidmannos, 1904), 636–37; cf. Franz Brunhölzl, *Geschichte der lateinischen Literatur des Mittelalters*, vol. 1, *Von Cassiodor bis zum Ausklang der karolingischen Erneurung* (Munich: W. Fink, 1975), 154. It survives in three ninth-century manuscripts now in Paris, BN MSS. lat. 1153 (the source of Winterfeld's edition); lat. 13377 (Dieter Schaller and Ewald Könsgen, *Initia carminum Latinorum saeculo undecimo antiquiorum* [Göttingen: Vandenhoeck & Ruprecht, 1977], no. 1335); and lat. 17655 (Hans Walther, *Das Streitgedicht in der lateinischen Literatur des Mittelalters*, intro. and indexes by Paul Gerhard Schmidt [1920; repr., Hildesheim: Georg Olms, 1984], 88).

[159] The relevant passages of the *EN* are printed in the apparatus to Winterfeld's edition.

of Juvencus by the editor of the Patrologia Latina,[160] contains an account of the Descent with narrative contours and speeches by Pluto, Adam, David, and Christ not unlike those of the EN. And yet few features of the poem can be unequivocally anchored in the apocryphon. If the poet took his inspiration from the DI, he chose to reproduce only its broad outlines, filling them with Christian and classical commonplaces. Two poems on the same subject by John Scotus Eriugena, "Emicat ex Erebo ..." and "Postquam nostra salus ...," both maintained in the classical and biblical idiom, are even further removed from the EN and almost devoid of its echoes.[161] So are the "descensus" parts of the tenth-century vision of Ansellus Scholasticus.[162] All three poets seem to have worked within the general tradition of the Harrowing of Hell informed by the EN, but not with the apocryphal text itself.

Even late medieval and renaissance poets, whose knowledge of the EN can be safely assumed, take a high degree of poetic licence in their treatments of the Harrowing and do not always follow the EN. While the "Sapphicon de inferorum vestatione et triumpho Christi" by Paulus Crosnensis Ruthenus,[163] first printed in 1513, like the "Triumphus" of pseudo-Juvencus, bears some broad resemblance to the EN, the connection between Erasmus's 1489 "Carmen heroicum de solemnitate paschali ..."[164] and the EN is more tenuous, even though Erasmus was almost certainly familiar with the apocryphon, which he mentions in his colloquium "Peregrinatio religionis ergo."[165]

The fact that the EN is not the immediate or easily recognizable source of the above-mentioned poems does not diminish its significance as a text crucial for the medieval conception of catabasis. Without it, the idea of the Descent might not have evolved into a coherent, dramatic legend of the Harrowing of Hell. However, the influence of the EN was often indirect, scattered, and diffused by intermediate

---

[160] PL 19:385–88.

[161] Ludovicus Traube, ed., Poëtae Latini aevi Carolini, vol. 3, MGH (Berlin: apud Weidmannos, 1896), 536, 543–44; Schaller and Könsgen, Initia carminum, nos. 1977, 4387, and 12269.

[162] [Édélestand Pontas] Du Méril, ed., Poésies populaires latines antérieures au douzième siècle (Paris: Brockhaus et Avenarius, 1843), 200–17; Walther, Carmina medii aevi, no. 9091.

[163] Paulus Crosnensis Ruthenus, Pauli Crosnensis Rutheni Carmina, ed. Maria Cytowska (Warsaw: Państwowe Wydawnictwo Naukowe, 1962), 172–79.

[164] Desiderius Erasmus, The Poems of Desiderius Erasmus, ed. C. Reedijk (Leiden: E. J. Brill, 1956), 190–201.

[165] Desiderius Erasmus, Opera omnia Desiderii Erasmi Roterdami, vol. 1, pt. 3, Colloquia, ed. L.-E. Halkin, F. Bierlaire, and R. Hoven (Amsterdam: North-Holland, 1972), 470–94.

sources, but also enhanced by parallel and consonant traditions transmitted in the writings of the fathers. Simultaneous diffusion and reinforcement gave many thematic or narrative strands of the *EN* quasi-independent, cross-textual existence.

One example of the diffusion of motifs associated with the *EN* through other texts is the literary career of the pseudo-Augustinian "Sermo 160," a composite piece that shares with *EN* 22–24 not only certain themes but phraseology as well. Before the eleventh century, a version of the "Sermo," amplified with passages from the sermons of Eusebius "Gallicanus" on the Pasch,[166] was apparently more influential than the *EN* itself. It resonates in several early liturgical hymns in verse and prose. A late seventh- or eighth-century abecedarius from Italy or Gaul, "Audite omnes canticum mirabile . . . ,"[167] includes two speeches derived from it. One of them (stanzas 3–9), by "tortores mali" ("evil torturers"), is modeled on the Eusebian fragments incorporated into the "Sermo"; the other, by "turbae beatae" ("blessed throngs"), is reminiscent, even at the lexical level, of the saints' speech in the fourth paragraph of pseudo-Augustine's sermon.[168] Similar utterances of infernal lament and saintly plea, all with echoes of the "Sermo," occur also in three tenth- to twelfth-century sequences from Limoges, "O beata et venerabilis virgo Maria alma . . . ," "Cantat omnis turba . . . ," and "Clara gaudia, festa paschalia. . . ."[169] Furthermore, the "Sermo" was quoted extensively by the author of the highly dramatic liturgy from the ninth-century Book of Cerne, in which the saints plead for deliverance in the words of pseudo-Augustine.[170] Widely disseminated in the latter half of the first millennium, the "Sermo" remained in active liturgical use well into the twelfth century, when it was adapted as lections for Easter Matins at the monastery at Prüfening.[171]

---

[166] Eusebius "Gallicanus," *Collectio homiliarum*, 1:141–50, 2:878–79.

[167] Edited by Karolus Strecker, *Poëtae Latini aevi Carolini*, vol. 4, pt. 2, MGH (Berlin: apud Weidmannos, 1923), 565–69; cf. Schaller and Könsgen, *Initia carminum*, no. 1352.

[168] PL 39:2061.

[169] Edited by Guido Maria Dreves, *Prosarium Lemovicense. Die Prosen der Abtei St. Martial zu Limoges aus Troparien des 10., 11. und 12. Jahrhunderts* (Leipzig: Fues's Verlag [R. Reisland], 1899), 65–66, 59, and 66–67, respectively. For the last one, see also Schaller and Könsgen, *Initia carminum*, no. 2337.

[170] Dumville, "Liturgical Drama," 374–406.

[171] Karl Young, "The Harrowing of Hell in Liturgical Drama," *Transactions of the Wisconsin Academy of Sciences, Arts, and Letters* 16, no. 2 (1909): 934–46. Outside liturgy, the "Sermo" was used extensively by Jacobus a Voragine in the *Legenda aurea*, chap. 54 (p. 242); it was known to Thomas Aquinas, who cites it, in the context of the discussion of Christ's Descent into Hell, in his *Summa theologiae* 3a, q. 52, ad 5 (vol. 54, ed. Richard T. A. Murphy [New York: Blackfriars in conjunction with McGraw-Hill Book Co., 1965], 166). The Eusebian fragment was placed at the head of the *EN* in several manuscripts of the *EN*, discussed above.

The *EN*'s connection with homiletic literature was perhaps stronger than with any other form of public worship, and consequently it is easier to document. Medieval preachers approached the apocryphal text in a variety of ways: they adapted it in its entirety to specific homiletic purposes, or transformed only portions of it—usually the story of Joseph and the Harrowing of Hell—into homilies, or quarried it for colorful, dramatic details. One of the earliest examples of homiletic adaptation of the entire *EN* is preserved, together with a Carolingian homiliary, in Grenoble, Bibl. mun. MS. 470, fols. 18r–26v (saec. XII). In this manuscript, the *EN* is introduced with a summary of the Creation and the Fall of humankind and ends with an account of the Last Judgement. As in the *Palestra*, the prologue sets the stage for the central events of the Redemption related in the *EN*, and the epilogue adds their ultimate completion at the end of time. Thus framed, the homily presents the scheme of sacred history as it has unfolded and as it will unfold itself in time.

Some homilists adapted only portions of the *EN*, especially those narrating the episodes not described in detail in the canonical gospels. A late medieval German preacher, Franciscus Woitsdorf (d. 1463), inserts the story of Joseph of Arimathea (*EN* 12–17) among his *Sermones de tempore*, preserved in at least three manuscripts.[172] When not incorporated verbatim, the same section of the *EN* served as a source or model for more independent homiletic accounts of the imprisonment and miraculous deliverance of Joseph, while its apocryphal continuation (*EN* 17–27) inspired sermons on the Harrowing of Hell.[173]

Predictably, the *EN* is often embedded in the midst of manuscript collections of sermons. Versions of the B type invited their placement and use as a homily through the opening apostrophe to a listening audience, "Audistis, fratres karissimi . . ." ("You have heard, most beloved brothers . . ."). In one of the oldest copies of that sort, Padova, Biblioteca Antoniana 473 Scaff. XXI, fols. 138v–47v (saec. XI–XII), the *EN*, entitled significantly *Sermo de passione*, is inserted, together with the apocryphal *Visio Pauli*, among miscellaneous sermons. Another copy of *EN* B, in a twelfth-century, possibly Spanish manuscript, London, BL MS. Addit. 29630, begins a series of sermons, and the word "sermones," written between the columns at the head of the text,

---

[172] Kremsmünster, Stiftsbibliothek MS. 311 (saec. XV); and Wrocław, Biblioteka Uniwersytecka MSS. I F 215 (saec. XV), and I F 725 (saec. XV/2).

[173] On Joseph, see for instance Honorius Augustodunensis, "De paschali die," in his *Speculum ecclesiae* (PL 172:932D–33A); on the Harrowing, see Bruno Segniensis, "In die resurrectionis," in *Maxima bibliotheca veterum patrum*, vol. 6 (Lyon: Apud Anissonios, 1677), 754, and the homily in Cambridge, St. John's College MS. C. 12, fol. 141va.

is its only title. But texts of type A also occur in the company of sermons, perhaps even more frequently: they are encountered, for instance, in such homiletic manuscripts as Kremsmünster, Stiftsbibliothek MSS. 3 (saec. XV/1) and 170 (saec. XV in.); London, BL MS. Addit. 17003 (saec. XV); and Oxford, Bodl. Lib. MS. Bodl. 406 (saec. XIII).

3.4. Conclusion

The *EN* reached the peak of its popularity as the Middle Ages were beginning to wane and new religious attitudes to assert themselves. Even as some scribes were willing to treat it with the respect usually accorded the greatest patristic authorities and to place it in the company of the canonical texts, others began to speak out against it. The main source of its enduring appeal—the imaginative, mythologized narrative of the Harrowing of Hell—became the target of impassioned criticism and ridiculing attacks.[174] Few critics went as far as Reginald Pecock (b. 1395, d. 1460), who denied the apostolic sanction for the belief in Christ's Descent.[175] Most, like the anonymous author of the English treatise *Speculum devotorum*, accepted the Descent as an article of faith but rejected what the *EN* suggests about the nature of the event because "hyt ys not autentyke & also for the forseyde doctur Lyre prouyth hyt euydently false be autoryte of holy wryt & seyingys of othyre doctorys"; the author will not put "sueche thynge here þat ys so vnsykyr & mygthte be cause of erroure to sympyl creaturys."[176]

As theological redefinitions of Christ's Descent into Hell became more entrenched with the work of Pico della Mirandola, Nicholas of Cusa, and others, the *EN* lost most of its ground and support. In the disputes concerning the nature of the Descent raging throughout the sixteenth century in Europe, the *EN* often bore the brunt of scorn and contempt. In his harangue against Richard Smith, an Oxford theologian, Christopher Carlile mocks the legendary account of the Harrowing of Hell which the former allegedly affirmed, and the *EN* with it. He derides his opponent:

---

[174] Dewey D. Wallace, Jr., "Puritan and Anglican: The Interpretation of Christ's Descent into Hell in Elizabethan Theology," *Archiv für Reformationsgeschichte* 69 (1978): 248–87.

[175] H. T. Riley, ed., *Registra quorundam abbatum S. Albani, qui saeculo XV^{mo} fluorere*, vol. 1, *Registrum abbatiae Johannis Whethamstede*, Rer. Brit. M. A. Script., vol. 28, pt. 6 (London: Longman, 1872), 281, 285.

[176] James Hogg, ed., *The Speculum devotorum of an Anonymous Carthusian of Sheen*, Analecta Cartusiana, vol. 13 (Salzburg: Institut für englische Sprache und Literatur, Universität Salzburg, 1974), 312.

The false Gospell ascribed to Nicodemus, testifieth as many absurdityes as you do. How that Orcus and Pluto reason, how they myght kepe CHRIST out of their kingdome, they be suche Prodigious fables as are in the dreames of Brigitta, and in many of ye schole men. Which are tedious to repeat, folishe to be committed to wryting, ridiculous to the wise, impossible to be credited, hurtfull to the symple, and engenderinge a thowsande absurdityes.[177]

By 1582, when Carlile's mockery of Smith and the *EN* was published, the apocryphon, together with other legendary accretions, had already been abjured by the Roman Catholic Church, striving to rid herself of fancy and superstition through the actions of the Council of Trent. Outside and inside pressures for reform ultimately resulted in the placement of the *EN* on the Index. It was officially condemned by the Louvain Index of 1558 as part of the *Orthodoxographa theologiae sacrosanctae ac syncerioris fidei Doctores numero LXXVI* . . . , originally edited by Johann Basilius Herold in 1555 and re-edited by Johann Jakob Grynaeus in 1569.[178] In the Trent Index of 1564 and the Liège Index of 1569, the *EN* is singled out by its own title.[179] The *EN* never recovered from these attacks on its reputation and never regained its former popularity and prestige.

---

[177] Christopher Carlile, *A Discourse, Concerning two diuine Positions, The first effectually concluding, that the soules of the faithfull fathers, deceased before Christ, went immediately to heaven. The Second sufficientlye setting forth vnto vs Christians, what we are to conceiue, touching the descension of our Sauiour Christ into hell: Publiquely disputed at a Commencement in Cambridge, Anno Domini 1552. Purposefuly written at the first by way of confutation, against a Booke of Richard Smith of Oxford, D. of Diuinity* . . . (London: Roger Ward, 1582), fols. 52v–53r.

[178] Cf. J. M. de Bujanda, ed., *Index de l'Université de Louvain 1546, 1550, 1558,* (Sherbrooke, Québec: Centre d'études de la renaissance, 1986), 339–40.

[179] Franz Heinrich Reusch, ed., *Die Indices librorum prohibitorum des sechzehnten Jahrhunderts* (1886; repr., Nieuwkoop: B. de Graaf, 1961), 272, 287.

The *Gospel of Nicodemus* in the Vernacular Literature of Medieval France

RICHARD O'GORMAN

O vere digna hostia
per quem fracta sunt tartara[1]

ld and Middle French literature experienced widespread influence from the apocryphal *Evangelium Nicodemi (EN)*.[2] This
indebtedness, broadly speaking, took two forms: direct translation or adaptation of the Latin text, and appropriation of individual
themes, motifs, or dramatic situations from the apocryphon.

1. Translations and adaptations

1.1. Three early verse translations

Identification of the precise recensions of the Latin work that found
their way to northern France in this period to provide models for vernacular translations will doubtless have to await the results of the
investigation now under way of the extensive Latin manuscript tradition.[3] What is certain, however, is that by the end of the twelfth century

---

[1] "Ad coenam agni providi ... ," in *Hymnarius Moissiacensis*, ed. Guido Maria
Dreves, Analecta hymnica medii aevi, vol. 2 (1888; repr., New York: Johnson
Reprint Corp., 1961), 46.

[2] Unless otherwise noted, all references to the Latin text will be to H. C. Kim,
ed., *The Gospel of Nicodemus: Gesta Salvatoris*, Toronto Medieval Latin Texts, vol. 2
(Toronto: Pontifical Institute of Mediaeval Studies, 1973). The text will be cited by
chapter and paragraph numbers.

[3] Zbigniew Izydorczyk, "The Unfamiliar *Evangelium Nicodemi*," *Manuscripta*
33 (1989): 169–91.

the matter was of great interest to popular writers and that versions of the apocryphon, complete with the *Descensus Christi ad inferos* and Pilate's letter to Tiberius (Claudius), began to appear in the vernacular.

First among these versions in French seems to have been a partial adaptation in octosyllabic rhymed couplets composed at Mont-Saint-Michel by a Norman poet, André de Coutances.[4] Proclaiming that all good Christians know of Christ's Passion and death from Holy Scripture, André skips the account of the trial before Pilate, begins with the events following the Crucifixion (*EN* 11), continues through the account of the Harrowing of Hell by Carinus and Leucius (vv. 815–1932), and concludes with the letter to Claudius that summarizes the events of the life of Christ (vv. 1933–2028). In the prologue, the poet confesses to having liked song and dance in his youth, but now, being of mature age, he wishes to turn his attention to more edifying matters (vv. 1–6). He must have had some education, doubtless in the schools of Paris, and he counts among his close friends, and perhaps family, the lady of Tribehou, to whom he addresses his poem. This family, prominent in the Cotentin in lower Normandy (département de la Manche) at the turn of the century, suggests perhaps that André was also of noble birth.

Also from the first half of the thirteenth century comes the second metrical Old French version of the *EN*,[5] that of a certain Chrétien, about whom practically nothing is known (he is certainly not to be identified with the famous champenois poet Chrétien de Troyes). His version of the apocryphon, a "work of simple, unpretentious piety,"[6] embraces the entire Latin text, though not without some compression (he devotes 840 verses to the *Descensus Christi ad inferos*, as against André de Coutances's 1214). It opens with a dedication to the Trinity and a prologue closely related in contents to that found in the *codex Einsidlensis* edited by Kim; it closes with the letter to Claudius and an epilogue in which Chrétien gives his name and states that he has translated the work, "De latin en romanz turnée" (v. 2186). Based on a

---

[4] This text, along with the two other metrical versions, has been published by Gaston Paris and Alphonse Bos, eds., *Trois Versions rimées de l'Évangile de Nicodème par Chrétien, André de Coutances et un anonyme*, Société des anciens textes français, vol. 22 (Paris: F. Didot, 1885), 73–136, from London, British Library (BL) MS. Addit. 10289. Paris (ibid., xxv) dates the poem to the very early thirteenth century, around the period of the annexation of Normandy by Philip Augustus in 1204. On André's version, see Walter Becker, "Die Sage von der Höllenfahrt Christi in der altfranzösischen Literatur," *Romanische Forschungen* 32 (1913): 903–12, and D. D. R. Owen, *The Vision of Hell: Infernal Journeys in Medieval French Literature* (New York: Barnes and Noble, 1970), 99–101.

[5] Text in Paris and Bos, *Trois Versions*, 1–69.

[6] Owen, *The Vision of Hell*, 101.

study of rhyme and meter, the editors localize the poet's region of origin to the east of Paris, perhaps in Champagne, although the manuscript they used (Florence, Biblioteca Laurenziana MS. Conventi suppressi 99) was copied in a marked Anglo-Norman hand. A second copy of Chrétien's poem was brought to light by Meyer—Cambridge, Fitzwilliam Museum MS. 123, a manuscript formerly the property of M. McLean. Meyer rejected Paris and Bos's localization of the author's dialect in eastern France: "Je ne vois pas de raison pour que le poème n'ait pas une origine anglaise ou normande" ("I see no reason why the poem should not be of English or Norman origin").[7]

A third verse translation of the *EN*, by an otherwise unknown Anglo-Norman writer, has been preserved in a single fourteenth-century manuscript, London, Lambeth Palace MS. 522.[8] This anonymous work dates in all probability from the second half of the thirteenth century, but the late manuscript that preserves the text shows considerable corruption: "il fourmille de fautes incroyables, qui attestent chez le copiste une ignorance presque complète du français et une rare insouciance du sens de ce qu'il écrivait" ("it is full of unbelievable faults which show that the scribe knew virtually no French and cared even less about the meaning of what he was writing").[9] It opens with the same prologue and dedication to the Trinity as in Chrétien's version, and, like the latter, the text contains all three parts of the apocryphon. The poet also concludes with Pilate's letter summarizing the events of the life of Christ, this time addressed to Tiberius: "A Cesar Tyberye ad conté Par lettre ..." (vv. 2066 ff.). But unlike his predecessors, the anonymous writer provides no epilogue, no revelations or personal touches about himself or his condition. He effaces himself completely from the text and, when mentioning his source, says merely: "Devums parler hardiement / De ceo ke nos veums escrit / De nostre sire Jhesu Crist" (vv. 4–6; "We must speak boldly about what we see written concerning our Lord Jesus Christ").

These three metrical versions of the *Évangile de Nicodème* are all associated in one way or another either with Normandy or with Anglo-Norman England. This suggests that the apocryphon was unusually popular in these regions, especially in the thirteenth century.[10] Its vogue in the Norman sphere of influence is sometimes

---

[7] Paul Meyer, "Note sur un nouveau manuscrit de la traduction en vers de l'Évangile de Nicodème par Chrétien," *Bulletin de la Société des anciens textes français* 24 (1898): 83.

[8] Paris and Bos, *Trois Versions*, 139–212.

[9] Ibid., xlviii.

[10] Two other copies of Chrétien's text, now lost, were apparently in existence in the Middle Ages, housed in Assumption Abbey in Leicester; see Madeleine

explained as a result of the serious and pious nature of much of Anglo-French verse during the period;[11] an alternative explanation, as I suggest below, may connect it with the growing popularity in England of the cult of St. Joseph of Arimathea.

The three verse translations lay little claim to literary merit, aiming rather at communicating to the faithful the truths relating to Christ's Passion, death, and Descent into Hell. This is especially true of the anonymous version, whose somewhat doggerel verse strove to reflect the Latin text (the so-called *EN* A) but managed from time to time to slip into a confused written expression. The version of André de Coutances is much more accomplished; also basing his text on the Latin version A, André handles the vernacular with skill, deviating from the original on occasion to impart a personal touch and to craft dialogue to relieve the monotony of third-person narrative. In comparison with André's poem, that of Chrétien is pedestrian, exhibiting few of the versifying techniques of the Norman poet: "It is a work of simple, unpretentious piety, such as we have come to associate with the Anglo-Normans rather than the continental writers."[12]

1.2. Prose versions

It was, however, with the rise of prose as a vehicle for serious literature in the early thirteenth century that versions of the *Évangile de Nicodème* experienced their most widespread diffusion, as attested by their rich and complex manuscript traditions, both in the north of France and in Occitania. In Old and Middle French alone, more than sixty manuscripts preserve, in whole or in part, the text of one version or another, and the pseudo-gospel's popularity extended into fifteenth- and even sixteenth-century printed editions.[13] I can do little more than summarize here this immense body of writing, especially since

Blaess, "Les Manuscrits français dans les monastères anglais au moyen âge," *Romania* 94 (1973): 356–57, nos. 98 and 931 of the catalogue.

[11] Owen, *The Vision of Hell*, 75–77.

[12] Ibid., 101.

[13] Two incunabula of the Middle French *Évangile* are known: *Passion N.-S.-Jésus-Christ*, printed in Paris by J. Trepperel in 1497 (see Richard Paul Wülcker, *Das Evangelium Nicodemi in der abendländischen Literatur. Nebst drei excursen ...* [Paderborn: F. Schöningh, 1872], 28), and a *Vie de Jesu Crist* printed in Brittany by Robin Foucquet in 1485 (see Émile Roy, *Le Mystère de la passion en France du XIV*^e *au XVI*^e *siècle*, Revue Bourguignonne, vols. 13–14 [1903–4; repr., Geneva: Slatkine, 1974], 325–27), both of which derive from a text of the long version attributed to Gamaliel, the *Passion selon Gamaliel*. A sixteenth-century edition, printed in Lyon by Jehan de Chandeney in 1510, is most likely from the Trepperel imprint, but this point remains to be verified.

the nature of these vernacular prose texts, relying to different degrees on particular Latin models, is extremely varied, and because we do not yet possess reliable editions. Further, the underlying tradition of the Latin manuscripts has not yet been established firmly enough to permit one to assign an individual vernacular prose rendition to a specific Latin recension.

The material quality of the various manuscripts that transmit the prose *Évangile* varies from the most wretched copies scribbled hastily on paper (e.g., Paris, Bibliothèque nationale [BN] MS. fr. 24438) to sumptuous vellum manuscripts containing large collections of saints' lives and other works copied with the greatest care and luxuriously illuminated (Paris, BN MSS. fr. 6260, 24209, etc.). Although some French copies of the apocryphon are found isolated with a few other texts in an individual manuscript (e.g., Paris, Bibliothèque de l'Arsenal MS. 5366), in most cases the *Évangile* figures as one element in larger compilations of pious material, sacred history, or hagiographical legends (Paris, BN MSS. fr. 187, 409, 1850, etc.), as well as in collections of a secular nature (Paris, BN MS. fr. 15219). Often it forms, with other pieces, a sort of prologue to a French "légendier" (Paris, BN MSS. fr. 411, 6447, 17229, etc.),[14] and it is frequently found introducing a French version of the apocryphal *Vindicta Salvatoris* (Paris, BN MSS. fr. 12445, 17229, Chantilly, Musée Condé MS. 38, etc.).[15] It is even substituted at times for Jean Belet's translation of the passion from Jacobus a Voragine's *Legenda aurea* (Paris, BN MSS. fr. 183, 184, 413; Brussels, Bibliothèque royale MS. 9225; London, BL MS. Addit. 17275, etc.).[16]

In its broadest outline, the manuscript tradition of the prose *Évangile* preserves two main forms of the text: the short version and the long one.

1.2.1. Short version (Latin EN A)

This version of the *Évangile de Nicodème* has been published by Alvin E. Ford according to what he considered to be two distinct traditions,

---

[14] Essentially Meyer's groups C^1 and D ("Légendes hagiographiques en français," in *Histoire littéraire de la France*, vol. 33, ed. Paul Meyer [Paris: Imprimerie nationale, 1906], 414–20), which combine the following works into an introduction to the "légendier" proper: (1) *La Nativité de Jesus*; (2) *L'Apparition* (Adoration of the Magi); (3) *La Purification de notre Dame*; (4) *La Passion du Christ et descente aux enfers*; (5) *La Conversion de Saint Paul*; and (6) *La Chaire de Saint Pierre*.

[15] One redaction of the prose *Vengeance*, Paris, BN MS. fr. 187, actually incorporates elements of Robert de Boron's prose *Joseph d'Arimathie* relating to Joseph; see Alexandre Micha, "Une Rédaction de la *Vengeance de Notre Seigneur*," in *Mélanges offerts à Rita Lejeune* (Gembloux: J. Duculot, 1969), 2:1291–98.

[16] See Meyer, "Légendes," 426–27.

A and B.[17] This edition leaves something to be desired.[18] For tradition A, Ford bases his text on Paris, BN MS. fr. 19525, and for tradition
B, on Paris, BN MS. fr. 6447, but he fails to provide a justification for
the filiation of the manuscripts of each tradition. Also, the variant readings are in such a tangle that it is difficult for readers to sort out the
various recensions. The editor does set forth the main differences
between the two traditions:[19] in addition to minor variation in expression, tradition B has compressed the text slightly in comparison with
A, causing the omission of several short passages. Moreover, B lacks
the entire prologue of A, which dates the work "al quinzime an que
Tyberie Cesar aveit esté enpereor de Rome" ("in the fifteenth year
when Tiberius Caesar was emperor in Rome") and attributes the composition to Nicodemus, who wrote it "en ebreu et en latin" ("in
Hebrew and in Latin").[20] Although there is a slight discrepancy in the
dating of the Passion, this prologue resembles the one in the *codex
Einsidlensis* but does not include the dedication to the Trinity or the reference to the discovery of the document by emperor Theodosius in
Jerusalem.[21]

TRADITION A. The identification of Ford's tradition A is not without
problems. First, to his list of seven manuscripts we must add:

> Aberystwyth, National Library of Wales MS. 5028c
> London, BL MS. Egerton 613
> Metz, Bibliothèque municipale (Bibl. mun.) MS. 262.[22]

---

[17] Alvin E. Ford, *L'Évangile de Nicodème: Les Versions courtes en ancien français
et en prose*, Publications romanes et françaises, vol. 125 (Geneva: Droz, 1973), 41–
81 and 83–106, respectively.

[18] See the reviews by C. R. Sneddon in *French Studies* 31 (1977): 441–42, and
Richard O'Gorman in *Cahiers de civilisation médiévale* 19 (1976): 59–61.

[19] Ford, *L'Évangile de Nicodème*, 28–30.

[20] Ibid., 41.

[21] Kim, *The Gospel of Nicodemus*, 13; Constantinus de Tischendorf, ed., *Evangelia apocrypha*, 2d rev. ed. (Leipzig: H. Mendelssohn, 1876), 314–15.

[22] Michel Zink, *La Prédication en langue romane avant 1300*, Nouvelle bibliothèque du moyen âge, vol. 4 (Paris: Champion), 64. And perhaps also Paris, BN
MS. fr. 6260, which Ford terms a "version hétéroclite" (Ford, *L'Évangile de Nicodème*, 27) but which opens with the prologue and the beginning of the text
according to tradition A. Jean Bonnard, *Les Traductions de la Bible en vers français
au moyen âge* (1884; repr., Geneva: Slatkine, 1967), 92–104, associates this manuscript, together with Paris, BN MS. fr. 9562, with the anonymous translation in
verse of the Old Testament. The Metz copy is acephalous, beginning: "... en
Jherusalem. Je vi donques Jhesum seoir sur asinum ..." (Ford, *L'Évangile de
Nicodème*, p. 42, l. 32, tradition A). I am indebted to Mme Geneviève Brunel-
Lobrichon of the Institut de recherche et d'histoire des textes in Paris for a notice
of this manuscript. A version belonging to tradition A was printed by Bengt

Second, as Shields points out,[23] two manuscripts from Ford's list of tradition A, Paris, BN MS. fr. 1850 (siglum *E*), and Oxford, Queen's College MS. 305 (siglum *F*), represent in fact either a variant recension within this version or else a completely different version, and they should doubtless have been edited separately (to the two can be added Dijon, Bibl. mun. MS. 525).[24]

The same distinct recension formed the basis for interpolations into two Old French prose romances. The post-Vulgate sequel to the *Roman de Merlin*, edited as the *Livre d'Artus*,[25] contains a text that derives directly from it. The *Livre* is extant in a single manuscript, Paris, BN MS. fr. 337. The *Évangile* begins:

Il auint fait li preudom u nonantiesme an de la segnorie Tiberij Cersar lempereur de Rome & u nonantiesme an de la segnorie Herode le fil Herode roi de Galilee....[26]

(It happened, the worthy man said, in the nineteenth year[27]

Lindström, ed., *A Late Middle English Version of the Gospel of Nicodemus Edited from British Museum MS Harley 149*, Acta Universitatis Upsaliensis, Studia Anglistica Upsaliensia, vol. 18 (Uppsala: Almqvist and Wiksell, 1974), 44–126, text B, from London, BL MS. Egerton 2710.

[23] Hugh Shields, "Bishop Turpin and the Source of *Nycodemus gospell*," *English Studies* 53 (1972): 499; idem, "Légendes religieuses en ancien français (MS. 951 de la Bibliothèque de Trinity College à Dublin)," *Scriptorium* 34 (1980): 66.

[24] Incipit (from *E*): "Il avint el nonantiesme an de la seignorie Tyberii Cesar, l'enpereor de Rome, el nonantiesme an de la seignorie Herode . . .''; explicit: "E ensi i a par tot .v. mile et .v. cenz anz''; see Meyer, "Légendes," 393. Lindström, *A Late Middle English Version*, 44–129, printed this recension from Paris, BN MS. fr. 1850 (his text C). Note the frequency, in Ford's variants to tradition A, with which his MSS. *E* and *F* agree against his base manuscript. Izydorczyk, "The Unfamiliar *Evangelium Nicodemi*," 183, identifies a late Latin recension of the *EN*, a fusion of his types A and C, which "strangely" dates the Passion to "anno nonagesimo" of Tiberius. This could well be the origin of the variant version of Ford's tradition A; see also Zbigniew Izydorczyk, "The Latin Source of an Old French Gospel of Nicodemus," *Revue d'histoire des textes* 25 (1995): 265–79. Finally, Shields, "Légendes religieuses," 66, concludes that another manuscript from Ford's tradition A, Dublin, Trinity College MS. 951, represents in fact the debris of a text "dont l'indépendence n'admet . . . aucun doute."

[25] H. Oskar Sommer, ed., *The Vulgate Version of the Arthurian Romances*, vol. 7 (Washington: Carnegie Institution, 1916).

[26] Ibid., p. 247, l. 27. A translation into Middle Dutch verse of *Le Livre d'Artus*, presumably with the interpolated *Évangile de Nicodème*, was joined in 1326 by Lodewijk van Velthem to Jacob van Maerlant's verse adaptation of Robert de Boron's prose *Joseph* and *Merlin*; see Roger Sherman Loomis, *Arthurian Literature in the Middle Ages: A Collaborative History* (Oxford: Clarendon Press, 1959), 445, and Richard O'Gorman, "La Tradition manuscrite du *Joseph d'Arimathie* en prose de Robert de Boron," *Revue d'histoire des textes* 1 (1971): 145–46.

[27] Kim, *The Gospel of Nicodemus*, 13: "in anno xviii imperatoris Tyberii Caesaris."

of the lordship of Tiberius Caesar, emperor of Rome, and in
the nineteenth year of the lordship of Herod, son of Herod
king of Galilee. . . .)

In the *Roman de Perceforest*, the author put the story of Joseph of Arimathea into the mouth of Alain le Gros.[28] While he amputated considerably the *Descensus* portion of this recension (everything after the
dialogue between Satan and Hades),[29] the author seems to have followed closely the first part of the apocryphon.[30] The excerpt in the
Roman opens:

> Il advint au dix neufiesme an de lempire Tibere Cesar de
> Romme et de Herode roy de Galilee, consul Rufibellionis, pro-
> cureur en Judee, Ponce Pilate fut le prince, provoyres des Juifs
> Joseph et Cayphas, Some et Sathain, Cormalie et Judas, Nevie
> et Nephtalim, Alexandre et Sirus et moult dautres des Juifs
> vindrent a Pylate alencontre Jesus, en laccusant en maintes
> manieres en disant. . . .[31]

> (It happened in the nineteenth year of the reign of the emper-
> or Tiberius Caesar of Rome and of Herod king of Galilee, in
> the consulate of Rufibellion, chief procurator in Judea being
> Pontius Pilate, high priests of the Jews Joseph and Cayphas,
> Some and Sathain, Cormalie and Judas, Nevie and Nephtalim,
> Alexandre and Sirus and many others of the Jews came to
> Pilate against Jesus accusing him of many things saying. . . .)

A future editor of this variant recension of the short version will
doubtless have to take into consideration these two interpolated texts,
along with the three extant manuscripts mentioned above.

TRADITION B. The list of sixteen manuscripts of Ford's tradition B[32]
can be lengthened considerably by addition of the following:

Paris, BN MS. fr. 413
Paris, BN MS. fr. 17229
Paris, Bibliothèque Sainte-Geneviève MS. 1302
Tours, Bibl. mun. MS. 1015 (acephalous)

---

[28] Jeanne Lods, *Le Roman de Perceforest*, Société de publications romanes et
françaises, vol. 32 (Geneva: Droz, 1951), 33–34.
[29] Becker, "Die Sage," 924.
[30] This voluminous romance is being edited by Jane H. M. Taylor and Gilles
Roussineau for the Textes littéraires français series, but the section containing the
Évangile de Nicodème has not yet appeared.
[31] Wülcker, *Das Evangelium Nicodemi*, 28.
[32] Ford, *L'Évangile de Nicodème*, 83–106.

Turin, Biblioteca Nazionale MS. L. I. 5
Brussels, Bibliothèque royale Albert Ier MS. 2306 (olim 9030–37)

Doubtless we can add as well Geneva, Bibliothèque publique et universitaire, MS. Comites Latentes 102, formerly Cheltenham, Phillipps MS. 3660,[33] sold at Sotheby's on 21 November 1972. This is the version of the *Évangile* often admitted into the Belet translation of Jacobus a Voragine's *Legenda aurea* (see Paris, BN MSS. fr. 183, 185, 413, etc.).

1.2.2. Long version (Latin EN B; sometimes entitled Le Livre ..., Passion ..., or Évangile selon Gamaliel)

Ford gives no information about this prose version except to list summarily nine manuscripts under the heading "Versions Longues" (27). He defers an edition of this text to a later date. To his nine manuscripts we can now add the following:

Bern, Bürgerbibliothek MS. A 260
Besançon, Bibl. mun. MS. 588
Paris, Bibliothèque de l'Arsenal MS. 5366
Toulouse, Bibl. mun. MS. 888
Vatican City, Biblioteca Apostolica Vaticana MS. Reg. lat. 1728
(short fragment from the beginning)

According to the Vatican manuscript, this version begins:

En celuy temps que Jhesucrist print mort et passion en la cité de Jherusalem soubz Ponce Pilate qui estoit seneschal de Jherusalem pour Julius Cesar, empereur de Romme, et avoit son lieu en Jherusalem et en Cesarie.... (Fol. 148r)

(At that time when Jesus Christ suffered death and torment in the city of Jerusalem under Pontius Pilate, who was procurator [seneschal] for Julius Caesar, emperor of Rome, and he governed in Jerusalem and in Caesarea....)

An edition of this long version was prepared by Madeleine Le Merrer as a "mémoire de maîtrise" at the Université de Caen; Mme Le Merrer writes that "la thèse ... a été transformée en 'thèse d'état' ... Soutenance prévue: 1991" ("the thesis ... has been transformed into a 'state doctoral thesis'.... Anticipated date of thesis defence: 1991").[34]

---

[33] Meyer, "Légendes," 421.
[34] Madeleine Le Merrer, ed., "Édition de la version en prose de l'Évangile de Nicodème d'apres cinq manuscrits du XIVe et XVe siècles" (Mémoire de maîtrise, Université de Caen, 1968). The *Livre de Gamaliel* and its Occitan source are discussed below by Josep Izquierdo, pp. 159–63.

1.3. Other adaptations

In addition to the short and long versions, Ford lists also "Trois Para-phrases": Paris, BN MS. fr. 15219, and London, BL MSS. Royal 20 B. V and Egerton 2781.[35] The *Évangile de Nicodème* contained in the first of these has nothing in common with the two London manuscripts but is in fact a summary of the events related in the *EN* as found in Vincent of Beauvais's *Speculum historiale*. It begins with the deposition from the cross and includes a much compressed account of the Harrowing of Hell narrated by Carinus and Leucius.[36] The other two manuscripts, supplemented by Cambridge, University Library MS. Dd. 4. 35,[37] rep-resent a composite Anglo-Norman work which links portions of the apocryphon to a *Complaint of Our Lady*, drawn largely from biblical sources. It is an emotionally charged lament in the first person in the tradition of the *Mater Dolorosa*. The *planctus* section first incorporates the episode of the imprisonment of Joseph (from chaps. 12 and 15 of the *EN*) and then adds, in third-person narrative, the material pertain-ing to Joseph from chapters 12–17. Both parts of this Anglo-Norman work were printed by Marx and Drennan in conjunction with their edi-tion of the Middle English text.[38] The editors suggest that this trun-cated version of the apocryphon might have come about in England because of the growing interest in Joseph of Arimathea as the apostle of Britain.[39] This might also explain the diminished role accorded the Harrowing of Hell, the account of Carinus and Leucius being here reduced to fewer than 200 words.[40]

Extensive material from the *EN* has been absorbed into yet another work brought to our attention by Alexandre Micha as "une autre

[35] Ford, *L'Évangile de Nicodème*, 27.

[36] This text, though greatly compressed, was taken directly from Vincent of Beauvais's *Speculum historiale* (see below, pp. 116–18). See the edition of this short text in Richard O'Gorman, "The Text of the Middle French *Évangile de Nicodème* from Paris, Bibliothèque Nationale, f. fr. 15219," *Medium Ævum* 61 (1992): 298–302.

[37] This is a late fifteenth-century fragment of two folios, bound at the begin-ning of a codex containing Latin texts. It represents the remains of the sequence *Complaint* and *Évangile de Nicodème*, although only a short fragment of the *Nicodème* was spared the mutilation (C. W. Marx and Jeanne F. Drennan, eds., *The Middle English Prose Complaint of Our Lady and Gospel of Nicodemus*, Middle English Texts, vol. 19 [Heidelberg: C. Winter, 1987], 118.10–19.9); see also C. William Marx, "A Newly Identified Fragment of the Anglo-Norman Prose *Complaint of Our Lady* and *Gospel of Nicodemus* in Cambridge University Library MS Dd. 4. 35," *Notes & Queries* 236 (1991): 157–58.

[38] Marx and Drennan, *The Middle English Prose Complaint*, 73–136.

[39] Ibid., 41; cf. Valerie M. Lagorio, "The Evolving Legend of St Joseph of Glastonbury," *Speculum* 46 (1971): 209–31; idem, "Joseph of Arimathea: The *Vita* of a Grail Saint," *Zeitschrift für romanische Philologie* 91 (1975): 54–68.

[40] Marx and Drennan, *The Middle English Prose Complaint*, 41.

[*Passion-Évangile de Nicodème*] encore plus longue."[41] Micha provides a list of six manuscripts of this work, known after its incipit as *Selon la sentence du philozophe Aristote:*

Lyon, Bibl. mun. MS. 864
Paris, BN MS. fr. 968
Paris, BN MS. fr. 969
Paris, BN MS. fr. 973
Paris, BN MS. fr. 975
Paris, BN MS. fr. 24438.

We must delete from this list BN MS. fr. 24438, a text closely related to the long version attributed to Gamaliel and edited by Le Merrer,[42] and add:

Bern, Bürgerbibliotek MS. 82[43]
Copenhagen, Kongelige Bibliotek MS. De Thott 132
Paris, Bibliothèque de l'Arsenal MS. 2076
Paris, Bibliothèque de l'Arsenal MS. 6869
Privas, Archives départementales de l'Ardèche MS. 4 (I. 3)

plus two incunabula described by Roy.[44] This list of manuscripts can surely be lengthened by a careful search of library catalogues. This text noticed by Micha is an extremely long work of a composite nature, unstudied, it would seem, by those working in the field. Though not, strictly speaking, a version of the *Évangile*, it is a Passion narrative combining a goodly amount of pious and moral material for meditation, drawn from a wide variety of sources, including the church fathers and medieval philosophers and theologians, with a liberal mixture of biblical narrative, canonical and apocryphal alike.[45] It traces the events of Holy Week from the raising of Lazarus in Bethany to the appearance of the risen Savior to his followers and the visit of the Holy Ghost at Pentecost. In the Copenhagen manuscript, the text fills no fewer than ninety-seven folios, including a summary of such events

---

[41] Micha, "Une Rédaction," 1291.

[42] Le Merrer, "Édition de la version en prose de l'Évangile de Nicodème." In fact, BN MS. fr. 24438 contains two Passion narratives: the passion composed for Isabeau de Bavière, which opens the manuscript (fols. 1r–82r) and is briefly discussed below, and the *Évangile selon Gamaliel* (fols. 140v–201v).

[43] Hermannus Hagen, *Catalogus codicum Bernensium* (Bernae: B. F. Haller, 1875), 99–100.

[44] Roy, *Le Mystère*, 255.

[45] There is, for example, an Œdipus-like story of Judas (MS. De Thott 132, fol. 61r–v), the account of the healing of Longinus (fol. 83r–v), and the message from Pilate's wife not to punish Jesus (his innocence was revealed to her in a dream; fol. 68v).

from the apocryphon as the interrogation by Pilate, the imprisonment of Joseph, and the Descent into Hell. The heading begins:

> Cy commence l'istoire de la passion nostre Seigneur Jhesucrist, le benoist Filz de Dieu et de la glorieuse Vierge Marie, le Sauveur du monde, laquelle il voult souffrir pour la redemption de l'umain lignaige, regnant Thiberien empereur de Romme, nommé Cezar, en l'an xviiime de son regne. . . .

> (Here begins the story of the Passion of Our Lord Jesus Christ, the blessed son of God, and of the glorious Virgin Mary, the Savior of the world, the Passion he willingly suffered for the Redemption of the human race, in the reign of Tiberius, emperor of Rome named Caesar, in the eighteenth year of his reign. . . .)

The incipit reads:

> Selon la sentence du philozophe Aristote en son premier livre de phisique: Qui veult avoir congnoissance d'aucune chose parfaittement, il doit premierement les causes enquerir et demander.[46]

> (According to the saying of the philosopher Aristotle in his first book of Physics: whoever desires knowledge of anything perfectly, he must first inquire and seek the causes.)

The account of Joseph's release from prison is found among the reported appearances of Jesus after his Resurrection:

> Comment nostre Seigneur delivra Joseph de la prison

> Nostre Seigneur Jhesucrist se departi d'elles et s'apparut a Joseph qui l'avoit enseveli, lequel les juifz avoient mis en prison pour le service qu'il avoit fait a nostre Seigneur Jhesucrist. Et estoit enclos en ung petit lieu moult estroictement seellé et fermé, et avoient conclud de l'occirre mais que le samedi fut passé. Adonc vint nostre Seigneur a lui et lui essuia ses yeulx qu'il avoit tous moueillez de lermes, et le visaige aussi, puis le baisa et le mist hors de celle prison sans ce que les seaulx ne les huis feussent despecez, et le ramena tout sain en son hostel.[47]

---

[46] Copenhagen, Kongelige Bibliotek MS. De Thott 132, fol. 1r.
[47] Ibid., fol. 90v.

(How Our Lord delivered Joseph from prison

Our Lord Jesus Christ took leave of them and appeared to Joseph, who had buried him, whom the Jews had cast into prison for the service that he had rendered Our Lord Jesus Christ. And he was shut up in a tiny place, tightly sealed and closed, and they had decided to kill him as soon as the Sabbath was passed. Then Our Lord came to him and wiped his eyes that were all moist with tears, and his face also, then he kissed him and freed him from that prison without breaking the seals or shattering the doors, and he returned him safely to his house.)

Since *Selon la sentence du philozophe Aristote* is likely to remain unedited for some time to come, I give in the appendix the entire *Descensus* section, again according to the Copenhagen manuscript. This account appears to derive from Jacobus a Voragine's *Legenda aurea*[48] or from one of the French translations of it.

Selon la sentence is said in fact to owe much to pseudo-Bonaventure's *Meditationes vitae Christi*,[49] an extremely popular work of Franciscan spirituality, which inspired also, more or less directly, an anonymous Passion narrative in French prose composed in 1398, at the behest of Isabeau de Bavière.[50] The *Passion Isabeau* recounts events in the life of Christ, from the resurrection of Lazarus to the Crucifixion and burial; a short excerpt is given by Roy.[51] In the first half of the fifteenth century, it presumably served as a basis for *Selon la sentence*. Since little is known about the various late medieval *Passions*, we shall have to await a thorough study of their texts to determine the indebtedness of the *Passion Isabeau* and *Selon la sentence* to the *Meditationes*, as well as their mutual relationships.[52]

---

[48] Jacobus a Voragine, *Jacobi a Voragine Legenda aurea vulgo Historia Lombardica dicta*, ed. Th. Graesse (Dresden: Impensis Librariae Arnoldianae, 1890), 242–44.

[49] Roy, *Le Mystère*, 250–55.

[50] Ibid., 250–54; Edelgard E. DuBruck, "The *Passion Isabeau* (1398) and Its Relationship to Fifteenth-Century *Mystères de la Passion*," *Romania* 107 (1986): 77–91.

[51] *Le Mystère*, 261–62. This text has now been edited by Edelgard E. DuBruck, *La Passion Isabeau: Une Édition du manuscrit Fr. 966 de la Bibliothèque Nationale de Paris* (New York: Peter Lang, 1990).

[52] A somewhat compressed Middle French adaptation of the *Meditationes* was made for Jean, Duc de Berry, sometime between 1380 and 1403. This *Vie de nostre benoit Sauveur Ihesuscrist*, often attributed to Jean Gerson because of a version of the Chancellor's sermon "Ad Deum vadit" interpolated into it, is extant in three manuscript copies (two complete) and partially in three incunabula. In the recent edition by Millard Meiss and Elizabeth H. Beatson, *La Vie de Nostre Benoit Sauveur Ihesucrist & La Saincte Vie de Nostre Dame* (New York: New York University Press,

Almost the entire *Évangile* was absorbed into yet another French work, a compilation of apocryphal legends in Paris, BN MS. fr. 95 (known as the Andrius manuscript), entitled by the recent editors *The Penitence of Adam.*[53] This work combines an account of the postlapsarian life of Adam and Eve with the *Évangile de Nicodème*, the two joined by a transitional quest of Seth and the story of the holy rood. Narrative unity is thus achieved: Adam's exile from paradise is brought to a conclusion with the return to paradise as a result of Christ's sacrifice on the cross and the Harrowing of Hell, fulfilling the promise of Redemption made to Seth. The typological relationship between Adam and Christ underlies the progression from Fall to Redemption, and the tree that sprang from the seed planted in Adam's mouth connects the tree of life with the wood of the cross. The *Évangile* section does not include the trial before Pilate (doubtless for reasons similar to those of André de Coutances) but begins with the descent from the cross and the imprisonment of Joseph, and it continues through Christ's Harrowing of Hell, as reported by "Carin et Lyoncel." The text concludes with Pilate's letter to Claudius.[54]

This brief outline only begins to give an account of the rich body of translations and adaptations of the apocryphal gospel in Old French. I have not even mentioned Jean de Vignay's unedited translations of Vincent of Beauvais's *Speculum historiale* and Jacobus a Voragine's *Legenda aurea*, both of which, extant in many manuscripts, contain long excerpts from the apocryphon.[55] Apparently unrelated to Jean's work is the Middle French redaction of that portion of Vincent's *Speculum*

1977), I have noted the influence of the *EN* in the following episodes: the miracle of the standards (Christ before Pilate is honored by the servant, and the standards lower in his presence [61–63]), Procula's dread (86), the mission to the underworld (110–15), the imprisonment of Joseph (115–16), and his release (119). When asked where Jesus was, the guard poses the usual condition: "Si nous rendez Joseph d'Abarimathe, et nous vous rendrons Jhesus de Nazareth" (126). See Geneviève Hasenohr, "À propos de la *Vie de Nostre Benoit Saulveur Jhesus Crist*," *Romania* 102 (1981): 352–91, who revises the accepted date of composition, authorship, and localization of the work and argues that the dedication to Jean de Berry is a fake, added many years later. A start in sorting out these various passion narratives in the tradition of the *Meditationes* has recently been made in the introduction to Sean Caulfield's dissertation, "An Edition of the Middle French Prose 'Resurrection nostre Saulveur Jhesucrist,' Based on Vatican, Reginensis Lat. 1728" (Ph.D. diss., University of Iowa, 1993).

[53] Esther C. Quinn and Micheline Dufau, eds., *The Penitence of Adam: A Study of the Andrius MS*, Romance Monographs, vol. 36 (University, Miss.: Romance Monographs, 1980).

[54] Ibid., 92–101.

[55] Monique Paulmier-Foucart and Serge Lusignan, "Vincent de Beauvais et l'histoire du *Speculum Maius*," *Journal des savants* (1990): 121–22; C. Knowles, "Jean de Vignay, un traducteur de XIVe siècle," *Romania* 75 (1954): 353–83.

historiale which summarizes the events from the deposition and en-
tombment to the account of the risen sons of Simeon, Leucius and
Carinus, witnesses to the Harrowing of Hell; it is preserved in Paris,
BN MS. fr. 15219, fols. 37r–40r. The following excerpts from Vincent's
Latin text (bk. 7, chap. 58)[56] and from the French translation may give
some idea of the faithfulness and skill of the anonymous translator:[57]

Haec audientes, omnes gauisi
sunt: Et euntes Annas, & Caiphas,
Nicodemus, & Ioseph, & Gamaliel,
non inuenerunt eos in sepulchris:
sed ambulantes in Arimathiam
inuenerunt eos ibi in oratione,
flexis genibus: & osculantes eos
cum omni veneratione, & timore
Dei perduxerunt eos Hierusalem
in sinagogam: clausisque ianuis
tollentes legem Domini, posue-
runt in manibus eorum, coniu-
rantes eos *per Deum Adonai, qui
per legem, & Prophetas locutus est,*
dicentes: Dicite si creditis, quod
ipse sit Christus, qui vos resusci-
tauit a mortuis: & enarrate nobis
quomodo resurrexistis.

Ces choses oyes, il se leverent,
c'est assavoir [39r] Annas, Cayphas, Nicodemus, Joseph, et Gamaliel, et alerent aux tumbeaux et
ne trouverent mie les corps.
Aprés ilz alerent a Abarimatie et
les trouverent a genoulx en oroi-
son. Adonc ilz les viserent a grant
reverance et devocion et les mene-
rent a Jherusalem en la signago-
gue. Et comme les portes furent
fermees, ilz apporterent la loy
Dieu et la misdrent en leurs mains
et les conjurerent en telle maniere:
—Nous vous conjurons, firent
ilz, de par le Dieu qui ceste loy
donna, que vous nous diez se
c'est mes Sire qui vous a ressusi-
tez, et nous racontez en quelle
maniere.

---

[56] Vincent of Beauvais, *Speculum historiale* (1624; repr., Graz: Akademische
Druck- u. Verlagsanstalt, 1965), 242.

[57] O'Gorman, "The Text," 301. (Translation of the French passage: Having
heard these things, they arose, that is Annas, Cayphas, Nicodemus, Joseph, and
Gamaliel, and went to the graves, but they did not find the bodies there. Afterwards, they went to Arimathea and found them kneeling in prayer. Then they
beheld them with great reverence and devotion, and they led them to the synagogue in Jerusalem. And when the doors were closed, they brought out the book
of the law of God and placed it in their hands and entreated them as follows:
—We entreat you, they said, by the God who wrote the law, that you tell us
whether it was my Lord who raised you up from the dead, and relate to us how
it was done.
Then Carinus and Leucius, for that was what they were called, when they
heard themselves entreated thus, began to tremble and sigh and, raising their
eyes to heaven, they made the sign of the cross on their tongues and began to
speak:
—Give us, they said, parchment and ink, and we shall write down those
things that we have heard and seen.)

Hanc ergo coniurationem audientes Carinus, & Leucius, contremuerunt corpore, & gemuerunt corde: simulque in caelum respicientes, feceruntque digitis suis signaculum crucis super linguas suas: & statim simul locuti sunt dicentes. Date nobis singulos tomos chartae, & scribemus, quae vidimus, & audiuimus.

Adonc Cari[n]us et Leucius, car ainsi estoient ilz appellez, quant il se virent ainsi conjurez, commencerent a trembler et a souppirer et puis leverent leurs yeulx au ciel et firent le signe de la croix sur leurs langues et commencerent a parler:

—Donnez nous, firent ilz, du parchemin et de l'ancre et nous escriprons ce que nous avons oy et veu.

Other literary works, too, await investigation for what they might reveal of apocryphal influence. For example, portions of the *Évangile* are likely to have been incorporated into a work known as the *Bible historiale*.[58] One such Bible, London, BL MS. Addit. 54325,[59] contains—according to the catalogue—a listing of two chapters possibly connected to the apocryphal story of Joseph of Arimathea: "La persecucioun Joseph de Arimathie" and "La pees Joseph de Arimathie." This and other biblical and pseudo-biblical texts might well yield a rich harvest of apocryphal material.

2. Appropriation of themes

Alongside this tradition of direct translation and adaptation of the *EN*, often connected with the incorporation of blocks of apocryphal material into longer pious or religious texts, some of its narrative elements were woven into secular or quasi-religious works, going back to the twelfth century, if not earlier. References to the apocryphon are found scattered throughout medieval French literature, appearing in Chrétien

---

[58] This work, preserved in numerous manuscripts (at least 20 in the BN alone), came from the pen of Guyart des Moulins. At the end of the thirteenth century, this Picard author translated the *Historia scholastica* of Peter Comestor and enriched it with material from the Bible to produce a truly popular biblical narrative; see Samuel Berger, *La Bible française au moyen âge* (Paris: Imprimerie nationale, 1884), 157–99; Bonnard, *Les Traductions*, 3–8; Hans Robert Jauss, ed., *La Littérature didactique, allégorique, et satirique*, Grundriss der romanischen Literaturen des Mittelalters, vol. 6, pt. 1 (Heidelberg: C. Winter, 1968), 29–30; R. P. McGeer, "Guyart Desmoulins, the Vernacular Master of Histories and His *Bible Historiale*," *Viator* 14 (1983): 211–44.

[59] Formerly Phillipps MS. 3202, sold at Sotheby's on 28 November 1967 (New Series III, Lot 96). The sale to the Huntington Museum was pre-empted by the British Library.

de Troyes's *Perceval*,[60] Rutebeuf's *Dist de Nostre Dame*,[61] the *Roman de la rose*,[62] and in numerous *credos* of the *chansons de geste*.[63] In the collection of pious tales known as the *Ci nous dit*,[64] we find a brief account of the imprisonment of Joseph ("comment li debonnaires Jesucriz desprisonna le bon Joseph d'Abarimatie," chap. 109), the Descent into Hell ("comment Garicius et Lancius qui furent filz saint Simeon ressussiterent," chap. 112), the story of Longinus ("ciz aveugles qui feri cest angoisseus coup," chap. 83a), and so on. While it is not certain whether all of these references betray direct influence from the *EN* (certainly the *Ci nous dit* does), they do attest to the popularity of the stories of Joseph of Arimathea and the doctrine of the Descent of Christ into Hell in Old French literature.[65]

In general, Old French romances tended to quarry the *EN*, especially chapters 11 to 16 (the second part of the *Gesta Pilati*), for the non-canonical elements connected with the figure of Joseph of Arimathea; in contrast, Passion narratives and dramatic texts usually concentrated on the story of Christ's Descent into Hell to free the righteous who had died prior to his sacrifice on the cross (the *Descensus Christi ad inferos*).

2.1. Old French romances

The apocryphal story of Joseph of Arimathea taken from the *Gesta Pilati* was first told on French soil by Gregory of Tours in an introductory chapter in his *Historia Francorum*,[66] testimony to the apocryphon's being known and read in sixth-century France. Gregory relates that Joseph was imprisoned by the chief priests but was freed by the risen Savior when the walls of his prison were suspended in air ("'nocte parietes de cellula . . . suspenduntur in sublimi'; "at night the

---

[60] Chrétien de Troyes, *Le Roman de Perceval ou le Conte du Graal*, ed. William Roach, 2d ed., Textes littéraires français (Geneva: Droz, 1959), vv. 585–88.

[61] Rutebeuf, *Œuvres complètes de Rutebeuf*, ed. Edmond Faral and Julia Bastin, 2 vols. (Paris: Picard, 1959–60), 1:238, vv. 76–82.

[62] Guillaume de Lorris and Jean de Meun, *Le Roman de la rose*, ed. Félix Lecoy, vol. 3, Classiques français du moyen âge, vol. 98 (Paris: Champion, 1979), vv. 18749–56.

[63] Pierre Ruelle, ed., *Huon de Bordeaux*, Université libre de Bruxelles: Travaux de la Faculté de philosophie et lettres, vol. 20 (Brussels: Presses universitaires, 1960), vv. 2036–38.

[64] Gérard Blangez, ed., *Ci nous dit: Recueil d'exemples moraux*, 2 vols., Société des anciens textes français (Paris: Picard, 1979–86).

[65] Widespread iconographic evidence further confirms the popularity of the two themes in twelfth- and thirteenth-century France; see Émile Mâle, *L'Art religieux du XIIIe siècle en France*, 8th ed. (Paris: A. Colin, 1948), 163–66.

[66] PL 71:171–73.

walls of the cell ... were suspended on high"). When the guards were
asked to produce the body of Christ, they answered: "Reddite vos
Joseph, et nos reddimus Christum" ("You return Joseph, and we shall
return Christ"), an echo of *EN* 13.2, where the soldiers say: "Ioseph
nos damus. Date vos Iesum" ("We shall give Joseph. You give us
Jesus"). The bishop of Tours was also familiar with Pilate's letter to
Tiberius: "Pilatus autem Gesta ad Tiberium Caesarem mittet, et ei tam
de virtutibus Christi, quam de Passione vel resurrectione ejus insinuat"
("And Pilate sent the Acts to emperor Tiberius, and informed him both
about Christ's virtues and about his Passion or Resurrection").[67] Since
Gregory omits the *Descensus* portion altogether, we might suppose that
his exemplar, like the palimpsest preserved in Vienna, was perhaps
representative of the earliest Latin form of the pseudo-gospel, before
the Harrowing of Hell was added to it.[68]

The legendary story of Joseph of Arimathea shaped the evolution
of the literature of the Grail. Around the turn of the twelfth century, a
Burgundian poet, Robert de Boron, composed *Le Roman de l'estoire dou
Graal*, better known as *Le Joseph d'Arimathie*. Moved by Chrétien de
Troyes's unfinished romance *Le Conte del Graal* (or the *Perceval*), but
puzzled presumably by the interpretation to be placed on Chrétien's
vessel—called here for the first time "graal"—Robert set out to write
its prehistory and in the process transformed the grail (with lower case
"g") into the Holy Grail. A stroke of real inspiration led Robert to the
remarkable idea that the Grail was first and foremost the cup or vessel
that Christ used to hold the wine while uttering the words of consecra-
tion at the Last Supper; it was subsequently employed by Joseph of
Arimathea to collect the blood of the Savior as it flowed from his
wounds during the preparation of his body for burial. This same
vessel, now twice hallowed, containing as it did first the transubstanti-
ated blood of Christ, then his *real* blood shed during his sacrifice on
the cross, became in Joseph's possession the centerpiece of a mystical
service, the prototype of the chalice of the mass, and, in later romances, the object of the quest for spiritual perfection by the knights
of the Round Table.

After the burial of Christ, Joseph was imprisoned by the Jews lest
he revealed the iniquity of their actions. If they were asked where
Jesus was, they would say that his body had been given to Joseph: "Se
vous Joseph ci nous rendez, / Par Joseph Jhesu raverez."[69] However,

---

[67] Ibid., 172.
[68] Izydorczyk, "The Unfamiliar *Evangelium Nicodemi*," 177; Guy Philippart,
"Les Fragments palimpsestes de l'Évangile de Nicodème dans le *Vindobonensis*
563 (Ve s.?)," *Analecta Bollandiana* 107 (1989): 171–88.
[69] Robert de Boron, *Le Roman de l'estoire dou Graal*, ed. William A. Nitze,

Joseph, instead of being released by Christ as in the *EN*, is miraculously sustained by the blood relic until the fall of Jerusalem many years later, when Vespasian discovers his whereabouts and sets him free. Together with his sister, brother-in-law, and a company of followers, Joseph with his vessel becomes the central figure in the establishment of a primitive Christianity, in which the Grail-chalice and its table-altar serve to mediate between God and humankind and produce for the righteous an ineffable sense of well-being. Joseph dies in the Holy Land, but his kinsmen and followers migrate west, to the Vales of Avalon, to establish Christianity on British soil. Joseph's table, founded in the distant lands of the primordial cult, looks back to the table of the Last Supper and forward to the Round Table established by Merlin, with the three tables now symbolic of the Holy Trinity.

Robert's vision led him to combine apocryphal elements of the Joseph story with other pseudo-canonical texts to produce a vast fictional canvas of the establishment of Christianity and its transfer to Britain, a sort of *translatio sacri*, to link up with the Arthurian legend in the process of elaboration at that time. It was Robert who conceived this remarkable idea of bridging the gap between Chrétien's *graal* and sacred history with a narrative centered on the figure of Joseph of Arimathea.[70]

Sometime during the first two decades of the thirteenth century, Robert's *Joseph d'Arimathie*, along with his *Roman de Merlin*, was turned into prose.[71] Combined with the prose *Perceval* (called the *Didot-Perceval*),[72] also thought to have come from the pen of Robert, the three romances form a trilogy of universal history, recounting events from the Creation and Fall of humankind to the disintegration of the Arthurian world. This prose cycle served in turn as the point of departure for a vast compilation of prose romances known collectively as the *Vulgate Version of the Arthurian Romances*.[73] In several of these works, the story of Joseph of Arimathea, as popularized by Robert de Boron, contributed to the organization of this huge body of fiction. Chronologically, the first of these romances is the *Estoire del Saint Graal*, a long,

Classiques français du moyen âge, vol. 57 (1927; repr., Paris: Champion, 1957), vv. 659–60.

[70] The account of Joseph's request for the body of Jesus, the deposition and burial with Nicodemus's assistance, and his imprisonment by the Jews is found in *Joseph d'Arimathie*, ibid., vv. 439–960.

[71] Richard O'Gorman, "The Prose Version of Robert de Boron's *Joseph d'Arimathie*," *Romance Philology* 23 (1970): 449–61; idem, "La Tradition."

[72] William Roach, ed., *The "Didot-Perceval" According to the Manuscripts of Modena and Paris* (Philadelphia: University of Pennsylvania Press, 1941).

[73] Edited in Sommer, *The Vulgate Version*.

rambling work based on the prose version of Robert's *Joseph*. The bare
bones of the story told by Robert, however, are here expanded into a
long, uneven, fictionalized narrative in which Joseph is no longer celi-
bate but has a wife and a son, Josephe; after numerous adventures, he
is finally transported to England with all his followers to become the
apostle of the British Isles.[74]

This basic story of Joseph of Arimathea was embroidered and
transformed in numerous ways and absorbed into many thirteenth-
century Grail romances. It appears interpolated into the *First Continuation* of Chrétien de Troyes's *Perceval*;[75] scattered through the *Perlesvaus*;[76] added in the Manessier continuation of Chrétien's *Perceval*;[77]
transformed into the strange and mysterious story of Joseph and the
Grail told in the *Sone de Nansai*;[78] and interpolated, doubtless, in
many others (see the discussion of the *Livre d'Artus* and the *Perceforest*
above).

Although, as we have seen, Robert de Boron used primarily the
apocryphal tradition of Joseph of Arimathea, his debt to the Harrowing
of Hell was also not insignificant. He recounts that, after Christ's
burial, "the true God . . . went directly to hell; he freed his friends, Eve
and Adam, their progeny that the fiend held in bondage, the saints
and all good folk, for he did not leave any sinless person behind, all
those whom he had redeemed, those for whom he was delivered up to
death."[79] Then, in the opening sequence of the second romance of the
cycle, *Merlin*,[80] Robert recapitulates this reference to the Harrowing
by returning to that point in the narrative where the devil bemoans the

---

[74] Ibid. 1:13–20.

[75] William Roach, ed., *The Continuations of the Old French "Perceval" of Chrétien de Troyes*, vol. 3, pt. 1, *The First Continuation* (Philadelphia: American Philosophical Society, 1952), vv. 17561–778.

[76] William A. Nitze and T. Atkinson, *Le Haut Livre du Graal: Perlesvaus*, vol. 2 (Chicago: University of Chicago Press, 1937), 185.

[77] William Roach, ed., *The Continuations of the Old French "Perceval" of Chrétien de Troyes*, vol. 5, *The Third Continuation by Manessier* (Philadelphia: American Philosophical Society, 1983), vv. 32689–770.

[78] Roger Sherman Loomis, *The Grail: From Celtic Myth to Christian Symbol* (Cardiff: University of Wales Press, 1963).

[79] Robert de Boron, *Le Roman*, vv. 593–609. For the teaching of twelfth-century theologians regarding those from postlapsarian times whom Christ saved, see Ralph V. Turner, " 'Descendit ad Inferos': Medieval Views on Christ's Descent into Hell and the Salvation of the Ancient Just," *Journal of the History of Ideas* 27 (1966): 179–87. Peter Lombard, for example, came to the conclusion that all of Adam's progeny departed from this life before the coming of Christ could, under certain conditions, have been saved (ibid., 194).

[80] Robert de Boron, *Merlin, roman du XIIIe siècle*, ed. Alexandre Micha, Textes littéraires français, vol. 281 (Paris: Droz, 1980).

loss of the "friends" of Christ. Here we see the influence of the *EN* (Tischendorf's Latin *Descensus* A, chap. 22):

> Mout fu li ennemis courciez
> Quant enfer fu ainsi brisiez,
> Car Jhesus de mort suscita,
> En enfer vint et le brisa.
> Adam et Eve en ha gité
> Ki la furent en grant viuté.
> O lui emmena ses amis
> Lassus ou ciel, en paradis.
> Quant deable ce aperçurent,
> Ausi cum tout enragié furent;
> Mout durement se merveillierent
> Et pour ce tout s'atropelerent
> Et disoient: "Qui est cist hon
> Qui ha teu vertu et tel non?
> Car nos fermetez ha brisies,
> Les portes d'enfer depecies." (Vv. 1–16)

(The devil was enraged when the gates of hell were shattered, for Jesus arose from the dead and went to hell and broke down the gates. Adam and Eve who lived in great wretchedness he set free. He led his friends with him into heaven above, to paradise. When the devils became aware of this, they were as if mad with rage; they were greatly astonished and they assembled saying: "Who is this man who has such power and authority, for he has knocked down our walls and shattered the gates of hell?")

Thus the stage is set for an infernal council (vv. 31–184), reminiscent of the deliberation in *EN* 20 between Hades and Satan. Assembled together, the devils lament the diminishing number of victims banished to the infernal region and decide, in order to regain the power over humankind that they lost through the sacrifice of Christ on the cross, to send one of their number to earth to engender an Antichrist.[81] (Another text, the dramatic *Jour du Jugement*, also exploits this theme of the infernal council, and again the devils' discussion leads to their decision to send one of their number, Angignars, to seduce a young woman who will give birth to the Antichrist.)[82]

---

[81] Olin H. Moore, "The Infernal Council," *Modern Philology* 16 (1918): 171–73. At the beginning of his *Joseph*, Robert reminds his readers that all people "great and small, king, prince, duke and count, the patriarchs and prophets, good and bad alike, went directly to hell" (*Le Roman*, vv. 11–20).

[82] Grace Frank, *The Medieval French Drama* (Oxford: Clarendon Press, 1954), 132.

2.2. Passion narratives

Prior to their absorption into dramatic literature, themes derived from
the *EN* first figured in verse narratives of the Passion, dating from the
dawn of literature in the vernacular. Let us begin then by considering
these narrative verse accounts of the Descent into Hell. From the most
archaic period in French literature comes a text known as the *Passion
du Christ*, preserved in a manuscript at Clermont-Ferrand, originating
in the north of the *langue d'oïl* but copied in the south by a scribe who
introduced into its text many Provençal traits:[83]

> Qua e l'enfern dunc asalit
> fort Satanan alo venguet:
> per soa mort si l'a vencut
> que contra homne non a vertud . . . .
>
> Equi era li om primers
> el soi enfant per son pecchiad . . .
>
> de cel enfern toz los livret,
> en paradis los arberget.
>
> (And he therefore assaulted hell / and vanquished Satan: / by
> his death he defeated him, / for he has no power over man.
> . . . There was found the first man, / and his progeny, on
> account of his sin . . . he delivered them all from that hell, /
> and brought them to dwell in paradise.)

In later narratives of the Passion, this brief allusion becomes increas-
ingly lengthened until, based on the apocryphon, a full narrative of the
Descent is developed. The most influential of these works is *La Passion
des jongleurs*,[84] itself an intermediary between narrative literature, perhaps homiletic in nature, and its representation "par personnages," i.e.,
in dramatic performance. The *Passion des jongleurs,* as interpolated by
Geufroi de Paris into his *Bible des sept estaz du monde,* opens with the
council of the Jews and closes with the scene of the three Marys at the
sepulcher. This octosyllabic verse narrative spanning all of Holy Week
incorporates elements drawn from a wide variety of pious stories and
legends, including many themes and motifs from the *EN* (the lowering
of the standards at the trial of Jesus [vv. 961–77], the accusation that
Jesus was an illegitimate son of Mary and Joseph [vv. 944–53], the
appearance of the devil to Pilate's wife [vv. 1198–257], and the name of

---

[83] Gaston Paris, ed., "La Passion du Christ," *Romania* 2 (1873): 94–97.

[84] Anne Joubert Amari Perry, ed., *La Passion des jongleurs,* Textes, dossiers,
documents, vol. 4 (Paris: Beauchesne, 1981).

Longinus [vv. 1624–723]). The story of Joseph of Arimathea, though brief, adheres closely to the apocryphal source (vv. 3753–76): he is imprisoned for his role in the burial of Jesus (vv. 3545–50), and when the Jews ask the soldiers to produce his body, one of them answers: "Rendez Joseph ... Et nous vous rendrons Jhesucrist" (vv. 3759–60; "Give back Joseph ... And we shall give back Jesus Christ"). But the author of the *Passion des jongleurs* goes even further: he borrows the entire *Descensus* section of the *EN* and retells it in vividly dramatic language (vv. 2356–3032). The soul of Jesus leaves his body while it hangs on the cross and descends into hell to free his "friends" (v. 2375); then the princes of hell, Enfer and Sathan, discuss fearfully the coming of Christ who, in a bright light, dispels the darkness and leads out of the infernal region Adam and the others (vv. 2899–901). On the way they meet Enoch and Elijah, who were spared death in order to combat the Antichrist, and the Good Thief Dismas, carrying his cross (v. 2967). This narrative passion, surviving in several versions and in many manuscripts, was immensely popular and provided many of the apocryphal elements that passed into the dramatic literature of late medieval France.[85]

2.3. Dramatic literature

The most pervasive influence of the Harrowing of Hell theme, however, is seen in the theatrical productions of medieval France—in the liturgical drama. The dramatic potential offered by the breaking of the gates of hell, the chaining of Satan, and the freeing of the righteous in a triumphal procession did not go unnoticed by writers responsible for the Easter cycles. Setting aside the fleeting references to the Descent or those derived simply from the creed, I shall concentrate on those

---

[85] The title *Passion des jongleurs* covers various versions of the narrative of the Passion and Descent. In addition to this version, adopted by Geufroi de Paris (and a similar one in Grenoble, Bibl. mun. MS. 1137; see Bonnard, *Les Traductions,* 181), there are two independent versions of the *Passion des jongleurs,* plus a third one interpolated into the *Roman de saint Fanuel,* the last preserving more faithfully the *EN* episodes (Becker, "Die Sage," 914–22; Owen, *The Vision of Hell,* 103–9). Frances A. Foster, ed., *The Northern Passion: Four Parallel Texts and the French Original,* 2 vols., EETS OS, vols. 145, 147 (London: Oxford University Press, 1913–16), 2:102–25, prints the *Passion des Jongleurs* according to Cambridge, Trinity College MS. O. 2. 14. Becker, "Die Sage," 923, also points out that Jean d'Outremeuse incorporated a prose version of the *Passion des jongleurs* into his *Myreur des hystors.* These texts are not to be confused with the *Livre de la Passion,* edited by Grace Frank (*Le Livre de la Passion: Poème narratif du XIV* siècle, Classiques français du moyen âge, vol. 64 [Paris: Champion, 1930]), a narrative intermediary between the *Passion des jongleurs* and the later *mystères,* which also contains episodes of the Harrowing (Owen, *The Vision of Hell,* 109–10).

works that expand the themes of the *EN* into major dramatic compo-
nents of the play.

The most dazzling pageant of the medieval stage was that showing
Christ, carrying the cross of victory, issuing from the monstrous jaws
of Leviathan spewing forth fire and smoke,[86] and leading the Old
Testament personages released from hell to everlasting joy, with Adam
and Eve in the lead, often followed by the prophets and other denizens
of the Old Law, sometimes even the entire human race, the "humain
linaige."[87] This dramatic scene may be indebted either directly to the
Descensus Christi ad inferos in one of its Latin or vernacular versions, or
to one of the narrative passions. While the defective manuscripts of an
Anglo-Norman play, *La Seinte Resureccion*, suggest that it originally
preserved a dramatic Harrowing of Hell,[88] the first extant text to
transmit such a scene seems to be the *Passion du Palatinus*, followed by
the *Biard* section of the *Passion d'Autun* (vv. 1866–1913), both deriving
from the narrative *Passion des jongleurs* discussed above.[89] The *Resurrection du Sauveur* from Paris, Bibliothèque Sainte-Geneviève MS. 1131,
presents a brief Harrowing scene in which souls in hell pray for their
release while Lucifer bewails their impending Redemption. Christ then

---

[86] The jaws of Leviathan, spoken of in Jb. 40–41 and identified with the
dragon of Rv. 12, and hence with Behemoth and Satan, represent the gaping
mouth of hell. "He who will open the gates of the mouth of Leviathan" (Mâle,
L'Art religieux, 425) designates Christ, who, in his Descent into Hell, has overcome
Satan. This is the origin of the iconographic tradition that represents the open
mouth of the beast as the entrance to hell. See Pamela Sheingorn, "Who Can
Open the Doors of His Face? The Iconography of Hell Mouth," in *The Iconography
of Hell*, ed. Clifford Davidson and Thomas H. Seiler (Kalamazoo: Publications of
the Medieval Institute of Western Michigan University, 1992), 1–19.

[87] Becker, "Die Sage," 976. On the elaborate and colorful staging of this scene,
see Gustave Cohen, *Histoire de la mise en scène dans le théâtre religieux français du
moyen âge* (Paris: Champion, 1926), 92–99; Donald Clive Stuart, "The Stage Setting
of Hell and the Iconography of the Middle Ages," *Romanic Review* 4 (1913): 330–
42; and Becker, "Die Sage," 961–67. Cohen notes, "À l'étage inférieur sur le plan
des échafauds, s'ouvre le *Limbe* où attendent les Pères et baye l'horrifique Gueule
ou Crapaut d'Enfer à travers laquelle on aperçoit les diables jetant les damnés à
la chaudière. Le déploiement de feux et de flammes de cet horrible lieu a contraint de le construire en maçonerie . . . ," *Le Théâtre en France au moyen âge* (Paris:
Presses universitaires de France, 1928), 60. A few medieval descriptions of continental productions are translated by Peter Meredith and J. E. Tailby, *The Staging
of Religious Drama in Europe in the Later Middle Ages: Texts and Documents in English
Translation* (Kalamazoo: Medieval Institute, Western Michigan University, 1983);
see especially pp. 73, 74, 81, 90, 91, 113. Cf. also Philip Butterworth, "Hellfire:
Flame as Special Effect," in *The Iconography of Hell*, 67–102.

[88] Frank, *The Medieval French Drama*, 88 n. 1.

[89] Grace Frank, *La Passion du Palatinus*, Classiques français du moyen âge, vol.
30 (Paris: Champion, 1922); idem, *La Passion d'Autun* (Paris: Société des anciens
textes français, 1934). Cf. Frank, *The Medieval French Drama*, 126–31.

appears to liberate the souls to the distress of the infernal creatures.[90] In a second *Passion* in the same manuscript, the events of the Harrowing follow very closely the *Descensus* narrative of the *EN*.[91] Direct offspring of these dramatic productions are the vast spectacles of the fifteenth century, referred to as *Mystères de la Passion*. Performances of these plays lasted for days—four in the case of Greban— and embraced a multitude of scenes and characters. The *Passion de Semur*, which translates entire chapters of the *EN*,[92] and the *Passion d'Arras*, by a certain Mercadé, seem to be the earliest of this group.[93] But the masterpiece was surely the *Passion* composed or, perhaps, compiled by Arnoul Greban in Paris ca. 1450 and performed there at least three times before 1473.[94] Using Mercadé's framework but treating his predecessor's material with much freedom, Greban infuses the entire production with a tenderness of feeling and a real sense of dramatic movement.[95] While the treatment of Joseph of Arimathea here is traditional, the scenes from the Harrowing of Hell are truly spectacular.[96]

But Greban's dramatic work had an even longer development in store for it. Just as Greban himself appropriated much of Mercadé's text, so did Jean Michel base his *Passion*, preserved only in printed editions, on Greban's play. According to Frank, "Michel stretches the events of Greban's second and third days ... to four, and devotes some 30,000 lines to them, thus expanding individual speeches to wearisome length."[97] The plays of Mercadé, Greban, and Michel were exploited well into the sixteenth century by all subsequent theatrical producers, who combined, adapted, shortened, and excerpted individual segments for separate performances.[98] However, a full discussion of these texts would go far beyond the scope of these few pages.

The extent of the *EN*'s influence on dramatic literature can be gleaned from the *Mystère de la Passion Nostre Seigneur*, from MS. 1131 of the Bibliothèque Sainte-Geneviève in Paris,[99] the first full-length

---

[90] Frank, *The Medieval French Drama*, 139.

[91] Ibid., 141; Becker, "Die Sage," 936–42.

[92] Roy, *Le Mystère*, 83.

[93] Becker, "Die Sage," 942–53.

[94] Arnoul Greban, *Le Mystère de la Passion d'Arnoul Gréban*, ed. Gaston Paris and Gaston Raynaud (Paris: F. Didot, 1878). Cf. Frank, *The Medieval French Drama*, 183.

[95] Frank, *The Medieval French Drama*, 181–89.

[96] On the work of Greban, see Pierre Champion, *Histoire poétique du quinzième siècle*, 2 vols., Bibliothèque du XVe siècle (Paris: Champion, 1923), 2:133–88.

[97] Frank, *The Medieval French Drama*, 187.

[98] A good example of such a derivative production is extant in *Le Mystère de la Passion de Troyes*, recently edited by Jean-Claude Bibolet, *Le Mystère de la Passion de Troyes*, 2 vols., Textes littéraires français, vol. 347 (Geneva: Droz, 1987).

[99] Graham A. Runnalls, ed., *Le Mystère de la Passion Nostre Seigneur du manu-*

Passion play of the French Middle Ages and a landmark in the evolution of the great mysteries of the fifteenth century. It contains 4477 octosyllabic verses and is generally believed to date from the mid-fourteenth century. Its performance was probably associated with a confraternity dedicated to the cult of Sainte-Geneviève, with its center at the church of Saint-Étienne-du-Mont.[100] With the exception of the canonical gospels, the EN represents the single most important source for the Sainte-Geneviève Passion, which draws extensively on a manuscript akin presumably to Tischendorf's Latin A.

The action of the play extends through Holy Week, from the anointing of Jesus and resurrection of Lazarus at Bethany (preceding the entry into Jerusalem) to the appearance of Jesus to the Magdalene. The playwright was influenced by the Gesta Pilati in several scenes:

(a) Pilate's family intercedes on behalf of Jesus (vv. 2162–275). Although the apocryphon does not mention the son and daughter as does the Passion, the nocturnal dream of Pilate's wife comes directly from the EN.

(b) The figure of Veronica (v. 2322) is probably taken from the EN, where she bears witness to her cure by Jesus at the interrogation before Pilate. In the Passion, however, the legend is fully developed to include the cloth imprinted with the features of Jesus at the time of his scourging (vv. 2320–47).

(c) Chapters 11 and 12 of the EN inspired the author of the Passion to place on stage the quarrel between the high priests and Joseph, not, however, without some influence from Robert de Boron's treatment of the same event. The entire scene of Joseph's petition for the body of Christ through to the Resurrection owes many details to the apocryphon (vv. 3167–857).

(d) The names of the Bad Thief, Gestas (v. 2746), and the soldier Longinus, who pierced the side of Jesus (v. 2981), are taken from the EN, but for the latter, the legend is fully developed: Longinus is blind and recovers his eyesight on contact with the blood of Jesus.

But a more thoroughgoing apocryphal influence occurs in the scene of the Harrowing of Hell, here placed after the Resurrection, as was not unusual in French texts of the period.[101] Runnalls documents these borrowings from EN 18–19, 21–23, 25:[102]

scrit 1131 de la Bibliothèque Sainte-Geneviève, Textes littéraires français, vol. 206 (Geneva: Droz, 1974).

[100] Ibid., 16–18.

[101] Zbigniew Izydorczyk, "The Inversion of Paschal Events in the Old English Descent into Hell," Neuphilologische Mitteilungen 91 (1990): 439–41.

[102] Runnalls, Le Mystère, 287–88.

(a) Satan and Beelzebub fearfully contemplate the coming of Jesus (vv. 3913–68).
(b) Christ summons the infernal princes to open the gates of hell (vv. 3969–4026).
(c) The gates of Hades are shattered, and the saints and prophets issue forth, with Adam and Eve bringing up the rear (vv. 4027–112).

The Old French theater, then, owed much to New Testament apocrypha, especially to the *EN*. With the obvious need to fill out scenes of dramatic force as the length of the Passion plays increased, playwrights naturally turned to the apocryphal account of the trial of Jesus for the pathos of his torment and Crucifixion and for additional information on the shadowy characters of Joseph of Arimathea and Nicodemus, who laid Christ to rest. The scenes of the Descent into the pit of hell are depicted with great dramatic effect: the breaking down of the gates of hell, the account of the sons of Simeon who, having returned to life, recount the events of the coming of Christ to hell, the chaining of Satan, and, finally, with all its theatrical possibilities, the procession of the redeemed emerging from the fiery mouth of the beast and ascending into heaven.

Although this necessarily brief sketch of the influence of the *EN* on French letters of the Middle Ages must leave much unsaid, the reader will, I hope, be able to assess the broad outlines of this influence on the various texts of the period, and the student will find here the canvas into which other elements can be inserted. Once the finishing touches have been applied to this picture, we shall doubtless be in a better position to assess the impact of the *Gospel of Nicodemus* on the literary period extending from the early thirteenth to the closing years of the fifteenth century. With the increasing prominence accorded of late to the study of popular culture, medieval vernacular translations of apocrypha will surely play an ever larger role in our assessment of the influence of popular texts on social attitudes.

Appendix

La Descente aux Enfers
(Excerpt from Copenhagen, Kongelige Bibliotek MS. De Thott 132)

[83v] S'ensuit en l'Istoire Saincte que Joseph d'Arimathie, qui estoit noble et estoit saint homme et occultement avoit esté disciple a Jhesucrist; quant il eust veu les signes, il s'enhardi et vint a Pilate et lui demanda le corps au doulx Jhesucrist, et Pilate lui octroya. Et doncques il osta, ou fist oster, le doulx Jhesucrist de la croix et lui avecques Nicodemus l'ensevelirent.

Comment Jhesucrist descendi ou limbe pour les racheter

Mais avant que nous mettons de sa sepulture, il nous fault ouir comment et par quelle maniere ses amis il racheta d'enfer. Pour quoy nous devons savoir que tantost que [84r] l'ame feust partie du corps il descendit en enfer, la maniere comment raconte Nicodeme en son euvangile; et dit que entre les autres qui aparurent aprés la mort de Jhesucrist les deux filz de Simeon le juste, Carinus et Leu[c]ius, furent ressuscitez, lesquelz en la presence de Nicodemus, de Anne, de Caiphas, de Joseph d'Arimathie et de Gamaliel raconterent comment Jhesucrist estoit descendu en enfer et avoit ses amis delivré, et le reciterent en telle maniere:
Comme nous estions en l'obscurté des tenebres d'enfer soubdainement vint une lumiere qui estoit doree et estoit aussi vermeille comme la poulpre. Adonc Adam le pere d'umaine creature devant tous s'esjouist et nous dit: "Sachiez que ceste lumiere est la promesse de nostre Createur qui nous avoit promis sa lumiere pardurable et son rayon pour noz tenebres enluminer." Vint aprés Ysaye qui nous dit: "Veci la lumiere de Dieu le Pere qui vient a nous, de laquelle, nous estant ou monde, j'avoie prophetisé en disant que le peuple habitant en tenebres recevroient en lumiere." Aprés seurvint nostre pere Simeon qui nous dit: "Glorifions et louons Dieu qui nous vient visiter, car moy estant ou monde en mes anciens jours je portai Jhesus le filz de la Vierge Marie entre mes bras quant il fut presenté ou temple, et fuz contraint par le saint Esperit dire que mon cuer estoit appaisié en veant et tenant le Sauveur qui devoit venir visiter son peuple comme la lumiere pour la gloire du peuple d'Israel."
Aprés vint ung habit de hermite qui nous dist: "Je suis Jehan nommé et sachiez que j'ai baptisé Jhesucrist et l'ai denoncé au monde et l'ai monstré du doi en disant: 'Veci l'aignel de Dieu qui vient oster les pechez du monde.'" Aprés vint Seth le filz de Adam qui nous dit: "Quant j'estoie au monde et vy que mon pere Ada[m] estoit griefve-

ment malade, je m'en alai aux portes de paradis et priai Dieu qu'il envoyast son ange pour me donner de l'uille de sa misericorde pour en oindre mon pere. Mais vint l'ange Michiel qui me dit: 'Filz, tu pers ta peine, car l'ange qui portera l'uille de misericorde pour guerir le monde ne [84v] sera envoyé jusques atant que v^m ii^c ans seront passez.'" Adonc les sains et anciens peres s'esjoïrent en disant que le temps estoit venu.

Et quant Sathan vit les peres esjouir, il se doubta et commanda que les portes d'enver feussent barrees et serrees. Et ainsi que Sathan parloit encores, veci la lumiere de Jhesus qui descendit et fit grant bruit comme tonnerre en tant que tout enfer trembla et fut ouye une telle voix: "Vous, princes d'enfer, ouvrez voz portes, si y entrera le Roy de Gloire!" Adant les ministres de Sathan coururent pour fermer et verroiller les portes et disoient: "Qui est cestui tant fort, tant puissant, tant cler et replandissant? Onc mais Enfer ne se doubta fors maintenant; oncques mes le monde ça jus ne nous envoya tel. Il ne vint pas comme prisonnier, mais pour les prisonniers delivrer. Nous le veons, nous, pas comme subget a nous, mais comme nostre juge," et se complaingnoient en disant: "O enfer, ou est ta puissance maintenant?"

Et ainsi que ceulx d'enfer fermoient leurs portes survint le roy David qui leur dist: "Seigneurs, pour quoy sarrez vous voz portes? J'avoie bien dit, moy estant [ou monde], que celui pour qui vous fermez voz portes seroit tant fort et puissant qu'i briseroit les huis d'enfer et que barre et verroil a sa puissance ne pourroit resister." Ainsi que David parloit la voix secondement fut ouye qui dit que: "Vous, princes d'enfer, ouvrez voz portes, si y entrera le Roi de Gloire!" Et Enfer respondi tout espouenté: "Qui est celui Roi de Gloire?" Respondit David: "C'est le Seigneur fort et puissant, redoubté en toutes batailles, a qui vous ne pourrez resister." Et ce dit, la puissance de Jhesus brisa portes, barres et verroilz et nous enlumina et resjouit. Et vint a Adam et le salua moult doulcement et lui dist: "Mon ami Adam, paix si te soit donnee et a tous tes enfans," et le print par la main, et lui et tous les autres il les delivra des peines d'enfer et de la puissance des ennemis et les mena hors. Et au jour de sa benoite ascencion en celle noble compaignie monta en paradis.

The *Gospel of Nicodemus* in Medieval Catalan and Occitan Literatures

JOSEP IZQUIERDO

he purpose of this essay is to examine four texts which contain Catalan or Occitan translations of the apocryphal *Evangelium Nicodemi* (*EN*); two of them, *Sens e razos d'una escriptura* and *E la mira car tot era ensems*, are in verse and two, *Lo Gènesi* and *Gamaliel*, in prose.

This study would have been greatly facilitated by a critical edition of the Latin *EN*, providing information about the archetypal Latin translation as well as its subsequent recensions. Without such an edition, it is impossible to determine exactly which of the many versions of the *EN* circulating in the Middle Ages served as sources for vernacular translations, or to ascertain whether the differences among vernacular texts are due to their use of different Latin traditions or to the initiative of individual translators or copyists. The profusion of fragmentary, abridged, and derivative Latin redactions compounds the problems.[1] The eclectic edition of the Latin *EN* published by Tischendorf

---

[1] The main secondary sources for vernacular translations of the *EN* are Jacobus a Voragine's *Legenda aurea* and Vincent of Beauvais's *Speculum historiale*. It is likely that biblical glosses and commentaries, too, served as sources for vernacular accounts of the Passion. The *Legenda aurea* (completed in 1260) was translated into Catalan in the last quarter of the thirteenth century, according to Joan Coromines, preface to *Vides de sants rosselloneses*, ed. Charlotte S. Maneikis Kniazzeh and Edward J. Neugaard, vol. 1 (Barcelona: Fundació Salvador Vives Casajuana 1977), xvii–xxii. Geneviève Brunel, "*Vida de sant Frances*. Versions en langue d'oc et en catalan de la *Legenda aurea*: Essai de classement des manuscrits," *Revue d'histoire des textes* 6 (1976): 263–64, proves that Occitan versions rely on this first Catalan translation. The Catalan translation of the *Speculum historiale* was begun in 1360 by the Dominican friar Jaume Domènec on the order of King Peter III, "el Cerimoniós"; twenty years after Jaume's death, Antoni Ginebreda, also a Dominican, was put in charge of its continuation; see Jordi Rubió i Balaguer, *Història de la literatura catalana*, vol. 1 (Barcelona: Publicacions de l'Abadia de Montserrat, 1984),

is clearly inadequate in light of Izydorczyk's work on its medieval manuscript tradition.[2] However, to the extent that it gives some indication of the apocryphon's textual range, Tischendorf's edition can still be useful, especially if supplemented by Kim's transcription of the *codex Einsidlensis*[3] and Izydorczyk's study of the manuscripts.

1. Sens e razos d'una escriptura

The Occitan poem beginning *Sens e razos d'una escriptura*, written towards the end of the thirteenth century, opens with a translation in 2144 verses of *EN* type B.[4] It then proceeds to relate the story of the apostles and disciples going forth to preach the Good News and elaborates the theme of iniquity and sin presaging the end of the world. There follow an account of future tribulations of mankind, announced in the words of the synoptic evangelists (Mt. 24:4–14, 29; Mk. 13:5–13, 24–25; Lk. 21:8–19, 25–26), a description of the coming of the Antichrist, a list of the fifteen signs which are to precede the Last Judgement, and, finally, a brief vision of the Last Judgement itself. The entire work amounts to a total of 2792 verses.

Sens e razos d'una escriptura is extant in two manuscripts:

A   Paris, Bibliothèque nationale (BN) MS. fr. 1745, fols. 105–24, saec. XIV in.[5]

B   London, British Library MS. Harley 7403, fols. 1–35; saec. XIV in. The first 1374 verses of the text are missing; other lacunae indicate that the manuscript has lost some of its subsequent

---

136, 138, 281, and Lola Badia, "Frontí i Vegeci, mestres de cavalleria en Català als segles XIV i XV," *Boletín de la Real Academia de Buenas Letras de Barcelona* 39 (1983–84): 194 n. 10.

[2] Constantinus de Tischendorf, ed., *Evangelia apocrypha*, 2d rev. ed. (Leipzig: H. Mendelssohn, 1876), 333–434; Zbigniew Izydorczyk, "The Unfamiliar *Evangelium Nicodemi*," *Manuscripta* 33 (1989): 169–91; idem, *Manuscripts of the "Evangelium Nicodemi": A Census*, Subsidia Mediaevalia, vol. 21 (Toronto: Pontifical Institute of Mediaeval Studies, 1993).

[3] H. C. Kim, ed., *The Gospel of Nicodemus: Gesta Salvatoris*, Toronto Medieval Latin Texts, vol. 2 (Toronto: Pontifical Institute of Mediaeval Studies, 1973).

[4] Edited in H. Suchier, *Denkmäler provenzalischer Literatur und Sprache*, vol. 1 (Halle: Niemeyer, 1883), 1–84, 481–95. In the margins, Suchier notes the correspondences between this text and the Latin version of the *EN* as edited by Tischendorf.

[5] Suchier, *Denkmäler*, 483–84; A. Jeanroy, *Bibliographie sommaire des chansonniers provençaux*, Classiques français du moyen âge, 2d series, Manuels, vol. 16 (Paris: Champion, 1916), 18; see also Clovis Felix Brunel, *Bibliographie des manuscrits littéraires en ancien provençal*, Societé de publications romanes et françaises, Publications, vol. 13 (Paris: Droz, 1935), no. 154.

folios as well.[6] The version of the fifteen signs (fols. 27–34) in this manuscript is similar to the one found in the Anglo-Norman *Mystère d'Adam* and was published by Suchier, who considered it a translation from the latter.[7]

The third manuscript, signaled by Suchier, Turin, Biblioteca Nazionale MS. L. VI. 36a, containing a partial French translation of the poem, was destroyed by fire.[8]

In the following discussion, I have limited my analysis to the two surviving manuscripts of the Occitan text. My aims are to characterize the poem's translation of the *EN* and its underlying source text, to ascertain the form and content of the original Occitan work, and to assess the relationship between the two manuscripts.[9] Two scholars who almost a century ago turned their attention to that last problem arrived at conflicting conclusions: Suchier proposed that MS. A was closer to the original, while Meyer suggested that MS. B represented a more primitive state of the text.[10]

To facilitate the discussion of the poem, I have subdivided it into three thematic sections, without, however, losing sight of the essential unity of the work. The sections are: (a) a translation of the *EN* (vv. 1–2144); (b) the legend of the Antichrist (vv. 2145–416); and (c) the fifteen signs before Doomsday and the Last Judgement (vv. 2417–792).

(a) A translation of the *Evangelium Nicodemi*

The text of *Sens e razos d'una escriptura* begins with a close translation of the B version of the *EN*, preceded by a prologue written by the translator (vv. 1–50). In the prologue, the translator makes clear his wish to be faithful to the original Latin (vv. 24–25, "car tornaray be verament / lo Lati em plana paraula," "since I will accurately translate / the Latin into the vulgar tongue"), and his intention not to manipulate the text (v. 26, "hon non aura bafa ni faula," "where there will be neither jokes nor fiction"). In verses 27–34, he outlines the contents of the work, making mention of the eschatological sections (Antichrist,

[6] Suchier, *Denkmäler;* see also Brunel, *Bibliographie*, no. 21.
[7] Suchier, *Denkmäler*, 156–64.
[8] H. Suchier, "Zu den altfranzösischen Bibelübersetzungen," *Zeitschrift für romanische Philologie* 8 (1884): 429.
[9] It has already been established by Suchier, *Denkmäler*, 494, that neither manuscript is a *descriptus* from the other.
[10] Ibid., 494–95; Paul Meyer, "Légendes pieuses en provençal," in *Histoire littéraire de la France*, vol. 32, ed. Paul Meyer (Paris: Imprimerie nationale, 1898), 104.

fifteen signs, Last Judgement), which do not belong to the *EN* but which follow the apocryphon in the poem. The regrettable absence of a critical edition of the Latin *EN* seriously impedes our ability to establish the precise source of the Occitan poetic translation. While there is no doubt that the underlying text belonged to type B, determining the exact nature of that text and its relationship to other witnesses of *EN* B is a difficult and complex task. The poem's dependence on tradition B is apparent from its inclusion of the so-called first prologue, beginning "Ego eneas hebreus ...";[11] the Occitan poet gives the substance of this prologue in vv. 51–60:

> Ieu Eneas Mayestre dic
> dels Ebrieus ay trobatz escrigz
> lo fagz que fero li Juzieu
> a Jhesu Cristz, lo fil de dieu,
> e Nicodemus que ho vi
> ho escrius tot em pargami
> en Ebrayc segon sa razo;
> pueys ieu en Grec, car mi fom bo,
> ho translatyey e ho escrys,
> si com la letra departys.

> (I, Master Eneas, declare that I have found a writing about the Hebrews, concerning the deed of the Jews against Jesus Christ, the Son of God. And Nicodemus, who was a witness to it, wrote it down on parchment in Hebrew, according to his understanding; after that I translated it and wrote it in Greek, according to the writing.)

Moreover, the poem furnishes—in the same way as do Latin B texts—the sentences missing from chapters 1.2 and 4.2 of the mainstream Latin tradition A.[12] Thus—to quote an example that will be useful also later on—the statement found exclusively in *EN* B, "Dic nobis, si quis Caesarem blasphemaverit, dignus est morte anne? Dicit eis Pilatus: 'Dignus mori' " (*EN* 4.2; " 'Tell us, if someone blasphemed against Caesar, is he worthy of death or not?' Pilate said to them: 'He is worthy to die' "),[13] is translated in the following manner:

---

[11] Rémi Gounelle, "Recherches sur le manuscrit CCCC 288 des *Acta Pilati*" (Mémoire présenté pour l'obtention de la maîtrise ès lettres classiques, Université de Paris X-Nanterre, 1989), 39. In the body of the essay, the *EN* will be cited by chapter and paragraph numbers.

[12] Izydorczyk, "The Unfamiliar *Evangelium Nicodemi*," 181.

[13] Tischendorf, *Evangelia apocrypha*, 350.

"Aras digas, senher Pilatz,
de sol aysso la veritatz,
si alcus homs per ren dizia
de Sezar alcuna folia,
non es dignes doncs de morir?"
"Si es" Pilatz lur pres a dir. (Vv. 509–14)

("Now, sir Pilate, tell only the truth about this: if somebody says something foolish about Caesar, does he not therefore deserve to die?" "Yes, he does," said Pilate to them.)

Finally, the narrative of Christ's Descent into Hell clearly reflects the *Descensus Christi ad inferos* B, as edited by Tischendorf.[14]

The manuscript tradition of *EN* B still remains to be worked out in detail. Hoffmann and Izydorczyk have noted the existence of two subgroups within this version, differing not only in lexical and stylistic features but also in the degree of completeness.[15] One subgroup, attested in four manuscripts, contains full texts of the *Gesta* and the *Descensus*, while another, more numerous, shows gaps extending from chapter 2.3 to 4.5 (covering the Jews' charges against Christ, the attempts of the twelve righteous Jews to protect him, and some further details of the trial before Pilate), and from chapter 9 to 11 (covering the release of Barabbas, the Crucifixion, and Christ's death, i.e., the sections most clearly related to the canonical gospels).[16] Since the Occitan poem translates the substance of these frequently excised chapters (vv. 311–555, 685–856), we may conclude that its author had at his disposal one of the complete texts of *EN* B. At this point we might ask, firstly, whether the full texts of *EN* B indeed form a homogeneous tradition, and, secondly, whether the readings of the full texts are consistently reflected in the translation. Assuming the translation is based on a single source text, the second question could be rephrased as a query about the nature of that text. The definitive answer to the first of the above questions must await a detailed study of all extant B manuscripts; I hope, however, that my attempt to address the second will throw some light also on the first.

In his doctoral dissertation, Werner Hoffmann proposed a stemma of the Latin witnesses of *EN* B, which not only differentiates between complete and incomplete manuscripts but further subdivides each sub-

---

[14] Ibid., 417–32.

[15] Werner J. Hoffmann, "Konrad von Heimesfurt. Untersuchungen zu Quellen, Überlieferung und Wirkung seiner beiden Werke *Unser vrouwen hinvart* und *Urstende*" (Ph.D. diss., Universität Trier, 1987); Izydorczyk, "The Unfamiliar *Evangelium Nicodemi*."

[16] Izydorczyk, "The Unfamiliar *Evangelium Nicodemi*," 182 and n. 25.

138   JOSEP IZQUIERDO

group on the basis of variant readings. For the purpose of comparing
EN B with the Occitan translation in *Sens e razos*, I have selected three
manuscripts. One of them, Venice, Biblioteca Nazionale Marciana MS.
4326 (Lat. XIV, 43; saec. XIV–XV),[17] represents the complete text B of
the apocryphon; the other two, Vatican City, Biblioteca Apostolica
Vaticana MSS. Vat. lat. 4578 (saec. XIV) and Vat. lat. 4363 (saec. XII),[18]
have expunged versions from two distinct lines of transmission.

In view of the completeness of the Occitan translation, one might
expect it to preserve the readings of the Venice manuscript. However,
a close comparison with the three Latin witnesses reveals that this is
not always the case. Starting with the prologue, the poem inclines
toward Vat. lat. 4363 rather than towards the Venice text. In the
former, the introductory homiletic opening, "Audistis, fratres dilectis-
simi, per sanctum evangelium quae acta sunt ..." ("You have heard in
the holy gospel, most beloved brothers, what took place ...")[19] is followed by a defense of the *EN* based on John 21:25 (where John
explains that he did not describe all the deeds of Christ because had he
done so, the whole world could not contain the books that would have
been written). Only after this apology does the typical B-text prologue
begin. In a similar fashion, the Occitan poem justifies the translation of
the apocryphon (vv. 35–44), pointing out that the substance of the *EN*
cannot be found in the Gospels of John or Matthew because many
things happened in those days which have not been recorded by the
evangelists. The relationship between the translation and the expunged
texts is further evidenced by many shared readings. One of them
occurs in chapter 1.5, in which both Vatican manuscripts read "Viden-
tes autem Iudaei signa quomodo se incurvaverunt et adoraverunt
Iesum ..." ("The Jews, seeing how the signs bent themselves and
adored Jesus ...");[20] this clause is absent from the Venice text, yet the
Occitan translator includes it, "Cant li juzieu ayso an vistz / d'aquels
signes, que adoro Cristz" (vv. 229–30). Occasionally, the translation
agrees with Vat. lat. 4578 against the other two. In chapter 15.4, Vat.
lat. 4363 and the Venice manuscript read, respectively, "Ideo te in carcerem missimus ..." ("Therefore we have put you in prison ...") and
"Ideo reclusimus te et posuimus custodes custodire ianuas ..."
("Therefore we have imprisoned you and set the guards to guard the
doors ...").[21] The Occitan text, however, has

---

[17] Cf. ibid., 174; Tischendorf's witness C.
[18] Tischendorf's witnesses A and B.
[19] Tischendorf, *Evangelia apocrypha*, 334, critical apparatus.
[20] Ibid., 341.
[21] Ibid., 380, critical apparatus.

e t'enclausem en la mayo
hon ueys, fenestra ni bojal
con avia, ni bo ni mal (vv. 1344–46)

(and we locked you in a house where there was no door,
window, or skylight, neither good nor bad),

a faithful translation of Vat. lat 4578, "Ideo inclusimus te in domo ubi
nulla erat fenestra . . ." ("Therefore we have imprisoned you in a house
where there was no window . . .").[22]

Evidence such as this suggests the Occitan writer had access to a
complete version of *EN* B but one that was textually close to the incomplete versions, especially to Vat. lat. 4363. This hypothesis needs,
however, to be further verified through a thorough and systematic
comparison of the Latin and Occitan texts.

Within the main body of the Occitan translation, the only important departure from the Latin *EN* is the inclusion of a *planctus* by the
Virgin Mary on the death of her son (vv. 897–948), a lyrical commonplace widely used in Occitan narrative and dramatic passions during
the late Middle Ages. This digression is inserted into the narrative after
Christ's death, and more precisely between the departure of spectators
and executioners and Joseph of Arimathea's request for the body of
Christ (i.e., between chaps. 11.2 and 11.3). It occurs, therefore, in an
especially weak portion of *EN* B, often excised on account of its similarity to the canonical accounts.[23] It may have been to embellish the
familiar story that the translator added the *planctus* as well as such
details as Longinus's blindness. The *planctus* in *Sens e razos* includes
some topoi characteristic of the genre; for example, Mary contrasts her
former happiness with her present pain caused by the simultaneous
loss—in the death of Christ—of her father, husband, and son,[24] and
she expresses her desire to die with Christ. The absence of other common themes, such as the *commendatio* of Mary to John, can probably be
explained by the apocryphal context to which it had been adapted and
which required certain thematic adjustments.

The text of *Sens e razos* in MS. B is incomplete, beginning only at
v. 1375, "vejas qui es parlar ab tu" ("behold who is speaking with
you"), words spoken by Christ when he appeared to Joseph of Arimathea imprisoned by the high priests. Throughout the rest of the

---

[22] Ibid., 380.
[23] Izydorczyk, "The Unfamiliar *Evangelium Nicodemi*," 181–82.
[24] The ultimate source of this motif is probably the *Planctus beatae Mariae*
(C. W. Marx, "The *Quis dabit* of Oglerius of Tridino, Monk and Abbot of Locedio," *Journal of Medieval Latin* 4 [1994]: 118–29), widely circulating and translated
into Occitan and Catalan during the Middle Ages.

translation, the texts in MSS. A and B coincide, although B, due to a loss of some folios, lacks vv. 1962–95 and 2130–60.[25]

(b) The legend of the Antichrist

An account of the Antichrist, the second major theme of *Sens e razos* in MS. A (vv. 2145–416), specifies that the Antichrist will come from the line of Dan, be born out of the union of a whore and the devil, and be brought up in Babylon (vv. 2267–72). He will subjugate all the peoples of the world, conquering those of noble birth by money, the humble by fear and by their own imitation of the nobles, priests by his knowledge and eloquence, and monks and hermits by performing miracles (vv. 2273–306). Those who do not follow him, he will kill. He will rebuild Jerusalem, and the Jews will adore him, believing that he is the Messiah (vv. 2306–32). After destroying Solomon's temple, he will rebuild it, forcing the people to worship him there (vv. 2333–42).

The tribulations of virtuous men will be like nothing that has happened since the beginning of the world. They will far exceed the Deluge, for then Noah at least was able to save himself and his family in the ark (vv. 2343–52). These tribulations will last for three and a half years; were they to last any longer, not a single believer would survive. At that time, God will return to earth two prophets, Enoch and Elijah, whom he had transported live into paradise, but they will be killed by order of the Antichrist (vv. 2353–73).

A short time before the coming of the Antichrist, one virtuous Christian king from the house of France will reign throughout the world. This king will make a pilgrimage to the holy places so that God will forgive his sins. On the Mount of Olives he will lay down his crown (vv. 2374–93); there will be no other king until the coming of the Antichrist. Towards the end of his reign, the Antichrist will climb the Mount of Olives to the place whence Christ ascended into heaven and will try to do the same. At that moment, Saint Michael, the avenging angel, will swoop down and slay him. On seeing this happen, the crowds will repent for having followed him and will ask for God's mercy; the Jews, Saracens, and Philistines will realize the futility of waiting for a new Messiah and convert (vv. 2393–416).

This story of the life of the Antichrist draws primarily on two sources. Verses 2267 to 2332 summarize the *Elucidarium*, book 3,

---

[25] Suchier, *Denkmäler*, 485, shows that gaps consist systematically of either 34 (twice) or 67 verses (once). Since each page in MS. B contains 17 verses and each folio 34, gaps are easily explained by the loss of one or two folios (the lacuna extending from v. 2130 to v. 2160 corresponds to a folio with 16 verses on one page and 15 on the other).

chapter 10, often ascribed to Honorius Augustoduniensis;[26] the remainder, including the reference to the last king from the house of France (vv. 2374–93), appears to be taken from the *De ortu et tempore Antichristi* by Adso Dervensis.[27] The reference to the universal flood in the context of the tribulations inflicted on mankind (vv. 2343–52) appears neither in Honorius nor in Adso. It may, however, be found in the *De sant Miquel Arcàngel*, part of the *Libre dels àngels* written in the latter half of the fourteenth century by a Catalan Franciscan, Francesc Eiximenis (b. ca. 1330, d. 1409).[28] Chapters 40 to 45 of Eiximenis's work include a description of the coming of the Antichrist and the Last Judgement, focusing on Saint Michael's intervention in these events. In this context, an allusion to the universal flood is introduced with the impersonal and uninformative "diu's," "it is said." Eiximenis's account seems to have been taken from numerous commentaries and glosses on the Holy Scriptures, which he knew most likely through "florilegia" or "summae."[29] It is, perhaps, not unreasonable to assume that the Occitan author of *Sens e razos* drew on an eschatological compilation similar to that used later by Eiximenis. His reference to the flood may, therefore, indicate a certain level of biblical learning and exegetical sophistication.

In MS. B, the conclusion of the translation of the *EN* and the beginning of the narration about the dispersion of the disciples (vv. 2130–63) are lacking due to a missing folio. Another gap of two folios occurs at a later point (vv. 2309–75) and explains the absence of other important parts of the story: the rebuilding of Jerusalem, the acceptance by the Jews of the Antichrist as the long-awaited Messiah, the

---

[26] PL 172:1163–64.

[27] Adso Dervensis, *De ortu et tempore Antichristi*, ed. D. Verhelst, CC CM, vol. 45 (Turnhout: Brepols, 1976); cf. Richard Kenneth Emmerson, *Antichrist in the Middle Ages* (Manchester: Manchester University Press, 1981), 74–107.

[28] Francesc Eiximenis, *De sant Miquel Arcàngel: el quint tractat del "Libre dels àngels,"* ed. Curt J. Wittlin (Barcelona: Curial, 1983).

[29] Eiximenis mentions the following writers in these chapters: pseudo-Methodius, Polimarchus (a commentator on the former), "Aymó" (Haymo Halberstatensis), "Rabanus" (Hrabanus Maurus), and "Strabus" (pseudo-Walafridus Strabo). In other words, he quotes the very best of the eschatological commentators, most of whom flourished in the ninth century; see D. Verhelst, "La Préhistoire des conceptions d'Adson concernant l'Antichrist," *Recherches de théologie ancienne et médiévale* 40 (1973): 88. This apparent preference for the ninth-century authors may be due to the fact that it was during the last centuries of the first millennium that the typology of the Antichrist came to be fixed. It remained unchanged throughout the Middle Ages, transmitted in "florilegia" citing the above-mentioned authors. On problems connected with identifying the sources used by Eiximenis, see Albert G. Hauf, *D'Eiximenis a sor Isabel de Villena: aportació a l'estudi de la nostra cultura medieval* (Barcelona: Institut de Filologia Valenciana – Publicacions de l'Abadia de Montserrat, 1990), 110–11.

destruction and rebuilding of Solomon's temple, the reference to the flood, and the arrival of Enoch and Elijah on earth to confront the Antichrist.

(c) The fifteen signs of Doom and the Last Judgement

The fifteen signs are the terrible natural portents which over the course of fifteen days are supposed to destroy the world and announce the Day of Judgement. Descriptions of the particular events of each day vary considerably in the two manuscripts of the Occitan poem.

Following some introductory verses (2417–24) and a heading ("Aysso desus es la passion de Jhesu Cristz. Et ausso son los XV signes que veno," "The text above is the passion of Jesus Christ. And these are the fifteen signs which are to come"), the A text begins by identifying St. Jerome as its source ("si co l'escrig san Jeronimes," "As saint Jerome wrote"). A new prologue is then introduced, which consists of forty verses (vv. 2431–32 and 2435–72) extracted from the description of the fifteen signs in the *Mystère d'Adam*,[30] an Anglo-Norman religious drama from the twelfth century.[31] The order and content of the signs in MS. A follow the account contained in Peter Comestor's *Historia scholastica*, chapter 141,[32] except that the poet intercalates into Comestor's account an additional forty-two verses, again from the Anglo-Norman text. This amplification is both purposeful and skilful, for it manages to expand and enhance the descriptions of the signs without destroying the coherence of the text.[33]

At the Last Judgement, its time hidden to all but the Almighty, the resurrected will be summoned to the valley of Josaphat by the sound of a trumpet, according to A (vv. 2707–92). Angels will carry Christ's cross and nails, and Christ will speak first to the righteous and then to the sinners. The rewards and punishments they have merited will be fixed forever. The author concludes by stating that he has completed the work as outlined at the beginning (vv. 27–34).

---

[30] Edited by P. Aebischer, *Mystère d'Adam* (Geneva: Droz, 1963).

[31] The *Mystère d'Adam* was an extensively diffused vernacular source for the motif of the fifteen signs; see Uda Ebel, "Die literarischen Formen der Jenseits- und Endzeitvisionen," in *La Littérature didactique, allégorique, et satirique*, ed. Hans Robert Jauss, 2 pts., Grundriss der romanischen Literaturen des Mittelalters, vol. 6 (Heidelberg: C. Winter, 1968), 1:194–96; 2, no. 4370.

[32] PL 198:1611–12.

[33] In MS. A, the only signs which do not include any verses from the Anglo-Norman text are the third, fourth, sixth, tenth, eleventh, and thirteenth. The signs for which texts A and B do not correspond include the fifth, ninth, tenth, twelfth, and fourteenth.

The description of the fifteen signs in MS. B differs noticeably from
that in A, as it has no title and translates faithfully the entire section on
the fifteen signs from the *Mystère d'Adam.*[34] Again there are textual
gaps caused by missing folios: the end of the first sign, the entire second and third, and the beginning of the fourth are missing, and so are
the conclusion of the fifteenth sign and most of the account of the Last
Judgement. The narrative is taken up again at what is verse 2758 in
MS. A.

Conclusions

As we have seen, the greatest difference between MS. A and B lies in
their varying accounts of the fifteen signs of Doom. According to
Suchier, the original narrative was based exclusively on Comestor. The
account from the *Mystère d'Adam* was substituted for the original narrative in an independent branch of the manuscript tradition. Manuscript
A is thus a result of merging these two traditions: its copyist must
have had before him both the original version following Comestor and
the version following the *Mystère,* and decided to expand Comestor's
text by interpolating eighty-two verses from the latter.[35] Paul Meyer,
on the contrary, writes:

> Nous inclinons à croire que le manuscrit de Londres [MS. B]
> nous donne l'état primitif des deux poèmes: d'abord l'Évan-
> gile de Nicodème augmenté d'un morceau sur l'Antechrist,
> ensuite le poème français des Quinze signes.[36]

> (It is our belief that the London manuscript records the early
> state of the two poems: first the Gospel of Nicodemus together
> with a fragment on the Antichrist, then the French poem on
> the fifteen signs.)

Meyer dismisses Suchier's theory with the statement that his reasons
"ne nous paraissent pas décisives" ("do not appear to us to be conclusive"). He rejects any argument for the unity of the Occitan work based
on similarities of style and versification in the fifteen signs and in the
translation of the *EN,* attributing these similarities to nothing more

[34] This version of the fifteen signs was edited separately in Suchier, *Denkmäler,* 156–64.
[35] Ibid., 492–95.
[36] Meyer, "Légendes," in *Histoire littéraire,* 32:104.

than the same "médiocre" quality of composition.[37] He also implies that the text in MS. B is earlier than that in A because it is shorter. In my view, it is Suchier's theory that offers a coherent explanation of the text as we have received it. Firstly, the unity of the work is beyond doubt. The plot is already outlined in the early verses (27–34) and reiterated at the end, making it impossible to speak, as Meyer did, of two different poems. Secondly, the narrative schema, which joins the story of the Passion of Christ with the story of the Antichrist, a description of the fifteen signs, and the Last Judgement, has French and Catalan counterparts.[38] Finally, the text in MS. B cannot be considered earlier merely because it is shorter than the one in MS. A, since its present brevity has been caused by loss of folios.[39]

Suchier's theory regarding the fifteen signs, although founded more on common sense than on material evidence, agrees fairly well with what the author himself tells us about the poem. In the prologue, the author explicitly states on two different occasions that he is translating from Latin into the vulgar tongue:

Sens e razos d'una escriptura
qu'ay atrobada sancta e pura
m'a mes e motz gran pessamen,
cossi la puesca solamen
de Lati en Romans tornar. (Vv. 1–5)

. . . .

la quarta faray de mo sen,
car tornaray be veramen
lo Lati en plana paraula,
hon non aura bafa ni faula. (Vv. 23–26)

(The meaning and explanations I found in a holy and pure treatise have made me think much about how I could translate it from Latin into Romance.)

. . . .

(in the fourth place, I shall use my mind, for I shall translate most faithfully from Latin into vulgar tongue, where there will be no jokes or fiction.)

---

[37] Ibid., 104–5. See Suchier, *Denkmäler*, 493, on the correspondence between verses in the two texts.

[38] On the French text (Paris, BN MS. fr. 1444), see E. Walberg, *Deux Versions inédites de la légende de l'Antéchrist* (Lund: C. W. K. Gleerup, 1928), xlviii–lxxv, 63–102. Walberg edits only the sections on the Antichrist, the fifteen signs, and the Last Judgement. For the Catalan texts, see part two of this essay.

[39] Suchier, *Denkmäler*, 485.

In spite of these declarations, Meyer assumes that a French version of the signs was part of the original text. In my view, it is unlikely that the Occitan author should have included in his work a translation from Anglo-Norman as this would have constituted a significant break in the linguistic consistency and continuity of his sources.

2. E la mira car tot era ensems

The Catalan poem which includes a translation from the *EN*, *E la mira car tot era ensems*, has not been the object of any studies of the same quality as Suchier's work on *Sens e razos d'una escriptura*; it has merited only a rather cursory transcription.[40]

The poem belongs to the genre of Romance Passion narratives in verse, which relate the events in the life of Jesus Christ from his capture to his Ascension. The simplest forms in this genre follow the canonical gospels literally, but more typically the passions include legendary stories (e.g., the legend of the tree of the cross, the story of Judas's thirty pieces of silver) and apocryphal themes from the *EN*.[41] Such is also the case with *E la mira car tot era ensems*. The poem is preserved in MS. 1029 of the Biblioteca de la Universitat de Barcelona, dated by Rosell to the second half of the fourteenth century.[42] The manuscript is badly damaged, and the poem has lost both the begin-

---

[40] E. Moliné i Brasés, ed., "Passió, mort, resurrecció i aparicions de N. S. Jesucrist," *Estudis universitaris catalans* 3 (1909): 65–74, 155–59, 260–64, 349–51, 459–63, 542–46; 4 (1910): 99–109, 499–508. Moliné i Brasés's work provides neither notes nor commentary and contains several errors in transcription. Verse numeration is irregular; eighty verses which were rendered illegible by damage to the manuscript are simply omitted from the numbering scheme. Pending the appearance of a new and more accurate edition, I relied directly on the manuscript, numbering every verse. The first verse, transcribed by Moliné i Brasés as "e s'*amira* car tot era ensems," is a mistaken reading for "e la mira car tot era ensems." Here "mira" means "myrrh." Jaume Massó i Torrents, *Repertori de l'antiga literatura catalana*, vol. 1 (Barcelona: Alpha, 1932), 43, 380–84, includes some remarks on Moliné i Brasés's transcription.

[41] The greatest number and variety of passions in verse are in French. See Paul Meyer, "Légendes hagiographiques en français," in *Histoire littéraire de la France*, vol. 33, ed. Paul Meyer (Paris: Imprimerie nationale, 1906), 355–56, 358; Walberg, *Deux Versions*, xlviii–lxxv, 63–102; Grace Frank, *Le Livre de la Passion: Poème narratif du XIVe siècle*, Classiques français du moyen âge, vol. 64 (Paris: Champion, 1930); Edith Armstrong Wright, *Ystoire de la Passion*, The Johns Hopkins Studies in Romance Literatures and Languages, vol. 45 (Baltimore: Johns Hopkins Press, 1944).

[42] F. Miquel Rosell, *Inventario general de manuscritos de la Biblioteca Universitaria de Barcelona*, vol. 3 (Madrid: Direcciones Generales de Enseññanza Universitaria y de Archivos y Bibliotecas, Servicio de Publicaciones de la Junta Técnica, 1961).

ning and the concluding portions; the surviving text totals 2506 verses in *noves rimades*. In spite of its incompleteness, the poem is an interesting, perhaps even original example of a Passion narrative in verse, for it interpolates, in a unique way, the tale of the Antichrist into a translation of the *Descensus* with features of *EN* C.[43]

To facilitate the following discussion, I have again divided the text into four major narrative sequences: (a) the trial, Passion, death and burial of Christ (vv. 1–492); (b) the Resurrection, the appearances to the disciples, and the imprisonment of Joseph of Arimathea (vv. 493–1220); (c) the Descent into Hell and the arrival of the Antichrist (vv. 1221–2329); and (d) the signs of the Last Judgement (vv. 2330–506).

(a) The trial, Passion, death, and burial of Christ

The first surviving pages of *E la mira car tot era ensems* provide a narrative of the sufferings of Christ (vv. 62–212), framed by the latter portion of a legend of Judas's thirty pieces of silver (vv. 1–61) and a legend of the discovery of the holy cross by Saint Helen (vv. 213–308). Both legends correspond verse for verse to the narratives which appear in the Catalan manuscript of the *Bíblia rimada* under a single title, *Dels diners on fo venut Jhesuchrist.*[44]

---

[43] Izydorczyk, "The Unfamiliar *Evangelium Nicodemi*," 183. There exists another Catalan text which follows the narrative design of passions in verse, the *Poema de la Passió*, but its importance for this study is slight since it does not directly draw any elements from the *EN* and devotes only 23 verses to the Descent into Hell. It recounts in 688 verses the story of the Passion, death, Resurrection, Descent into Hell (vv. 205–228), Ascension, arrival of the Antichrist (vv. 477–516), and Last Judgement (vv. 517–668). The text is acephalous and dates from the fifteenth century; it is preserved in Paris, BN MS. esp. 472, fols. 1r–21r. It has been edited by Pere Bohigas, "El repertori de manuscrits catalans de la Institució Paxtot: Missió de Paris, Biblioteca Nacional (1926–1927)" in two successive issues of *Estudis universitaris catalans* (1930–31) and reprinted in *Sobre manuscrits i biblioteques* (Barcelona: Curial edicions – Publicacions de l'Abadia de Montserrat, 1985), 247–56. The manuscript is described in A. Morel-Fatio, *Bibliothèque nationale. Catalogue des manuscrits espagnols et des manuscrits portugais* (Paris: Imprimerie nationale, 1892), no. 637.

[44] This manuscript, now in the Biblioteca Colombina de Sevilla, MS. 7-7-6, consists of: a) a translation in *noves rimades* of the *Historia scholastica* by Peter Comestor (the *Bíblia rimada* in the strict sense, from the late thirteenth century); b) a prose translation by fra Romeu Sabruguera of the Book of Psalms (end of the thirteenth century); and c) five poems, again in *noves rimades*, relating the legends of New Testament characters (fourteenth century), the last of which is *Dels diners on fo venut Jhesuchrist*. See Joan Coromines, ed., "Les llegendes rimades de la Bíblia de Sevilla," in *Lleures i converses d'un filòleg* (Barcelona: El pi de les tres branques, 1971), 216–45. On problems connected with contents and dating, see Catherine Ukas, "New Research on the *Bíblia rimada*: the Apocryphal Legends," in *Actes del tercer colloqui d'estudis catalans a Nord-Amèrica (Toronto, 1982): Estudis*

Until recently considered unique in Catalan, the *Bíblia rimada* account of *Dels diners on fo venut Jhesuchrist* might appear to preserve a text more faithful to the archetypes of the two legends than *E la mira car tot sera ensems*. For example, where the *Bíblia rimada* reads "estremonià," ("wizard"),[45] verse 4 of *E la mira car tot era ensems* gives "somiador" ("dreamer"). Proper names in *E la mira car tot era ensems* often suffer from the same kind of corruption; for instance, "Derminià" and "Eusebi"[46] become "Sermina" and "Humfebià" (vv. 8 and 294). However, the fact that the *Bíblia rimada* groups the two under a single title, which refers only to the first, and joins them only superficially by means of a highly compressed story of the Crucifixion, suggests that they must have been extracted from a longer text in which they were suitably contextualized within the complete story of Christ's Passion and separated by a detailed description of the Crucifixion. The only Catalan text which meets these conditions is, in fact, *E la mira car tot era ensems*. I am, therefore, inclined to believe that the legends as they appear in the *Bíblia rimada* were extracted from an earlier and fuller copy of the text we are concerned with.

Following the legend of the discovery of the holy cross by Saint Helen, the poetic narrative resumes at the point where Longinus wounds Christ with a lance (v. 308). In verses 317–30, the narrator effects a curious *planctus*—curious because while it is not unusual to find in this type of narrative a *planctus* in which Mary grieves over the death of her son,[47] it is unusual for the narrator himself to deliver the lament. The fragment relating the burial of Christ by Joseph of Arimathea (vv. 420–78) appears to be corrupt. Verses 479–92 announce the Descent of Christ into Hell, which receives full treatment later. Except for the two legends and this tiny anticipation of the *Descensus*, this first portion of *E la mira car tot era ensems* is based entirely on the canonical gospels.

(b) The Resurrection, the appearances to the disciples, and the imprisonment of Joseph of Arimathea

This narrative sequence, relating the angel's announcement of the Resurrection to Mary Magdalene and the disciples' journey to Galilee after hearing the news (vv. 493–549), is also based on the canonical

---

en honor de Josep Roca-Pons, ed. Patricia Boehne, Josep Massot i Muntaner, and Nathanael B. Smith (Barcelona: Publicacions de l'Abadia de Montserrat, 1982), 123–38.

[45] Coromines, "Les llegendes," v. 1144.

[46] Ibid., vv. 1146 and 1288.

[47] *Sens e razos d'una escriptura,* vv. 897–948, may serve as an example.

gospels. In the following segments, in which Caiaphas summons the soldiers who guarded the sepulcher and the Jews express their anger at Joseph of Arimathea for having buried Christ's body (vv. 550–613), the author combines an abridgement of *EN* 13.2–3 with the canonical narrative of Matthew 28:11–15.

After describing Christ's appearance to the two disciples on the road to Emmaus (vv. 614–62), the poet recounts several episodes with counterparts in the *EN* 12–13.3: the testimony of Joseph of Arimathea before the high priests; his imprisonment, death sentence, and flight; and the evidence given by the guards of the sepulcher and their bribery to spread the rumour that the disciples have stolen the body of Christ (vv. 663–752). The poem continues to rely on the *EN* in vv. 753–895, narrating the arrival in Jerusalem of the three rabbis from Galilee, who claim to have seen Christ preach to his disciples (*EN* 14.1), and moves smoothly to the account of Christ's appearances to Thomas (Jn. 20:19–20) and to the disciples on the Sea of Galilee (Jn. 21:1–12). To this is added a speech by Christ, in which he announces to his disciples the coming of the Holy Spirit and in which he sends them to spread his teaching throughout the world. This part of the poem ends with a description of the Ascension (vv. 896–927).

The succeeding segments are drawn exclusively from the *EN*. The three rabbis are bribed to refrain from making public what they have seen and to return to Galilee (vv. 928–51; *EN* 14.2). Some of the Jews lament bitterly, but the high priests insist that the apostles must have stolen the body of Christ (vv. 952–86; *EN* 14.3). At Nicodemus's suggestion, they search for Christ and find Joseph of Arimathea instead. They send him a letter inviting him to speak to them. Joseph accepts the invitation and explains to them how Christ appeared to him in prison and set him free (vv. 987–1131; *EN* 15). The Jews' lament continues as they become more and more convinced of the truth of Christ's Resurrection. One of them, Levi, remembers the time when he witnessed the presentation of the child Jesus in the temple. The three rabbis are summoned again to confirm their declaration that Christ has truly risen (vv. 1132–221; *EN* 16).

(c) The Descent into Hell and the arrival of the Antichrist

Although it arranges material in the fashion characteristic of *Descensus* A, *E la mira car tot era ensems* contains Tischendorf's chapter 28 (vv. 1221–2329), typical of *EN* C.[48] In this sequence, Joseph of Arimathea

---

[48] Tischendorf, *Evangelia apocrypha*, 409–12; cf. Zbigniew Izydorczyk, "The Latin Source of an Old French Gospel of Nicodemus," *Revue d'histoire des textes* 25 (1995): 265–79.

and Nicodemus tell Pilate about Carinus and Leucius. Pilate has their words put into writing and subsequently orders all the wise men, princes of the priests, doctors, and scribes to meet in the temple so that he may ascertain from them whether the book they so secretly guard in the temple has announced the arrival of Christ. All those assembled admit the divinity of Jesus but make excuses for not having recognised him previously. They relate the prophecies concerning the coming of the Messiah which are found in the Bible.[49]

Like the Occitan *Sens e razos d'una escriptura*, the Catalan *E la mira car tot era ensems* includes the legend of the Antichrist, but its insertion into the text is more adroit from a narrative point of view. It is related not directly by the narrator but by Elijah, who enlarges upon the comments made by Enoch in the *Descensus* (vv. 1909–2083). The body of the legend is taken from the *De ortu et tempore Antichristi* by Adso Dervensis, albeit with some variations and omissions. It is worth noting, however, that in the Catalan version, the figure of the virtuous last emperor who lays aside his crown on Golgotha is omitted. This figure, probably inspired by the *Revelationes* of pseudo-Methodius,[50] was fully incorporated into eschatological texts from the ninth century onwards and indeed appears in *Sens e razos d'una escriptura*. A possible explanation for its absence from the Catalan poem might lie in the intrinsic logic of its narrative. The Occitan text follows a strict chronological order (Passion, Crucifixion, Descent, appearances to the disciples, persecution of Christians, reign of the last emperor, coming of the Antichrist), which would be incomplete without the last emperor episode. In contrast, the Catalan text includes the legend of the Antichrist because the meeting of Elijah and Enoch invites it as a foreshadowing of their future fate. The account of the last emperor is omitted because it is not germane to their story and is not required to complete a chronological sequence.

Due to damage caused by humidity, the thirty-seven lines from verse 2293 to 2329 (fol. 41cd) are almost illegible. The translation from the *EN* ends with these lines, at a point approximately half way through what is Tischendorf's chapter 28.

---

[49] The same chapter 28 occurs in a French translation of *EN* (cf. Alvin E. Ford, ed., *L'Évangile de Nicodème: Les Versions courtes en ancien français et en prose*, Publications romanes et françaises, vol. 125 [Geneva: Droz, 1973], 71 [MS. E]); however, a systematic comparison of French and Catalan translations reveals that the two are not directly related.

[50] Verhelst, "La Préhistoire," 92–96.

(d) The signs of the Last Judgement

At verse 2330 (fol. 42a) the text turns suddenly to a description of some extraordinary human beings, tiny in stature, whose life functions are over in a very short time; the women marry at four, have children at five and die at ten, and the men die at fifteen. Their enemies are cranes (vv. 2337–42). This description corresponds to the ancient and medieval image of pygmies, as indeed they are described by Pliny.[51] We must assume that between fols. 41 and 42 some folios were lost, although, given the sorry state of the manuscript, this is rather difficult to prove. However, the facts that fol. 41 leaves the sequence incomplete and that the next verse on fol. 42 bears no relation to the previous verse on fol. 41b strongly support such an assumption. The lost fragment would have comprised the conclusion of the translation from the *EN* and a transition to the description of the pygmies. There are unfortunately no clues as to what this link might have been. Verse 2356 situates the pygmies geographically to the East: "delay estan enves orient"; given the eschatological context, the text might be describing the peoples of Gog and Magog, who accompany the Antichrist, also from the East. If this were the case, however, it would be the only instance known to us in which the peoples of Gog and Magog are identified with the pygmies.[52]

In verses 2359–62, the poet or a copyist states that he has translated "aço" (v. 2361; "this thing") from Latin. It is difficult to know whether by "aço" he means the whole work or just the preceding description of the pygmies. Directly following this line is a short account of the life of Sibyl and her dream of the signs before Doomsday. The final pages of the manuscript are missing, the text ending with the twelfth day.

The sources for the account of the fifteen signs are several. The prologue explaining the story of the Sibyl and her predictions to the Roman Senate is extracted from pseudo-Bede.[53] The description of the signs themselves is similar to that found in the *Legenda aurea* of Jacobus a Voragine.[54] The twelfth sign of the Catalan text, "les fembres qui seran prius / el ventre cridaran l'infant" ("children will cry in the

---

[51] Claude Kappler, *Monstruos, demonios y maravillas a fines de la Edad Media* (Madrid: Akal, 1986), 151.

[52] In another fourteenth-century Catalan manuscript, pygmies appear to be located geographically in close proximity to the peoples of Gog and Magog but are not in any other way associated with them; see Abraham Cresques, *Atlas Català* (Barcelona: Diàfora, 1975), 137.

[53] PL 90:1181–86.

[54] Walberg, *Deux Versions*, xiii–xlviii and 3–61, esp. 12, vv. 285–86.

wombs of pregnant women"), is a characteristic element of the first sign in the *Mystère d'Adam*,[55] later disseminated in other works as well.

Conclusions

E la mira car tot era ensems is an eclectic text, compiled from several different sources. Although we do not explicitly find here, as in the Occitan poem, internal references which confirm the unity of the work, the fact that it clearly belongs to a specific genre, the passion in verse, surely reveals a desire for unity on the part of the author or compiler. It is true that all the elements which comprise the Catalan poem exist as separate works—*Legendes rimades*, canonical gospels, *EN*, the legends of the Antichrist and of the fifteen signs—but the compiler has expended a considerable effort to link the materials narratively, for instance, by having Elijah in the *Descensus* relate the legend of the Antichrist.

It is more difficult to know whether the compiler drew only on Latin texts or whether he also made use of vernacular translations. The account of the fifteen signs appears to have been adapted from a vulgar version, for while some sequences are clearly drawn from Latin, at least one, the account of the children who will cry from their mothers' wombs, seems to have been taken from the Anglo-Norman *Mystère d'Adam*. The remark that "aço" was translated from Latin (v. 2361) could have been present in the poet's vernacular source.

The inclusion of Tischendorf's chapter 28, characteristic of *EN* C, by the author of the Catalan text adds weight to Izydorczyk's hypothesis concerning its Hispanic origin, or, at least, the importance of its diffusion in the kingdom of Aragon, especially since one of its early manuscripts is associated with the Catalan monastery of Ripoll (Barcelona, Archivo de la Corona de Aragón MS. Ripoll 106). Indeed there is nothing to indicate that there was not a Catalan translation of the complete C version of the *EN* which the compiler of *E la mira car tot era ensems* might have used as his main source.

3. *Lo Gènesi* and *Gamaliel*

In addition to the poetic translations discussed above, portions of Catalan and Occitan renditions of the apocryphal *Evangelium Nicodemi* are

---

[55] The Catalan poem follows Jacobus a Voragine, although with some transpositions: Voragine's fifth sign is split between the fifth and tenth signs in the Catalan poem, and the first part of Voragine's twelfth sign is split between the sixth and seventh. Voragine's seventh sign is the ninth in the Catalan text and the sixth is the eleventh, to which the poem adds the second part of Voragine's twelfth.

preserved in two prose texts, *Lo Gènesi* and *Gamaliel*. Since the two texts were diffused equally in both vernaculars, I shall discuss the Catalan and Occitan versions of each simultaneously.

(a) *Lo Gènesi*

Lo Gènesi is a universal chronicle, based on the historical books of the Bible, covering the time from the Creation of the world up to emperor Constantine.[56] It survives in nine manuscripts: five in Catalan, three in Occitan, and one in Italian. They include:

A   Paris, Bibliothèque Sainte-Geneviève MS. 24; saec. XIV ex.; Occitan.[57]

B   Paris, BN MS. esp. 205, fols. 199v–205r; the text corresponding to the chapter entitled "De l'escrit de Nicodemus" in the other manuscripts; written in 1400; Catalan.[58]

C   Florence, Biblioteca Laurenziana MS. Redianus 149; saec. XV med.; fragmentary; Catalan.[59]

D   Paris, BN MS. fr. 6261; saec. XV in.; Occitan.[60]

E   Paris, BN MS. esp. 541; written in 1451; Catalan. Used by Amer.[61]

---

[56] In his study of the sources of *Lo Gènesi*, Paul Rohde, "Die Quellen der romanischen Weltchronik," in Suchier, *Denkmäler*, 589–638, paid most attention to those in Latin. His findings should probably be revised to take into account possible vernacular intermediaries between the Latin texts and the chronicle. One case in point might be the *EN*, which may have been adapted by the chronicler from an Occitan translation rather than from the original Latin.

[57] Brunel, *Bibliographie*, no. 247. Fols. 69a–75a are edited in Suchier, *Denkmäler*, 386–97.

[58] Morel-Fatio, *Biblothèque nationale*, no. 80; see also Bohigas, "El repertori de manuscrits," 100. It is edited in Suchier, *Denkmäler*, 398–461.

[59] Description and edition in Suchier, *Denkmäler*, 398–461, 495–96.

[60] Brunel, *Bibliographie*, no. 174. Description and edition in Suchier, *Denkmäler*, 398–461, 496.

[61] Bohigas, "El repertori de manuscrits," 139–40. This manuscript was used by Miquel Victorià Amer, *Compendi historial de la Biblia que ab lo títol de "Genesi de Scriptura" trelladá del provençal a la llengua catalana mossen Guillem Serra en l'any M. CCCC. LI.* (Barcelona: Biblioteca Catalana, 1873). One of the flaws of Amer's edition, pointed out already by Morel-Fatio in his review of it (*Romania* 4 [1875], 481), is the confusion of the copyist with the translator of the work. Another error occurs in the title given to the chronicle, which should read *Lo Gènesi* and not *Gènesi de Scriptura*. This misunderstanding resulted from an imperfect transcription and interpretation of the colophon, "Fon acabat lo present libre, apellat Gènesi, de scriura, a XXIIII del mes de Octobra en l'any MCCCCLI, par mans de mi Guillem Serra, rector de sent Julià de Montseny, diocesis Barchinone." The following is a correct translation of this closing statement: "The transcription of the present book, called *Gènesis*, was completed on the 24th of October in the year 1451 by me, Guillem Serra, priest of Sant Julià in Montseny, diocese of Barchinone."

F   Paris, BN MS. esp. 46; saec. XV ex.; Catalan.[62]
G   Paris, BN MS. n. a. fr. 4131; saec. XV; Occitan.[63]
H   Florence, Biblioteca Riccardiana MS. 1362; written in 1444; Italian.[64]
I   Barcelona, Archivo de la Corona de Aragón, Codicum Fragmenta 5; last decade of saec. XIV; a single folio that served as a cover, the top side much deteriorated; 305mm x 221mm, writing space 221mm x 188mm; written in two columns, 38 lines each. Text begins on fol. 1a, "Diu al libre de Jènesi que en lo comensement del mont creà Déus lo cel e la terra. E la terra era buyde e tot lo mont era tenebras, e l'esperit de Déu anava sobra les aygas …" ("The Book of Genesis says that in the beginning of the world God created the heavens and the earth. And the earth was empty and all the world was darkness, and the spirit of God floated over the waters …"); it concludes on fol. 1d, "Lo segon pecat fo desobadiència, con trespesà lo manament de Nostre Seyor. E per açò totes les coses qui eren sotsmeses a el li foren desobadiens, així com pecats devorar. Lo tercer paccat fo avarícia, com el cobaagà més que no li era atorgat, e per aquest paccat perdé" ("The second sin was disobedience, for he transgressed the commandment of our Lord. And, therefore, all that was under him disobeyed him, as though devoured by sin. The third sin was greed, for he wanted more than was granted to him, and because of this sin he perished").[65]

Suchier edited the part of *Lo Gènesi* corresponding to chapters 12 to 27 of the *EN* and studied its manuscripts.[66] His study might serve as a foundation for a critical edition of the text, but, unfortunately, such an edition has not yet materialized. In his study, Suchier establishes the existence of two branches in the manuscript tradition of *Lo*

---

[62] Morel-Fatio, *Bibliothèque nationale*, no. 8. Described and edited in Suchier, *Denkmäler*, 398–461, 496.

[63] Edited in V. Lespy and P. Raymond, *Récits d'histoire sainte en béarnais*, 2 vols. (Pau: Société des bibliophiles du Béarn, 1876–77).

[64] Described and partially edited in Suchier, *Denkmäler*, 497–98, 573–88.

[65] A curious thing about this folio is that it does not come from a manuscript of a complete text but is an exercise copy, left incomplete at the end of the last column. The copyist did not finish the last phrase even though there is room to do so; to fill in the empty space in the line, he just drew a continuous line. My dating of this folio is based on the similarity of its calligraphy to that of autograph letters of Bartomeu Sirvent, belonging to that period. This fragment of *Lo Gènesi* has been discovered by Mr. Jaume Riera i Sans, who advised me of its existence and for whose kind assistance I am most grateful.

[66] Suchier, *Denkmäler*, 387–461, 495–506.

Gènesi, one represented by the Occitan MS. A, and the other by MSS. B, C, D, E, F (D, even though in Occitan, coincides textually with the Catalan manuscripts).[67] Suchier signals also the presence in MS. A of corrupted readings which may be explained as misreadings of a Catalan original. For instance, the sentence "E demanderon Elizeu per Elias e giqueron lo filh que el l'avian receuput la neuch e que el l'avian pausat en paradis terrenal," which occurs in A,[68] makes sense only if one realizes that "filh que" ("son who") is a misinterpretation of the Catalan "fins que" ("until"). This and other details suggest that the Occitan MS. A is in fact a translation of the original Catalan work. The scant attention accorded *Lo Gènesi* so far is perhaps responsible for the persistence of the unexamined notions about its Occitan origin.[69] The chronicle is clearly in need of an exhaustive textual study, with a strong emphasis on patterns of its diffusion, as well as of a full edition; only such intensive investigation may throw some light on its obscure beginnings and resolve doubts about the nature and extent of its influence.

Most likely Catalan in origin, *Lo Gènesi* was widely disseminated in the fourteenth and fifteenth centuries. I have located over fifty references to it in late medieval inventories of manuscripts; one of the oldest copies belonged in 1331 to Joan de Mitjavila, a merchant of València.[70] In Mitjavila's book, *Lo Gènesi* occurs together with a text on vices and virtues; elsewhere, fragments of *Lo Gènesi* were inserted into didactic collections, perhaps to add to a sense of thematic closure, as is the case in MS. B, which contains only the chapter "De l'escrit de Nichodemus," transcribed as a continuation of the Catalan prose translation of the *Breviari d'amor* by Matfre Ermengaud. This practice of including fragments of one didactic compilation in another was not unusual in the later Middle Ages.[71]

---

[67] Manuscript G was not studied by Suchier.

[68] Suchier, *Denkmäler,* p. 391, ll. 15–19; *EN* 15.1.

[69] See Guy De Poerck and Rika Van Deyck, "La Bible et l'activité traductrice dans les pays romans avant 1300," in *La Littérature didactique, allégorique, et satirique,* 1:39.

[70] "Item I libre en pergamí scrit, ab cubertes vermelles, de Gènesi et de Vicis e Virtutes" ("Likewise a book written on parchment, with crimson covers, concerning Genesis and concerning Vices and Virtues"); see Luz Mandigorra Llavata, "Leer en la Valencia del trescientos. El libro y la lectura en Valencia a través de la documentación notarial (1300–1410)" (Ph.D. diss., Universitat de València, 1989), 2:71–72. The inventory was previously published by J. Mas, "Notes documentals de llibres antichs a Barcelona," *Boletín de la Real Academia de Buenas Letras de Barcelona* 8 (1915): 240.

[71] See Lola Badia, "L'aportació de Ramon Llull a la literatura en llengua d'oc: per un replantejament de les relacions Occitània – Catalunya a la baixa Edat Mitjana," in Lola Badia, *Teoria i pràctica de la literatura en Ramon Llull* (Barcelona:

An analysis of the contents of *Lo Gènesi* with respect to the *EN* reveals that the apocryphon was adapted in two distinct sequences. The first occurs in the context of the trial of Jesus and combines elements of the four canonical gospels and the *EN*. The author always specifies which of the five texts served as the basis for his account of a particular episode. In the section entitled "Com los juheus crucificaren Jhesucrist,"[72] the narrative of the trial before Pilate follows closely the *EN* and incorporates chapters 1 and—in this order—2.5, 6, 7, 5, and 9 of the apocryphon.[73] All these passages are unambiguously attributed to Nicodemus with statements such as "Diu Nichodemus en son scrit ...," "Atressí diu Nichodemus ...," and "Aquestes coses tro assí diu Nichodemus."[74] The second sequence of borrowings from the *EN*, entitled "De l'escrit de Nichodemus," is found after an account of the Resurrection and fully covers chapters 12 to 27 of the apocryphon.[75]

Each of these two adapted sequences appears to be based on a different version of the Latin *EN*, the first on version A, and the second on B. That the vernacular account of the trial follows the Latin A text is suggested by the cursor's reply to Pilate, justifying his display of reverence for Christ when summoning him to appear before the procurator of Judea (*EN* 1.3). In *EN* A, the cursor refers to his trip to one Alexander in Jerusalem ("Quando misisti me Hierosolimam ad Alexandrum ..."),[76] perhaps the same Alexander who earlier appears among the accusers of Christ (*EN* A 1.1). *EN* B makes no reference to Alexander either in the list of Christ's accusers or in the cursor's speech. *Lo Gènesi* clearly reflects at this point the text of A: "Senyor, com vos me trametés a Alexandri en Jherusalem, viu aquest hom qui anava cavalcant en una somera" ("Lord, as you sent me to Alexander in Jerusalem, I saw this man riding on a donkey").[77]

The remainder of this first part of the apocryphon's adaptation is so condensed as to make it difficult to identify other characteristics and the exact shape of the source. Such radical abbreviation of the *EN* is not unusual in Catalan texts. A Catalan life of Jesus in BN MS. esp. 486, fols. 220c–90a,[78] combining canonical and apocryphal sources,

---

Quaderns Crema, 1992), 141–71, on the insertion of chapters from Ramon Llull's *Doctrina Pueril* into a Catalan translation of the *Somme le Roi*.

[72] Amer, *Compendi historial de la Biblia*, 197–207.

[73] Ibid., 197–200, 200–202.

[74] Ibid., 197, 199, 202.

[75] Ibid., 238–60.

[76] Kim, *The Gospel of Nicodemus*, 14.

[77] Amer, *Compendi historial de la Biblia*, 198.

[78] See Bohigas, "El repertori de manuscrits," 78–79; Ramón Miquel y Planas, *Estudi històrich y crítich sobre la antiga novela catalana* (Barcelona, 1912), 54–58.

contains a highly compressed account of the Descent, possibly indebted to *EN* A. Such compilations of abbreviated texts enjoyed considerable vogue in the Middle Ages.

At the close of the last century, Suchier pointed out a relationship between the translation of *EN* 12–27 in *Lo Gènesi* and verses 965–2144 of the Occitan poem *Sens e razos d'una escriptura*, based on the apocryphal tradition B. That relationship may be illustrated by the following texts, relating Adam's response to Satan in *EN* 20.1:

EN B	*Sens e razos*	*Lo Gènesi*
Audiebantque sancti dei contentionem satane et inferni. sed ipsi adhuc minime inter se recognoscentes. nichilominus erant cogniti. Sed sanctus pater noster adam. ita sathane respondens per omnia. Dux mortis quid formidas? Dominus ecce venit. qui omnia figmenta tua destruet. captus ab eo religatusque eris per secula.	Cantz Adam au la contenso / que fan essems li duy gloto, / dis al Satan en aut mot fort: / "O enemic, seynher de mort, / que me enganiestz em deceupistz, / e paradis tu mi tolguistz, / puys m'aduysistz en ta preyo, / cantz ieu fis la menespreyo, / enganatz iestz e deceuputz, / sempre seras tostz cofondutz. / Qui me formetz, ve ti que ve! / Per mi iestz mortz; que ayssi cove / que mi traga de ta preyo, / em menara a guerizo. / Enganatz iestz que m'enganiestz, / e cofundutz quem cofondiestz. / Tu enemic em breu perdras / tota la forsa que tu as. / Morta es mortz, e vida vieu / et es tornada essom briu. / Per mortz es vida reviscuda. / Tu mortz iestz tota cofonduda."	E quant Adam oý la contesa que lo diable havia ab Infern, dix al diable a grans veus, molt esforsadament: "E tu, enemich, príncep de mort, qui m'enguanest en paradís terrenal e puys metistme en ta presó per tal com jo menyspresé lo manament de nostro senyor passant-lo, e enguanest-me, mas enguanat seràs; e confunits-me, mas confús seràs per tostemps. Cor vet aquell qui'm formà, qui és per mi mort en la creu, e axí convenia ésser fet, e traurà'm d'esta presó e menar m'ha en la glòria sua. E tu, enemich maleyt, vuy perts tot ton poder; que la mort és morta e la vida és viva, e per la mort és vida resuscitada, e la mort per la vida és offegada."[79]

[79] *EN* B is quoted from Gounelle, "Recherches sur le manuscrit CCCC 288," 73; *Sens e razos*, vv. 1819–40, from Suchier, *Denkmäler*; and *Lo Gènesi*, from Amer, *Compendi historial de la Biblia*, 255. The spelling and punctuation of Amer's edition of *Lo Gènesi* have been systematized.

(*EN* B: And the saints of God heard the contention between Satan and Hell, but they still hardly recognized one another; nevertheless they were known. But our holy father Adam answered Satan in all respects: Why are you terrified,

Without a doubt, *Sens e razos* and *Lo Gènesi* reflect the same version of
the *EN*. It is also clear that *Sens e razos* is not dependent on *Lo Gènesi*,
since the former translates the entire *EN* and the latter does not. The
possibility of reverse dependence is also precluded by several textual
differences, one of the most significant occurring in the passage to
which I have already alluded when discussing the relationship between the Catalan and Occitan versions of *Lo Gènesi*. That passage
occurs at *EN* 15.1, where Nicodemus adduces the example of Elijah's
ascension into paradise. Here are the relevant texts:

EN B	*Sens e razos*	*Lo Gènesi*
Et sicut docet nos scriptura sacri libri. quia sanctus elyas assumptus est in celis. Et heliseus clamavit voce magna. et proiecit helias melotem suum. super helyseum. Et iterum helyseus projecit melotem illum super iordanem. et transiit in ierico. et occurrerunt illi filii prophetarum et dixerunt ad heliseum. Ubi est dominus tuus Helias? et dixit quia assumptus est	Que aysso nos mostra l'escrigz, / que Helyas si fon raubitz / et Helyzeu lo cieu sirvens / cridet: Payre, co no m'atens? / Tro flum Jorda ayssil seguetz; / aqui Helyas si gitetz / ad Helyzeyu pres so mantell, / et ell fes li pon bo e bell / sus en l'ayga si l'estendetz, / com per um pon desus passetz. / Pueys en apres tan lo segui, / tro que nol saup ni non lo vi, / et	Cor la scriptura nos diu que Elies hy serà vist, e aquell cridava: "Elies, pare meu, no'm vulles desemparar!" E sabem que gità lo seu pali a Eliseu quant li demanava que romangués en la sua gràcia. E dix-li Elies: "si tu pots veure que jo me'n vaja, serà't atorgat ço que demanes." E quant la nuu rebé Elies, viu-lo Eliseu, e lavors cridà: "pare meu, pare in

prince of death? Behold, here comes the Lord who will destroy everything you
have made. You will be captured by him and bound for ever.)

(*Sens e razos:* When Adam heard the contention made between the two
gluttons, he said to Satan loudly, raising his voice: "O enemy, lord of death, you
who deceived me and stole paradise from me, and locked me in your prison
when I committed the offence! You have been tricked and deceived, you will
always be confounded. Oh, my Maker, I see you coming! For me you died; and
so it is fitting that he release me from your prison and lead me to salvation. You
who deceived me have been deceived; you who confounded me have been confounded. You, enemy, will soon lose all the strength you have. Death is dead, and
Life lives and has recovered its strength. Through death is Life restored; you,
Death, have been completely confounded.")

(*Lo Gènesi:* And when Adam heard the contention made between the devil
and Hell, he said to the devil, raising his voice, very loudly: "Hey you, enemy,
prince of death, you who deceived me in the earthly paradise and then locked me
up in your prison because I had despised the commandment of our Lord,
transgressing it! You deceived me, but you will be deceived; and you confounded
me, but you will be forever confounded. For, behold, here is my Maker, who has
been killed on the cross for me, and thus must it be; and he will deliver me from
this prison and will bring me to his glory. And you, damned enemy, today will
lose all your power, for Death is dead and Life lives, and through death is Life
resuscitated, and Death is conquered by Life.")

celum. et dixerunt ad helyseum. Nunquid et preses [leg. spiritus] rapuit eum; et proiecit eum in unum ex montibus sed magis tollamus pueros nostros nobiscum. et requiramus. eum. Et confirmaverunt helyseum. et ibat cum illis. et quesierunt eum tribus diebus noctibus. et [non] invenerunt eum. quoniam vere assumptus est.

Helyzieu si fo marritz, / ayssi co nos retras l'escrigz, / et encontret si ab de gens. / Cil li demando belamens: / On es Helyas? Ell respon: / el cel s'en pojava amon. / Doncs dissero aquill trastugz: / esperitz l'a raubitz, som cugz, / el l'a pauzatz en un dels puegz, / aral quiyram, tro sia nuegz. / Il lo quero motz tostz ades, / nol trobero ni luny ni pres. / Adoncs saupro que raubitz es, / em paradis l'en a dieus mes.

meu". E ladonchs li gità lo pali Elies, e hac Eliseu aytal gràcia com hac Elies. E sabem que vingueren los fills dels prophetes, qui eren en aquella terra, a Eliseu, e demanaren-lo de per Elies, e cercaren-lo, tro que seberen que per cert que l'havia rebut la nuu, e l posa en paradís terrenal.[80]

---

[80] *EN* B is quoted from Gounelle, "Recherches sur le manuscrit CCCC 288," 56–57; *Sens e razos*, vv. 1215–40, from Suchier, *Denkmäler*; and *Lo Gènesi*, from Amer, *Compendi historial de la Biblia*, 243–44.

(*EN* B: And as the Scriptures of the Holy Book teach us, holy Elijah was taken up into heaven. And Elisha cried out with a loud voice, and Elijah cast his cloak upon Elisha. And again Elisha cast that cloak upon Jordan and crossed into Jericho. And the sons of prophets met him and said to Elisha: Where is your lord Elijah? And he said that he was taken up into heaven. And they said to Elisha: Has the spirit not caught him up and thrown him upon one of the mountains? But rather let us take our boys with us and look for him. And they reassured Elisha, and he went with them. And they sought him for three days [and] nights and [did not] find him because he was truly taken up.)

(*Sens e razos*: Thus the Scripture demonstrates that Elijah was carried off, and his servant Elisha cried: "Father, why do you not wait for me?" He followed him in this way to the river Jordan. Here Elijah threw his mantle to Elisha, and it became a good bridge to him: he spread it over the waters and passed over it as he would over a bridge. Then he continued to follow him until he lost sight of him, and Elisha grieved, as the Scripture tells us. And he met some people; they asked him courteously, "Where is Elijah?" He replied, "He was raised into the sky." So the people said, "A spirit has carried him off, I so believe, and has set him on a mountain; let us look for him until the night comes." They searched for him far and wide, but they could not find him. So they learned that he has been carried off, and God has put him in paradise.)

(*Lo Gènesi*: Thus the Scripture tells us that Elijah will be seen this way, and he cried: "Elijah, my father, do not abandon me!" And we know that he threw his mantle to Elisha when he asked him to remain in his grace. And Elijah said to him: "If you can see how I leave, you will receive what you ask for." And when the cloud took Elijah, Elisha saw it, and so he cried: "My father, my father." And so Elijah threw his mantle to him, and Elisha received as much grace as Elijah had. And we know that the sons of the prophets who were in the land came to Elisha, and they asked him about Elijah, and they looked for him until they became convinced that a cloud had taken Elijah and set him in the earthly paradise.)

Sens e razos follows here the text of the *EN* very closely, but the same cannot be said of *Lo Gènesi*, which gives at this point one of its most problematic passages, varying from manuscript to manuscript. However, *Lo Gènesi* preserves at least one characteristic of the Latin text that does not appear in *Sens e razos:* in both the *EN* and *Lo Gènesi* Elisha meets the "sons of the prophets" ("filii prophetarum," "los fills dels prophetes"), while in *Sens e razos* he meets unspecified "people" ("encontret si ab de gent," "he met some people"). *Lo Gènesi* cannot, therefore, be directly dependent on the Occitan poem, and its author must have had direct access to the textual tradition of the *EN*. To account for the general correspondences between *Sens e razos* and *Lo Gènesi* one might postulate, with Suchier,[81] that the two shared a common source text of the *EN*, which each author treated with some degree of freedom.

Another textual problem in *Lo Gènesi*, which will also surface in *Gamaliel*, is connected with Leucius and Carinus, the two characters brought back to life who recount the Harrowing of Hell. In *Lo Gènesi*, they appear as "Alexandri" and "Rufo," assuming the names of the sons of Simon of Cyrene, according to the *Historia scholastica*. It should be noted that neither *EN* B nor *Sens e razos* mentions the father of Leucius and Carinus, who in *EN* A is identified as Simeon. The onomastic changes in *Lo Gènesi* may, perhaps, be partly explained by variability in the spelling of the names of the two revived characters in the Occitan poem and by the association of one of those spellings ("le nsimon," v. 1556) with Simon of Cyrene.[82]

(b) *Gamaliel*

Gamaliel is a narrative of the trial, death, and Resurrection of Jesus Christ, in which Nicodemus and his uncle, Gamaliel, are among the principal characters. Gamaliel, a teacher of law and a member of the Jewish council, not only plays an important part in the story but is also its narrator. The text arose from the confluence of various traditions associating Nicodemus with Gamaliel and from the interaction of those traditions with the *EN*, supposedly written by Nicodemus. Nicodemus and Gamaliel, nephew and uncle, appear together in the legend of the finding of the relics of St. Stephen—it was they who buried St. Stephen, and their bodies were discovered lying beside him. This legend and the widespread cult of St. Stephen account for the popularity of Nicodemus and Gamaliel in Catalonia and Occitania. The prose *Gama-*

---

[81] Suchier, *Denkmäler*, 506–8.
[82] Ibid., 508.

liel, presenting a new version of the trial before Pilate with a special focus on those two familiar characters, met with wide acceptance in France, Occitania, and the Kingdom of Aragon: it survives in fourteen French, three Occitan, and two Catalan manuscripts.[83] The text was printed frequently during the latter part of the fifteenth century and the first thirty years of the sixteenth; it was also translated from Catalan into Castilian (1522) and into Latin (1525) by Juan de Molina.[84]

The Occitan manuscripts of *Gamaliel* include:

A   Paris, BN MS. fr. 1919; saec. XV.[85]
B   Paris, BN MS. fr. 24945, fols. 92–126; saec. XV (olim St. Victor 880).[86]
C   Rodez, Bibliothèque municipale MS. 60, fols. 48–98; saec. XV.[87]

The two Catalan manuscripts are:

A   Vatican City, Biblioteca Apostolica Vaticana MS. Reg. 2056; written in 1454.
B   Barcelona, Biblioteca de Catalunya MS. 325; saec. XVIII (a copy of a fifteenth-century manuscript).

Madaleine Le Merrer argues, on the basis of the oldest French manuscript (Grenoble, Bibliothèque municipale MS. 468, ol. 50; saec. XIV) and the Occitan MS. B, in favor of the precedence of the Occitan version over the French.[88] Numerous corrupt readings of the French text corroborate this opinion, accepted also by G. Hasenohr.[89] The Catalan recension is, in all probability, also related to the Occitan and not to the French, as it does not share the erroneous readings of the latter.

---

[83] The small number of Catalan manuscripts is compensated for by numerous references to *Gamaliel* in medieval inventories of manuscripts, which clearly show that the text was well known in Catalonia.

[84] The incunabulum is described by J. Ribelles Comín, *Bibliografía de la lengua valenciana* (Madrid: Tipografia de la Revista de Archivos, Bibliotecas y Museos, 1929), 1:450–57, and the 1510 edition by F. J. Norton, *A Descriptive Catalogue of Printing in Spain and Portugal 1501–1520* (Cambridge: University Press, 1978), 72.

[85] Brunel, *Bibliographie*, no. 158.

[86] See ibid., no. 197, and Meyer, "La Traduction provençale de la *Légende dorée*," *Romania* 27 (1898): 129.

[87] Brunel, *Bibliographie*, no. 262; idem, "Notice du ms. 60 de la Bibliothèque de la Ville de Rodez," *Bibliothèque de l'École des chartes* 94 (1933): 1.

[88] Madeleine Le Merrer, "D'une source narrative occitane de la Passion provençale et des mystères rouergats: l'*Évangile de Gamaliel*," in *La Vie théâtrale dans les provinces du Midi, Actes du IIe colloque de Grasse, 1976* (Tübingen: Y. Giraud, 1980), 47–48.

[89] Geneviève Hasenohr, "À propos de la *Vie de Nostre Benoit Saulveur Jhesus Crist*," *Romania* 102 (1981): 378.

That an originally Occitan text should be so widely diffused in French translations is not surprising: *Gamaliel* may serve as an illustration of the process of linguistic substitution under way in Occitania in the fourteenth and fifteenth centuries which caused a slow abandonment of texts written in Occitan in favor of those in French. A text composed in Occitan and subsequently translated into French continued to be read by Occitan speakers in French.

The principal source of *Gamaliel* was the Occitan poem *Sens e razos d'una escriptura*. It may be instructive to compare the following passage from *Gamaliel* with the excerpts cited above on p. 156:

E quant Adam ohí la veu de Jesuchrist en infern, començà a tremolar de pahor que hac de la gran contesa que infern avia de Jesuchrist, e començà a cridar altament dient: "Ay enemich e senyor de mort! tu m'enganist, e·m deçebist, e de paradís me getist, e puys me metist en ta presó, quant me aguist fet fallir contra lo manament que m'avia donat aquell qui·m formà: e tu m'enganist, e est deçebut, e enganat e confús. Vet que aquell qui·m formà per mi és mort, car així convenia per què·m gitàs de ta presó! Ay enemich, perduda has ta força e ton poder! Morta és mort, e vida viu, e és venguda per aquell que nos avem ohit."[90]

(And when Adam heard the voice of Jesus Christ in hell, he started to tremble, fearing the great struggle between hell and Jesus Christ, and he started to cry loudly, saying, "Alas, enemy and lord of death! You misled me and deceived me and threw me out of paradise, and then you locked me up in your prison after you made me break the commandment that my Maker had given me. And you misled me, and you have been deceived and confused. Now my Maker has died for me, for thus by necessity you cast me out of your prison! Alas, enemy, you have lost your strength and your power! Death is dead, and Life lives, and it has come about through him whom we have heard.")

This passage is almost identical with the corresponding sections of both *Lo Gènesi* and *Sens e razos* and, without further evidence, could easily be derived from either. However, in the following fragment—to be compared with the texts on pp. 157–58—*Gamaliel* clearly follows the Occitan poem, moving away from the Catalan chronicle:

---

[90] Pedro Armengol Valenzuela, ed., *Obras de S. Pedro Pascual, Mártir, obispo de Jaen y religioso de la Merced*, vol. 1, *Nueve leyendas o contemplaciones, el Libro de Gamaliel, la Destrucció de Jerusalem* (Rome: F. Cuggiani, 1905), 145. I have systematized the spelling and punctuation of Armengol's edition.

Car nós trobam en nostra scriptura que Elias rabí que ell e un
de sos dexebles, li dix: "pare, com no'l sperats?" E seguit-lo
entrò al flum Jordà, e aquí Elias gità son mantell sobre l'aygua
e anà desús lo mantell axí com per un pont, e seguí'l tant fins
que no'l poch pus veure; e quant l'hac perdut de vista los
juheus foren fort irats. E isqué de l'aygua e encontrà's ab
gents, que demanaren on era Elias, e los jueus respongueren
que sus al cel se n'era pujat; e lavors digueren: "creem bé que
spirits l'agen pres, e que l'agen posat sobre qualque puig." E
anaren-lo sercar per les montanyes e per les valls, e no'l po-
gueren trobar; e lavors arbitraren-se que pres era stat, e que
Déu l'avia mes en paradís, e que axí ho trobaven en scrit.[91]

(Because we find in our Scripture that rabbi Elijah, that he and
one of his disciples, he said, "Father, why do you not wait for
him?" And he followed him to the river Jordan, and here
Elijah threw his mantle over the water, and he walked over
the mantle as over a bridge, and he followed him until he
could see him no more; and when he lost sight of him, the
Jews became very angry. And he went away from the water,
and he met some people who asked where Elijah was, and the
Jews answered that he had risen up into the sky. And so they
said, "We believe that spirits have carried him away and set
him on some mountain." And they went to search for him
through the mountains and valleys, and they could not find
him; and so they considered that he had been carried away,
and that God had placed him in paradise, and that thus they
found it written.)

In spite of the obvious proximity of this passage to the text of *Sens e
razos*, certain details pose, as in *Lo Gènesi*, problems of textual transmission. The text of *EN* B, "quia sanctus elyas assumptus est in celis et
heliseus clamavit ...," correctly translated in *Sens e razos* as "que
Helyas si fon raubitz et Helyzeu lo sieu sirvens cridet ...," appears in
Gamaliel as "que Elias rabi que ell e un de sos dexebles li dix" (note
the parallel between "raubitz" and "rabi"); *Lo Gènesi* renders the same
clauses as "que Elies hy serà vist, e aquell cridava." The omission of
Elisha's name in *Gamaliel* and *Lo Gènesi* results in faulty sentences and
incomplete sense. Another problematic detail in *Gamaliel* is the identity
of Leucius and Carinus's father: his name appears as "Fulli" in the
Catalan version and "Ruben" or "Simeon" in French texts (in *Sens e
razos* he is not named at all). Problems such as these highlight the

<hr>

[91] Ibid., 150.

complex nature of the relationships among the three vernacular texts and urge a thorough study of their textual background to dispel the air of uncertainty and controversy that still hangs about them.

One other textual feature of *Gamaliel* deserves notice as it relates to the *EN* and possibly to another related text: the presence of a character named Jafel de Jaffa (or Japhet de Casse in the French versions). Jafel is invited by the council of the Jews to produce three credible witnesses to confirm the truthfulness of the testimonies concerning Christ's divinity. The three witnesses he brings forth are named Abraam, Rubén, and Jacob; they appear after the account of the Descent into Hell and adapt the testimonies of Addam, Finees, and Legias as related in *EN* B 14.1.[92] The character of Jafel appears also in an important and widely disseminated Romance work, *La Destrucció de Jerusalem.*[93] Since he does not appear in any other religious or didactic work known to me, there may be some link between this work and *Gamaliel;* an in-depth study of the relationship between *Gamaliel* and *La Destrucció de Jerusalem* might, therefore, throw some new light on both texts.

5. Conclusion

One of the reasons for the *EN*'s success during the Middle Ages was, doubtless, its testimony to an otherwise poorly attested article of faith, the Descent of Christ into Hell. However, most references to the Descent in Catalan and Occitan works are not based directly on the apocryphal *Descensus Christi ad inferos,* which was the ultimate rather than the immediate source. Catalan and Occitan writers of the late Middle Ages usually owed their knowledge of the matter of the *EN* to the *Legenda aurea* and the *Speculum historiale.* Also, the tradition of Franciscan spirituality encouraged—through the examples of works such as the *Meditationes vitae Christi* and the *Meditationes de passione Christi*—affective and meditative reshapings of the narrative elements of the *EN.*

---

[92] Ibid., 157–62.

[93] See C. Chabaneau, "La Prise de Jérusalem ou la vengeance du sauveur," *Revue des langues romanes* 32 (1888): 581–608; 33 (1889): 31–46, 600–609; Josep Hernando i Delgado, ed., "La destrucció de Jerusalem. La venjança que féu de la mort de Jesuchrist Vespesià e Titus son fill," in *Miscel·lània de textos medievals* 5 (1989): 1–116; Alvin E. Ford, ed., *La Vengeance de Nostre-Seigneur. The Old and Middle French Prose Versions: the Version of Japheth,* Studies and Texts, vol. 63 (Toronto: Pontifical Institute of Mediaeval Studies, 1984).

Nevertheless, through its successive transformations and adaptations, such as those discussed in this essay, the *EN* exerted strong
influence on Catalan and Occitan literatures. Without its inspiration,
mediated by those textual refashionings so extensively diffused in the
fifteenth century, Sor Isabel de Villena (b. 1430, d. 1490) would have
been unable to add to her *Vita Christi* one of the most effective elaborations of the theme of the Descent in late medieval Catalan literature.[94]
She devotes almost one hundred and eighty pages to the glorification
of Christ's victory over death and relates in detail Christ's reception of
the saints with full courtly splendor and grand speeches and the final
procession to paradise.

Translated by Josep Izquierdo
and Zbigniew Izydorczyk

---

[94] Isabel de Villena, *Vita Christi*, ed. Ramón Miquel i Planas (Barcelona: Biblioteca Catalana, 1916), 3:5–182.

The *Gospel of Nicodemus* in Medieval Italian Literature: A Preliminary Assessment[1]

AMILCARE A. IANNUCCI

he *Evangelium Nicodemi* (*EN*) consists of two rather loosely con-
joined parts: the first gives an account of Christ's trial, Passion,
and Resurrection, with the story of Joseph of Arimathea woven
into the narrative (*Gesta Pilati*); the second relates Christ's Descent into
the underworld (*Descensus Christi ad inferos*).[2] Although the work
never gained the status of a canonical gospel, it enjoyed great authority
and prestige in the Middle Ages. For instance, in the early thirteenth
century, Vincent of Beauvais justified his summary of it in his widely
read *Speculum* by stating that "some works are considered apocrypha
because they are contrary to truth ... others simply because their
authors are unknown, although they contain pure truth." The *Evangelium Nicodemi*, Vincent suggests, belongs to the latter category.[3]

---

[1] This essay is a revised version of "The *Gospel of Nicodemus* in Medieval Italian Literature," which appeared in *Quaderni d'italianistica* 14, no. 2 (1993): 191–220.
[2] The standard edition of the *Evangelium Nicodemi* is that in Constantinus de
Tischendorf, ed., *Evangelia apocrypha*, 2d rev. ed. (1876; repr., Hildesheim:
G. Olms, 1966), 333–434. All my references are to chapter and paragraph numbers
of this edition unless otherwise stated.
[3] Vincent of Beauvais, *Speculum naturale*, Prologus (1624; repr., Graz: Akademische Druck- und Verlagsanstalt, 1964), col. 8: "Quaedam enim reputantur
Apocrypha, quia veritati aduersantur, vt sunt libri haereticorum. Quaedam vero,
quia auctores eorum ignorantur, licet puram veritatem contineant, vt est Euangelium Nazaraeorum." In the Middle Ages, the *Evangelium Nicodemi* was known by
a variety of names, including *Evangelium Nazaraeorum*, which Vincent uses in the
Speculum naturale. In the *Speculum historiale*, on the other hand, he repeatedly calls
the work *Evangelium Nicodemi*. See, for example, *Speculum historiale*, bk. 7, chap. 40
(1624; repr., Graz: Akademische Druck- und Verlagsanstalt, 1965), 236. The popularity of Vincent's encyclopedia probably contributed to the wide dissemination
of this title—*Evangelium Nicodemi*—which became the most common way of referring to the apocryphon in the later Middle Ages.

The pseudo-gospel's immense popularity stemmed precisely from
the fact that it added further information to the canonical accounts of
Christ's death and Resurrection, and spelled out in great detail a
story—Christ's Harrowing of Hell—which was only vaguely alluded
to in the Old and New Testaments. The story of Christ's Descent into
Hell and defeat of the forces of evil captivated the medieval mind.
Although the *Gospel of Nicodemus* (*GN*) was not the only source of the
Harrowing story, it was certainly the most dramatic and influential
version of it.

The Harrowing of Hell has, of course, long been an object of
intense study, yet its major source, the *GN*, has only recently begun to
attract sustained scholarly interest. Much of the attention has focused
on the origin, dissemination, and textual characteristics of the Latin
version, or rather versions, of the apocryphon.[4] However, as the
essays in this volume indicate, its interaction with various medieval
European literatures has not been entirely neglected. In addition, new
medieval translations have recently been discovered and some have
been published.[5]

Despite lively critical discussion of the *GN*, its presence in and
impact on medieval Italian literature remain almost completely unexplored. My preliminary research on the subject indicates that the
apocryphon was widely known in Italy, not only in its Latin versions,
but also in several Italian translations. The manuscript tradition testifies to this. Moreover, from the second half of the thirteenth century
on, its influence is seen repeatedly in longer literary and quasi-literary
works and echoed in countless shorter compositions. In this essay I
shall provide a preliminary assessment of the situation, indicating
areas which deserve further exploration.

Because of a dearth of critical literature on the subject, research
must be based almost exclusively on primary sources, many of which

---

[4] Zbigniew Izydorczyk, "The Unfamiliar *Evangelium Nicodemi*," *Manuscripta*
33 (1989): 169–91, and idem, *Manuscripts of the "Evangelium Nicodemi": A Census*,
Subsidia Mediaevalia, vol. 21 (Toronto: Pontifical Institute of Mediaeval Studies,
1993).

[5] See, for example, Alvin Ford, ed., *L'Évangile de Nicodème: Les Versions courtes
en ancien français et en prose*, Publications romanes et françaises, vol. 125 (Geneva:
Droz, 1973); C. William Marx and Jeanne F. Drennan, eds., *The Middle English
Prose Complaint of Our Lady and Gospel of Nicodemus*, Middle English Texts, vol. 19
(Heidelberg: C. Winter, 1987); Achim Masser, ed., *Dat ewangelium Nicodemi van
deme lidende vnses heren Ihesu Christi: Zwei mittelniederdeutsche Fassungen*, Texte des
späten Mittelalters und der frühen Neuzeit, vol. 29 (Berlin: E. Schmidt, 1978); and
Achim Masser and Max Siller, eds., *Das Evangelium Nicodemi in spätmittelalterlicher
deutscher Prosa: Texte*, Germanische Bibliothek, 4th ser., Texte und Kommentar
(Heidelberg: C. Winter, 1987).

are unpublished. This is certainly true of the Italian translations of the *EN*. Of the dozen or more known to me, only two have actually been published, both in rare nineteenth-century editions with little or no critical apparatus. There are probably more early Italian translations waiting to be discovered. One of the problems in tracking them down is that the Italian versions of the apocryphon, like the Latin, appear under different names. In addition to the many variations on *Il vangelo di Nicodemo*, they can be called *Storia della passione di Yhesu Christo, La passion del nostro Signor Giesu Christo,* and *Passio di Nicodemo,* to name just a few examples. These translations must be carefully studied to ascertain the date and place of composition, and, if possible, the identity of the translator and/or scribe, in order to reconstruct the cultural context in which each translation was executed, and to determine its sphere of influence. It appears that most of the translations are in Tuscan, but at least two were rendered into Venetian. One of these, contained in a rather late manuscript, written by a certain "Dominicus filius nobilis viri Nicolai de Cartrano" in 1465, seems to have been made from a Tuscan original.[6]

It is also important to establish which Latin form of the text each Italian translation is based on. As is well known, there are at least two major manuscript traditions of the Latin text, which scholars refer to as *EN* A and B. The two diverge in many ways. For instance, the *Descensus Christi ad inferos* of the B text is somewhat shorter and differs from its more common counterpart in selection, arrangement, and wording. The B text also has no meeting with Enoch and Elias, an episode which occupies chapter 25 of the A text. Of the two published Italian versions, one is based on the Latin text A, the other on B. *Il Passio o Vangelo di Nicodemo* was published in 1862 by Cesare Guasti in the "Scelta di curiosità letterarie inedite o rare" series, from a fifteenth-century manuscript owned by Giuseppe Ceppi of Prato.[7] It closely follows *EN* A until chapter 20, when it breaks off abruptly in the middle of the speech in which Hell points out to Satan the special nature of Christ's salvific power. The man who is about to descend into hell has, through the power of his Word, already rescued several souls from his realm, including Lazarus. Indeed, the text ends just before the mention of the revival of Lazarus's lifeless body.

Some twenty years later, in 1883, Hermann Suchier published *El*

---

[6] See Giulio Porro, *Catalogo dei codici manoscritti della Trivulziana* (Turin: Fratelli Bocca, 1884), 190, and Caterina Santoro, *I codici medioevali della Biblioteca Trivulziana* (Milan: Biblioteca Trivulziana, 1965), 123.

[7] Cesare Guasti, ed., *Il Passio o Vangelo di Nicodemo, volgarizzato nel buon secolo della lingua, e non mai fin qui stampato,* Scelta di curiosità litterarie inedite o rare dal secolo XIII al XIX, vol. 12 (Bologna: Romagnoli, 1862).

Vangielo di Nicchodemo from Florence, Biblioteca Riccardiana, MS. 1362 (formerly P. III. 14), as an appendix in *Denkmäler provenzalischer Literatur und Sprache.*[8] This translation in prose contains the last five chapters (12 to 16) of the *Gesta Pilati* and all eleven chapters (17–27) of the B text of the *Descensus Christi ad inferos,* although this material has been condensed somewhat. In other words, it focuses on the story of Joseph of Arimathea, which unfolds principally in the last chapters of the *Gesta,* and the Harrowing of Hell. Suchier associates this Italian translation with several Provençal and Catalan prose versions of the *EN,* which are similarly abridged.[9] Moreover, he suggests that these may in turn depend on a complete Provençal verse translation of the apocryphon.[10] Whatever the case, there is absolutely no doubt that the ultimate source for all these vernacular renderings is *EN* B.

The cluster of texts published by Suchier—Provençal, Catalan, and Italian—illustrates the dynamic and productive quality of the *EN.* Neither geography nor language could constrain it, nor could its status as a quasi-sacred text prevent it from being altered in its passage from one language to another. The Italian translation differs from the B text, and, in some cases, from its Provençal and Catalan counterparts in a couple of interesting ways.

The Archangel Gabriel replaces Michael as the "keeper of paradise" in the episode in which Adam sends his son Seth to ask for the "oil of mercy" to anoint his sick body (chap. 20 in the B text). This seems an odd substitution. Michael's role in casting out the great dragon, "he whom we call the devil or Satan," from heaven (Rv. 12:7–9) would seem to make him a more appropriate choice. Indeed, in the A text Michael is given an even more prominent role: in addition to this episode (chap. 19.1), he also appears in several other scenes (chaps. 25.1; 27.1–2; 28.3–4, etc.). Perhaps the change was suggested by the prophetic nature of the angelic words spoken to Seth. I quote from the Italian translation (chap. 20.3): "L'angiolo Gabriello allora mi disse: Set, tu adomandi olio di misericordia per ugniere tuo padre, e ancora non è tenpo, ma verrà tenpo ch'egli n'arà" ("Then the Angel Gabriel said to me: Seth, you ask for the oil of mercy to anoint your father; the time has not yet come, but the time will come for him to have it"). It is worth noting that of the texts published by Suchier, the Italian is the only one which puts forward Gabriel. The Provençal verse translation

[8] Hermann Suchier, ed., *Denkmäler provenzalischer Literatur und Sprache,* vol. 1 (Halle: Niemeyer, 1883), 573–88. Cf. the comments on *Lo Gènesi* by Josep Izquierdo, earlier in this volume, pp. 152–59.

[9] Suchier, *Denkmäler,* 387–461.

[10] Ibid., 1–84; notes on 481–515.

remains completely faithful to the B text and retains Michael. In the shorter Provençal and Catalan prose versions, the heavenly figure is unnamed, referred to simply as "l'angel" or "l'angel Cherubin."

The second deviation is even more intriguing and may actually be an attempt to make the work conform more closely to the canonical account. It deals with the two non-biblical figures who are freed from hell by Christ along with the patriarchs and who are entrusted with the important task of bearing witness to the event. Each writes his own account, independently of the other. The two stories match perfectly. Their textual adventure is not quite as seamless.

In the Greek *Descensus*, these two figures are not named; they are simply identified as the sons of Simeon. The Simeon in question is the one in Luke 2:25–35, who received the child Jesus in his arms in the temple. There is no indication in this passage or elsewhere that he had sons. Elements of the Luke episode and Simeon himself are also recalled in the last chapter of all the various versions of the *Gesta Pilati*. In the Latin A text of the *Descensus*, the sons of Simeon are given the names of Karinus and Leucius. In the B text they are also called Karinus and Leucius but are no longer linked to Simeon, who is not mentioned. Commentators are uncertain about the origin of these names but usually conclude that they "are somehow connected with Leukios Charinos, the Gnostic author of the Acts of John."[11]

In our Italian text, Karinus and Leucius became "Allexandro e Ruffo, figliuoli di Simone Cireneo" (chap. 17.1; "Alexander and Rufus, the sons of Simon of Cyrene"). The Simeon of Luke 2:25–35 is still present in chapter 16.1 (i.e., the last chapter of the *Gesta*), but in the very next chapter (the first of the *Descensus*) his place is usurped by Simon of Cyrene, the man who was compelled to carry Jesus' cross, according to several gospel passages (Lk. 23:26, Mt. 27:32, and Mk. 15:21). In the passage from Mark, he is identified as "the father of Alexander and Rufus." Simon of Cyrene and his sons do not normally figure as characters in the Latin versions of the apocryphon, but they do make a brief appearance in the expanded chapter 10 of the Greek recension B of the *Gesta Pilati*. It is interesting to note that the Greek *Descensus* always follows this version of the *Gesta*, which is rather late, no manuscript containing it being older than the fourteenth century. Chapter 10 deals with Christ's Crucifixion and death, and in the longer

[11] Felix Scheidweiler, "The Gospel of Nicodemus," in *New Testament Apocrypha*, vol. 1, *Gospels and Related Writings*, ed. Edgar Hennecke, English trans. ed. R. McL. Wilson (Philadelphia: Westminster Press, 1963), 476; cf. Montague Rhodes James, *The Apocryphal New Testament* (1924; repr., Oxford: Clarendon Press, 1975), 95, and Mario Erbetta, ed., *Gli apocrifi del Nuovo Testamento*, vol. 1, pt. 2, *Vangeli: Infanzia e passione di Cristo. Assunzione di Maria* (Turin: Marietti, 1981), 237.

Greek version, Mark 15–21 is simply appropriated, without altering in any way the roles of the characters. How Alexander and Rufus came to supplant Karinus and Leucius in our Italian text is an interesting question but one which is impossible to answer definitively on the basis of the evidence at hand. On the other hand, their presence does seem to confirm the close affiliation between our Italian text and the abridged prose Provençal and Catalan versions of the apocryphon in which Alexander and Rufus also prevail. In this case too the Provençal verse translation remains faithful to the Latin B text. I have lingered over these two peculiar details because traces of them can be seen in some Italian adaptations of the work, which I shall discuss in a moment.

The diffusion of these translations remains to be determined, but one thing is certain: the *GN*, whether in Latin or in Italian, left its mark on a wide range of Italian texts, from *laude* and *sacre rappresentazioni* to religious *cantari* and sermons. To be sure, this mark is sometimes faint, discernible only through the filter of a number of other texts: it is not always possible in brief allusions to a *GN* theme to cite the apocryphon as the immediate or sole source. Much of the *Gesta Pilati* is a reworking of materials in the canonical gospels. As for the *Descensus Christi ad inferos*, although it was the most influential source for the Harrowing theme, there were other accounts, such as the pseudo-Augustine sermon "De pascha II," which also circulated freely in the Middle Ages.[12] Moreover, in the early thirteenth century, Vincent of Beauvais summarized the *EN* in his widely read *Speculum historiale* (bk. 7, chaps. 40–63). Later in that century, Jacobus a Voragine epitomized the apocryphon in his equally successful *Legenda aurea* (chap. 54).[13] Some of the *EN*'s content also found its way in a less systematic fashion into the extremely popular early fourteenth-century *Meditationes vitae Christi* (esp. chaps. 80–89), once attributed to Saint Bonaventure.[14] In this light, it is obvious that unless there is a specific verbal echo, philologically demonstrable, or unless the structural imprint of the apocryphon is sufficiently clear, many passages from medieval Italian texts evoking characters, images, or scenes from the *EN* cannot definitively be attributed to it. What can be said of these passages with a degree of certainty is that their authors were probably familiar with a constellation of texts which, in addition to the *EN*, included the *Legenda aurea*

---

[12] Pseudo-Augustine, "Sermo 160. De pascha II," PL 39:2059–61.

[13] Jacobus a Voragine, *Jacobi a Voragine Legenda aurea vulgo Historia Lombardica dicta*, ed. Th. Graesse (1890; repr., Osnabrück: O. Zeller, 1969).

[14] Pseudo-Bonaventure, *Meditationes vitae Christi*, in *S. R. E. Cardinalis Bonaventurae . . . Opera omnia*, ed. A. C. Peltier, vol. 12 (Paris: L. Vivès, 1864), 509–630.

and later the pseudo-Bonaventurian *Meditationes vitae Christi*. The latter work was especially influential: quickly translated into Italian, it circulated widely. Indeed, one of the oldest manuscripts (second half of the fourteenth century) containing the Italian *Meditationes* also includes, immediately following, an Italian version of the *EN* (Florence, Biblioteca Riccardiana, MS. 1286).[15] With this caveat in mind, let us now turn to some medieval Italian texts which were, directly or indirectly, touched by the *GN*.

As I have already indicated, the *Gesta Pilati* retells, and in some cases expands, several episodes in the canonical gospels dealing with the trial, Passion, and Resurrection of Christ. The most important of the amplified episodes is that of Joseph of Arimathea, whose story comes to the fore in the last chapters of the *Gesta*. But there are other such altered episodes which also proved to be extremely popular. Among them are the episode of the two Thieves (chap. 10.1–2; cf. Mt. 27:38, Mk. 15:27, but especially Lk. 23:32–44) and that of the soldier who pierces Christ's side with a spear (chap. 16.4; cf. Jn. 19:34). In both cases the *Gesta*'s major elaboration consists in naming the characters, who are left anonymous in the canonical gospels. Jacobus a Voragine specifically notes this fact with reference to the two Thieves: "... unus conversus, scilicet Dismas, qui erat a dextris, sicut dicitur in evangelio Nicodemi, et alius damnatus, scilicet Gesmas, qui erat a sinistris" ("... one of them, Dismas, who was crucified at Christ's right side, was converted, as we read in the *Gospel of Nicodemus*, and the other, Gesmas, on the left side, was condemned").[16]

The soldier who wounds Christ on the cross seems also to have been identified for the first time in the *Gesta*. He is called Longinus. Erbetta notes, "Il nome Longino, noto pure dalla lettera di Pilato a Erode, deriva forse dall'assonanza con il greco *lonché* = lancia" ("The name Longinus, known also from the letter of Pilate to Herod, derives perhaps from the assonance with the Greek word *lonché* meaning spear").[17] The episode is recalled fleetingly in the last chapter of the *Gesta* (16.4): "et lancea latus eius perforavit Longinus miles" ("and Longinus the soldier pierced his side with a spear"), but in some Latin manuscripts it is also referred to earlier, in chapter 10.1: "Accipiens autem Longinus miles lanceam aperuit latus eius, et continuo exivit

---

[15] See Salomone Morpurgo, *I manoscritti della R. Biblioteca Riccardiana di Firenze*, vol. 1 (Rome: n.p., 1900), 345–46, and Arrigo Levasti, ed., *Mistici del Duecento e del Trecento* (Milan: Rizzoli, 1935), 997–99.

[16] Jacobus a Voragine, *Legenda aurea*, chap. 53. For the translation, see Jacobus de Voragine, *The Golden Legend: Readings on the Saints*, trans. William Granger Ryan (Princeton: Princeton University Press, 1993), 1:203.

[17] Erbetta, *Gli apocrifi*, 255 n. 76.

sanguis et aqua" ("Taking the spear, the soldier Longinus opened his side, and immediately blood and water flowed out").[18] However, Longinus's adventures do not end here. Apparently he repented of his deed, converted to Christianity, and died a saint. His full story is told by Jacobus a Voragine in the *Legenda aurea* (chap. 47; cf. Vincent of Beauvais, *Speculum historiale*, bk. 7, chap. 47). A capsule version of it also appears in the *Meditationes vitae Christi:* "Unus autem, Longinus nomine, tunc impius et superbus, sed post conversus, et martyr et sanctus, porrigens lanceam de longe, eorum preces et rogamina contemnens, latus Domini Jesu dextrum vulnere grandi aperuit, et exivit sanguis et aqua" (chap. 80; "And one called Longinus, who was then wicked and proud but later converted and became a martyr and a saint, extended a spear from afar, and, ignoring their prayers and entreaties, he opened a large wound on his right side from which blood and water poured out").

References to Longinus abound in medieval Italian literature, in both religious and nonreligious texts. For example, he manages to make his way into such diverse texts as a *canzone* by the Florentine poet Pacino Angiulieri lamenting the death of his beloved,[19] an entertaining parody of the Passion by Ruggieri Apugliese in which he represents himself as being falsely accused and crucified by the Sienese ecclesiastical authorities,[20] and Uguccione da Lodi's *Il Libro* (vv. 219–21), a long didactic poem about sin, punishment, and repentance.[21] His cruel act is also recalled in the *Passione lombarda* (vv. 164–65), a significant early *lauda*,[22] a genre of religious poetry which I shall return to in a moment. I have purposely limited myself to thirteenth-century texts. Longinus's presence in subsequent centuries is so pervasive, especially in *laude*, that to track him further would be pointless. Just one more example, this one from a fourteenth-century collection of *laude* from Cortona,[23] a small city in Umbria which produced a large number of them, including some of the earliest examples of the genre. There are no traces of the *EN* in the earliest of these, contained in a thirteenth-century manuscript, but several in the later collection mentioned above.[24] The Longinus episode is evoked in five separate

---

[18] See Tischendorf, *Evangelia apocrypha,* 362.

[19] Gianfranco Contini, ed., *Poeti del Duecento,* vol. 1 (Milan: Ricciardi, 1960), 389–92.

[20] Ibid., 402–6.

[21] Ibid., 597–624.

[22] Giorgio Varanini, ed., *Laude dugentesche* (Padua: Antenore, 1972), 107–20.

[23] Giorgio Varanini, Luigi Banfi, and Anna Ceruti Burgio, eds., *Laude cortonesi del secolo XIII al XV,* 4 vols. (Florence: Olschki, 1981–85).

[24] These are contained in vol. 2 of *Laude cortonesi,* edited by Anna Ceruti Burgio.

laude,[25] and on two occasions his name is actually mentioned.[26] The difference here is that the *Meditationes* has come into play as a subtext and references to Longinus are filtered through it. This is especially obvious in *Lauda* 32: "Un fel Giudeo, che Longino è chiamato" ("A wicked Jew called Longinus").[27] But the *Gesta Pilati* continues to lurk in the background, and is recalled in at least one other *lauda*. Verse 60 of *Lauda* 28, "ed è un vero maguo (mago) et rio" ("and he is a real sorcerer and he is evil"), echoes several passages in the *Gesta Pilati* (chaps. 1.1, 2.1, 2.5) where the Jews accuse Christ of being a sorcerer, a "magus."[28] One *lauda*—number 4—also alludes to the Harrowing of Hell: "gytto n'è em Lenbo a ffare aquisto, / a i sancti padri trar di presgione" (vv. 9–10; "He went to limbo to redeem, / the holy fathers he set free from prison"). Although the reference is too general to indicate the *Descensus Christi ad inferos* as the specific source, it seems very likely that the author or authors of these *laude* from Cortona were familiar with both parts of the *EN*. The same may be said of Uguccione da Lodi and the author of the *Passione lombarda*.

In *Il Libro*, Uguccione da Lodi briefly evokes Christ's Descent into Hell (vv. 227–29) immediately after his reference to the Longinus episode (vv. 219–21). Despite its name, the *Passione lombarda* narrates all the major events of Christ's life from the Annunciation to the Resurrection, including, in two short verses, his Harrowing of Hell: "per nu descende Cristo a l'inferno, / per trar nui de tenebria" (vv. 177–78; "for us Christ descends into hell, / to pull us out of darkness"). As in the *laude cortonesi* and *Il Libro*, there is not enough here to claim the *Descensus* as the unique point of reference. Indeed, in this particular case we have little more than the clause from the Apostles' Creed, "descendit ad inferos." On the other hand, there is absolutely no doubt of the provenance of a Harrowing passage in another significant *lauda* from the *Duecento*, this one from the Abruzzi region in south-central Italy. This archaic *lauda*, usually called the *Lamentatio beate Marie de filio*, is composed of thirty mono-rhythmic quatrains, six of which are dedicated to the Harrowing of Hell.[29] The sequence focuses on the binding of Satan and the release of the patriarchs from hell, in other words, the material of chapters 24 and 25 of *Descensus B*, which the author of this important *lauda* must have had before his eyes:

---

[25] Ibid., nos. 3, vv. 99–102; 15, v. 23; 26, vv. 23–26; 31, vv. 11–14; 32, vv. 59–62.
[26] Ibid., nos. 31, v. 11; 32, v. 59.
[27] Cf. *Meditationes*, chap. 80.
[28] See Ceruti Burgio's note to this passage.
[29] This *lauda* is printed in Francesco A. Ugolini's *Testi volgari abruzzesi del Duecento* (Turin: Rosenberg & Sellier, 1959), 8–50.

Poy ke na croce   Christo spirao,
Bivaçamente   a lu fernu annao.
Da poy ke gio,   dentro n'entrao
Et lu Malignu   scì 'ncatenao.

Da poy ke ll' abe   strictu legatu,
E mmultu forte   l'ay menacçatu:
"Iammay non fay   lo teu usatu!
Ore te sta co-   scì 'ncatenatu."

Lu gran Siniore   scì prese a ffare:
Tuctu lu fernu   prese a ccercare,
Li soy fedili   prese a ciamare
E ttucti quanti   li fa 'dunare.

Gionne ad Adam   k' ipsu creao;
Levase Adam,   scì favellao:
"Ecco le mani   ke mme plasmaru,
Lu gran Siniore   ke mme creao."

Ore favella   l'altu Siniore
A ttuti sancti   con grande amore:
"Pro vuy sostinni   la passione:
Venite a 'rrcepere   le gran corone."

En paradisu   ne l'ay menati
E ttuti quanti   l'ay coronati:
"Co lo meu sangue   vv'aio accattati;
Ore vedete   k' i' vv'aio amati." (Vv. 65–88)

(After Christ died on the cross, he
immediately descended into hell.
When he got there, he entered
and chained the evil one.

After he had bound him tightly,
he chastised him greatly:
"You will never again do what you used to do!
Now you will be chained forever."

The great Lord proceeded in this manner:
he started searching all of hell,
summoning his faithful, and then
he made them all gather together.

He went to Adam, whom he had created.
Adam got up and said: "Here are
the hands that shaped me, here is
the great Lord that created me."

Then the mighty Lord spoke
to all the saints with great love:
"For you I suffered the passion;
come to receive the great crowns."

He led them into paradise
and crowned them all: "With my blood
I redeemed you; now you can see
how much I have loved you.")

Verse 79 ("Ecco le mani ke mme plasmaru") translates exactly Adam's words to Christ in chapter 25 of *Descensus B* ("Ecce manus quae plasmaverunt me"). According to Ugolini, this *lauda* is the most ancient example of the "literary type" of the "Pianto per la passione di Cristo" ("Lament for the Passion of Christ"),[30] which flourished in the thirteenth, fourteenth, and fifteenth centuries. Poems belonging to this well-defined group, like the noted *Il Pianto delle Marie* (vv. 243–47),[31] often call up the Harrowing, but never as explicitly as their prototype. In the universally recognized masterpiece of the type, Jacopone da Todi's *Donna de Paradiso*, also known as *Il Pianto della Madonna*, there is no mention of it.[32] Indeed, I could detect no clear reference to the GN in any of Jacopone's poems.

The most famous composer of *laude* seems to have shunned our apocryphon, but other less celebrated, mostly anonymous writers of *laude* used it as one of their favorite source books. The religious poems known as *laude* could take either a dramatic or nondramatic form, and were sung by lay confraternities in cities throughout Italy, starting in the second half of the thirteenth century. Most of the *laude* that I have referred to so far are of the nondramatic type, often referred to as "lyrical *laude*," even though they could be quite long and narrative in character, like the *Passione lombarda* and the *Lamentatio abruzzese*. The lyrical type developed earlier and eventually adopted the metrical scheme of the profane love ballad. However, the imprint of the apocryphon can best be seen in the *laude* of the dramatic sort. Although there is some controversy concerning the lyrical type, there is general agreement that the dramatic kind first flourished among the *Disciplinati* of Perugia,[33] a lay religious movement which traces its beginnings to the

---

[30] Ugolini, *Testi volgari abruzzesi*, 10.

[31] For the text, see ibid., 116–40.

[32] For the text, see Jacopone da Todi, *Laude*, ed. Franco Mancini (Bari: Laterza, 1977), 201–6.

[33] See Ignazio Baldelli, "La lauda e i Disciplinati," in *Il movimento dei Disciplinati nel settimo centenario dal suo inizio (Perugia – 1260)*, *Convegno internazionale: Perugia 25–28 settembre 1960, Appendice al Bollettino, n. 9* (Spoleto: Deputazione di Storia Patria per l'Umbria, 1962), 338–67.

great spiritual upheaval of 1260 led by Raniero Fasani. The movement
quickly spread outside of Perugia into the rest of Umbria, and it was
not long before confraternities of *Disciplinati* were established in cities
throughout central and northern Italy. The *Disciplinati* combined self-
flagellation with the singing of *laude*. In Perugia, probably under the
influence of the Dominicans, the singing of *laude* was organized
around the liturgical calendar, and soon became an integral part of
their "liturgy," as De Bartholomaeis explains:

> Nel margine della liturgia ufficiale, venne a formarsi una
> liturgia nuova, con un cerimoniale suo proprio, con una sua
> propria melodia; la quale, in origine, era stata la melodia
> popolare della canzone da ballo, ora rielaborata da' nuovi
> contrappuntisti che i Disciplinati assoldarono.[34]

> (A new liturgy, with a ceremonial all of its own and with its
> own melody, came into existence on the fringes of the official
> liturgy. This melody, which had originally been the popular
> melody of the ballad, was later re-elaborated by the new
> contrapuntists recruited by the *Disciplinati*.)

Some days were dedicated to the singing of lyrical *laude*, others to
dramatic ones, also referred to as *devozioni*. Initially, the *laude*, whether
lyrical or dramatic, were simply sung in the oratory. Later dramatic
representations of the Passion and other sacred episodes were performed for the people in church and eventually in public squares. The
dramatic form seems to have come into its own as a genre during the
first half of the fourteenth century.[35]

The *laude* of the *Disciplinati* of Perugia are preserved in two fourteenth-century collections, discovered by Monaci in the 1870's.[36] They
both contain about 160 *laude*, half of which are of the dramatic variety.
There is no critical edition of the *laudario perugino*. However, a good
selection of Perugian dramatic *laude* can be found in volume one of
Vincenzo De Bartholomaeis's *Laude drammatiche e rappresentazioni sacre*,
still the most extensive anthology of early Italian drama.[37] In De
Bartholomaeis's collection there are several *devozioni* which clearly

---

[34] Vincenzo De Bartholomaeis, *Origini della poesia drammatica italiana*, 2d ed.
(Turin: Società Editrice Internazionale, 1952), 220.
    [35] See Angela Maria Terruggia, "In quale momento i Disciplinati hanno dato
origine al loro teatro?" in *Il movimento dei Disciplinati*, 434–59.
    [36] Ernesto Monaci, "Uffizj drammatici dei Disciplinati dell'Umbria," *Rivista
di filologia romanza* 1 (1872): 235–71; 2 (1875): 29–42.
    [37] Vincenzo De Bartholomaeis, ed., *Laude drammatiche e rappresentazioni sacre*,
3 vols. (Florence: Le Monnier, 1943).

draw on the *EN*. For the Perugian Passion *lauda*, De Bartholomaeis cites the *Meditationes vitae Christi* (chaps. 75–83) as the sole source,[38] but the *Gesta Pilati* seems also to be present, even if somewhat further removed. The fact that the very next *lauda*, the one for Holy Saturday, is fashioned on the *Descensus* supports this claim. I shall deal with this important *lauda* in a moment. First, I would like to discuss briefly another *lauda* also drawn from the *Descensus*. It is the short *devozione*— 56 verses in all—for the third Sunday of Advent.[39] Set in limbo, it recreates the patriarchs' sense of expectation before the arrival of Christ. The *lauda* begins with David's prophecy in chapter 21 of the A text (22 in the B):

> Presso è l'avenimento
> de quil signore de cuie io profetaie:
> trarrane d'este guaie
> e serim fuor de tanta tenebria (vv. 1–4)

> (The coming of the Lord about whom
> I prophesied is near; he will free us
> from these misfortunes
> and we will be out of this darkness)

and ends with Adam and Eve announcing their imminent release from hell and ascent into paradise:

> Noie che l'antico pasto
> mangiammo prima, prendiamo conforto,
> puoia che sem presso al porto
> d'andare en Cielo a quilla gerargia. (Vv. 53–56)

> (We who first ate the ancient meal,
> let us rejoice for the time is near
> for us to go into heaven
> to join that hierarchy.)

In between Isaias, Geremia and Abel have speaking parts. Of these, Abel appears in neither the A nor the B text, and Eve is present only in B, but there is no doubt that the *lauda* takes the *Descensus* as its point of departure. However, it develops no further than the prophet's talk of Redemption. The event—Christ's Harrowing of Hell—alluded to in the conversation of the patriarchs never takes place in this *lauda*. To be sure, the Harrowing motif is evoked in another Perugian *lauda*

---

[38] Ibid. 1:232–43. Cf. Paolo Toschi, ed., *L'antico dramma sacro italiano* (Florence: Libreria Editrice Fiorentina, 1926), 1:153–70.
[39] For the text, see De Bartholomaeis, *Laude drammatiche*, 1:53–55.

from the Advent period, not included in De Bartholomaeis's collection. It is published by Giuseppe Galli in *Laude inedite dei Disciplinati umbri.*[40] It is a curious *lauda*, also quite short (78 verses). The sinners of hell plead with Christ to have mercy on them. However, cross in hand, he rebuffs them. Then he turns to the just and leads them out of hell:

> Figluogle mieie, meco venite
> Benedecte dal mio Pate;
> El regno mio possederite
> Tucte quante ensiememente,
> El quale a voie fo ordenato
> Puoie ch'el mondo fo 'dificato. (Vv. 73–78)

> (My children, blessed by my Father,
> come with me; all of you together
> will attain my realm.
> This was ordained for you
> when the world was created.)

The content of these two *devozioni* was probably suggested by the liturgy, which, during Advent, reverberates with allusions to the *Descensus* themes. Within the *laudario perugino* they anticipate the Holy Week *lauda* in which the material of the *Descensus* is given full expression.

The orthodox view, upheld by the majority of theologians, including Aquinas in the *Summa theologiae* (3a, q. 52, ad 3), was that Christ descended into hell immediately upon his death, while his body was still suspended on the cross. There was, however, another popular tradition which maintained that Christ did not descend into hell until the night before his Resurrection. This view was sustained by the many actions and words recalling the Descent in the liturgy for Holy Saturday and Easter Sunday. The *Elevatio crucis* ceremony celebrated before matins on Easter Sunday often included a dramatic representation, based on the Vulgate Psalm 23, of the Harrowing. I mention all of this because the Perugian Harrowing *lauda* was in the beginning probably two separate *laude.*[41] The first, performed on Holy Saturday, focused on the patriarchs in limbo. The second, for Easter, represented their release from hell and the ascent into paradise, where they met Enoch and Elijah, and the Good Thief. Later, the two were combined and assigned to Holy Saturday. The resultant *devozione* is considered to

---

[40] Giuseppe Galli, ed., *Laudi inedite dei Disciplinati umbri scelte di sui codici più antichi* (Bergamo: Istituto Italiano d'Arti Grafiche, 1910), 105–7.

[41] Cf. Toschi, *L'antico dramma sacro*, 1:200, and De Bartholomaeis, *Origini della poesia drammatica*, 305.

be one of the masterpieces of early Italian drama[42] and has been published several times.[43]

In its simplicity and linearity, it does have a certain charm and power. As the Hebrew patriarchs and prophets wait in limbo, a ray of light suddenly pierces the engulfing darkness and fills them with hope. The long-awaited Messiah has finally come to liberate them from their infernal prison:

> Quisto lume mo venute
> procedon da quilla fontana
> che ne promise la salute
> de tutta quanta gente umana;
> però ciascuno aggia buon cuore
> ché quisto è l'alto suo splendore. (Vv. 1–6)

> (This light which has just arrived
> springs from that fountain
> that promised us salvation
> for all human kind;
> so every one take heart
> for this is his high splendor.)

Satan boasts to Hell of his previous victories over Christ (vv. 67–72) but at the same time warns Hell to prepare for a struggle against the Son of God:

> Tosto t'apparecchia, Enferno,
> per quillo che s'è già gloriato
> ch'è figliuol de Dio Eterno
> ed hanne el popol mio turbato,
> e fese tristo molto forte
> vedendo appressare la morte. (Vv. 43–48)

> (Get ready at once, Hell,
> for the one who has already been glorified,
> the son of God eternal;
> his coming has perturbed my people
> and made them sad,
> for they see death approach.)

---

[42] See, for instance, Mario Bonfantini, ed., *Le sacre rappresentazioni italiane* (Milan: Bompiani, 1942), 69, and Baldelli, "La lauda e i Disciplinati," 364.

[43] See Galli, *Laudi inedite*, 60–71; Toschi, *L'antico dramma sacro*, 1:181–200; De Bartholomaeis, *Laude drammatiche*, 1:242–58; Bonfantini, *Le sacre rappresentazioni*, 69–87; and Emilio Faccioli, ed., *Il teatro italiano. Dalle origini al Quattrocento*, vol. 1 (Turin: Einaudi, 1975), 90–112.

Recalling the wounds it suffered when Christ resurrected Lazarus from
the dead (vv. 97–102), Hell at once rebuffs Satan and urges him to har-
ness the forces of darkness in order to secure the gates against assault:

> Or Satan, or te departe
> tosto da la sedia mia,
> e combatte con tuoie arte
> ch'el re de gloria qui non sia,
> ed alcuno chiude quille porte
> quanto se può far forte. (Vv. 109–14)

> (Now Satan, now depart immediately
> from my abode, and fight
> with all your means so that
> the King of glory may not enter
> here; someone close those
> doors as securely as possible.)

The pace of the action quickens. Satan orders his troops of demons to
station themselves for combat:

> O dilette miei legione,
> contraste a quisto passo;
> ciascun piglie el suo cantone
> chi più alto e chi più basso. (Vv. 115–18)

> (Oh my beloved legions,
> oppose this act of force;
> everyone pick a spot,
> some up high and some down low.)

Tension builds quickly as the Hebrew fathers demand repeatedly that
Hell open its gates, adapting the "Attolite portas" formula from Psalm
23:7 as in *Descensus* A, chapter 5:

> Aprite tosto e non chiudete,
> ché mo venire lo vedrete!
> . . . .
> Apre, Enferno, ché se' vinto! (Vv. 119–20, 127)

> (Open up immediately and
> do not shut the gates
> for you will see him come now!
> . . . .
> Open up, Hell, for you are conquered!)

True to the script, Hell responds by reformulating the "Quis est iste
rex gloriae?" passage:

Chi è l'uom cusì fervente,
qual'è re de gloria ditto? (Vv. 145–46)

(Who is this man who is so fervent,
who is called the King of glory?)

At this point, an angel's voice cries out to Hell:

O voie, principe de male,
aprite quiste vostre porte!
Comando a voie, porte eternale,
che levare siate acorte,
che quell'Alto gloria Rene
per entrare qua entro viene. (Vv. 157–62)

(Oh you, prince of evil,
open these gates of yours!
I command you, eternal gates,
to be ready to open
because that mighty King of glory
is about to come here to enter.)

Then suddenly Christ, bearing the cross, arrives and smashes Hell's gates. Stunned, Hell shrieks a series of desperate questions (cf. *Descensus* A, chap. 6):

Chi se' tu che me descioglie,
quil che el mortal peccato lega?
Chi se' tu, ch'el Limbo spoglie,
enverso te ciascun si priega?
Chi se' tu tal combattetore,
ch'haie vento el nostro gran furore? (Vv. 205–10)

(Who are you who unlocks me,
I who mortal sin contain?
Who are you who despoils limbo,
and to whom everyone kneels?
Who are you, mighty warrior,
who have overwhelmed our great furor?)

Christ overpowers Satan, binds him, and banishes him to the furthest reaches of hell:

Satan, tu haie data nulla pena
a l'uom molto temporale,
legar te voie con mia catena
che tu non faccia a lor più male!
Enfin al novissimo dine
per mia virtù starai cusine. (Vv. 229–34)

(Satan, you have caused
frail, timebound man much grief;
I want to tie you with my chain
so that you will no longer hurt him!
Until Judgement Day you will remain
this way by virtue of my power.)

Then he extends his hand to the just of the Old Testament, starting
with Adam, and takes them out of hell:

E voie, sante miei, venite,
quil ch'a mia 'magene fatte sete!

JESUS ad sanctos:

Voie sarete recomparate
per lo legno cruciato,
ch'eravate prima dannate
per lo legno già vetato.
O Adam, mo pace sia
a te colla tua compagnia!

Iterum:

E voie, che foste el primo pate,
vien de fuore emprimamente,
e voie, figliuoglie, el seguitate;
Abel, Abeth, buon servente,
David, Aronne, e Moises,
Isaia cogli altri quagiù messe. (Vv. 251–64)

(And you, my saints, come, you
who are made in my image!

JESUS to the saints:

You will be redeemed
by virtue of the wood of the Crucifixion,
you who had been damned
because of the wood of the forbidden tree.
Oh Adam, may peace now accompany
you and yours.

He continues:

And you, who were the first father,
come out first,
and you, my children, follow him;
Abel, Abeth, good servant,

David, Aaron and Moses,
Isaiah and all the others down here.)

At this climactic point (v. 265), with the transition from "tristitia" to "gaudium," the solemn *passionale* mode gives way to the celebratory *pasquale* manner.[44]

> Alleluia cantiamo
> ché noie andiam con Cristo Salvatore!
> Tutte te confessiamo
> che se' encarnato per noie Redentore;
> o benegno Signore,
> che per le peccator sangue haie versato,
> al mondo quisto canto
> tu fa' sentir, che tanto t'è costato. (Vv. 297–304)

> (Let us sing alleluia
> because we are going with Christ the Savior!
> We all confess to you
> who became man in order to be our Redeemer;
> oh kind Lord,
> who have shed your blood for sinners,
> let this song, which has cost you so much,
> be heard throughout the world.)

The scene now shifts to paradise: Christ hands the just to the Archangel Gabriel (and not Michael as in the *Descensus*) to be led into "l'alto regno." There they meet Enoch and Elijah and then Dysmas, the Good Thief. The *lauda* ends with Christ announcing his imminent visit to his mother, who along with Mary Magdalene has been weeping for him at the sepulcher. The two Perugian Resurrection *laude*[45] both begin with Mary in tears at Christ's tomb. The second of the two ends with a reference to Christ's triumph in limbo (vv. 75–76).

As this brief summary indicates, this *devozione* closely follows *Descensus* A, chapters 2–10 (i.e., *EN* A, chaps. 18–26). It deviates from the chronology of this text on two occasions only. It does away completely with the Seth episode (chap. 3) and introduces a new scene (vv. 163–98) involving the Good and Bad Thieves immediately before Christ's Descent into limbo. There is no such scene in *Descensus* A. In *Descensus* B (chap. 7) the Good Thief precedes Christ into hell and announces his imminent arrival. However, the new scene in our *lauda* has little to do with the episode in *Descensus* B. Rather it seems to be

---

[44] De Bartholomaeis, *Origini della poesia drammatica*, 223–24.
[45] For the text, see De Bartholomaeis, *Laude drammatiche*, 1:259–69.

an imaginative elaboration of chapter 10 of the *Gesta Pilati*. In the *lauda* it is the Bad Thief, Gestas, identified by name, who precedes Christ into hell. Lamenting his fate, he is led by demons to Satan, who greets him ironically: "Ben venga Gestas, el mio deletto! / voie che tu gode del mio regno" (vv. 181–82; "Do come oh Gestas, my beloved! / I want you to enjoy my kingdom"). The scene shifts to Christ on the cross, who sends the Good Thief, Dysmas, to paradise. He is met there by the Archangel Gabriel, who admits him into the heavenly realm: "Volentier t'apro e sta' en buon cuore" (v. 197; "I open the gates gladly and welcome you"). At the very end of the *lauda* (vv. 345–60), the just find the Good Thief in paradise and converse with him. This final sequence follows *Descensus* A, chapter 10, and is in the right chronological slot. Nonetheless, there seems to be considerable confusion as to how the Good Thief got to paradise, since in verses 289–96 he is harrowed out of hell along with the Hebrew fathers. The fusion of two separate *laude* may account for the presence in this *devozione* of two versions of the Good Thief's assumption into heaven. Despite these anomalies, the *devozione* is remarkably faithful to *Descensus* A, which seems to be its only source. De Bartholomaeis makes the odd suggestion that the authors of this *devozione* used Jacobus a Voragine's summary in the *Legenda aurea* as a guide for the exclusion of episodes in their dramatization of the apocryphon.[46] The only substantial portion of the *Descensus* that the Perugian *devozione* excludes is the Seth episode, which the *Legenda aurea* includes.

I have devoted some time to the *laudario perugino* because of its acknowledged position at the head of the Italian religious dramatic tradition and because of its enormous influence on the *laudari* of other cities. Also, as we have seen, it did much to popularize the *EN*, the *Descensus* portion in particular. The Perugian Holy Saturday *lauda* became a source for subsequent Harrowing *laude* and Harrowing sequences in Passion and Resurrection plays. At least two other major collections of *laude* containing separate Harrowing plays have come down to us: one from Orvieto,[47] the other from L'Aquila in the Abruzzi.[48] In 1405 Tramo Da Lonardo put together an anthology of *laude* of the *Disciplinati* of Orvieto, referred to as *ripresentationi* or *devotioni*. The Descent into Hell was presented on Easter. Unfortunately, the first part of this *devozione* is missing, but its dependence on the Perugian *lauda*

---

[46] De Bartholomaeis, *Origini della poesia drammatica*, 305.

[47] For the text, see Annibale Tenneroni, ed., *Sacre rappresentazioni per le fraternite d'Orvieto nel Codice Vittorio Emmanuele 528* (Rome: Tipografia del Senato di Giovanni Bardi, 1914), 57–60.

[48] For the text, see Vincenzo De Bartholomaeis, ed., *Il teatro abruzzese del medio evo* (Bologna: Zanichelli, 1924), 32–40.

is obvious. For instance, at the moment of the liberation of the patriarchs from hell, the meter changes from the *passionale* to the *pasquale*
mode, as it does in the Perugian *lauda*.[49] The next *devozione* for Easter
Monday on the apparition of Christ to the Virgin also resonates with
echoes of the Harrowing.[50] The theme was obviously an important
one in Orvieto.

The *laudario* of the *Disciplinati* of San Tommaso of L'Aquila was
compiled during the second half of the fifteenth century, but contains
pieces which are much earlier. One of these is a Harrowing *lauda*, *La
devotione della festa de Pasqua*, which probably dates from the end of the
fourteenth century or the beginning of the fifteenth. The Perugian
lauda's influence on it is less pronounced, and certainly not of a metrical order. The *Disciplinati* of San Tommaso did away completely with
the *pasquale* mode. They also altered the verse form of the *sestina*,
discarding the octosyllabic verse in favor of the hendecasyllable. These
metrical changes facilitated the speaking of parts. In L'Aquila the
devozione was no longer a ritual, closely tied to the liturgy, as it was in
Perugia, but a spectacle, spoken rather than sung, for special feast
days. Consequently, the staging became more elaborate, and the
performance in due course moved out of the Church and into the
square.

The *Disciplinati* of San Tommaso's attitude toward sources was
also quite different. A comparison between the Perugian Harrowing
lauda and the L'Aquila *devozione* for Easter will bring this into focus. As
I have already noted, the Perugian *lauda* depends almost exclusively on
Descensus A, from which it rarely strays. It is a dramatic verse adaptation, sometimes almost a translation, of a single text. Moreover, the
sequence of scenes, except for the spurious scene (vv. 163–68) involving the two Thieves, follows exactly the narrative of *Descensus* A. On
the other hand, the *devozione* from L'Aquila is sustained by many texts,
the most important of which is almost certainly an abridged Italian
translation of *EN* B, very similar to one found in the Riccardiana
manuscript published by Suchier.[51] For instance, Adam's words in
stanza 44 clearly echo the B text (cf. *Descensus* B, chap. 9.1): "Questa è
la mani del mio Criatore / che è venuto al Limbo ad liberarne!" ("This
is the hand of my Creator / who came to limbo to free me!"). Moreover, in the Easter *devozione* from the Abruzzi, as in the Riccardiana
GN, Karinus and Leucius become Alexander and Rufus. However, in

---

[49] De Bartholomaeis, *Origini della poesia drammatica*, 258.
[50] For the text, see Tenneroni, *Sacre rappresentazioni*, 60–65; also published in
Toschi, *L'antico dramma sacro*, 1:201–15.
[51] Suchier, *Denkmäler*, 573–88.

the *devozione,* the role of the mute narrators of the *Descensus* is expanded: they become characters in the action with speaking parts.

The subject matter of the *Descensus* dominates the *devozione* (51 of
74 stanzas), but this material is framed by the last chapters (12 to 15 in
particular) of the *Gesta Pilati,* which deals with the various other (indirect) accounts of Christ's Resurrection (that of the three rabbis from
Galilee, that of the soldiers guarding the sepulcher, and that of Joseph
of Arimathea). The *devozione* begins with the arrest and imprisonment
of Joseph of Arimathea (sts. 1–5). Then the scene shifts abruptly to the
arrival of the Good Thief in paradise, where he is greeted by an angel
(sts. 6–9). Next we are plunged into limbo, where, we are told by
Adam, the patriarchs have been in a state of high expectation ever
since John the Baptist announced to them the coming of Christ (sts. 10–
12). Several patriarchs and prophets (Isaiah, Simeon, John the Baptist,
Noah, Seth, Moses, David, Aaron, and Joshua), not all of whom appear
in the *Descensus,* step forward and recall the words with which they
prophesied this event (sts. 13–33). Next a messenger arrives and warns
Satanasso of Christ's approach (sts. 34–36):

> Quisto scì è quillo che Laçaro suscitòne:
> Verrà quagiù lo Limbo a despogliare,
> Se tu no fay bona provisione;
> Lu Limbo et lu Inferno fa bene inserrare;
> Se non te providi, vì che tte llo dico,
> Serray legato chomo sou inimicho. (St. 35)

> (This man is the one who raised Lazarus
> from the dead: he will descend to despoil limbo
> if you do not make good provisions;
> it would be wise to lock limbo and hell;
> if you do not act, as I am telling you,
> you will be made his prisoner.)

The *Descensus* figures of Satan and Hell (*Inferus*) are somewhat blurred
in this passage. However, it is clear that Satanasso in the *devozione*
is Hell. The Satan of the *Descensus,* on the other hand, is referred to
as Luciferu, but he does not speak. He is present only to be bound.
Needless to say, the dispute between the two infernal princes which
precedes Christ's arrival in hell in the *Descensus* is absent from the
devozione.

In the next scene, Christ arrives and binds Lucifer (sts. 37–42). The
patriarchs are then freed, starting with Adam (sts. 43–45). As Christ
instructs an angel to take the patriarchs into heaven, Rufus moves
forward and begs that he and his brother, "figlioly del devoto tuo
Simone" ("the sons of the devout Simon"), be released. Christ obliges

and commands them to make his deed known to the world (sts. 46–47):

> Per quella carità c'abbe Simone,
> Voglio che nel mundo ritornete;
> Dentro nel Templo ne fayte mentione,
> Ad tucto el populo parlete:
> "El Limbo delly boni à spolliatu,
> In eterno Lucibello à incatenatu!" (St. 47)

> (By virtue of that charity that Simon had,
> I want you to return to the world;
> you are to mention this in the temple,
> and to everyone you will announce:
> "The good have been freed from limbo;
> Lucifer has been chained for all eternity!")

A stage direction explains that Rufus and Alexander remain in their tomb until Joseph of Arimathea is freed. This happens next (sts. 48–50), and Rufus and Alexander go to the Hebrew authorities to tell their story (sts. 51–54). Rufus's account of the Harrowing echoes Dante's brief evocation of the event in *Inferno* 4 (vv. 55–63):

> Trassene Adamo el primo parente,
> Abraam, Aaron, David et Zaccharìa,
> Moyses che fó tanto hobediente,
> Simone, Sette, Johanni et Jsaya;
> Et Patriarcha con altri Beati
> Tucti io li vidi insemi liberati. (St. 54)

> (He freed from limbo Adam, the first father,
> Abraham, Aaron, David and Zachariah,
> Moses who was so obedient,
> Simon, Seth, John and Isaiah;
> the patriarchs with other blessed ones,
> I saw them all freed together.)

Caiaphas and Annas accuse the two brothers of heresy and have them arrested.

A series of short scenes now follows in quick succession. Caiaphas and Annas order that Joseph be brought before them to be punished, but Joseph, his house still under lock and key, has disappeared (sts. 55–60). Some pilgrims arrive in Jerusalem and are brought to Caiaphas and Annas to be questioned. The pilgrims, whose role recalls that of the three rabbis in *Gesta Pilati*, chapter 14, declare that Christ has risen from the dead and is now among his disciples in Galilee (sts. 61–65). As Annas refutes their claim, the soldiers guarding Christ's sepulcher (cf. *Gesta Pilati*, chap. 13) enter and confirm Christ's Resurrection (sts.

66–69). On hearing this, Caiaphas and Annas decide that it would be undesirable for this news to be spread. They bribe the soldiers and the pilgrims to keep quiet (sts. 70–72; cf. *Gesta Pilati*, chaps. 13 and 14). The final two stanzas deal with the release of Rufus and Alexander from prison by an angel. Christ's words in the last stanza (74) are identical to those he pronounced in stanza 47 after freeing the two from limbo. This may indicate that these stanzas are misplaced in the manuscript,[52] but at this point in the *devozione* the two brothers are, in fact, in prison (cf. st. 56). Whatever the case, the action seems to be incomplete, although the *devozione* is duly concluded, as is typical in this collection, with a lyrical *lauda*.

With reference to the play's sources, we are far from the simple intertextuality of the Perugian *lauda* with its uncompromising fidelity to *Descensus* A. Here the scope has been widened to include the last chapters of the *Gesta Pilati*, but this material has been dismantled and redistributed. Large portions have been eliminated. Other texts have come into play to contaminate the primary source, which is almost certainly, as I have indicated, an abridged B text of the *EN*, even though the order of the *Descensus* sequences sometimes suggests the A text. This is probably due to the influence of the Perugian Harrowing *lauda*. Interestingly, however, the Perugian *lauda*'s presence is strongest in the Good Thief episode, which is out of place. In addition to Dante's *Commedia*, another probable source is the *Lamentatio abruzzese*.

In the lyrical *lauda* (sts. 75–82) that concludes the *devozione*, the freeing of the patriarchs from hell becomes a metaphor for the Redemption:

> Laudemo tucti el Criator Superno,
> Oggi ci liberòne dallo Inferno;
> In Paradiso menonci.
> . . . .
> O summo Dio, eterno Redemptore,
> De questa terra caccia via lu errore!
> O Signor, perdonancy! (Sts. 75, 82)

> (Let us all praise the supreme Creator,
> who today freed us from hell
> and led us into paradise.
> . . . .
> Oh mighty God, eternal Redeemer,
> banish sin from this world!
> Oh Lord, forgive us!)

---

[52] De Bartholomaeis, *Origini della poesia drammatica*, 306.

Given the triumphal nature of the Harrowing theme, this association was not uncommon,[53] but here it is expressed in rather simple terms. On the other hand, in a late fourteenth- or early fifteenth-century Florentine play, entitled *Il contrasto di Belzabù e Satanasso*, the idea takes on a theological dimension. This play is significant from several perspectives, including the history of medieval Italian theater, once identified exclusively with the Florentine *sacra rappresentazione* which flourished in the second half of the fifteenth century. Written in *sestine* of hendecasyllables, like the *devozione* from L'Aquila, it stands midway between the Perugian *laude* and the Florentine *sacre rappresentazioni* in *ottava rima*.

Despite its title, we are dealing essentially with a Descent into Hell play, drawn from *Descensus B* and perhaps other Harrowing plays like those from Perugia and L'Aquila. What distinguishes the Florentine play is that the *Descensus* has come into contact with the genre of the *piato* or dispute, and, in particular, with *Il Piato ch'ebbe Dio col Nemico*, published by Roediger along with *Il contrasto di Belzabù e Satanasso* in *Contrasti antichi: Cristo e Satana*.[54] *Il Piato* takes its cue from the *Descensus*. The opening scene has Christ dying on the cross and descending into limbo, where he remains until Easter morning, forty hours later, at which time he delivers the patriarchs out of hell.[55] The devil ("lo dimonio") is present throughout the Passion monitoring events, moving back and forth from limbo several times:

> Essendo Christo crocifixo in su la croce, lo nimico ne facea grande allegressa; andando et tornando molto spesso dal limbo, vide l'alegressa de li santi: incontenente congnoue la sua confuxione. (Ll. 4–7)

> (After Christ had been crucified on the cross, his enemy was extremely happy; he came and went often from limbo, and saw the happiness of the saints: his confusion knew no limits.)

The rest—the work is 261 lines long—consists of an animated theological discussion between God and the devil concerning the justice of the Redemption. The devil argues that with Original Sin he has acquired legal rights over man:

---

[53] Jean Monnier, *La Descente aux enfers, étude de pensée religieuse, d'art et de littérature* (Paris: Fischbacher, 1904), discusses this association.

[54] See Friedrich Roediger, *Contrasti antichi: Cristo e Satana* (Florence: Alla Libreria Dante, 1887), 35–48, 49–72.

[55] Ibid., 31–33.

Disse lo dimonio: Io prouo che l'omo de' essere mio per legge
vsata et anticata che non mi de' mai essere tolto. (Ll. 22–24)

(The demon said: I maintain that, in accordance with established and ancient law, man belongs to me and he can never
be taken away from me.)

The *Descensus*, of course, does not concern itself explicitly with theological issues. It is principally a glorification of Christ, who descends
into hell and defeats the forces of evil. These submit to his power; they
do not argue the legality of his action.[56]

More than the content, *Il Piato* determines the shape of *Il contrasto*.
The play begins with a debate between Belzabù and Satanasso, who
correspond to Satan and Hell (*Inferus*), respectively, in the *Descensus*.
This scene is based on the episode in the *Descensus* where the two
infernal princes argue about what action is to be taken in preparation
for Christ's arrival in hell. However, this episode, completely suppressed in the *devozione* from L'Aquila, is here greatly expanded and
moved to a position of prominence, at the beginning of the play (sts.
1–18). Belzabù, like *lo dimonio* in *Il Piato*, moves back and forth between
earth and limbo, reporting on Christ's trial, Crucifixion, and death.
This technique of reporting events rather than representing them is
highly effective, and allows the author to contextualize the situation
quickly by bringing into the picture events narrated in the *Gesta*. The
next sixteen stanzas (19–34) deal with the prophecies of the patriarchs,
the opening of the gate, and the liberation of the just. The triumphant
element is understated: there is, for instance, no binding of Belzabù.
Rather the focus is on the significance of the Passion. Christ's death on
the cross is seen as the ransom price to be paid for the Redemption of
man, who with Original Sin had fallen under the devil's control:

> Io son Giesù per nome chiamato,
> morto so'stato in sulla dura crocie
> per riconp(e)rare d'Adamo il peccato:
> (chè) tu-llo ingannasti, nimico ferocie.
> Ronpete le porti et gittatele via,
> sicchè entri dentro il figliuol(o) di Maria! (St. 31)

> (I am called Jesus,
> I died on the hard cross
> to redeem the sin of Adam:
> you tricked him, fierce enemy.
> Break down the gates and cast them aside
> so that the son of Mary may enter.)

---

[56] Cf. Ibid, 55.

It is the so-called Latin or "juridical" theory of the Redemption which
is being put forward here.[57] In this context, it is not surprising that
Adam and Eve are given more attention than in other Harrowing plays:

> O Adamo che da me fusti creato
> et dettiti Eva per tua compagnia,
> poi commettesti qvel tale peccato,
> ch'io ne sono oggi morto in qvesta dia,
> la vostra colpa è oggi rimessa,
> ora venite alla patria promessa. (St. 32)

> (Oh Adam, whom I created
> and to whom I gave Eve as your companion,
> you committed that sin,
> for which I have died on this day;
> your sin has been redeemed today,
> now come to the promised land with me.)

In the last part of the play (sts. 35–50), the influence of *Il Piato* is
strongest. Adam and Eve and the other patriarchs have been delivered
(st. 34), but Christ is detained in hell by Satanasso, who insists that a
great injustice is being committed against him:

> Tu-ssai ben, Yesù, ch'io guadagniai
> Adamo, primo vom(o), per mio sapere.
> Lasciato posseder(e) tu sì me l'ài,
> Sanza niuna lite o qvistione avere:
> Adamo con costoro ò posseduto,
> et mai a-tte non renderon(o) trebuto. (St. 37)

> (Jesus, you know well that I gained
> power over Adam by virtue of my knowledge.
> You allowed me to possess him
> without resistance or debate:
> I have jurisdiction over Adam and the others;
> they have never paid tribute to you.)

Christ refutes this claim:

> Non per saper(e) gli auesti; (ma) per inganni
> Adamo ed Eva, anzi gl'ingannasti;
> promettendo lor ben(e) desti lor danni,
> del paradiso cacciar(e gli) procurasti. . . . (St. 38)

---

[57] On this subject, see Gustav Aulén, *Christus Victor* (London: S. P. C. K.,
1970), 81–100.

(You did not gain control over them
through knowledge but through deception.
In fact, you deceived Adam and Eve
by promising them good, but instead you gave them
only grief, and you caused them
to be banished from the earthly paradise....)

The tone of the debate soon drops: the juridical gives way to the comical. Realizing that he has no chance of prevailing, Satanasso stoops to bargain. Christ can have the souls of limbo, but he is to keep the living: "qve(gl)i del mondo lasciami possedere" (st. 41). The offer is promptly rejected. Satanasso now becomes more and more pathetic and ridiculous. One final, absurd proposal: take the men but leave the women in hell (st. 49). Christ will have none of this: "Nè femmina nè vomo aver potresti / di qvesta giente ch'aueui serrate" (st. 50; "You may keep neither the women nor the men of those people whom you have locked up"). Soon afterward, in mid-stanza, the play breaks off incomplete, but my impression is that the anonymous author had come to the end of his inspiration.

There are documents recording representations of other Harrowing plays now lost. For instance, we know that a representation "di Cristo quando spogliò l'Inferno" ("of Christ's Harrowing of Hell") was performed in Rome in 1473,[58] and that among the edifizi or stage settings that circulated in Florence during the festival of John the Baptist there was one for limbo.[59] Another index of the Harrowing's enormous popularity was that it often made its way into Passion and Resurrection plays. Of course, these same plays often also echoed, directly or indirectly, the Gesta Pilati. However, as I have already noted, it is more difficult to pinpoint the Gesta's presence in these texts, since so much of it is drawn from the canonical gospels. In this sense it is much easier to track the Descensus and the themes associated with it.

I shall now move on to some Passion and Resurrection plays where the Harrowing of Hell is either recalled or actually represented. This list is not intended to be complete;[60] it includes only those plays which are immediately accessible to me.

In the laudari we have discussed, the Descent into Hell was represented either on Holy Saturday (Perugia) or on Easter day (Orvieto, L'Aquila). In other words, it was associated more with the Resurrection

[58] Alessandro D'Ancona, Origini del teatro italiano (Turin: Loescher, 1891), 1:289.
[59] Ibid. 1:217–44.
[60] For a bibliography of Italian sacred drama, see Alfredo Cioni, Bibliografia delle sacre rappresentazioni (Florence: Sansoni Antiquariato, 1961).

than with the Passion. I am aware of only one major Good Friday *devozione* in which the Harrowing theme is pervasive. To be sure, the Descent into Hell is not represented directly; rather the details of the event are recounted in the speeches of various characters. The *devozione*, along with one for Maundy Thursday, is contained in a Venetian manuscript from the last quarter of the fourteenth century.[61] The language is shot through with Venetian, but the two *devozioni* may be Umbrian in origin. The Good Friday *devozione* begins with the flagellation and ends with the placement of Christ's body in the tomb by Joseph of Arimathea and Nicodemus. It also includes a moving lament of the Virgin, consoled by the Archangel Gabriel. The Harrowing dominates two important scenes. In the earlier scene (vv. 201–44), two souls are resuscitated from the dead through the power of the Passion. One of them addresses Christ on the cross and tells him in language reminiscent of Dante (*Inf.* 4.55–63) that the patriarchs anxiously await his arrival in limbo:

> Adamo primo nostro parente
> Sta aparechiato te aspetando;
> Abel, Noè, e Abraam obediente,
> Isaac e Iacob con ipso stando,
> Isaì, Ieremia e David fervente,
> Elia e altri prophete mercè chiamando,
> Et Moises legistro con lo vostro precursore
> Stano aspectando a vui, dolce Signore. (Vv. 233–40)

> (Adam our first father is ready
> and is waiting for you;
> Abel, Noah, and the obedient Abraham,
> Isaac and Jacob are with him
> as are Isaiah, Jeremiah and the fervent David,
> Elijah, and other prophets, all calling for mercy:
> and Moses the legislator with your precursor,
> they are waiting for you, oh sweet Lord.)

The other scene is more elaborate (vv. 362–428). As Christ is about to expire, Satanas ("lo Demonio") arrives and places himself on the right arm of the cross. He has come for Christ's soul, but first attempts to bargain with his foe (vv. 387–88). Christ rejects the proposal, and an animated debate ensues between the two, during which the main

---

[61] For the text of these two *devozioni*, see Alessandro D'Ancona, "Le devozioni del giovedì e del venerdì santo," *Rivista di filologia romanza* 2 (1875): 1–24, and Toschi, *L'antico dramma sacro*, 2:315–67. See also D'Ancona's discussion in *Origini del teatro italiano*, 1:184–207.

elements of the Harrowing (the storming of the gates, the binding of Satan, and the liberation of the just) are summarized (vv. 389–428).

In the course of the fifteenth century the ritual of performing *devozioni* throughout the liturgical year was gradually abandoned. Confraternities concentrated their efforts on a few major productions, at least one of which inevitably focused on the dramatic events of Easter week. This gave rise to the great Italian Passion plays of the fifteenth and sixteenth centuries from the Abruzzi, Rome, and Florence. Indeed, according to the statutes of the Confraternity of the Gonfalone, one of its principal functions was to "represent the Passion of Christ."[62] Founded in 1486, the Arciconfraternita del Gonfalone combined several Roman associations of *Disciplinati*. In addition to the Passion play elaborately staged at the Colosseum on Good Friday, the Roman Confraternity put on a Resurrection play at Saint John Lateran or Saint Peter's. Later, in the sixteenth century, the Resurrection play too was staged at the Colosseum. These plays usually compressed and combined several existing shorter dramas treating episodes leading up to and following the Passion. By far the most famous of the Italian Passion plays was *La passione del Colosseo*. In its early versions this play contained a scene set in limbo, but this episode was excised in later versions. It does not appear, for instance, in the version in octaves which bears the names of Giuliano Dati and others. First printed in 1496, this version was republished several times during the sixteenth century.[63] Unfortunately, the limbo scene is also missing from the archaic version in *sestine*, published by De Bartholomaeis.[64] However, here its absence is due simply to the fact that the only surviving copy of an early popular edition of the play used by De Bartholomaeis is mutilated.

The Dati version of *La passione del Colosseo* is 179 stanzas; the Abruzzese *passione* is over 300 stanzas. The longest of the Italian Passion plays at 600 octaves is a highly derivative Florentine play contained in a late fifteenth-century compilation.[65] This Passion play should not be confused with the more modest (85 stanzas) *La rappresentazione della cena e passione* by Castellano Castellani, which has been

[62] De Bartholomaeis, *Origini della poesia drammatica*, 365.

[63] See Fabrizio Cruciani, *Teatro nel Rinascimento: Roma 1450–1550* (Rome: Bulzoni, 1983), 263–70; for the text, see Girolamo Amati, ed., *La passione di Cristo in rima volgare secondo che recita e rappresenta da parola a parola la dignissima compagnia del Gonfalone di Roma il venerdì santo in luogo detto il Colosseo* (Rome: Sinimberghi, 1866).

[64] *Laude drammatiche*, 2:154–83.

[65] De Bartholomaeis, *Origini della poesia drammatica*, 404–8.

published several times.[66] These plays are huge if compared with the *devozioni* of the fourteenth century, which averaged 300 to 400 verses, but they are insignificant if measured against *La passione di Revello*, which stands in a category by itself.[67] It is as close as Italy comes to the massive French mystery plays. Presented over a three-day period in 1490, the Revello Passion spans some 13,000 verses. Despite its name, the play covers the whole history of man's Redemption through to the Resurrection. A certain Fra Simone seems to have been entrusted with the drafting of the text. Well-versed in theology if not in poetry, Fra Simone taps a large number of sources to realize his vision.[68] One of these is the *GN*. The *Gesta Pilati* is extensively used in Day Two, from verse 1282 on, and a condensed *Descensus A*, complete with a scene in paradise with Enoch and Elijah, is reenacted on Day Three (vv. 1936–2051) near the end of the play, i.e., within the context of the Resurrection. The position of the Harrowing sequence in *La passione di Revello* underscores the fact that the Descent into Hell is more easily absorbed into Resurrection than Passion plays.

There is a short but interesting Harrowing sequence (vv. 781–834) in the Roman Resurrection Play.[69] It begins with the holy fathers in limbo singing a song in praise of God. As soon as their song ends, Christ appears and knocks on the infernal gates. Satan arrogantly rebukes him, demanding to know who it is that has come to disturb his realm. Christ exclaims:

Che tardi tu, Satan perché non apri
A me che voglio il Limbo dispogliato? (Vv. 799–800)

(What are you waiting for, Satan, why won't you open the gates for me who want to despoil limbo?)

Satan remains defiant. At this point the apocryphon is pushed aside and the words of Psalm 23:9–10 in Latin are called forth and dramatized:

CRISTO *batte un'altra volta e dice:*

Attollite portas, Principes, vestras, et elevamini, portae aeternales, et introibit Rex gloriae.

---

[66] See, for instance, Luigi Banfi, ed., *Sacre rappresentazioni del Quattrocento* (Turin: UTET, 1963), 325–72.
[67] Anna Cornagliotti, ed., *La passione di Revello* (Turin: Centro Studi Piemontesi, 1976).
[68] These sources are listed by Cornagliotti in the introduction to her edition of *La passione di Revello*, xxxiv–xlvii.
[69] De Bartholomaeis, *Laude drammatiche*, 2:183–96.

SATAN *risponde:*

Quis est iste Rex gloriae?

CRISTO *risponde:*

Dominus fortis est in praelio, ipse est Rex gloriae! (Vv. 803–5)

(CHRIST *knocks again and says:*

Lift up your gates, Princes, and raise up the eternal gates, and the King of glory shall come in.

SATAN *answers:*

Who is this King of glory?

CHRIST *answers:*

The Lord mighty in battle, he is the King of glory!)

Then quickly Christ forces the gates open, chains Satan, and frees the holy fathers. "Vien fuora" ("Come out") he cries repeatedly as he leads them out of hell. Freed from the abyss, the holy fathers kneel and sing "Adoramus te."

The *Festum Resurrectionis,*[70] a short (120 verses in all) fifteenth-century Resurrection play from Pordenone in the Veneto region, similarly appropriates Psalm 23. The action in the thirteen-verse Harrowing sequence, with which the play begins, is reduced to its bare essentials. It takes its cue from chapter 2 of *Descensus* A. A light pierces the engulfing darkness of limbo, and Adam exclaims:

> Quest'è la luce del Segnore mio,
> quest'è lo lume del Figliuol de Dio!
> Noi te avemo pur chiamato tanto,
> che hai udito il nostro amaro pianto.
> O Redentore de l'umana carne,
> tu se' venuto pur a liberarne. (Vv. 1–6)

> (This is the light of my Lord, this
> is the light of the Son of God!
> We have called you so much
> that you have heard our sad cries.
> Oh Redeemer of man, you have
> now come to free us.)

---

[70] For the text, see De Bartholomaeis, *Laude drammatiche,* 2:297–302.

Isaiah relates his prophecy concerning this light by quoting Isaiah 9:2. Here Italian gives way to Latin, preparing the stage for the dramatic exchange between Christ and Infernus taken from Vulgate Psalm 23:9–10. The sequence ends here. A stage direction informs us that Christ despoils hell.

The Harrowing episode in an anonymous fifteenth-century Florentine Resurrection Play[71] is almost as long as the whole of the *Festum Resurrectionis*. It occupies 15 of 106 octaves (sts. 10 to 24). The episodic structure of this *sacra rappresentazione* indicates that it is a reworking of several shorter plays or *laude*. The Harrowing episode is clearly indebted to the Perugian Holy Saturday *devozione* or one very similar to it. The original model—*Descensus A*—is further in the background. The anonymous author may not even have known the apocryphon directly. The narrative has been shortened, but some new details have been added for dramatic effect. Christ carrying a banner figuring the cross and flanked by two angels appears suddenly and announces his intention to free the souls of limbo. Then he descends into hell and ties Satanasso. Unlike the Roman Satan, the Florentine Satanasso is not defiant. He acknowledges the power of Christ and acquiesces:

> Dapoi che tanto onore t'è concesso,
> per forza tremo, e te Signor confesso. (St. 14)

> (Since so much honor has been granted to you,
> I tremble before your strength, and acknowledge you as
>   Lord.)

He seems to be a conflation of the figures of Satan and Inferus in the *Descensus*. Christ calls the patriarchs to himself and leads them to freedom.

> Adam, vien fuor del limbo e di prigione,
> e tu, Abram, principal patriarca,
> ancor tu Josuè, cor di leone,
> e tu, Noè, che fabricasti l'arca.
> Esca qua fuor il forte Gedeone,
> e David, re de' profeti, monarca.
> E tutti gli altri con gran festa e riso
> venitene al terrestre paradiso. (St. 15)

> (Adam, come out of limbo and prison,
> and you, Abraham, the principal patriarch,
> and you too, Joshua, the lion-hearted,

---

[71] For the text, see Banfi, *Sacre rappresentazioni del Quattrocento*, 373–422.

and you, Noah, who built the ark.
Come out, strong Gideon and David,
King of the prophets and monarch.
And all the others, with joy and laughter,
come with me to the earthly paradise.)

Adam thanks him on behalf of them all. Next several of the patriarchs
step forward and speak. Each bears in hand an object which identifies
him. Noah, for example, carries an ark. Turning to the others he says:

> Questo legno de l'arca sublimato
> dimostra nostra grande esaltazione. (St. 17)

> (This wood representing the ark
> demonstrates our great exaltation.)

David, holding a psalter, says:

> Questo saltér letifica il cor mio;
> sonando io canterò le laude a Dio. (St. 17)

> (This psalter delights my heart;
> by playing it, I praise the Lord.)

Then he begins to sing, "Misericordias domini in eternum cantabo."
The others join in as they proceed to the earthly paradise. A stage
direction tells us that it is located on top of a mountain and is guarded
by an angel with sword in hand. This detail betrays the influence of
Dante, visible elsewhere in the play. There they meet the Good Thief
and then Enoch and Elijah. Like the Umbrian *lauda*, the episode ends
with Christ announcing his intention to visit and console his mother:

> Restate ch'i' vo' prima visitare
> mia madre santa, e quella consolare. (St. 24)

> (Stay here while I go to visit
> my saintly mother and console her.)

There is no doubt that the *EN*'s impact—and that of the *Descensus*
in particular—was greatest in drama, but the work, as I have already
indicated, also left its mark on other areas of medieval Italian literature. Federico Frezzi, for example, dedicates a chapter to "Limbo and
Original Sin" with a Harrowing sequence in *Il Quadriregio* 2.4, an uninspired imitation of Dante's *Commedia*.[72] However, with the exception
of Dante, whom I shall discuss in a moment, the most ambitious and

---

[72] Federico Frezzi, *Il Quadriregio*, ed. Enrico Filippini (Bari: Laterza, 1914).

complex adaptation of the *Descensus* belongs to the fourteenth-century Sienese poet, Niccolò Cicerchia. The first part or *cantare* (85 octaves) of his long narrative poem entitled *La Risurrezione* is an imaginative amplification of *Descensus A*, which he probably knew in an Italian translation. The second part, which deals more specifically with the events of the Resurrection proper, adapts portions of the *Gesta Pilati*—chapter 12 (sts. 3–15) and chapter 15 (sts. 120–26) in particular—but its major sources are the canonical gospels and the ubiquitous *Meditationes*. *La Risurrezione* was written sometime after 1364, the date of composition of *La Passione*, Cicerchia's other, more fortunate narrative poem in *ottava rima*. It too taps the *Gesta Pilati* (see st. 107, for instance), but not as extensively or as obviously. *La Passione*'s enormous popularity during the Renaissance was due, in part, to the fact that it was attributed during this period to either Petrarch or Boccaccio. Some work has been done on Cicerchia's sources, in particular by Varanini in his edition of *La Passione* and *La Risurrezione*,[73] but the Sienese poet's complex appropriations from the *EN* need to be investigated further.

Themes from the *EN*, especially the Harrowing, were also summoned up in sermons. Franco Sacchetti, for instance, better known to literary historians for his *Trecentonovelle*, dedicates the sermon for Holy Saturday to the Descent into Hell in his *Sermoni evangelici* (no. 46).[74] The presence of the apocryphon is even more frequent in what De Bartholomaeis aptly calls "sermoni semidrammatici" ("semidramatic sermons").[75] In this genre, which evolved in the fourteenth and fifteenth centuries, the preacher punctuated his sermon with dramatic *laude* and at times with other forms of poetry. This kind of preaching was used especially by the Franciscans in the remote mountainous regions of the Abruzzi. Alessandro de Ritiis was a proficient practitioner of the genre, as the selection from his *Sermonale* in the appendix to De Bartholomaeis's *Il teatro abruzzese del medio evo* illustrates.[76] His sermons are punctuated by dramatic *laude* and dramatizations of passages from Cicerchia's poems, which de Ritiis believed to be by Petrarch. However, this practice is by no means limited to the Abruzzi. The *Passione di Revello* incorporates sermons by Fra Simone. Perhaps the best example of this procedure from our perspective is the Venetian *devozione* for Good Friday, in which there are several indications

---

[73] Niccolò Cicerchia, "*La Passione* and *La Risurrezione*," in *Cantari religiosi senesi del Trecento*, ed. Giorgio Varanini (Bari: Laterza, 1965), 307–447. Varanini discusses Cicerchia's sources on pp. 542–51.

[74] Franco Sacchetti, *I sermoni evangelici*, ed. Ottavio Gigli (Florence: Le Monnier, 1857).

[75] *Origini della poesia drammatica*, 325–35.

[76] Pp. 317–28.

in the text that the action is suspended to give way to preaching: "Dito
questo, lo Predicatore predica" ("Having said this, the preacher begins
to preach"). This particular interruption comes in the midst of the animated debate between Christ and Satanas which I referred to earlier.
There is no doubt that the *EN* was a very dynamic and productive
text in the Italy of the Middle Ages and the early Renaissance. Both the
A and the B text were translated several times, it would appear. Moreover, it was repeatedly adapted, especially in dramatic form. Sometimes great care was taken not to deviate from the original too much;
at other times, it was elaborately reworked, bringing other sources into
play or redefining the material in relation to another genre. It was
amplified, and it was compressed to be inserted into a longer work.
But no one used the material more imaginatively and boldly than
Dante.

Dante knew the content of the *EN* from various sources. He had
probably read Vincent of Beauvais's and Jacobus a Voragine's summaries of the work, and was certainly familiar with theological accounts
of the Descent into Hell like that of Aquinas in the *Summa theologiae*
(3a, q. 52, ad 3). He may also have come into contact with a version of
the original text. Several details point in this direction. For instance, in
limbo he describes Christ at the Harrowing as "un possente, / con
segno di vittoria coronato" ("a mighty one, / crowned with the sign of
victory" [*Inf.* 4.53–54]).[77] The phrase "segno di vittoria" seems to echo
"signum victoriae," used in both *Descensus* A (chap. 8.1) and *Descensus*
B (chap. 10.1) to refer to Christ's cross. The souls of limbo plead with
Christ to leave it in hell as a sign of his victory over the forces of evil
and death. The reference to the blessed as "bianche stole" in *Paradiso*
30.129 recalls two passages in the Apocalypse in which St. John speaks
of the "white garments" of the elect (Rv. 3:5 and 7:13; cf. *Par.* 25.95),
but the metaphor may also have been suggested by the "stolas albas"
of *Descensus* A, chapter 11.1, i.e., the white robes that the souls harrowed by Christ from hell received after being baptized in the River
Jordan. In some versions of *Descensus* A, chapter 7.1, Beelzebub is
described as having three heads.[78] Dante's Lucifer, whom he also
calls Beelzebub in *Inferno* 34.127 is, of course, three-headed. More generally, Dante's representation of Lucifer as a grotesque, ice-bound creature banished to the bottom of hell's pit may have been influenced, in

[77] All quotations from Dante's *Commedia* are from Dante Alighieri, *La Commedia secondo l'antica vulgata*, 4 vols., ed. Giorgio Petrocchi (Milan: Mondadori, 1966–
67).
[78] Tischendorf, *Evangelia apocrypha*, 400; cf. Luigi Moraldi, ed., *Apocrifi del
Nuovo Testamento*, Classici delle religioni, sezione 5 (Turin: UTET, 1971), 633.

part, by the Satan of the *Descensus*, who after his defeat is chained and thrust into the abyss.

Traces of the *Gesta Pilati* are more difficult to discover. However, I would like to propose that the mysterious "colui / che fece per viltà il gran rifiuto" (*Inf.* 3.59–60; "the one who made, because of cowardice, the great refusal"), usually identified as Celestine V by the commentators,[79] may be a reference to Pilate and his vile act of washing his hands of Christ's fate. To be sure, Pilate's candidature has been put forward before[80] but not on the grounds that at this point in the poem Dante's major subtext, along with *Aeneid* 6, is the *EN*. In other words, the intertextual context of *Inferno* 3 and 4 strongly suggests Pilate as the unnamed soul who committed the "great refusal." The intertextual link between the *Commedia* and the apocryphon functions not only at the level of details, but also in a wider structural sense. I have argued elsewhere that Dante's two major narrative models in the *Inferno* are Book 6 of Virgil's *Aeneid* and the *Descensus Christi ad inferos.*[81] The canonical gospels offered no clear narrative pattern for him to follow in constructing his *poema sacro*. The *Descensus* was the closest thing to a Christian narrative epic that Dante could find. Thus Dante appropriated the Harrowing story, with its powerful dramatic imagery, artfully combined it with his classical narrative model, and generally used it to pattern his own descent into hell. He also turned to it to define structurally three of his most important episodes in the first *cantica.*

The structure of Dante's *Commedia* could not, of course, accommodate a direct representation of the Harrowing. Nevertheless, the most logical place to stage the Descent into Hell, using all the stock images available in the *Descensus* and other traditional accounts, would be *Inferno* 4. Dante's treatment of limbo, however, is unique. Taken as a whole, it departs completely from the preceding tradition, both theological and poetic. By creating the "nobile castello" ("noble castle"), which contains the virtuous pagans, Dante breaks with the concept of limbo that had evolved in the West from the New Testament through St. Augustine and Gregory the Great to St. Thomas. Dante also overturns the usual poetic representation of limbo by shifting the emphasis from the Harrowing of Hell to the "nobile castello."

---

[79] See Francesco Mazzoni's summary of the criticism on the subject in *Saggio di un nuovo commento alla Divina Commedia, Inferno, Canti I–III* (Florence: Sansoni, 1967), 390–415.

[80] See Mazzoni again for the summary of the criticism, ibid.

[81] Amilcare A. Iannucci, "Dottrina e allegoria in *Inferno* VIII, 67 – IX, 105," in *Dante e le forme dell'allegoresi*, ed. Michelangelo Picone (Ravenna: Longo, 1987), 99–124.

In his representation of limbo, Dante is interested in neither the "limbus puerorum" nor the "limbus patrum" and the Harrowing of Hell. He is concerned rather with the "limbus paganorum integrorum" or the "nobile castello," which he created to dramatize the tragic consequences of the Fall in that unredeemed period of time between Adam and Christ. Dante's stark evocation of the Harrowing in *Inferno* 4 is stripped of the bold agonistic imagery which vivifies traditional representations:

> ... Io era nuovo in questo stato,
> quando ci vidi venire un possente,
> con segno di vittoria coronato.
>   Trasseci l'ombra del primo parente,
> d'Abèl suo figlio e quella di Noè,
> di Moïsè legista e ubidente;
>   Abraàm patrïarca e Davìd re,
> Israèl con lo padre e co' suoi nati
> e con Rachele, per cui tanto fé,
>   e altri molti, e feceli beati.
> E vo' che sappi che, dinanzi ad essi,
> spiriti umani non eran salvati. (Vv. 52–63)

> (... I was new-entered on this state
> when I beheld a Great Lord enter here;
> the crown he wore, a sign of victory.
>   He carried off the shade of our first father,
> of his son Abel, and the shade of Noah,
> of Moses, the obedient legislator,
>   of father Abraham, David the king,
> of Israel, his father, and his sons,
> and Rachel, she for whom he worked so long,
>   and many others—and He made them blessed;
> and I should have you know that, before them,
> there were no human souls that had been saved.)[82]

The Harrowing is no longer the focal point of Dante's limbo. Its primary function is to set in dramatic relief the tragedy of the virtuous pagans. In its new context, the Harrowing announces not so much victory as defeat, for in his representation of limbo Dante transfers the poetic axis from those whom Christ released from the prison of hell to those who were left behind. By shifting the focus from comedy to

---

[82] The translation is by Allen Mandelbaum, *The Divine Comedy of Dante Alighieri. Inferno* (New York: Bantam Books, 1982).

tragedy, he succeeds in creating in his limbo one of the most gripping and poignant episodes in the entire *Commedia*. The poetic power of Dante's limbo lies precisely in the unexpected juxtaposition of two images—the Harrowing of Hell and the "nobile castello"—one an image of release and fulfilment, the other of confinement and melancholy, one of comedy and the other of tragedy. In order to emphasize the tragedy of unredeemed time, Dante deliberately dramatizes it in a context traditionally used by poets and theologians alike to represent the "comic" turning-point in history. Dante's limbo is a place not of jubilation but of sadness and the melancholy which results from the knowledge that one can never attain spiritual fulfilment: "sanza speme vivemo in disio" (*Inf.* 4.42; "without hope we live in desire"). In short, in *Inferno* 4 Dante downplays the imagery connected with the Descent into Hell because he wants to depict not the fullness of time—"plenitudo temporis"—but the emptiness of time.[83]

Dante is too alert to the dramatic possibilities of the imagery traditionally associated with the Harrowing of Hell to abandon it altogether. Instead he reworks it, blending Christian elements with pagan ones, and presents them in a new setting. Dante gives the revitalized imagery full play in the terrifying drama which takes place in front of the walls of the City of Dis (*Inf.* 8.67–9.105). Demons try to prevent Dante's and Virgil's entry into the city, and are supported by the three Furies and indeed the Medusa herself, who lurks menacingly in the background. Virgil, i.e., Reason, is unable to overcome the forces of evil unaided. But soon a divine being, an obvious analogue of Christ, descends from heaven to help them. He puts the devils and the Furies to flight, and then forces open the gate of the city (*Inf.* 9.88–90). The "messo" compares his mission to that of Hercules, who overpowered Cerberus when he rescued Theseus from Hades (*Inf.* 9.91–99). But obviously the pagan archetype is fused with the Christian one, for the "messo's" action also recalls that of Christ, who 1266 years earlier had unlocked that "less secret door" at the mouth of hell's pit:

> Questa lor tracotanza non è nova;
> ché già l'usaro a men segreta porta,
> la qual sanza serrame ancor si trova.
> Sovr' essa vedestù la scritta morta. (*Inf.* 8.124–27)

---

[83] For a more complete discussion of Dante's limbo from this perspective, see Amilcare A. Iannucci, "Limbo: The Emptiness of Time," *Studi danteschi* 52 (1979–80): 69–128.

(This insolence of theirs is nothing new;
they used it once before and at a gate
less secret—it is still without its bolts—
the place where you made out the fatal text.)[84]

The whole episode is an original and powerful stylistic reworking of the Harrowing of Hell, governed by the laws of Dante's cultural syncretism. Nonetheless, the inner meaning of the episode remains same as that of the Harrowing. This adaptation of the Descent, like the traditional version, celebrates the victory of the forces of good over the forces of evil, and man's release from the slavery of sin. Here it is Dante, and hence everyman, who is "harrowed" from hell. Actually, the divine messenger intervenes to make it possible for the pilgrim to descend into lower hell, into the mosqued City of Dis, as he must do if he is to ascend Mount Purgatory and rise into Paradise.[85]

The little *sacra rappresentazione* before the City of Dis illustrates how Dante injects new life into the familiar story simply by recasting it and presenting it in a new and unexpected context. In *Inferno* 2, Dante taps the motif if not the imagery of the Harrowing in a more subtle manner. In this episode Beatrice is not just a figure of her earthly self, or an allegory of revelation; rather she fulfils the role of Christ-figure she assumed in the *Vita Nuova*. Christ's last act in his first coming was to harrow hell. Beatrice's descent into limbo completes the analogy to Christ in his first coming established in the *Vita Nuova*. It should be noted that there is complete temporal (within the liturgical time frame of the poem) and spatial correspondence between Beatrice's descent into hell and Christ's. But in *Inferno* 2 the underlying structural model—the Harrowing of Hell—is not reinforced with the dramatic imagery usually associated with the theme. Instead, Beatrice's descent into limbo is presented in lyrical terms reminiscent of the *dolce stil nuovo*, which Dante used to describe her in the *Vita Nuova*. Nonetheless, Beatrice too enters hell triumphantly, although the imagery surrounding her descent is very subdued. Beatrice, like Christ, is not subject to the devil's power or hell's torment (*Inf.* 2.88–93). Moreover, Beatrice too "harrows" hell. She frees Dante and, by extension, mankind from the constraints of their self-made terrestrial hell, objectified in the metaphor of the "selva oscura" ("dark forest"). After all, it is she who overcomes the three beasts which collectively embody the sins of hell, and in particular the "lupa" ("she-wolf"), which was let loose by Satan himself (*Inf.* 1.111).

---

[84] Translation by Allen Mandelbaum.
[85] For a more detailed study of this episode, see Iannucci, "Dottrina e allegoria."

One more point. In traditional harrowings, as we have seen, Christ liberates Adam from hell first. This symbolic gesture emphasizes Christ's redemptive power and establishes a clear link between the man who first cast mankind into sin and the man who released us from it. Here it is Dante, who at one level of the prologue's allegory is an Adamic figure and at another everyman, who is set free by Beatrice.[86]

Despite the *Commedia's* immense influence and prestige, Dante's treatment of the apocryphon is so unique that it leaves few traces on the subsequent literature, except for the verbal echoes which I have signalled in the course of this essay. Post-dantesque representations of limbo remain, for the most part, tied to the *Evangelium Nicodemi,* and in Italy they never quite surpass the simple and naive beauty of the Perugian Holy Saturday *lauda.*

[86] For a more detailed study of this episode, see Amilcare A. Iannucci, "Beatrice in Limbo: A Metaphoric Harrowing of Hell," *Dante Studies* 97 (1979): 23–45.

The *Gospel of Nicodemus* in
Old English and Middle English[1]

C. W. MARX

his essay is concerned with questions of use, status and influence of the *Gospel of Nicodemus* in Old English and Middle English.[2] An important measure of influence and status is use, and use can be investigated through examining how materials have been organized in manuscripts, the compilation of sequences—be they narrative, meditative, devotional, or all three—and the adaptation and appropriation of texts to different genres of writing. But it is the manuscripts which have the most to tell us about how the *Gospel of Nicodemus* was used; and so, where possible, it is from the manuscripts that this essay draws much of its evidence.

Old English prose

The earliest manuscript containing an English text of the *Gospel of Nicodemus* is Cambridge University Library (CUL) MS. Ii. 2. 11, an Old

[1] I would like to acknowledge financial assistance from the Pantyfedwen Fund of University of Wales, Lampeter, which allowed me to consult manuscripts in various British repositories. I am grateful to Miss Suzanne Eward, Librarian and Keeper of Muniments at Salisbury Cathedral, and Mr. Roger Custance, Fellows' Librarian, Winchester College, for assistance with manuscripts in their collections. I would like to thank Dr. Janet Burton, Dr. Nicole Crossley-Holland, Prof. Zbigniew Izydorczyk, Prof. Derek Pearsall, and Dr. Oliver Pickering for their help in the preparation of this essay.

[2] Abbreviated *GN* when used generically or with reference to English and other vernacular versions. For the Latin text of the *Evangelium Nicodemi*, abbreviated *EN*, H. C. Kim's edition, *The Gospel of Nicodemus: Gesta Salvatoris*, Toronto Medieval Latin Texts, vol. 2 (Toronto: Pontifical Institute of Mediaeval Studies, 1973), is used throughout; the text is cited in the order of chapter, paragraph, and line number(s). Reference is made occasionally to the *EN* texts in Constantinus de Tischendorf's *Evangelia apocrypha*, 2d rev. ed. (Leipzig: H. Mendelssohn, 1876), 333–434.

English gospel book from the third quarter of the eleventh century.
The first item (fols. 2r–173r) is a translation of the gospels into West-
Saxon;[3] this is followed by the OE prose *Gospel of Nicodemus* (fols.
173v–93r)[4] and the last item (fols. 193r–202r), the *Vindicta Salvatoris* in
OE prose.[5] The manuscript was among the donations of Bishop Leofric (d. 1072) to Exeter Cathedral and can be identified in his list as
"þeos Englisce Cristes-boc"; as N. R. Ker and Max Förster have shown,
the copy of the donation list now in the Exeter Book originally belonged to this manuscript.[6] The status of the *GN* here is ambiguous: it
might be seen as a fifth gospel, and yet the way it is presented in the
manuscript suggests that it was of secondary importance. The beginnings of the four gospels are signalled by rubricated Latin incipits, and
each starts on a recto even though the facing verso has had to be left
blank for Mark (fol. 54v), Luke (fol. 84v) and John (fol. 132v). The *GN*,
on the other hand, begins at the top of fol. 173v, the verso of the last
page of John's gospel. The initial letter is enlarged to two lines and
illuminated; the text opens as follows:

On þære halgan þrynnysse naman, her ongynnað þa gedonan
þyng þe be urum hælende gedone wæron, eall swa Þeodosius
se mæra Casere hyt funde on Hierusalem on þæs Pontiscan

[3] Edited by Benjamin Thorpe, *Ða Halgan Godspel on Englisc: The Anglo-Saxon Version of the Holy Gospels* (London: J. G. F. and J. Rivington, 1842), and recently by R. Liuzza, *The Old English Version of the Gospels*, EETS OS, vol. 304 (London: Oxford University Press, 1994). Cf. N. R. Ker, *A Catalogue of Manuscripts Containing Anglo-Saxon* (Oxford: Clarendon Press, 1957), 28–31, no. 20; P. R. Robinson, *Catalogue of Dated and Datable Manuscripts c. 737–1600 in Cambridge Libraries*, 2 vols. (Cambridge: D. S. Brewer, 1988), 1:34, no. 55.
[4] Edited by W. H. Hulme, "The Old English Version of the Gospel of Nico-demus," *PMLA* 13 (1898): 457–542; the text from this manuscript is presented on pp. 471–515 in parallel with that in London, British Library (BL) MS. Cotton Vitellius A. XV. For editions based on the Cambridge manuscript, see S. J. Crawford, ed., *The Gospel of Nicodemus*, Anglo-Saxon Texts, vol. 1 (Edinburgh: I. B. Hutchen, 1927), and Thomas Powers Allen, ed., "A Critical Edition of the Old English Gospel of Nicodemus" (Ph.D. diss., Rice University, 1968); cf. also Jackson J. Campbell, "To Hell and Back: Latin Tradition and Literary Use of the *Descensus ad Inferos* in Old English," *Viator* 13 (1982): 112–14, and A. di Paolo Healey, "Anglo-Saxon Use of the Apocryphal Gospel," in *The Anglo-Saxons: Synthesis and Achievement*, ed. J. D. Woods and D. A. E. Pelteret (Waterloo, Ont.: Wilfrid Laurier University Press, 1985), 95–98. I am aware of but have not had the opportunity to consult the forthcoming work by Professor J. E. Cross *et al.* on the Latin exemplar of the OE prose *GN*.
[5] Edited by Bruno Assmann, *Angelsächsische Homilien und Heiligenleben* (1889; repr. with introduction by Peter Clemoes (Darmstadt: Wissenschaftliche Buchge-sellschaft, 1964), xxxiv, 181–92.
[6] Ker, *A Catalogue*, 28–31; Max Förster, "The Donations of Leofric to Exeter," in *The Exeter Book of Old English Poetry*, intro. R. W. Chambers, Max Förster, and Robin Flower (London: P. Lund, 1933), 10–14.

Pilates domerne, eall swa hyt Nychodemus awrat eall myd
Ebreiscum stafum on manegum bocum þus awryten. (Fol. 173v)[7]

(In the name of the Holy Trinity, here begins [the account of]
the deeds which were performed by our Savior, just as Theodosius, the famous emperor, discovered it, among many
books, in Jerusalem in the judgement hall of Pontius Pilate,
[and] just as Nicodemus wrote it, set out entirely in Hebrew
script.)

The only other enlarged initial in the *Gospel* begins the text proper,
immediately following this. The above, although it is not rubricated, is
the incipit for the *GN* and is abbreviated from the Latin prologue (*EN*
Prol.1–14); it serves the same purpose as the incipits for the four
gospels, but is less prominent and less a signal for a major division in
the manuscript. The *GN* ends on fol. 193r; after one blank line is a two-
line illuminated initial "O" beginning the *Vindicta Salvatoris*. The division here is like that used between chapters in the canonical gospels.
There is no explicit for the *GN* and no incipit of any kind for the
Vindicta Salvatoris, which might be taken as an additional chapter of
the *Gospel*.

The status of the manuscript itself is uncertain. As Förster argued,[8] it has some of the features of a sacred liturgical book. For
example, rubricated titles or instructions signal when a gospel passage
is appointed in the liturgy; these are in OE and followed by a brief
Latin incipit of the passage in the same ink as the main OE text. But
what status did the manuscript have? It contrasts with the other gospel
book in Leofric's donation, Oxford, Bodleian Library (Bodl. Lib.) MS.
Auct. D. 2. 16; this is in Latin, is organized and decorated as a liturgical book, and contains no additional texts, apart from the prefaces of
Jerome and Eusebius.[9] Would a compiler have been as ready to include apocryphal materials in a Latin gospel book such as this? Despite
the prestige of the vernacular in Anglo-Saxon England, the *GN* was
probably placed beside the gospels in the Cambridge manuscript
precisely because it was a vernacular compilation. Further, it is difficult to imagine the OE manuscript being used as a liturgical book in
the strict sense; it may have had some allied function for study or
reading aloud in other contexts. The sequence in CUL MS. Ii. 2. 11 of

---

[7] Hulme, "The Old English Version," 471.1–5.

[8] Förster, "The Donations," 13–17.

[9] F. Madan and H. H. E. Craster, *A Summary Catalogue of Western Manuscripts
in the Bodleian Library at Oxford*, vol. 2, pt. 1 (Oxford: Clarendon Press, 1922), 511–
12, no. 2719; Otto Pächt and J. G. Alexander, comps., *Illuminated Manuscripts in the
Bodleian Library, Oxford*, vol. 1 (Oxford: Clarendon Press, 1966), 33, no. 427.

the four gospels, the *GN*, and the *Vindicta Salvatoris* points to the use of apocryphal texts to supplement and extend the account of the life of Christ up to and including the destruction of Jerusalem. As we shall see, this is a recurring feature of the manuscript history of the *GN*. The rescuing of the souls from hell and the vengeance of Christ were seen as crucial to the working out of the history of the Redemption. The manuscript's function was probably not so much liturgical but more that of a repository of sacred history.

The nature of the OE *Gospel of Nicodemus* itself goes some way to support this argument. It is derived from the textual tradition of *EN A*, and it is useful to compare it with Kim's edition from the *codex Einsidlensis*. The OE text shows close translation, paraphrase, compression, and omissions. Some of the omissions can be attributed to mechanical error either in the Latin exemplar or by the translator. For example, the OE has no counterpart for *EN* 4.3.11–4.4.2;[10] this was clearly lost through eyeskip. The same explanation accounts for the loss of *EN* 15.6.13–17.[11] But other omissions are probably intentional, even if they reflect some clumsy editing; whether this occurred in the Latin tradition or the Old English is not clear. The episode of the standards as it appears in *EN* 1.5.1–1.6.17 is compressed into this short passage:

> Se rynel hyne wæs swyðe byddende þæt he sceolde in ofer his hrægl gan, ond se leofa hælend hyne wearð geeaðmedende. Ac onmang þam þe he wæs ingangende, hyne wæron fæla manna geeaðmedende ond heora heafdo to hym onhyldende. (Fol. 175r)[12]

> (The messenger earnestly beseeched him to walk over his garment, and the beloved Savior humbly complied. But among those [in the place] where he entered, many men worshipped him and bowed their heads to him.)

The editor or translator is aware of the episode, but he has distorted it so that its significance is lost to the context. The largest omission is the counterpart to *EN* 5.1.6–11.3.3; this could reflect intervention in the Latin. The OE text is sewn together in this way:

> Þa stod þar to foran þam deman an Iudeisc wer þæs nama wæs Nychodemus, ond cwæð to þam deman, "La leof, ic bydde þe for þynre myltse þæt ðu læte me sprecan ane feawa worda." Þa cwæð Pilatus, "Gea sprec." Þa cwæð Nichodemus,

---

[10] Cf. Hulme, "The Old English Version," 480.12.
[11] Cf. ibid., 492.22.
[12] Ibid., 474.5–9.

"Ic secge eow ealdron ond mæssepreostum ond diaconum ond ealre þyssre Iudeiscan mænigeo þe her on geferscype syndon; ic axie eow hwæt ge wyllon æt þyson men habban." Swylce word he þær forðlet swylce ær nan oðer ne dorste. Þa wæs hym þær neh sum wer standende se wæs Iosep genemned, wæs god / wer ond ryhtwys, ond næs næfre hys wylles þær man þone hælend wregde on nanum gemange. He wæs of þære ceastre þe ys genemned Arimathia ond he geanbidiende wæs Godes ryces oð þæt ðe Cryst wæs ahangen ond he æt Pilate þa Crystes lychaman abæd ond hyne of þære rode genam ond on clænre scytan befeold ond hyne on hys nywan þruh alede on þære þe nan oðer man ær on ne læg. (Fol. 178r–v)[13]

(Then stood there before the judge a Jewish man whose name was Nicodemus, and he spoke to the judge, "Indeed, dear sir, I pray you, through your mercy, that you allow me to speak a few words." Then Pilate said, "Yes, speak." Then Nicodemus said, "I speak to you elders and priests and deacons and to all this multitude of Jews who are here in a company; I ask you what you desire from this man." He spoke such words there as no other dared before. Then was there standing beside him a certain man who was called Joseph, a good and righteous man, and it was never his wish that they should denounce the Savior in any assembly. He was from the city which is called Arimathea, and he was waiting for the kingdom of God—until Christ was crucified—and he asked Pilate for the body of Christ, and took it from the cross and wrapped it in a clean sheet and laid it in his new tomb in which no other man had lain.)

This passage begins with material from chapter five, down to "hwæt ge wyllon æt þyson men habban" (*EN* 5.1.1–6), which is followed by a reference to Nicodemus's speech in defense of Jesus (*EN* 5.1.6–18). The next clause, "þa wæs hym þær neh sum wer standende," is editorial and places Joseph with Nicodemus at the trial of Christ. The remainder is from *EN* 11.3.3–10, the context of which is the deposition and burial. The phrase "oð þæt ðe Cryst wæs ahangen" is editorial and is designed to account for the events between the trial and death of Christ; it is syntactically awkward, and how it functions is not clear. The omissions from the *Gospel* are the accounts given in his defense of the miracles of Christ, the decision to release Barabbas, the flagellation,

---

[13] Ibid., 480.16–32.

and the Crucifixion. It has been argued that this lacuna reflects the loss of folios from the original OE manuscript,[14] but another explanation, in the light of what has been discussed so far, is that the text—possibly the Latin recension which was the exemplar of the OE translation—has been subject to editorial work designed to compress it, and more importantly to remove material which duplicates the gospels.[15] There are other omissions, but they are less extensive in the latter part of the text where the narrative depends less on the biblical source.[16] The *GN* in CUL MS. Ii. 2. 11 reflects the processes not only of translation but of adaptation. Although the text in this manuscript is not the original,[17] it is probable that the OE *Gospel of Nicodemus* was designed for a very similar context, a vernacular gospel book with additional apocryphal narratives providing a record of early Christian history.

This translation of the *GN* is found in two other manuscripts, both about 100 years later. Here the contexts suggest different "readings" of the apocryphal *Gospel*. London, BL MS. Cotton Vitellius A. XV is a composite manuscript: the portion (fols. 4r–93v) which contains the *GN* is dated by Ker to the middle of the twelfth century; the other (fols. 94r–209v) is the *Beowulf*-manuscript dated saec. X/XI.[18] The *GN* (fols. 60r–86v) is the second item and is missing a little more than two pages at the beginning.[19] It was copied independently of the Cambridge manuscript and preserves some clearly "better" readings. It is preceded by a paraphrase in OE of the *Soliloquia of St. Augustine*[20] attributed to King Alfred (fols. 4r–59v) and followed by the prose *Solomon and Saturn* (fols. 86v–93v),[21] and a homily on St. Quintin (fol. 93v).[22]

---

[14] W. H. Hulme, ed., "The Old English Gospel of Nicodemus," *Modern Philology* 1 (1903–4): 582–83; Michael Swanton, ed. and trans., *Anglo-Saxon Prose* (London: Dent, 1975), 144.

[15] Hulme, "The Old English Version," 517, had earlier suggested editorial intervention; Allen, "A Critical Edition," 7–13, describes a process of editing but suggests no purpose for it.

[16] The most extensive, *EN* 16.1.6–16.3.16, occurs at Hulme, "The Old English Version," 492.29; this is testimony concerning the recognition of Christ by Simeon and repetition of aspects of the Passion and burial of Christ.

[17] Ibid., 540–41; Campbell, "To Hell and Back," 114.

[18] Ker, *A Catalogue*, 279–83, nos. 215 and 216.

[19] This text is printed in parallel with that in the Cambridge manuscript by Hulme, "The Old English Version," 471–515.

[20] Edited by Thomas A. Carnicelli, *King Alfred's Version of St. Augustine's "Soliloquies"* (Cambridge, Mass.: Harvard University Press, 1969).

[21] Edited by James E. Cross and Thomas D. Hill, *The Prose "Solomon and Saturn" and "Adrian and Ritheus": Edited from the British Library Manuscripts with Commentary*, McMaster Old English Studies and Texts, vol. 1 (Toronto: University of Toronto Press, 1982); see also Ker, *A Catalogue*, 279–80.

[22] Edited by Max Förster, "Zur altenglischen Quintinus-Legende," *Archiv für das Studium der neueren Sprachen und Literaturen* 106 (1901): 258–59.

The manuscript is damaged and a contents list compiled for Cotton indicates that between items one and two there was a portion of a legend of St. Thomas the Apostle. Here the *Gospel* has become part of an anthology of didactic and wisdom literature. Thomas Shippey has pointed out that the *Solomon and Saturn* text in this manuscript, although it has a place in wisdom literature, is also curiously literal and factual in the questions it asks and the answers it gives.[23] It was perhaps this taste for the factual which attracted the compiler to the *Gospel;* it provided answers to nagging questions, such as what did Christ do between his death and Resurrection, and what was the fate of those who lived before his coming. In the late thirteenth century, the manuscript was in the library of St. Mary's, Southwick, Hampshire, a priory of Augustinian canons founded in 1133, and it is possible that it originated there.[24]

The same association with didactic literature is found in the other mid-twelfth-century manuscript of this translation, London, BL MS. Cotton Vespasian D. XIV;[25] it consists of texts for teaching theology, many but not all of which are homilies of Ælfric.[26] There is no evidence as to its ownership, but Ker tentatively located it to Canterbury or Rochester on the basis of the handwriting. More recently Rima Handley has argued that the original compilation was made at Canterbury.[27] The *Gospel,* here entitled *De resurrectione Domini,* is item 31 (fols. 87v–100r) and shows extensive revision when set against the other two manuscript texts of the translation. It opens in this way:

> Ðæs dæiges þe ure Hælend for ure alesednysse geðolede pine
> on þær halgen rode, þa wæs þære neh sum were standende,
> se wæs Joseph genæmned, and he wæs god were and rihtwis,
> and næs næfre his willes, þær me þone Hælend forwreigde,

[23] Thomas Shippey, *Poems of Wisdom and Learning in Old English* (Cambridge: D. S. Brewer, 1976), 21.

[24] N. R. Ker, ed., *Medieval Libraries of Great Britain. A List of Surviving Manuscripts,* 2d ed., Royal Historical Society Guides and Handbooks, vol. 3 (London: Offices of the Royal Historical Society, 1964), 181; Carnicelli, *King Alfred's Version,* 31.

[25] This version has been edited by Hulme, "The Old English Gospel of Nicodemus," 591–610, and by Rubie D.-N. Warner, *Early English Homilies from the Twelfth-Century MS Vesp. D. XIV,* EETS OS, vol. 152 (London: K. Paul, Trench, Trübner, 1917), 77–88. See also Healey, "Anglo-Saxon Use of the Apocryphal Gospel," 98–99.

[26] Ker, *A Catalogue,* 271–77, no. 209; Malcolm Godden, ed., *Ælfric's Catholic Homilies: the Second Series,* EETS SS, vol. 5 (London: Oxford University Press, 1979), xl–xlii.

[27] Rima Handley, "British Museum MS. Cotton Vespasian D. XIV," *Notes and Queries* 219 (1974): 243–50.

on nanen gemange. He wæs of þære ceastre þe is genæmned
Barimathia. He onbad on Jerusalem forð þæt se Hælend wæs
ahangen, and to þan æfene he eode to Pilate, and abæd æt
him Cristes lichame. . . . (Fol. 87v)[28]

(On the day on which our Savior, for our Redemption, suffered torture on the holy cross, then was there standing nearby a certain man who was called Joseph, and he was a good
and righteous man, and it was never his will that men should
accuse the Savior in any assembly. He was of the city which is
called Arimathea. He remained in Jerusalem until the Savior
was crucified, and in the evening he went to Pilate and asked
him for the body of Christ. . . .)

There are verbal echoes of the passage from the Cambridge manuscript
given earlier,[29] but the text has been shaped so that it effectively
begins at EN 11.3.3; there is none of the awkwardness of the transition
from the events of the trial to those of the deposition. This version is
what its Latin title declares it to be, an account of the Resurrection. The
text is characterized by compression, paraphrase, and a general freedom with the original;[30] it even contains some preacherly asides:

Eala, mæn þa leofeste, hwu laðlic and hwu grislic wæs þære
deoflene gemot, þa seo Helle and se Deofel heom betweonen
cidden! (Fol. 96r)[31]

(Alas, most dear people, how horrible and dreadful was that
council of the devils, when Hell and the Devil quarrelled
between themselves.)

Eala mæn, hwu grislic hit wæs þa þa seo deo/fellice Helle
þone feond Beelzebub underfeng, and hine fæste geheold! For
þan se Deofol wæs ær þære helle hlaford, and eallra þære
deofellicre þingen þe hire on wæron. (Fol. 98r–v)[32]

(Alas, people, how dreadful it was when the devilish Hell
took charge of the fiend Beelzebub, and held him securely! For
that Devil had been the lord of hell and of all the devilish
possessions which were in it.)

---

[28] Warner, Early English Homilies, 77.
[29] Hulme, "The Old English Version," 480.24–29.
[30] Hulme, "The Old English Gospel of Nicodemus," 582–83. Handley, "British
Museum MS. Cotton Vespasian D. XIV," 243–50, states that this is a feature of
many of the texts in the compilation.
[31] Warner, Early English Homilies, 85.
[32] Ibid., 86.

Again the text is being used for a purpose. There is some uncertainty as to the function of the manuscript, whether it can be seen as a homiliary in a very strict sense. Handley prefers to characterize it as "a teaching manual for young religious."[33] Nevertheless, a large number of homilies have been used to compile this manuscript, and Hulme needlessly cavils at the notion that this version of the GN can also be called a homily, in the broader sense implied by this context.[34] His argument that the two passages given above may have been added by the compiler does more to support than to deny the hypothesis. The text has been edited and adapted to this new, didactic context, and was probably designed as a "temporale" sermon on the Resurrection.[35]

This text of the GN was copied independently of the other two manuscripts and is followed by the story of Titus and Vespasian, an abbreviation of the *Vindicta Salvatoris* (fols. 100v–102r).[36] That these two texts should appear in sequence is likely to be the result of design, and both have been subject to the same type of revision, possibly by the same scribe. It is probable that the model for the sequence is reflected in the Cambridge manuscript. The linking of the two texts in Cotton Vespasian D. XIV gives support to the earlier suggestion that the lost original manuscript was in nature and content very much like CUL MS. Ii. 2. 11.

The OE prose translation of the GN is thought to date from the early to mid-eleventh century, possibly as early as the mid-tenth century.[37] Apart from this, there are many texts in OE verse and prose which use the subject of the Harrowing of Hell. J. J. Campbell has argued that there is no evidence to show that any of these owes a debt to the *Gospel* and that they are based on a variety of sources such as sermons, commentaries, hymns, and theological writings. This conclusion is endorsed by Greenfield and Calder.[38] Campbell has failed, however, to take account of a passage in the seventh Blickling Homily.[39] A major source for this homily is the pseudo-Augustinian "Sermo 160: De

---

[33] Handley, "British Museum MS. Cotton Vespasian D. XIV," 247.

[34] Hulme, "The Old English Gospel of Nicodemus," 580.

[35] Handley's argument ("British Museum MS. Cotton Vespasian D. XIV," 245–46) that Judgement Day is the organizing theme of quire block D, where the GN appears, is strained.

[36] Edited by Assmann, *Angelsächsische Homilien*, 193–94.

[37] Hulme, "The Old English Gospel of Nicodemus," 6–7; Campbell, "To Hell and Back," 112–13.

[38] Stanley B. Greenfield and Daniel G. Calder, *A New Critical History of Old English Literature* (New York: New York University Press, 1986), 199.

[39] The manuscript is dated saec. X/XI (Ker, *A Catalogue*, 451–55, no. 382). For the edition of the seventh Blickling Homily, see Richard Morris, ed., *The Blickling Homilies of the Tenth Century*, EETS OS, vol. 73 (London: N. Trübner, 1880), 82–97.

pascha II,"[40] or, as seems likely, a version of the Latin which included additional material.[41] What has not been noticed is that the third paragraph of "Sermo 160" shows close verbal parallels with *EN* 22 and 23. The precise relationship of these two texts is open to question, but it is likely that the *EN* is the source for the homily.[42] Paragraph three of the pseudo-Augustinian sermon appears as part of the seventh Blickling Homily:

"Hwonon is þes þus strang, & þus beorht, & þus egesfull? ... Nu he hafaþ on his hidercyme ealle scyldige fordemde & gehynde."[43]

("From where is this one, so strong and so bright and so terrifying? ... Now, by his coming here he has condemned and humbled all the guilty.")

A homily in Oxford, Bodl. Lib. MS. Junius 121, of the third quarter of the eleventh century, makes use of another text of pseudo-Augustine's "Sermo 160," and this also contains a translation of paragraph three.[44] In an important sense, however, Campbell's argument remains intact, for it is only through the vehicle of the pseudo-Augustinian homily that this portion of the *EN* found its way into the vernacular. Other OE homilies contain lively accounts of the Harrowing and present themes found in the *GN*,[45] but Campbell's investigations do not suggest that it is used in these texts. He admits, however, that authors may have

---

[40] PL 39:2059–61; see Eligius Dekkers and Aemilius Gaar, *Clavis patrum latinorum* (Steenbrugis: In Abbatia Sancti Petri, 1961), 89.

[41] David N. Dumville, "Liturgical Drama and Panegyric Responsory from the Eighth Century? A Re-examination of the Origin and Contents of the Ninth-Century Section of the Book of Cerne," *Journal of Theological Studies* 23 (1972): 374–88; Campbell, "To Hell and Back," 131–34, 136–43. Sources for the homily include Eusebius "Gallicanus," "Homilia XII, De pascha, I," and "Homilia XIIA (Homilia XII ampliata), De pascha, IA," in his *Collectio homiliarum, de qua critice disseruit Ioh. Leroy*, ed. Fr. Glorie, CC SL, vol. 101 (Turnhout: Brepols, 1970), 141–50.

[42] I drew attention to this parallel with the *EN* in my Ph.D. dissertation, C. W. Marx, "The Devil's Rights and the Deception of the Devil: Theological Background and Presentations in Middle English Literature, with an Edition of the *Devils' Parliament*," 2 vols. (Ph.D. diss., University of York, 1981), 1:52–53; see also Zbigniew Izydorczyk, "The Unfamiliar *Evangelium Nicodemi*," *Manuscripta* 33 (1989): 180. The relationship between the two texts needs further investigation, but I am not convinced that it is crucial to the argument that the homily pre-dates by quite a considerable time the earliest surviving manuscript of the *Descensus Christi ad inferos*.

[43] Morris, *The Blickling Homilies*, 85, 87.

[44] Edited by Anna Maria Luiselli Fadda, " 'De Descensu Christi ad Inferos': Una inedita omelia anglosassone," *Studi medievali* 13 (1972): 1002–1004.82–99; Campbell, "To Hell and Back," 138–41.

[45] Campbell, "To Hell and Back," 134–36, 141–42.

been at some distance from their sources. The kinds of variations in speeches and ideas these texts introduce do not preclude the ultimate influence of the *GN*, although firm evidence is so far lacking.[46]

The *Middle English Harrowing of Hell* and the thirteenth-century context

Treatments of materials based on the *Gospel of Nicodemus* reflect the new linguistic, literary, and doctrinal climates of the twelfth and thirteenth centuries. At least four influences need to be taken into account: the use of French as first a dominant and then a rival literary language, the emergence of the sentiment and the literature of affective piety, the effects of the Fourth Lateran Council of 1215 on the provision of popular, instructional writing, and finally changes in the doctrine of the Redemption, a subject with which the *Gospel* is intimately bound up. We can catch a glimpse of its status in the late thirteenth century through some remarks in a Latin text which had profound influence on the literature of popular piety, the *Legenda aurea* of Jacobus a Voragine. In the chapter on the Passion, Jacobus cites the *EN* for the names of the two Thieves and details of Christ's dispute with Pilate.[47] In the chapter on the Resurrection, the *EN* is referred to in this way:

> De septimo autem et ultimo hic considerando, qualiter sanctos patres, qui erant in limbo, Christus eduxit et quid ibi egit, evangelium aperte non explanavit. Augustinus tamen in quodam sermone et Nicodemus in suo evangelio aliquatenus hoc ostendunt.[48]

> (Concerning the seventh and last issue that needs to be considered here, namely how Christ led out the holy fathers who were in limbo and what he did there, the gospel has declared

---

[46] See the homily of the mid to late eleventh century printed by Hulme, "The Old English Gospel of Nicodemus," 610–14, from Cambridge, Corpus Christi College (CCCC) MS. 41, pp. 295–301 (Ker, *A Catalogue*, 43–45, no. 32). An unpublished version of this homily appears in CCCC MS. 303, pp. 72–75 (saec. XII; Ker, ibid., 99–105, no. 57). On this homily, see Sara Cutforth, "Delivering the Damned in Old English Homilies: An Additional Note," *Notes and Queries* 238 (1993): 435–37; Ms. Cutforth is preparing an edition in which she assesses the evidence for the use of the *GN*.

[47] Jacobus a Voragine, *Jacobi a Voragine Legenda aurea vulgo Historia Lombardica dicta*, ed. Th. Graesse (1890; repr., Osnabrück: O. Zeller, 1969), 223, 226. This text, or parts of it, are thought to have reached England in the 1270s; see Manfred Görlach, *The Textual Tradition of the South English Legendary*, Leeds Texts and Monographs, n.s., vol. 6 (Leeds: School of English, 1974), 28.

[48] Jacobus a Voragine, *Legenda aurea*, 242; the section on the Harrowing of Hell appears on pp. 242–45.

nothing openly. Nevertheless, Augustine in a certain one of his sermons and Nicodemus in his own gospel have revealed something of this.)

The absence of clear testimony about the Harrowing of Hell in the canonical gospels does not mean that there is no truth to the episode: the *EN* and the sermon of Augustine are the authorities for it. The sermon referred to is in fact the pseudo-Augustine, "Sermo 160: De pascha," and the extracts from it include that portion of paragraph three which has parallels with the *EN* 22 and 23. The apocryphal gospel is, by implication, endorsed twice.

One indication of the different directions in which treatments of the *GN* were moving in the thirteenth century is provided by London, BL MS. Harley 2253, located to Herefordshire.[49] It is a trilingual miscellany in two parts: the first four quires (fols. 1–48) are "written in a professional textura of the late thirteenth century"; the rest of the manuscript (fols. 49–140) is dated to the fourth decade of the fourteenth century.[50] The manuscript usefully shows two quite different treatments of the *Gospel*. The first four quires, which are wholly in French, contain a prose *GN* (item 3, fols. 33va–39rb) as part of what can be termed a legendary;[51] fols. 55v–56v have a text of the verse *Middle English Harrowing of Hell*.[52] The prose text in this manuscript

[49] Reproduced by N. R. Ker, intro., *Facsimile of British Museum MS. Harley 2253*, EETS OS, vol. 255 (London: Oxford University Press, 1965); for a description of the manuscript, see pp. ix–xxiii. Its dialect is discussed in Angus McIntosh, M. L. Samuels, and Michael Benskin, *A Linguistic Atlas of Late Medieval English*, 4 vols. (Aberdeen: Aberdeen University Press, 1986), 1:111; 3:175, linguistic profile 9260 (hereafter cited as *LALME*). Carter Revard, "Richard Hurd and MS Harley 2253," *Notes and Queries* 224 (1979): 199–202, has identified the scribe as one who "worked in and around Ludlow during the years 1314–1349"; cf. idem, "Three More Holographs in the Hand of the Scribe of MS Harley 2253 in Shrewsbury," *Notes and Queries* 226 (1981): 199–200, and idem, "Scribe of MS Harley 2253," *Notes and Queries* 227 (1982): 62–63.

[50] Ker, *Facsimile*, xvi and xxi–xxiii.

[51] Ibid., ix–x. The *GN*, which is in Ford's "Tradition A" (Alvin E. Ford, ed., *L'Évangile de Nicodème: Les Versions courtes en ancien français et en prose*, Publications romanes et françaises, vol. 125 [Geneva: Droz, 1973], 22), is followed by legendary texts (fols. 39va–41va) for which there are parallels in another AN manuscript of the *Gospel*, London, BL MS. Egerton 2710; see below, n. 53.

[52] Edited in W. H. Hulme, *The Middle English Harrowing of Hell and Gospel of Nicodemus*, EETS ES, vol. 100 (London: K. Paul, Trench, Trübner, 1908), 1–23; cf. Carleton Brown and Rossell Hope Robbins, *The Index of Middle English Verse* (New York: Columbia University Press, 1943), nos. 185, 1258 (hereafter cited as *IMEV*). Discussions, with bibliographies, of ME treatments in verse and prose of texts related to the *GN* are found in Frances A. Foster, "Legends of Jesus and Mary," in *A Manual of the Writings in Middle English 1050–1500*, ed. J. Burke Severs, vol. 2 (The Connecticut Academy of Arts and Sciences, 1970), 448–50, 640–42.

is only one among a number of the *Gospel* found in Anglo-Norman manuscripts from the thirteenth century onwards, and French verse treatments of it also appear in Anglo-Norman contexts.[53] These facts are in no way surprising, but they need to be kept in mind when assessing the popularity of the text and sources for English versions.

In origin the *Middle English Harrowing of Hell* is also thirteenth-century and appears in the important miscellany Oxford, Bodl. Lib. MS. Digby 86 (fols. 119r–20v), dated to between 1272 and 1282 and located to south Worcestershire.[54] This is another trilingual miscellany, and here French is the dominant language. The third manuscript containing the *Middle English Harrowing of Hell* is Edinburgh, National Library of Scotland MS. 19. 2. 1 (fols. 35v–37r), the Auchinleck Manuscript, dated to the period 1330–40, and almost entirely in English. The text is in "Hand A," the language of which has been localized to the London/Middlesex border.[55] Although there are differences in detail,

---

[53] Paris, Bibliothèque nationale (BN), MS. f. fr. 19525, fols. 50c–59a: the text is in Ford's "Tradition A" (*L'Évangile de Nicodème*, 21). London, BL MS. Egerton 2710, fols. 126ra–32rb: the text is in Ford's "Tradition A" (ibid., 21–22) and is followed by the letter of Pilate, the healing of Tiberius, the condemnation of Pilate, the Veronica legend and the story of Simon Magus (fols. 132rb–34rb). On these two manuscripts see Paul Meyer, "Notice du ms. Egerton 2710 du Musée Britannique," *Bulletin de la Société des anciens textes français* 15 (1889): 72–97, and D. W. Russell, ed., *La Vie de Saint Laurent: An Anglo-Norman Poem of the Twelfth Century*, Anglo-Norman Texts, vol. 34 (London: Westfield College Press, 1976), 1–4. Cambridge, Emmanuel College MS. 106, fols. 193r–96v: dated to the fourteenth century and localized to Worcestershire (?); see M. R. James, *The Western Manuscripts in the Library of Emmanuel College: A Descriptive Catalogue* (Cambridge: Cambridge University Press, 1904), 90–94. This text is fragmentary but is in Ford's "Tradition A" (*L'Évangile de Nicodème*, 22). Another AN text appears in London, BL MS. Egerton 613, fols. 13v–21r; this covers *EN* 12–28, and the sequence continues with legendary material such as the healing of Tiberius, the destruction of Jerusalem, the Veronica legend, and the finding and exaltation of the holy cross (fols. 21r–29v); see Betty Hill, "British Library MS. Egerton 613," *Notes and Queries* 223 (1978): 398–401. On manuscript contexts in England for versions of the *Gospel* in French verse, see Gaston Paris and Alphonse Bos, eds., *Trois Versions rimées de l'Évangile de Nicodème par Chrétien, André de Coutances et un anonyme*, Société des anciens textes français, vol. 22 (1885; repr., New York: Johnson Reprint Corp., 1968), iv–v, xvi–xvii, xlvi–xlvii; see also Cambridge, Fitzwilliam Museum MS. McClean 123, described by Nigel Morgan, *Early Gothic Manuscripts [II]: 1250–1285*, A Survey of Manuscripts Illuminated in the British Isles, vol. 4 (London: H. Miller Publishers – Oxford University Press, 1988), 193–95, item 187.

[54] The contents are given in Gulielmus D. Macray, *Catalogi codicum manuscriptorum Bibliothecae Bodleianae, pars nona, codices a viro clarissimo Kenelm Digby, Esq. Aur., anno 1634 donatos, complectens* (Oxford: Clarendon Press, 1883), 91–97; see also B. D. H. Miller, "The Early History of Bodleian MS. Digby 86," *Annuale mediaevale* 4 (1963): 23–56, and Andrew G. Watson, *Catalogue of Dated and Datable Manuscripts c. 435–1600 in Oxford Libraries*, 2 vols. (Oxford: Clarendon Press, 1984), 1:68. For dialect, see *LALME*, 1:147, 3:150–51, linguistic profile 7790.

[55] Derek Pearsall and I. C. Cunningham, intro., *The Auchinleck Manuscript*,

in terms of their broad outlines and structure the three versions are quite similar; the main differences are in the prologue. Where the French text of the *Gospel* in Harley 2253 is conservative and faithful to the Latin, the *Middle English Harrowing of Hell* is innovative and shows an intelligent response to developments in devotion and doctrine. The *Middle English Harrowing of Hell* and its innovations are the result of the fresh ways in which the Harrowing of Hell is conceived. One of the most important changes is that traditional themes of the *Gospel* as well as some new ones appear in speeches of Christ. The *Middle English Harrowing of Hell* uses Christ's words at the entry into hell, "Hard gates haui gon" (v. 27, Digby 86; *EN* 21.1.3–4, 21.2.2–3, 21.3.4–5), but the speech is extended into an account of the life, suffering, and Passion of Christ; for example:

> Men duden me so muchel same;
> Wiþ wounden stronge makede me lame;
> Hi nomen me wiþouten sake,
> Bounden min honden to mi bake,
> Hi beten me þat I ran ablode,
> And suþþen me duden one þe rode;
> For Adam sunful, iwis,
> Al haui þoled þis. (Vv. 35–42; Digby 86)

There is no reference in the *GN* to the suffering of Christ, certainly nothing to generate compassion, but incorporated into this speech is an aspect of the literature of affective piety, which is all the more compelling for being so restrained. At the entry into hell in the *GN*, Satan recounts the life of Christ and his preparations to put him to death (*EN* 20.1–2); the overriding theme is his ignorance of Christ's true nature. In the *Middle English Harrowing of Hell* it is Christ who expresses this theme in a speech to Satan (vv. 53–70, Digby 86), which in turn leads on to their debate (vv. 71–136, Digby 86), another feature for which there is no counterpart in the *GN*.

Because of the amount of direct speech and debate, the *Middle English Harrowing of Hell* has been thought by some to be a short drama or a quasi-dramatic text, or possibly a text for recitation.[56] That scholars

---

National Library of Scotland Advocates' MS. 19. 2. 1 (London: The Scolar Press in association with The National Library of Scotland, 1977), vii–xxiv; *LALME* 1:88, 3:305–6, linguistic profile for "Hand A" 6510.

[56] Richard Axton, *European Drama of the Early Middle Ages* (London: Hutchinson University Library, 1974), 114; Alfred W. Pollard, ed., *English Miracle Plays Moralities and Interludes*, 8th ed. (Oxford: Clarendon Press, 1927), xxi, 166–72 (text); Carter Revard, "*Gilote et Iohane:* An Interlude in B. L. MS Harley 2253," *Studies in Philology* 79 (1982): 128–29.

have speculated in this way indicates that it fits uneasily into precon-
ceived notions of medieval genres. It was adaptable and could be used
in different contexts as its three manuscripts show. But it was not only
the possibilities offered by dramatic or quasi-dramatic forms that dictated the nature of the *Middle English Harrowing of Hell*. Developments
in the doctrine of the Redemption show their influence in the debate
between Christ and Satan, which is at the center of the text, and these
as much as anything account for the different way in which the Harrowing is conceived. The *Middle English Harrowing of Hell*, through the
debate (vv. 71–136, Digby 86), offers a view of the Redemption which is
in line with Anselmian ideas and which has parallels in Latin writing.[57]

Abbreviated Middle English prose versions and the literature of the Passion

The literature of affective piety influenced AN and ME versions of the
Gospel of Nicodemus in other important ways. London, BL MSS. Royal
20 B. V and Egerton 2781 contain an AN prose sequence made up of
two texts: an account of the Passion of Christ narrated by Mary, the
Complaint of Our Lady, and an account of the Resurrection drawn from
chapters 12–17 of the GN. The sequence may date from between 1380
and 1390. L. F. Sandler,[58] however, on the basis of the stylistic evidence of the illuminations, places Egerton 2781 between 1340 and 1350,
in which case the sequence could date from the early fourteenth century.[59] It was translated into ME sometime before 1390 and in this
form survives in three manuscripts, each of which contains different
versions: Cambridge, Magdalene College MS. Pepys 2498 (saec.

---

[57] C. W. Marx, "An Edition and Study of the *Conflictus inter Deum et Diabo-
lum*," *Medium Ævum* 59 (1990): 16–40. The doctrinal context is set out in C. W.
Marx, *The Devil's Rights and the Redemption in the Literature of Medieval England*
(Cambridge: D. S. Brewer, 1995), 84–88.

[58] Lucy Freeman Sandler, *Gothic Manuscripts 1285–1385*, A Survey of Manuscripts Illuminated in the British Isles, vol. 5 (London: H. Miller Publishers –
Oxford University Press, 1986), 2:127–29.

[59] An edition of the AN texts appears in parallel with the ME translations in
C. W. Marx and J. F. Drennan, eds., *The Middle English Prose Complaint of Our Lady
and Gospel of Nicodemus*, Middle English Texts, vol. 19 (Heidelberg: C. Winter,
1987). For the argument that these texts form a narrative sequence, see C. W.
Marx, "Beginnings and Endings: Narrative-linking in Five Manuscripts from the
Fourteenth and Fifteenth Centuries and the Problem of Textual 'Integrity,'" in
Manuscripts and Readers in Fifteenth-Century England, ed. Derek Pearsall (Cambridge: D. S. Brewer, 1983), 70–81; on the problem of dating the sequence, Marx
and Drennan, *The Middle English Prose Complaint*, 14–16.

222 C. W. MARX

XIV/2); Leeds, University Library, Brotherton Collection MS. 501 (saec. XV med.); and San Marino, Henry Huntington Library MS. HM 144 (saec. XV/XVI). Although the two texts are distinguished in the manuscripts, it is probable that the sequence was conceived as a whole; incorporated into Mary's narrative is the account from GN 12 and 15 of the imprisonment and release of Joseph of Arimathea, and the text of the Gospel in the sequence begins where the episode of the imprisonment finishes. The AN Gospel of Nicodemus is surprisingly brief over the Harrowing of Hell, which is summarized in little more than 200 words. This was no doubt purposeful: the Resurrection narrative is designed to emphasize the figure of Joseph of Arimathea, and a number of changes are made in order to give him more prominence.[60]

The Complaint, which occupies approximately three-quarters of the sequence, grew out of the literature of affective piety. Mary's account modulates between a chronicle-like narrative, using curial prose style, and highly charged emotional responses to the suffering of Christ at each stage of the Passion; the first mode serves to authenticate the second. The purpose of the text is to generate compassion, a profound sympathy with Mary and Christ. Something of this emotionalism is carried over into the GN.[61] How is the Gospel being used in this context? Jeanne Drennan argued that the Gospel is at the basis of the sequence and that the compiler replaced its trial and Crucifixion sections with the Complaint.[62] This hypothesis deserves consideration, but needs to be modified. It can be restated in this way: the compiler had available to him a number of texts, including a complete GN; he selected from it only those parts concerned with Joseph of Arimathea and the Resurrection. For the Passion he used texts such as the Quis dabit, the pseudo-Anselmian Dialogus, and the Meditationes vitae Christi, or material related to them.[63] This hypothesis suggests that, in response to contemporary taste for the literature of compassion, the compiler regarded large portions of the GN as obsolete.

Royal 20 B. V is a composite manuscript in three parts, with the majority of items in French and the rest in Latin. The Complaint and Gospel appear in the first part and together are the fifth item (fols. 147r–56r). The first is the New Testament in French, which is followed by Latin hymns from the Sarum Breviary, with parallel French translations. The manuscript is a miscellany of mainly devotional material,

---

[60] Marx and Drennan, The Middle English Prose Complaint, 38–42.
[61] Ibid., 42.
[62] J. F. Drennan, "The Complaint of Our Lady and Gospel of Nicodemus of MS Pepys 2498," Manuscripta 24 (1980): 164–70.
[63] Marx and Drennan, The Middle English Prose Complaint, 26–37.

and we may speculate on the basis of its contents that it was owned by a secular household rather than a religious institution. Egerton 2781 is a book of hours, small in size (110mm x 170mm), with many accretions of a devotional nature in Latin and French. The manuscript is heavily illustrated and decorated; in the sequence of the *Complaint* and *Gospel* alone, which together form the last item (fols. 131r–89v), there are thirty-six historiated initials. This type of manuscript would have been privately owned, and it is a great compendium of verbal and visual popular piety.[64]

Pepys 2498 has been located on linguistic grounds to the area around Waltham Abbey in Essex.[65] The sequence of the *Complaint* and *Gospel* is the second last item in the manuscript (pp. 449a–63b). All the major texts are religious prose and many are translations from French: the *Pepysian Gospel Harmony* (from French; pp. 1a–43a), the ME translation of Robert Gretham's AN *Miroir* (pp. 45a–212b), a ME translation from AN of the *Apocalypse* (pp. 226b–63b), a ME prose version of the Psalter (pp. 263b–370a), and the *Ancrene Riwle* (pp. 371a–449a). Comparisons are invited between Pepys 2498 and the Vernon and Simeon manuscripts, but this is altogether a more specialized compilation. It is a large volume (340mm x 240mm), and its contents are carefully organized with couplets introducing each text, a feature found in some French manuscripts.[66] It is a useful indicator of the demand for didactic and devotional texts in English. H. Leith Spencer has argued that the ME *Mirror* was intended specifically for private lay reading,[67] and A. Ian Doyle has suggested that the manuscript as a whole was designed for a devout lay community, possibly a large household[68]— an assessment that fits with the impression gained from the nature of the contents.

Brotherton 501 has been localized to south Lincolnshire, and is a collection of religious prose and verse, including portions of the *Prick of Conscience* and the *South English Legendary*. Carelessness in rebinding

---

[64] For accounts of the AN manuscripts, see ibid., 8–9. A fragment of a third manuscript, of the late fifteenth or early sixteenth century, has come to light; see C. W. Marx, "A Newly Identified Fragment of the Anglo-Norman Prose *Complaint of Our Lady and Gospel of Nicodemus* in Cambridge University Library MS Dd. 4. 35," *Notes and Queries* 236 (1991): 157–58.

[65] Marx and Drennan, *The Middle English Prose Complaint*, 10–11; *LALME* 1:64, 3:124–25, linguistic profile 6260.

[66] Meyer, "Notice," 73.

[67] H. Leith Spencer, *English Preaching in the Late Middle Ages* (Oxford: Clarendon Press, 1993), 36 and *passim*.

[68] A. Ian Doyle, "A Survey of the Origins and Circulation of Theological Writings in English in the 14th, 15th and Early 16th Centuries," 2 vols (Ph.D. diss., Cambridge University, 1953), 1:106, 2:66–67.

has disrupted the order of the folios. The text of the sequence is closely related to that in Pepys 2498, but it has been compressed and considerably reduced. The purpose of the manuscript is not evident, but it may have been a private commonplace book of popular instruction and devotion.[69] Huntington HM 144, approximately one hundred years later than Pepys 2498 and tentatively located to the Berkshire-Surrey region, contains texts of a mainly religious nature and includes Chaucer's *Tale of Melibee* and *Monk's Tale* and Lydgate's *Churl and the Bird*.[70] Here the sequence has undergone major revisions, and in the *GN* portion the Harrowing has been expanded from the roughly two hundred words of paraphrase in the AN and its ME translation to a narrative.[71] It reveals knowledge of the *GN*, but it is clear as well that the reviser developed the dialogue between Christ and Satan based on Psalm 23:7–10 from the Latin of the Vulgate. As a gloss on the traditional narrative, the revision emphasizes that the choruses of the saints are prophecies of the deliverance from hell, and in addition to those figures referred to in the *GN*, the list includes Abraham, Isaac, and Jacob. But the major revision is that new textual boundaries have been established in the sequence so that the account of the imprisonment and release of Joseph of Arimathea, which appears as part of Mary's narrative in the earlier version, is identified as "the stori of Ioseph of Aramathye and Nicodemus."[72] This new division may be the result of knowledge of the *GN* from which the account was originally drawn. The larger context of the sequence in the manuscript is also significant: following the *Gospel* are excerpts from Caxton's printing of the *Polychronicon* (fols. 54v–64r) which refer to events following the Resurrection up to the destruction of Jerusalem. The revisions to the *Complaint* and *Gospel* may have been designed to accommodate them to an encyclopedia or legendary, one that was partly devotional but mainly narrative.

Another sequence of two texts shows a similar use of the *GN* and competition between narrative and devotional impulses. This survives in three manuscripts: London, BL MS. Egerton 2658; Manchester, John Rylands University Library English MS. 895; and Stonyhurst College

[69] Marx and Drennan, *The Middle English Prose Complaint*, 11–12. The latest discussion of the manuscript is by O. S. Pickering, "Brotherton Collection MS 501: A Middle English Anthology Reconsidered," *Leeds Studies in English*, n.s., 21 (1990): 141–65; for the dialect, see *LALME* 1:97, 3:258–59, linguistic profile 69.

[70] Marx and Drennan, *The Middle English Prose Complaint*, 12–13.

[71] Cf. ibid., 134.ME.4–135.ME.2 and 201.50–202.45.

[72] Ibid., 194.

MS. 43, fols. 21r–96v; all are of the fifteenth century.[73] In Egerton 2658 (fol. 15va) the first item is identified as the "liber Aureus de passione et resurreccione Domini per dominum Bonaventuram Cardinalem," which immediately links it to pseudo-Bonaventure's *Meditationes vitae Christi*.[74] The identification, however, obscures the eclecticism of the text: it is based on chapters 70–98 of the *Meditationes vitae Christi*, but uses many other sources including the *GN*. After a brief prologue summarizing the miracles and ministry of Christ, there follows a translation of chapter one of the *GN:*

> Then aftyr it drow fast toward Estryn, Annas & Cayphas byss-
> hopys and princis of prestis ordeynyd for þat ȝere, Dome,
> Datan, Gamabel, Iudas, Levy, Neptalim, Alysaunder & othyr
> folk of þe Iewys comen to Pylatis & maden hem partys aȝens
> Ihesu & acusyd hym of many dyuerse poyntis & sayden to
> Pylate. . . . (Stonyhurst College MS. 43, fol. 21r)[75]

The sequence begins, therefore, with a portion of the trial of Christ before Pilate and the miracle of the standards in *EN* 1.5–6, but here these events are placed before Palm Sunday, and Pilate releases Jesus. This expands the episode of the conspiracy of the Jews (Jn. 11:47–53), but the effect is to create a second, earlier trial for which there is no precedent in the canonical gospels.

The trial proper in the *Meditationes vitae Christi* (chap. 76) is brief, but in this ME text it is expanded with an account of the dream of Pilate's wife, a version of the trial drawn from the gospels and the *GN*, and the remorse and suicide of Judas (Egerton 2658, fols. 5vb–6rb). In

---

[73] For descriptions of these manuscripts, see British Museum, London, *Catalogue of Additions to the Manuscripts in the British Museum in the Years 1882–1887* (1889; repr., London: Trustees of the British Museum, 1968), 378; Frank Taylor, *Supplementary Hand-List of Western Manuscripts in the John Rylands Library* (Manchester: The Manchester University Press, 1937), 28; G. A. Lester, *The Index of Middle English Prose: Handlist II* (Cambridge: D. S. Brewer, 1985), 64–65; The Royal Commission on Historical Manuscripts, "The Manuscripts in the Library of Stonyhurst College, Belonging to the Society of Jesus," in *Second Report of the Royal Commission on Historical Manuscripts* (London: G. E. Eyre and W. Spottiswoode, 1871), 144. An edition of only the ME *Gospel of Nicodemus* in these three manuscripts and Oxford, Bodl. Lib. MS. Bodley 207, has been prepared by Alan W. Holden, "The Gospel of Nicodemus in Middle English Prose from British Museum MS Egerton 2658, John Rylands English MS 895, Bodleian Library MS Bodley 207, Stonyhurst MS XLIII" (Master's thesis, University of London, 1951). I am preparing a critical edition of the whole sequence for the Early English Text Society.

[74] *Meditationes vitae Christi*, in *Opera Omnia S. Bonaventurae*, ed. A. C. Peltier, vol. 12 (Paris, 1868), 509–630.

[75] Quotations and references will be mainly to the text in Egerton 2658, but the manuscript is damaged at this point and the text illegible.

the midst of *Meditationes* chapter 77, the compiler has included a scene of the mocking, which is only hinted at in the Latin text, and the legend of the holy rood (Egerton 2658, fols. 6vb–7ra). The latter has its origins in the *GN*, but the version given here reflects the development of the legend long after it had become independent of that text. Into *Meditationes* chapter 84 the compiler has introduced a long passage on the fears of the Jews and their imprisonment of Joseph of Arimathea; some of this is from the gospels, but most is taken from the *EN* 12.1. *Meditationes* chapter 85 concerns Christ's Descent into Hell, but in the ME text there are indications of the use of the *GN*: "Thanne oure Lord Ihesus sende hem into Paradys by Mychael þe Archaungel as it is more fully declarid herafter" (Egerton 2658, fol. 11va). Michael is not mentioned in the *Meditationes*, but what is more significant is the reference to a fuller account of the Harrowing which is to follow: namely, the version of the *GN* which appears as the second text in the sequence. *Meditationes* chapter 89 opens with a reference to the release of Joseph of Arimathea from prison; in this ME version, this is a cue to use details of the episode from the *GN* (15.6; Egerton 2658, fol. 12va). Finally, after the explicit of this first text, the *Gospel* begins in this way:

> Now turne we aȝen to þe proces aforhonde, how it bifell of Ioseph of Aramathye whiche þe Iewes hadde enprisoned þe Saterday. Þe morwe vpon her Sabot day þei forȝat not Ioseph of Aramaþie whiche þei hadde yputte ynto þe stronge stonen house. Þei gadred hem togedres yn here temple and toke here rede to slee Ioseph.... (Egerton 2658, fol. 15va).

This is precisely the point in the Latin *EN* (12.2) where the earlier account of the imprisonment of Joseph left off, and the opening sentence is careful to link what follows to that episode. This version of the *Gospel* is based quite closely on the Latin text, certainly much more so than that in Egerton 2781 and Royal 20. B. V. It consists of translation and paraphrase; probably for reasons of economy, but possibly because of the exemplar, portions of the original are omitted.[76] The text concludes with material from *EN* 27 and an allusion to the letter of Pilate (*EN* 28; Egerton 2658, fol. 18ra–rb).

    In comparison with the AN/ME prose sequence discussed earlier, the *Gospel* is here more prominent: a major element in the compilation of the first part and more faithfully represented in the second. What, however, is the relationship between the two texts, and how was the sequence conceived? As it stands, there are two accounts of the release

---

[76] For example, *EN* 16.1.1–9 and 17.1.7–12 are linked; cf. Egerton 2658, fol. 16va.

of Joseph of Arimathea, and, while the compiler freely adds new materials, he stops short of incorporating the full narrative of the Harrowing from the GN at the point where it is signalled in the *Meditationes*. So, might the sequence as we have it be a later idea and the *Gospel* an addition to the eclectic Passion narrative? The internal cross-references, however, and the frequent use of the GN in the first text, suggest that the second is more than an appendix, and that the sequence was probably conceived as a whole. The texture of this sequence is different from the first one we discussed, at least in its AN and earlier ME forms; it purposely incorporates more narrative and legendary elements into what is essentially a devotional text. At the same time, however, some additions are clearly meant to increase compassion. This sequence is more diverse than the AN one, and although it does not show the radical developments found in the version in HM 144, it shares something of its encyclopedic character. And this is one of the recurring uses of the GN, to fill in gaps and supplement the narrative provided by the canonical gospels and other texts.

Egerton 2658 contains only this sequence. It is a large format manuscript: there is evidence of some cropping, and the present page size is approximately 330mm x 230mm; in its original form, it probably had the same dimensions as Pepys 2498. It consists of 18 medieval folios, probably a gathering of 8 and a bifolium: fol. 1r is badly worn, and the text has been rubbed away; fol. 18v is blank and shows signs of wear. The evidence suggests that the manuscript had a long history of independence from a larger compilation and may well have been originally published in the form in which it has survived. The script is neat and regular, with much gold decoration on illuminated initials, and the Latin passages are rubricated. It is not a deluxe manuscript, but it is careful and impressive. Assigning a context is difficult: it would be equally at home in a religious institution or lay household. John Rylands MS. English 895, which is in one hand and located to Wiltshire,[77] is a more workaday manuscript, but it too consists only of this sequence. The loss of folios at the beginning of the manuscript and at the point of conjunction of the two texts means that we do not know how or if they were identified or differentiated; Lester argues that they appeared as separate items.[78] Stonyhurst 43 is in one hand but shows three different kinds of language located to "W. Norfolk near the Ely border."[79] It is another workaday volume, 170mm x

---

[77] *LALME* 1:138, 3:545, linguistic profile 5331.

[78] Lester, *The Index*, 65.

[79] See *LALME* 1:165, 3:323–24, linguistic profile 649, where, curiously, Stonyhurst 43 is referred to as Stonyhurst 8.

120mm, and our sequence appears with other items:[80] (1) Life of St.
Katherine (fols. 1r–19v);[81] (2) the Passion and Resurrection sequence
(fols. 21r–96v); (3) a popular prayer in ME verse (fols. 96v–97v), beginning "Ihesu for þi wurthy wounde / That went to þi hert rote;"[82]
(4) a short prose text on events leading to the Assumption of the
Virgin (fols. 97v–98r); (5) *The Charter of the Abbey of the Holy Ghost* (fols.
99r–121v).[83] The volume is a modest collection of popular piety. The
Passion and Resurrection sequence is identified with a rubric on fol.
21r as "Passio Domini nostri Ihesu Christi, sit nostra salus & pro-
tectio." Throughout the text rubrics identify different parts of the
narrative, and that which introduces the GN is typical of these: "Quomodo Iudei in die Pasche pariter congregauerunt et fecerunt consilium
ad interficiendum Ioseph ab Armamathia" (Stonyhurst 43, fol. 83r;
"How the Jews on the day of the Passover gathered together and
devised a plan to kill Joseph of Arimathea"). But there is no firm
boundary between the two main parts of the sequence which appear
in the manuscript as one text. The explicit reads as follows:

> Explicit iste liber a quibusdam vocatus testamentum Nichodemi
> in quo continetur passio Domini nostri Ihesu Christi, resurectio,
> ascencio, pentecoste, et qualiter libro Carynes & Levynes scrip-
> cerunt in templo de Ierusalem quomodo Dominus noster Ihesus
> Christus intrauit Infernum & lyberauit Adam et Euam & alios
> sanctos, et postmodum quomodo Pylatus fecit libros de pre-
> dictis materiis in pretorio de Ierusalem et misit vnam epistolam
> imperatori Tyberyo Rome de passione Domini nostri Ihesu
> Christi facta per Iudeos in Ierusalem, in modo ut scripbitur in
> libro isto. (Stonyhurst 43, fol. 96r–v)

> (Here this books ends which is called by certain ones the
> Testament of Nicodemus; in it is contained the Passion of our
> Lord Jesus Christ, his Resurrection, Ascension, Pentecost, and
> how in the temple of Jerusalem, Carynes and Levynes wrote
> in a book how our Lord Jesus Christ entered into hell and
> freed Adam and Eve and other saints, and afterwards how
> Pilate ordered records of the foresaid matters to be kept in the
> palace in Jerusalem, and sent a letter to the emperor Tiberius
> at Rome concerning the Passion of our Lord Jesus Christ

---

[80] ME prose texts are identified by their index number in R. E. Lewis, N. F.
Blake, and A. S. G. Edwards, *Index of Printed Middle English Prose* (New York: Garland, 1985), cited as *IPMEP*; verse texts by their index number in *IMEV*.

[81] *IPMEP* 29.

[82] *IMEV* 1752.

[83] *IPMEP* 590.

which was caused by the Jews in Jerusalem, just as will be written in this book.)

This reviews the contents of what has gone before and identifies the whole sequence as the *GN*, an indication, possibly, of its authority in the popular imagination.

This text of the *GN* is found also in Oxford, Bodl. Lib. MS. Bodley 207, fols. 120v–26r;[84] the manuscript has been located to Surrey and may have been in the possession of Newark Priory. The text of the *Gospel* is independent of the ME version of the *Meditationes vitae Christi* with which it is found in the other three manuscripts, and follows instead Nicholas Love's translation (1410).[85] Unlike the other three manuscripts, this includes the letter of Pilate to Claudius (*EN* 28) and a text of the *Cura sanitatis Tiberii* (fols. 124r–26r). The *Gospel* comes after the rubricated memorandum attached to the *Meditationes* on fol. 120v, but there is no incipit or explicit to identify the text. Three hands using a similar language have been identified in the manuscript, and the *Gospel* and the texts which follow it are coincident with the third. The execution is not of the same standard as the other two, as if the *Gospel* were an afterthought. The manuscript is generally in gatherings of eight, and fols. 119–26 form the last one. The *Meditationes* finishes on the verso of the second folio of the gathering, so the *Gospel* and its related texts may have been used to fill it in. The question of the presence of this text of the *Gospel* in this manuscript, given its literary relations elsewhere, is tantalizing. That it is found in a manuscript of a different version of the *Meditationes* is probably not coincidence but a reflection of an association between the two texts in the period before Love. Further, the presence of this *Gospel* in a manuscript of the Love text suggests how the officially sanctioned translation made other versions obsolete. At the very least, it reveals that even if a sequence of texts had been conceived as a whole, scribes or editors still freely used parts of it for their own purposes.

A third sequence involving literature of affective piety and the *GN* appears in Harley 1740 (fols. 5ra–22rb).[86] It is identified by the simple

---

[84] Madan and Craster, *A Summary Catalogue*, 167–68, no. 2021.

[85] For this ME translation of the *Meditationes*, see Nicholas Love, *Nicholas Love's "Mirror of the Blessed Life of Jesus Christ,"* ed. Michael G. Sargent (New York: Garland, 1992). See also Elizabeth Salter, *Nicholas Love's "Myrrour of the Blessed Lyf of Jesu Christ,"* Analecta Cartusiana, vol. 10 (Salzburg: Institut für englische Sprache und Literatur, Universität Salzburg, 1974). For the dialect of Bodley 207, see *LALME* 1:146, 3:494, linguistic profile 5641.

[86] British Museum, London, *A Catalogue of the Harleian Manuscripts in the British Museum*, 4 vols. (London: Printed by Command of His Majesty King George III, 1808–12), 2:193.

rubric "Passio Domini Nostri Ihesu Christi" and conceived in a way similar to the *Quis dabit*, that is, as a revelation in answer to a prayer for knowledge of the suffering of Christ:

> Ther was a man of religion þat after his holi deuocion was riȝt diligent in his prayers afore Matyns & after, and had an vsage custommabli to wake whan his breþerin slept. And so he stablid in his holi deuocion a brennyng desire to knowe þe sondre paynes & anguysches þat our Lorde Ihesu Criste sufferd for mankynde. (Harley 1740, fol. 5ra)

The revelation of the Passion begins, after a brief reference to the Last Supper, with the events of the agony in the garden and the betrayal. The suffering of Christ is elaborated in great detail, in ways similar to those found in other Passion texts, and the compilation frequently combines emotional response with doctrinal issues. The Harrowing of Hell is introduced to illustrate the idea that Christ's body and soul retained their divinity after they were separated at his death. The account of the Harrowing begins in this way:

> And anone he descendid to hel, riȝt briȝt and ferdful to þe feendis. And whan he was come to þe ȝates of brasse of hell, he said, "Open ȝoure ȝatis, ȝe princes of hell; he shall enter, þe kynge of glory." And when [he] herd þis, þan þus seid tho Sathan þe prince, "Departe fro me; lo, go oute of my sightes; if ȝow be euyl fighters howe schall ȝowe fighte aȝens hym and chase hym." Then seid Sathan to his euyll workers, "Shett ȝoure ȝates of brasse; put þerto ȝour barres, and bere þere aȝenst fersly þat we be not taken with our pray þat we haue herein." (Harley 1740, fol. 20ra)

This passage is drawn from *EN* 21.1, and the Harrowing uses material selectively from this point up to and including *EN* 25.1–4 (Harley 1740, fol. 20vb). Altogether its purpose is to form part of the account of the Resurrection. The narrative concludes like a gospel harmony but with emphasis on Christ's appearance to Mary (Harley 1740, fol. 22rb).

In the conclusion no mention is made of the narrative framework, that is, the revelation, but immediately following in the same hand is a text with the rubric: "Item de passione Christi bona contemplacio" (Harley 1740, fol. 22rb–24ra).[87] This is a spiritual exercise addressed to a female figure. It fits neatly with the previous narrative, which high-

---

[87] Edited in C. W. Marx, "British Library Harley MS. 1740 and Popular Devotion," in *England in the Fifteenth Century*, ed. Nicholas Rogers, Harlaxton Medieval Studies, vol. 4 (Stamford: P. Watkins, 1994), 207–22.

lights the suffering of Christ; it organizes the events of the Passion and the instruments of the Passion into a systematic exercise which aims to establish spiritual and moral discipline. The two texts are meant to be read together, and they complement each other. In its original form the manuscript contained only these two texts; a later hand has added a third item, a ME sermon on the Latin text "Homo quidam fecit cenam magam & vocauit multos" (fols. 24rb–29va).[88] As a whole, the sequence contains four important features of the *Meditationes vitae Christi,* that is, narrative, doctrine, episodes designed to create compassion, and instructions for meditation. It is the last feature, lacking from the two sequences we discussed earlier, which argues for the greater sophistication of this compiler.

In this context, as in the other two we have discussed, the *GN* is used selectively; only certain episodes are generally relevant, mainly the imprisonment and release of Joseph of Arimathea and the Harrowing of Hell. Both are testimony of the Resurrection and were used for that reason. In these contexts a general preoccupation with emotional responses to Christ's suffering has rendered irrelevant large portions of the *Gospel.* Its account of the trial of Christ, the prolonged disputes over his identity, and the testimony of the witnesses to his life and work must have seemed abstract and legalistic, too lacking in feeling, in the light of the potential offered by the literature of affective piety.

Instructional literature

Another thirteenth-century context for the *Gospel of Nicodemus* is the literature of instruction which developed in response to the injunctions of the Fourth Lateran Council (1215) to preach and teach. The *South English Legendary,* a vast and amorphous network of *temporale* narratives and saints' lives, is a manifestation of just such a response.[89] In the *South English Legendary* only one text uses the *GN* at all extensively, the *Harrowing of Hell and Destruction of Jerusalem,* which survives in a fifteenth-century manuscript located to southeast Norfolk, St. John's College, Cambridge, MS. B. 6, fols. 73r–79r. This contains mainly early forms of *temporale* narratives such as the *Ministry and Passion,* and the *Harrowing of Hell and Destruction of Jerusalem* is part of this thirteenth-

---

[88] Veronica M. O'Mara, "A Checklist of Unedited Late Middle English Sermons That Occur Singly or in Small Groups," *Leeds Studies in English,* n.s., 19 (1988): 157.

[89] Derek Pearsall, *Old English and Middle English Poetry,* The Routledge History of English Poetry, vol. 1 (London: Routledge & K. Paul, 1977), 102–5; Görlach, *The Textual Tradition.*

century group.[90] The text consists of 542 lines and depends for the most part on *GN* chapters 11–27 for vv. 1–320, the story of Joseph of Arimathea and the Harrowing of Hell, and on *Legenda aurea*, chapter 67, "De sancto Jacobo apostolo," for vv. 321–542, the destruction of Jerusalem. Fewer than ninety lines have no basis in these two sources, which the compiler reproduces quite closely but not uncritically. Joseph of Arimathea is the link between the two narratives—an idea probably suggested by a passage in chapter 67 of the *Legenda aurea*:

> In evangelio tamen Nicodemi dicitur, quod cum Judaei ipsum [Joseph] reclusissent, Christus resurgens eum inde eripuit et in Arimathiam duxit. Potest dici, quod cum eductus a praedicatione Christi non cessaret, a Judaeis iterum est reclusus.[91]

> (However, in the gospel of Nicodemus it is said that although the Jews had imprisoned Joseph, the risen Christ released him and brought him to Arimathea. It is possible that he was imprisoned a second time because, having been released, he would not cease from preaching about Christ.)

This occurs at the end of the account of the destruction of Jerusalem in the *Legenda aurea* and serves to explain the discovery of Joseph imprisoned in the city. In linking the two narratives, the *Harrowing of Hell and Destruction of Jerusalem* follows a well established pattern, but the focus on Joseph makes the text seem as much a *sanctorale* as a *temporale* narrative.

Why the account of the Harrowing should occur outside the main *temporale* narratives of the ministry and Passion of Christ in the *South English Legendary*, particularly the *Ministry and Passion*, deserves consideration. The *Harrowing of Hell and Destruction of Jerusalem* shares small passages with the larger narratives, such as the episode of the dream of Pilate's wife, which is more logically located in this text than in the *Ministry and Passion*.[92] The best explanation for the indepen-

---

[90] The *Harrowing of Hell and Destruction of Jerusalem* is listed in *IMEV* as item 3706; it is edited in C. W. Marx, ed., *The Devils' Parliament and the Harrowing of Hell and Destruction of Jerusalem*, Middle English Texts, vol. 25 (Heidelberg: C. Winter, 1993), 115–57. For descriptions and discussions of the manuscript and text, see M. R. James, *A Descriptive Catalogue of the Manuscripts in the Library of St. John's College Cambridge* (Cambridge: University Press, 1913), 37–38, no. 28; O. S. Pickering, "The Temporale Narratives of the South English Legendary," *Anglia* 91 (1973): 425–55; idem, ed., *The South English Ministry and Passion*, Middle English Texts, vol. 16 (Heidelberg: C. Winter, 1984), 61–73; Marx, *The Devils' Parliament*, 116–17; for the dialect, *LALME* 1:64, 3:354–55, linguistic profile 4646.

[91] Jacobus a Voragine, *Legenda aurea*, 302–3.

[92] Pickering, *The South English Ministry and Passion*, 38–40; Marx, *The Devils' Parliament*, 127–31.

dence of the *Harrowing of Hell and Destruction of Jerusalem* from the *Ministry and Passion* and its related narratives is that the account of the imprisonment and release of Joseph of Arimathea followed by the Harrowing of Hell (*EN* 11–27) was too much of a piece and too extensive to be incorporated into a text like the *Ministry and Passion* and would have overbalanced it. It is only a highly ambitious project, such as the *Cursor mundi*, which could absorb the *GN* either in part or in its entirety.

The *Cursor mundi* is dated to around 1300, and includes as part of its vast narrative chapters 12–28 of the *GN*, including the letter of Pilate (vv. 17289–18582);[93] the exemplar, at least for this portion, was probably fairly closely related to *EN* A. The verse rendering is remarkably faithful to the details of its source, with only minor homiletic additions, such as vv. 17447–62 on the greed of the soldiers who are offered a bribe to suppress their testimony about the Resurrection (*EN* 13.3) and vv. 17575–94 on the idea that Jesus is to be sought in the spirit ("et quaerentes non inuenerunt Iesum"; *EN* 15.1.18–19). The Redemption forms the thematic context for the *GN*. The verse translation from the *Gospel* comes after a number of passages which follow the burial of Christ and which reflect on the meaning of the Crucifixion and the reactions of Mary (vv. 16913–17288). The narrative is introduced with the themes of the Redemption and defeat of the Devil,

> Þat ranscuning wald i of tell,
> Þou spede me, lauerd! for-to spell
> Hu mighteli þou harud hell,
> And queld him þat all wald quell (Cotton, vv. 17265–68),

and is prefaced by an address to Christ which attributes the account to the testimony of Nicodemus. Between the end of the *Gospel* and the account of the post-Resurrection appearances is an interlude which, like the preface, takes up the significance of the death of Christ and the Harrowing of Hell, and concludes with the bestiary imagery of Christ the lion (vv. 18585–660). The theme is not presented in a self-consciously doctrinal fashion, but chapters 12–28 of the *GN* are introduced into the *Cursor mundi* to dramatize the Redemption.

Like the *Cursor mundi* but on a less ambitious scale is the *Stanzaic Life of Christ*, which is placed in the late fourteenth century and is from Chester.[94] It runs to 10840 lines and was compiled mainly from the

---

[93] Edited by Richard Morris, *Cursor mundi (The Cursor of the World)*, pt. 3, EETS OS, vol. 62 (London: K. Paul, Trench, Trübner, 1876), 992–1065. See also Pearsall, *Old English and Middle English Poetry*, 106–7; John Thompson, "Textual Interpolations in the Cotton Manuscript of the *Cursor Mundi*," *Neuphilologische Mitteilungen* 92 (1991): 23–24.

[94] Edited by Frances A. Foster, *A Stanzaic Life of Christ*, EETS OS, vol. 166

Polychronicon and the *Legenda aurea*. The *Stanzaic Life of Christ* makes no special claims for itself other than, as two early stanzas indicate (vv. 9–16), to translate Latin instructional writing into English. It uses the portion of the chapter in the *Legenda aurea* on the Resurrection which deals with the Harrowing of Hell. As we have seen already, the *Legenda aurea* cites two authorities for the Harrowing, the *EN* and the pseudo-Augustinian "Sermo 160: De pascha," which includes parallels with *EN* 22 and 23. The *Legenda aurea*'s text of the *EN* begins in chapter 18 with the opening of the narrative of Leucius and Carinus. It is highly selective for reasons that reflect certain strategies. More of the text is retained where it reflects the theme of fulfilment of prophecies, chapters 18 and 19 and 26 (the meeting with the Good Thief), or where there is an apocalyptic theme, chapter 25, the meeting with Enoch and Elijah. The main episodes of the *EN* appear in some form, including much of chapter 20, the dispute between Inferus and Satan on the nature of Christ. Omitted entirely are chapters 22 and 23 on Christ's conquest of the devils and the reproaches of Inferus to Satan for bringing about the death of Christ. But these two chapters are represented in the extracts from the pseudo-Augustine "Sermo 160" given earlier. Their omission probably reflects the astute observation by the compiler that they would be repetitious. The dramatic action is reduced to essential details, and because of the omission of *EN* 22 and 23, Christ's entry into hell (*EN* 21) is linked directly to the leading out of the saints (*EN* 24); these episodes form one sentence. This version ends with a brief reference, from *EN* 27, to the transfiguration of Carinus and Leucius.

The *Stanzaic Life of Christ* follows the *Legenda aurea* faithfully and includes even the introductory sentences on the subject and its authorities (vv. 7801–8). The extracts from the pseudo-Augustinian sermon appear in vv. 7809–64 and from the *EN* in vv. 7865–8108. The reader is reminded of the nature of the source because the text is interspersed with key Latin phrases, such as the command to open the gates of hell, but these are translated into ME as well. The translator took few liberties with his source, and additions are designed primarily to make its sense more explicit; for example, compare the Latin with the ME in this instance: "... et, cum haec loqueretur, facta est vox ut tonitruum dicens" ("and, when he said that, there came a voice like thunder saying")[95]

(London: H. Milford, 1926); *IMEV* 1755. See also Ian Johnson, "Prologue and Practice: Middle English Lives of Christ," in *The Medieval Translator: The Theory and Practice of Translation in the Middle Ages*, ed. Roger Ellis (Cambridge: D. S. Brewer, 1989), 69–85.

[95] Jacobus a Voragine, *Legenda aurea*, 244.

whil Sathan spake to Helle so
And Helle to Sathanas Aȝayn,
a voice as thonour made was tho
that all hell dred & had dedayne. (Vv. 7997–8000)

Nothing is left to chance, and stanzas are very often filled out with detail designed to clarify meaning or context. At one point, however, the translator forgets that the two sons of Simeon are narrating the account and uses the formula "as rede we" (v. 7985). The *Stanzaic Life of Christ* is entirely functional, an avenue which, as part of a larger program of compilation, makes portions of the GN available in the vernacular for instructional purposes.

The *Metrical Life of Christ* is similar in scope to the *Stanzaic Life of Christ* but only half its length.[96] It is dated to the early part of the fifteenth century, and the author's language was an East Midlands type.[97] The manuscript (London, BL MS. Addit. 39996) is in one hand located to Leicestershire.[98] Scholars have been uncertain whether the *Metrical Life of Christ* was originally one work, but there is little reason not to regard it as a single compilation in the form in which it survives. Formulae of direct address and lines such as "As ȝe seen bifore ȝow here / Þe encense brenne in þe censere" (vv. 439–40) suggest that it was designed for reading in church. Two portions of the *Metrical Life of Christ* reflect the influence of the GN. The first (vv. 3300–449) appears in the context of reports of the Resurrection (vv. 3221–99) and uses as its framework the story of the sons of Simeon, that is, GN 17–27. The compiler is using the *Gospel*, but, where the *Stanzaic Life of Christ* slavishly reproduces its source, the *Metrical Life of Christ* presents a lively, brisk, and in many ways independent account of the Harrowing. The compiler is prepared to adapt materials from the GN to new purposes. He takes Satan's speech on the conflict between himself and Christ, addressed to Inferus (*EN* 20.1), and uses it to show that Satan realized the identity of Christ only at the Crucifixion (vv. 3352–61); his return to hell in this version is to announce the defeat of the devils (vv. 3362–65). This is a major reinterpretation of the *Gospel*. There are other additions but the most important is Christ's extended speech (vv. 3388–407) in which he explains the Redemption and the fate of the devils in hell. In the GN Christ says little at the Harrowing of Hell, so this speech represents an important innovation. It does not have the same implications as the debate between Christ and Satan in the *Mid-*

---

[96] Edited by Walter Sauer, *The Metrical Life of Christ*, Middle English Texts, vol. 5 (Heidelberg: C. Winter, 1977).

[97] Ibid., 9–11.

[98] *LALME* 1:102, 3:237–38, linguistic profile 300.

dle English Harrowing of Hell, but it creates a more human Christ who is also a teacher of doctrine. The *Metrical Life of Christ* does not go as far as the *Middle English Harrowing of Hell* in reinterpreting the Harrowing of Hell in the *GN*, but it shows a freedom in the use of the source, which makes the vernacular tradition seem less of a slave to the Latin.

The second part of the *Metrical Life of Christ* to use the *GN* is the account of the imprisonment and release of Joseph of Arimathea (vv. 4138–307). This comes after the post-Resurrection appearances of Christ and the making of the creed. It uses the source freely to develop the theme of the treachery of the Jews against Joseph: vv. 4138–83 are based loosely on *EN* 12.1, his imprisonment; vv. 4184–211 on *EN* 15.6, his release; vv. 4212–51 on details in *EN* 12.2, the discovery that he was not in the prison, and *EN* 15.2–5, his return to Jerusalem; and vv. 4252–77 on *EN* 14, the bribing of the witnesses to the Resurrection. The rest of the episode (vv. 4278–307) has no basis in the *Gospel* but uses the idea found in the *Legenda aurea* and the *Harrowing of Hell and Destruction of Jerusalem* that Joseph was imprisoned a second time. Like the other two texts, the *Metrical Life of Christ* narrates the discovery of Joseph by Titus fifty years later at the destruction of Jerusalem, but this is treated separately (vv. 4788–821). For the compiler of the *Metrical Life of Christ* the integrity of the source clearly took second place to larger narrative strategies.

The *GN* appears in ME verse in a version independent of other narratives and including episodes from the trial to the Harrowing.[99] The ME *Stanzaic Gospel of Nicodemus*, because it is known to have been used in the York cycle, can be dated to before 1378 and is probably as early as the first quarter of the fourteenth century.[100] It survives in four manuscripts, all with some variations: London, BL MSS. Cotton Galba E. IX, fols. 57v–66v (G); Harley 4196, fols. 206r–15r (H); Addit. 32578, fols. 116v–40v (A); and London, Sion College Arc. L. 40. 2/E. 25, fols. 13r–38v (S). The forms of language of G, H, and S are characterized as "fully northern," while that of A is located to "north east Lancashire, or possibly extreme west Yorkshire."[101] The stanza form

---

[99] Edited in W. H. Hulme, *The Middle English Harrowing of Hell*, 22–136; *IMEV* 512.

[100] Pearsall, *Old English and Middle English Poetry*, 297; Foster, "Legends," 448–49, 640–41.

[101] On Cotton Galba E. IX, see Robert E. Lewis and Angus McIntosh, *A Descriptive Guide to the Manuscripts of the "Prick of Conscience,"* Medium Ævum Monographs, n.s., vol. 12 (Oxford: Society for the Study of Medieval Languages and Literature, 1982), 58–59; on Harley 4196, ibid., 66–67, and Saara Nevalinna, ed., *The Northern Homily Cycle: The Expanded Version in MSS Harley 4196 and Cotton Tiberius E VII*, vol. 1, *From Advent to Septuagesima*, Mémoires de la Société néophilologique de Helsinki, vol. 38 (Helsinki: Société néophilologique, 1972), 5–11;

is 12 lines rhyming a. b. a. b. a. b. a. b. c. d. c. d. The text is a translation of the *GN* related to the version in Ford's French manuscripts "E"
(Paris, BN MS. f. fr. 1850, fols. 78r–92v, saec. XIII) and "F" (Oxford,
Queen's College MS. 304, fols. 1c–5c, saec. XV/2): there are at least
seven instances where lines in the *Stanzaic Gospel of Nicodemus* have
parallels in passages peculiar to this French recension.[102] Lindström
states that these passages have no counterparts in known Latin manuscripts, but Izydorczyk's brief account of what he identifies as the Latin
EN C shows two parallels.[103] Further work on this Latin recension
might reveal that all the passages identified by Lindström as unique to
the French have a basis in it; and in a recent article, Zbigniew Izydorczyk assembles evidence to show the close links between a Latin
recension intimately related to *EN* C and the recension of the French
translation represented by Ford's manuscripts "E" and "F."[104] This
would open up the question of the origin of the ME text, the linguistic
evidence for which is obscured by the nature of the translation itself.
Nevertheless, it can be associated with a specific textual tradition.

The translation is not literal, and the source is often simplified.
One strategy was to substitute a sustained speech for passages of argument with frequent changes of speaker. For example, the dispute
between Christ and Pilate about the nature of truth is cut short, and
Christ is given a speech on the theme (vv. 349–60; *EN* 3.2.13–18).[105]
The same feature is apparent in vv. 423–32, where the translator has
overridden the dialogue in which Pilate questions the actions of the

---

on Addit. 32578, see Lewis and McIntosh, *A Descriptive Guide*, 76–77; on Sion College Arc. L. 40. 2/E. 25, see ibid., 82–83, and N. R. Ker, *Medieval Manuscripts in
British Libraries*, vol. 1, London (Oxford: Clarendon Press, 1969), 289. For dialects,
see *LALME* 1:101, 106, 113, 137; 3:213, linguistic profile 365 for "A," 670–71, linguistic profile 481 for "Hand B" in "S."

[102] The French text of the *GN* in Paris, BN MS. f. fr. 1850 ("E") is printed as
text "C" in Bengt Lindström, ed., *A Late Middle English Version of the Gospel of
Nicodemus Edited from British Museum MS Harley 149*, Acta Universitatis Upsaliensis, Studia Anglistica Upsaliensia, vol. 18 (Uppsala: Almqvist & Wiksell, 1974),
44–129. "E" and "F" are collated with the base text of "Tradition A" in Ford,
L'Évangile de Nicodème, 41–71; see also ibid., 22–23. The correspondences are: vv.
121–28 (Lindström, *A Late Middle English Version*, 48."C".22); vv. 387–92 (ibid.,
58."C".11–13, and 132); vv. 455–64 (ibid., 61."C".18–62."C".25, and 133); vv. 511–
16 (ibid., 65."C".1–66."C".2, and 134); vv. 661–68 (ibid., 74."C".17–18, and 136);
vv. 691–712 (ibid., 76."C".2–10, and 136); vv. 1409–20 (ibid., 111."C".22–29 and
111."C".1, and 144). An eighth parallel is probably vv. 423–28 (ibid., 59."C".24–
60."C".26, and 133).
[103] "The Unfamiliar *Evangelium Nicodemi*," 182.
[104] I am grateful to Zbigniew Izydorczyk for allowing me to consult his essay,
"The Latin Source of an Old French Gospel of Nicodemus," before it appeared in
Revue d'histoire des textes 25 (1995): 265–79.
[105] Lindström, *A Late Middle English Version*, 57."C".19–24.

Jews; they simply assert their reasons for condemning Christ (EN 4.4–5).[106] Another strategy is wholesale abbreviation. The third paragraph of EN 20 is omitted, but the command of Inferus not to bring Christ into hell has been moved in the translation from that context to replace the opening sentence of the second paragraph, vv. 1309–14.[107] This policy to compress and abbreviate is most evident in the latter part of the text, where, for example, vv. 1533–36 summarize a large portion of EN 24: "ilk prophet þus gan tell / of þaire awin prophecy / how he suld hery hell / how he suld for þam dy" (G; EN 24.3.1–13).[108] The style of the Harrowing of Hell sequence in the Latin EN is less sparse and more complex than that of the earlier part; the translator may have found that his skill was stretched in this area of his source and, therefore, sought ways to bypass large portions of text.

But not all the variations from the source are omissions. In some instances the translator would appear to be adding to the text as the result of various sorts of pressures. The account of the flagellation of Christ is embellished in vv. 601–12 under the influence of well established traditions of affective piety: "a crown of thorn ful sare / to threst þai haue bygun / on his heuid, till þe hare / was all of blude biron" (G, vv. 609–12; EN 10.1.1–4);[109] and the speech of Isaiah in hell is expanded to emphasize the theme of the fulfilment of prophecy (vv. 1195–200; EN 18.1.13–19).[110] In places the translator simply failed to understand the source text: he does not keep the distinction between Satan and Inferus ("Sone efter þat spak satanas / þat mayster was in hell," G, vv. 1285–86) and must use some vague figures referred to as "þai," presumably devils, to take on the speeches of Inferus.

The texts in the four manuscripts differ in some ways. G and H have an additional stanza (vv. 181–92) which attributes the dream of Pilate's wife to the Devil. It is impossible to determine if this stanza is original or later embellishment, but it indicates the extent to which this explanation of the episode was current and exerted pressure on a version of the GN.[111] The closing part of the text shows the most variation among the four manuscripts. The source included the rare "chapter 28," which does not appear in the codex Einsidlensis but which Tischendorf gives in his edition: here the Jews calculate the time at which Christ was due to appear and find that Jesus has fulfilled the

---

[106] Ibid., 59."C".19–60."C".29 and "C".1–4.

[107] Ibid., 106."C".3–107."C".17.

[108] Ibid., 119."C".14–23.

[109] Ibid., 71."C".16–20.

[110] Ibid., 99."C".2–100."C".8.

[111] An account of the Latin tradition of commentary on the dream appears in C. W. Marx, The Devil's Rights, 52–53.

prophecy. The translator began with this at v. 1661, and G, H, and S follow it to the end: v. 1747 in G and H and v. 1746 in S.[112] The final stanza in S (vv. 1741–52) represents probably the original ending, with the last six lines (vv. 1747–52) composed to provide a conclusion. G and H contain additional lines, two half stanzas: vv. 1748–54 use the prophecy of Isaiah 11:1, and vv. 1755–56 ("þan may we se, sir, þus-gates est / he was god sun of mightes maste," G) can be linked to another textual tradition of the *EN*.[113] G and H, vv. 1748–56, may reflect a variant text of the *GN* which a later compiler used. A summarizes vv. 1717 to the end in two lines, "He was gods son verray / þat we gaffe dedys wounde" (A, vv. 1715–16). These create the context for the letter of Pilate to Claudius as the conclusion, but vv. 1717–28 describing the remorse of Pilate add an emotional element not found in the *EN*. The letter itself (A, vv. 1729–812) appears in versions of the Latin (*EN* 28) and follows the *GN* in OF and AN manuscripts.[114] The letter of Pilate clearly remained closely associated with the *GN*, and its influence was such that at least one compiler was provoked to this kind of extensive revision.

Even this brief discussion of the *Stanzaic Gospel of Nicodemus* shows that it is much more eclectic than Hulme suggested;[115] the translator was adapting the source in the light of his skills and contemporary tastes. But what function did the text have? The manuscripts offer some suggestions. G and H, both from the end of the fourteenth century, are large professional, if not commercial, productions (G, 114 fols., 355mm x 215mm; H, 258 fols., 380mm x 265mm), carefully written in double columns. A and S, dated respectively to 1405 and the turn of the fourteenth to the fifteenth centuries, are smaller, more pedestrian manuscripts but substantial nevertheless. The *Prick of Conscience* is common to all four, and this aligns the *Stanzaic Gospel of Nicodemus* with the popular theological and instructional literature which that text reflects.[116] The *Prick of Conscience* (vv. 6529–46) itself uses the *GN* as an authority for the pains of hell, and this is a further indication of how the apocryphon was read. Much of the other contents of these four manuscripts is also instructional and didactic verse, for example the *Expanded Northern Homily Cycle* and *Tractatus de legenda*

[112] Tischendorf, *Evangelia apocrypha*, 409–12; Lindström, *A Late Middle English Version*, 126–29.
[113] Tischendorf, *Evangelia apocrypha*, 412, apparatus for D.
[114] For example, London BL MSS. Egerton 2710, fol. 132rb–va, and Harley 2253, fol. 39rb–va.
[115] Hulme, *The Middle English Harrowing of Hell*, xv–xvi.
[116] Lewis and McIntosh, *A Descriptive Guide*, 1–5.

sanctorum in H,[117] the creed poem[118] and *Templum Domini*[119] in A, and the verse treatise on shrift[120] and *Lamentations of Our Lady to Saint Bernard*[121] in S. Only G shows any variety, but this miscellany includes religious as well as secular literature.[122] The manuscripts suggest that this version of the GN was used for instructional purposes in the manner of homiletic and legendary texts as well as popularizing treatises on doctrine. It is not difficult to imagine how this ME *Gospel of Nicodemus* could be seen to fulfil all these purposes. A measure of the success with which it made the Latin *Evangelium Nicodemi* accessible is its use in vernacular drama.

Middle English drama

Texts like the *Stanzaic Gospel of Nicodemus* and the *Stanzaic Life of Christ* were originally of interest to scholars because they could be shown to have been used in the composition of the English mystery plays. Their importance as reflections of popular piety was secondary. It has been argued that much of the Harrowing of Hell play in the Chester mystery cycle[123] can be traced to the *Stanzaic Life of Christ*.[124] Apart from a few lines of narrative-linking, the Chester Harrowing play uses material corresponding to *Stanzaic Life of Christ* vv. 7893–8104, that is, from the speech of Adam in hell to the entry of the saints into paradise. In their commentary on this play, Lumiansky and Mills present a confusing picture of the sources, but the evidence of vv. 169–76 is decisive: the ordering of Satan to leave his seat and fight on behalf of the devils has no counterpart in the *Legenda aurea* or *Stanzaic Life of Christ* but is based on EN 21.1.5–8.[125] This suggests that the playwright knew the GN in some form apart from the *Legenda aurea* or *Stanzaic Life of Christ* and turned to it when he needed lines for a dramatic episode. More importantly we see the value of a text like the

---

[117] Ibid., 66–67; Nevanlinna, *The Northern Homily*, 6.

[118] *IMEV* 2700.

[119] Ibid., 967.

[120] Ibid., 557.3.

[121] Ibid., 771 and 1869.

[122] Pearsall, *Old English and Middle English Poetry*, 122 and 297.

[123] R. M. Lumiansky and David Mills, eds., *The Chester Mystery Cycle*, 2 vols., EETS SS, vols. 3 and 9 (London: Oxford University Press, 1974–86), 1:325–39; 2:262–76.

[124] Robert H. Wilson, "The *Stanzaic Life of Christ* and the Chester Plays," *Studies in Philology* 28 (1931): 413–32.

[125] Lumiansky and Mills, *The Chester Mystery Cycle*, 2:270.

Stanzaic Life of Christ to a dramatist: it was more convenient to work from a précis and only occasionally turn to the original. Other additions are aimed at highlighting the Redemption by using the language of popular theology, such as ransom and the four daughters of God (vv. 61–62; 68–70; 215–20); and Satan's admission in vv. 181–82 of guilt for Adam's Fall has doctrinal implications.[126] The episode of the alewife at the end of the play (vv. 277–336), however, serves only dramatic purposes.[127] For the most part the play relies heavily on material from the GN mediated through the *Legenda aurea* and the *Stanzaic Life of Christ*, but its doctrinal themes have been updated.

The GN appears in a very different way in the York cycle, where it is used in a series of plays beginning with "Christ before Annas and Caiaphas" and ending with "the Resurrection."[128] For the most part it supplies only episodes and incidents, although it is the main source for the Harrowing of Hell play. There is general agreement that the compiler used the ME *Stanzaic Gospel of Nicodemus*; verbal echoes are evident in at least six plays: 29 "Christ before Annas and Caiaphas," 30 "Christ before Pilate 1: The Dream of Pilate's Wife," 33 "Christ before Pilate 2: The Judgement," 36 "The Death of Christ," 37 "The Harrowing of Hell" (also, Towneley 25), 38 "The Resurrection" (also, Towneley 26).[129] These are relatively few but sufficient to confirm that this is a version which the dramatist used and to suggest some-

---

[126] C. W. Marx, "The Problem of the Doctrine of the Redemption in the ME Mystery Plays and the *Cornish Ordinalia*," *Medium Ævum* 54 (1985): 24–25.

[127] R. M. Lumiansky, "Comedy and Theme in the Chester Harrowing of Hell," *Tulane Studies in English* 10 (1960): 5–12; Axton, *European Drama*, 183–84.

[128] Richard Beadle, ed., *The York Plays*, York Medieval Texts, 2d ser. (London: E. Arnold, 1982), 242–355.

[129] Martin Stevens and A. C. Cawley, eds., *The Towneley Plays*, 2 vols., EETS SS, vols. 13 and 14 (London: Oxford University Press, 1994). Scholars have not always given the same list of the York plays which use the *Stanzaic Gospel of Nicodemus*. W. A. Craigie, "The *Gospel of Nicodemus* and the York Mystery Plays," in *An English Miscellany Presented to Dr. Furnivall in Honour of His Seventy-fifth Birthday* (Oxford: Clarendon Press, 1901), 54, cites York 37, vv. 229–31, as a borrowing from the *Stanzaic Gospel*, vv. 25–27, but fails to notice the obvious borrowing of the same lines in York 29, vv. 52–55. Other lines of this part of the play can be traced back to the *Stanzaic Gospel*: compare York 29, vv. 35–55, and *Stanzaic Gospel*, vv. 21–44. E. G. Clark, "The York Plays and the *Gospel of Nichodemus*," *PMLA* 43 (1928): 153, includes York 39 "Christ's Appearance to Mary Magdalene" in her list but not York 29; however, in her discussion (158), even though she repeats the error, she clearly intends York 29. Grace Frank, "On the Relation between the York and Towneley Plays," *PMLA* 44 (1929): 315, perpetuates Clark's error and includes York 39 among the plays which use the *Stanzaic Gospel*; she says nothing about York 29. York 39, vv. 38–149, and Towneley 26, vv. 580–659, may be related, but they contain nothing from the GN. The Towneley plays figure in this discussion only where they share with York.

thing about his practice of compilation: he probably knew his sources thoroughly—possibly even from memory—and used them mainly as cribs; he was more independent than the compiler of the Chester cycle. Certain substantial episodes, even if they show only a few verbal parallels and are extensively embellished, are ultimately based on the GN. The episode of the beadle and the miracle of the standards is dramatized over two plays (30, vv. 307–97, and 33, vv. 138–293),[130] and 33 continues with details of the trial from the GN.[131] The "Harrowing of Hell" (play 37) is firmly rooted in the Stanzaic Gospel of Nicodemus, vv. 1160–568, that is, from the chorus of the saints at the entry of Christ into hell to the entrusting of the souls to Michael.[132] Most of the episodes in the play find parallels in the Stanzaic Gospel, although the compiler treated some familiar ones in different ways. The first dispute among the devils (vv. 97–120) is modelled on GN 20, but the terms are different. The second dispute (vv. 133–80) concerns the identity of Christ and shows thematic parallels with GN 20. As we have pointed out already, the Stanzaic Gospel has omitted chapter 20.3, and therefore all mention of the raising of Lazarus; the play, however, has two references to it (vv. 161–62, 171–72). The compiler therefore did not use only the Stanzaic Gospel but had access to another version. The major innovation in the play is the debate between Jesus and Satan (vv. 213–334), which replaces the dispute among the devils in GN 23. This effectively changes how the doctrine of the Redemption is presented so that more modern ideas become part of the drama. In this respect the play of the Harrowing is like the Middle English Harrowing of Hell in that it is a reinterpretation of the episode.[133]

The presence of the GN in the N-Town Passion Play is less easy to detect; indeed, a recent editor is inclined to see little direct influence.[134] This view, however, ignores the debt which some episodes and ways of dramatizing themes owe to the GN. The prologue in which Demon recounts Christian history (47–51, vv. 1–124) develops the theme of the Devil's confusion over the identity of Christ and his

[130] Stanzaic Gospel, vv. 61–176; EN 1.2–6; Lindström, A Late Middle English Version, 46."C".26–50."C".14.
[131] York play 33, vv. 296–327; Stanzaic Gospel, vv. 217–24, 301–24; EN 2.2 and 3.1; Lindström, A Late Middle English Version, 52."C".23–26 and 55."C".5–56."C".11.
[132] Lindström, A Late Middle English Version, 98."C".21–121."C".4; EN 18–25.
[133] Marx, "The Problem of the Doctrine of Redemption," 20–32.
[134] Peter Meredith, ed., The Passion Play from the N. Town Manuscript (London: Longman, 1990), 22. All subsequent references are to Meredith's edition. Another edition was prepared for the Early English Text Society by Stephen Spector, ed., The N-Town Play: Cotton MS Vespasian D. 8, 2 vols., EETS SS, vols. 11 and 12 (Oxford: Oxford University Press, 1991).

plot against him (48–49, vv. 25–60). This aspect of the prologue is based ultimately on two speeches of Satan in the *GN* before Christ enters hell (*EN* 20.1 and 20.2.13–19); in "Passion Play 1" the theme is given a new context and is much expanded, but the debt is obvious. A portion of the speech of Satan in the episode of the dream of Pilate's wife in "Passion Play 2" (109, vv. 499–523) is even more clearly based on the passage in the *GN* just referred to. The Devil's order to Satan not to bring Christ into hell (110, vv. 524–27) is derived from the speech of Inferus in the *Gospel* (*EN* 20.3.12–26). The scene continues with Satan's change of mind and attempt to prevent the Crucifixion through the dream, something which does not appear in the *Gospel* but which is developed in this context in other texts which use it, most notably the *Harrowing of Hell and Destruction of Jerusalem*.[135]

The Harrowing of Hell is treated in two parts in "Passion Play 2" (130–31, vv. 993–1042, and 144–46, vv. 1368–439). To say that "more than in any of the cycles it arises from a traditional understanding of the incident"[136] is misleading. The compiler was familiar with the *GN*, and it provided a pattern for some of the episodes in the two parts: the entry of Christ into hell (130–31, vv. 1017–26; *EN* 21), the recognition by the devils of Christ's identity and that they have been overcome by him (131, vv. 1027–34; *EN* 22), Christ's taking the souls from hell, and the chorus of the saints (144–45, vv. 1368–407; *EN* 24). The figure of Christ is central to both parts, and his speeches carry the doctrinal import; this contrasts with the *GN*. The second part reflects the theme of *GN* 24, Christ taking the souls from hell, but, except for v. 1368 (cf. *EN* 24.1.2), there are no verbal echoes, and the chorus of the saints includes Eve, John the Baptist and Abraham. The presence of Eve among the saints (144, vv. 1384–91) and the episode of the binding of Satan (vv. 1408–31) recall the variant text, Tischendorf's Latin B.[137] On the other hand, vv. 1440–41 and 1443 (146) appear to be based on the *Middle English Harrowing of Hell*, and this text may be the source of some of the features of the episode not found in the more common version of the *GN*.[138] More so than any of the others, this presentation is a radical reinterpretation of the Harrowing, both dramatically and doctrinally.[139]

---

[135] Marx, *The Devils' Parliament*, 128–29; 138, vv. 197–210.

[136] Meredith, *The Passion Play*, 22.

[137] Ibid., 145; Tischendorf, *Evangelia apocrypha*, 429–30.

[138] It is generally agreed (Meredith, *The Passion Play*, 220) that vv. 1440–41 and 1443 are based on the *Middle English Harrowing of Hell*, vv. 43–44 and 45 (Auchinleck). See *Middle English Harrowing of Hell*, vv. 115–256, Digby 86.

[139] Marx, "The Problem of the Doctrine of Redemption," 20–24.

Piers Plowman and *The Devils' Parliament*

For all its distinctiveness *Piers Plowman* is in part a product of the
didactic tradition to which we have been referring in connection with
the drama. Langland's knowledge of the *GN* in some form is not in
doubt, but he used it mostly for general themes and structures. The
speech of Book shows that Langland knew the story of the two sons of
Simeon, although he made no use of them as narrators:

> Loo, hell myhte nat holde, bote opened tho god tholede
> And lette out Symondes sones to sen hym honge on rode.
> (C 20.258–59; cf. B 18.249–50)[140]

Langland's version of the Harrowing (B 18.261–406 / C 20.269–449) follows the outlines of *GN* 18–27. After the command to open the gates of
hell (B 18.261–65 / C 20.269–73), there is a dispute among the devils
(B 18.266–315 / C 20.274–349). Apart from Christ's commands and
some brief phrases, however, only the following speech of Satan,
which occurs in the dispute, echoes even faintly a substantial passage
in the *GN*:

> Suche a lyht aȝenes oure leue Lazar hit fette;
> Care and combraunce is come to vs all.
> Yf this kyng come in, mankynde wol he fecche
> And lede hit þer Lazar is and lihtliche me bynde.
> Patriarkes and prophetes haen parled herof longe
> That such a lord and a lihte shal lede hem all hennes.
> (C 20.275–80; cf. B 18.267–72)

These lines recall the speech of Inferus in *EN* 20.3. Skeat suggested that
Langland may have used the account of the Harrowing in the *Legenda
aurea*, but here Langland follows what is explicit in the *EN* and only
implicit in the abbreviated version of the speech in the *Legenda*, namely
Satan's fear that if Christ enters hell he will rescue mankind.[141] In the
course of the dispute in *Piers Plowman*, the devils come to realize that
through the actions of Lucifer they will lose their power. This is the
theme of *GN* 20 and 23, but the terms of the arguments are different.

---

[140] Quotations are from William Langland, *Piers Plowman: An Edition of the
C-Text*, ed. Derek Pearsall, York Medieval Texts, 2d ser. (Berkeley: University of
California Press, 1978); references to version B are to William Langland, *Piers
Plowman: The B Version*, ed. George Kane and E. Talbot Donaldson (London: The
Athlone Press, 1975).

[141] William Langland, *The Vision of William Concerning Piers the Plowman*, ed.
W. W. Skeat, 2 vols. (Oxford: Clarendon Press, 1886), 2:247; Jacobus a Voragine,
Legenda aurea, 243–44.

Langland then compresses several episodes into eleven lines (B 18.316–26 / C 20.359–69): the second command of Christ, a dialogue between Christ and Lucifer, the breaking of the gates, references to speeches by the saints in hell and John the Baptist, the blinding of Lucifer, and finally Christ drawing the saints to him. Only some of these have counterparts in the *GN*, but the speeches of the saints echo briefly *EN* 18.1.16–18 and 18.3.6–8:

> Patriarkes and profetes, *populus in tenebris,*
> Songen with seynt Iohan *"Ecce agnus dei!"*
> (C 20.366–67; cf. B 18.323–24)

Christ then enters hell and, in his speech to Lucifer, justifies the Redemption (B 18.327–403 / C 20.370–446). Langland's version of the Harrowing, while it uses some aspects of the *GN*, is a reinterpretation of the episode in the light of ideas on the Redemption which followed in the tradition of Anselm. This more than anything else accounts for the differences of substance between the treatments of the Harrowing in *Piers Plowman* and the *GN*, a feature of Langland's thought which recent discussions of the episode have failed to appreciate.[142]

In terms of its theology, Langland's version is similar to the *Middle English Harrowing of Hell* and the York and Towneley play of the Harrowing. Something which remains puzzling, however, is why Langland did not present Christ disputing with Lucifer or Satan as in these two texts and others. One answer may be that, even if Langland did not use the theology of the *GN*, he followed its dramatic structure. In the *Gospel* the devils, Satan, and Inferus dispute with each other, not with Christ, and they come to realize they will lose their power. Christ's entry into hell is then a show of force which demonstrates his conquest. Langland's version has a similar pattern: after a dispute among the devils, Christ enters as the victor and, although he makes a speech justifying the release of man, he does not engage in argument.

A reinterpretation of the Harrowing along similar lines appears in the *Devils' Parliament*, probably of the first half of the fifteenth century and located to the East Midlands.[143] There are two medieval manu-

---

[142] These include Malcolm Godden, *The Making of "Piers Plowman"* (London: Oxford University Press, 1990), 138–51; James Simpson, *"Piers Plowman": An Introduction to the B-text* (London: Longman, 1990), 208–16; R. A. Waldron, "Langland's Originality: The Christ-Knight and the Harrowing of Hell," in *Medieval English Religious and Ethical Literature: Essays in Honour of G. H. Russell,* ed. Gregory Kratzmann and James Simpson (Cambridge: D. S. Brewer, 1986), 66–81. On Langland's treatment of the Redemption, see Marx, *The Devil's Rights,* 100–113.

[143] *IMEV* 3992.

scripts; the language of London, BL MS. Addit. 37492, has been tentatively located to Essex, while the language of London, Lambeth Palace
Library MS. 853, is mixed, with elements from South Huntingtonshire,
East Northamptonshire or North Bedfordshire predominating.[144] The
Devils' Parliament is a verse sermon and survives in two versions. It
uses the Harrowing of Hell as a climax for a narrative by the Devil of
the life of Christ. This text is indebted to the *GN* for at least three passages: (1) the command at the gates of hell and the question and reply
concerning the identity of Christ (A 259–68 / B 251–60; *EN* 21.3.3–12),
(2) the second command to open the gates and the rescuing of Adam
and Eve (A 321–28 / B 353–60; *EN* 21.3.3–5, 21.3.16–19, and 24.2.1–6),
and (3) part of the chorus of the saints as Christ is about to take them
out of hell. This third instance illustrates how material from the *Gospel*
is used with other sources:

> Quod Dauid, "Y tolde of on ful grym
> That schuld tobrestyn brasyn ʒatys,"
> Quod Zacarye, "& visite hys folke & out nyme
> And leue behynde that hym hatys,"
> Quod Symeon, "Lyʒt ys folke in dym;
> Lo derkenys leseth hys statys."
> Quod Baptyst, "Thys lombe Y tolde of hym
> That the worldys synne abatys." (A 337–44; cf. B 369–76)

The first two and last two lines alone can be traced to the *GN* and then
in only the most general terms (*EN* 21.2.3–8 and 18.3.6–8). The rest of
the stanza is derived from Luke 1:68, 71, and 79, the song of Zacharias,
the liturgical *Benedictus*. Zacharias, father of John the Baptist, has no
role in the *GN*, and although Simeon appears, he has a different
speech. This stanza shows the eclectic nature of the *Devils' Parliament*
and how, as a source, the *GN* is used in a piecemeal fashion, possibly
even from memory. But if debts for specific passages are rare, the conception of the *Devils' Parliament* owes much to the *GN*, for the idea of
casting the Devil in the role of narrator of the life of Christ, and as one
who is unsure of Christ's identity and who has plotted his death,
appears in embryo in Satan's speeches to the devils in hell (*EN* 20.1

---

[144] The A and B texts are edited in parallel by Marx, *The Devils' Parliament*,
11–114; a transcription of B appears in Frederick J. Furnivall, ed., *Hymns to the
Virgin and Christ, "The Parliament of Devils" and Other Religious Poems ...*, EETS
OS, vol. 24 (London: K. Paul, Trench, Trübner, 1867), 41–57. On the problems of
localizing Addit. 37492, see Marx, *The Devils' Parliament*, 13–14; on Lambeth 853,
see *LALME* 1:118; no linguistic profile is given. My own analysis of Lambeth 853
suggests that north Buckinghamshire can be added to the probable area of origin
of the manuscript.

and 20.2.13–19). In this respect the *Devils' Parliament* is similar to the prologue of Demon in "Passion Play 1" of N-Town. At the same time, the *Devils' Parliament* has at its center a debate between Christ and Lucifer on the issue of the Redemption (A 277–320 / B 269–352). This has no precedent in the *GN* but is a reflection of the change in theological ideas which resulted from the twelfth-century controversy over the issue of the Devil's rights. The *Middle English Harrowing of Hell*, the York and Towneley play of the Harrowing, *Piers Plowman* B 18 / C 20, and the *Devils' Parliament* are essentially reinterpretations of the Harrowing of Hell. They reflect a new reading of the *GN* and a new response to the issues raised by the text in the light of theological and didactic concerns.[145]

Middle English prose translations from Latin

While the *Gospel of Nicodemus* makes its first appearance in English in OE prose, there are no examples of it complete in ME prose until the late fourteenth century. John Trevisa (b. ca. 1342, d. ca. 1402), vicar of Berkeley and chaplain to Thomas IV lord of Berkeley in Gloucestershire, produced what is probably the earliest known ME prose translation of the *Gospel*.[146] There are two contexts for this work that need to be taken into account, the production of the translation, and the three manuscripts in which it survives: London, BL MS. Addit. 16165, fols. 94v–114v (A); Salisbury Cathedral MS. 39, fols. 129v–47r (S); Winchester College MS. 33, fols. 74r–93v (W); all are of the fifteenth century.[147] A is a Shirley manuscript, and recent research has dated the part which includes the *GN* to around 1425.[148] The attribution of

---

[145] On this issue, see Marx, "The Problem of the Doctrine of Redemption"; idem, "An Edition and Study of the *Conflictus*"; idem, *The Devil's Rights*.

[146] Edited by H. C. Kim, "The Gospel of Nicodemus Translated by John Trevisa" (Ph.D. diss., University of Washington, 1963). See also David C. Fowler, "New Light on John Trevisa," *Traditio* 18 (1962): 289–317, and Aaron J. Perry, ed., *Dialogus inter Militem et Clericum, Richard FitzRalph's Sermon: 'Defensio Curatorum' and Methodius: 'þe Bygynnyng of þe World and þe Ende of Worldes,' translated by John Trevisa*, EETS OS, vol. 167 (London: Oxford University Press, 1925), xci–xciv.

[147] They are described in British Museum, London, *Catalogue of Additions to the Manuscripts in the British Museum in the Years 1846–1857* (London: Printed by Order of the Trustees, 1864), 155–56; Salisbury Cathedral, *A Catalogue of the Library of the Cathedral Church of Salisbury* (London: Spottiswoode, 1880), 9–10; Norman Davis, ed., *Non-Cycle Plays and the Winchester Dialogues: Facsimiles of Plays and Fragments in Various Manuscripts and the Dialogues in Winchester College MS. 33*, Leeds Texts and Monographs, Medieval Drama Facsimiles, vol. 5 (Leeds: University of Leeds, School of English, 1979), 135–39.

[148] R. J. Lyall, "Materials: the Paper Revolution," in *Book Production and Pub-*

the translation to Trevisa which has not so far been questioned rests on two types of evidence. In the versified table of contents in A, Shirley identifies Trevisa as the translator,[149] and in the top margin of A fols. 94v–95r is written, "þe passyoun of oure lord ihesu translated by mayster Iohan Trevysa."[150] This attribution comes at most twenty years after Trevisa's death. The translation also contains interpolations which are glosses on "Olympias" (EN Prol.10) and "Amen" and "Alleluia" (EN 24.2.11). The first finds a parallel in Trevisa's translation of the Polychronicon, but only in A is it identified specifically with him, and this may be the work of Shirley; but the second interpolation is associated with him in A and S.[151]

The translation is based on EN A.[152] Apart from the interpolations already mentioned, Trevisa's chapter 2 has a variation and an addition of roughly fifty words which serve to create two episodes from one: in Trevisa's text the miracle of the standards (chap. 1) is an episode separate from the main trial before Pilate.[153] There is no known precedent for this in the Latin manuscripts, but at least two vernacular texts show a similar treatment of the miracle of the standards, the ME prose sequence of the Passion and GN found in Egerton 2658 etc., which we discussed earlier, and the OF translation and adaptation of the Meditationes vitae Christi made for Jean de Berry.[154] It is possible that Trevisa was aware of a tradition of treating the episode of the miracle of the standards in this way and adapted his text accordingly.[155]

We should see the production of this text of the GN in the context of the other translations produced by Trevisa and his colleague John Walton for the Berkeley family; as R. F. Green remarks, "a list of their

---

lishing in Britain, 1375–1475, ed. Jeremy Griffiths and Derek Pearsall (Cambridge: Cambridge University Press, 1989), 16–19.

[149] At fol. 2v; the verse preface is printed in Eleanor Prescott Hammond, ed., "John Shirley: Two Versified Tables of Contents," in English Verse between Chaucer and Surrey, ed. Eleanor Prescott Hammond (Durham, N.C.: Duke University Press, 1927), 194–96.

[150] The attribution also appears in the explicit of the Boethius; see A, fol. 94r.

[151] A, fols. 94v and 112r; S, fols. 129v and 144v; W, fols. 74r and 90v; see also the beginning of book 4 of Trevisa's translation of Ralph Higden's, Ranulphi Higden monachi Cestrensis Polychronicon . . . , vol. 4, ed. Joseph Rawson Lumby, Rer. Brit. M. A. Script., vol. 41 (London: Longman, Trübner, 1872), 253.

[152] Kim, "The Gospel of Nicodemus Translated by John Trevisa," xxi–xxx.

[153] Ibid., 8–9.

[154] Millard Meiss and Elizabeth H. Beatson, eds., La Vie de Nostre Benoit Sauveur Ihesuscrist & La Saincte Vie de Nostre Dame (New York: New York University Press, 1977), 61–63.

[155] Kim, "The Gospel of Nicodemus Translated by John Trevisa," xxiii–xxvii, considers it to be the result of an error.

translations reads almost like a prospectus of works essential for the formation of a basic aristocratic library."[156] The *Polychronicon*, one of Trevisa's major translation projects, is full of biblical and early Christian history but lacks a sustained account of the trial, Crucifixion, and Resurrection of Christ. The translation of the GN may have been meant to fill this deficiency. What is significant about Trevisa is that he takes over the *Gospel* as a whole; he does not follow the contemporary fashion of the literature of affective piety to displace its trial and Crucifixion episodes and retain only the account of Joseph of Arimathea and the Harrowing of Hell. Trevisa's translation points to a view of the *Gospel* as an authority for sacred history. This is reflected in a remark by John Wyclif in *De veritate Sacrae Scripturae:*

> Item multi preter quatuor ewangelistas scripserunt ewangelia, ut patet de Nichodemo, cuius autoritas videtur racionabiliter debere capi, et quia fuit fidelis et sanctus et quia interfuit.[157]

> (Indeed, apart from the four evangelists, many wrote gospels, as is obvious in the case of Nicodemus, whose authority it seems ought reasonably to be accepted, because he was faithful and holy and because he was present [at the time when Christ lived].)

The GN is not questioned as a record of events.

The three surviving manuscripts suggest a variety of uses for Trevisa's translation. In A the *Gospel* is described in the top margins and in the explicit as a Passion text, "the Passion as translated by Trevisa" and "the Passion of Christ by Nicodemus." In the light of the contemporary literature of affective piety, anything less like a Passion narrative would be hard to find. This label, which appears on other versions of the *Gospel* as well, was probably used for want of something better. The GN is the second item in A; it is preceded by Chaucer's translation of Boethius's *Consolation of Philosophy* (fols. 4r–94r) and followed by *The Mayster of the Game* (fols. 115r–90r) by Edward, duke of York, who died in 1415, and a variety of other texts, many of which are by Lydgate. It is difficult to agree with R. F. Green that the manuscript reflects a kind of antiquarian project;[158] whether or not it was produced for commercial reasons, it has the air of a generally up-to-date collection enhanced by the work of known personalities.[159] It

---

[156] Richard Firth Green, *Poets and Princepleasers: Literature and the English Court in the Late Middle Ages* (Toronto: University of Toronto Press, 1980), 154.

[157] John Wyclif, *De veritate Sacrae Scripturae*, ed. Rudolf Buddensieg, Wyclif Society, 3 vols. (London: Trübner, 1905–7), 1:237.

[158] Green, *Poets and Princepleasers*, 132.

[159] Green, *Poets and Princepleasers*, 132, is questioned in A. S. G. Edwards,

should be remembered that Trevisa's translation of the *GN* was an innovation; the text was well known as an authority, but his was probably the first complete English prose translation since the eleventh century. Here it has a prominent place in a compilation of contemporary or near contemporary literature.

No such importance attaches to the *Gospel* in S, where it is the last and only vernacular item in a manuscript which is a collection mainly of Latin meditative and didactic texts; its English language has been located to Wiltshire.[160] It was owned by Thomas Cyrcetur (b. ca. 1376, d. 1453), whose donation appears at the end (fol. 147r), following the *Gospel*. He was a canon of Salisbury Cathedral and is associated with an anti-Wycliffite tradition; he emerges as one who was essentially conservative in theology and ministry.[161] The list of his bequests reads like a standard collection of medieval popular theology and learning, and includes Chaucer's translation of the *Consolation of Philosophy*, the *Legenda aurea*, the *Historia scholastica* of Peter Comestor, and the *Veritas theologiae*.[162] It is instructive to see the *GN* in the context of the collection as a whole; it appears among standard late medieval learned texts. W is made up of six sections. Only the first four (fols. 1–109), the main part of the manuscript of the mid- to late fifteenth century, need concern us; fols. 110–15 and fols. 116–19 are later additions of the sixteenth century. The first four sections make up a series of booklets, and the *Gospel* occupies the third, which is composed of a gathering of 8 and a gathering of 12 (fols. 74r–93v).[163] The

---

"Lydgate Manuscripts: Some Directions for Future Research," in *Manuscripts and Readers in Fifteenth-Century England*, ed. Derek Pearsall (Cambridge: D. S. Brewer, 1983), 20–21. On A and Shirley generally, see Lyall, "Materials," 16–19; Julia Boffey and John J. Thompson, "Anthologies and Miscellanies: Production and Choice of Texts," in *Book Production and Publishing in Britain, 1375–1475*, 284–88; and Julia Boffey, *Manuscripts of English Courtly Love Lyrics in the Later Middle Ages* (Woodbridge, Suffolk: D. S. Brewer, 1985), 15–17.

[160] Three hands are detectable, and the manuscript may be composite. There are only four items: the first (fols. 1r–10v) is a series of short Latin texts; that on fol. 4v has a marginal note *meditationes beati Bernardi*; item two (fols. 11r–19r) is identified as the Latin text of the *Speculum sacerdotum*; item three (fols. 19v–129v) is John de Waldeby's treatise in Latin on the Lord's Prayer, *Ave Maria* and Apostles' Creed; the fourth item is the *GN* (fols. 129v–47r). Kim, "The Gospel of Nicodemus Translated by John Trevisa," used S as the basis for his edition. *LALME* 1:161, identifies "three hands in a similar language" in fols. 129v–47r (see also 3:546, linguistic profile 5371).

[161] R. M. Ball, "Thomas Cyrcetur, a Fifteenth-Century Theologian and Preacher," *Journal of Ecclesiastical History* 37 (1986): 205–39; Anne Hudson, *The Premature Reformation: Wycliffite Texts and Lollard History* (Oxford: Clarendon Press, 1988), 423, 453.

[162] See Salisbury Cathedral MSS. 13, 36, 39, 40, 55, 81, 84, 113, 126, 167, 170, 174.

[163] See Davis, *Non-Cycle Plays*. This text, unknown to Kim, was first noticed

first two booklets contain extracts from the *South English Legendary* and the Winchester dialogues *Lucidus and Dubius* and *Occupation and Idleness*, and the fourth contains the *Abbey of the Holy Ghost* (fols. 94r–108v). The same hand appears in the four booklets, so although they were probably not copied in close succession, they form the work of a single compiler. Here the prose *Gospel* is part of a collection of didactic literature and might even be considered as part of the legendary; in both the incipit and explicit, it is described not simply as an account of the Passion but as covering the history of Christ through to the Ascension. These three manuscripts of Trevisa's translation show different ways in which the text was read and a growing interest in the complete *Gospel* in prose in the fifteenth century.

Worcester Cathedral Library MS. F172, dated to roughly the third quarter of the fifteenth century,[164] contains another ME prose *GN* translated from Latin (fols. 4r–12r); like Trevisa's, it is based on *EN* A.[165] The manuscript has been damaged, and in its present state the *Gospel* is the first item, beginning imperfectly at *EN* 9.5.3 ("aduersus Iesum . . ."). The translation is very literal, more like a gloss on the Latin, and would seem to have been made, along with others, for the manuscript. One example illustrates some of its features:

If he be so myghti in manhod trewly I sey to the he is almyghti and the power of hym may noman resiste ne withstande and if he sey hymsilf to drede deth and wil take the woo shalbe to the in euerlastyng worldis in preiudice. (Fol. 8v)

Si talis potens est in humanitate, uere dico tibi omnipotens est in diuinitate, et potentiae eius nemo potest resistere. Et si dicit se mortem timere, capere te uult et ue tibi erit in sempiterna secula. (*EN* 20.2.7–10)

The translator misses the accusative and infinitive construction, translates "resistere" using a doublet, and fails to appreciate the sense of

by Kathleen H. Power, "A Newly Identified Prose Version of the Trevisa Version of the Gospel of Nicodemus," *Notes and Queries* 223 (1978): 5–7. The special features of the text have been discussed in David C. Fowler, "The Middle English Gospel of Nicodemus in Winchester MS 33," *Leeds Studies in English*, n.s., 19 (1988): 67–83.

[164] John Kestell Floyer, *Catalogue of Manuscripts Preserved in the Chapter Library of Worcester Cathedral*, ed. Sidney Graves Hamilton (Oxford: J. Parker, 1906), 96–98.

[165] The manuscript has been discussed in a number of places, but see Doyle, "An Unrecognized Piece of *Piers the Ploughman's Creed* and Other Works by Its Scribe," *Speculum* 34 (1959): 430–32, and C. Paul Christianson, "Evidence for the Study of London's Late Medieval Manuscript-Book Trade," in *Book Production and Publishing in Britain, 1375–1475*, 101 and n. 43.

"capere" in this context, "to deceive." The *Gospel* finishes on fol. 12r, where it corresponds to the end of Kim's text (*EN* 28.36). Following this, after a mid-line paragraph mark and running to fol. 12v, is a summary of the history of Joseph of Arimathea and the destruction of Jerusalem, the interrogation and execution of Pilate, and the events following his death. There are fifteen blank lines on fol. 12v; then, on fols. 13r–16r is the ME prose translation from Latin of the *Legend of the Cross before Christ*.[166] At the end of this text is written "Explicit Passio Nichodemi" (fol. 16r). This explicit more strictly should appear on fol. 12r, but its presence here reflects the way in which certain texts became associated with the *GN*, almost as if it were the center of a network of legends. This legend of the cross in its Latin form appears with the *EN* in a number of manuscripts, and it is likely that the ME sequence is drawn from such a source. F172 as a whole is an important collection of practical instruction and contemplative works, such as Hilton's *Scale of Perfection* (book 1) and Rolle's *Mending of Life*.[167] The use of the vernacular for many of the texts and the way in which they are translated are the most striking features of the manuscript; they probably functioned as reference works, or as Ian Doyle characterizes them, "as cribs for consultation."[168] This context reinforces the impression of the importance attached in the fifteenth century to the complete *Gospel* in ME prose.

Middle English prose translations from French

In addition to Latin, French versions of the *Gospel of Nicodemus* provided a source for ME prose translations. One example is found in Library of Congress MS. Faye-Bond 4 (formerly, pre-Ac 4), fols. 37v–63v. The language and hands of the two scribes of fols. 1r–63v have been localized to West Essex and dated between 1395 and 1415, so the text is roughly contemporary with Trevisa's. This part of the manuscript was probably produced at the Benedictine Priory at Hatfield Broad Oak (Hatfield Regis) and intended for the nunnery of Castle Hedingham in north-eastern Essex, even if it did not remain at—or possibly even reach—its destination.[169] The text generally follows Ford's "Tradition

---

[166] Edited by Betty Hill, "The Fifteenth-century Prose Legend of the Cross before Christ," *Medium Ævum* 34 (1965): 203–22.

[167] No adequate description of F172 has been published; for texts printed from it, see *IPMEP* 36, 61, 119, 255, 379, 397, 411, 528, 540, 651.

[168] Doyle, "An Unrecognized Piece," 431.

[169] This version of the *GN* has been edited by Betty Hill, "The Middle English Prose Version of the *Gospel of Nicodemus* from Washington, Library of Congress

A," which concludes with only a reference to Pilate's letter to Claudius (fol. 56r–v); then follows a narrative which includes the healing of Tiberius, the condemnation of Pilate, the Veronica legend, and the story of Simon Magus during the reign of Nero (fols. 56v–63v).[170] What follows the *Gospel* here also appears in an AN manuscript of the second half of the thirteenth century, Egerton 2710 (fols. 132rb–34rb).[171] The ME material beginning with the *Gospel* can be regarded as a translation of the kind of AN sequence found in this manuscript; and Library of Congress MS. Faye-Bond 4, fols. 37v–63v, probably reflects an older French compilation in which the *Gospel* formed part of a legendary of early Christian history. The other contemporary contents are a ME translation from French of the *Rule of Saint Benedict* adapted for the use of nuns (fols. 1r–36r) and an "Injunction for Nuns" (fols. 36v–37v). The compilation is a product of the changing linguistic climate of the fourteenth century and the needs of a female religious community.[172]

Another translation of the *GN* from French appears in London, BL MS. Harley 149.[173] The manuscript is dominated by *Dives and Pauper* (fols. 7r–182v), the extended commentary on the Ten Commandments. This is written by three hands, but the rest of the manuscript (except for the last folio, fol. 281) is in one hand (the fourth) throughout. The *GN* appears after (1) "an English version of Jacques Legrand's *Livre de Bonnes moeurs*" (fols. 183r–252r)[174] and (2) an account of the Last Supper (fols. 252r–54v). Apart from the last folio (fol. 281), the rest of the manuscript is taken up with the *GN* and related material (fols.

---

pre-Ac 4," *Notes and Queries* 232 (1987): 156–75; the manuscript is described in Seymour De Ricci and W. J. Wilson, *Census of Medieval and Renaissance Manuscripts in the United States and Canada*, vol. 1 (1935; repr., New York: Kraus Reprint Corp., 1961), 180–81. Evidence that the text is translated from French is given by Hill, "The Middle English Prose Version," 158. See also Jeanne Krochalis, "The Benedictine Rule for Nuns: Library of Congress MS 4*," *Manuscripta* 30 (1986): 21–34; Betty Hill, "Some Problems in Washington, Library of Congress MS Faye-Bond 4," in *In Other Words: Transcultural Studies ... Presented to H. H. Meier*, ed. J. L. MacKenzie and R. Todd (Dordrecht: Foris, 1989), 35–44; *LALME* 1:165, 3:122, linguistic profile 6210 [hand B], and 123, linguistic profile 6230 [hand A].

[170] Hill, "The Middle English Prose Version," 171–75.

[171] See above, n. 53. I am grateful to my colleague Dr. Nicole Crossley-Holland for examining Egerton 2710; she confirms that the ME legendary material is a close and accurate translation of the text as it is found in the French manuscript.

[172] A fourth item on the creed (fols. 64r–78r) is in a later hand.

[173] Edited in Lindström, *A Late Middle English Version;* for the manuscript, see British Museum, London, *A Catalogue of the Harleian Manuscripts*, 1:44. Evidence that this is a translation from French is given by Lindström, *A Late Middle English Version*, 11–14.

[174] Lindström, *A Late Middle English Version*, 33.

254v–80v). The text of the *Gospel* is a holograph and is dated to the fourth quarter of the fifteenth century, although it may be later. The translator conflated two recensions of Ford's "Tradition A," one related to Egerton 2710 and the other to BN MS. f. fr. 1850;[175] the latter manuscript is of the same recension as the one we discussed in connection with the source for the ME *Stanzaic Gospel of Nicodemus.* There are some additions not found in the French, such as references to Judas Iscariot and the dream of Pilate's wife as the work of the Devil.[176] Further, the making of the creed (fol. 267r–v) is introduced in the midst of the account of Joseph of Arimathea returning to Jerusalem (cf. *EN* 15.4). Lindström does not print this addition, but even if it appears to be "extra-contextual," it was clearly intended as part of this version of the *GN.*

The compiler's conception of the *Gospel* is indicated by the divisions he imposes on it and the links he makes with other texts. An incipit appears on fol. 254v which describes it as a "story of þe passyoun," and at the top of fol. 263r is the explicit, "here endyth the passyoun of Ihesu Cryst and folowyth serteyn storyes of thynges done aftyr hys passyoun." This introduces the episode of the Centurion reporting the miracles at the death of Christ (*EN* 11.2). Unlike those who refer to the whole *Gospel* as an account of the Passion, this compiler has here recognized some of the problems of this label. What follows from here to fol. 280v is the Resurrection and post-Resurrection narrative. The equivalent of the end of the *Gospel* comes on fol. 276r with "Et sic est finis deo gratias, here aftyr foloweth a story of þe veronycle." The rest of the text is based on the same source as the account in Library of Congress MS. Faye-Bond 4, fols. 56v–63v,[177] without the letter of Pilate. It is an independent translation and differences of substance may be the result of changes in the French tradition as well as conflation of two or more texts by the translator. Nevertheless, the continuation is derived from a manuscript related to Egerton 2710. Sections of the narrative are further signalled with headings, which reflect practices elsewhere in the sequence. The translator has presented this latter part as a legendary, and what we think of as the *GN* has been used in this larger compilation.

---

[175] Ibid., 11–15.
[176] Ibid., 16–19.
[177] Hill, "The Middle English Version," 172–75.

Early printed texts

A striking indication of the continued popularity of the *Gospel of Nicodemus* in the late fifteenth and early sixteenth centuries is its appearance, in whole or in part, in printed form. The first instance of the printing of material from the *Gospel* in English is in Caxton's text of the *Legenda aurea*, the extracts from *GN* 18–27 in the chapter on the Resurrection. The earliest edition dates from 1483, and there were subsequent ones in the fifteenth and sixteenth centuries.[178] The English *GN* appeared as an independent text first in 1507 and was printed eight times by three publishers down to 1537.[179] The efficiency and closely-knit nature of the printing trade meant that one version became the standard text and all others were ignored, at least in this medium. This independent status makes it more difficult to find clues as to how the *Gospel* might have been read; nevertheless, the form gives it authority as a record of sacred history. Anne Hudson has found that at least one of these early printed texts was in the possession of an individual associated with Lollardy, but she detects nothing to link it with the movement itself.[180]

The earliest printing is by Julian Notary (1507)[181] and consists of 22 leaves without pagination. Wynkyn de Worde's edition of 1509[182] has 26 leaves without pagination; it is a reprint but not a line-for-line reprint of Notary's text. Wynkyn de Worde did not take over the text in a wholly uncritical way. There is evidence of modernization and correction of faulty or awkward readings in Julian Notary's edition.[183] With this Wynkyn de Worde established the format for all subsequent printings down to 1537, including those by John Scot. The text is a translation from French of the recension of Ford's "Tradition

---

[178] A. W. Pollard and G. R. Redgrave, *A Short-Title Catalogue of Books Printed in England, Scotland, and Ireland and of English Books Printed Abroad 1475–1640*, 2d ed., revised and enlarged by W. A. Jackson, F. S. Ferguson and K. F. Pantzer, 3 vols. (London: The Bibliographical Society, 1976–91), 24873–80 (cited as *STC*). The extracts from *GN* 18–27 appear in the first Caxton printing, *STC*, 24873, on fols. 20vb–21vb.

[179] *STC* 18565 (Julian Notary, 1507); *STC* 18566–68 and 18570 (Wynkyn de Worde, 1509, 1511, 1512, 1518, 1532); and *STC* 18569 and 18570a (J. Skot, 1529, 1537?). A fuller account of the early printings appears in C. W. Marx, "Julian Notary, Wynkyn de Worde, and the Earliest Printed Texts of the Middle English *Gospel of Nicodemus*," *Neuphilologische Mitteilungen* 96 (1995) 389–98.

[180] Hudson, *The Premature Reformation*, 483–84 and n. 222.

[181] *STC* 18565.

[182] *STC* 18566.

[183] This accords with what we know of Wynkyn de Worde's practices elsewhere; see Carol M. Meale, "Wynkyn de Worde's Setting-Copy for *Ipomydon*," *Studies in Bibliography* 35 (1982): 156–71.

A" represented by Paris, BN MS. f. fr. 1850, and Oxford, Queen's College MS. 305, the version which, as we pointed out earlier, is related to what Izydorczyk has identified as *EN C*, and which is at the basis of the ME *Stanzaic Gospel of Nicodemus* and the text in Harley 149. The identification in the prologue (p. 2) of "bysshop Turpyn" as the translator, however, has been shown to be the result of a palaeographical error.[184] It is generally thought that Julian Notary was French, and he probably acted as both translator and publisher; in this respect he would have been following the practices of Caxton.[185] Some features of this version do not appear to derive from the French textual tradition. These may have been present in a lost manuscript, or the translator may have used two sources. Another possibility is that these additional features reflect contemporary expectations of texts which deal with the Passion and Resurrection of Christ. There is, for example, a long interpolation of the legend of Syndonia, who wove the cloth which Joseph of Arimathea purchased to bury Christ in ([pp. 18–20]). The legend is not widespread, but its presence reflects the practice of adding materials of this kind to Passion narratives.[186] The flagellation is developed as a separate episode in Julian Notary's text ([p. 15]),[187] and it was probably added in response to the long established tradition of writing on the Passion of Christ.

One feature of these editions which offers some suggestion of how the text was perceived, or how readers were encouraged to perceive it, is the illustrations. All the printings of the *Gospel* down to 1537 contain two types of illustrations: events in the Passion of Christ, and what can be called conversational groups made up of conventional figures to whom names are assigned with labels. The use of scenes from the Passion, particularly on the title-page, aligns the text with devotional

[184] See Lindström, *A Late Middle English Version*, 14–15; Ford, *L'Évangile de Nicodème*, 22–23; Hugh Shields, "Bishop Turpin and the Source of *Nycodemus gospell*," *English Studies* 53 (1972): 497–502. Lindström prints the text in BN MS. f. fr. 1850 as "text C." Shields gives evidence that the translation is from French.

[185] E. Gordon Duff, *A Century of the English Book Trade. Short Notices of All Printers, Stationars, Bookbinders, and Others Connected with It from the Issue of the First Dated Book in 1457 to the Incorporation of the Company of Stationers in 1557* (London: The Bibliographical Society, 1948), 112–14; James Moran, *Wynkyn de Worde: Father of Fleet Street*, 2d ed. (London: Wynkyn de Worde Society, 1976), 35; Henry R. Plomer, *Wynkyn de Worde and His Contemporaries* (London: Grafton, 1925), 163–76; N. F. Blake, "Wynkyn de Worde: the Later Years," in *Gutenberg-Jahrbuch* (Mainz: Verlag der Gutenberg-Gesellschaft, 1972), 129; on Caxton as translator, idem, *Caxton and His World* (London: London House & Maxwell, 1969), 125–50.

[186] Lindström, *A Late Middle English Version*, 15; Marx and Drennan, *The Middle English Prose Complaint*, 65.

[187] Marx, "Julian Notary," 390, gives the text from Julian Notary's printing.

literature and suggests parallels with what must have been the most common symbol of private devotion, the book of hours. The other type of illustration reflects what is a more central feature of the *GN*, namely, that it is a text about disputes over the nature and identity of Jesus.

A Reformation response

The latest English manuscript text of the *Gospel of Nicodemus*, one which post-dates the printed texts, is of interest mainly for the context in which it appears: CUL MS. Mm. 1. 29, of the late sixteenth century —after 1564.[188] It is a paper manuscript with modern binding (1972), guarding, and repair, and consists of, in order: 1 modern flyleaf; 1 sixteenth-century flyleaf (160mm x 195mm); 1 modern flyleaf; 59 paper folios of different dimensions with modern repairs and foliation; and 1 modern flyleaf at the end. On the sixteenth-century flyleaf, the antiquarian Humphrey Wanley identified the manuscript as a notebook of "Thomas Earl, minister of S Mildreds Bred street," compiled during his incumbency 1564–1600. In addition to ecclesiastical notes, it is also a commonplace book with extracts concerning Puritan and Catholic issues.[189] The *Gospel* appears on fols. 8r–16v and is based on the Latin *EN* 11.3.3–27.1.2, that is, from Joseph asking Pilate for the body of Christ to a brief mention of Karinus and Leutius at the end of the narrative. The text is prefaced by comments in at least three hands; Hulme gives most of them in his description,[190] but there are some errors in his transcription of the following, which is written in the hand of the main text:

> Because thee fable of that Romain papall sinagogue ys not now exstaunt thowght somtym impryntid in the Inglishe tounge under the tytle of Nychodemus Ghospell I have agayn written thee same ovt of their oude postills as Iohn Herolt sermones discipulij sermo 146 /I/, sermones dormi secure sermo 30, Iacobus de Voragine De Resurrectione domini, whose wordes follow thus. (Fol. 8r)[191]

---

[188] University Library, Cambridge, *A Catalogue of the Manuscripts Preserved in the Library of the University of Cambridge*, 6 vols. (Cambridge: University Press, 1856–67), 4:122; Hulme, *The Middle English Harrowing of Hell*, lv–lvii.

[189] For contents, see Hulme, *The Middle English Harrowing of Hell*, lv.

[190] Ibid., lvi.

[191] Hulme's reading "146, 1 F" is an error; "/I/" is probably an index mark in a volume without pagination. What Hulme gives as superscript "iii" is a caret mark indicating where "Iacobus de Voragine" should appear.

The reference to the printing of the *Gospel* is probably to one of the sixteenth-century editions. Three authorities are cited here. The third is the chapter on the Resurrection in the *Legenda aurea*, which contains extracts from *EN* 18–27, but this is not the source for the version in this manuscript. The reference to *John Herolt* is to Johannes Herolt, a Dominican friar active at Basel during the first half of the fifteenth century; his *Sermones Discipuli de tempore et de sanctis* was widely circulated, and a large number of printings survive from the fifteenth and sixteenth centuries, including one by Julian Notary (1510).[192] His "sermon 146," entitled "De articulis fidei," under the fifth article "descendit ad inferna," deals with issues surrounding Christ's Descent into Hell, the liberation of the saints, and the parts of hell.[193] The sermon contains, however, no extracts from the *Gospel*. The "sermones dormi secure" are the *Sermones dominicales* of Joannes de Verdena, which were frequently printed in the fifteenth and sixteenth centuries, occasionally along with the sermons of Johannes Herolt.[194] "Sermon 30" is for "dominica prima post octauas pasche" and is based on the text "Ego sum pastor bonus et cognosco oues meas" (Jn. 10:14), but there is nothing to suggest a link with the *GN*. "Sermon 35" on the Ascension contains references to Christ rescuing the souls from hell and uses Psalm 23:7 and 9 (Vulgate), which also appear in *GN* 21. This sermon is closest thematically to the *Gospel* and may be the intended reference.[195] Since the manuscript text is based on the *Gospel* and not one of these authorities, the compiler may have cited them not as sources but as precedents. So, in the clause "I have agayn written thee same ovt of their oude postills as Iohn Herolt . . . ," "as" may have the sense "in the manner of." Whatever his purpose, he locates the *Gospel* in a popular Latin and Catholic tradition.

What follows the *GN* is more revealing of the compiler's views; fols. 16v–19r contain a series of attacks on the text as "popishe." He questions Christ's personal Harrowing of Hell and argues for purity of

---

[192] *STC* 13226; Joannes Herolt, *Miracles of the Blessed Virgin Mary*, trans. C. C. Swinton Bland, intro. Eileen Power, Broadway Medieval Library (London: G. Routledge & Sons, 1928), 2–3. Ten editions of works by Herolt appear in Bodleian Library, Oxford, *Bodleian Library Pre-1920 Catalogue: Incunabula* (Oxford: Bodleian Library, 1988), 262–63.

[193] I have used the text of this sermon in a 1511 edition of Joannes Herolt's *Sermones Discipuli de tempore et de sanctis: et Quadragesimale eiusdem: cum diuersis tabulis [quam] necessariis* (Rouen: Petrus Oliuerius, 1511); the volume is without pagination.

[194] Ten editions of works by Joannes de Verdena appear in *Bodleian Library Pre-1920 Catalogue*, 303.

[195] I have consulted Joannes de Verdena, *Sermones dominicales* (Cologne: C. Winters, 1477); this volume is without pagination.

doctrine and belief.[196] This response to the GN is perhaps not untypical of Protestant attitudes. But it is paradoxical that such a hostile compiler should bother to copy out the text. The GN perhaps retained a deep-rooted fascination which even the Reformation could not destroy.[197]

---

[196] Hulme, *The Middle English Harrowing of Hell*, lvii, transcribes a small portion of this commentary.

[197] Although it is beyond the scope of this essay, it is interesting to note that there has recently come to light a manuscript dating from around 1660 of an English translation of the GN which may be the work of a recusant; see Irma Taavitsainen and C. W. Marx, "A Seventeenth-Century English Manuscript of *The Gospel of Nicodemus* in Royal Library of Stockholm, MS Huseby 71," *Notes and Queries* 239 (1994): 150–55.

The Influence of the *Evangelium Nicodemi* on Norse Literature: A Survey[1]

KIRSTEN WOLF

ntercourse between the centers of learning on the continent and in Britain and the monasteries and cathedrals of medieval Scandinavia led to the translation of an astonishing number of devotional and doctrinal books. That these books gained immense popularity is shown by their many manuscripts, as well as by the entries in the catalogues of libraries of monasteries and bishoprics in Scandinavia. Much of this ecclesiastical literature has undoubtedly been lost, especially the older manuscripts written presumably on vellum, a fact which made them particularly useful for purposes that eventually led to their destruction. Law codices, leech-books, and the like were preserved because of their continued usefulness, but the religious literature had less of a chance of survival.

The *Evangelium Nicodemi* (*EN*) comprises two originally independent Greek works, in Latin named *Gesta* (or *Acta*) *Pilati* and *Descensus Christi ad inferos* (*DI*), which were joined in an apocryphal gospel probably in the fifth century under the title *Passio Domini* or *Gesta Salvatoris* and later renamed *Evangelium Nicodemi* (a title popularized by Vincent of Beauvais's *Speculum historiale* and Jacobus a Voragine's *Legenda aurea*) after its alleged author Nicodemus, who assisted Joseph of Arimathea in preparing Christ's body for burial (Jn. 19:39–40). The work evidently enjoyed great popularity in Scandinavia, just as it did elsewhere in pre-Reformation Europe. We still possess the gospel in several manuscripts, despite the attempts of the reformers to exclude such hagiographic literature from their own developing corpus of doctrines and texts.

---

[1] Reprinted from *Mediaeval Studies* 55 (1993): 219–42, by permission of the publisher. Copyright 1993 by the Pontifical Institute of Mediaeval Studies, Toronto.

The present survey of the Norse translations, adaptations, and paraphrases of the *EN* falls naturally into two main parts: West and East Norse, representing a geographical and linguistic distinction between Norway and Iceland, on the one hand, and Denmark and Sweden, on the other.

1. West Norse

The oldest rendering of the *Evangelium Nicodemi* into a Norse language is the Old Norse-Icelandic *Niðrstigningarsaga*, a translation of the *Descensus Christi ad inferos*. The translation, which is commonly dated to the twelfth century, survives in four medieval Icelandic manuscripts.[2] The oldest of these manuscripts is Copenhagen, Arnamagnæan Institute (AM) 645 4°, which contains the complete text. It is a collective volume of Latin ecclesiastical literature translated into Icelandic, and *Niðrstigningarsaga* belongs to the so-called younger part written in all probability in the beginning of the thirteenth century.[3] The other three manuscripts are defective. AM 623 4°, which has been dated to about 1325, lacks the beginning.[4] AM 233a fol., from 1350–1360, consists of the inner column of a leaf in a collective volume. AM 238 fol. V, dated to the fifteenth century, is a single leaf most probably also from a collective volume. As Magnús Már Lárusson has shown, an additional source text, Reykjavík, Jón Sigurðsson Collection (JS) 405 8°, is a copy of a medieval manuscript, made by the farmer Ólafur Jónsson í Arney (ca. 1722–1800) in 1780, which contains the complete text of *Niðrstigningarsaga*; in addition, it includes a long chapter connecting *Niðrstigningarsaga* with the story of the Passion, which, as Magnús Már Lárusson demonstrates, cannot have been composed before 1540, the year in which Oddur Gottskálksson's Icelandic translation of the New Testament was published.[5] The four medieval manuscripts have been

---

[2] Magnús Már Lárusson ("Um Niðurstigningarsögu," *Skírnir* 129 [1955]: 159–68) dates it to the time of the first bishop of Hólar, Jón Ǫgmundarson (d. 1121). He does not present any argumentation for his hypothesis, but his view is shared by Ian J. Kirby (*Bible Translation in Old Norse*, Université de Lausanne, Publications de la Faculté des lettres, vol. 27 [Geneva: Droz, 1986], 35). See also Otto Gschwantler, "Christus, Thor und die Midgardschlange," in *Festschrift für Otto Höfler zum 65. Geburtstag*, ed. Helmut Birkhan and Otto Gschwantler (Vienna: Notring, 1968), 145–68.

[3] See Ludvig Larsson, ed., *Isländska handskriften No 645 4° i den Arnamagnæanske Samlingen på Universitetsbiblioteket i København i diplomatarisk aftryck utgifven: I. Handskriftens äldre del* (Lund: Malmstöm, 1885), ii–iii.

[4] See Den Arnamagnæanske Kommission, *Ordbog over det norrøne prosasprog: Registre* (Copenhagen: Den Kommission, 1989), 339.

[5] Magnús Már Lárusson, "Um Niðurstigningarsögu," 167, bases his conclu-

edited separately by C. R. Unger;[6] AM 623 4° has also been edited by Finnur Jónsson,[7] and AM 645 4° appears in a facsimile edition with an introduction by Anne Holtsmark.[8] JS 405 8° has not been edited. On the basis of a number of Norwegianisms in AM 645 4°, Eugen Mogk, Didrik Arup Seip, and Hans Bekker-Nielsen make a claim for a Norwegian origin of the translation.[9] Magnús Már Lárusson, however, considers an Icelandic provenance more likely, and although the question of the translation's national origin may never be answered, it is worth noting that the four medieval manuscripts are all Icelandic.[10] The relationship among the manuscripts has been debated. G. Turville-Petre notes that the differences among the four medieval texts of the saga are not great and that they are clearly to be traced to the same original translation.[11] His view is supported by two interpolations, which are found neither in the Latin texts nor in related vernacular translations, but which appear in all four manuscripts.[12] Turville-Petre also notes that in the translation the original triad of Christ-Satan-Inferus is reduced to a dualism between Christ and Satan, while Inferus is transposed to a host of devils ("jǫtnar," giants; "djǫflar," devils; "ríkistrǫll," mighty trolls; "helvítisbúar," inhabitants of hell; "ríkisdjǫflar," mighty devils; "kappar," champions; "illar vættir," evil beings; "helvítisfolk," hell folk; "hǫfuðdjǫflar," principal devils). Inferus appears personified only in AM 238 fol. V, the youngest text, which leads Turville-Petre to conclude that this is probably due to a revision by a learned scribe. Although it is not explicitly stated, he

sion on the reading "Eli, Eli lama asapthani," which appears in both texts. JS 405 8° has not been the subject of a textual, critical discussion.

[6] C. R. Unger, ed., *Heilagra manna søgur: Fortællinger og legender om hellige mænd og kvinder*, 2 vols. (Oslo: Bentzen, 1877), 2:1–20. This edition will be cited by page and line number. A new edition is in preparation by Odd Einar Haugen (see n. 15 below).

[7] Finnur Jónsson, ed., *AM 623, 4°: Helgensagaer*, Samfund til udgivelse af gammel nordisk litteratur, vol. 52 (Copenhagen: Jørgensen, 1927), 1–9.

[8] Anne Holtsmark, ed., *A Book of Miracles: MS No. 645 4to of the Arna-Magnæan Collection in the University Library of Copenhagen*, Corpus Codicum Islandicorum Medii Aevi, vol. 12 (Copenhagen: Munksgaard, 1938).

[9] Eugen Mogk, *Geschichte der norwegisch-isländischen Literatur*, 2d rev. ed. (Strassburg: Trübner, 1904), 890; Didrik Arup Seip, *Nye studier i norsk språkhistorie* (Oslo: Aschehoug, 1954), 84, 135; Hans Bekker-Nielsen, "Nikodemusevangeliet," in *Kulturhistorisk Leksikon for nordisk middelalder*, vol. 12 (Copenhagen: Rosenkilde and Bagger, 1967), cols. 308–9.

[10] Magnús Már Lárusson, "Um Niðurstigningarsögu," 166.

[11] G. Turville-Petre, *Origins of Icelandic Literature* (Oxford: Clarendon Press, 1953), 127.

[12] AM 645 4°: pp. 4.18–33, 5.1–12; AM 623 4°: pp. 10.12–25, 10.32–11.2; AM 233a fol.: pp. 14.27–15.8; AM 238 fol. V: pp. 19.33–20.8, 20.17–24.

appears to suggest that AM 238 fol. V is furthest removed from the
original, that it has two or more sources, and that, therefore, the stemma
is contaminated. Magnús Már Lárusson considers AM 623 4° closest to
the original text, although it is a poor copy of only a section of the
text.[13] Gary L. Aho agrees with Turville-Petre that all four manuscripts go back to a common original (*X).[14] AM 238 fol. V he sees as
the most faithful witness to *X, whereas AM 645 4°, AM 623 4°, and
AM 233a fol. are in his view sister-copies presenting a separate recension derived from a nonextant first redaction of *X (*X1). The most
exhaustive analysis of the filiation of the manuscripts was undertaken
by Odd Einar Haugen.[15] Haugen agrees with Turville-Petre and Aho
that AM 238 fol. V represents a separate recension as opposed to AM
645 4°, AM 623 4°, and AM 233a fol., and that these three manuscripts
derive from a common source (*X). Contrary to Magnús Már Lárusson's theory, he claims that there is no evidence for any hierarchy
among the three manuscripts and points out that in most cases AM 238
fol. V renders the Latin more accurately than the other three manuscripts. Haugen demonstrates that consistent argumentation can be
given in favor of both Turville-Petre's stemma, i.e., that the recension
represented by AM 238 fol. V is contaminated, and Aho's stemma, i.e.,
that the recension is not contaminated, and argues that other criteria,
such as extratextual ones, must be utilized in order to make a qualified
choice. He refers to Turville-Petre's observation that AM 238 fol. V follows the Latin in translating the personified Inferus with the neuter
form "helvíti" ("hell") and argues that it is more probable that a
revision would attempt to correct the text as in AM 238 fol. V rather
than vice versa as in AM 645 4°, AM 623 4°, and AM 233a fol. He supports his hypothesis by pointing out that the archaic language of AM
645 4° and AM 623 4° suggests that their common source, *X, belongs
to the twelfth century, and that this leaves little margin for a supposed
redactión between AM 645 4°, AM 623 4°, AM 233a fol., and the first
translation (as argued by Aho). He also draws attention to the dates of
the four manuscripts and notes that it would seem peculiar that the
fifteenth-century AM 238 fol. V was the oldest textual witness to the

---

[13] Magnús Már Lárusson, "Um Niðurstigningarsögu," 159.

[14] Gary L. Aho, "A Comparison of Old English and Old Norse Treatments of
Christ's Harrowing of Hell" (Ph.D. diss., University of Oregon, 1966), 156.

[15] Odd Einar Haugen, "The Evaluation of Stemmatic Evidence. Recension and
Revision of Niðrstigningar saga," in The Sixth International Saga Conference 28.7. –
2.8.1985, Workshop Papers, 2 vols. (Copenhagen: The Arnamagnaean Institute,
1985), 1:423–50, esp. 428–38. This analysis is further developed in idem, "Stamtre
og tekstlandskap: Studiar i resensjonsmetodikk med grunnlag i Niðrstigningar
saga" (Ph.D. diss., University of Bergen, 1992).

original translation and that the other older manuscripts were representative of a secondary redaction. Finally, he refers to the two interpolations which do appear in AM 238 fol. V, but which fit in better with the free rendering of the three older manuscripts. Haugen demonstrates that none of the three older manuscripts can be the source of AM 238 fol. V, although there are striking similarities between AM 645 4° and AM 238 fol. V, and that, therefore, the exemplar of AM 238 fol. V must be a manuscript placed on a higher node in the stemma.

Although *Niðrstigningarsaga* contains only the story of the Descent into Hell, the opening and concluding lines suggest that the translator had access to the whole text of the *EN*.[16] The translation is based on the so-called A-group of texts in Tischendorf's edition (the version that was no doubt most widely used in Western Europe),[17] though, of course, with the two interpolations added in the middle of the text and with some drastic modifications in the first and last chapters. The translator begins with a note saying that, although this book has not been given the same prominence as other sacred writings, it contains nothing dubious ("Segia menn samsett hava Nichodemum lerisvein drotens," p. 1.10–11)[18] and then begins the story at chapter 2 (*EN* 18) in the Latin ("Nos autem cum essemus cum omnibus patribus nostris . . ."). The ending also differs considerably from the Latin. The Norse translator ignores the doctrinal character of his source text and concludes with the statement that Charinus and Leucius were not found in their graves after Christ's Resurrection, and that their book passed through many hands before it finally ended up in Constantinople. This omission of doctrinal elements in the Latin is one of the characteristics of the Norse translation as is the omission or simplification of repetitive or very detailed accounts. Thus, instead of rendering all five verses of Psalm 30 (*DI* 7.2 [*EN* 24] in the Latin), the translator renders only one and mentions that four more verses of that psalm were recited (".iiii. vers søng hann af þeim salm framan," p. 7.14–15).[19] In general, the omissions and simplifications are restricted to descriptions that appear superfluous to the movement of the story, although *Niðrstigningarsaga* is not completely consistent in this respect. A number of

---

[16] Magnús Már Lárusson, "Um Niðurstigningarsögu," 161.

[17] Constantinus de Tischendorf, ed., *Evangelia apocrypha*, 2d rev. ed. (1876; rpt., Hildesheim: G. Olms, 1966). The chapter and paragraph numbers in this edition will be given for references to the Latin text (A-group). For a recent discussion of the manuscripts and editions of the *EN*, see Zbigniew Izydorczyk, "The Unfamiliar *Evangelium Nicodemi*," *Manuscripta* 33 (1989): 169–91.

[18] "Men say that Nicodemus, the Lord's disciple, composed it."

[19] See Gary L. Aho, "*Niðrstigningarsaga*: An Old Norse Version of Christ's Harrowing of Hell," *Scandinavian Studies* 41 (1969): 150–59, esp. 157.

rhetorical passages are retained; the Enoch and Elijah story, for example, which is a digression, remains in the translation, and only a few of the many direct and indirect speeches in the Latin are reduced. Some omissions or simplifications include instances in which the translation attempts to be more literal. Thus, figurative language is avoided; the metaphor "oriens" ("dayspring") for Christ in the Latin is left out [20] as is the simile comparing Lazarus to an eagle (*DI* 4.3 [*EN* 20]).[21] Related to this interest in the tangible as opposed to the abstract is, as noted above, the transformation of the triad of Christ, Satan, and Inferus to an opposition between Christ, on the one hand, and Satan, on the other, while Inferus is represented by a host of giants, devils, and trolls.

Direct signs of Latin influence are found in *Niðrstigningarsaga* in the retention of Latin words or phrases, usually in the form of commands or pronouncements, ranging in length from a single word to several lines of printed text, usually with no accompanying translation.[22] Indirect signs of Latin influence are found in a number of "learned style" elements.[23] These include the substantive use of adjectives ("Slict it sama sungo aller helger" [p. 7.15];[24] "Þa gerþi siþan dominus crossmarc ifer Adam oc ollom helgom oc toc i hønd Adams oc ste up or helvite með her miclom, oc fylgþo drotne aller helger" [p. 7.20–22])[25] and the use of reflexive verbs expressing the passive (". . . oc mun þat miscunnarsmior þeim, er endrgetasc af vatne oc helgom annda, verþa endrgetnaðr at eilifre sælo" [p. 3.8–10])[26] as well as the

---

[20] ". . . ipse oriens filius dei" (*DI* 2.3 [*EN* 18]; "even the dayspring, the Son of God") > "ipse filius dei" (p. 2.19; "the Son of God"); AM 238 fol. V: "sialfr guds son" (p. 17.23). Translations of quotations from the Latin *Descensus* A are based on M. R. James, *The Apocryphal New Testament* (1924; repr., Oxford: Clarendon Press, 1986).

[21] "Nec ipsum Lazarum tenere potuimus, sed excutiens se ut aquila per omnem agilitatem et celeritatem salivit exiens a nobis, et ipsa terra quae tenebat Lazari corpus mortuum statim reddidit vivum" ("Neither could we keep Lazarus, but he, like an eagle shaking himself, leaped forth with all agility and swiftness, and departed from us, and the earth also which held the dead body of Lazarus straightway gave him up alive").

[22] In AM 238 fol. V there is, however, a tendency to translate the Latin words and phrases.

[23] See Jónas Kristjánsson, "Learned Style or Saga Style?" in *Specvlvm norroenvm: Norse Studies in Memory of Gabriel Turville-Petre*, ed. Ursula Dronke et al. (Odense: Odense University Press, 1981), 260–92.

[24] "All the holy [people] sang the same."

[25] "Then the Lord made the sign of the cross over Adam and all the holy [people] and took Adam's hand and rose from hell with a large army, and all the holy [people] followed the Lord." AM 623 4°: "Slict et sama sungo allir helgir" (p. 12.35); AM 623 4°: "Þa blezaþi drottinn Adam oc alla helga. Þa tok guþ i ha/nd Adami oc ste up meþ hann til paradisar, oc fylgþo drottni allir helgir" (p. 13.1–3).

[26] "and may that be the oil of mercy to those who are born again from water

extensive use of the present participle. On the whole, the translation makes few attempts to retain literary embellishments, but in a few instances alliteration in the Latin is reproduced (although alliteration in the Latin is not especially noticeable), e.g., "creatorem omnium creaturarum" (*DI* 10 [*EN* 26]) > "scapare allrar scepno" (p. 8.11).[27] Similarly, the translator manages in a few instances to duplicate Latin parallelisms, e.g., "Claudite portas crudeles aereas et vectes ferreos supponite et fortiter resistite" (*DI* 5.1 [*EN* 21]) > "Taket er, greypet oc byrget nu hliþen aull oc føret fyrer iarngrindr oc iarnbranda, oc verezc hart oc standet viþ vel" (p. 5.15–17).[28] But *Niðrstigningarsaga* is not a slavish translation of the Latin original. As Turville-Petre notes, the translator has often improved upon the source text in his accounts of the inhabitants of Inferus by using words and expressions from Norse mythology, which even in the twelfth century must have seemed archaic (see above).[29] Further native stylistic elements are the stereotyped linguistic formulae used to introduce a new episode and to resume a suspended episode ("En ec tec fra þvi at segia, er þa gørþisc en fleira til stormerkia" [p. 4.18–19]; "Nu scal þar til mals taca, er ec hvarf aþr fra" [p. 4.34]); "En nu tek ec þar til mals at segia þat, hvat þeir hava til tekit i helvite, siþan er Satan for ut" [p. 5.13–14])[30] as well as the use of decidedly native words like "þinga" ("hold a meeting") and "kappi" ("champion").

---

and the Holy Spirit to become reborn to eternal bliss." AM 623 4°: "... oc mon þat misconnarsmior þeim, er endrberasc af vattni oc helgom anda, verþa til eilifrar sølo" (p. 9.11–12); AM 238 fol. V: "... ok mun þetta myskunar vidsmior vera til endrgetningar þeim, er fa muno af vatni ok helgum anda i eilift lif" (p. 18.19–21).

[27] "the maker of all creatures." AM 623 4°: "scapari allrar scepno" (p. 13.34); AM 233a fol.: "skapari allrar skepnu" (p. 16.27).

[28] "Shut ye the hard gates of brass and put on them the bars of iron and withstand stoutly." AM 623 4°: "Takeþ er nu grimmir, oc byrgiþ hliþ oll ramliga meþ iarnhurþom oc latiþ slagbranda viþ innan, oc verizc hart oc standiþ vel viþ" (p. 11.4–6); AM 233a fol.: "Takit þer nu ok byrgit hlið ꜵll, ok setit fyrir iarngrindr ok iarnbranda, oc verit hart ok standit vid vel" (p. 15.12–13).

[29] Turville-Petre, *Origins*, 128; see also Fredrik Paasche, *Norges og Islands litteratur inntil utgangen av middelalderen*, rev. ed. by Anne Holtsmark, in Francis Bull et al., *Norsk Litteraturhistorie*, vol. 1 (Oslo: Aschehoug, 1957), 299.

[30] "But I am neglecting to say that more great wonders took place"; AM 623 4°: "Nu mun ec segia fra stormerkiom þeim, er þa gørþosc" (p. 10.12); AM 238 fol. V: omitted.

"Now we must return to where we earlier left off"; AM 623 4°: "Nu scal þar til taka, er ver hurfom aþan fra" (p. 10.26); AM 233a fol.: "Nu er fra þvi at segia, hvat þeir hofduz at i helviti, sidan er Sathan for ut" (p. 15.10–11); AM 238 fol. V: "En þa er þau tauludo med sier, sem fyrir sagt" (p. 20.9).

"But now I begin to tell what they did in hell after Satan had gone out"; AM 623 4°: "Nu scal segia fra atburþom þeim er i helviti varo" (p. 11.3).

The translator frequently amplifies the text in order to enliven the
narrative and to give it a more dramatic effect. As Fredrik Paasche
notes, the translator must have been greatly involved in the story.[31]
Thus, "... Satan princeps et dux mortis" (DI 4.1 [EN 20]; "Satan the
prince and chief of death") is expanded as follows:

... Satan iotunn helvitis hofðingi, er stundom er meþ .vii.
høfðom en stundom með .iii., en stundom i dreka like þess, er
omorlegr er oc ogorlegr oc illegre a allar lundir." (P. 3.16–18).[32]

Many of the additions, large or small and seemingly insignificant when
analyzed individually, serve to give the story a militant tone. One such
example is the rejoicing of "omnes sancti" (DI 8.2 [EN 24]; "all the
saints") after Christ's Descent, which in the translation is altered to
"með her miclom" ("with a big army," p. 7.22). As Aho notes, the
translator consistently represents Christ's descensus as a military action,
a harrowing of Hell.[33]

As mentioned above, Niðrstigningarsaga contains two interpolations, one connected with Revelation 19, the other with Job 41. They
relate that Christ rides forth in majesty upon a white horse, his eyes
burning, wearing a gown, and wrapped in a blood-drenched banner.
Satan, deceived into believing Christ to be fearful of death and thus
easy prey, transforms himself into the shape of the world serpent, the
Miðgarðsormr, and tries to swallow him. But Satan is snagged on "the
hook of divinity," we are told, "like a fish on a hook or a mouse in a
trap or a fox in a snare." Satan is then bound, and angels are commanded to guard him. As James W. Marchand notes, Christ's strata-
gem reflects the medieval motif of pia fraus, according to which Christ

---

[31] "Oversætteren har vært tatt av emnet" (Paasche, Norges og Islands litteratur,
299). Paasche is of the opinion, however, that the Latin Descensus text is even
more powerful ("... tross alt må det sies at slagkraften er større i Descensus; til
det opptrin av vill majestet som skildres i legenden om nedfarten passer i særskilt
høy grad latinens svære masser").
[32] "Satan, the giant chieftain of hell, who sometimes has seven heads and
sometimes three, and who is sometimes in the shape of a dragon, who is horrible
and awful and evil in all respects" (AM 623 4°: "... Sathan heims hofþingi, er
stundom er þar met .vii. ha/fþom eþa .iii. i hreþiligo dreka liki oc omorligo á allar
lundir" [p. 9.18–19]; AM 238 fol. V: "... helvitis hofdingi leidtogi daudra i liking
hrædilegs dreka ok miog auskurlegs, sa er stundum syndiz þeim med sio hof-
dum, en stundum med .iii., stundum i mannz liki" [p. 18.27–29]). Aho, "A Comparison," 171, notes that the amplification is more than just a colorful addition,
because later on in the translation, Satan does change into a dragon.
[33] Aho, "Niðrstigningarsaga," 156–57. The phrase just mentioned is omitted in
AM 623 4°.

was allowed to use human cunning to defeat his enemy.[34] The first interpolation appears just before Satan is driven out of Inferus:

Þat var mioc i þat mund døgra, er himennen opnaþisc, þar com fram fyrst hestr hvitr, en hofðingi sa reiþ hesti þeim, er morgom hlutom er gofgari en gørvaster aller aþrer, augo hans varo sem elldz logi, hann hafði corono a høfði, er morg sigr-merki mate of syna, hann hafði cleþi þat umb aunnor utan, er bloþstoket var; a cleþi hans yfer mioþmenni voro orþ þessi riten: rex regum et dominus dominorum; hann var solo biar-tare; hann leide efter ser her mikinn, aller þeir, er honom fylgþo, riþo hestom hvitom, oc voro aller cledir silki hvito oc voro lioser mioc. Sa inn ricsti allvalldr leit þa til Jorsalaborgar oc melte: "Gilldra su er at Jorsolom er gør verþi miþgarþsormi at scaþa." Hann fal þa øngul, þann er horvenn var agni oc eigi sia mate, i ezlino, þvi er i gilldrona var lagit, oc sva vaþinn gat hann folget, svat eigi of mate sia. Þa bauþ hann nøcqerom dyrlingom sinom at fara fyrer ser oc gøra vart viþ como sina til helvitis. (P. 4.19–33).[35]

The second interpolation is about Satan's journey to Jerusalem to cap-ture the crucified Christ, so that he can prove Christ's human nature:

Þa er Satan com ut, þa sa hann englaliþ mikit vera comet til helvitis, en gec eigi til fundar viþ ða, oc sneide hann þar hia. Þa bra hann ser i dreca like oc gørðiz þa sva mikill, at hann þotesc liggia mundo umb heimen allan utan. Hann sa þau tiþennde at Jorsolom, at Jesus Cristr var þa i andlati, oc for þangat þegar oc ætlaþi at slita ondina þegar fra honom. En þa er hann com þar oc hugþez gløpa mundo hann oc hafa með

---

[34] James W. Marchand, "Leviathan and the Mousetrap in the Niðrstigningar-saga," Scandinavian Studies 47 (1975): 328–38, esp. 333.

[35] "In an instant it became bright daylight, as the heavens opened. There came forward first a white horse, and the chieftain who rode it was in many re-spects nobler than the most accomplished of all others. His eyes were like burn-ing flames. He had a crown on his head and many tokens of victory were visible. He had a blood-drenched banner wrapped around himself, and on it were writ-ten these words: Rex regum et dominus dominorum. He was brighter than the sun. He led a great army and all those who accompanied him rode white horses and were clothed in white silk and were very bright. That one, the most powerful leader, then looked toward Jerusalem and said, 'The trap which is ready at Jeru-salem is destined to maim the world-serpent.' He hid the hook inside the bait so that it could not be seen; thus was it laid upon the trap. The fishing line he was also able to hide, so that it could not be seen. Then he requested several of his holy companions to go before him and make known His coming to hell" (Aho, "Niðrstigningarsaga," 153).

ser, þa beit øngullinn godomsens hann, en crossmarkit fell a
hann ovan, oc varþ hann þa sva veidr sem fiscr a øngle eþa
mus under treketi, eþa sem melraki i gilldro, epter þvi sem
fyrer var spat. Þa for til dominus noster oc bat hann, en qvade
til engla sina at varþveita hann. (P. 5.1–11).[36]

Aho views the interpolations as containing original material and connects them with the story of Þórr's fishing expedition because of the
use of the term "Miðgarðsormr."[37] Marchand, however, argues
against this theory, claiming that the interpolation of the allegory of
Christ as the bait on the hook of the cross with which Leviathan was
taken is a medieval commonplace considerably older than the Þórr and
Miðgarðsormr theme.[38] He follows Magnús Már Lárusson in drawing
attention to the fact that elsewhere in Old Norse Leviathan and the
Miðgarðsormr are equated,[39] and he refers to the Icelandic Hómilíubók,
which mentions the theme of Leviathan on the hook in a section taken
from Gregory the Great's homily on Mary Magdalen.[40] The interpola-

---

[36] "Then when Satan came out, he saw a large force of angels had come to hell,
but he did not go to meet them. He turned aside. Then he changed himself into the
shape of a dragon and made himself so huge that it seemed he would encircle the
entire earth. He saw those events in Jerusalem and that Jesus Christ was near death
and he went there immediately and intended to tear the soul from him. But when
he came there and thought that he would swallow him and carry him away, then
the hook of divinity snagged him and the cross fell down upon him and he was
caught like a fish on a hook or a mouse in a trap or a fox in a snare, as had been
foretold. Then our Lord came forward and bound him and told his angels to guard
him" (Marchand, "Leviathan and the Mousetrap," 328).

[37] Aho, "Niðrstigningarsaga," 154–55. Gschwantler, "Christus, Thor und die
Midgardschlange," 158, also notes, "In der oben ausgehobenen Stelle der Niðrstigningar saga heißt es, daß sich der Teufel in die Gestalt eines Drachen verwan-
delte und so groß wurde, daß man meinte, er liege außen um die ganze Welt
herum. Daß hier der Übersetzer an die Midgardschlange gedacht hat, die sich um
den ganzen Erdkreis schlingt, ist nicht zu bezweifeln."

[38] Marchand, "Leviathan and the Mousetrap," 333. See also Gschwantler,
"Christus, Thor und die Midgardschlange," 149.

[39] Magnús Már Lárusson, "Um Niðurstigningarsögu," 164–65.

[40] Theodor Wisén, ed., Homiliu-bók: Isländska Homilier efter en handskrift från
tolfte århundradet (Lund: Gleerup, 1872), 75–76: ". . . oc sté hann þa yver ᴇɴ forna
fiánda es hann lét ofriþar mᴇɴ beriasc i gegn sér. þat sýnde drotᴛᴇɴ þa es hann
mælte viþ ᴇɴ sǽla iób. Mᴏɴ eigi þu draga leviaþan ['miþgarþsormr' is written
superscript] a ǫngle eþa bora kiþr hans meþ baúge. Sia gléýpande hvalr merker
gróþgan anskota þaɴ es svelga vill allt maɴkyn i dauþa. Agn es lagt a ǫngol en
hvass broddr leýnesc. þeɴa orm tók almáttegr guþ a ǫngle. þa es hann sende son
sɪɴ til daúþa sýnelegan at líkam en osýnelegan at guþdóme. Diabolus sa agn
likams hans þat es hann beit oc villde fyrfara. en guþdoms broddr stangaþe hann
svasem ǫngoll. A ǫngle varþ hann tekᴇɴ. þuiat hann beidesc at gripa lícams agn
þat es hann sa. en vass guþdóms brodr sa es leýndr vas sǽrþe hann. A ǫngle
varþ hann tekᴇɴ. þuiat hann fek scaþa afþui es hann beít. oc glataþe hann þeim
es hann hafþe áþr vellde yver. þuiat hann treýstesc at gripa þaɴ es hann hafþe

tor or translator of *Niðrstigningarsaga* could, therefore, have appropriated the theme from a number of sources, including the *Hómilíubók*. Because of this interpolation, scholars have seen influence from *Niðrstigningarsaga* in Eysteinn Ásgrímsson's *Lilja* from the mid-fourteenth century.[41] In one hundred stanzas in *hrynhent* meter, the poem tells of the history of the world from the Creation to the Annunciation, of the life and death of Christ, of the Ascension and the Day of Judgement. The last section contains the poet's confessions and prayers to Virgin Mary, the Lily. Paasche, Magnús Már Lárusson, and Thomas D. Hill draw attention to stanza 60, in which the poet refers to the image of Christ's humanity as the bait and his divinity as the hook by which Leviathan ("ormrinn bjúgi," i.e., the Miðgarðsormr) is caught:[42]

> En í andláti Jésú sæta
> oss er flutt, at gægz á krossinn
> fjandinn hafi ok frétt at syndum
> færaglǫggr, ef nǫkkur væri;
> hlægir mik, at hér mun teygjaz
> hans forvitni sér til vansa,
> eigi mun nú ormr enn bjúgi
> agn svelgjandi á króki fagna.[43]

---

etke vellde igegn" ("... and he rose above the Ancient Enemy when he let violent men attack him. This the Lord revealed when he spoke to Blessed Job: 'You cannot draw out Leviathan [the miðgarð serpent] with a hook or pierce his jaw with a ring.' This voracious whale signifies the greedy Devil who wishes to swallow all mankind in death. The bait is put on the hook and the sharp point is hidden. Almighty God took the serpent with a hook when he sent His Son to die, visible in body, but invisible in divinity. The devil saw the bait of His body which he bit upon and wished to destroy, but the point of divinity snagged him like a hook. He was taken on a hook, because he was enticed to seize the bait of the body, which he saw. But the sharp point of divinity which was hidden wounded him. He was taken on a hook, because he was hurt by that on which he bit. And he lost that over which he previously had power, because he sought to seize the One against Whom he had no power" [Marchand, "Leviathan and the Mousetrap," 331–32]). The section is a free rendering of *Homiliae in evangelia*, lib. 2, hom. 25 (PL 76:1194B–96C); see Gschwantler, "Christus, Thor und die Midgardschlange," 151 n. 45, and Marchand, "Leviathan and the Mousetrap," 332. The section occurs also in AM 684c 4°; see Magnús Már Lárusson, "Um Niðurstigningarsögu," 164, and Marchand, "Leviathan and the Mousetrap," 336 n. 16.

[41] Finnur Jónsson, ed., *Den norsk-islandske skjaldedigtning*, A1–2 (tekst efter håndskrifterne) and B1–2 (rettet tekst) (1908–15; repr., Copenhagen: Gyldendal, 1967 [A] and 1973 [B]), A2:363–95, B2:390–416.

[42] Fredrik Paasche, *Lilja. Et kvad til Guds moder* (Oslo: Aschehoug, 1915); Magnús Már Lárusson, "Um Niðurstigningarsögu," 166; Thomas D. Hill, "Number and Pattern in *Lilja*," *Journal of English and Germanic Philology* 69 (1970): 561–67, esp. 563.

[43] Finnur Jónsson, *Den norsk-islandske skjaldedigtning*, B2:406. "And at the death of dear Jesus, we heard that the keen-sighted devil was eager at the cross

Because of the appearance of the theme elsewhere in Old Norse-Icelandic literature, it is, however, as Marchand points out, unnecessary
to assume a direct connection between *Niðrstigningarsaga* and *Lilja*.[44]
The motif of the falling cross as a mousetrap in *Niðrstigningar-*
saga—which, according to Aho, is also Northern—is, as Magnús Már
Lárusson, Gschwantler, and Marchand note, a patristic commonplace
too, which has its origin in Augustine.[45] Marchand claims that "the
mention of the mousetrap of the cross is perfectly *à propos* in this part
of the story." He reiterates C. I. Minott's understanding of the mousetrap as a means of overcoming the devil and forcing him to relinquish
the captive souls. The reference to the mousetrap in *Niðrstigningarsaga*,
therefore, suggests deft handling and clear understanding of the doctrinal underpinning of the topos on the part of the interpolator or the
author of his source text. Marchand also notes that there is nothing
"Northern" about making the devil into a fox; it is just another patristic commonplace.

There are indications that in the sixteenth century there was in
existence a different medieval translation of the *EN* or else a fuller
redaction of *Niðrstigningarsaga*. AM 727 4° II, *Tijdfordrijf Edur Lijtid*
Annals Kuer by Jón Guðmundsson lærði (1574–1658), written in 1644,
contains extracts from earlier literary works and Jón Guðmundsson's
own notes and comments. A large portion of his commentary is
devoted to the *EN*, and in comparison with the extant manuscripts of
Niðrstigningarsaga his account is more detailed.[46] Thus, whereas *Niðr-*

---

and sought for sins—whether there might be any there—but I rejoice that his
curiosity enticed him there for his disgrace. For the crooked serpent, swallowing
the bait, will not have any joy in the hook."

[44] Marchand, "Leviathan and the Mousetrap," 331.

[45] Magnús Már Lárusson, "Um Niðurstigningarsögu," 166; Gschwantler,
"Christus, Thor und die Midgardschlange," 155; Marchand, "Leviathan and the
Mousetrap," 333–34. Augustine, "Sermo 130," par. 2 (PL 38:726). Gschwantler
says, "Wenn der isländische Übersetzer wirklich die Formulierung des Augustinus vor sich hatte, was natürlich nicht der Fall zu sein braucht, so gewährt
gerade diese Stelle einen interessanten Einblick in seine Übersetzungstechnik: Er
wußte, daß 'muscipula' im Zusammenhang mit dem Kreuz nicht Mausefalle
bedeuten kann, sondern einfach Falle. Daher läßt er das Kreuz auf den Teufel
herabfallen, doch die ursprüngliche Bedeutung von 'muscipula' rief in ihm die
Vorstellung der Mausefalle hervor und so fügte er das Bild von der Maus in der
Mausefalle dem vom Fisch an der Angel und dem Fuchs in der Schlinge hinzu.
Übrigens kommt das Kreuz als Falle auch noch in den Sententiarum libri quattuor
(Distinctio XIX) des Petrus Lombardus vor: In seiner stark von Anselm und
Abälard beeinflußten Erlösungslehre gibt er ganz unvermittelt die oben ange-
führte Stelle aus Augustinus wieder. Sollte die Niðrstigningar saga in der zweiten
Hälfte des 12. Jhs. entstanden sein, so muß man auch mit Petrus Lombardus,
dessen Werke überaus große Verbreitung fanden, als Vermittler rechnen."

[46] This section is found in Mariane Overgaard, ed., *The History of the Cross-*

stigningarsaga merely states that Charinus and Leucius wrote an account of Christ's Descent ("Karinus oc Leucius ... rito þenna þot niþrstigningar Crisz, af ðvi at þeir villdo eki viþ menn mela, oc leto bocena coma i hendr Nicodemo oc Joseph [p. 8.28–31]),[47] Jón Guðmundsson follows the Latin and tells that Charinus and Leucius each and in separate places wrote an account of Christ's Descent and that when the two accounts were compared, they were identical.[48]

Two translations of the *EN* survive in a number of Icelandic manuscripts from the mid-eighteenth century to the end of the nineteenth century: (1) Magnús Grímsson's translation (Reykjavík, National Library [Lbs.] 509 4°) from the middle of the nineteenth century, and (2) an anonymous and somewhat older translation preserved in two recensions: A (Copenhagen, Royal Library [NkS; now in Lbs.] 68 4°, Lbs. 786 8°, Lbs. 1036 8°, Lbs. 1258 8°, Lbs. 2144 8°, JS 36 4°, JS 219 8°; and Reykjavík, Icelandic Literary Society [ÍB] 212 8°) and B (Lbs. 526 8°, Lbs. 1160 8°, Lbs. 1333 8°, Lbs. 2636 8°, JS 280 4°, JS 456 8°, ÍB 98 8°, and ÍB 393 8°).[49] Mariane Overgaard has examined the oldest of these manuscripts, Lbs. 1258 8° from 1751, and notes that the manuscript contains an account of Charinus and Leucius which agrees with Jón Guðmundsson's. She is, however, of the opinion that the late character of the language would seem to preclude that the translation is identical with the one which was copied by the priests when Jón Guðmundsson was a child, and which he himself refers to ("þeir nynæmustu nyju sida prestar skrifudu sier N. G. i barndæmi mynu").[50] She concludes: "He would thus seem to have been familiar either with a now-lost medieval translation of the Gospel of Nicodemus or else with a fuller redaction of Niðrstigningar saga than that which now survives."[51] Since there are no verbal similarities between *Niðrstigningarsaga* and *Tijdfordrijf* and since there is no other (conclusive) evidence of a fuller

---

Tree down to Christ's Passion: Icelandic Legend Versions, Editiones Arnamagnæanæ, Series B, vol. 26 (Copenhagen: Munksgaard, 1968), 79–82.

[47] "Karinus and Leucius ... wrote this tale about Christ's Descent because they did not want to speak with men, and let the book come into the hands of Nicodemus and Joseph."

[48] "þeir Joseph og Nichodemus bàdu þessa ij menn og upprisu votta ad lata þeim epter skrifadann þeirra vitnizburd. adur þeir skylldust ad. og þeir jatudu þui. langt var i millum þeirra borga. enn þegar þær bækur voru samanbornar. fanst ecki einu ordi fleira nie færra og eingin annar mismunur, helldur öll sòmu ord i badum þeim bokum. um nidurstignijng vorz herra" (Overgaard, *The History of the Cross-Tree*, 85).

[49] Here and in the following, see Kirsten Wolf, "Om en 'tabt' islandsk oversættelse af Nikodemusevangeliet," *Arkiv för nordisk filologi* 107 (1992): 167–79.

[50] "the priests of the most novel new faith wrote N. G. in my childhood."

[51] Overgaard, *The History of the Cross-Tree*, cxx–cxxi.

redaction of *Niðrstigningarsaga*, the latter suggestion can probably be rejected. The former suggestion seems more likely, especially since both Lbs. 1258 8° and JS 280 4°, the second-oldest manuscript from 1779, contain errors suggesting that neither is a copy of the original translation. It appears more probable that both manuscripts are derived from a copy of the original text and that between this copy and the two manuscripts there are missing links. Whether or not the original translation is identical with the translation that was copied by the priests when Jón Guðmundsson was a child cannot be ascertained, but the possibility cannot be excluded.

A poetic paraphrase of *EN* material is found in the late medieval *Niðurstigningsvísur*,[52] which Jón Þorkelsson, Finnur Jónsson, Páll Eggert Ólason, Jón Sigurðsson and Guðbrandur Vigfússon, and Gschwantler all ascribe to the last Catholic bishop in Iceland, Jón Arason of Hólar, who was executed in 1550.[53] Apart from Eysteinn Ásgrímsson, Jón Arason was no doubt the most celebrated poet of pre-Reformation times, though it may well be that his fame has caused him to be credited with more verse than he actually composed. While there is no doubt of his authorship of *Píslargrátur* and *Davíðsdiktur*, his association with *Niðurstigningsvísur* as well as a number of other poems has been

[52] This is the title in the oldest manuscript of the *vísur* (AM 713 4°); in the other manuscripts (except group D, which has no title), it is called either *Niðurstigningsvísur* or *Niðurstigningarvísur*. The poem was first edited by Jón Sigurðsson and Guðbrandr Vigfússon, *Biskupa sögur*, 2 vols. (Copenhagen: Möller, 1858–78), 2:546–57, later by Finnur Jónsson, *Jón Arasons religiøse digte*, Det Kongelige Danske Videnskabernes Selskab, Historisk-filologiske Meddelelser, vol. 2, pt. 2 (Copenhagen: Høst & Søn, 1918), 58–69, and most recently by Jón Helgason, *Íslenzk miðaldakvæði: Islandske digte fra senmiddelalderen*, vol. 1, pt. 2 (Copenhagen: Munksgaard, 1936), 221–38. The present discussion of the poem is based on Jón Helgason's edition. The poem survives in a large number of manuscripts, which Jón Helgason (212–21) divides into nine groups (A–I). These nine groups go back to just as many mutually independent recordings from oral tradition, perhaps with the exception of C and D. That C and D are related is evident from stanzas 2–3, which are recast in a Lutheran spirit (e.g., "dogling himna stræta" [3.5] for "drottins uisit mæta"). A is the oldest manuscript and most probably the best, but it is not without errors. The mistake in "lasu lofspar hreinar" (33.3), probably under the influence of "lokur ok lasa alla" (34.3), provides evidence of its basis in oral tradition. B is close to A, but there appears to be no written textual relationship between the two groups. H presents a redaction which in a number of places is deliberately recast in order to eliminate Catholic elements and in order to clarify unclear phrases.
[53] Jón Þorkelsson, *Om digtningen på Island i det 15. og 16. Århundrede* (Copenhagen: Høst, 1888), 328; Finnur Jónsson, *Den oldnorske og oldislandske Litteraturs Historie*, 3 vols. (Copenhagen: Gad, 1920–24), 3:129; Páll Eggert Ólason, *Menn og menntir siðskiptaaldarinnar á Íslandi*, vol. 1 (Reykjavik: Bókaverzlun Guðm. Gamalíelssonar, 1919), 419; Jón Sigurðsson and Guðbrandr Vigfússon, *Byskupa sögur* 2:546 n. 1; Gschwantler, "Christus, Thor und die Midgardschlange," 158.

questioned. He is mentioned as author only in the title of manuscripts of the H-group (see n. 52 above), and his association with the poem may, therefore, be inaccurate.[54] Finnur Jónsson, however, has drawn attention to verbal similarities between *Niðurstigningsvísur* and *Píslargrátur* and *Ljómur*, which has also been ascribed to Jón Arason, and claims that these point to one and the same poet.[55]

Although there is no formal division other than the stanzas, the poem falls naturally into four parts. (1) Stanzas 1–4 form an introduction in which the poet laments his sins and calls upon the Divinity to help him compose a poem of praise. In stanza 2, the poet addresses the Virgin Mary directly (cf. "kuædit þitt," "your poem"), which suggests that the poem is dedicated especially to her, and in stanza 4 the poet turns to Christ himself with a similar prayer. (2) Stanzas 5–9 give an account of the birth of Christ and the flight to Egypt.[56] In stanza 10, the Jews' anger is mentioned, and in stanza 11, the poet refers directly to the *Gesta Salvatoris*, evidently as his (ultimate) source for the account of Christ's Harrowing of Hell (sts. 24–37).[57] Stanzas 12–23 give an account of Judas's treason, the trial, and the Crucifixion.[58] (3) Stanzas 24–37 then describe Christ's Descent into Hell. (4) The conclusion (sts. 38–42) consists of a prayer for moral strength and guidance and for mercy.

Only stanzas 15–37 of the poem bear any relation to the *EN*. Moreover, the section corresponding to the *Acta Pilati* (sts. 15–23) bears no

---

[54] See Jakob Benediktsson, "Kristdigte," in *Kulturhistorisk Leksikon for nordisk middelalder*, vol. 9 (Copenhagen: Rosenkilde and Bagger, 1964), cols. 292–94, esp. col. 293; Jón Helgason, *Íslenzk miðaldakvæði*, 219.

[55] *Jón Arason religiøse digte*, 23.

[56] Finnur Jónsson, *Jón Arason religiøse digte*, 22, draws attention to stanzas 7.6–8 ("'kuinnan kom til ydar ein / med vngan suein / er bar hun áá briosti sinu," "the woman came to you alone / with a young boy / whom she carried by her breast"), i.e., the story about the poor woman's child, Dysmas, whom Virgin Mary nursed. According to the legend, this child was to become one of the two robbers who were crucified together with Christ (cf. Lk. 23:42–43). The story is found in Old Norse in *Maríu saga* (C. R. Unger, ed., *Mariu saga: Legender om Jomfru Maria og hendes jertegn* [Oslo: Brögger & Christie, 1871], 39).

[57] "Nichodemus nadi / nefnilegur ad greina liost / dyrstur drottin spadi / Dauids kongs fyrer munn ok briost / med prophetum ok prudum eingla choris / grædarans pinu glosa tok / ok giordi áá bok / gesta saluatoris."

[58] Finnur Jónsson, *Jón Arason religiøse digte*, 22, notes that the same account is found in *Píslargrátur* (sts. 12–23) and that the source is the same: stanza 13.5–8 echoes Lk. 22:48, Mk. 14:14; stanza 14 echoes Jn. 18:10–11, etc.; stanza 16.5–8 echoes Mk. 14:50; and stanza 19.6 echoes Jn. 19:2. He also notes details not mentioned in *Píslargrátur*, e.g., Judas's treason (sts. 12–13; mentioned also in *Ljómur*, st. 10), the cutting off of the ear of the high-priest's servant (st. 14), and the flight of the disciples (st. 16). Páll Eggert Ólason, *Menn og menntir*, 419, suggests that this section of *Niðurstigningsvísur* (sts. 12–23) may have influenced Hallgrímur Pétursson's *Passiusálmar*.

more semblance to the *EN* than to the scattered accounts in the Vulgate. The trial itself is described in stanzas 17–18, but they give few details and do not tell of Pilate's predicament, and Nicodemus and the people healed by Christ, who come forward on his behalf, are not mentioned. The story of the Crucifixion is rendered in stanzas 19–23, though with no mention of Gestas and Dysmas and of Joseph of Arimathea. Stanzas 24–27 correspond to *Descensus Christi ad inferos* or *Niðrstigningarsaga*, but the frame that contains the central story is substantially reduced and changed. It is not presented as being recorded by Charinus and Leucius, who, in fact, are not mentioned at all; instead the poem begins at the words of Satan (*DI* 4.1 [*EN* 20]; *Niðrstigningarsaga*, p. 3.15). The dialogue between Satan and Inferus, who—as in the three older manuscripts of *Niðrstigningarsaga*—is not personified but represented as "djǫflar" ("devils"), is recorded in stanzas 24–26, the debate about the opening of the gates and Christ's entrance is described in stanzas 29–32, and the account of Christ's presence in Inferus is given in stanzas 33–37.

In spite of the reference in stanza 11 to the *Gesta Salvatoris*, the relationship between the *EN* and the *Niðurstigningsvísur* appears to be only a thematic one. The relationship between *Niðrstigningarsaga* and the poem is more difficult to determine. Magnús Már Lárusson is of the opinion that the poem is based on the saga, but he offers no argumentation for his hypothesis.[59] Finnur Jónsson is more cautious and suggests that it may be based on memory or on a text different from the extant *Niðrstigningarsaga*.[60] There are no verbal similarities between the two works, and although the poet may have been acquainted with the saga, it is doubtful whether it served as a direct literary source. A curious similarity between the two works is, however, the reference to the "ormr" in the last three lines of stanza 27, which echoes the interpolations in *Niðrstigningarsaga* and, in particular, stanza 60 of *Lilja*: "upp á krossinn ormuren skreid / ok andlatz beid / salina suelgia uilldi."[61] Magnús Már Lárusson draws attention to two manuscripts of *Lilja*, London, British Museum (BM) 4892 and AM 622 4°, which have the reading "a krossi fagna" ("have joy in the cross")

---

[59] Magnús Már Lárusson, "Um Niðurstigningarsögu," 165.

[60] ". . . enten er fremstillingen, som den foreligger i udgaven i Heil[agra] m[anna] s[ǿgur], vilkårlig behandlet (mulig efter hukommelsen?) eller også en noget forskellig tekst benyttet . . . , i alle tilfælde er fremstillingen naturligvis stærkt forkortet" (*Jón Arason religiøse digte*, 22–23).

[61] "Up the cross the serpent crawled and died wanting to swallow the soul." "Ormrinn" / "Ormrinn bjúgi" is mentioned or alluded to also in *Kristbálkur* (sts. 13 and 45), *Krossvísur* II (st. 15), and *Krosskvæði* (st. 24). All three poems are edited in Jón Helgason, *Íslenzk miðaldakvæði*, 144–56, 262–66, 277–85.

instead of "á króki fagna" ("have joy in the hook"). The reading in these two manuscripts resembles the reading in *Niðurstigningsvísur*.[62] The Harrowing of Hell motif appears widely in Old Norse-Icelandic religious prose and poetry, though it is important to bear in mind that the *EN* was not the only source of the Harrowing of Hell theme and that the motif may not necessarily be derived directly or even indirectly from the *EN* (or *Niðrstigningarsaga*). Aho has examined a great number of homilies, saints' lives, and sagas of the apostles, and he has noted that references to the Harrowing are common but that none of them is particularly striking, and that they are undoubtedly derivative from standard Latin conceptions and treatments of the theme. Usually, the Harrowing is mentioned in a single phrase or sentence as merely one aspect of Christ's career.[63]

In poetry, the Harrowing is alluded to in two lines of stanza 4 in Einarr Skúlason's *Geisli*, a *drápa* in *dróttkvætt* meter on the death and miracles of St. Óláfr Haraldsson, delivered in the cathedral of Niðaróss (Trondheim) in 1153 or 1154, where it is stated that a multitude of deceased rose with Christ ("veitk, at mildr frá moldu / meginfjǫlði reis hǫlða").[64] A further reference appears in *Leiðarvísan*, a *drápa* in *dróttkvætt* meter from the latter half of the twelfth century on the observance of Sunday, which tells (st. 31) that Christ himself bound the devil.[65] Finally, *Líknarbraut*, a *drápa* also in *dróttkvætt* meter, written by an anonymous monk some time after 1300, on the Passion, the Descent, the Resurrection, and the Ascension, relates (st. 22) that Christ descended into hell to visit with the devils.[66]

---

[62] Gschwantler, "Christus, Thor und die Midgardschlange," 156, notes, "Rein sprachlich ist es natürlich möglich, die Stelle so aufzufassen wie dies Jón Arason in seinen Niðrstignings vísur getan hat . . . , daß die Schlange auf das Kreuz gekrochen sei. Ob die Form 'a krossi' nun ursprünglich ist oder sekundär, es scheint hier eine alte Variante der Allegorie vom geköderten Leviathan vorzuliegen, in der das Kreuz mit der Angel gleichgesetzt wird."

[63] Aho, "A Comparison," 189, and "*Niðrstigningarsaga*," 155, however, draws attention to *Tveggja postola saga Jons ok Jacobs* (C. R. Unger, ed., *Postola sögur: Legendariske fortællinger om apostlernes liv deres kamp for Kristendommens udbredelse samt deres martyrdød* [Oslo: Bentzen, 1874], 536–711), which says that after the Crucifixion Christ went "heriandi . . . til helvitis . . . með hvellum hamri" (559.10–12). According to Aho, "*Niðrstigningarsaga*," 155, "[a]n Old Norse audience would immediately associate this Christ with Þórr, who used Mjǫlnir, his wondrous hammer, to slay many an evil giant in just such a fashion."

[64] Finnur Jónsson, *Den norsk-islandske skjaldedigtning*, A1:459–73, B1:427–45, quotation at B1:427, st. 4.5–6.

[65] "Dag reis sinn með sigri / snjallastr faðir allra / (sjóli huggaði seggi / sólar hauðrs) af dauða, / áðr batt flærðar—fróðan / fjandi heilagr andi / fast ok fyrða leysti / fremðar—styrkr ór myrkrum" (ibid., A1:618–26, B1:622–33, quotation at B1:630). See also Fredrik Paasche, *Kristendom og kvad. En studie i norrøn middelalder* (Oslo: Aschehoug, 1914), 105.

[66] "Kvaliðr sté, ǫllum æðri, / ítr gramr til helvítis / dægra láðs ept dauða /

References in late medieval poems include stanza 116 of *Rósa* (another of Virgin Mary's many symbolic names), modelled on *Lilja*. A sixteenth-century manuscript, AM 622 4°, attributes the poem to Sigurður blindur, though, in reality, his name is associated with another poem in the manuscript, the poem known as *Milska*, in which the Harrowing is alluded to in stanza 58. The theme is mentioned also in *Píslardrápa* (sts. 24–26), *Blómarós* (sts. 196–200), and *Ljómur* (sts. 14–17),[67] which was very popular in Iceland and in the Faroe Islands.[68] Further references are found in *Kristbálkur* (sts. 48–49), *Krossvísur I* (sts. 18–25),[69] and *Krosskvæði* (st. 26).[70]

In secular literature a reference to the Harrowing appears in the Apostolic Creed contained in the Christian law section (*Kristindómsbǫlkr*) of the *Landslǫg* of King Magnús Hákonarson lagabœtir (reigned 1263–1280): "fór nidr til helvítis at leysa þaðan alla sína menn."[71] The anonymous author of the so-called *Fourth Grammatical Treatise*, a handbook of grammar and rhetoric composed towards the middle of the fourteenth century, was clearly also acquainted with the story of the Harrowing and makes a reference to it in stanza 21.1–4.[72]

Textually far removed from but thematically related to the *EN* is the story of the life of Pontius Pilate in *Gyðinga saga*, a mid-thirteenth-century compilation recording the history of the Jews from 175 BC to AD 44, by Brandr Jónsson, bishop of Hólar (d. 1264).[73] Although the

---

djǫfla rann at kanna; / leysti sinn at sǫnnu / sólhallar gramr allan / lýð fyr lífstré þjóðar / liknar-styrkr frá myrkrum" (Finnur Jónsson, *Den norsk-islandske skjaldedigtning* A2:150–59, B2:160–74, quotation at B2:166). See also Paasche, *Kristendom og kvad*, 128, and Magnús Már Lárusson, "Um Niðurstigningarsögu," 166.

[67] See *Jón Arason religiøse digte*, 20, and Páll Eggert Ólason, *Menn og menntir*, 417.

[68] The Faroese version has been edited and discussed by R. Jensen, "Ljómur," *Aarbøger for nordisk oldkyndighed og historie* (1869): 311–88, and Jón Helgason, "Færøiske studier: I. Den eldste optegnelse av færøiske kvad. – II. Ljómur på Færøiene," *Maal og minne* (1924): 29–48.

[69] See *Jón Arason religiøse digte*, 23, and Páll Eggert Ólason, *Menn og menntir*, 417.

[70] All poems are edited in Jón Helgason, *Íslenzk miðaldakvæði*, 6–35, 38–58, 59–64, 69–111, 122–39, 144–56, 253–60, 277–85.

[71] "went down to hell to release all his men." R. Keyser and P. A. Munch, eds., *Norges gamle love indtil 1387*, 5 vols. (Oslo: Det Kgl. Norske Videnskabers Selskab, 1846–95), 2:306.

[72] "Pindr reis vpp með anda / angrleystv herfangi / hlyrna gramr til himna / hrein sotti guð drottinn." Björn Magnússon Ólsen, ed., *Den Tredje og Fjærde Grammatiske Afhandling i Snorres Edda tilligemed de Grammatiske Afhandlingers Prolog og To Andre Tillæg*, Samfund til udgivelse af gammel nordisk litteratur, vol. 12 (Copenhagen: Knudtzon, 1884), 144.

[73] Kirsten Wolf, ed., *Gyðinga saga* (Reykjavík: Stofnun Árna Magnússonar, 1995). The text of the Pilate legend is found on pp. 171–80 and 187–216. The Pilate

Pilate legend is ultimately derived from the *Gesta Pilati*, the direct source of the story in *Gyðinga saga* appears to be an immediate precursor of the one in Jacobus a Voragine's *Legenda aurea*.[74] Parts of the Pilate legend are found also in *Stephanus saga* in Stock. Perg. fol. nr. 2 in the Royal Library, Stockholm (saec. XIV), and AM 661 4° (saec. XV).[75] The text of the Pilate sections in *Stephanus saga* is on the whole identical to the text of the Pilate legend in *Gyðinga saga*, but in some places it is more detailed and the rendering of the Latin more accurate. Accordingly, it has been argued that the Pilate section in *Stephanus saga* is derived from a fuller and nonextant version of *Gyðinga saga*.[76] Pilate material appears also in *Stephanus saga* in Stock. Perg. fol. nr. 3,[77] a collection of twenty-five legends from ca. 1525, presumably based on the *Passionael*, one of the revised and expanded translations of the *Legenda aurea* into Low German, though in the case of *Stephanus saga* Widding and Bekker-Nielsen argue that the Icelandic translator drew most of his material from the older version in Stock. Perg. fol. nr. 2 and AM 661 4° and only occasionally supplemented his material from the *Passionael*.[78] From the late seventeenth century to the nineteenth century there are numerous Icelandic manuscripts containing versions of the Pilate legend, only three of which have been edited.[79] Generally, these stories are longer than the medieval ones; they are augmented with matter drawn from the Bible, and commonplaces of a

---

legend had previously been edited in Unger, *Postola sögur*, 151.12–53.4 and 154.35–59.20.

[74] Jacobus a Voragine, *Jacobi a Voragine Legenda aurea vulgo Historia Lombardica dicta*, ed. Th. Graesse (1890; repr., Osnabrück: Zeller, 1965). The Pilate legend appears in chapter 35, "De passione Domini," and in chapter 57, "De sancto Jacobo apostolo." See Jón Helgason, "Gyðinga saga i Trondheim," in *Opuscula*, vol. 5, Bibliotheca Arnamagnæana, vol. 31 (Copenhagen: Munksgaard, 1975), 343–76, esp. 362; and Kirsten Wolf, " 'Lífssaga Pilati' in Lbs. 4270 4to," *Proceedings of the PMR Conference* 12/13 (1987–88): 239–62, esp. 243.

[75] Unger, *Heilagra manna søgur* 2:287–309.

[76] Jón Helgason, "Gyðinga saga," 370–71; Wolf, " 'Lífssaga Pilati,' " 244.

[77] Agnete Loth, ed., *Reykjahólabók: Islandske helgenlegender*, 2 vols., Editiones Arnamagnæanæ, Series A, vols. 15–16 (Copenhagen: Reitzel, 1969–70). *Stephanus saga* is found in 1:213–45.

[78] Ole Widding and Hans Bekker-Nielsen, "En senmiddelalderlig legendesamling," *Maal og minne* (1960): 105–28, esp. 116; idem, "Low German Influence on Late Icelandic Hagiography," *The Germanic Review* 37 (1962): 237–62, esp. 251.

[79] AM 629 4° from 1697, the oldest of these manuscripts, is edited by Howard Martin ("The Legend of Pontius Pilate in Icelandic and Middle Low German: An Edition of Two Manuscripts" [Ph.D. diss., University of Wisconsin-Madison, 1971], 69–84); sections of Lbs. 4280 4° from 1791 are edited by Wolf (" 'Lífssaga Pilati,' " 246–54); and Lbs. 714 8° from the end of the eighteenth century by Kirsten Wolf, "An Extract of *Gyðinga saga* in Lbs. 714 8vo," in *Opuscula*, vol. 9, Bibliotheca Arnamagnæana, vol. 39 (Copenhagen: Reitzel, 1991), 189–202.

pious nature to edify the audience are frequently inserted. We are here dealing with a version or versions that have as their source not the Latin versions of the eleventh or twelfth centuries, nor vernacular translations of these, but rather, as Howard Martin points out, "a more detailed source which evolved from the merging of several traditions, both biblical and legendary."[80] Although there is some discrepancy among these late Icelandic versions in wording and style, the content is usually more or less the same, and it is clear that they all go back to the Latin versions of the eleventh and twelfth centuries and that they—like the medieval versions—are derived ultimately from the *Gesta Pilati*.

2. East Norse

One fragment of an Old Danish poetic rendering of the *Evangelium Nicodemi* has survived: Stockholm, Royal Library (SKB) A 115 from ca. 1325.[81] The manuscript consists of two adjacent leaves, both of which have been damaged. (The top margin has been trimmed to such an extent that the first line on both leaves has been eliminated, and on the second leaf the outer margin has been cut, and the bottom is torn.) The home of the anonymous author and the origin of the manuscript are considered to be Lund or its close vicinity. From a number of scribal errors it is clear that SKB A 115 does not present the original but is a copy of an older manuscript. Whether the older manuscript presented the original or was also a copy cannot be ascertained, but it is assumed that it was written in the same Scanian linguistic form as SKB A 115.

The poem, written in *knittel*, the normal form of mainland Scandinavian epic in the Middle Ages, appears to be based on Tischendorf's D^a group of texts (see above), i.e., Fabricius's text, to which reference will be made in the following,[82] but in a couple of instances there are readings that appear closer to other redactions. Johs. Brøndum-Nielsen suggests that the poem may to some extent be relying on a nonextant

---

[80] Howard Martin, "The Legend of Pontius Pilate," *Amsterdamer Beiträge zur älteren Germanistik* 5 (1973): 95–188, quotation at 117.

[81] Johs. Brøndum-Nielsen, ed., *Et gammeldansk Digt om Christi Opstandelse efter Fragment Stockh. A 115 (c. 1325)*, Det Kongelige Danske Videnskabernes Selskab, Historisk-filologiske Meddelelser, vol. 35, pt. 1 (Copenhagen: Munksgaard, 1955). The poem had previously been edited by Isak Collijn, "Nyfunna fragment af fornsvenska handskrifter bland räkenskapsomslagen i Kammararkivet," *Samlaren* 34 (1913): 275–93. The following discussion of the poem is essentially a resumé of Brøndum-Nielsen's exhaustive analysis of the work.

[82] Johannes Albertus Fabricius, ed., *Codex apocryphus Novi Testamenti* (Hamburg: Schiller, 1703).

German poetic adaptation of the *EN*; he bases his argument on the fact
that the two almost unrhymed lines of verse "ænghen stath mughu ui
ihesum spøria. / Num ioseph sagho ui i arymathia" (vv. 27–28) may
point to a Middle High or Low German poem with the rhyme "(er)v-
ragen – (in arymathia wi[r]) sagen."

The poem contains altogether 103 lines of verse and covers the
conclusion of the *Gesta Pilati* ("Congregati ergo sunt omnes Judæi ...
[*EN* 14]) and the beginning of the *Descensus Christi ad inferos* ("... et
scribemus vobis omnia quæ vidimus" [*EN* 17]). Its original size remains unknown. The text of the fragment appears to presuppose
earlier (nonextant) accounts of Nicodemus's defense of Christ, of
Joseph of Arimathea, who requested from Pilate the body of Christ and
gave it burial, of the guardians at the grave, who brought the news of
Christ's Resurrection, and of the three men of Galilee who witnessed
the Ascension on the Mount of Olives. Definite or probable allusions
to these accounts appear in the fragment. Other sections of the *EN*, such
as the Jews' charges against Christ, Pilate's inquiry, and the account of
Charinus and Leucius of the events in Inferus would appear to have
been an obvious part of the poem. It is possible, perhaps probable, that
the manuscript contained a gathering consisting of six to seven double-
leaves, of which the surviving fragment formed the middle leaf.

Although the rhymes reveal a poor prosodic routine, the work is
not unpoetic. Several words or phrases suggest a poetic stylistic tradition, whether native or foreign, such as the asyndetic "yuir biargh dala
scogha thranga" (v. 22) as opposed to the common literary syndetic
"gothe clærka. riddara oc suena" (v. 16), where influence from courtly
style is discernible in the vocabulary, the literary simile in "thætt hiarta
ryghe s[ua hart sum eet] staal" (v. 64), and the ballad-like "gotha
l[økko oc cranka] bathe" (v. 76). But on the whole the style is straightforward, e.g., "oc mana [tho them um guth o]c alt thætt guth scop" (v.
94) and "Sighir [um thæn sum ith]ær resde af døth. / ær thæs guzs [sun
sum os thæsse] logh bøth" (vv. 95–96). Brøndum-Nielsen concludes
that both usage and diction are close to prose and spoken language,
although sometimes the style does suggest a literary tradition.[83]

The translator (or adaptor) has rendered the Latin text freely. In a
couple of instances he appears to follow the Vulgate rather than the
EN. Thus, in the poem (v. 18) and in 4 Kings 2:17, Eliseus sends men
out to seek Elias, whereas in the *EN* Eliseus (Helisæus) himself goes

---

[83] "Ordbrug og Diktion ... staar gerne Prosaen og Talesproget nær, men
hæver sig stundom ogsaa til en højere Stil med Præg af litterær Tradition.
Jævnheden giver Digtet et tiltalende Særpræg" (Brøndum-Nielsen, *Et gammeldansk
Digt*, 13–14).

out to seek Elias. In "Han bedes af [guth att han thær] til lifthe. / att han mate ihesum i thæ[tta lif hitta]" (vv. 71–72)[84] the poem seems closer to Luke 2:26 ("Et responsum acceperat a Spiritu sancto, non visurum se mortem, nisi prius videret Christum Domini").[85] Moreover, a few additions and amplifications are found; apart from the couplet "Att ihesus ær op standen af døth. thætt sighia æi the ena. / Num thæt uittna gothe clærka. riddara oc suena" (vv. 15–16),[86] for which no parallel is found in the Latin text, these do not contain factual information and are most probably caused by the rhyme, e.g., "mittamus viros in montes Israel" (EN 15) > "Sua latum ui nu oc mæn um cring ganga. / yuir biargh dala scogha thranga" (vv. 21–22).[87] Similarly, the "thre dagha" (v. 25; "three days") is probably the translator's own addition, added as a parallel to the preceding "Thre dagha" in verse 19. In relation to the Latin, there are also several omissions and simplifications. Thus, the words of Annas, Caiphas, and Nicodemus to Joseph (EN 15) are omitted, the speech of Annas and Caiphas is simplified (EN 14 > vv. 9–12), and the same applies to the content of the letter to Joseph (EN 15 > vv. 33–34) and Joseph's praise of God (EN 15 > vv. 35–36). From verse 57 onwards the translator tightens the narrative considerably. After Christ's words to Joseph ("...usque in quadragesimum diem non exeas de domo tua. Ego autem ambulo ad discipulos meos" [EN 15]),[88] the EN tells of the Jews' dismay, of "quidam Levita" ("a certain Levite") who gives an account of the aged and devout Simeon, who took the infant Christ in his arms in the Temple and blessed him, of the three men of Galilee who repeat the account of the Ascension, and of Joseph, who relates to the Jews that Simeon's two sons also arose from their graves. In the poem, the references to both "quidam Levita" and the three men of Galilee are omitted, and their words are put into the mouth of Joseph, who thus assumes a more leading role in the narrative.[89] Moreover,

---

[84] "The requests from God / that he will live to meet Jesus in this life."

[85] Biblia Sacra iuxta Vulgatam Clementinam, ed. Albertus Colunga and Laurentius Turrado, 5th ed. (Madrid: La Editorial Catolica, 1977). "It had been disclosed to him by the Holy Spirit that he would not see death until he had seen the Lord's Messiah"; The New English Bible with the Apocrypha: Oxford Study Edition (New York: Oxford University Press, 1976).

[86] "Not only they say that Jesus is arisen from death. / Good clerics, knights, and swains testify to that."

[87] "let us send men into the mountains of Israel" > "Then let us now send men to walk / over mountains, valleys, dense forests."

[88] "...do not go out of your house until the fortieth day. But I am going to my disciples."

[89] See Tue Gad, Legenden i dansk middelalder (Copenhagen: Dansk Videnskabs Forlag, 1961), 253.

according to the poem (vv. 57–59), Joseph himself went to the Mount of Olives on the fortieth day and was one of the witnesses of the Ascension.

An Old Swedish prose translation of the entire *EN* survives in three manuscripts. The oldest of these is SKB A 110 ("Codex Oxenstiernianus") from Vadstena. It consists of 300 leaves and is not a single book as such, but rather a collection of six manuscripts. The Swedish *Sermo angelicus*, a collection of miracles, and a translation of the Acts of the Apostles form a unit, the oldest, from 1385. The second book is incomplete and somewhat younger; it contains a translation of *Vitae Patrum* and a life of St. Bridget. The translation of the *EN* is found along with a section of St. Bridget's revelations and a number of saints' lives in the third book, written in a hand no later than the beginning of the fifteenth century.[90] The second manuscript, Codex Skokloster 3 4° (also called "Passionarius," now in Stockholm, Royal Archive [SRA]) from 1450–1470, is presumably also from Vadstena.[91] It contains the *Old Swedish Legendary* (*Fornsvenska legendariet*), a collection of legends in chronological order from the beginning of Christianity until the mid-thirteenth century, composed probably by a Dominican friar no later than ca. 1300.[92] It is believed that the translation of the *EN* did not originally belong to the *Old Swedish Legendary*, since it is not found in the two older manuscripts of the legendary, SKB A 34 and Upps. C 528.[93] The third manuscript, SKB A 3, from Vadstena, was written in

---

[90] G. E. Klemming, ed., *Klosterläsning*, Samlinger utgifna af svenska fornskriftsällskapet, vol. 15 (Stockholm: Norstedt & söner, 1877–78). The *EN* translation is on pp. 377–419. The references in the following are to this edition.

[91] Vilhelm Gödel (*Sveriges medeltidslitteratur. Proveniens* [Stockholm: Nordiska bokhandeln, 1916], 46) draws attention to the fact that from some comments at the end of the manuscript it is clear that in 1531 it was owned by a certain Anna at Aspenäs in Upland, the wife of Sten Thuresson Bielke. This might suggest that the codex is from that area, though he also notes that it gives the impression of being from Vadstena.

[92] Georg Stephens, ed., *Ett forn-svenskt legendarium innehållande medeltids kloster-sagor om helgon, påfvar och kejsare ifrån det I:sta till det XIII:de århundradet*, 2 vols., Samlingar utgifna af svenska fornskrift-sällskapet, vol. 7, pts. 1–2 (Stockholm: Norstedt & söner, 1847–58). Sections from SRA 3 4° are edited on pp. 965, 994, 999–1006. Other manuscripts of textual significance containing this legendary are SKB A 34 (Codex Bureanus) from 1350; Uppsala, University Library (Upps.) C 528 (Codex Bildstenianus) from the early fifteenth century; and SKB A 124, a fragment from ca. 1300–1350. For a discussion of the filiation of these manuscripts, see Valter Jansson, *Fornsvenska legendariet: Handskrifter och språk*, Nordiska texter och undersökningar utgivna i Uppsala av Bengt Hesselman, vol. 4 (Stockholm: Geber, 1934).

[93] The *EN* translation is found in G. E. Klemming, ed., *Svenska medeltidens bibelarbeten*, 2 vols., Samlingar utgifna af svenska fornskrift-sällskapet, vol. 9 (Stockholm: Norstedt & söner, 1848–55), 2:373–411.

1502. It originally consisted of a three-volume lectionary arranged according to the Church year for the nuns of Vadstena. The first volume contained the time from Simon and Judas (28 October) until the octave of Christmas, the second from the octave of Christmas until Trinity Sunday, and the third from Trinity Sunday until Simon and Judas. Volumes one and three were written by the sisters Katarina Gudhmundi and Anna Girmundi and prepared by Elseby Gjordsdotter under the direction of the abbess Anna Fickesdotter Bylow; volume two, about which little is known, is designated as "modher syster Märitta bok." Volume one is still extant, volume two is lost, and only six leaves are preserved of volume three. In volume one, fols. 13–19, chapters 1–9 of the *EN* translation are found under the title "Thetta är läst nichodemi." The rest of the translation appears on fols. 72–80 under the title "Thetta är aff nichudemi läst som enkannelika röre wars herra opstandilse."[94] These sections of SKB A 3 4° have not been edited.

Like the Danish poetic adaptation, the Swedish text is based on Tischendorf's Dᵃ-group of texts,[95] but unlike the Danish, the Swedish presents a very literal rendering of the Latin. In a few instances Latin phrases are retained (though with accompanying translations), especially in the rendering of biblical quotations, e.g., "Nunc dimittis domine &c" (Lk. 2:29; p. 402.22–23).[96] Whereas omissions and simplifications are minor and generally rare, amplifications and expansions are common. They include doublet renderings (e.g., "honorabilis" [*EN* 15] > "hedhirlikin ok älskelikin" [p. 400.9]),[97] explanatory notes (e.g., "ab Arimathia" [*EN* 11] > "af aramathia swa hetande stadh i iudhalande" [p. 393.31]),[98] as well as amplifications in order to create a more dramatic effect (e.g., "Ego nec unam culpam invenio in Jesum" [*EN* 4] > "Nw for stund sagdhe iak idhir, himil oc iordh oc sool hawir iak til tygh at iak ey finna kan ena minzsta sak mz ihesu" [p. 384.16–18]).[99] Now and then factual information (from the biblical story, here from Jn. 19:29) is added, e.g., "... oc blandadhan dryk mz ätikkio oc galla oc bitra mirram gutu the i swamp oc opsändo thz for hans mun

---

[94] A list of the contents of volume one is given by G. E. Klemming, ed., *Bonaventuras betraktelser öfver Christi lefverne: Legenden om Gregorius af Armenien*, Samlinger utgifna af svenska fornskrift-sällskapet, vol. 15 (Stockholm: Norstedt & söner, 1859–60), xii–xxiii.

[95] See Brøndum-Nielsen, *Et gammeldansk Digt*, 9.

[96] SRA 3 4° has "Nunc dimittis domine in pace seruum tuum quia viderunt oculi mei salutare tuum" (Klemming, *Svenska medeltidens bibelarbeten*, 2:396.12–14).

[97] "honorable" > "honorable and lovable."

[98] "from Arimathea" > "from a place in Judea called Arimathea."

[99] "I find not any one fault in Jesus" > "I told you that I have heaven, earth, and the sun as a testimony that I cannot find the smallest fault in Jesus."

at han skulle thz drikka" (p. 391.12–15). Although the translator
adheres closely to the Latin text, native idiomatic expressions are
found, e.g., "ex fornicatione" (*EN* 2 and 9) > "af frillo säng" (p. 382.24)
/ "i hordom" (p. 388.28),[100] "occidere" (*EN* 3) > "af daghom taka"
(p. 383.21).[101] A slight mistranslation occurs in the rendering of "...
dicentes: Si ipsum esse creditis Jesum, qui vos suscitavit à mortuis,
dicite nobis quod vidistis, et quomodo resuscitati estis à mortuis" (*EN*
17) > "... vm i tron oppa ihesum som idhir opreste af dödha" (p.
404.17–18).[102] Finally, in the Swedish text (as in the Danish and in the
Vulgate) Eliseus sends men out to seek Elias: "... wtuäliom os män
som vmgange israels biärgh. oc vanlica the finna han" (p. 399.13–16).
   Allusions to the Descent appear in Swedish and Danish prayer
books from the late Middle Ages. In the Swedish prayer books, a reference is found in prayer no. 23,[103] and in the Danish books references
appear in prayers nos. 23, 87, 209, and 341.[104] The Danish prayer
book *Visdoms spejl*, nos. 527–836, preserved in AM 784 4° and AM 782
4°, contains a direct allusion to the *EN* among the seventy-five Easter
prayers.[105]
   As in Old Norse-Icelandic literature, there are also in Old Danish
and Swedish literature stories of the life of Pilate which are, at least
thematically, related to the *Gesta Pilati* section of the *EN*. In Swedish,
a Pilate legend, based on the *Legenda aurea*, is found in the *Old Swedish
Legendary* (see above). Another Swedish version of the legend appears
in *Siælinna thrøst* from around 1420, which survives in SKB A 108 from
ca. 1438–1442.[106] The work is a translation of a Low German adaptation of the *Legenda aurea*, *Der große Seelentrost*, from the mid-fourteenth
century, but augmented with material drawn from the Vulgate, Peter
Comestor's *Historia scholastica*, and a number of Swedish works. It con-

---

[100] "through fornication" > "from a concubine's bed" / "in adultery."
[101] "kill" > "take away from days."
[102] "saying: Believe ye that it is Jesus which raised you from the dead? Tell
us how ye have arisen from the dead" > "if you believe in Jesus who raised you
from the dead." See Brøndum-Nielsen, *Et gammeldansk Digt*, 102.
[103] Robert Geete, ed., *Svenska böner från medeltiden*, Samlingar utgifna af
svenska fornskrift-sällskapet, vols. 131, 133, 135 (Stockholm: Norstedt & söner,
1907–9), 63–66; see also Tue Gad, "Kristus," *Kulturhistorisk Leksikon for nordisk middelalder*, vol. 9 (Copenhagen: Rosenkilde and Bagger, 1964), cols. 365–77, esp. col.
376.
[104] Karl Martin Nielsen, ed., *Middelalderens danske bønnebøger*, 4 vols. (Copenhagen: Gyldendal, 1945–63), 1:101–2, 2:80–81, 300–301.
[105] Ibid. 3:179–473. See Gad, *Legenden*, 278, and "Kristus," 376.
[106] Sam. Henning, ed., *Siælinna thrøst. Første delin aff the bokinne som kallas
Siælinna thrøst*, Samlingar utgifna af svenska fornskrift-sällskapet, vol. 59 (Uppsala:
Almquist & Wiksell, 1954). The Pilate legend is on pp. 265–72.

sists in the main of an exposition of the Ten Commandments, which are explained through various biblical and profane legends, miracles, and the like. The Pilate legend is found in the exposition of the Fifth Commandment, and it is clear that the translator or compiler was acquainted with the *EN* ("Tho scrifwer nichodemus at tha war herra war upstandin aff dødha ..." [p. 272]),[107] though the source is here Upps. C 528 (*Old Swedish Legendary*, see n. 92), which refers to the *EN* on the same occasion. A translation from the original of the Swedish *Siælinna thrøst* into Danish (*Siæla trøst*) survives in the fragments Upps. C 529 and SKB A 109, both from around 1425, but only the middle section of the Pilate legend is extant.[108]

Conclusion

The *Evangelium Nicodemi* and its subject enjoyed widespread popularity in Scandinavia throughout the Middle Ages and well into modern times. It is represented by a variety of translations ranging from very literal (the Old Swedish translation) to free renderings (the Old Norse-Icelandic *Niðrstigningarsaga*), and from prose to poetry (the Old Danish poem and the Icelandic *Niðurstigningsvísur*). Allusions to one of the main themes of the work, the Harrowing of Hell, are found widely both in poetry and prose, mostly within the religious literature of medieval Scandinavia, but significantly also in secular literature, King Magnús's *Landslǫg*, and *The Fourth Grammatical Treatise*. The theme was of particular interest to medieval writers, and its varied, at times innovative, treatment combined with powerful imagery and doctrinal content provided writers and audiences alike with an absorbing, dramatic story concerning redemption and judgement.

---

[107] "Nicodemus writes that when our Lord had arisen from the dead...." See ibid., 272.

[108] Niels Nielsen, ed., *Sjælens Trøst* ("*Siæla trøst*"), Universitets-jubilæets Danske Samfund (Copenhagen: Schultz, 1937–52), 28–30.

The *Gospel of Nicodemus* in High German Literature of the Middle Ages[1]

WERNER J. HOFFMANN

Ⅰn German-speaking countries, the *Evangelium Nicodemi (EN)* was undoubtedly the most popular and widely disseminated of the New Testament apocrypha. Its popularity in the Middle Ages is amply demonstrated by the large number of prose and verse adaptations, which began to appear in the thirteenth century. In addition, the *EN* profoundly influenced vernacular writing. It provided biblical epics, Passion tracts, chronicles, sermons, legends, and especially religious plays with imaginative motives, themes, and scenes, especially for the depiction of the Harrowing of Hell.

1. Verse adaptations of the *Evangelium Nicodemi*

The full text of the *Evangelium Nicodemi* was rendered into Middle High German verse three times: by Konrad von Heimesfurt at the beginning of the thirteenth century, by Gundacker von Judenburg at the close of the same century, and by Heinrich von Hesler around 1300.[2] None of these renderings is an exact verse translation of the *EN*,

---

[1] This essay was completed in 1992. I should like to thank Dr. Zbigniew Izydorczyk for information on Latin manuscripts of the *Evangelium Nicodemi*.

[2] Throughout this essay, Latin *EN* A is cited from H. C. Kim, ed., *The Gospel of Nicodemus: Gesta Salvatoris*, Toronto Medieval Latin Texts, vol. 2 (Toronto: Pontifical Institute of Mediaeval Studies, 1973), unless otherwise noted; references are to chapter, paragraph, and line numbers. The Middle High German verse adaptions of the *EN* have been discussed by Richard Paul Wülcker, *Das Evangelium Nicodemi in der abendländischen Literatur. Nebst drei excursen ...* (Paderborn: F. Schöningh, 1872), 34–50, and Achim Masser, *Bibel- und Legendenepik des deutschen Mittelalters*, Grundlagen der Germanistik, vol. 19 (Berlin: E. Schmidt, 1976), 117–24.

but each revises the apocryphal source in an idiosyncratic manner; what they all have in common, however, is the extensive use of the canonical gospels in addition to the *EN*. Gundacker and Heinrich von Hesler also append—probably following their Latin sources—versions of the legend of Pilate and Veronica.

1.1. The *Urstende* of Konrad von Heimesfurt

The first German adaptation of the *EN*, the *Urstende* (2162 verses),[3] was composed possibly as early as the first decade of the thirteenth century. Its author, Konrad von Heimesfurt, inscribes his name in an acrostic; he can probably be identified with a ministerial of the same name from Eichstätt, who between 1198 and 1212 appears four times in the lists of witnesses on the documents of Bishop Hartwig von Eichstätt. In its sole surviving manuscript, Vienna, Österreichische Nationalbibliothek (ÖNB) MS. 2696, fols. 20vb–35ra (ca. 1300), Konrad's rendition of the pseudo-gospel bears the title "deu vrstende" ("The Resurrection"), which, however, reflects only part of the poem's contents. Before the *Urstende*, Konrad had already written another verse narrative based on an apocryphal source, *Unser vrouwen hinvart* (1209 verses), a free translation of pseudo-Melito's *Transitus Mariae*. In both these poems, he is strongly influenced by the Middle High German tradition of courtly epic and especially by Hartmann von Aue.[4]

As author of the apocryphal source of the *Urstende* Konrad names not Nicodemus but a Jew, "Enêas" (v. 54). Thus it is clear that the Latin antecedent of the poem should be sought among the rare manuscripts in which the *EN* begins with the "Eneas" prologue, that is, among the manuscripts of *EN* B. A comparison of the *Urstende* with versions A and B of the *EN* shows, however, that Konrad used the longer B version only for the *Gesta Pilati* (*EN* 1–16); for the *Descensus Christi ad inferos* (i.e., *EN* 17–27), he turned to the A version.[5] Such a

---

[3] Konrad von Heimesfurt, *Unser vrouwen hinvart und Diu urstende*, ed. Kurt Gärtner and Werner J. Hoffman, Altdeutsche Textbibliothek, vol. 99 (Tübingen: Niemeyer, 1989), 53–129; all subsequent references will be to this edition. Idem, *Diu urstende*, ed. Kurt Gärtner and Werner J. Hoffman, Altdeutsche Textbibliothek, vol. 106 (Tübingen: Niemeyer, 1991), is a teaching edition.

[4] On Konrad von Heimesfurt, see Werner Fechter, "Konrad von Heimesfurt," in *Die deutsche Literatur des Mittelalters. Verfasserlexikon*, 2d rev. ed., ed. Kurt Ruh (hereafter cited as Ruh, *Verfasserlexikon*), vol. 5 (Berlin: W. de Gruyter, 1985), 198–202, and the introduction to the scholarly edition of Konrad's poems, which contains a complete bibliography.

[5] For a discussion of Konrad's Latin model, but without the knowledge of the Salzburg manuscript discussed below, see Werner J. Hoffmann, "Konrad von

combination of *Gesta* B with *Descensus* A is found, as far as I know, in only one Latin manuscript, Salzburg, Erzabtei St. Peter MS. a V 27, fols. 111r–39v (saec. XII ex.).[6] The conclusion that the Salzburg manuscript preserves the Latin model of the *Urstende* is further supported by several variant readings of that manuscript, absent from other copies of *EN* B but present, through German equivalents, in the *Urstende.*

Konrad's other sources, in addition to the *EN*, included the canonical gospels and the Acts of Apostles. In fact, the events of the New Testament provide a framework for his narrative. His story begins with the events that led up to Jesus' trial before Pilate (vv. 69–258; Palm Sunday, the decision to kill Jesus, the betrayal by Judas, and Jesus' arrest); the consequences of the trial—the Crucifixion and the burial—are treated very briefly (vv. 743–822); a somewhat longer section on the Ascension and Pentecost (vv. 1111–224) prepares the conclusion. Into this New Testament frame, Konrad inserts the incidents recorded in the *EN:* Jesus' trial before Pilate (vv. 259–742), his Resurrection and the deliverance of Joseph of Arimathea (vv. 823–1074), and the questioning of the witnesses to Jesus' Resurrection and Ascension and to his Descent into Hell (vv. 1225–2148).

Whenever Konrad draws on the New Testament, he remains faithful to his source, even if at times considerably condensing the canonical matter. He treats with greater freedom the material derived from the *EN*, which lies at the very heart of the poem, freely omitting, abbreviating, transposing, expanding, combining, or changing motives for actions. As a result, his account of the trial before Pilate (vv. 259–742) is much more lucid and concise than that of the *EN*. Firstly, unlike the *EN*, it alternates the speeches of the prosecution and the defense; secondly, for the sake of clarity, it omits large portions of the original narrative (the messenger scene, Pilate's conversations with different witnesses, with Jesus, and with the leaders of the Jews); and thirdly, it remodels certain episodes, borrowing details from medieval German judicial procedures.[7] In the next segment of the poem (vv. 823–1074),

---

Heimesfurt. Untersuchungen zu Quellen, Überlieferung und Wirkung seiner beiden Werke *Unser vrouwen hinvart* und *Urstende"* (Ph.D. diss., Universität Trier, 1987), chap. 3.2.

[6] Closely related to the Salzburg manuscript is Munich, Bayerische Staatsbibliothek (BSB) Clm 17181, fols. 103r–12r (saec. XI), which preserves only the *Gesta* up to chap. 16.1. The *Somnium Neronis* appended to the *EN* in the Salzburg manuscript has been edited by Wolfgang Speyer, "Neue Pilatus-Apokryphen," *Vigiliae Christianae* 32 (1978): 53–59. The Salzburg text represents also the exact model of the German prose translation G; see below, pp. 316.

[7] Cf. Erich Klibansky, *Gerichtsszene und Prozeßform in den erzählenden deutschen Dichtungen des 12.–14. Jahrhunderts*, Germanische Studien, vol. 40 (1925; repr., Nendeln, Liechtenstein: Kraus Reprint Corp., 1967), 9–16.

the deliverance of Joseph of Arimathea is more closely linked with the Resurrection of Jesus than in the *EN*, and the parallels between the two events receive greater emphasis. Moreover, the scenes involving the guards of the sepulcher contain more dialogue, while the discovery of Joseph's empty prison cell by the Jews is described vividly and realistically. Both the threats of the Jews against Joseph at the opening of the prison, which are only hinted at in the *EN* with "cum iniuriis multis" ("with many insults"),[8] and the Jews' surprised reactions to the disappearance of the captive are given in direct speech. The final two episodes, concerned with Joseph of Arimathea and the sons of Simeon, Karinus and Leoncius (vv. 1225–2148), show clearly Konrad's indebtedness to Middle High German courtly literature of about 1200, for this part of the poem is dominated by courtly ceremonies associated with arrivals, greetings, and farewells. The two episodes—the questioning of Joseph by the Jewish leaders regarding his liberation and the interview with the two sons of Simeon regarding Jesus' Descent into Hell—have essentially the same structure, even though such parallelism is absent from the *EN*. They both include the following elements: a) a festive welcome to the witnesses (vv. 1289–95, 1568–73); b) negotiations behind closed doors, from which the "tumben" ("the uneducated") are excluded (vv. 1320–31, 1574–80); c) expressions of respect and submission (vv. 1357–80, 1586–605); d) Nicodemus's role as spokesman for the Jews and his request that the witnesses recount their experiences (vv. 1390–425, 1606–67). The three witnesses to the Ascension, Addas, Finees, and Egeas, are only briefly mentioned, and their appearance (vv. 1493–544) serves primarily to connect the other incidents involving questioning of witnesses (the confirmation of Joseph's statements and the reference to the two sons of Simeon). The report on the Descent into Hell (vv. 1693–2116), which in the *Urstende* is introduced with the *Canticum triumphale* ("Cum rex gloriae Christus . . ."), is—like the trial before Pilate—structurally simplified in comparison with the *EN*; however, Seth's account of his journey to paradise (vv. 1868–2020) is substantially enlarged and embellished with descriptions of the difficult path and the wonderful fragrance of paradise.

Characteristic of Konrad's handling of the apocryphal source is his unceasing attempt to simplify the plot and reduce it to its essentials. He focuses, to a greater extent than does the *EN*, on the witnesses' reports concerning Jesus, on the testimonies and miracles stressing the truth of his Resurrection, and on the Jews' reactions to the attestations. Most of the departures from the *EN* result from this concern with the testimonies about Jesus. All events not directly tied to these attesta-

---

[8] *EN* B 12.2; Salzburg, Erzabtei St. Peter MS. a V 27, fol. 120r.

tions are either omitted or sharply reduced; incidents in which the witnesses are questioned are embellished; the witnesses' reports are elaborated whenever they concern the actions of Christ; and the reliability of the witnesses and the truthfulness of their testimonies are emphasized. After each attestation (a report of a witness or a miracle, such as the standards bowing before Jesus or Joseph's empty prison), the reaction of the Jews—more clearly dismissive or unbelieving than in the *EN*—is described. Even more antisemitic than the Latin apocryphon, the *Urstende* depicts the Jews in a consistently negative light; this is evident, for instance, from such epithets as "mortgîten," "gotes widerwinnen" ("bloodthirsty," "foes of God"). Moreover, each of the three main sections of Konrad's work concludes with a polemical statement against the Jews: the account of the trial ends with a tumultuous scene, in which the Jews are compared to dogs (vv. 729–42); the section on Joseph of Arimathea closes with a digression on the unbelief of the Jewish people (vv. 1075–110); and the epilogue that follows the story of the Descent is similar in tone and content (vv. 2149–62).[9]

Although it has been preserved in a single complete manuscript, the *Urstende* exerted a significant influence on later authors who dealt with the same material. Approximately one third of the poem was incorporated into Heinrich von München's compilation of the *Weltchronik*; it was also used by Gundacker von Judenburg, Hawich der Kellner, the author of the *Befreiung der Altväter*, and the Alemannic translator of the *EN* (Alemannic version E).[10]

1.2. Gundacker von Judenburg's *Christi Hort*

Toward the end of the thirteenth century, Gundacker von Judenburg (Steiermark) composed the poem *Christi Hort* (5294 verses).[11] The title of this work is attested in its only complete manuscript, Vienna, ÖNB MS. 15225 (saec. XIV in.): "daz pǔch haizt Christz hort." Nothing certain is known about the author, who identifies himself in the poem (vv. 188–89) and who may have been a priest.[12]

---

[9] For a detailed comparison of the sources, see Hoffmann, "Konrad von Heimesfurt," chaps. 3.3 (continuous commentary on the sources) and 3.4 (summary of Konrad's treatment of his sources). The structure of the *Urstende* is represented in tabular form in the introduction to its 1989 edition, Konrad von Heimesfurt, *Unser vrouwen hinvart*, xlv–xlvi.

[10] Cf. sects. 1.2, 1.4, 2.3, and 3 below.

[11] *Gundackers von Judenburg "Christi Hort" aus der Wiener Handschrift*, ed. J. Jaksche, Deutsche Texte des Mittelalters, vol. 18 (Berlin: Weidmannsche Buchhandlung, 1910).

[12] Werner Fechter, "Gundacker von Judenburg," in Ruh, *Verfasserlexikon*, vol. 3 (1981), 303–6; Kurt Stübiger, *Untersuchungen zu Gundacker von Judenburg*, German-

The *Christi Hort* consists of several distinct sections so heterogeneous in content and style that earlier scholars wondered whether they
might not have been penned by different authors. It begins with an
introduction on the history of salvation (vv. 1–170), followed by the
first prologue, in which the poet mentions his own name (vv. 171–250),
and by an account of the life of Jesus (through to his capture) in the
form of a prayer (vv. 251–1304). Each of the twenty-three subsections
into which this narrative prayer is divided opens with an appeal to
Jesus, "ich man dich" ("I remind you"), and evokes a particular scene
in his life. Only then, ushered by another prologue (vv. 1305–26), does
the main account of the Passion, Resurrection, and Pentecost begin (vv.
1327–4044). In this latter part of the poem, Gundacker used not only
the *EN* and the Bible but other sources as well, including a Latin
liturgy and a *planctus Mariae*. The poem concludes with an extended
version of the legend of Pilate and Veronica (vv. 4045–5294).[13]

In the second prologue, Gundacker identifies "Nichodemus" as the
main source of his Passion story (vv. 1305–13); he claims that his
source is reliable because Nicodemus was present at all of the events
as an eyewitness: "der berichtet uns da von sus wie ez alles ergie unt
wie ez geschach, want er ez allez horte unt sach" (vv. 1310–12; "he
reports to us how it all took place and how it happened, because he
heard and saw it all"). He emphasizes the authenticity of the events as
recounted in the *EN* on another occasion as well, namely in his account
of the miraculous deliverance of Joseph of Arimathea: "swie ez doch
nicht geschriben ist an dem ewangelio, so ist ez doch benam also. ez
ist endlichen war" (vv. 2276–79; "even though it is not written in the
gospel, it is nevertheless actually so. It is absolutely true").

The Latin *EN* that lies behind Gundacker's poem must have belonged to version A, as evidenced by his dating of the Passion (vv.
1381–95; cf. prologue in A). More specifically, his source manuscript
must have stemmed from the textual tradition which appended to *EN*
A two additional texts, the *Somnium Neronis* and the *Signa in eversione
Iherusalem*, which have survived only as addenda to the Latin apocryphon. Chapters 1 and 2 of their joint edition by Ernst von Dobschütz
provided the basis for vv. 3903–4044 of the poem.[14] Gundacker's

ische Studien, vol. 15 (1922; repr., Nendeln, Liechtenstein: Kraus Reprint Corp., 1967).
[13] Stübiger, *Untersuchungen*, 79–123.
[14] Ernst von Dobschütz, "A Collection of Old Latin Bible Quotations: *Somnium Neronis*," *Journal of Theological Studies* 16 (1915): 12.1–15.9. Dobschütz mentions
Gundacker on pp. 7–8. For a note on the source of this section of Gundacker's
poem, see also Stübiger, *Untersuchungen*, 106–14, who, however, was unaware of
Dobschütz's edition; cf. also the partial edition of the *Somnium* by Johann Carl
Thilo, *Codex apocryphus Novi Testamenti* (Leipzig: F. C. G. Vogel, 1832), cxl n. 139.

Latin manuscript may have also contained a source of the poem's concluding section, the Latin prose legend of Pilate composed in Germany in the twelfth century and usually titled *Historia apocrypha of the Legenda aurea* because Jacobus a Voragine refers to it repeatedly in his hagiographical compilation.[15]

Gundacker reproduces the substance of the *EN* with its addenda much more faithfully than does Konrad von Heimesfurt, even though his rendition is, for the most part, condensed and abbreviated. In some sections in which he embellishes his source, he follows such literary models as the *Urstende* and the *Mai und Beaflor*.

In the account of the trial before Pilate, Gundacker strictly separates the apocryphal from the canonical. The first part of that account (vv. 1396–704) relies solely on the *EN* and adopts, although not without considerable compression, its apocryphal sequence of events. Gundacker expands only the messenger scene and the miracle of the standards (vv. 1420–561); those chapters of the *EN* which agree with the canonical gospels (2.5–6, 3, 4.1–2) he ignores here completely. The second part of the poem's account of the trial (vv. 1705–914) is based entirely on the canonical gospels.

Gundacker grounds his narrative of the events that followed Christ's death on the cross (vv. 2145–3032) on well-known scriptural material (from the burial up to the miracles at Pentecost) and fits excerpts from the *EN* (the scene with the guards of the sepulcher and the arrest of Joseph of Arimathea) into this canonical setting. It is noteworthy that Christ's Descent into Hell and the deliverance of Joseph of Arimathea are briefly recounted (vv. 2247–92) first after the burial, that is, at the chronologically "correct" point; later they are presented again, just as in the *EN*, in the form of eyewitness accounts. One motif of Gundacker's description of Joseph's empty prison cell is not found in the *EN*: he mentions that a spring broke to the surface in

---

All other writers on Gundacker, including Karl-Ernst Geith, "Eine Quelle zu Gundackers von Judenburg *Christi Hort*," *Zeitschrift für deutsches Altertum* 97 (1968): 57–68; and idem, review of *Das Evangelium Nicodemi in spätmittelalterlicher deutscher Prosa. Texte*, edited by Achim Masser and Max Siller, *Arbitrium* 7 (1989): 286–89, seem not to have been aware of the *Somnium*, which is essential for study of the sources of the *Christi Hort*.

[15] For proof that the *Historia apocrypha* was a source of Gundacker's work, see Ernst von Dobschütz, *Christusbilder. Untersuchungen zur christlichen Legende*, Texte und Untersuchungen zur Geschichte der altchristlichen Literatur, vol. 18, N.F., vol. 3 (Leipzig: J. C. Hinrichs, 1899), 300*, no. 42; for a complete edition of this Latin prose text on Pilate, see Joachim Knape, "Die Historia apocrypha der Legenda aurea (dt.)," in Joachim Knape and Karl Strobel, *Zur Deutung von Geschichte in Antike und Mittelalter*, Bamberger Hochschulschriften, vol. 11 (Bamberg: Bayerische Verlagsanstalt, 1985), 113–72. Cf. also idem, *Pilatus*, in Ruh, *Verfasserlexikon*, vol. 7 (1989), 673–74.

the prison and that Jesus used it to baptize Joseph (vv. 2423–28; cf. also vv. 3354–57). According to Stübiger, this may be an allusion to the well-known legend from the *Martyrium Petri*, according to which Peter caused a spring to break to the surface in his prison, so that he could baptize his prison guards.[16]

Having dealt with the events of Pentecost (vv. 2885–3032), Gundacker turns his attention to the examination of the witnesses by the Jewish leaders (vv. 3033–612). From this point onward (after v. 3033), he follows exclusively the *EN* (14–27), yet time and again he models individual incidents on Konrad von Heimesfurt's *Urstende*. In particular, he embellishes with details of courtly ceremony the incidents involving Joseph of Arimathea and the two sons of Simeon, Karinus and Leoncius.[17] Gundacker's dependence on Konrad shows also in the report on the Descent into Hell (vv. 3613–864), most notably in Seth's description of his journey to paradise (vv. 3686–742). On the whole, however, Gundacker's version of the Descent is a faithful, albeit again highly compressed, representation of the *Descensus*. It ends, as in the *EN*, with Joseph and Nicodemus handing over the written report of the two brothers to Pilate (vv. 3885–902), but then adds a touch of its own by making Pilate send the same report—not his own letter, as in the *EN*—to King Claudius in Rome (vv. 3903–5).

The mention of Pilate's dispatch to Rome forms, just as in Gundacker's Latin source, a transition to the appendix comprising the *Somnium Neronis* and the *Signa in eversione Iherusalem*. The appendix relates how Claudius gave Pilate's "prieve" ("letters") to Nero, and how Christ appeared to Nero in a dream and commanded him to avenge his death. Moved by this vision and by Pilate's letter, Nero orders Vespasian to wreak vengeance on the Jews (vv. 3906–42). This episode is followed by a listing of the seven omens foreshadowing the destruction of Jerusalem (vv. 3943–4044).

The redaction of the *EN* which served as Gundacker's model—the *EN* proper augmented with the *Somnium*—probably concluded with the omens. Gundacker, however, continues his story with a detailed account of the legend of Pilate and Veronica (vv. 4045–5294). Here, his source is the Latin prose legend of Pilate, the so-called *Historia apocrypha of the Legenda aurea*.[18] On the whole, the poet follows the narrative structure of the *Historia* relatively closely,[19] (in his retelling of the legend, Tiberius's

---

[16] Stübiger, *Untersuchungen*, 103–4.

[17] The influence of the *Urstende* on Gundacker is discussed by Hoffmann, "Konrad von Heimesfurt," chap. 4.2.3.

[18] Knape, "Die Historia apocrypha," 149.67–55.182. Knape edited a German translation of this prose text on Pilate, together with the Latin original, placed below the German text (pp. 146–65). I am citing the line numbering of the Latin.

[19] Vv. 4045–348, the healing of Vespasian, correspond to pp. 149.67–51.107 of

messenger is called Columban, not Albanus); however, he fleshes out the brief narrative of his source with detailed descriptions of the councils, of the selection and arming of messengers, of ocean voyages, and of receptions and greetings. The most important model for these descriptions was a courtly romance in verse, *Mai und Beaflor*.[20]

Gundacker certainly did not use a German prose translation of the *Historia apocrypha* as the basis of his legend of Pilate and Veronica. The German text alleged by Geith[21] to have been Gundacker's source is, in fact, a prose redaction of Gundacker's version, inserted into the so-called *Klosterneuburger Evangelienwerk*; it was first identified by Gärtner.[22] That this German text is dependent on Gundacker and not the reverse can be easily demonstrated, for Gundacker remains much closer to the Latin exemplar than does the prose text. The prose includes not only the legend of Pilate and Veronica but also the conclusion of the *EN* (27.5; presentation of the letters to Pilate) and the appendix to the *EN* with the *Somnium Neronis* and the omens foreshadowing the destruction of Jerusalem. While Gundacker recounts the events of the appendix exactly in the sequence of his Latin source, the author of the prose text divides them up and inserts them at various points in the legend of Pilate and Veronica.[23] Like Gundacker, he presents the conclusion of the *EN* and Nero's vision,[24] but he places Nero's orders to Vespasian to punish the Jews in the middle of the Pilate-Veronica legend,[25] and the seven omens toward the end.[26]

---

the prose text; vv. 4349–5088, the healing of emperor Tiberius, to pp. 151.108–55.175; and vv. 5089–5294, the death of Pilate, to p. 155.176–82.

[20] Werner Fechter, "Gundacker von Judenburg und *Mai und Beaflor*," *Amsterdamer Beiträge zur älteren Germanistik* 7 (1974): 187–208.

[21] Geith, "Eine Quelle"; idem, review of *Das Evangelium Nicodemi in spätmittelalterlicher deutscher Prosa*, 287–88.

[22] Kurt Gärtner, "Klosterneuburger Evangelienwerk," in Ruh, *Verfasserlexikon*, vol. 4 (1983), 1248. This work has been edited as an appendix to a German translation of the *EN*, version H, in Achim Masser and Max Siller, eds., *Das Evangelium Nicodemi in spätmittelalterlicher deutscher Prosa. Texte*, Germanische Bibliothek, 4th ser., Texte und Kommentar (Heidelberg: C. Winter, 1987), 428–44.

[23] Geith, "Eine Quelle," 63 n. 1, and Masser and Siller, *Das Evangelium Nicodemi*, 35, and n. 42, also identify these differences in the sequence of events between Gundacker and the German prose text, but they explain them incorrectly—being unaware of the Latin source used by Gundacker—as alterations made by Gundacker.

[24] Masser and Siller, *Das Evangelium Nicodemi*, 428.11–20; cf. *Christi Hort*, vv. 3885–920.

[25] Masser and Siller, *Das Evangelium Nicodemi*, 440.336–42; cf. *Christi Hort*, vv. 3925–38.

[26] Masser and Siller, *Das Evangelium Nicodemi*, 442.395–44.441; cf. *Christi Hort*, vv. 3943–4044.

1.3. The *Evangelium Nicodemi* of Heinrich von Hesler

The third Middle High German verse redaction of the *EN* was composed by Heinrich von Hesler, probably around 1300.[27] Heinrich was presumably a native of Burghesler in Thuringia, west of Naumburg an der Saale. In addition to the *Evangelium Nicodemi* (5392 verses),[28] he is responsible for two other poems, the *Apocalypse* (his most ambitious composition in 23254 verses) and the *Erlösung* (surviving only in fragments). Although he identifies himself as author in the latter two poems, no such self-identification accompanies the *Evanglium Nicodemi;* his authorship of the translation is, however, certain because it shows marked similarity in language, vocabulary, rhyming patterns, and style to the two signed poems, as demonstrated by Amersbach and de Boor.[29] Wiedmer's study of Heinrich's theological thought further confirms this conclusion.[30]

The writings of Heinrich von Hesler are generally associated with the literature of the Teutonic Knights[31] as they were disseminated mainly among the members of that order; the *Apocalypse* is even connected with a pictorial cycle which originated within the order.[32] However, there is no clear evidence that Heinrich's poems were commissioned by the Teutonic Knights or that he himself belonged to the order, although we know that he was a knight (cf. *Apocalypse*, v. 16480).

In his *Evangelium Nicodemi*, Heinrich tries—like Konrad von Heimesfurt and Gundacker—to combine the events related in his apocryphal source with those recorded in the canonical gospels and thereby to make his account more comprehensive. However, unlike his

---

[27] Cf. Achim Masser, "Heinrich von Hesler," in Ruh, *Verfasserlexikon*, vol. 3 (1981), 749–55.

[28] Heinrich von Hesler, *Das Evangelium Nicodemi*, ed. Karl Helm, Bibliothek des Litterarischen Vereins, vol. 224 (1902; repr., Hildesheim: G. Olms, 1976).

[29] Karl Amersbach, *Über die Identität des Verfassers des gereimten Evangeliums Nicodemi mit Heinrich Hesler*, 2 vols., Schulprogramm Gymnasium Konstanz (Konstanz: F. Stadler, 1883–84); Helmut de Boor, "Stilbeobachtungen zu Heinrich von Hesler," in *Vom Werden des deutschen Geistes. Festgabe Gustav Ehrismann*, ed. Paul Merker and Wolfgang Stammler (Berlin: W. de Gruyter, 1925), 124–48.

[30] Peter Wiedmer, *Sündenfall und Erlösung bei Heinrich von Hesler. Ein Beitrag zum Verständnis der deutschen Bibelepik des späten Mittelalters*, Basler Studien zur deutschen Sprache und Literatur, vol. 53 (Bern: Francke, 1977), 11–20.

[31] Karl Helm and Walther Ziesemer, *Die Literatur des Deutschen Ritterordens*, Gießener Beiträge zur deutschen Philologie, vol. 94 (Gießen: W. Schmitz, 1951), 75–91.

[32] Gerhard Bott and Udo Arnold, eds., *800 Jahre Deutscher Orden. Ausstellung des Germanischen Nationalmuseums Nürnberg ...* (Gütersloh: Bertelsmann Lexikon Verlag, 1990), 99–100, nos. II.7.6 and II.7.7.

predecessors, he does not recount the canonical narrative through to the miracles at Pentecost, but rather confines himself to the events of the Passion (up to the placing of the guards at Jesus' tomb); he recounts them in two long passages (vv. 393–678 and 1418–2284), striving to present the canonical material as exhaustively as possible.

The entire poem is structured in the following manner: vv. 1–300, introduction to the Fall of Man; vv. 301–92, prologue (with an invocation of the Holy Spirit and a list of sources); vv. 393–678, Passion events prior to the trial (decision by the Jews to kill Jesus, the Last Supper, Gethsemane, Jesus' arrest, Peter's denial); vv. 679–1417, Jesus' trial before Pilate (based on EN 1–9); vv. 1418–2284, Jesus' appearance before Herod, the death sentence, the Crucifixion, the laying of Jesus in the grave, the placing of guards at the tomb (based on the canonical gospels, with some sections from the EN); vv. 2285–841, questioning of the witnesses (based on EN 12.1 to 16); vv. 2842–3779, report on the Descent into Hell; vv. 3780–803, reaction to the report and Pilate's letter; vv. 3804–4713, legend of Pilate and Veronica and a brief account of the destruction of Jerusalem; vv. 4714–5392, extended invective against the Jews.

At several points, Heinrich reflects on the relationship between the EN and the canonical gospels and offers reasons why the testimony of Nicodemus is particularly important. In the prologue (vv. 369–92), he points out that "durch tumme lute" ("because of uneducated people") the four evangelists passed over many things in their gospels, which were "voltriben" ("expanded," "completed") by a "meister," namely Nicodemus. Nicodemus was well acquainted not only with the leaders of the Jews but—according to John 18—with Jesus as well: "die rehten waren mere beidenthalp er wiste" (vv. 382–83; "he knew the true news from both sides"). Similar thoughts are expressed again at the beginning of the trial (vv. 679–711): Nicodemus, "tougen Cristes kneht" ("secretly a servant of Christ"), was present at Jesus' trial as an ear- and eyewitness, unlike the disciples who had all fled for fear of the Jews. He knew the secrets of the Jewish leaders, who did not conceal anything from him and dared not harm him (he was "des kunnes also starc," "from a powerful family") when he argued in court on Jesus' behalf.

Discussing the words of Jesus on the cross, Heinrich remarks on the discrepancies among the four evangelists and on their relation to the account of Nicodemus (vv. 2166–91). He notes that only Mark (15:34) and Matthew (27:46) include Christ's words "Eli, Eli, lamma sabacthani? hoc est: Deus meus, Deus meus, ut quid dereliquisti me?" ("that is to say: My God, my God, why hast thou forsaken me?"). Luke and Nicodemus agree—against Mark and Matthew—in a different wording: Nicodemus gives the Hebrew phrase, "Via alach, hoe fricole" (vv. 2185–86), and Lucas translates it, "Vater ich bevele in dine hant mine sele!" (vv. 2188–89; "Father, into thy hands I commend my spirit"). In contrast to the three synoptic evangelists and Nicodemus, John gives neither of the two utterances: "Johannes die rede vorswigen hat, sin passio sunder titel stat" (vv. 2171–72; "John omitted this statement; a *titulus* [i.e., such an utterance by Christ] is missing in his account of the Passion").

Heinrich's model was a manuscript with the usual A version of the *EN;* this may be amply demonstrated, for he translates the Latin text (Tischendorf's group D of the *Gesta* and version A of the *Descensus*) quite faithfully.[33] That model belonged to a large manuscript family, attested by numerous Latin witnesses and by four German translations, in which the *Cura sanitatis Tiberii* is appended to the *EN* and forms with it a textual whole.[34] Heinrich's version of the Pilate-Veronica legend (vv. 3804–4713) is based on version B of the *Cura* (cf. vv. 4530 ff. and the *Cura*, chap. 14), which extends as far as chapter 14. However, it also contains passages that can be traced to another text on Pilate, the *Historia apocrypha of the Legenda aurea.*[35] They include: the sending of Pilate's messenger, Adrianus, and the healing of Vespasian (vv. 3890–4225); the sending of Albanus by Tiberius (Albanus is Tiberius's second messenger, for according to the *Cura* Tiberius had earlier dispatched Volusianus; vv. 4226–34); and a short account of the destruction of Jerusalem (vv. 4596–713). Finally, several details of Hesler's legend of Pilate and Veronica and the destruction of Jerusalem are quarried from the *Sächsische Weltchronik* ("der konige buchen," v. 4718, "the book of kings").[36]

Masser is of the opinion that Hesler's direct source was a compilation from the *EN* and the canonical gospels; it belonged, according to Masser, "to a well documented recension of the *Evangelium Nicodemi,* attested also in German manuscripts; this recension was characterized by digressionary additions based on the canonical accounts of the Passion and by the inclusion of legendary material from other sources."[37] By "a well documented recension ... attested also in German manuscripts" Masser certainly means the Alemannic prose version E of the *EN,* which he discovered and edited, but which has little in common

---

[33] Karl Helm, *Untersuchungen über Heinrich Heslers Evangelium Nicodemi,* Habilitationsschrift (Halle a. S.: E. Karras, 1899), 34.

[34] Edited in Dobschütz, *Christusbilder,* 157**–203**.

[35] Cf. ibid., 300*–301*, no. 43, where the author identifies a "mixture" of 8 (i.e., *Historia apocrypha*) and 2 (i.e., *Cura sanitatis Tiberii*). Helm's investigation of the sources, *Untersuchungen,* 42–49, is somewhat confusing.

[36] Heinrich von Hesler, *Das Evangelium Nicodemi,* xxx–xxxi; Helm, *Untersuchungen,* 58–59.

[37] Masser, "Heinrich von Hesler," 753; cf. idem, *Bibel- und Legendenepik,* 121.

with Hesler's work as far as the extensions beyond the Latin text are concerned. As long as no Latin manuscript of the compilation postulated by Masser has been identified, his assertion, though emphatic, remains an unproven hypothesis and a rather improbable one at that. There is no reason why one should doubt that an author who was so well versed in the four gospels as to compare them (as the digression on the words of Jesus on the cross shows [vv. 2166–91]) could also have independently borrowed material from them to expand the *EN* (as did Konrad von Heimesfurt and Gundacker).

Altogether, Heinrich von Hesler translated the *EN* more faithfully and more completely than either Konrad von Heimesfurt or Gundacker von Judenburg.[38] This is particularly true with respect to the account of Jesus' trial, in which Heinrich's version hardly differs in content or structure from his apocryphal source. He makes only a few minor additions, such as the explanation of the significance of the court standards as signs of the imperial judicial authority (vv. 835–51) or the inclusion of Lazarus in the ranks of those healed by Jesus (vv. 1249–65).

Heinrich shortens and alters parts of the middle section of the *EN*, the questioning of the witnesses by the High Council. The two episodes dealing with the guards of the sepulcher and with Joseph's empty prison—which in the *EN* are independent of each other (chaps. 12 and 13)—are here linked closely together, and their content is substantially changed (vv. 2285–449). When questioned by the Jews, the guards report that they saw Joseph of Arimathea with Jesus at the grave; only after the guards' assertion that Joseph is no longer in prison do the Jews visit his cell and find it empty. In the episode that follows, the guards are bribed by the Jews. Joseph's report of his liberation (vv. 2588–678) is expanded to include a description of Jesus' Ascension, which Joseph claims to have witnessed.

In his rendering of the *Descensus* (vv. 2842–3779), Heinrich considerably enlarges upon his source as he describes Christ's forceful entry into hell in much greater detail and with greater drama. The cry "Tollite portas" is repeated three times in the poem (in the *EN* only twice). It first resounds during the conversation between the devil and his helpers, terrifying the lesser demons until the devil pacifies them again (vv. 3062–80). The effects of the second cry are described at some length: it illuminates hell as bright as day, and cleanses the souls of their flecks of sin (vv. 3150–273). With the third "Tollite portas," Christ himself appears in the underworld. The doors of hell break apart, the

[38] For an overview of the sources of Heinrich von Hesler's *Evangelium Nicodemi*, see Helm, *Untersuchungen*, 33–42.

fire of hell is extinguished, a soothing wind blows, and the sufferings of the souls cease (vv. 3274–309).

Heinrich attempts—more emphatically than does his source—to place the Descent in the context of salvation history extending from the Fall to the Redemption. Reflections on the Fall and on salvation are central to all three of Heinrich's works. In his introduction to the *Evangelium Nicodemi*, he pursues the question of why God, knowing the weakness of human beings, permitted the Fall. Heinrich explains that God wanted the Fall in order to make possible, out of his love for humankind, the Incarnation of his Son, whereby he joined himself to human weakness. Similar thoughts can be found in other extended digressions (vv. 1670–764, 1929–2165, 3905–4193).[39]

However, in his version of the Descent, Heinrich explores soteriological themes not through digressions but through speeches of participating characters, especially of the devil and his helpers. The Harrowing of Hell is presented as a triumphal climax to a crafty legal dispute between God and Satan. According to this legal scenario, the salvation of humankind was possible only through deception of the devil. Through the Fall, the devil acquired a legal claim to humankind, which he could not forfeit unless he violated God's law. The devil committed such a violation when he brought about the death of God's son on the cross. But in order to make the devil transgress divine law, Christ had to conceal his transcendental nature under his human one. The notion that the salvation of humankind was the outcome of divine duplicity is present in the *EN*, but Heinrich develops it with greater clarity and gives it a wider scope.[40]

Already the first dialogue between Satan and his helpers—still closely dependent on *EN* 20—reveals that Christ has concealed his divinity under the cloak of his human nature (vv. 3011–149). After the second "Tollite portas" cry, the devil realizes that he has let himself be deceived by the human "brode" of Christ, and that he has lost his dominion (vv. 3230–45). His helpers reproach him for not recognizing Christ's true nature at the moment of his birth, for then Christ was ministered by angels (vv. 3246–73). These two speeches—one by the devil and the other by his minions—have no counterparts in the *EN*. When Christ forces his way into hell, Satan admits that he has been conquered and describes the marvel of the Incarnation, in which the divine "stete und des menschen val" ("permanence and human decline") have joined together (vv. 3328–86; cf. *EN* 22). The following

---

[39] For a detailed interpretation of these digressions, see Wiedmer, *Sündenfall und Erlösung*, 25–83.

[40] Ibid., 73–79.

tirade of the "hellemenie" ("inhabitants of hell") against Satan (vv. 3387–463; cf. *EN* 23) shows that even in contriving the Fall, the devil was only an instrument in God's plan of salvation. Quite inadvertently, the devil spoke the truth when he promised Adam that he would be like God, for with Christ's Incarnation, God united Himself with the weakness of human nature.

Heinrich evokes the Fall repeatedly in his account of the Descent— not only in the speeches of the devil and his helpers (cf. vv. 3008–9, 3201, 3220–21, 3316–17)—and always links the Fall to the Redemption of humankind through Christ's Passion and Harrowing of Hell. Upon arriving in hell, Christ proclaims to the saints that he has gained for them on the tree of the cross the eternal life that Adam had lost through another tree (vv. 3470–89, elaborated on the basis of *EN* 24.1.1–5). Seth's earlier report (vv. 2914–3010) is expanded in comparison to *EN* 19 by inclusion of the statement, taken from the legend of the cross, that the tree of the cross had grown from a branch of the tree in the Garden of Eden. Seth had received the branch from the Archangel Michael, and Adam had planted it in the earth (vv. 2956–61, 2992–3000).

The two sons of Simeon conclude their report of the Descent with a speech (vv. 3696–777) in which they admonish the Jews to do penance and to accept baptism (cf. *EN* 27.2, "paenitentiam agite, et misereatur uestri"; "do penance and he will show mercy to you"). However, the Jews were "so verhartet" ("so obstinate"), the two brothers note, that they were unwilling to change their ways and were, therefore, condemned to eternal damnation. Only the Jews living at the end of times will convert: "zu des jungesten tages zit, so werdet ir blinden sende, die heiligen schrift vorstende, als daz urteil wirt naende, und werdet danne gaende zur martre und zur toufe, als der hirz in sime loufe zu dem frischen brunnen tut" (vv. 3750–57; "Around the Day of the Judgement, you blind will see and understand the Holy Bible as the Judgement draws nearer; and then you will go to your passion and your baptism, just as the stag runs to the fountain of fresh water").[41] Similar thoughts cast in a similar idiom (cf. vv. 4738–43) occur in Heinrich's extensive anti-Jewish digression (vv. 4714–5392) at the end of the poem. There, he exhorts German princes to hold the Jews in "drucke" (i.e., to suppress them), to curb their profiteering, and to force them to accept Christianity.

The *Evangelium Nicodemi* of Heinrich von Hesler was much more successful than the other two verse adaptations of the *EN*. Whereas the complete texts of the *Urstende* and the *Christi Hort* survive each in a

---

[41] Cf. Ps. 41:2; Wiedmer, *Südenfall und Erlösung*, 12–18.

single manuscript, Heinrich's poem is extant in four more or less complete copies, seven fragmentary ones, and a number of excerpts.[42] These manuscripts were distributed primarily throughout eastern Germany. This is evident not only from the provenance of manuscript S (Schwerin, Wissenschaftliche Allgemeinbibliothek, Bestandszentrum, no shelf-mark, saec. XIV), on which Helm's edition is based, but above all from the transmission history of the fragments. One of them, the East Central German manuscript E, a *codex discissus* written around 1300, is of special importance, for it is the oldest textual witness to the poem.[43] Furthermore, in several manuscripts, Hesler's *Evangelium Nicodemi* is compiled with the *Marienleben* composed by Brother Philipp for the Teutonic Knights.[44]

The wide dissemination of Heinrich's German redaction of the apocryphon, suggested by a large number of its manuscripts, is further confirmed by its subsequent influence on several late medieval texts, including the *Weltchronik* compiled by Heinrich von München, a manuscript (E^3) of the Alemannic prose version E of the *EN*, the *Weihenstephaner Chronik*, and the plays of the *Tiroler Passion*.[45]

1.4. The three verse redactions of the *Evangelium Nicodemi* in Heinrich von München's *Weltchronik*

Heinrich von München's *Weltchronik* is a monumental historical compilation, written probably in the second quarter of the fourteenth century. It is based on older world chronicles that deal with only parts of the Old Testament (such as the chronicle of Rudolf von Ems or the *Christherre-Chronik*) but continues the historical narrative to Heinrich's own times with the help of many other works, mostly in German verse. Heinrich's *Weltchronik* is preserved in nineteen manuscripts and several fragments, all dating from the second half of the fourteenth to the fifteenth century, primarily of Bavarian-Austrian provenance. The extant texts vary substantially in both content and length (up to 100,000 verses);[46] interestingly, some of them preserve, in the sections

---

[42] Cf. Heinrich von Hesler, *Das Evangelium Nicodemi*, i–xix; Achim Masser, "Eine unbekannte Handschrift vom Evangelium Nicodemi Heinrichs von Hesler," *Zeitschrift für deutsche Philologie* 91 (1972): 321–36; Kurt Gärtner, "Neue Fragmente von Heinrichs von Hesler *Evangelium Nicodemi*," *Zeitschrift für deutsches Altertum* 107 (1978): 206–15.

[43] Gärtner, "Neue Fragmente," 207–8.

[44] Ibid., 215. Bruder Philipp, *Bruder Philipps des Carthäusers Marienleben*, ed. Heinrich Rückert, Bibliothek der gesamten deutschen National-Literatur, vol. 34 (1853; repr., Amsterdam: Rodopi, 1966).

[45] See below, sects. 1.4, 2.3, 4, and 5.1.

[46] For a detailed study of Henrich von München's *Weltchronik*, with addi-

devoted to the New Testament history and based on the *Marienleben* of Brother Philipp, an extensive compilation of the three German verse renditions of the *EN*.[47] On the basis of the strongly divergent manuscripts of the *Weltchronik*, the structure of this rhymed compilation of the vernacular *EN* texts can be reconstructed roughly as follows. Gundacker's *Christi Hort* (beginning at v. 1381) provided the framework into which portions of the other two redactions were interpolated: from Konrad von Heimesfurt's *Urstende*, almost the entire trial before Pilate and small portions of the Descent into Hell; and from Heinrich von Hesler's *Evangelium Nicodemi*, primarily a large part of the Pilate-Veronica legend. The events preceding the trial and the initial stages of the proceedings before Pilate (the messenger scene, the miracle of the standards) were recounted in a collage of short, even minute excerpts from all three translations, supplemented with the compiler's own verses.

This composite of the three German verse adaptations of the apocryphon did not originate in the *Weltchronik;* rather, it goes back to an even older compilation, which survives in only two early fourteenth-century fragments, both dealing with the legend of Pilate and Veronica.[48] Five manuscripts of Heinrich's chronicle have preserved the compilation in varying degrees of completeness and in different relationships to the other texts constituting the chronicle, especially to Brother Philipp's *Marienleben*. The compilation is best preserved, albeit with large gaps, in two manuscripts, Wolfenbüttel, Herzog August Bibliothek (HAB) Cod. Guelf. 1.5.2. Aug. fol. (saec. XIV/2), and Gotha, Forschungsbibliothek MS. Chart. A 3 (written in 1398). Fuller but more heavily reworked is the text in a group of manuscripts stemming from Heinz Sentlinger (Munich, BSB Cgm 7330, dated 1394; Wolfenbüttel, HAB Cod. Guelf. 1.16. Aug. fol., dated 1399; Graz, Universitätsbibliothek MS. 470, written by Johannes von Ezzlingen in 1415 [a copy of the

---

tional bibliographic information, see Gisela Kornrumpf, "Die Weltchronik Heinrichs von München. Zu Überlieferung und Wirkung," in *Festschrift für Ingo Reiffenstein zum 60. Geburtstag*, ed. Peter K. Stein, Andreas Weiss, and Gerold Hayer, Göppinger Arbeiten zur Germanistik, vol. 478 (Göppingen: A. Kümmerle, 1988), 493–509.

[47] Hoffmann, "Konrad von Heimesfurt," chap. 4.1.2; Paul Gichtel, *Die Weltchronik Heinrichs von München in der Runkelsteiner Handschrift des Heinz Sentlinger*, Schriftenreihe zur bayerischen Landesgeschichte, vol. 28 (Munich: Beck, 1937), 164–68.

[48] The two fragments (Vienna, ÖNB MS. Ser. nova 4818; Budapest, Országos Széchényi Könyvtár MS. Germ. 54) have been edited by Edward Schröder, "Fragmente aus Gundacker von Judenburg und Heinrich von Hesler. Mitgeteilt von Ferdinand Menčik," *Zeitschrift für deutsches Altertum* 50 (1908): 386–91, and H. von Kleinmayr, "Handschriftliches zur Pilatuslegende," *Zeitschrift für deutsches Altertum* 62 (1925): 241–50.

Munich manuscript]). Traces of the compilation can also be found in a number of additional manuscripts which either omit the events of the New Testament completely or else replace them entirely with an unaltered text of Philipp's *Marienleben;* the apocryphal texts surface in the chapters dealing with the omens of the destruction of Jerusalem (Gundacker) and with Vespasian's siege and conquest of Jerusalem (Heinrich von Hesler).

The New Testament section of Sentlinger's adaption of the *Weltchronik,* in a version closely akin to Wolfenbüttel, HAB Cod. Guelf. 1.16. Aug. fol., served as the basis for an early-fifteenth-century *Historienbibel* (a biblical history in prose), entitled *Die Neue Ee,*[49] extant in over thirty manuscripts and eight early printed editions. Its author rendered the *Weltchronik* into prose, preserving its contents largely intact. Through *Die Neue Ee,* freely revised material from the old verse adaptations of the *EN*—and especially from Gundacker's—enjoyed wide circulation as late as the fifteenth century, side by side with the numerous prose translations.

2. Prose translations

From the beginning of the fourteenth century on, there appeared a number of High German prose translations of the *EN,*[50] most of which were first made available in a comprehensive edition by Masser and Siller. The editors designate individual translations with alphabetic sigla from A to I; the first German printed text (referred to below as the "printed edition") has not been given any siglum. The text edited as version I (445–47) cannot, however, be counted among independent translations of the *EN* because it is an excerpt from the *Deutsche Chronik* of Twinger von Königshofen.[51] Two additional versions should be added to those published by Masser and Siller: K in The Hague, Koninklijke Bibliotheek MS. 73 E 25, fols. 75r–95v (saec. XV ex.),[52] and M in Berlin, Staatsbibliothek Preußischer Kulturbesitz (SBPK) Mgo 387,

---

[49] Hans Vollmer, ed., *Die Neue Ee, eine neutestamentliche Historienbibel,* Materialien zur Bibelgeschichte und religiösen Volkskunde des Mittelalters, vol. 4 (Berlin: Weidmannsche Buchhandlung, 1929); cf. Kurt Gärtner, "Die Reimvorlage der *Neuen Ee.* Zur Vorgeschichte der neutestamentlichen deutschen Historienbibel," *Vestigia Bibliae* 4 (1982): 12–22.

[50] Albert Viktor Schelb, "Evangelium Nicodemi," in Ruh, *Verfasserlexikon,* vol. 2 (1980), 659–63.

[51] Werner J. Hoffmann, "Die ostmitteldeutsche Übersetzung des *Evangelium Nicodemi* in der Den Haager Handschrift 73 E 25 (Übersetzung K), Untersuchungen und Text," *Vestigia Bibliae* 9/10 (1987/88, published in 1991): 271 n. 60.

[52] Edited by Hoffmann, "Die ostmitteldeutsche Übersetzung."

fols. 193r–244r (saec. XVI). If one counts the text compiled with version E in Karlsruhe, Badische Landesbibliothek MS. St. Georgen 83 (saec. XV; siglum E³) as a separate translation, there are altogether twelve prose translations of the *EN* dating between the fourteenth and the early sixteenth centuries.

Only four (H, A, E, and F) of these twelve were widely diffused; all others, except for the printed edition, survive in unique copies. For the most part, the prose translations are straightforward, although the degree of adherence to the Latin varies considerably; only version E takes considerable liberty with the Latin model, for it contains amplifications derived from the canonical gospels and from legendary sources. Two versions (F and K) begin only with the second section of the *EN* (in chaps. 11 and 12, respectively) and omit the trial part entirely.

In general, the German prose translations are based on the standard text of *EN* A. The only exceptions are texts G (a combination of *Gesta* B and *Descensus* A), K (based on version A with interpolations from *Gesta* B and *Descensus* B), and the printed edition (rendered from the Latin version that included Tischendorf's chapter 28, a mixture of A and C).

The *EN* is almost always extended with various addenda. Besides Pilate's letter, missing only in E and in the printed edition, the *Cura sanitatis Tiberii* is the most frequent appendix; it forms the conclusion to the *EN* in four translations (A, B, C, and K). With respect to the *Cura*, the translations reflect the transmission pattern of the Latin, for the *Cura* seems to have been appended to the Latin *EN* most frequently in the German speaking areas. In a few translations, however, different versions of the legend of Pilate and Veronica are added: in F, the so-called *Historia apocrypha of the Legenda aurea*; and in H and E³, prose redactions of the German verse translations by Gundacker and Heinrich von Hesler, respectively. Other appendices include the *Somnium Neronis* in G and Tischendorf's chapter 28 in the printed edition. All these additions, fully integrated with the *EN* both in the Latin and in the vernacular traditions, are of particular importance in determining the Latin sources of individual translations. In a few cases (in particular, in translations B and G), the addenda make it possible to identify precisely the branches of the Latin manuscript tradition which underlie the translations.

2.1. Version H (*Klosterneuburger Evangelienwerk*)

The earliest German prose translation of the *EN* can be found as part of the *Klosterneuburger Evangelienwerk*, written probably around 1330.[53] The author, an unnamed Austrian from the diocese of Passau, was—according to his own testimony—a layman and composed his work with the help "of outstanding, religious, and learned people" ("erberger vnd geistlicher vnd wol gelerter leut"),[54] so that "the uneducated laymen are ... improved and made firm in the Christian faith" ("di vngelerten leyen ... an cristenlichem gelauben gepessert vnd geuestent werden"; fol. 6ra–rb). In addition to the *Evangelienwerk*, other works are ascribed to the same author, including a partial translation of the Old Testament (the so-called *Schlierbacher Bibel*).

Eighteen manuscripts of the *Evangelienwerk*, dating from the fourteenth and fifteenth centuries, are known to exist. With one exception, they all come from the Bavarian-Austrian area; five contain the complete text, six fragments, and seven excerpts only.[55] One of the manuscripts, Schaffhausen, Stadtbibliothek MS. Generalia 8 (saec. XIV/1), is illustrated throughout and includes a series of miniatures depicting the contents of the *EN*.[56]

The *Klosterneuburger Evangelienwerk* is a translation of the gospels (extending to the beginning of the Acts of Apostles), harmonized and divided into pericopes. Detailed explanatory glosses follow each section of the gospels. Incorporated into these glosses or appended to them are prose redactions of German verse texts, such as Konrad von Fußesbrunnen's *Kindheit Jesu* or Gundacker's *Christi Hort*, and transla-

---

[53] On the *Evangelienwerk*, see Gärtner, "Klosterneuburger Evangelienwerk." This translation of the *EN* is edited in Masser and Siller, *Das Evangelium Nicodemi*, 396–444.

[54] Klosterneuburg, Stiftsbibliothek MS. 4, fol. 7va–vb

[55] The transmission of this work is discussed by Gärtner, "Klosterneuburger Evangelienwerk," 1248–49; Masser and Siller, *Das Evangelium Nicodemi*, 85–99; Gisela Kornrumpf, "Das *Klosterneuburger Evangelienwerk* des österreichischen Anonymus. Datierung, neue Überlieferung, Originalfassung," *Vestigia Bibliae* 9/10 (1987/88, published in 1991): 115–31, who notes four new manuscripts; and Kurt Gärtner and Bernhard Schnell, "Die Neisser Handschrift des *Klosterneuburger Evangelienwerks*," *Vestigia Bibliae* 9/10 (1987/88, published in 1991): 155–67. In addition to the seventeen manuscripts identified in these publications, Gärtner discovered a fragment on a piece of parchment, Graz, Steiermärkisches Landesarchiv, no shelf-mark. The entire textual tradition of the *Klosterneuburger Evangelienwerk* will be discussed in a forthcoming dissertation by Wilfried Hebeda (Eichstätt).

[56] Gärtner and Schnell, "Die Neisser Handschrift," discuss a fifteenth-century copy of this manuscript, also illustrated, of which only some old photographs and fragments survive.

tions of narrative chapters from such Latin texts as the *Legenda aurea*
and the *Vita beate virginis Marie et Salvatoris rhythmica*.
Already in the prologue the author acknowledges his use of the
EN as a source supplementing the four gospels and evokes the names
of both Nicodemus and Joseph of Arimathea:

> vnd han zu den heiligen ewangelien gesaczt ze glos—das ist
> zu bedeutnůsse—etleicher seligen herren schrift, die bei Jhesu
> Cristo warn vnd im dinten vntz in die juden marterten vnd
> tŏtten; das ist besonderlich ein herre der heiset Nichodemus.
> ... Das ander was der edel herre Joseph von Aromathia.[57]

> (and I added to the sacred gospels as a gloss—that is as an
> explanation—the writings of a number of blessed men, who
> were with Jesus and served him, until he was tortured and
> killed by the Jews. I am referring particularly to a man named
> Nicodemus. ... The other was the noble man Joseph of Arima-
> thea.)

Later, in the section dealing with the trial, he defends the writings of
Nicodemus by referring to the final sentence of the Gospel of John (Jn.
21:25): "wand sand Johanns ewangelist selbe geschriben hat. daz vnser
herre. vil zaichen getan hat. die an seinem puech niht geschriben sint.
Da von sol des herren Nychodemi schrift niemen fŷr lug haben"
(400.147–50; "for St. John the Evangelist himself wrote that our Lord performed many signs but that they are not recorded in his book. For this
reason no one should consider the writings of Nicodemus untrue").[58]

The anonymous writer gives an almost complete translation of the
EN, based on a manuscript of the Latin A version with Pilate's letter
(to Tiberius); however, he splits the apocryphal text into several parts
and then inserts them into his narrative at the thematically appropriate
points. The part dealing with the trial (396.1–408.432; *EN* 1–9) forms a
relatively self-contained unit, although punctuated with numerous
additions. The following chapters of the *EN* (10–13; 409.433–14.599) are
heavily fragmented and spread throughout the account of the Passion
and Resurrection. A continuous, straightforward translation covers
only chapters 14–27 (415.600–27.1008); there follows a report of the
Ascension. The whole work concludes with a somewhat rearranged
prose rendition of the Pilate and Veronica section from Gundacker's
Christi Hort.

---

[57] Klosterneuburg, Stiftsbibliothek MS. 4, fol. 7vb.

[58] For the sake of clarity and convenience, all citations from this and other
translations of the *EN* edited in Masser and Siller, *Das Evangelium Nicodemi*, will
be identified in the body of my essay by page and, whenever appropriate, line
numbers, unless otherwise noted.

The author of the *Klosterneuburger Evangelienwerk* translates the *EN* into fluent German prose. At times he condenses his Latin model: chapters 15, 22, and 23 are substantially shortened. He constantly includes explanatory remarks, especially in the account of the trial, where the *EN* closely follows the content of the canonical gospels (for example, in the dream of Pilate's wife [399.131–400.137, 400.141–53] and in the Barabbas episode [405.306–6.341]). Often these glosses contain polemics against the unbelief of the Jews and sometimes observations about the differences between the canonical gospels and the *EN*, revealing the author's detailed knowledge of the relevant texts as well as his theological competence.[59]

2.2. Version A (*Augsburger Bibelhandschrift*)

Like H, version A has been transmitted along with a translation of the Bible, but unlike H, it is a self-standing text.[60] Nine manuscripts of version A have been identified, including one not listed by Masser and Siller, Augsburg, Universitätsbibliothek Cod. III. 1. 2° 9, fols. 319r–40v (from Bamberg, Heiliggrab-Kloster; written in 1443; siglum A⁹).[61] By far the oldest is Augsburg, Staats- und Stadtbibliothek 2° Cod. 3 (siglum A¹), the so-called *Augsburger Bibelhandschrift*, whose first part (the gospels, Apocalypse, Catholic letters, and a lectionary) was written in 1350.[62] The section that contains the *EN* (fols. 315va–37vb)—but which also includes the letters of Paul (fols. 251va–315va)—cannot be much later. The language of A¹ is East Swabian, and in the fifteenth century the manuscript was owned by a resident of Augsburg. The remaining manuscripts, almost all of them from the first half of the fifteenth century, are—as far as the owners can be determined—from the northern Bavarian and East Frankish dialectical areas (Nürnberg, Coburg, Bamberg). With two exceptions (Bamberg, Staatsbibliothek MS. Msc. hist. 155, fols. 23rb–29ra, written in 1473 [siglum A⁸], and A⁹),

---

[59] He remarks (401.193–402.198), for instance, that the answer to Pilate's question "Quid est veritas?" ("What is truth?"), absent from Jn. 18:38, has been recorded and transmitted only by Nicodemus (*EN* 3.2).

[60] Edited in Masser and Siller, *Das Evangelium Nicodemi*, 121–64. For a characterization of the translation, see ibid., 20–23.

[61] Eight manuscripts have been described by Masser and Siller, ibid., 52–64. For a description of the ninth manuscript, see Karin Schneider, *Deutsche Handschriften der Universitätsbibliothek Augsburg. Die Signaturengruppen Cod. I.3 und Cod. III. 1* (Wiesbaden: O. Harrassowitz, 1988), 163–66.

[62] The translation of the canonical gospels in this manuscript has been studied by Elke Donalies, *Die Augsburger Bibelhandschrift und ihre Überlieferung. Untersuchung und Text der vier Evangelien* (Münster: Waxmann, 1992).

the *EN* appears in these manuscripts in the context of biblical translations, usually amid the same texts as in A[1].
The model for A was the Latin vulgate version of the *EN* with
Pilate's letter and the complete B version of the *Cura sanitatis Tiberii*.
Three among the manuscripts of the *Cura* studied by Dobschütz come
close to the hypothetical source of A,[63] namely those numbered 3, 5,
and 6 (compare the phrase "vnd liez nach sinem tode Claudium"
[162.189], "and after his death he left Claudius [as his successor],"
from the German Pilate-Veronica legend with the variants of the *Cura*
given by Dobschütz).[64]
Version A adheres to its source very closely, often imitating Latin
participial constructions or retaining Latin word order. The translator
clearly treated the *EN* as a biblical text, which was to be changed as
little as possible when rendered into the vernacular.
In manuscripts A[1] to A[7], translation A has been copied faithfully,
notwithstanding the remark in A[5], "Daz ewangelio Nycodemus gehört
nicht zu dem text der wybel" ("the gospel of Nicodemus does not
belong to the text of the Bible"). However, in the two manuscripts with
non-biblical contexts, A[8] and A[9], it has been subject to significant revisions. The changes in the former—modernization of vocabulary and
smoothing of syntax—are restricted to the beginning and the end of
the text. The redactor of the latter altered the whole text more thoroughly, systematically eliminating all syntactic Latinisms and effecting
fluent, easily comprehensible prose style.

2.3. Version E

Version E was also made in the fourteenth century; the oldest of its
nine manuscripts,[65] Engelberg, Stiftsbibliothek MS. 243, fols. 81ra–85va
(siglum E[4]), was written by a Lucern burgher, Johannes Ottenrütti, in
1383 or shortly thereafter. Manuscript E[8], previously in the possession
of R. P. Wülcker but not otherwise identified by Masser and Siller,[66]
is now Toruń, Uniwersytet Mikołaja Kopernika, Biblioteka Główna Rps
11/I (High Alemannic, saec. XV ex.).[67] The E version was disseminated

[63] Dobschütz, *Christusbilder*, 158**.
[64] Ibid., 182**.8–11; see also Hoffmann, "Die ostmitteldeutsche Übersetzung,"
234–35.
[65] Described by Masser and Siller, *Das Evangelium Nicodemi*, 67–75.
[66] Ibid., 75.
[67] I was referred to this manuscript by Zbigniew Izydorczyk and was able to
consult a microfilm copy of it. The manuscript reached Toruń via the University
Library of Königsberg (Kaliningrad). It now contains only the *EN* (55 leaves), the
other two texts previously found in it having been lost (Sibylline prophecy and

primarily in the south and west of the Alemannic speaking area, but it
also found its way into the East Swabian (Munich, BSB Cgm 523, fols.
189rb–95va, written in 1471; siglum E[5]) and even into the Low German
(Wolfenbüttel, HAB Cod. Guelf. 430 Helmst., fols. 131va–55vb; from
1456; siglum W) regions. Inscriptions of its medieval owners suggest
that it was read predominantly in Benedictine and reformed Dominican female convents.

E is a very loose adaptation of the *EN* (without Pilate's letter).[68]
Its author not only rendered the *EN* freely, mostly paraphrasing and
fleshing it out, but also enlarged it with additions from other sources.
A passage introducing Nicodemus (249.1–19) serves as a preface. In an
evening conversation, Jesus converted Nicodemus to his teaching (Jn.
3:1–5), and for this reason Nicodemus defended Jesus before Pilate,
assisted at Jesus' burial, and eventually wrote his *Evangelium*. The
narrative proper begins with the Passion events according to the
canonical gospels (249.20–53.129): the decision by the Sanhedrin to kill
Jesus, the Last Supper, Jesus' arrest, the interrogation before Annas,
and Judas's suicide. After this, the story of the *EN* begins, frequently
augmented with canonical passages, especially in the account of the
Crucifixion (265.432–68.515). In addition to the gospels, the author of
E drew also on other works to amplify the *EN*. For the story of the
marriage of Mary and Joseph (257.226–41), only alluded to in the *EN*
2.4, he used the apocryphal *Infancy Gospel of Pseudo-Matthew*; for
Enoch's report on the Antichrist (300.1161–302.1202; *EN* 25), he relied
on Adso of Montier-en-Der's *De ortu et tempore Antichristi*. It is particularly noteworthy that the redactor's sources included also either an
adaptation of Konrad von Heimesfurt's *Urstende*, or a verse translation
of the *EN* with borrowings from the *Urstende*. E shows extensive
borrowings from the *Urstende* in two places, in the questioning of the
two sons of Simeon with a long speech by Nicodemus (278.744–80.810)
and in Seth's detailed description of his journey to paradise (285.884–
88.945). Brief quotations from the *Urstende* are scattered throughout the
text, especially in the account of the Descent into Hell.[69]

The textual history of version E is very complicated. Only five of
its nine manuscripts contain the full text, best preserved in Solothurn,
Zentralbibliothek MS. S 194, fols. 1r–58r (saec. XV/2; siglum E[6]), the
manuscript on which Masser and Siller based their edition; closely

---

a play of the Last Judgement). For a discussion of the manuscript, see Wülcker,
Das Evangelium Nicodemi, 51–54.

[68] Edited in Masser and Siller, *Das Evangelium Nicodemi*, 249–305.

[69] The relevant passages are printed in the second apparatus to the critical
edition of the *Urstende*; see Konrad von Heimesfurt, *Unser vrouwen hinvart*.

related to E⁶ are Berlin, SBPK MS. Germ. quart. 167 (saec. XV/2; E¹), and St. Gallen, Stiftsbibliothek MS. 1142 (saec. XV med.; E²). A slightly revised redaction of the same text appears in E⁸, which is in turn close to what must have been the model of the Low German text W.⁷⁰ Two manuscripts contain only the Descent into Hell: E⁴ and E⁵. E⁴, the oldest manuscript, is particularly important because it has preserved many rhymes of its poetic source which are not found in the other copies. The East Swabian manuscript E⁵ contains the Descent into Hell in a heavily revised, somewhat foreshortened form.⁷¹

Manuscripts E³ and E⁷ compile the E version with some non-biblical texts. The former, Karlsruhe, Badische Landesbibliothek MS. St. Georgen 83, fols. 58r–101v (saec. XV), partly replaces the loose adaptation of the *EN* characteristic of E with an otherwise undocumented faithful translation of the Latin.⁷² The E text remains nearly intact only in the section dealing with the Descent; elsewhere it surfaces only sporadically. The *EN* is extended with a version of the legend of Pilate and Veronica, consisting of two partially overlapping texts: one (324.1–26.79), a substantially abridged prose redaction of the corresponding section of Heinrich von Hesler's *Evangelium Nicodemi*; and the other (326.80–29.200), a partial translation of the legend of St. James the Less from the *Legenda aurea* (the healing of Vespasian and the destruction of Jerusalem).⁷³

In E⁷, Colmar, Bibliothèque de la ville MS. 306 (second decade of the fifteenth century, written possibly in Colmar), the *EN* forms part of a monumental compilation of Passion texts.⁷⁴ This composite Passion treatise, entitled in the manuscript "spiegel des lidens cristi" ("mirror of Christ's Passion"), comprises primarily a translation of large portions of Ludolph of Saxony's *Vita Christi*, amplified with borrowings from a number of additional texts. Most important among them—besides an otherwise unidentified *passion marie*—is the German version

---

⁷⁰ Edited in Achim Masser, *Dat ewangelium Nicodemi van deme lidende vnses heren Ihesu Christi. Zwei mittelniederdeutsche Fassungen,* Texte des späten Mittelalters und der frühen Neuzeit, vol. 29 (Berlin: E. Schmidt, 1978), 61–97.
⁷¹ Edited in Masser and Siller, *Das Evangelium Nicodemi,* 330–37.
⁷² For an edition of E³, see ibid., 306–23 (from the very beginning to chap. 17 of the *EN*) and 324–29 (legend of Pilate and Veronica); the *Descensus* portion of E³ is given in the apparatus to the edition of E.
⁷³ Masser and Siller (ibid., 42–43) do not identify the source of the latter.
⁷⁴ I was able to examine a microfilm copy of this manuscript. This manuscript has been studied from the point of view of art history by Karin Jänecke, *Der spiegel des lidens cristi. Eine oberrheinische Handschrift aus dem Beginn des XV. Jahrhunderts in der Stadtbibliothek zu Colmar (Ms. 306)* (Hannover: [Gebr. Jänecke], 1964). Masser and Siller, *Das Evangelium Nicodemi,* 74, were aware of the E text in this manuscript only from the excerpts printed by Jänecke, pp. 162–65.

E of the pseudo-gospel.[75] Except for two passages (249.1–19, 261.337–63.390), the compilation incorporates the entire redaction E in two large textual units (253.113–65.436, the trial before Pilate; and 272.614–305.1253, Joseph's deliverance and the Descent, beginning in chap. 14) and fourteen excerpts, mostly very short and always identified with the inscription "vsser deme passion Nicodemi" ("from the passion of Nicodemus"). The manuscript is decorated with numerous colored line drawings and includes a series of illustrations for the *EN* (among them, two miniatures of the miracle of the standards).[76]

In the prologue, the compiler of the *Spiegel* names as one of his main sources—in addition to the four evangelists—"nicodemus der do ein heimlicher Junger cristi was" ("Nicodemus, who was a secret disciple of Christ"). He emphasizes Nicodemus's reliability: "Dar umbe es milteklich ze glŏbende ist das es also sige als er das gescriben hăt" (fol. 1va; "so that one can readily believe that this was exactly the way he wrote it"). Later, at several points in the narrative of the trial before Pilate, the compiler provides critical comments about the contents of the *EN*: concerning the miracle of the standards, for example, he remarks that he has read about it only in the "passion nycodemi" (fol. 80ra). He makes a similar remark regarding the tale of the marriage of Jesus' parents, which he knows from "andren bewerten bŭchern" (fol. 81r; "other reliable books"), and notes that never before has he encountered it mentioned in connection with the trial. In another context a more critical attitude causes him to omit a passage[77] with the following explanation: "die rede schrib ich hie nit. won ich andertswo nit gelesen han dz die rede also vor pylato geschech" (fol. 83ra; "I do not write this speech down because I have not read anywhere else that this speech was held before Pilate").

Masser holds a completely different view of the origin and textual history of E from the one sketched above; in particular, he sees the relationship between E and Konrad von Heimesfurt's *Urstende* differently.[78] Starting with the correct observation that E is not a prose redaction of the *Urstende* and that E contains also verses reflecting the contents of the *EN* but not of the *Urstende*, he concludes that E and the *Urstende* must have had a common source. This alleged source would have been a

---

[75] I was able to identify the following additional sources: Heinrich Seuse, *Büchlein der ewigen Weisheit; Visio Pauli;* Hugo Ripelin of Strasbourg, *Compendium theologicae veritatis;* an account of Jean de Mandeville's travels translated by Otto von Diemeringen.

[76] Cf. illustration 6 (fol. 78r) in Jänecke, *Der spiegel des lidens cristi.*

[77] Masser and Siller, *Das Evangelium Nicodemi,* 261.337–63.390, the defense of Jesus by Nicodemus and the testimonies of those who had been healed by Jesus.

[78] Ibid., 24–32.

poem composed around 1200 and dealing exclusively with the Descent into Hell because, according to Masser, only the Descent part of E contains rhymes. This rhymed antecedent of the Descent in E was supposedly rendered into prose. Only E⁴ and E⁵, Masser argues, preserve the prose version in its original scope; in the other manuscripts, it was augmented with an introduction, or, rather, with two independent introductions, one in E³ and the other in E⁶ and related manuscripts.

Masser's hypothesis of a lost poetic version of the Descent into Hell as the basis for E and the *Urstende* does not withstand careful scrutiny. The assertion that the verse passages in E are confined to the Harrowing of Hell, that is, to the section transmitted in E⁴ (which begins with the second chapter of the *Descensus*) is verifiably untrue. The most striking correspondences with the *Urstende* occur, in fact, in the passages that directly precede the Descent into Hell (278.748–80.810), and these are missing in E⁴ (and E⁵). The assumption that the introductory portion of E³ is independent of the normal E text cannot be maintained either (cf. the prologue and the narrative of the events preceding the trial.)

It is more likely that at the beginning of the textual tradition of E there stood a complete, unified text, a fairly free rendition of the Latin *EN*, amplified at various points with excerpts from other writings, including a text in verse. About the form of this poem, whose importance as a source of E is clearly overestimated by Masser, one can at best make only conjectures because E preserves only its small fragments. It certainly contained more than the Descent into Hell, and it was not simply an adaption of the *Urstende*. It was probably a verse translation of the *EN*, occasionally inlaid with revised fragments of the *Urstende*. Various circumstances support the priority of the *Urstende* and argue against the *Urstende* being based on the hypothetical poem; not least among them is the fact that the specific Latin source of the *Urstende* has now been identified. It is only from this source, a rare Latin version of the *EN*, that verses 1625–67 of the *Urstende* (Nicodemus's speech to the two sons of Simeon)—reproduced partly verbatim in E (279.785–80.795)—can be derived.

2.4. Version F

There are seven known manuscripts of version F: to those described by Masser and Siller must be added Wolfenbüttel, HAB Cod. Guelf. 28.4. Aug. 2 fol., fols. 306v–17v (written in 1480; Swabian, with Bavarian scribal features; siglum F⁷).[79] Translation F was probably made in the

---

[79] Ibid., 33–34, 75–83. The Wolfenbüttel manuscript was first identified by

vicinity of Lake Constance around 1400. It was disseminated primarily in the southern and eastern regions of the Alemannic speaking area (Engelberg, Zürich, Pfäfers, St. Gallen), but also in the western reaches of the Bavarian dialect (Scheyern). The oldest manuscript, used by Masser and Siller for their edition of this version,[80] Munich, BSB Cgm 640, fols. 61va–67rb (F[1]), was written around 1425 in the Bavarian Benedictine monastery of Scheyern.

Version F does not contain the complete text of the *EN* but begins only at chapter 11.1 (the miracles at the Crucifixion). It includes, as an appendix, the legend of Pilate and Veronica, based on the *Historia apocrypha of the Legenda aurea*,[81] which covers the healing of Vespasian by Pilate's messenger Adrianus, the Veronica legend (mentioning Tiberius's messenger named Albanus), and the death of Pilate and the fate of his corpse. The author of F renders the *EN* quite freely into fluent, vibrant German prose. He usually abridges the Latin text and omits a few chapters (e.g., chaps. 20–23, the conversations among the devils). On one occasion, however, he makes an interesting addition: after the testimony of Joseph of Arimathea regarding the two sons of Simeon (chap. 17.1), he adds a short report—based probably on the *Legenda aurea*—describing how Joseph was imprisoned by the Jews a second time and freed by Vespasian and Titus at the time of their conquest of Jerusalem (343.146–44.151).

Only four (F[1], F[2], F[3], F[7]) of the seven manuscripts contain the complete text of this translation. The other three have only the appendix: F[4] begins with Pilate's letter, while F[5] and F[6], in which the text appears in combination with the legends of the apostles from the *Elsässische Legenda aurea*,[82] open with the legend of Veronica (the second part of the appendix).[83] In both F[5] and F[6], the text has been substantially revised, usually augmented; in one instance (364.140–65.156), the content has been enlarged with a report on the destruction of Jerusalem taken probably from the *Legenda aurea*'s legend of James the Less.

Konrad Kunze in his review of *Das Evangelium Nicodemi in spätmittelalterlicher deutscher Prosa. Texte*, edited by Achim Masser and Max Siller, *Anzeiger für deutsches Altertum* 99 (1988): 196–97.

[80] Masser and Siller, *Das Evangelium Nicodemi*, 338–58.

[81] Knape, "Die *Historia apocrypha*," 146–65.

[82] Werner Williams-Krapp, *Die deutschen und niederländischen Legendare des Mittelalters. Studien zu ihrer Überlieferungs-, Text- und Wirkungsgeschichte*, Texte und Textgeschichte, vol. 20 (Tübingen: Niemeyer, 1986), 40–41, 46.

[83] F[5] has been edited in Masser and Siller, *Das Evangelium Nicodemi*, 359–66.

2.5. Other prose translations

Whereas the four translations discussed above were widely disseminated—H in the Bavarian-Austrian area, A in northern Bavaria, E in the western and southern Alemannic regions, and F in the south-eastern Alemannic area—the other translations survive in single manuscripts. Two versions come from western Central Germany (B and C), two from eastern Central Germany (K and M), and two from Bavaria (D and G). With two exceptions (B of the late fourteenth and M of the sixteenth centuries), all manuscripts belong to the fifteenth century. Three versions, C, D, and M, are based on the usual Latin vulgate version of *EN* A with Pilate's letter, but C includes also the *Cura sanitatis Tiberii* (incomplete version B, extending only to Dobschütz's chap. 14). Translations B and G are derived from the less common Latin versions of the *EN* with characteristic addenda, and K offers a particularly interesting textual form of the apocryphon. Because the Latin models of the last three versions can be clearly identified, I will discuss the three (B, G, K) in greater detail.

Translation B (Heidelberg, Universitätsbibliothek Cpg 118, fols. 90v–126v, West Central German, saec. XIV ex.)[84] is based on *EN* A with Pilate's letter, and includes the rare A version of the *Cura sanitatis Tiberii*. Most characteristic of B is a short text inserted between Pilate's letter and the *Cura:*

> Czu prime do machten sy eren rad weddir en; Czu tercien czijd do wart her gegeyßelt; Czu sexten czijd wort her gehangen an das cruce; Czu none gab her synen geyst vff; An der czenden stunde steyk her czu der helle; Completa, so ist alle dink vollenbracht; metten, wente czu metten czijd stunt der here vff von tode. (196.772–76)

> (In the first hour, they took counsel against him; in the third hour, he was scourged; in the sixth hour, he was hanged on the cross; in the ninth hour, he rendered up his spirit; in the tenth hour, he went down into hell; at compline all things were completed; matins [is so called] because at the time of matins the Lord arose from the dead.)

This short description of the Passion according to the canonical hours can also be found (again inserted after Pilate's letter) in some Latin manuscripts of the *EN*.[85] The Latin manuscripts with that addition

---

[84] Edited ibid., 173–200.

[85] *Prima hora consilium fecerunt iudei. . . . Matutina dicitur quia Dominus mane surrexit.* Bordeaux, Bibliothèque municipale MS. 111, 275vb–85vb; Eutin, Kreisbib-

contain, like the German translation B, the less common and more ancient version A of the *Cura* (extending to chap. 14, expl., "defunctus est in stratu suo in pace," "he died peacefully in his bed").[86] They also show characteristic agreements with translation B in various passages, such as, for instance, Adam's greeting in chapter 24 (Trier manuscript, "Tunc adam dixit ad dominum Ecce manus que me plasmauerunt"; translation B, "Do sprach Adam czu dem heren: 'sich dyt sint dy hende dy mych geschufen' " [192.651–52], "Then Adam spoke to the Lord, 'Look, these are the hands that created me' "), which until now has been known in precisely the same wording only in *Descensus* B.

The model of translation G in Munich, BSB Cgm 7240, fols. 2ra–18va (Bavarian; written in 1447),[87] has been identified with the Latin text preserved in Salzburg, Erzabtei St. Peter MS. a V 27, fols. 111r–39r (last third of the twelfth century). This Latin manuscript has exactly the same combination of texts as G: a) chapters 1–16 (*Gesta Pilati*) of the rare, longer B version, with the prologue of Eneas; b) chapters 17–27 (*Descensus Christi ad inferos*) and Pilate's letter, based on the vulgate *EN* A; c) the *Somnium Neronis* through to the sentence introducing the omens of the destruction of Jerusalem.[88] The importance of the Salzburg manuscript consists in the fact that, together with Munich, BSB Clm 17181, fols. 103r–12r (saec. XI), which stops at chapter 16.1, they are the only surviving texts of the Latin *EN* B from the German-speaking territory. A comparison of G with the Salzburg manuscript shows that the translator adhered closely to the Latin model and often imitated Latin constructions in his German prose style. However, a few instances show that he did not use the Salzburg manuscript itself as his immediate source but rather a manuscript closely related to it.

Translation K, The Hague, Koninklijke Bibliotheek MS. 73 E 25, fols. 75r–95v (East Central German; saec. XV ex.),[89] provides further evidence that the rare Latin *EN* B was not altogether unknown in the German-speaking regions. This German redaction, which opens with chapter 12.1 (arrest of Joseph of Arimathea), is based mainly on the

---

liothek MS. II, pp. 1–26; Göttingen, Niedersächsische Staats- und Universitätsbibliothek 4° Cod. Ms. Theol. 153, fols. 86ra–97va; Hannover, Niedersächsische Landesbibliothek MS. I 247, fols. 1r–21r (only the addenda of this version); Leipzig, Universitätsbibliothek MS. 819, fols. 92v–111v; Trier, Stadtbibliothek MS. 200/1190 8°, fols. 53r–70r. I was able to examine the last-named manuscript.

[86] Dobschütz, *Christusbilder*, 181**.9.

[87] Edited in Masser and Siller, *Das Evangelium Nicodemi*, 365–95. Cf. ibid., 83; Williams-Krapp, *Die deutschen und niederländischen Legendare*, 220.

[88] Dobschütz, "A Collection," 12.1–13.9. For an edition of the *Visio Neronis* from the Salzburg manuscript (without the knowledge of Dobschütz's edition), see Speyer, "Neue Pilatus-Apokryphen."

[89] Edited by Hoffmann, "Die ostmitteldeutsche Übersetzung."

typical *EN* A with the complete *Cura;* however, it contains numerous interpolations from *EN* B, including a few from the first chapter of *Descensus* B (*EN* 17). No Latin manuscript with the same textual configuration is known at present, but it might be worth investigating whether any of the extant Latin texts beginning at chapter 12 preserves the model of *Gesta* K.

Independent of the various manuscript versions discussed above is the German printed edition, reissued several times during the first half of the sixteenth century.[90] Its title announces that the *EN* supplements the canonical gospels and does not contradict them: "Euangelium Nicodemi / auß dem Latein ins Teütsch gebracht / in welchem vil hüpscher puncten / die die andern Euangelisten nit setzen / begriffen werden (doch jnen nit wider) fast nützlich zulesen" ("The gospel of Nicodemus translated from Latin into German, in which many good points are included which the other evangelists do not include [without contradicting them], very worthwhile to read"). This edition, like the Low German translation L and the Dutch translation D, is a rendition of the Latin *EN* with Tischendorf's chapter 28. According to Thilo, the direct source of this printed version was probably the Latin edition published by a Leipzig printer, Melchior Lotter, in 1516.[91]

3. Reception of the *Evangelium Nicodemi* in poetry

The motif of Christ's Harrowing of Hell, in the later Middle Ages popularized by the *EN*, has a long history in German literature. References to it can be found as early as Otfrid von Weißenburg's *Evangelienbuch*,[92] the first major poem in German (ca. 863–871). The speech by an angel who announces to the women at the grave that Christ has risen contains a brief report of how Christ conquered the devil in the underworld, freed the righteous from hell, and led them to his kingdom (bk. 5, chap. 4, vv. 49–56).

The motif of the Harrowing is also employed in several Early Middle High German poems, but like Otfrid's work, they present no evidence of direct use of the pseudo-gospel. The spoliation of hell in the *Ezzolied* (written in 1064/65; vv. 299–310)[93] is based on an interpre-

[90] Described and edited in Masser and Siller, *Das Evangelium Nicodemi,* 107–10, 468–92.

[91] Thilo, *Codex apocryphus,* clii–cliii.

[92] Otfrid von Weißenburg, *Otfrids Evangelienbuch,* ed. Oskar Erdmann, 6th ed. prepared by Ludwig Wolff, Altdeutsche Textbibliothek, vol. 49 (Tübingen: Niemeyer, 1973).

[93] Edited in Albert Waag, *Kleinere deutsche Gedichte des XI. und XII. Jahrhun-*

tation of Luke 11:21–22 (the defeat of the devil, the "fortis armatus," by someone stronger). The probable source for the treatment of the Descent into Hell in other works is pseudo-Augustine's "Sermo 160," itself related to the EN.[94] It underlies the *Leben Jesu*, written by Frau Ava before 1127 (vv. 1732–83),[95] the *Hochzeit*, composed around 1160 (vv. 985–1050),[96] and the *Anegenge*, dated between 1170 and 1180 (vv. 3157–260).[97]

A detailed treatment of the Harrowing of Hell can also be found in the Silvester legend of the *Kaiserchronik* of the mid-twelfth century.[98] During the disputation between pope Silvester and twelve Jewish scholars concerning the truth of the Christian religion, the Jewish scholar Jubal directs the conversation to Christ's Descent. He maintains that, like any other person, Christ must have been subject to the devil during his sojourn in the netherworld (vv. 9702–25). Silvester wins the argument, as he does many others in the disputation, by citing an Old Testament passage, Psalm 23:7–10 ("Tollite portas . . ."), to prove the truth of the Harrowing. Then he gives a detailed account of the event in two parts corresponding to the two central scenes of the liturgical plays of the Harrowing (see below, sect. 5.1): the dialogue between the angels and the devils, and the prophets' song of joy. In the former, the angels twice demand, with the "Tollite portas," that the gates of hell be opened, while the devils ask in amazement who is seeking entry; in the latter, the prophets intone the "Advenisti desiderabilis" (vv. 9726–807).

None of the poems antedating the thirteenth century can be convincingly shown to have been inspired directly by the EN. Thus Konrad von Heimesfurt, the author of the early thirteenth-century *Urstende*, is both the first writer to translate the full text of the EN into German verse and the first German literary figure who can be shown to have been intimately familiar with the apocryphon. The other two verse renditions—by Gundacker and Heinrich von Hesler, respectively —aside, thematic material from the EN found its way into a number of

---

derts, 2d ed., Altdeutsche Textbibliothek, vol. 10 (Halle a. S.: Niemeyer, 1916), 1–16.

[94] PL 39:2059–61. Cf. Edward Schröder, *Das Anegenge. Eine litterarhistorische Untersuchung*, Quellen und Forschungen zur Sprach- und Culturgeschichte der germanischen Völker, vol. 44 (Strasbourg: K. J. Trübner, 1881), 54–55.

[95] Frau Ava, *Die Dichtungen der Frau Ava*, ed. Friedrich Maurer, Altdeutsche Textbibliothek, vol. 66 (Tübingen: Niemeyer, 1966).

[96] Waag, *Kleinere deutsche Gedichte*, 87–123.

[97] Edited by Dietrich Neuschäfer, *Das Anegenge. Textkritische Studien. Diplomatischer Abdruck. Kritische Ausgabe. Anmerkungen zum Text*, Medium Ævum, Philologische Studien, vol. 8 (Munich: Fink, 1966).

[98] Edited in Edward Schröder, *Die Kaiserchronik eines Regensburger Geistlichen*, MGH, Dt. Chron., vol. 1, pt. 1 (1892; repr., Munich: Monumenta Germaniae Historica, 1984).

poetic texts composed between the end of the thirteenth and the fifteenth century. Only rarely, however, do those poems reveal first-hand knowledge or use of the Latin apocryphon.

Two poems, the *Erlösung* and the *Von unsers herren liden*, deal only with the Harrowing of Hell. A characteristic feature of both is their profound similarity to the corresponding scenes in Easter and Passion plays. The *Erlösung*, an epic poem (7022 verses) written at the beginning of the fourteenth century in the Rhine Frankish dialect, presents the whole story of salvation from the Creation, through the Fall and the divine decision to save mankind, to the Last Judgement.[99] Its Descent episode is structured around the two liturgical hymns typical of dramatic elaborations of the theme, the "Tollite portas" and the "Advenisti desiderabilis" (vv. 5375–586). The first part of that episode, culminating in the "Tollite portas," consists of a discussion among the devils, in which they reveal their lack of knowledge about the Christ who has just died on the cross, followed by a dialogue between Christ, seeking admission to hell with the words of Psalm 23, and the ignorant devils (vv. 5375–461). The second part, concluding with the "Advenisti desiderabilis," includes the joyous songs of several patriarchs and prophets (vv. 5462–577), followed only by a brief account of how Christ led the "lobeliche schar" ("praiseworthy group") into paradise (vv. 5578–86). This condensed, characteristically structured account of the Harrowing in the *Erlösung* betrays strong affinity to the EN only in the devils' discussion (report on Jesus' miracles) and in the prophecy of Isaiah (reference to light dispelling the darkness of hell).

The *Von unsers herren liden* (941 verses)[100] is an unassuming fif-teenth-century poem in Swabian dialect, summarizing the events of Christ's Passion, sentence, death, burial, Descent into Hell, and Resurrection. The Descent, which occupies a third of the whole work (vv. 200–484), is structured from the following incidents: a discussion among the devils, Christ's entrance into hell and the binding of Luci-fer, the joyous songs of the patriarchs, and the translation of the redeemed into paradise. The most conspicuous structural correspon-dence between this poem and the dramatic texts consists in the place-ment of the prophets' speeches *after* the arrival of Christ. It is possible that the author used a Passion play as a source for his treatment of the

[99] Edited by Friedrich Maurer, *Die Erlösung: Eine geistliche Dichtung des 14. Jahrhunderts*, Deutsche Literatur, Reihe Geistliche Dichtung des Mittelalters, vol. 6 (1934; repr., Darmstadt: Wissenschaftliche Buchgesellschaft, 1964).

[100] Edited by C. T. Carr, *Von unsers herren liden: A Middle High German Poem, Edited from the British Museum Manuscript, Additional 24946*, Publications of the University of Manchester, Germanic Series, vol. 3 (Manchester: University Press, 1929).

Descent, but no such dramatic source has yet been identified. The phrasing of the poem shows no relationship to the *EN*.

Two other works, the *Befreiung der Altväter* and Hawich der Kellner's *Stephanslegende*, quarry Konrad von Heimesfurt's *Urstende* for the apocryphal material of the *EN*. The *Befreiung der Altväter*, extant in three manuscripts (two East Central German and one Alemannic) of the fifteenth century, is devoted exclusively to the Harrowing of Hell.[101] It shows the same thematic arrangement as the corresponding section of the *Urstende*. Particularly interesting in its brief poetic narrative of the Descent is Seth's detailed account of his journey to paradise (vv. 137–266). The poet based this account on the *Urstende*, whose substance and wording he followed closely (especially in the description of the wilderness outside paradise) as well as on the opening sections of the rood-tree legend.

Toward the middle of the fourteenth century, Hawich der Kellner, a ministerial of the Domstift St. Stephan in Passau, wrote his *Stephanslegende* (5245 verses).[102] Early in the poem (up to v. 1272), the questioning by the Jewish High Council of the various witnesses (Joseph of Arimathea, the eyewitnesses to Christ's Ascension, Carinus and Leucius) regarding Jesus' Resurrection and Ascension is reported in great detail. Hawich's source was not the Latin *EN* but, besides the Scriptures, only the *Urstende*, from which he takes over verbatim entire groups of verses. More typically, however, he liberally embellishes the scenes borrowed from the *Urstende*. His main purpose in introducing them was to enrich the legendary material concerning Saint Stephen, about whose life even the legends say little more than what is known from Acts 6:1–8:2. According to Hawich, Stephen took part in the questioning of the two sons of Simeon in the temple. It was he who told the people waiting outside the temple what Carinus and Leucius had reported. This public announcement of the report on the Descent marks the beginning of Stephen's preaching and converting, activities that aroused anger of the Jewish leaders and ultimately led to his being stoned. Stephen refers to the Descent also in the context of his proclamations of faith in two later sections of the poem, one adapting

---

[101] Edited by Leopold Zatočil, "Befreiung der Altväter," *Sborník Prací Filosofické Fakulty Brněnské University, Řada Literárně Vědná* 14, no. D 12 (1965): 75–93; cf. Werner Williams-Krapp, "Befreiung der Altväter," in Ruh, *Verfasserlexikon*, vol. 1 (1978), 667. For a discussion of the textual tradition of the poem and its dependence on the *Urstende*, see Hoffmann, "Konrad von Heimesfurt," chap. 4.2.4.

[102] Edited by Reginald J. McClean, *Havich der Kellner, Sankt Stephans Leben. Aus der Berliner Handschrift*, Deutsche Texte des Mittelalters, vol. 35 (Berlin: Weidmannsche Buchhandlung, 1930); cf. Karl-Ernst Geith, "Hawich der Kellner," in Ruh *Verfasserlexikon*, vol. 3 (1981), 561–63. Regarding Hawich's dependence on the *Urstende*, see Hoffmann, "Konrad von Heimesfurt," chap. 4.2.2.

the legend of Pilate and Veronica (vv. 1273 ff., probably a free adaptation of the *Cura sanitatis Tiberii*) and the other relating a disputation
between Stephen and some heathen scholars (vv. 2269 ff.).

The treatment of the pseudo-Nicodemean matter in the *Passional*,[103] written at the end of the thirteenth century, is based wholly on
the *Legenda aurea*. The chapter on the Resurrection (89.83–102.51) is
found in the first book, a combination of a life of Jesus with a life of
Mary, and contains accounts of the imprisonment and deliverance of
Joseph of Arimathea (95.76–96.33) and of the Descent into Hell (97.36–
102.51). In contrast to the *Legenda aurea*, there is no clear reference to
the *EN* in either account, only a vague allusion in the Joseph-episode
to tradition: "ovch haben die meistere vns kunt getan" (95.76; "the
scholars also made it known to us"). The poet merged the two descriptions of the Descent that follow each other in the *Legenda aurea* (pseudo-Augustine's "Sermo 160" and the *EN*) into a single report by insert-
ing the two sections of the sermon into the body of the *EN*-based
narrative.

Of some importance for the dissemination of the apocryphal
substance of the *EN* is the *Vita beate virginis Marie et Salvatoris rhythmica*,[104] composed in the first half of the thirteenth century. Three translations of this Latin poem into Middle High German verse survive: one
by Walther von Rheinau (Alemannic, second half of the thirteenth
century), another by the Swiss poet Wernher (Alemannic, before 1382),
and the third by Brother Philipp (beginning of the fourteenth century).
Because the focus of the *Vita rhythmica* is on the life of Mary, its
borrowings from the *EN* are of secondary importance. Nevertheless, on
six occasions the author identifies the *EN* as his source with an explicit
reference to "Ev. Nic.": 1) vv. 5114–21, different reactions to the erect-
ing of the cross; 2) vv. 5838–45, the songs of the patriarchs in praise of
Christ; 3) vv. 5848–67, the miracle of the standards; 4) vv. 6042–61, the
Harrowing of Hell; 5) vv. 6142–45, the appearance of Jesus to Joseph of
Arimathea in prison; and 6) vv. 6426–29, the introduction of the patriarchs into the heavenly paradise. The seventh borrowing is not acknowledged: vv. 6126–29, the mention of Pilate's letter to the Roman
caesar. The account of the miracle of the standards, included within a

---

[103] Edited by K. A. Hahn, *Das Alte Passional* (Frankfurt a. M.: H. L. Brönner,
1857).

[104] Edited by Adolf Vögtlin, *Vita beate virginis Marie et Salvatoris rhythmica*,
Bibliothek des Litterarischen Vereins, vol. 180 (Tübingen: Gedruckt für den Litte-
rarischen Verein in Stuttgart, 1888). One should also consult Max Päpke, *Das
Marienleben des Schweizers Wernher. Mit Nachträgen zu Vögtlins Ausgabe der Vita
Marie rhythmica*, Palaestra, vol. 81 (Berlin: Mayer & Müller, 1913), who prints
glosses and source references missing from Vögtlin's edition.

list of the miracles that occurred during the Passion of Jesus, is rather unusual. According to the *Vita*, it was a Jewish custom on high holidays to carry twelve banners in a festive procession around the temple; as the procession passed the scourged Jesus, the banners bowed, as if they wished to worship him.

All passages associated with the *EN* were incorporated, essentially unaltered, by Walther von Rheinau and the Swiss poet Wernher in their *Marienleben*; Wernher slightly extends only the section dealing with Joseph of Arimathea.[105] Philipp, however, whose poem is a very free adaptation of the *Vita*, includes only the two passages concerned with the Harrowing of Hell (vv. 7956–61) and with Joseph of Arimathea (vv. 8028–51), respectively. He considerably reduces the former but, like Wernher, amplifies the latter, expanding the *Vita's* brief reference to Joseph's Christophany by retelling how Joseph was freed and brought back to his house and how, on the following day, the Jews found the prison empty.

4. Reception of the *Evangelium Nicodemi* in prose texts

The *EN* was particularly popular with authors of prose narratives on the life of Jesus, and especially on his Passion. Two such narratives have already been discussed: the *Neue Ee*, which drew its *EN* material from the three German verse adaptations, and the *Spiegel des lidens Cristi*, indebted to the Alemannic prose redaction E. Of the other texts making extensive use of the *EN*, only the Passion tract *Do der minnenklich got* has been edited and carefully studied.[106] It was written around 1400 in the Alemannic dialect (probably in the vicinity of Strasbourg) and preserved in nine manuscripts (two have now been lost) from the early fifteenth to the mid-sixteenth century;[107] the extant copies differ from one another considerably both in wording and in substance. This long tract, beginning with the events of the eve of Palm Sunday, gives a detailed and—whenever possible—complete account of the Passion events through to Pentecost, augmented with

[105] Edited by Max Päpke, *Das Marienleben des Schweizers Wernher aus der Heidelberger Handschrift*, Deutsche Texte des Mittelalters, vol. 27 (Berlin: Weidmannsche Buchhandlung, 1920).

[106] Albert Viktor Schelb, "Die Handschriftengruppe *Do der minnenklich got*. Ein Beitrag zur spätmittelalterlichen Passionsliteratur" (Ph.D. diss., Freiburg, 1972); idem, "Passionstraktat *Do der minnenklich got*," in Ruh, *Verfasserlexikon*, vol. 7 (1989), 353–55.

[107] For a hitherto unknown manuscript of this text, see Schneider, *Deutsche Handschriften*, 282.

teachings on the Redemption and various edifying embellishments. It contains passages of largely unabridged translation from the *EN* as well as shorter fragments adapted freely from the apocryphon.[108] The following portions of the *EN* have been inserted into the tract in the form of translations: almost the entire trial before Pilate (*EN* 1.1–3.2, corresponding to 250.30–57.18; 4.1–2, to 261.19–29; 4.5–6.2, 7, and 8, to 272.15–74.24);[109] the Jews' explanation of the eclipse of the sun at Jesus' death (11.2, corresponding to 328.25–29.3); and the opening of Joseph's prison cell and the report of the guards of the sepulcher concerning the Resurrection (12.2–13.3, corresponding to 352.23–53.33). They have been transmitted by only one group of manuscripts; most probably, they did not belong to the original text and should be viewed as later interpolations. What all manuscripts have in common are the passages in which the *EN* is freely adapted: a brief mention of Jesus' defenders at his trial (272.9–14; 275.1–5, with a reference to the source, "Es stot öch geschriben in Nicodemus ewangelio," "It is also written in the gospel of Nicodemus"); the report of Joseph's arrest and his release by Jesus, expanded with an announcement of the death of Nicodemus (338.10–39.5), taken from a legend of the discovery of Saint Stephen; and the Harrowing of Hell, with a relatively short description of how the soul of Jesus, accompanied by many angels, freed the patriarchs from limbo (325.13–28.6). Both in the short account of the defenders of Jesus and in the description of the Descent, one can find exact correspondences with the Middle Dutch *Passie* edited by Indestege.[110]

Johannes von Zazenhausen (a Franciscan of Mainz; after 1362 suffragan bishop in Trier; d. 1380) uses the *EN* only sparingly in his story of the Passion, *Erit vita quasi pendens ante te* (Deut. 28:66),[111] composed between 1362 and 1371, even though he mentions the *EN*

---

[108] For a discussion of the passages taken from the *EN*, see Schelb, "Die Handschriftengruppe," 434–38. Schelb does not consider the possibility that the translated portions could be later interpolations.

[109] Page and line references are to Schelb, "Die Handschriftengruppe."

[110] Luc Indestege, ed., *Die Passie Jhesu naar een zestiende-eeuws handschrift in het Provinciaal Museum te Hasselt* (Maaseik: H. van der Donck, 1948), 73–74. A comparison of the passages on the defenders of Jesus in both passion tracts (Indestege, *Die Passie*, 41.7–12; Schelb, "Die Handschriftengruppe," 272.9–75.5) shows that, in Schelb's passion, only the portions freely adapted from the *EN* (272.9–14, 274.1–5) correspond to Indestege's tract and that only those must have belonged to the original text; the sections more rigorously translated from the *EN* were probably added by a later editor.

[111] Cf. Kurt Ruh, "Johannes von Zazenhausen," in Ruh, *Verfasserlexikon*, vol. 4 (1983), 827–30. Livarius Oliger, "Die deutsche Passion des Johannes von Zazenhausen O. F. M. Weihbischofs von Trier († c. 1380)," *Franziskanische Studien* 15 (1928): 245–48, reprints the Latin prologue to this work.

directly after the gospels in his list of sources. He places special emphasis on the interpretation of the "sensus historicus" and draws on a large number of theologians, Nicolaus of Lyra being the most recent, to enhance this line of exegesis. It is to clarify the "sensus historicus" that several passages from the EN are quoted. In connection with Pilate's question "Quid est veritas" (Jn. 18:38), the author first discusses why the canonical gospel does not give Jesus' answer, and then reports the answer as recorded in the EN (3.2; Trier, Stadtbibliothek MS. 818/1715, fol. 23r). The discussion of the reports that many of the departed rose with Jesus from the dead (Mt. 27:52–53) alludes to the two sons of Simeon (fol. 50v); it does not include their account of the Descent but focuses on the question whether those resurrected with Jesus also ascended with him into heaven, or whether they died again. An extremely brief treatment of Christ's Descent, inserted directly after the account of his burial (60v), indicates that, in spite of its incidental contributions, the EN was of secondary importance to the author of this treatise.

Two other Passion texts indebted to the EN in varying degrees can be mentioned here. Claus Schulmeister's treatise on the Passion survives in the holograph manuscript of 1396 (Engelberg, Stiftsbibliothek MS. 339). Claus, a city clerk in Lucerne between 1378 and 1402, was strongly influenced by German mysticism; in his work, he relied primarily on Ludolph of Saxony's *Vita Jesu Christi* but drew on other sources as well, including the EN.[112] Another treatise of Swiss provenance, the life of Jesus entitled *Induimini dominum* (Rom. 13:14; Engelberg, Stiftsbibliothek MS. 244, saec. XV in.), is a gospel harmony that makes ample use of glosses from church fathers and occasionally from the EN.[113]

Since the extensive field of late medieval German Passion literature still remains largely unexplored, one may surmise that, in addition to the four texts indicated above, there were many others which quoted, adapted, or alluded to the EN. A thorough analytical description of manuscript texts of the already known and studied Passion tracts could furnish further proof of the EN's pervasive influence. Kurt Ruh's dissertation on the large textual tradition of Heinrich von St. Gallen's tract *Extendit manum* (Gen. 22:10; approximately 180 manuscripts) may serve as an example. While describing primarily the

---

[112] Kurt Ruh, "Der Passionstraktat des Heinrich von St. Gallen," 2 vols. (Ph.D. diss., Zürich, 1940), 2:27–29; idem, *Bonaventura deutsch. Ein Beitrag zur deutschen Franziskaner-Mystik und -Scholastik*, Bibliotheca Germanica, vol. 7 (Bern: Francke, 1956), 271 n. 2.

[113] Kurt Ruh, "Leben Jesu *Induimini dominum*," in Ruh, *Verfasserlexikon*, vol. 5 (1985), 635–36.

manuscripts preserved in Swiss libraries, Ruh discovered that two of them—Zürich, Zentralbibliothek MS. B 288, fols. 23r–24v, 32r–33v, and 45r–50r (written in 1498), and Einsiedeln, Stiftsbibliothek MS. 284, pp. 409–14 (saec. XVI)—excerpted and incorporated into Heinrich's work fragments of vernacular adaptations of the *EN*.[114]

Narrative elements of the *EN* were also occasionally absorbed by late medieval German chronicles. In the *Straßburger Weltchronik* of Jacob Twinger von Königshofen, dated between 1380 and 1414, the material adapted from the *EN* occurs at the beginning of the third chapter ("von allen bebsten," "concerning all the popes"), inserted between a brief listing of the most important stations in the life of Jesus (with a polemic against the apocryphal text "genant 'unsers herren kintheit,'" "titled 'our Lord's childhood,'" probably to be identified with Philipp's *Marienleben*) and the beginning of a list of the popes.[115] Twinger's immediate source was, at his own admission, Vincent of Beauvais's *Speculum historiale*: "Vincencius schribet in sime buche genant speculum historiale, eine hübesche rede von der urstende, die etwas frömede ist" (501.11–13; "in his book *Speculum historiale*, Vincencius writes a fine account of the Resurrection, which is rather strange"). Although the *Speculum* was one of his most important sources, Twinger mentions it explicitly only once more.[116] Because the story of the Resurrection from the *EN* was the only narrative interpolation into the events of the New Testament, otherwise presented through short, chronicle-like notes, he probably felt obliged to ensure its credibility through an explicit reference to his source; after all, he himself refused to give credence to the narratives of the childhood of Jesus (see above). Beginning with Jesus' burial and Joseph's incarceration, Twinger gives (501.15–6.17) a short resume of Vincent's corresponding chapters (bk. 7, chaps. 48 and 56–63; *EN* 11–26). Most noteworthy in his rendition of Vincent's account are the changes he makes in the chronology of events. The report of the Descent into Hell comes directly after the burial of Jesus, and the liberation of Joseph is placed right after the Resurrection. The interrogation of several witnesses by

[114] Ruh, "Der Passionstraktat," 1:xcv–xcviii. The sources of the excerpts in the Zürich manuscript, not identified by Ruh, include the *Neue Ee* (fols. 23–24, 32–33) and the *Deutsche Chronik* of Jakob Twinger von Königshofen (fols. 45r–50r).

[115] Jacob Twinger von Königshofen, *Straßburger Weltchronik*, in *Die Chroniken der oberrheinischen Städte. Straßburg*, vol. 2, Die Chroniken der deutschen Städte vom 14. bis ins 16. Jahrhundert, vol. 9 (1871; repr., Göttingen: Vandenhoeck & Ruprecht, 1961).

[116] Rudolf Weigand, "Elements of the *Speculum historiale* in German Universal Chronicles of the Late Middle Ages," in *Vincent de Beauvais: Intentions et réceptions d'une œuvre encyclopédique au moyen âge*, ed. Monique Paulmier-Foucart, Serge Lusignan, and Alain Nadeau (Saint-Laurent, Quebec: Bellarmin, 1990), 401.

the Sanhedrin, which thematically belongs after the Ascension but whose chronology is not specified in the *EN*, is moved to Easter: the questioning of Phynees, Adda, and Aggeus takes place "am ostertage vor ymbeße" ("on Easter Sunday before the meal"), and the questioning of Joseph of Arimathea and the two sons of Simeon "noch ymbeße" ("after the meal").

Like Twinger's *Weltchronik*, the *Weihenstephaner Chronik* (Bavarian, written after 1433) offers the basic story of the *EN*, beginning with the arrest of Joseph of Arimathea.[117] The main source of this chronicle of emperors and popes was the *Flores temporum;* an important secondary source, particularly for the extended account of Charlemagne, was the rhymed German *Weltchronik* by Jansen Enikel. For the apocryphal material (90.20–93.23), the author of the *Weihenstephaner Chronik* turned to Heinrich von Hesler's German version of the *EN;* he used it also for the legend of Pilate and Veronica (93.24–96.28), a fact apparently overlooked by earlier scholars.[118] The *Chronik* only briefly summarizes the text of Heinrich's poem; consequently, its dependence on Hesler is apparent less from the coincidence in wording than from the reproduction of Hesler's idiosyncratic deviations from his Latin sources. These deviations include the curious linking of the report of the soldiers guarding the sepulcher with the opening of Joseph's empty prison cell (91.16 ff., the Jews first learn about Joseph's deliverance from the guards); the concluding words of the two sons of Simeon in their account of the Harrowing of Hell (93.3–9), exhorting the Jews and alluding to their conversion at the end of times; and the appearance of Lazarus as a witness on Jesus' behalf in the legend of Pilate and Veronica (95.31–32).

From the twelfth century on, Christ's Descent into Hell was frequently used as a theme in Easter sermons.[119] Homiletic accounts of the episode are usually short and based, as in early Middle High German verse compositions, mainly on the "Advenisti desiderabilis" anti-

---

[117] Edited by Sigrid Krämer, *Die sogenannte Weihenstephaner Chronik. Text und Untersuchung*, Münchener Beiträge zur Mediävistik und Renaissance-Forschung, vol. 9 (Munich: Arbeo-Gesellschaft, 1972).

[118] Krämer (ibid., 260–62) establishes the dependence of the *Chronik* on Heinrich von Hesler only with regard to the *EN* proper, not to the legend of Pilate and Veronica that follows. Although the section from the *EN* is preserved in only one of the three manuscripts of the chronicle, it certainly belonged to the original text of the *Chronik,* for all three also contain the legend of Pilate and Veronica. The excerpts from the *EN* are deliberately omitted in one manuscript and are absent (together with part of the legend) from another due to the loss of some folios.

[119] See Carl v. Kraus, *"Vom Rechte" und "die Hochzeit." Eine literar-historische Untersuchung*, Sitzungsberichte der Kaiserlichen Akademie der Wissenschaften in Wien, Phil.-hist. Kl., vol. 123, no. 4 (1891), 125.

phon (the greeting of Christ by the patriarchs) and on the pseudo-Augustinian "Sermo 160" (the speeches of the devils at the arrival of Christ). The *Kuppitsch'sche Predigtsammlung* (twelfth century, Upper German)[120] and the *St. Pauler Predigten* (first half of the thirteenth century, Bavarian)[121] contain good examples of such sermons.

A detailed retelling of the Descent into Hell can be found in the Easter sermon of the "Schwarzwälder Prediger" ("Preacher of Schwarzwald"),[122] active around the turn of the fourteenth century. It is introduced with a translation of Mark 16:1–7, a statement of the theme—how often Christ appeared to his disciples after his Resurrection—and a quotation from Peter of Riga's *Aurora*, which links the five wounds of Christ to his five appearances at Easter. Then it translates and augments those parts of the *Legenda aurea* which deal with Christ's appearances and the Harrowing of Hell. The "Preacher of Schwarzwald" quotes the speeches from his sources in Latin before translating them into German. As in the *Legenda aurea*, the account of the Descent consists of two parts: the excerpt from the sermon of pseudo-Augustine and the summary of the *Descensus*. Unlike the *Legenda aurea*, the Preacher ascribes not only the first but also the second part to Augustine: "Nu scribet uns S. Augustinus mê von der urstendi unsers herren. uñ sprichet . . ." ("Now St. Augustine writes us more about the Resurrection of our Lord and says . . .").[123]

Also through the Easter section in the *Legenda aurea*, the EN reached a number of German prose legendaries.[124] The most widely disseminated among the *Legenda*'s High German translations, albeit almost exclusively in southwestern Germany, was the *Elsässische Legenda aurea*,[125] made in Strasbourg ca. 1350. Its winter part, which

[120] Edited in Franz Josef Mone, "Altteutsche Predigten," *Anzeiger für Kunde der teutschen Vorzeit* 8 (1839): 525–27; cf. Dagmar Ladisch-Grube, "Kuppitsch'sche Predigtsammlung," in Ruh, *Verfasserlexikon*, vol. 5 (1985), 452–54.

[121] Edited by Adalbert Jeitteles, *Altdeutsche Predigten aus dem Benedictinerstifte St. Paul in Kärnten*, Altdeutsche Handschriften aus Oesterreich, vol. 1 (Innsbruck: Wagner'sche Universitäts-Buchhandlung, 1878), 75–78; new ed. and bibliography in Norman E. Whisnant, "St. Pauler Predigten," in Ruh, *Verfasserlexikon*, vol. 7 (1989), 366–69.

[122] Edited in Franz Karl Grieshaber, *Deutsche Predigten des XIII. Jahrhunderts* (1844; repr., Hildesheim: G. Olms, 1978), 137–50.

[123] Ibid., 145; cf. 149–50;

[124] For a discussion of German translations of the *Legenda aurea*, see Konrad Kunze, "Jacobus a Voragine," in Ruh, *Verfasserlexikon*, vol. 4 (1983), 460–63; for the transmission of the *Legenda*'s Easter section, see Williams-Krapp, *Die deutschen und niederländischen Legendare*, 446.

[125] Ulla Williams and Werner Williams-Krapp, eds., *Die Elsässische Legenda aurea*, vol. 1, *Das Normalcorpus*, Texte und Textgeschichte, vol. 3 (Tübingen: Niemeyer, 1980), 268.35–69.2 (the story of Joseph of Arimathea), and 269.7–72.17 (Christ's Descent into Hell).

includes the texts for Easter, survives in fifteen manuscripts.[126] More-over, five other translations of the *Legenda* (two in the East Central German and three in the Upper German dialects, all from the fifteenth century) preserve the same material, but none of them enjoyed wide circulation, each surviving in only one or two manuscripts.

The most popular German legendary was *Der Heiligen Leben*, written by a Dominican in Nuremberg around 1400 and extant in approximately two hundred manuscripts and forty-two early printed editions.[127] It is based on a variety of German and Latin sources (such as the *Passional*, the *Märterbuch*, and the *Legenda aurea*), but it is a purely hagiographical collection and does not contain any texts for Easter or other high festivals. Only a few of its manuscripts and all eight Low German printed editions include texts for such festivals (including Easter).

5. The *Evangelium Nicodemi* in liturgical drama

5.1. The Harrowing of Hell

A representation of Christ's Descent into Hell forms part of numerous medieval plays (Passion, Easter, and Corpus Christi plays).[128] It is usually placed *after* the Resurrection, and only rarely—in a dogmatic-ally more correct fashion—*before*.[129] Common to all the plays is the use of specific Latin liturgical hymns: Psalm 23:7–10 ("Tollite portas principes vestras ... Quis est iste rex gloriae ..."), the *Canticum trium-phale* ("Cum rex gloriae Christus ... Advenisti desiderabilis ...") from the liturgy *Elevatio crucis* celebrated on Easter morning, and the anti-phon "Venite benedicti patris mei," based on Matthew 25:34. These hymns, according to Thoran,[130] form the "Latin scaffolding" of the

---

[126] Ibid., xxx–xxxi; Williams-Krapp, *Die deutschen und niederländischen Legendare*, 35–52.

[127] Cf. Williams-Krapp, *Die deutschen und niederländischen Legendare*, 188–345.

[128] Cf. Rolf Bergmann, *Katalog der deutschsprachigen geistlichen Spiele und Marienklagen des Mittelalters* (Munich: Beck, 1986), index, 530.

[129] Cf. Zbigniew Izydorczyk, "The Inversion of Paschal Events in the Old English *Descent into Hell*," *Neuphilologische Mitteilungen* 91 (1990): 441. The sources of the descent episode in German plays have been studied by Georges Duriez, *Les Apocryphes dans le drame religieux en Allemagne au moyen âge*, Mémoires et travaux publiés par des professeurs des Facultés catholiques de Lille, vol. 10 (Lille: R. Giard, 1914), 44–68; Karl W. Ch. Schmidt, *Die Darstellung von Christi Höllenfahrt in den deutschen und den ihnen verwandten Spielen des Mittelalters* (Marburg: H. Bauer, 1915), 16–66; and Barbara Thoran, *Studien zu den österlichen Spielen des deutschen Mittelalters (Ein Beitrag zur Klärung ihrer Abhängigkeit voneinander)*, 2d ed., Göppin-ger Arbeiten zur Germanistik, vol. 199 (Göppingen: A. Kümmerle, 1976), 131–232.

[130] Thoran, *Studien*, 132–202.

episode, and already provide the main incidents of the Descent: the command to the devil and his helpers to open the gates; the joy of the patriarchs at Christ's arrival; and Christ's greeting of the patriarchs. The influence of the *EN* on this basic dramatic structure of the Descent is only indirect: the *Canticum triumphale* is modeled on a sermon by pseudo-Augustine, which is in turn based on the *EN*.[131]

The basic dramatic structure of the Descent inherent in the Latin hymns is developed to a greater or lesser extent in almost all the plays by means of additional scenes representing the prophets' joyous antici-pation, the discussions among the devils, the securing of the gates of hell, the greetings exchanged between Christ and the prophets, the binding of Lucifer, the condemnation of the wicked, or the translation of the prophets into paradise.[132] Other critics maintain that the au-thors of these plays borrowed the additional scenes from the *EN*.[133] However, a comparison with the *EN* reveals that, except for a few plays discussed below, the plays of the Harrowing of Hell exhibit no textual similarity to the apocryphon. In fact, the differences in the manner of presentation between the plays and the *EN* are conspicuous: the prophets named in the plays do not coincide with those in the *EN*, the dramatic lists of prophets include non-prophetic figures, and the prophecies do not correspond to those rehearsed in the *EN*. The *EN* provides only the underlying "idea"[134] of the patriarchs' rejoicing at Christ's arrival in their dim abode. One cannot speak here of the *use*, in the full sense of the term, of the *EN* as a textual source.

The frequently expressed opinion[135] that these plays are based on the Latin *EN* B must definitely be rejected. Current scholarship regarding the Latin textual tradition of the *EN* suggests that *Descensus* B was little known in German-speaking areas.[136] One can assume that the scenes allegedly taken from *Descensus* B, such as the binding of Lucifer or the condemnation of the wicked, originated in the widely disseminated popular conceptions of the Harrowing, and one need not necessarily derive them from a specific textual source.

---

[131] Ibid., 133 n. 88.

[132] Ibid., 202–28.

[133] Duriez, *Les Apocryphes*, 44–68; Schmidt, "Die Darstellung," 55–58; Thoran, *Studien*, 202–28.

[134] Achim Masser, "Das Evangelium Nicodemi und das mittelalterliche Spiel," *Zeitschrift für deutsche Philologie* 107, no. 1 (1988): 54–55.

[135] Schmidt, "Die Darstellung," 57–58; Duriez, *Les Apocryphes*, 56, 61; Thoran, *Studien*, 159–60, 221, 224, 227; Masser, "Das Evangelium Nicodemi und das mit-telalterliche Spiel," 57.

[136] Hoffmann, "Die ostmitteldeutsche Übersetzung," 227; Zbigniew Izydor-czyk, "The Unfamiliar *Evangelium Nicodemi*," *Manuscripta* 33 (1989): 181–82.

Only three plays, or groups of plays, occasionally borrowed the wording or the structure of the *EN* in their depictions of the Harrowing and can be properly said to have used the *EN* as a textual source: the *Tiroler Passion* (represented by a whole group of plays), the *Redentiner Osterspiel*, and the *Münchner Osterspiel*. All three share a common feature derived from the *EN:* the actual Harrowing is followed by a scene in paradise with Enoch, Elijah, and the Good Thief. Besides these three, only the *Alsfelder Passionsspiel*[137] and the *Augsburger Passionsspiel*[138] show occasional similarity in wording to the *EN*.

In the *Tiroler Passion*,[139] the Harrowing of Hell (vv. 3166–455) begins—after the introductory "Cum rex gloriae" and the "Tollite portas"—with a conversation between Lucifer and five devils (vv. 3168–241). This is followed by prophecies of the patriarchs (Adam, Isaiah, Simeon, John the Baptist, Seth, and David) concerning the coming of the Savior (vv. 3242–309). Both the infernal conversation and the prophecies are closely modeled on the *EN* (20–21.1 and 18–19). The subsequent scenes, Christ's forceful entry into hell and the greeting by the patriarchs (vv. 3310–93), do not show any close relationship to the *EN*. However, the conclusion of the Harrowing, the entry of the prophets into paradise and their encounter with Enoch, Elijah, and the Good Thief (vv. 3394–403; 3414–55), returns to the apocryphon. The author of the *Tiroler Passion* used not only the Latin *EN*, from which he lifted, in addition to the Descent, the incidents involving Joseph of Arimathea (see below, sect. 5.3), but also the rhymed *Evangelium Nicodemi* of Heinrich von Hesler, from which he copied almost verbatim parts of the prophets' speeches.[140] The *Villinger Passionsspiel* of

---

[137] Edited in Richard Froning, *Das Drama des Mittelalters*, 3 vols., Deutsche National-Litteratur, vol. 14 (1891–92; repr., Darmstadt: Wissenschaftliche Buchgesellschaft, 1964), 2:547–864; cf. the speeches by Ysaias, Symeon, and Johannes Baptista (vv. 7189–214), which correspond to *EN* 18.1–3.

[138] Edited in August Hartmann, *Das Oberammergauer Passionsspiel in seiner ältesten Gestalt* (1880; repr., Schaan, Liechtenstein: Sändig, 1982), 1–100; cf. Lucifer's monologue (vv. 2371–402) and Adam's speech (vv. 2419–28), corresponding to chapters 22.1 and 18.1 of the *EN*.

[139] Edited in Josef Edward Wackernell, *Altdeutsche Passionsspiele aus Tirol mit Abhandlungen über ihre Entwicklung . . .* (1897; repr., Walluf bei Wiesbaden: Sändig, 1972), 201–17. The Tirol group of plays consists of a large number of closely related play texts. Their earliest manuscripts belong to the end of the fifteenth century, but their origin can be traced back to the first half of that century, based on the reports of performances; cf. Rolf Bergmann, "Spiele, Mittelalterliche geistliche," in *Reallexikon der deutschen Literaturgeschichte*, ed. Paul Merker and Wolfgang Stammler (Berlin: W. de Gruyter, 1984), 82–83, §30, "Die Tiroler Spielgruppe."

[140] This relation was demonstrated by Masser, "Das Evangelium Nicodemi und das mittelalterliche Spiel," 55–56, and n. 27. The speeches by Symeon and Johannes Baptista (vv. 3252–79) correspond particularly closely to those in

1600[141] as well as its predecessor, preserved in the Berlin *Sündenfall und Erlösung*,[142] are partly dependent on the Descent scene of the *Tiroler Passion*.[143] It is indicative of the *EN*'s dramatic appeal that the author of the *Villinger Passionsspiel*, who throughout most of his play follows literally the Reformation play of Jacob Rüff (see below, sect. 5.2), includes specifically those sections from the *Tiroler Passion* which are based on the apocryphon (speeches by Seth, Simeon, and John the Baptist, as well as the conversation among the devils).

The *Redentiner Osterspiel*,[144] originating probably in Lübeck and preserved in a manuscript dating from 1464, adheres more closely to the *EN* in its representation of the Descent into Hell (vv. 261–754) than does the *Tiroler Passion*. Its Harrowing of Hell opens with the same sequence of events as the apocryphon: the utterances of the prophets (vv. 261–372; *EN* 18–19), followed by the dialogue between Satan and Lucifer (vv. 373–486; *EN* 20). The series of prophecies is augmented only by a speech of Abel and by a second appearance of Isaiah, while the infernal altercation includes a mention of Judas's betrayal. The central incidents of the Harrowing, with the breaking of the gates of hell, the binding of Lucifer, and the joyful greeting of the Savior by the patriarchs (vv. 487–617), are represented in the traditional manner through liturgical hymns. After a burlesque scene in which the devils attempt to hold John the Baptist in hell (vv. 618–46), and a complaint by Puck and Lucifer (vv. 647–68; freely modeled on *EN* 22–23), the concluding scene—again closely tied to *EN* 25–26—shows Michael leading the patriarchs into paradise, where they meet Enoch, Elijah, and the Good Thief (vv. 669–754).

The *Münchner Osterspiel*,[145] written for performance before an

---

Hesler's *Evangelium Nicodemi* (vv. 2880–913).

[141] Edited by Antje Knorr, *Villinger Passion. Literarhistorische Einordnung und erstmalige Herausgabe des Urtextes und der Überarbeitungen,* Göppinger Arbeiten zur Germanistik, vol. 187 (Göppingen: A. Kümmerle, 1976).

[142] Edited in Werner Williams-Krapp, *Überlieferung und Gattung. Zur Gattung "Spiel" im Mittelalter. Mit einer Edition von "Sündenfall und Erlösung" aus der Berliner Handschrift mgq 496,* Untersuchungen zur deutschen Literaturgeschichte, vol. 28 (Tübingen: Niemeyer, 1980).

[143] Knorr, *Villinger Passion,* 120–24; Thoran, *Studien,* 206–12, 216–20, 229–32; Williams-Krapp, *Überlieferung,* 39–42.

[144] Edited and translated by Brigitta Schottmann, *Das Redentiner Osterspiel.* Mittelniederdeutsch und Neuhochdeutsch, Reclams Universal-Bibliothek, vol. 9744–47 (Stuttgart: Philipp Reclam jun., 1975).

[145] Edited by Barbara Thoran, *Das Münchner Osterspiel (Cgm 147 der Bayerischen Staatsbibliothek München),* Litterae, vol. 43 (Göppingen: A. Kümmerle, 1977). Previously edited (without verse numbering) by A. Birlinger, "Ein Spil von der Urstend Christi," *Archiv für das Studium der neueren Sprachen und Literaturen* 39 (1866): 367–400. All subsequent references will be to Thoran's edition.

aristocratic audience, is preserved in a late sixteenth-century manuscript designed for reading only. Its Harrowing of Hell (vv. 36–467)
surpasses even the *Redentiner Osterspiel* in its faithfulness to the *EN*,
both with respect to the sequence of the events and to the wording of
individual speeches; in fact, it can be seen as an abridged verse translation of the corresponding section of the apocryphon. In comparison
with the *EN*, the play makes only a few additions, including the
obligatory liturgical hymns, a few utterances (Zacharias, Moses, Abraham), and the greeting of Christ by Eve. Unique to the *Münchener
Osterspiel* is the appearance of the two sons of Simeon, Carinus and
Leucius, as characters on stage; it is they who speak with Enoch, Elijah,
and the Good Thief. Also unusual for the German dramatic tradition
is the enactment on stage of the questioning of the two sons of Simeon
by the Sanhedrin in Jerusalem (vv. 468–557), which follows the Descent
into Hell. Every person named in *EN* 17.2, "Annas et Cayfas, Nichodemus et Ioseph et Gamaliel," makes a speech. Whereas in the *EN* the
two sons of Simeon remain silent and present their report in writing,
in the play Carinus answers the questions of Annas and Caiphas by
describing the beginning of the Descent (based on *EN* 18.1). After the
speeches by Nicodemus, Joseph, and Gamaliel, Leucius briefly reports
all that transpired in hell.

5.2. The interrogation of Jesus before Pilate

Dramatic representations of Jesus' trial before Pilate[146] rely on the *EN*
only in the textually closely related Passion plays of the Hessian
group. This group includes the following:[147] the early fourteenth-
century *Frankfurter Dirigierrolle*, which gives only stage directions and
the beginnings of speeches and hymns;[148] two fragments (not discussed here because they do not deal with the trial before Pilate) and
one other *Dirigierrolle*;[149] and three substantial plays from the late fifteenth and the early sixteenth centuries,[150] namely, the *Frankfurter*

---

[146] Duriez, *Les Apocryphes*, 11–35.
[147] Bergmann, "Spiele," 80–81, § 28, "Die hessische Spielgruppe."
[148] Edited in Froning, *Das Drama*, 2:340–74; cf. Bergmann, *Katalog*, 113–16,
no. 43.
[149] For the *Fritzlarer Passionsspielfragment* (ca. 1460) and the *Friedberger
Dirigierrolle* (fifteenth century), see Bergmann, *Katalog*, 131–32, no. 53, and 129–31,
no. 52, respectively. A recently discovered fragment (first half of the fourteenth
century) has been edited and discussed by Helmut Lomnitzer, "Ein Textfund zur
Frankfurter Dirigierrolle," in *Deutsche Handschriften 1100–1400. Oxforder Kolloquium
1985*, ed. Volker Honemann and Nigel F. Palmer (Tübingen: Niemeyer, 1988),
590–608.
[150] Cf. Bergmann, *Katalog*, 110–13, no. 42; 169–73, no. 70; and 148–51, no. 62.

Passionsspiel (1493), the *Alsfelder Passionsspiel* (performed in 1501, 1511, and 1517), and the *Heidelberger Passionsspiel* (1514). With the aid of these three plays, the original text underlying the *Frankfurter Dirigierrolle* can be partially reconstructed, although the extant plays all contain a remarkable number of idiosyncratic variants and extensive additions. To the same group of texts belongs also the biblical epic *Erlösung*, written at the beginning of the fourteenth century in the Mainz region, which frequently shares the wording with the aforementioned plays. Most likely, this epic was one of the main sources for the Ur-play of the Hessian group.[151]

In its representation of the trial before Pilate, that original play attested in the *Dirigierrolle* and partly recoverable from later plays followed primarily the canonical gospels. However, two speeches at the beginning of the trial are borrowed from the *EN*. In one, Caiphas introduces as one of the charges against Jesus the allegation of his illegitimate birth (*EN* 2.3): "dar zu ist er ein kebisch kint: das wissen alle, die hie sint" ("furthermore, he is an illegitimate child: everyone who is here knows that"; *Frankfurter Passionsspiel*, vv. 2739–40; *Alsfelder Passionsspiel*, vv. 3700–3701). In the other, Nicodemus defends Jesus by pointing out that Jesus' parents were legally married, a fact well known to many (cf. *EN* 2.4; *Frankfurter Passionsspiel*, vv. 2743–52; *Alsfelder Passionsspiel*, vv. 3704–13). That both speeches in which the Frankfurt and Alsfeld plays agree belonged to the original Frankfurt play is evident from the stage direction for and the incipit of the first speech ("Kayphas respondeat: Eya rihter und herre," "Kayphas shall answer: Oh judge and master"), as well as from the stage direction (standing on erasure) for the second speech ("Nychodemus respondeat," "Nychodemus shall answer") of the *Frankfurter Dirigierrolle* (lines 192–93). These two borrowings from the *EN* are absent from the *Heidelberger Passionsspiel* and from the *Erlösung*.

Substantial but mutually unrelated are other *EN*-based additions to the trial in the *Alsfelder Passionsspiel* and the *Frankfurter Passionsspiel*.[152] The Alsfeld play has two scenes dependent on the *EN*. One

---

The *Frankfurter Passionsspiel* has been edited in Froning, *Das Drama*, 2:375–534; the *Alsfelder Passionsspiel*, ibid., vols. 2–3, pp. 547–864; and the *Heidelberger Passionsspiel* in Gustav Milchsack, *Heidelberger Passionsspiel*, Bibliothek des Litterarischen Vereins, vol. 150 (Tübingen: Litt. Verein, 1880).

[151] For proof of the dependence of these plays on the *Erlösung*, see Rolf Bergmann, *Studien zu Entstehung und Geschichte der deutschen Passionsspiele des 13. und 14. Jahrhunderts*, Münstersche Mittelalter-Schriften, vol. 14 (Munich: Fink, 1972), 136–68. Ursula Hennig, "Erlösung," in Ruh, *Verfasserlexikon*, vol. 2 (1980), 599–602, assumes that there was a common source for the *Erlösung* and the Hessian plays, and provides additional literature.

[152] Duriez, *Les Apocryphes*, 11–35, quotes the corresponding passages, but he

of them shows Pilate's messenger ("cursor") escorting Jesus to the trial
(vv. 3776–835; *EN* 1.2–4); in the other, the banners bow miraculously
before Jesus (vv. 3836–983; *EN* 1.5–6). The latter scene enhances the
dramatic effect of the play by giving speaking parts to individual standard bearers, all of them named: after the miracle of the standards, each
of the twelve Roman "signiferi" confirms that the "baner" bowed against
his will. When the twelve Jewish men take over the banners, they boast
of their physical strength and announce their determination to hold them
firmly. But having failed, they too describe in vivid detail how the banners were pulled down from them by force. These two scenes (the initial
miracle and its aftermath) do not belong to the basic text of the *Alsfelder
Passionsspiel* used for a performance in 1501, but are part of an addendum
written by Henrich Hültscher of Alsfeld (d. 1547).[153]

The *Frankfurter Passionsspiel* is more heavily influenced by the *EN*
as it adapts the greater part of the *EN*'s account of the trial. The
following scenes are taken from the pseudo-gospel: the complaints of
the Jews (vv. 2943–88; *EN* 1.1); the "cursor" scene (vv. 2989–3124; *EN*
1.2–4); the dream of Pilate's wife (vv. 3125–200; *EN* 2.1); the dialogue
between Pilate and Jesus (vv. 3201–8; *EN* 2.2); the second accusatory
speech by the Jews and the defense by Nicodemus (vv. 3209–24; *EN*
2.3–4); Nicodemus's plea on behalf of Jesus (vv. 3280–99; *EN* 5.1–2);
and the reports of those who were healed by Jesus (vv. 3300–43; *EN* 6–7).
On the whole, the author of the *Frankfurter Passionsspiel* retains the
EN's sequence of events, although he omits the miracle of the standards, possibly because of technical difficulties in staging it. At times
he borrows from the apocryphon almost verbatim, but more typically
he abridges his source. He also foregrounds the character of Nicodemus, who, in the play, takes the place of the twelve righteous Jews
defending Christ's legitimate birth (*EN* 2.4), and who advises Pilate to
set Jesus free, reminding him about the Jewish practice of releasing a
prisoner at Easter (vv. 3350–61).

These scenes derived from the *EN* are introduced just before the
second interrogation of Jesus before Pilate; they follow the questioning
of Jesus by Herod and the meeting between Pilate and Herod (vv.
2823–942). In the first scene of interrogation before Pilate (vv. 2705–
822), the *Frankfurter Passionsspiel* agrees for the most part with the other
plays of the Hessian group, yet even here one speech, the first charge

---

does not remark on the totally different treatments of the material in the two
plays and does not consider their earliest version, which accounts for their agreements.

[153] Hansjürgen Linke, "Hültscher, Henrich," in Ruh, *Verfasserlexikon*, vol. 4
(1983), 293–94.

against Jesus (that he refers to himself as God, even though his father was Joseph the carpenter, vv. 2719–28), is drawn from the *EN* (1.1).[154]

In conclusion, it is worth noting that two other plays from the sixteenth century show familiarity with the trial section of the *EN*: the Protestant Passion play by Jacob Rǔff, published in Zürich in 1545, and the *Villinger Passionsspiel,* which in the pertinent scenes wholly depends on Rǔff. In the title of his play, Rǔff identifies the canonical gospels as his only source, and the plot of the third act, devoted entirely to the trial, is indeed based exclusively on the scriptural texts. However, the names of the Jewish accusors who come individually to speak before Pilate are taken from *EN* 1.1: "Cayphas, Annas, Simeon, Dathan, Gamaliel, Rabi Iudas, Leui, Neptalim, Alexander, Iairus." Moreover, the author resorts to the *EN* when dating Christ's Passion in the prologue to his play.[155]

5.3. The arrest and deliverance of Joseph of Arimathea

Scenes dealing with Joseph of Arimathea (*EN* 12, 15.6) are found only in the *Heidelberger Passionsspiel* (1514) and in the plays that belong to the *Tiroler Passion.*[156] While the former enacts only the imprisonment of Joseph, the latter includes three scenes of Joseph's arrest, his deliverance, and the opening of his empty prison.

In the *Heidelberger Passionsspiel,* the scene of Joseph's imprisonment (vv. 6040–125; *EN* 12.1) is preceded by those of the burial of Christ by Joseph and Nicodemus and of the appointing of the guards at the grave. The imprisonment begins with Annas's detailed report that Joseph and Nicodemus removed Jesus from the cross and buried him. These actions prompted the Jews to place a watch at the grave and precipitated the death sentence on Joseph (vv. 6040–67). At this point enter Joseph and Nicodemus, each introduced with a slightly shortened and modified Latin quotation from the *EN* (vv. 6068–77). The dialogue between Joseph and the Jews, reported in the apocryphon, is omitted here. Instead, there follows a discussion between Annas and Caiphas in which they decide to imprison Joseph and instruct the

---

[154] Cf. the *Alsfelder Passionsspiel,* vv. 3680–89, and the *Heidelberger Passionsspiel,* vv. 4575–84.

[155] The above quotation comes not from Rǔff's *Passion* but from the *Villinger Passionsspiel,* edited by Knorr, with which it agrees verbatim. In the *Villinger Passionsspiel* the date of the Passion is indicated in vv. 235–41 of the prologue; the names of the Jewish accusors are found in act 3, scene 2 ff., vv. 2528 ff. For a discussion of the dependence of the *Villinger Passionsspiel* on Jacob Rǔff, see Knorr, *Villinger Passion,* 67–102, esp. 84.

[156] Cf. Duriez, *Les Apocryphes,* 36–43.

guard to secure the prison (vv. 6078–99). This scene concludes with a detailed dramatization of the precautions taken during the locking of the prison: the prison guards attach wax seals to the door, bring one key to Caiphas and the other to Annas, and admonish them to keep the keys in safe places (vv. 6100–6125). Since this scene ends, in fact, the entire play, it appears that the surviving play-text is incomplete: the detailed description of the locking of Joseph's prison anticipates a resolution—the deliverance of Joseph by the risen Christ—which the play does not provide.

Independent of the *Heidelberger Passionsspiel*, the Joseph scenes in the *Tiroler Passion*[157] are inserted at three different points in the play. The first scene (vv. 2778–815; *EN* 12.1), introduced after the removal of Jesus from the cross by Joseph and Nicodemus in the presence of Mary and John, consists of a brief conversation in which Joseph defends his actions and accuses the Jews, while Caiphas and Annas threaten him and arrange for his imprisonment until Easter. The second scene (vv. 3404–13) is placed between Christ's Descent into Hell and the meeting of the patriarchs with Enoch and Elijah. It includes a brief and considerably altered dramatization of Christ releasing Joseph from prison and leading him to paradise (not to Arimathea, as in *EN* 15.6). Some four hundred lines later, in the scene of the opening of Joseph's prison (vv. 3792–837), the narrative account of the *EN* (12.2) is transposed into direct speech. "Raby Moyses" and another Jew remind Caiphas that Joseph is still in prison. Thereupon Caiphas gives instructions to bring Joseph forth from the place of his confinement (here referred to as a "turris," "tower"). When the Jews sent to execute these orders express their amazement at finding the prison empty, the "Famulus turris" ("keeper of the tower"; the phrase taken from Joseph's own account of his liberation in *EN* 15.6) tells them what has happened. The opening of the empty prison is followed by the report of the guards of the sepulcher concerning Christ's Resurrection and by the bribing of the guards (vv. 3838–951). As in the *EN*, Joseph's deliverance is also mentioned in this scene, an exact verse translation of *EN* 13.1–3.

Translated by Linwood DeLong
and Zbigniew Izydorczyk

---

[157] Wackernell, *Altdeutsche Passionsspiele*, 174–76, 214–15, 246–53. For a discussion of the divergent sections of the *Haller Passion*, see ibid., 337–39.

The *Gospel of Nicodemus* in Dutch and Low German Literatures of the Middle Ages[1]

WERNER J. HOFFMANN

The *Evangelium Nicodemi* *(EN)*[2] enjoyed the widest diffusion in Dutch-speaking countries during the fifteenth century. While only one verse adaptation dates back to the fourteenth century, four different prose translations, plus an originally Low German version subsequently rendered into Dutch, belong to the fifteenth. The *EN* reached the height of its vogue in the late fifteenth century when it was incorporated into, and thus disseminated through, *Dat Lyden ende die Passie Ons Heren Jhesu Christi,* a frequently printed Middle Dutch Passion narrative.

1. The *Evangelium Nicodemi* in Middle Dutch verse

1.1. The *Evangelium Nicodemi* in *Der leken spieghel* of Jan van Boendale

The only complete translation of the *Evangelium Nicodemi* *(EN)* into Middle Dutch verse is found in the didactic poem *Der leken spieghel* ("Mirror of the Laity") by Jan van Boendale (b. in Tervuren in 1279, d. ca. 1350 in Antwerp). Jan van Boendale was appointed chief town clerk ("scepenclerc") in Antwerp in 1314 and held that position for thirty

---

[1] I am indebted to the following scholars for useful advice and additional information: J. A. A. M. Biemans (Leiden), Jan Deschamps (Brussels), Zbigniew Izydorczyk (Winnipeg, Canada), Bob Miller (Oxford), and Fransjosef Pensel (Berlin).

[2] H. C. Kim, ed., *The Gospel of Nicodemus: Gesta Salvatoris,* Toronto Medieval Latin Texts, vol. 2 (Toronto: Pontifical Institute of Mediaevel Studies, 1973); the *EN* will be cited by chapter, paragraph, and line numbers.

years. During that period he wrote two works in addition to *Der leken spieghel*: the *Brabantsche Yeesten*, a chronicle of the dukes of Brabant in more than 16,000 verses, completed before 1316, and the *Jans teesteye*, a didactic dialogue on theological topics, finished before 1333. He is considered the second most important representative of Middle Dutch didactic poetry after Jacob van Maerlant, whose tradition he continued and whom he regarded as the "vader der dietscher dichtren algader" ("father of all Dutch poets").[3]

Boendale wrote his major work, *Der leken spieghel* (over 20,000 verses),[4] between 1325 and 1330 at the request of Rogier van Leefdale, burggrave of Brussels, and the burggrave's wife, Agnes von Kleve. In it, he discusses a wide variety of topics in theology, moral philosophy, and church history. He divides his work, which is expressly addressed to the laity, into four books, sequenced to reflect the history of salvation. Book 1 ("vander ouder eewen ...," "concerning the Old Testament ...") is devoted to the events of the Old Testament: it begins with the Creation of the world and deals with Adam, Noah, Abraham, Moses, David, Solomon, and the first Roman emperors. It also discusses the nature of God, the angels, the cosmos, purgatory, hell, the teachings regarding marriage, respect for parents, obedience, the Ten Commandments, and so on. Book 2 ("vander nuwer ewen ...," "concerning the New Testament ...") narrates the story of the Virgin Mary and the childhood of Jesus to the age of twelve, as well as his Passion, Resurrection, and Ascension into heaven. There follows a history of the church to the time of Charlemagne, with explanations of important church practices and doctrines: the Lord's Prayer, the Ave Maria, the creed, the mass, liturgical vestments, and so on. Book 3 ("Scone zeden ende manieren, Die dat volc sal hantieren ...," "Exemplary customs and rules for the conduct of life, which people should follow ...") offers general moral philosophy. It covers topics such as the relationship between husband and wife and the rearing of children, the duties of a sovereign, the four estates (clergy, nobility, peasants, merchants), and the four types of love. Of particular note in this book is the first recorded poetics of Middle Dutch. Book 4 ("Hoe aertrike sal inden ...,"

---

[3] A. v. Buuren and H. van Dijk, "Boendale, Jan van," in *Lexikon des Mittelalters* (Munich: Artemis Verlag, 1983), 2:307–8.

[4] Its only edition, Jan van Boendale, *Der leken spieghel, leerdicht van den jare 1330, toegekend aan Jan Deckers, klerk der stad Antwerpen*, ed. M. de Vries, 4 pts. (Leiden: D. du Mortier (en zoon), 1844–48), based on The Hague, Koninklijke Bibliotheek MS. 73 E 63 (saec. XIV med.), includes facsimiles of the beginning of the pseudo-gospel from two manuscripts; cf. E. Verwijs and J. Verdam, eds., *Middelnederlandsch Woordenboek*, vol. 10, *Bouwstoffen. Tweede gedeelte (G–Z)*, by G. I. Lieftinck (The Hague: M. Nijhoff, 1952), 365, no. 857.

"How the world will end . . .") reaches the end of time: the conquest of Jerusalem by a Christian sovereign, the coming of the Antichrist, and the Last Judgement. Boendale used a large number of sources: for book 1, the Book of Sidrac and the *Natuurkunde des geheelals;* for book 2, various New Testament apocrypha (described below), the *Rationale divinorum officiorum* of Wilhelm Durandus, and the *Chronicon pontificum et imperatorum* of Martin von Troppau; for book 3, the *Disticha Catonis* and the *Facetus;* and for book 4, the Book of Sidrac, besides other texts. Boendale's *Der leken spieghel* was relatively widely distributed: four complete manuscripts, ten fragments and four excerpts are still extant.[5]

The translation of the *EN* is contained in book 2 (over 10,000 verses), for whose opening sections Boendale relies almost exclusively on the apocryphal writings of the New Testament. The first part of the book (chaps. 1–34) provides detailed accounts of the life of Mary from her birth to her marriage to Joseph, the Annunciation and the birth of Jesus, the flight of the Holy Family to Egypt, their stay in Nazareth, and the miracles Jesus performed as a boy. The sources for these stories are—besides the *Legenda aurea*—*Pseudo-Matthew* and the *Infancy Gospel* edited by M. R. James.[6] In the tenth chapter, Boendale presents a thorough defense of the value and usefulness of New Testament apocrypha (in particular, of *Pseudo-Matthew,* which in its Latin manuscript tradition was usually ascribed to Jerome), using arguments similar to those found in other writings of the time (for example, in the prologues to the *Vita beate Marie virginis et Salvatoris rhythmica*). He states that although the apocryphal writings have not been authorized by the church, one may read them as long as they do not contradict the faith, and especially if their authors are known. It is very unlikely, he adds, that Jesus did not perform miracles in his youth, notwithstanding the evangelists' silence about them.

Boendale relates the life of Jesus only up to his twelfth year and compresses his public ministry into a brief summary of the miracles (chap. 35); then he continues with the story of the Passion, following a single apocryphal source—the *EN.* To explain why he passes over the events attested in the canonical gospels, he points out (chap. 35, vv. 7–18) that Jesus' life had already been excellently expounded by Jacob

[5] Jan Deschamps, *Middelnederlandsche handschriften uit Europese en Amerikaanse bibliotheken . . . Catalogus,* 2d ed. (Leiden: Brill, 1972), 116–18.

[6] M. R. James, ed., *Latin Infancy Gospels: A New Text, with a Parallel Version from Irish* (Cambridge: University Press, 1927), 2–95. The sources are discussed by J. J. Mak, "Boendale-Studies, III. Boendale en *Pseudo-Petrus,*" *Tijdschrift voor Nederlandse Taal- en Letterkunde* 77 (1959): 65–111; new manuscripts of James's *Infancy Gospel* have been signaled by Jan Gijsel, "Les 'Évangiles latins de l'enfance' de M. R. James," *Analecta Bollandiana* 94 (1976): 289–302.

van Maerlant in his rendering of the *Historia scholastica* (the *Rijmbijbel*). There is certainly not enough evidence to conclude, as Mak does,[7] that Jan van Boendale attached little value to the Bible; rather, the opening of book 2 must be seen as a completion of Maerlant's *Rijmbijbel* with the aid of apocryphal sources. The poet provides a further justification for his decision to omit the canonical material in the sentence that introduces his translation of the *EN:*

> Ende want ghi alden dach
> Uut den ewangelien hoort doen ghewach,
> Die die ewangelisten scriven,
> So laet ic u die achter bliven,
> Ende sal u maken memorie
> Van Nichodemus hystorie,
> Die hi bescrijft herde scone
> Van Cristum, den Gods zone. (Chap. 35, vv. 109–16)

(And since every day people hear readings from the gospels, as the evangelists wrote them down, I shall omit them and shall remind you of the story [historical account] about Christ, the son of God, written so well by Nicodemus.)

In the 2092 verses of chapter 36, Boendale gives a complete and very close translation of the *EN,* under the title "Die jeeste ons behouders, die de keyser Theodosius vant te Jherusalem in Pylatus vierscare, inden ghemenen boeken" ("The deeds of our Savior, which emperor Theodosius found in Jerusalem in the public records in Pilate's courthouse"), rendering literally the common Latin heading, "Gesta Salvatoris...." His translation omits only the prologue; otherwise it shows no deletions or insertions. The *EN* proper is continued in chapter 37 (98 verses) with the letter of Pilate to Claudius and with a brief explanation of Pilate's motive for writing to the Roman emperor, namely, to preempt Jewish attempts to blame him for the death of Jesus (vv. 69–80). Brief mentions of Pilate's suicide and of the destruction of Jerusalem (vv. 81–98)—the latter described in detail in Maerlant's *Rijmbibel*—conclude the chapter. The immediate source of Boendale's translation was a Latin vulgate text of the *EN,* possibly in a composite manuscript that also contained the *Infancy Gospel* edited by James.

Boendale's faithful adherence to the Latin of the *EN* may be related to the fact that he regarded Nicodemus's account as a particularly authentic, historical source for the last days of Jesus' life. In his

---

⁷ J. J. Mak, "Boendale en de Bijbel," *Nederlands Archief voor Kerkgeschiedenis,* n.s., 43 (1960): 221–49.

introduction to chapter 36, he specifically remarks—as does Heinrich von Hesler—that Nicodemus observed the events that followed Jesus' arrest at very close range, unlike the disciples who had all fled (vv. 1–16). Two chapters later, he lists the events that Nicodemus does not report—the Last Supper, the betrayal by Judas, the arrest and the interrogation by Annas and Cayphas—and explains that Nicodemus did not witness them personally. Nicodemus's story begins only at the moment he becomes involved in the proceedings against Jesus, that is, at the beginning of the trial before Pilate; he thus recounts only what he has actually seen (chap. 38, vv. 1–76). Boendale uses the example of Nicodemus and his fidelity to truth as an occasion to polemicize against contemporary fellow poets who uncritically included everything in their histories, whether it was true or false. He urgently admonishes the writers of "hystorien" to restrict themselves to authentic accounts because the term "hystoria," he reminds them, is derived from the Greek word *hystoron*, which means "zien" ("to see"; chap. 38, vv. 77–112).

1.2. The *Evangelium Nicodemi* in Jacob van Maerlant's *Spiegel Historiael* and *Historie van den grale*

Even before Jan van Boendale, his model, Jacob van Maerlant (b. ca. 1235, d. ca. 1300), had briefly treated the substance of the pseudo-gospel in his monumental poem *Spiegel Historiael*,[8] an adaptation, begun in 1283, of Vincent of Beauvais's *Speculum historiale*. In the seventh book of part 1, chapters 33 and 36–39, Maerlant relates the arrest and freeing of Joseph of Arimathea, the report of the soldiers who guarded the sepulcher, the three witnesses to the Ascension, and the Descent into Hell as narrated by the two sons of Simeon. He summarizes and highly abbreviates his source, the *Speculum historiale* 7.48 and 7.56–63; concluding the *Descensus*, he remarks,

> Daer dit aldus was bescreven.
> Ende daertoe wonderliker dinc,
> Dat ic cortelike overghinc. (Chap. 39, vv. 46–48)

(where [i.e., in the reports of the two sons of Simeon regarding the Descent] all these things were described, together with more marvellous things that I have omitted in the interest of brevity.)

---

[8] Jacob van Maerlant, *Jacob van Maerlant's Spiegel Historiael* . . . , ed. M. de Vries and E. Verwijs, pt. 1 (Leiden: Brill, 1863). For bibliography, see Deschamps, *Middelnederlandsche handschriften*, 93–95, no. 27.

Although it frequently refers to *Nychodemus Ewangelie,* Maerlant's *Spiegel* is not based directly on the *EN;* rather, those references, like the rest of the text, are derived from Vincent's *Speculum.* The poet ends his narrative of the apocryphal events with a critical comment about the lies that Grail romances have spread concerning Joseph of Arimathea:

> Van desen Joseph van Arimathien
> Maken hare favelien
> Die logenaren vanden Grale,
> Dat ic vor niet houde altemale. (Chap. 39, vv. 61–64)

(Those who lie about the Grail make up their fables concerning this Joseph of Arimathea. I do not believe any of them.)

These verses should be viewed in the context of numerous polemics in Maerlant's *Spiegel Historiael* against French Grail romances.[9] They pertain especially to the *Roman du Saint-Graal* of Robert de Boron, which deals with the origin of the Grail, the chalice of the Last Supper filled by Joseph of Arimathea with Christ's blood at the time of the deposition from the cross. Maerlant himself translated the prose version of that work into Dutch verse in his *Historie van den Grale* as early as 1261.[10]

In his prologue to the *Historie van den Grale,* Maerlant complains that his French source contains many historical untruths ("Ick wille dat gij des zeker zijt / Dat ick de historie vele valsch / Ge vonden hebbe in dat walsch," vv. 20–22; "I want you to be convinced that the story I found in the French source was totally false"). He, therefore, makes substantial corrections to the contents of that source,[11] drawing on the *EN,* the *Cura sanitatis Tiberii,* and Josephus, in addition to the Bible. Thus, for instance, he criticizes Robert's assertions that the Last Supper and the arrest took place in the house of Simon the Leper and that Joseph of Arimathea was Pilate's soldier because both these assertions contradict the Bible.

Maerlant departs from his source most substantially in the story of the imprisonment of Joseph of Arimathea. According to Robert de Boron, the Jews imprisoned Joseph so that he might not steal the body of Jesus. In his prison cell, Joseph was visited by Christ, who gave him the chalice of the Last Supper and taught him about the mysteries of

---

[9] J. te Winkel, "De Boron's Joseph d'Arimathie en Merlin in Maerlant's vertaling," *Tijdschrift voor Nederlandsche Taal- en Letterkunde* 1 (1881): 355–63.

[10] Jacob van Maerlant, *Historie van den Grale und Boek van Merline,* ed. Timothy Sodman, Niederdeutsche Studien, vol. 26 (Cologne: Böhlau, 1980), 115–60, vv. 1–1607. For an account of Robert's version, see above, pp. 120 ff.

[11] te Winkel, "De Boron's Joseph d'Arimathie," 332–42.

the Eucharist and the Grail. Joseph was not delivered from prison, Robert maintains, until the conquest of Jerusalem by emperor Vespasian. From Robert's narrative, Maerlant accepts as credible only Jesus' visit to Joseph's prison, the gift of the Grail, and Jesus' teaching. The rest of the story he dismisses as improbable because if it were to be true, Joseph would have had to spend forty-two years in jail. Instead, following the suggestion of the *EN* ("de ware lesse," v. 431; "the true account"), Maerlant maintains that, immediately after the Resurrection, Jesus delivered Joseph from prison and that the guards of the sepulcher pointed out to the Jews that Joseph had been freed (vv. 424–70; *EN* 12, 13, 15.6). He also replaces Boron's account of the events leading to Joseph's liberation by Vespasian (the healing of Vespasian afflicted with leprosy by Veronica's icon of Christ and Vespasian's expedition against Jerusalem)—not only irrelevant in his own work but also discredited as unhistorical—with two stories of greater relevance and credibility. He bases his versions of these stories on the Pilate-Veronica legend as told in the *Cura sanitatis Tiberii* and on Josephus's description of the destruction of Jerusalem.

1.3. Christ's Harrowing of Hell in the *Van den levene ons Heren*

The *Van den levene ons Heren,* perhaps the most important Middle Dutch scriptural poem, was written possibly in the first half of the thirteenth century.[12] In barely 5000 verses, it tells the life and suffering of Jesus, drawing mainly on the gospels. It is usually considered the earliest witness to the reception of the *EN* in Middle Dutch because it contains a detailed section describing Christ's Descent into Hell (vv. 3931–4503).[13] However, that section shows little resemblance to the *EN*. Before relating the Harrowing of Hell, the poet gives an impressive description—not unlike those found in visions of the otherworld, such as the *Visio Pauli* or the *Visio Tnugdali*—of various infernal torments (vv. 3931–4160). The actual Descent he treats rather briefly, in slightly over a hundred verses (vv. 4161–276). This episode, perhaps influenced by iconography, begins with the soul of Jesus destroying with his cross the gates of hell and illuminating the underworld (vv. 4161–76). Other motifs follow in quick succession: the joyful greeting of Jesus by Adam and the patriarchs and prophets; Jesus' explanation that he has suffered death for their sake; and the patriarchs' departure

---

[12] Edited by W. H. Beuken, *Van den levene ons Heren,* 2 pts., Zwolse drukken en herdrukken, vols. 60A and 60B (Zwolle: W. E. J. Tjeenk Willink, 1968).

[13] Cf. Beuken, *Van den levene ons Heren,* 2:189. Beuken's opinion (ibid., 98–99) that the description of the Crucifixion was influenced by the *EN* is erroneous.

from hell amid songs in praise of the Savior (vv. 4177–276). A long altercation between Jesus and the devil (which faintly foreshadows later *processus Satanae*, such as Jacobus de Theramo's *Belial*) forms the conclusion to the poem's Descent section. The altercation begins when Satan, in the company of his minions, pursues Jesus and the saints; he charges that Jesus stole the spoils which since the Fall of man had rightfully belonged to him and accuses Jesus of breaking the law. Thereupon Jesus explains to him that through his Incarnation and his death on the cross, he redeemed all those who had been prisoners in hell (vv. 4277–503).

2. Prose translations

Prose translations of the *EN* into Middle Dutch and Middle Low German date from approximately the beginning of the fifteenth century. Four different Dutch translations (A, B, C, D) and one Low German (L) are still extant. Two of the Dutch versions have already been edited: B by Jacobs, and both A and B by Cumps;[14] an edition of the Low German translation has been published by Masser.[15] Unlike most High German translations, the Dutch and Low German texts are based on Latin models that did not contain the Pilate-Veronica legend as an addendum: three of them (A, B, C) used the common A type of the *EN* with the letter of Pilate, and the remaining two (D and L), a version that incorporated Tischendorf's chapter 28.

Translation A exists in two North-West Dutch manuscripts dating from the first half of the fifteenth century:[16]

[14] J. Jacobs, ed., "Een nieuw Mnl. handschrift van het Evangelie van Nicodemus," in *Verslagen en Mededelingen der Koninklijke Vlaamse Academie voor Taal- en Letterkunde* (Gent: Erasmus, 1926), 546–87; Jan Cumps, ed., "De Middelnederlandse prozavertalingen van het *Evangelium Nicodemi*" (Licentiaatsverhandeling, Leuven, 1963).
[15] Achim Masser, ed., *Dat ewangelium Nicodemi van deme lidende vnses heren Ihesu Christi. Zwei mittelniederdeutsche Fassungen*, Texte des späten Mittelalters und der frühen Neuzeit, vol. 29 (Berlin: E. Schmidt, 1978).
[16] Cumps, "De Middelnederlandse prozavertalingen," 67–96, printed the text of A2 and variants from A1 (139–62). See G. I. Lieftinck, *Codices Manuscripti V. Codicum in finibus Belgarum ante annum 1550 conscriptorum qui in bibliotheca universitatis asservantur pars I, Codices 168–360 societatis cui nomen Maatschappij der Nederlandsche Letterkunde* (Leiden: Brill, 1948), 93–94, 137–38, and Cumps, "De Middelnederlandse prozavertalingen," 31–35, for descriptions of manuscript A2; and Werner Williams-Krapp, *Die deutschen und niederländischen Legendare des Mittelalters. Studien zu ihrer Überlieferungs-, Text- und Wirkungsgeschichte*, Texte und Textgeschichte, vol. 20 (Tübingen: Niemeyer, 1986), 77, for A1.

A1   Leiden, Bibliotheek der Rijksuniversiteit (BRU) MS. Ltk 280, fols.
      1ra–9vb; from the convent of St. Barbara in Amsterdam (Sisters
      of the Third Order of St. Francis);
A2   Leiden, BRU MS. Ltk 316, fols. 65r–99r.

In A1, the *EN* occurs at the beginning of a legendary. In A2, it is preceded by a Passion tract of Heinrich von St. Gallen and followed by
several short texts (the letter of pseudo-Lentulus describing Jesus'
physical appearance, the five "bloetstortinghen" ["sheddings of
blood"] of Jesus, etc., partly excerpted from the *Pseudo-Bonaventura-
Ludolfiaanse Leven van Jesus*). Translation A follows the Latin text very
closely but remains fluent and free of imitations of Latin syntax. Its
source must have been a Latin manuscript fairly similar to that edited
by Kim.[17] The arrangement of the texts in A is noteworthy: first
comes Pilate's letter and only then the actual *EN* (with the prologue).
In both manuscripts, the *EN* ends at chapter 27.1.11; a large section of
the final chapter (the end of the report on the Descent and the reactions to it) is, therefore, missing. As a result of these two changes—the
placement of Pilate's letter at the beginning and the omission of the
concluding section—the entire *EN* appears as Pilate's report to the
Roman emperor. Only A2 contains a heading for the entire text, which
draws attention to the apocryphal nature of the *EN*: "nicodemus
ewangeli dat geheten is die verholen passie" ("the Gospel of Nicodemus, which is called the hidden passion"). A1 contains instead two
headings, one for Pilate's letter, "Een epistel die pylatus tot claudium
die keyser screef" ("A letter that Pilate wrote to emperor Claudius")
and one at the beginning of the *EN* proper, "Vander passien ons heren
ende verrisenisse" ("Regarding the Passion and Resurrection of our
Lord"). A1, but not A2, divides the *EN* into consecutively numbered
chapters. In the fifteenth century, a copy of this translation may have
also been owned by the monastery of St. Barbara in Delft (Sisters of the
Third Order of St. Francis), for a medieval catalogue of the *studierboe-
ken* of this convent lists a Middle Dutch translation of the *EN* under the
title "Nicodemus ewangelien" ("Gospels of Nicodemus").[18]

The Middle Dutch translation B probably originated in the southeast of the Dutch-speaking area because all its extant manuscripts
come from that region:[19]

[17] Kim, *The Gospel of Nicodemus.*
[18] W. Moll, "De boekerij van het St. Barbara-Klooster te Delft in de tweede
helft der vijftiende eeuw . . . ," *Kerkhistorisch Archief* 4 (1866): 224, 241.
[19] Jacobs, "Een nieuw Mnl. handschrift," 552–87, prints the text of B2; Cumps,
"De Middelnederlandse prozavertalingen," 98–136, prints the text of B1 and gives
variants from B2 and B3, 165–223. For descriptions of the manuscripts, see ibid.,

B1   Leuven-Heverlee, Abdij van Park MS. 17, fols. 31r–74r; ca. 1400,
      from the Carthusian monastery of Zelem near Diest;
B2   Diest, Kruisherenklooster (Canons Regular of the Holy Cross),
      no shelf-mark; ca. 1450; probably from the Begijnhof in Diest;
B3   Utrecht, Bibliotheek der Universiteit MS. 2 D 23 (1032), fols.
      112v–43v; ca. 1470, Beghards of Maastricht.

All three manuscripts are very small in format. B2 contains only the
EN; in the other two, the apocryphon is found within the context of
other Passion texts: a translation of pseudo-Bede's *De meditatione passionis Christi per septem diei horas libellus* precedes it in B1, and a variety
of Passion texts (among them the *Brigitten passie* and the Passion from
a gospel harmony) accompanies it in B3. The close connection between
the *EN* and Passion texts is also indicated by its title: "Nycodemus
passi" ("Passion of Nicodemus").

    B translates the *EN* very loosely and tries to achieve clarity and
comprehensibility through numerous amplifications (factual explanations, motives for actions, double translations). As in sermons, many
biblical quotations, in particular sayings of the prophets pertaining to
the Descent, are first given in Latin and then translated. Some longer
additions occur in the story of the Passion, especially in the scenes of
the flagellation, the crowning with thorns, and the Crucifixion. It is
noteworthy that the writer has completely omitted chapter 2, probably
on dogmatic grounds. He may have taken exception to the content of
this chapter, which includes the statements of the twelve witnesses to
the marriage of Joseph and Mary. Later, in chapter 12.1, he hints at
what the twelve would have testified—their testimony agreeing here
with the teaching of the church but not with the *EN*—namely that
Jesus was born of a virgin: "die .xii. die ghetuicht hadden. Dat Jhesus
van ghenen mans toe doen gheboren en weer. mer vanden heilghen
gheest. in der reinre maecht liif ontfanghen weer" ("the twelve who
confirmed that Jesus was not born of any man but was conceived by
the Holy Ghost in the womb of the pure virgin").[20]

    Translation C survives in only one manuscript, The Hague,
Koninklijke Bibliotheek MS. 73 H 10, fols. 3r–11v (in Limburg dialect,

---

36–46 (B1 and B2); Jan Deschamps, in *Handschriften uit Diestse kerken en kloosters,*
Diestsche Cronycke, vol. 6 (Diest: Vrienden van het Stedelijk Museum en Archief
Diest, 1983), 144–46 (B2, with a reproduction of fol. 1r), and 180–81 (B1);
P. A. Tiele and A. Hulshof, *Catalogus codicum manu scriptorum Bibliothecae Universi-
tatis Rheno-Trajectinae,* vol. 1 (Utrecht: Kemink et Fil., 1887), 252 (B3); and Jan
Deschamps, *Tentoonstelling van Middelnederlandse handschriften uit beide Limburgen.
Catalogus* (Hasselt: Provinciale Bibliotheek te Hasselt, 1954), 43–44 (B3).
    [20] Cumps, "De Middelnederlandse prozavertalingen," 112.431–34.

from the Augustinian nunnery of St. Agnes near Maaseik).[21] The second part of this manuscript (fols. 12–159), which contains the *Pseudo-Bonaventura-Ludolfiaanse Leven van Jesus*, was written in 1427; the first part, containing the *EN*, is somewhat later. The manuscript preserves only the Descent portion of the *EN* (chaps. 17.2–27.5) and the letter from Pilate to Claudius. It is not clear whether or not this is only a fragment of a complete translation of the *EN*. Apart from the introductory sentence ("Men leset inden ewangelio van nycodemus wye ons heer die helle schoerden ende nam dar wt sijne vrinde," "One reads in the Gospel of Nicodemus how our Lord destroyed hell and removed his friends from there") and the beginning based loosely on *EN* 17.2 and relating how the two sons of Simeon were brought to Jerusalem, the surviving text is a straightforward, unadulterated translation of the last section of the *EN*, without any noteworthy omissions or insertions. The translator clearly attempted to formulate simple, easily comprehensible sentences, especially where the syntax of the Latin original is opaque or complicated.

Translation D, heretofore unknown to scholars, survives in two manuscripts:[22]

D1   Leiden, BRU MS. B. P. L. 61, fols. 163ra–69rb; North-West Dutch, written ca. 1490;

D2   Linz, Bundesstaatliche Studienbibliothek MS. 194 (new 224), fols. 143r–74r; Rhenish Franconian, from the area around Kaiserslautern; dating from 1529.

The Dutch manuscript D1 contains only a portion of the translation, beginning at *EN* 11.1 (heading: "die verrysenisse ons heren wt nycodemus ewangelium," "the Resurrection of our Lord, from the Gospel of Nicodemus"); D2, on the other hand, transmits the complete text (heading: "Nicodemus ewangelium von der passien vnsers herren Jhesu Christi," "The Gospel of Nicodemus regarding the Passion of our Lord Jesus Christ") but in a Rhenish Franconian rendition. Nevertheless, it is certain that this translation was made not in a German but

---

[21] I was able to examine a microfilm copy of the *EN* section of this manuscript. The manuscript is described in the Koninklijke Bibliotheek, The Hague, *Catalogus codicum manuscriptorum Bibliothecae Regiae*, vol. 1, *Libri theologici* (The Hague, 1922), no. 700, and by Jan Deschamps, "Handschriften uit het Sint-Agnesklooster te Maaseik," in *Album M. Bussels* (Hasselt: Federatie der Geschieden Oudheidkundige Kringen van Limburg, 1967), 173.

[22] I was able to examine microfilms of both manuscripts. I was directed to D1 through the work of W. Williams-Krapp (*Die deutschen und niederländischen Legendare*). I am grateful to Prof. Zbigniew Izydorczyk for informing me of the existence of D2. D1 is discussed below in section 3. There is only one unpublished, typewritten description of D2.

rather in a Dutch-speaking territory, because D2 shows a large number
of Middle Dutch elements—expressions that are found only in Middle
Dutch, such as "vierschare" (for the Latin "tribunal / praetorium,"
hall of judgement), "discipel" ("discipulus," disciple), "blixem" ("ful-
gur," lightening)—at times pairing them in double translations with
their German equivalents, as in "volburt oder consent" (consent),
"persecucien oder liden" (persecution or suffering), "hermite oder eyn
einsiedel" (hermit), "passien oder martel" (passion). Translation D was
probably completed in the first half of the fifteenth century, notwithstanding the late dates of the manuscripts, since it was used as a
source by the author of the Middle Dutch Passion story *Dat Lyden ende
die Passie* (see below, sect. 3). The translator based his work on the
Latin text which named Theodosius as its patron and which included
Tischendorf's chapter 28. He rarely translates word for word, frequently paraphrasing only the sense of the Latin original.

The Low German translation (L) has been edited by Masser on the
basis of only one manuscript: Lüneburg, Ratsbücherei MS. theol. 2° 83,
fols. 134ra–45rb (saec. XV med., from the Benedictine monastery of St.
Michael in Lüneburg; siglum L1).[23] Three additional manuscripts
prove that this translation was known not only in the Low German but
also in the Limburg and Ripuarian dialectal areas:

L2   Lübeck, Stadtbibliothek MS. theol. germ. fol. 9, fols. 103ra–20vb;
       1475, from the Sisters of Common Life, Lübeck;[24]
L3   The Hague, Koninklijke Bibliotheek MS. 133 E 6, fols. 237r–69v;
       ca. 1470, in northern Limburg dialect, from the Augustinian
       nunnery of Jerusalem in Venray;[25]

---

[23] Edited in Masser, *Dat ewangelium Nicodemi*, 30–60. The manuscript is
described ibid., 9–15. The text of L1, printed by Masser, contains numerous
lacunae; a complete, although by no means error-free, text is preserved in the
Lübeck manuscript, L2, now again available to scholars.

[24] I have consulted a microfilm of L2. Since World War II, the manuscripts of
Stadtbibliothek Lübeck were kept in the Soviet Union (Leningrad, Moscow); most
of the German manuscripts, including MS. theol. germ. fol. 9, were returned to
Lübeck in 1990. For a brief description of L2, see Paul Hagen, *Die deutschen theologischen Handschriften der Lübeckischen Stadtbibliothek*, Veröffentlichungen der
Stadtbibliothek der freien und Hansestadt Lübeck, vol. 1, pt. 2 (Lübeck:
M. Schmidt, 1922), 6–7. A detailed but unpublished description by Hagen,
preserved in Handschriftenarchiv des Zentralinstituts für Sprachwissenschaft der
Akademie der Wissenschaften of the former GDR in Berlin, had made it possible
to identify this text even before the manuscript was returned to Lübeck. I am very
grateful to Dr. Fransjosef Pensel for sending me a copy of this manuscript
description.

[25] I have identified this text on the basis of a microfilm copy. Cumps, "De
Middelnederlandse prozavertalingen," 25, incorrectly links this manuscript to
translation A. For descriptions of the manuscript, see Williams-Krapp, *Die*

L4   Darmstadt, Hessische Landes- und Hochschulbibliothek MS. 1848, fols. 197v–237r; ca. 1500, Ripuarian, probably from the Augustinian nunnery of St. Maria Magdelena in Cologne.[26]

In both Low German manuscripts L1 and L2, two brief texts translated from the *Legenda aurea*, one on the appearances of the risen Christ and the other on his Ascension, are appended to the *EN*; in L1, they are further extended with a Passion story based on the *Historia scholastica*. In L3, the *EN* concludes a legendary for the months of December and January (a mixture of the northern and southern Middle Dutch *Legenda aurea* and the additional legends). L4 is a composite manuscript with a large number of texts on the Passion; its *EN* is preceded by a legend of the cross.

The author of L translated his source—the same Latin redaction with chapter 28 which was used as the basis for translation D—most literally, closely adhering to the Latin word order and copying Latin syntax. The translation is best preserved in L2 and L1, although the latter has many lacunae. It is slightly revised in terms of style in L3 and somewhat abbreviated in L4. It appears to have originated in the Low German linguistic area because the only manuscripts to contain the unrevised text are the two genetically distant Low German manuscripts L1 and L2; furthermore, the Limburg and Ripuarian manuscripts, L3 and L4 respectively, show some textual misunderstandings which can be explained only on the basis of Low German models.

The *EN* preserved in a Low German manuscript now at the Herzog-August-Bibliothek in Wolfenbüttel, Cod. Guelf. 430 Helmst., fols. 131va–55vb (written in 1456, from the monastery of Klus near Gandersheim),[27] is not a reflex of any original Dutch or Low German translation; rather, it is a Low German adaptation of a High German version of the apocryphon, the Alemannic version E.

---

deutschen und niederländischen Legendare, 74, and L. Scheurkogel, "Dat ander Pasenael, de Noordnederlandse vertaling van de *Legenda aurea*" (Ph.D. diss., Groningen, 1990), 34–35.

[26] I was able to examine a microfilm copy of this manuscript, brought to my attention by Bob Miller (Oxford). It is described by Kurt Hans Staub and Thomas Sänger, *Deutsche und niederländische Handschriften. Mit Ausnahme der Gebetbuchhandschriften* (Wiesbaden: O. Harrassowitz, 1991), 97–103.

[27] Described and edited by Masser, *Dat ewangelium Nicodemi*, 15–19; 61–97.

3. *Dat Lyden ende die Passie Ons Heren Jhesu Christi*

It was through the Passion treatise entitled *Dat Lyden ende die Passie Ons Heren Jhesu Christi* ("The suffering and the Passion of our Lord Jesus Christ")[28] that the subject matter of the *EN* was most extensively diffused in large numbers of Middle Dutch manuscripts and printed books.[29] This work gives an account of the Passion of Christ, together with the events that preceded and followed it. The *Lyden* begins with the attempt by the Jews to stone Jesus (Jn. 10:22), the raising of Lazarus from the dead, and the decision by the Jewish leaders to kill Jesus; it continues through to Pentecost. There follows an examination by the Jews of the witnesses to Christ's Ascension and Descent, as recorded in *EN* 14–27. The *Lyden* concludes with an extended meditation and hymns in praise of Jesus.

The printed versions of the *Lyden* open with the following heading:

> Hier beghint dat lyden ende die passie ons heren Jhesu Christi. ende die teykenen ende die miraculen die hy dede nae dien dat hi ghecruust was alsoe die vier euangelisten bescreuen hebben ende Joseph van Aromathia ende Nycodemus getughet hebben. gelijkerwijs als sy seluer gesien hebben ende gehoert. (1.1–6)

> (Here begins the suffering and Passion of our Lord Jesus Christ and the signs and miracles he performed after he was crucified, as the four gospel writers described it and as Joseph of Arimathea and Nicodemus testified according to what they themselves saw and heard.)

One might be tempted to infer from this heading that the author relied primarily on the canonical gospels and the *EN* as his sources. However, a detailed examination of his sources leads to a totally different conclusion:[30] the main text that underlies and links the whole *Lyden*

---

[28] Hereafter referred to as *Lyden*. Edited by Alfred Holder, *Dat Lyden ende die Passie ons Heren Jhesu Christi*, Bibliotheek van Middelnederlandse Letterkunde, vol. 19 (Groningen: J. B. Wolters, 1877).

[29] In the manuscript on which Holder based his edition—Karlsruhe, Badische Landesbibliothek MS. 701, fols. 6r–164r (ca. 1510)—a whole quire is missing after fol. 133. In addition, fols. 150–57 have been rearranged during binding; their original sequence must have been as follows: 152, 153, 150, 151, 156, 157, 154, 155. These defects in the original manuscript, unnoticed by Holder, explain the absence from Holder's edition of a substantial portion of the text after p. 69.6 (fol. 133; the entire account of the Ascension of Jesus) and the confused state of the text between pp. 77.32 and 82.13 (fols. 150–57; the Descent into Hell and the beginning of the closing meditation).

[30] I can only summarize here the results of my examination of the sources. I

is the Middle Dutch *Pseudo-Bonaventura-Ludolfiaanse Leven van Jesus* (hereafter *Leven*), chapters 22–53.[31] Both the opening section of the *Lyden*, relating the events leading up to Holy Tuesday of the Passion Week, and the conclusion, concerned with the deposition from the cross, the burial, up to the miracle at Pentecost, correspond almost exactly to the *Leven*.[32] The *Leven*, a meditation that invites readers to pious reflection on all stations of Christ's Passion, is here transformed into a purely narrative text, from which all meditative passages have been purged. A few short, entirely narrative chapters of the *Leven* (e.g., most of the chapters on the appearances of Jesus after his Resurrection) have been incorporated by the author of the *Lyden* almost without change. In the Passion story itself, from Holy Wednesday to the Crucifixion, there are only occasional verbatim borrowings from the *Leven*, but even here the meditative treatise functions as a continuous thread connecting the narrated events.

The author of the *Lyden* must have also consulted the gospels, although it is often difficult to determine in exactly what form. For the episode with the disciples on the road to Emmaus (64.4–65.17), he used a Middle Dutch gospel harmony, borrowing from it verbatim.[33] In addition, he turned to at least one other source for details of the mistreatment of Jesus, his nailing to the cross, etc., absent from the canonical narratives. Unlike many other Passion texts of the period, the *Lyden* does not dwell on the descriptions of the cruelties inflicted on Jesus by the Jews; instead, its emphasis falls on the compassion of Mary.

The *EN* available to the author of the *Lyden* was not a Latin version but rather an earlier Dutch translation, version D. At various points he inserts excerpts from this translation: at the beginning of the trial before Pilate (30.7–35.34; *EN* 1.1–3.2, 5.1–2), at the arrest of Joseph of Arimathea (53.1–54.12; *EN* 12.1–2), and at the opening of the empty prison and the report of the guards of the sepulcher (57.12–58.28; *EN* 12.2–13.3). He also intercalates the complete conclusion of the *EN*

---

intend to publish their complete analysis in the near future.

[31] Edited by C. C. de Bruin, *Tleven Ons Heren Ihesu Cristi. Het Pseudo-Bonaventura-Ludolfiaanse Leven van Jesus*, Corpus Sacrae Scripturae Neerlandicae Medii Aevi, Miscellanea, vol. 2 (Leiden: Brill, 1980).

[32] *Lyden*, pp. 1.17–13.3, corresponds to *Leven*, chaps. 22–25 (124.24–41.4); *Lyden*, pp. 47.35–71.26, to *Leven*, chaps. 34–53 (185–220). The concluding meditation of the *Lyden* (80.1–85.24) is based partly on the *Leven* (224.14–27.9; a translation of pseudo-Bernard's song "Jesu dulcis memoria").

[33] He seems to have used a combination of the Liège and the later Cambridge diatessarons. Both have been edited by C. C. de Bruin in 1970 (*Het Diatessaron van Cambridge*, Corpus Sacrae Scripturae Neerlandicae Medii Aevi, Series Minor, vol. 1, pt. 3 [Leiden: Brill, 1970]; *Het Luikse Diatessaron*, Corpus Sacrae Scripturae Neerlandicae Medii Aevi, Series Minor, vol. 1, pt. 1 [Leiden: Brill, 1970]).

(14.1–27.5) between his account of the events of Pentecost and the
closing meditation (71.28–80.1). For the most part, he adapts his source
freely, at times making substantial changes. Thus the twelve witnesses
who in *EN* 2.4 testify on behalf of Jesus at the trial before Pilate ("die
goede Joden," "the good Jews") reappear in his concluding section. It
is they who ensure that Joseph of Arimathea is questioned by the High
Council and, at the end, communicate to the apostles the story of the
Descent (74.2 ff.; 79.24 ff.).

The actual report of the two sons of Simeon is only briefly summarized (79.3–15) because the Descent is discussed directly after Christ's
death (55.25–57.2). The model for the Descent was not the *EN* but
rather the *Leven* (194.20–95.10, with additions). Similarly, the references
to Jesus' repeated visits to the patriarchs in paradise after their deliverance from hell and to their translation from paradise to heaven shortly
before his own Ascension are borrowed from the *Leven*. Finally, the
story of the deliverance of Joseph of Arimathea (62.26–34), derived ultimately from the *EN*, is also taken directly from the *Leven* (220.16–24).

The extraordinary popularity of the *Lyden*, a straightforwardly narrative, simple text that describes the Passion, death, Resurrection, and
Ascension of Christ, is attested above all by the large number of its
printed editions. Even as a handwritten text, it was widely disseminated. One can identify three different versions of the *Lyden:* a brief,
original version, preserved primarily in early prints (*Lyden* 1); and two
longer, more elaborate texts that exist only in manuscript redactions
(*Lyden* 2 and *Lyden* 3).

Lyden 1. There are at least twenty printed editions of this version (see
above for the heading; incipit: "Hier beghinnet alsoe als die Joden in
haren rade vergaderden om Jhesum te doden," "Here begins [the
story] of how the Jews convened in their council in order to kill Jesus")
published between 1477 and ca. 1528.[34] In the seventeenth century, it
was reprinted twice more, in 1665 and 1671, under the title *'t Wonderlyk Euangelium van Nicodemus*, together with an anti-Catholic polemical
treatise by Arnoldus Montanus.[35] In addition, the following manuscripts transmit its unabridged text:

---

[34] Cf. M.-F.-A.-G. Campbell, *Annales de la typographie néerlandaise au XVe siècle*
(The Hague: M. Nijhof, 1874), 324–28, nos. 1153–68; idem, *Annales de la typographie
néerlandaise au XVe siècle. 2. supplément* (The Hague: M. Nijhoff, 1884), 28;
W. Nijhoff and M. E. Kronenberg, *Nederlandsche Bibliographie van 1500 tot 1540*
(The Hague: M. Nijhoff, 1923), 2:695, nos. 3678–80, and vol. 3, pt. 2, pp. 49–50, no.
4381.

[35] Cf. D. Grosheide, " 't Wonderlyk Euangelium van Nicodemus," *Het Boek*,
Derde Reeks, 34 (1961): 133–41.

Antwerp, Museum Plantin-Moretus MS. 182, fols. 104r–213r; saec. XVI in.;
Brussels, Bibliothèque royale Albert Ier MS. 10765–66, fols. 8r–114r; saec. XV ex.;
Karlsruhe, Badische Landesbibliothek MS. 701, fols. 6r–163v; ca. 1510.[36]

Two further manuscripts contain an abbreviated version that begins only with the Last Supper (16.8–78.12):

Amsterdam, Universiteitsbibliotheek MS. I G 5, fols. 23r–81v; ca. 1430;
olim Leuven, Universiteitsbibliotheek MS. 145.[37]

Lyden 2. The full text of this redaction is found in one manuscript (Gh), and portions of it occur in three others (Am, Ld1, Dü):[38]

Gh   The Hague, Koninklijke Bibliotheek MS. 73 H 8, fols. 1r–190v; ca. 1460, from the Augustinian nunnery of St. Agnes near Maaseik. Incipit: "Alle die ghene die mynne hebben van dat liden ons heren te horen die soelen horen syn op doen" ("All those who would like to hear about the suffering of our Lord should open their minds").

Am   Amsterdam, Universiteitsbibliotheek MS. I E 27, fols. 111r–93r; dated 1469, from the Sisters of the Third Order of St. Francis, 's-Hertogenbosch ("susteren van sunte Elyzabeth ten bloemen camp"). Heading: "Hier volghet na vander passien ende liden ons lieuen heren ihesu cristi. ende vanden werken die voer der passien geschieden. ende sonderlinghe vanden werken die onse here dede vanden palmsondach totten witten donredach toe" ("Here follows [the story] of the Passion and the suffering of our dear Lord Jesus Christ and of the deeds that occurred before the Passion, and especially of the deeds that our Lord performed from Palm Sunday to Maundy Thursday"). The text preserved here extends only to the Descent into Hell; it corresponds to fols. 1r–122r of Gh. The *Leven*, chapters 1–22, precedes the *Lyden*.[39]

---

[36] Printed by Holder, *Dat Lyden ende die Passie.*
[37] This list of manuscripts is based on the unpublished material from the catalogue of the *Bibliotheca Neerlandica Manuscripta*, the central bibliographic resource for Middle Dutch literature, located at Bibliotheek der Rijksuniversiteit in Leiden.
[38] I have consulted microfilm copies of manuscripts containing redactions 2 and 3, with the exception of Am, which I used in the original. For information regarding other manuscripts that may also preserve this version, see n. 41 below.
[39] This manuscript is mentioned by de Bruin, *Tleven ons Heren*, xxii.

Ld1   Leiden, BRU MS. Ltk 318, fols. 67ra–69rb and 120va–61ra; dated
       1476, from the Birgittine nunnery in Gouda.[40] Heading: "In dit
       boeck is bescreuen een deel van dat lyden ons heren ihesu cristi
       ende vanden miraculen die ghescieden in syn doot ende in syn
       verrisenisse also alst die vier ewangelisten bescriuen ende som-
       myghe puynten die in nycodemus passie staen" ("This book
       describes part of the Passion of our Lord Jesus Christ and the
       miracles that occurred at his death and Resurrection, as the four
       gospel writers have described it, and a few details that are found
       in the passion of Nicodemus"). This manuscript is a homiliary
       and contains only the beginning and concluding portions of
       Lyden 2. The first scribe copied the beginning of the text but
       stopped after a few pages (fols. 67ra–69rb, corresponding to Gh,
       fols. 1r–6r). Another scribe wrote the next section, which origi-
       nally stood at the end of the manuscript; it begins with the tract
       "O ghi allen die daer gaet biden weghe" ("Behold, all ye that
       pass by this way"; Lam. 1:12),[41] which covers the whole Pas-
       sion up to the burial of Jesus (fols. 70ra–120va), and which is
       continued with the conclusion of *Lyden* 2 (fols. 120va–61ra, corre-
       sponding to fols. 101r–90v of Gh).
Dü   Düsseldorf, Universitätsbibliothek MS. C 25, fols. 2ra–16vb; ca.
       1500, from Canons Regular of the Holy Cross, Marienvrede

---

[40] For a description of this manuscript, see G. C. Zieleman, *Middelnederlandse Epistel- en Evangeliepreken* (Leiden: Brill, 1978), 112–15.

[41] This Passion treatise, which is essentially a reworking of a tract by Heinrich von St. Gallen, is found in several additional manuscripts (cf. J. Reynaert,
*Catalogus van de Middelnederlandse handschriften in de bibliotheek van de Rijksuniver-
siteit te Gent*, vol. 1, *De handschriften verworven vóór 1852* [Gent: Rijksuniversiteit te
Gent, 1984], 100 n. 175, who gives further literature):

  Berlin, Staatsbibliothek Preußischer Kulturbesitz Mgq 1397; saec. XV;
  Brussels, Bibliothèque royale Albert Ier MS. IV 177; written in 1477;
  Gent, Universiteitsbibliotheek MS. 220; saec. XV/2;
  Strasbourg, Bibliothèque nationale et universitaire MS. 2932 (all. 724); saec.
  XV ex.

At least the Gent manuscript seems to include, as continuation, also a portion of
Lyden 2. Reynaert cites a whole series of manuscripts with texts on the Passion
related to the Gent manuscript; among them are the manuscripts of *Lyden* 2 (discussed above) as well as those of the *O ghi allen die daer gaet*. On two of the
manuscripts named by Reynaert, Bonn, Universitätsbibliothek MS. S 2052, and
Haarlem, olim Bisschoppelijk Museum MS. 101 (now Utrecht, Rijksmuseum Het
Catharijnekonvent), I have no further information, so it is unclear to me which of
the two texts they contain.

monastery near Wesel.[42] Heading: "Hijr geet aen die vpuersten-
tenisse ons heren ihesu cristi als nycodemus beschrijft" ("Here
begins the Resurrection of our Lord Jesus Christ, as it is described by Nicodemus"). The manuscript contains only an
excerpt from *Lyden* 2 (corresponding to Gh, fols. 108v–53v),
describing the events between the burial of Jesus and his Ascension. The excerpt is followed by an Easter sermon (fols. 17ra–
18vb), the account of the Descent from the *Legenda aurea* (fols.
18vb–20va, entitled "Collacie ter vesper wt nycodemus ewangelium," "A sermon for vespers, from the Gospel of Nicodemus"),
and by sermons for the days after Easter.

Lyden 3. Only one manuscript of this version survives:

Ld2   Leiden, BRU MS. B. P. L. 61, fols. 107ra–63ra; North-West Dutch,
ca. 1490.[43] Heading: "Dit boec dat is vanden lyden ons heren
ihesus cristus Ende vanden myrakelen dien hi in siin leuen dede
Ende hoe dat hi ter hellen daelde ende hoe dat hi siin vrienden
daer wt verloste Ende hoe dat hi verrees vander doet ende siin
vrienden vertroestede Ende hoe dat hi den heilighen gheest
neder sende" ("This book is about the suffering of our Lord
Jesus Christ and about the miracles that he performed in his life,
and how he descended into hell and liberated his friends from
there, and how he rose from the dead and comforted his friends,
and how he sent down the Holy Ghost"); incipit: "Alle die
ghene die minne hebben totten liden ons heren te horen die
sellen die dinghen verstaen die in desen boec ghescreuen siin"
("All those who wish to hear about the suffering of our Lord
should understand the things that are written in this book"). The
Lyden is followed by the Middle Dutch translation D of the *EN*
11–28, as well as by some additional New Testament apocrypha
(the legend of Pilate and Veronica, and the Assumption of the
Virgin, both largely based on the *Legenda aurea*) and an unidentified account of the destruction of Jerusalem.

---

[42] For a description of the manuscript, see Zieleman, *Middelnederlandse Epistel-
en Evangeliepreken*, 116; cf. also H. Vollmer, "Das Evangelium Nicodemi in
deutscher Prosa," *Bibel und deutsche Kultur* 6 (1936): 203.
[43] This manuscript, described by Zieleman, *Middelnederlandse Epistelen Evangeliepreken*, 49–50, and Williams-Krapp, *Die deutschen und niederländischen Legendare*, 76, 92–100, 128, consists of three parts: fols. 1ra–104vb, South Middle Dutch
translation of the *Legenda aurea*, nos. 1–50 with additional legends (no. 51 is Good
Friday); fols. 107ra–94vb, *Lyden* 3, with additional texts; fols. 195ra–282va, *Die
ewangelien ende die episteln in die vasten* ("The gospels and the epistles for Lent").

A comparison of these three versions of the *Lyden* with their Middle Dutch sources, particularly with the *Leven*, shows that the printed redaction, *Lyden* 1, is closest to the original text, whereas *Lyden* 2 and 3 expand it considerably. Both longer versions derive from a common earlier source, as is clear from their common secondary variations, additions, and transpositions, as well as from their almost identical incipits. However, the two differ substantially in specific detail. *Lyden* 2 expands the text with more or less extensive additions, including some long interpolations (Gh, fols. 24r–44r, the Bethany scene and the Last Supper) from Heinrich von St. Gallen's Passion tract *Extendit manum*.[44] Version 3 is a rather free revision of the *Lyden;* it inserts into the events preceding the Passion large chunks of the canonical gospels, such as a translation of John 5–11 (with the legend of the cross added after Jn. 5:4) at the outset of the narrative. It also omits some episodes from the *EN* with a comment that they can be found more accurately related in the translation of the apocryphon at the end of the manuscript.

It is impossible to be definitive about the time or place of the *Lyden's* origin. What is certain, however, is that this Passion text was not prepared especially for printing because some manuscripts that belong to the derivative version 2 antedate the first printed edition (Gheraert Leeu, Gouda 1477). The *Lyden* may have stemmed from the circles of the *devotio moderna,* for its main source, the *Leven,* received considerable attention there.[45] The most likely place of its origin is the northwestern part of the Netherlands.

4. The reception of the *Evangelium Nicodemi* in Middle Dutch prose

The preceding discussion has shown that translations of the *EN* are frequently found among the texts on the Passion and that the *EN* was used primarily to supplement the canonical information concerning the Passion of Christ. In addition, some Passion texts have absorbed certain themes from the *EN*. Two works widely used in the fifteenth century in the Netherlands illustrate this phenomenon. In the *Pseudo-Bonaventura-Ludolfiaanse Leven van Jesus,* ca. 1400,[46] a translation of a

---

[44] Kurt Ruh, "Der Passionstraktat des Heinrich von St. Gallen," vol. 1 (Ph.D. diss., Zürich, 1940), 4.4–30.29.

[45] The reception of the *Leven* is discussed by C. C. de Bruin, "Middeleeuwse Levens van Jesus als leidraad voor meditatie en contemplacie III," *Nederlandsch Archief vor Kerkgeschiedenis* 63 (1983): 144–45.

[46] Edited by de Bruin, *Tleven ons Heren.*

Latin text based on Ludolph of Saxony's *Vita Jesu Christi* and pseudo-Bonaventure's *Meditationes vitae Christi*, the *EN* is cited as a source for the account of the release of Joseph of Arimathea: "Hoe hi Joseph openbaerde, is ghescreven in Nycodemus ewangelie" (chap. 51; "How he appeared to Joseph is related in the Gospel of Nicodemus"; the actual account occurs in chap. 41). Similarly, the report on the liberation of the patriarchs from hell and the mention of Enoch and Elijah (chap. 36) echo the *EN*. In the translation of the *Articuli LXV de passione Domini* of Jordanus of Quedlinburg, preserved in over twenty Middle Dutch manuscripts, the *EN* is cited as a source seven times.[47] Details from the *EN* can also be found in the *Passie Jhesu*, a compilation of older Passion texts edited by Indestege from a Limburg manuscript dated 1575.[48] This treatise briefly mentions, in connection with the trial before Pilate, those healed by Jesus, who weep during the trial and attempt to help their healer (41.7–12, based on *EN* 4.5 and 6). It also contains a heavily abbreviated account, taken from the *EN*, of the soul of Christ freeing the prophets from limbo after his death on the cross (73.1–74.27).[49]

The substance of the *EN* was also partially transmitted through translations of Jacobus a Voragine's *Legenda aurea*, whose chapter 54 on the Resurrection ends with an account of the Descent into Hell adapted from the *Descensus Christi ad inferos*. The *Legenda* was translated into Dutch twice, once in 1359 by an anonymous Carthusian from the southern Dutch-speaking area and again, probably at the beginning of the fifteenth century, in the northern Dutch-speaking region.[50] Inde-

---

[47] This Latin work has not yet been edited. For a description of its contents and sources, see Robrecht Lievens, *Jordanus van Quedlinburg in de Nederlanden. Een onderzoek van de handschriften*, Koninklijke Vlaamse Academie voor Taal- en Letterkunde, Reeks 6, vol. 82 (Gent: Secretarie der Academie, 1958), 13–19.

[48] The text edited by Luc Indestege, *Die Passie Jhesu, naar een zestiende-eeuws handschrift in het Provinciaal Museum te Hasselt* (Maaseik: H. van Donck, 1948), occurs also, almost in its entirety, in Strasbourg, Bibliothèque nationale et universitaire MS. 2932 (All. 724; saec. XV ex.), where it is included in a Passion story whose beginning is based on *O ghi allen die daer gaet*; cf. note 41 above.

At least the beginning and the conclusion of the *Passie Jhesu* are taken from older sources. The Mount of Olives scene (Indestege, *Die Passie Jhesu*, 17–20) is taken from the passion edited by Holder, *Dat Lyden ende die Passie*; the conclusion (83–85) corresponds verbatim to the *Pseudo-Bonaventura-Ludolfiaanse Leven van Jesus* (chap. 36).

[49] Both these sections of Indestege's passion correspond remarkably to the Alemannic treatise *Do der minnenklich got*, edited by Albert Victor Schelb, "Die Handschriftengruppe Do der minnenklich got. Ein Beitrag zur spätmittelalterlichen Passionsliteratur" (Ph.D. diss., Freiburg, 1972). The two tracts come very close to each other elsewhere, too. It is possible that Indestege's passion is dependent on the text published by Schelb.

[50] Cf. Williams-Krapp, *Die deutschen und niederländischen Legendare*, 53–187.

pendent of these two is a translation of the Harrowing of Hell from the *Legenda aurea* contained in MS. C 25 of the Düsseldorf Universitätsbibliothek, fols. 18vb–20va.[51]

The account of the Descent into Hell in the *Tafel van den kersten ghelove* ("A Tablet of Christian Faith") of the Dominican Dirc van Delf, an extensive treatise on scholastic theology for the laity written in 1404, is likewise heavily indebted to the *Legenda aurea*. In the *Somerstuk 9* ("Van dat onse lieve heer clam ter hellen neder om die te breken ende der ouder vaderen te verlossen ende den duvel daerin te vanghen, te binden ende te besluten," "How our dear Lord descended into hell in order to destroy it and to liberate the patriarchs and to catch, bind, and lock up the devil there"),[52] Dirc explores the reasons why the soul of Christ had to descend into hell after his death and describes the topography of hell, all according to Hugh of Strasbourg's *Compendium theologicae veritatis*. He then proceeds to retell the Harrowing of Hell, drawing on the *Legenda aurea* but taking considerable liberty with it. Dirc's *Tafel* was the main source for the *Tafelboec* published ca. 1480 in Utrecht, which presents the lives of Jesus and Mary, dividing the material into readings for seven days of the week and for seven periods of each day. The Descent into Hell is placed under Matins and Prime of Saturday.[53]

5. Conclusion

To sum up, the only Middle Dutch verse translation of the *EN* is found in book 2 of the didactic poem *Der Leken spieghel*, composed by Jan van Boendale between 1325 and 1330. Boendale offers a complete and exceptionally accurate translation of the apocryphal gospel because he regards it as an authentic historical source, whose author, Nicodemus, was an eye-witness to all the events recounted in the apocryphon. Boendale's literary model, Jacob van Maerlant, had also emphasized the historical credibility of the *EN* and had used it, directly or indirectly, as a source for two of his works: the *Historie van den grale* (1261) and the *Spiegel Historiael* (begun in 1283). In both these works, Maerlant polemicizes against the mendacious tales concerning Joseph of Arima-

---

[51] See above, pp. 354–55.

[52] Meester Dirc van Delf, *Tafel van den Kersten Ghelove*, pt. 3A, *Somerstuc*, ed. L. M. Fr. Daniels, Tekstuitgaven van Ons Geestelijk Erf, vol. 6 (Antwerp: Centrale boekhandel "Neerlandia," 1938), 148–61.

[53] For a detailed description of the contents of the *Tafelboec*, see Dirc van Delf, *Tafel van den Kersten Ghelove*, pt. 1, *Inleiding en registers*, ed. L. M. Fr. Daniels, Tekstuitgaven van Ons Geestelijk Erf, vol. 4 (Antwerp: Centrale boekhandel "Neerlandia," 1939), 102–10.

thea, which, he claims, were spread by the French romances of the Grail, especially by the *Roman du Saint-Graal* of Robert de Boron. Although Maerlant used this romance as the main source for his early work, the *Historie van den grale*, he replaced large portions of Boron's work, which he regarded as historically unreliable, with material from other sources, including the *EN*, on which he based his account of the freeing of Joseph of Arimathea. While Jan van Boendale and Jacob van Maerlant were demonstrably acquainted with the *EN* itself, the thirteenth-century biblical poem *Van den levene ons Heren*, part of which deals with Christ's Descent into Hell, shows only distant resemblance to the corresponding section of the *EN*.

From the fifteenth century, five Middle Dutch and Middle Low German prose translations of the *EN* have survived. With one exception, they are extant in multiple manuscripts. These translations vary in scope and character, and include a free adaptation amplified with material from the canonical gospels, which originated in the southeast of the Dutch speaking area (B; 3 MSS.); a rather exact but fluent translation from the northwest (A; 2 MSS.); a translation that clings very closely to the wording of the Latin original, made in the Low German area but diffused also in the Limburg and Ripuaric regions (L; 4 MSS.); a rendition of which only the conclusion is preserved in a Dutch manuscript (D; the whole text exists in a Rhine Frankish translation); and, finally, a translation of the *Descensus* section (C; 1 MS). In manuscripts, the prose translations of the *EN* are usually found in close proximity to texts that deal with the Passion of Christ (e.g., MSS. B1, B3, A2, C, L4); less common is their association with legends (A1, L3). In contrast to the poems of Maerlant and Boendale, the prose versions, like the Passion tracts, provide additional material, beyond the gospels, for pious reflection on the Passion and Resurrection of Jesus Christ. The manuscripts of the prose translations all originated in monasteries, primarily convents closely linked to the movement of *devotio moderna*, whose importance for the creation and dissemination of religious literature in the fifteenth century can hardly be overestimated. However, the prose translations of the *EN* were not central to this devotional movement: compared to manuscript traditions of other translations sponsored by it, the extant manuscripts of the apocryphon are relatively few. One might, perhaps, detect in this paucity of manuscripts a somewhat critical or reserved attitude toward the *EN* in the circles of *devotio moderna*.

The material derived from the *EN* was most widely distributed through the Passion text *Dat Lyden ende die Passie Ons Heren Jhesu Christi*, preserved in a number of manuscripts and printed no fewer than twenty times between 1477 and ca. 1528. The main source of this straightforward narrative of Jesus' Passion, Resurrection, and Ascension, and of the events of Pentecost was the Middle Dutch *Bonaventura-Ludolfiaanse Leven van Jesus;* the *EN* found its way into the *Lyden* via the Middle Dutch prose version D, whose abbreviated sections appear incorporated at various points in the treatise.

Finally, several Passion texts—especially those translated from Latin, such as the *Bonaventura-Ludolfiaanse Leven van Jesus* and the translations of Jordanus von Quedlinburg's *Articuli LXV de passione Domini*—contain brief references to or details from the *EN*. Several others derive their apocryphal material from the *Legenda aurea* rather than directly from the *EN*.

Translated by Linwood DeLong
and Zbigniew Izydorczyk

The *Gospel of Nicodemus* in Ireland

ANN DOOLEY

℟he elaboration of a sustained narrative which fills out the chronology and provides additional details of Christ's trial before
Pilate, his Crucifixion, the events surrounding his Resurrection
and the witnesses thereto, and, finally, his triumphal visit to the
underworld had taken definite textual form in the Latin West by the
ninth century.[1] The *Gospel of Nicodemus* (GN) is a composite text made
up of an original Greek account of Christ's trial before Pilate, the so-
called *Acts of Pilate* (version A), to which was added a narrative of
Christ's Descent into Hell. The *Acts* are possibly as old as the second
century and were in circulation certainly by the fifth. The origin and
early format of the Harrowing of Hell segment are still matters of
scholarly debate. The Latin title by which the apocryphon is commonly
known, *Evangelium Nicodemi* (EN), is first found in manuscripts of the
twelfth century and after.[2]

The culture of learning in early Christian Ireland was demonstrably interested in apocrypha.[3] Given the exegetical method favored by
early Irish monastic learning, which emphasized the literal meaning of

---

[1] The Greek and Latin texts of the *Gospel of Nicodemus* have been edited by
Constantinus de Tischendorf, *Evangelia apocrypha*, 2d rev. ed. (Leipzig: H. Mendelssohn, 1876), 210–434, and the Latin version from the *codex Einsidlensis* by
H. C. Kim, *The Gospel of Nicodemus: Gesta Salvatoris*, Toronto Medieval Latin Texts,
vol. 2 (Toronto: Pontifical Institute of Mediaeval Studies, 1973); unless I indicate
otherwise, I quote the Latin text from Kim's edition and refer to it by chapter
and paragraph numbers. For an English translation, see Edgar Hennecke, *New
Testament Apocrypha*, vol. 1, *Gospels and Related Writings*, ed. W. Schneemelcher,
English translation edited by R. McL. Wilson (Philadelphia: Westminster Press,
1963), 444–81.

[2] The Latin manuscript tradition of the *EN* and the apocryphon's alternative
titles have been discussed by Z. Izydorczyk in the present volume, pp. 46–54, 77.

[3] For a discussion and catalogue of apocrypha in Ireland, see Martin McNamara, *The Apocrypha in the Irish Church* (Dublin: Dublin Institute for Advanced
Studies, 1975); the early use of apocrypha in the Irish Church has been studied by
David N. Dumville, "Biblical Apocrypha and the Early Irish: a Preliminary Investigation," *Proceedings of the Royal Irish Academy* 73C (1973): 299–338.

Scripture, it is natural that the expansion of the pool of "historical" information on the Passion and Resurrection of Christ afforded by the *GN* would have made this text an ideal candidate for Irish attention.[4] However, evidence for the early reception of the apocryphon in Ireland is unclear, although there is certainly plentiful evidence, both textually and iconographically, for a strong focus in insular Christianity on the saving acts of Christ, the natural doctrinal base for such an uncanonical interest.

Something of the general context for the interest in the Passion, within which we might expect the *EN* to have circulated, may be suggested by the following witnesses. As early as the first half of the seventh century, we find a tradition that among the relics preserved at Armagh was a cloth saturated with the blood of Christ.[5] This would imply, at the least, an appreciation on the part of Armagh of the prestige afforded by a particular devotion to the place and circumstances of Christ's Passion and entombment. In terms of liturgical devotion, a prayer at the Office of None in the *Antiphonary of Bangor* associates the descent from the cross with wonders revealed to Christ's followers, "qua cultoribus tuis divina monstrantur miracula" ("which divine marvels are revealed to your followers"), though there is no way of knowing whether these "marvellous things" were part of canonical or apocryphal Passion tradition.[6] The hymn "Precamur Patrem," found in the *Antiphonary of Bangor*, which has been ascribed to Columbanus by Howlett and to the Bangor circle of the young Columbanus by Curran,[7] draws on a tradition of the Descent into Hell for its inspiration in describing the effects of Christ's Passion.

> Conrosum nodis annis fere milibus
> extricat senis inferi feralibus.
> Tunc(?) protoplaustum lacrimosa(?) suboli

---

[4] For a discussion of the use of apocryphal material in early Irish exegetical writings, see the seminal article by Bernhard Bischoff, "Wendepunkte in der Geschichte der lateinischen Exegese in Frühmittelalter," *Sacris Erudiri* 6 (1954): 189–281; see also McNamara, *The Apocrypha*, 6.

[5] *Liber Angeli*, pars. 18–19, in *The Patrician Texts in the Book of Armagh*, ed. Ludwig Bieler, Scriptores Latini Hiberniae, vol. 10 (Dublin: Dublin Institute for Advanced Studies, 1979), 186; noted by C. Doherty, "The Cult of St. Patrick and the Politics of Armagh in the Seventh Century," in *Ireland and the Northern France: AD 600–850*, ed. Jean-Michel Picard (Dublin: Four Courts, 1991), 69.

[6] F. E. Warren, ed., *The Antiphonary of Bangor*, 2 vols., Henry Bradshaw Society, vols. 4 and 10 (London: Harrison and Sons, 1893), 2:21, no. 30; Michael Curran, *The Antiphonary of Bangor and the Early Irish Monastic Liturgy* (Blackrock, Co. Dublin: Irish Academic Press, 1984), 100–101, 175.

[7] David Howlett, "The Earliest Writers at Home and Abroad," *Peritia* 8 (1994): 1–10; Curran, *The Antiphonary*, 54–58.

abiecta mala morte saeua ultrice
Quemque antiquum paradiso incolam
Recursu suo clementer restituit.
Exaltans caput uniuersi corporis
In Trinitate locauit ecclesiae.
In hoc caelitus iubet portas principes
Regi cum sociis aeternales pandere.[8]

(He frees the man gnawed for thousands of years by the fatal knots of hell. Then (?) he liberates the first man with his tearful (?) offspring after casting down evil cruel avenging death. By his own return he has mercifully restored the ancient dweller in paradise. Raising up the head of the universal body of the Church he has placed him in the Trinity. On this [day] he orders princes to open eternal gates for the king with his companions.)

Curran remarks that this section of the hymn is not dependant on the accounts of the Descent found in other early liturgical hymns, with the exception of a possible echo of Prudentius.[9] He ascribes the treatment of the theme to the author's having drawn on the *Gospel of Nicodemus* and having given it an "original rendering."[10] We have no knowledge of the development of the *Descensus* part of the *EN* before the ninth century; thus, in this example and in a number of examples that follow below, it is difficult to be confident of the type of texts to which the community of Bangor might have had access. But the fact that the hymn can be dated to the sixth century makes it an extremely important early witness to the liturgical use of the apocryphal tradition of the Descent into Hell—indeed, Lapidge has suggested that the hymn was intended specifically for the vigil of Holy Saturday.[11]

---

[8] I have followed Curran, *The Antiphonary*, 214–15, in his conservative treatment of the text in retaining the manuscript readings "fere, ecclesiae."

[9] Ibid., 56.

[10] Ibid., 54.

[11] Michael Lapidge, "Columbanus and the 'Antiphonary of Bangor,' " *Peritia* 4 (1985): 104–16. The reference in the hymn to the eternal gates seems here to belong not to the *EN* tradition of the gates of hell but to the prior tradition which sees the usage of the verse "Attolite portas, principes vestras . . ." of Ps. 24 as a reference to Christ's Ascension; see A. Rose, " 'Attolite portas, principes, vestras . . .' Aperçus sur la lecture chrétienne du Ps. 24 (23) B," in *Miscellanea liturgica in onore di Sua Eminenza il cardinale Giacomo Lercaro acivescovo di Bologna* (Rome: Desclée, 1966), 1:453–78. In addition, the resurrection homily in the *Catechesis Celtica* interprets the references to "principes" in that verse as pertaining not to Satan's minions as in the *EN* but to Christ's victorious return to heaven. This passage, part of the Easter homily "In nomine Dei summi," is composed from segments of a commentary of Manchianus, and so the currency of this variant

In Irish homiletic writings, there are various "praeconia paschale" which refer to the theme of the Harrowing of Hell and place it in a totalizing eschatological perspective. Thus a homiletic piece on Easter from the late eighth- or early ninth-century *Catechesis Celtica*,[12] with a typically Irish heading, "In nomine Dei summi," declares the following: "Facta sunt in hac die multa beneficia, quia in hac die resurrexit Christus, Filius Dei uiui post uastationem inferni, et solutionem humani generis de ore diaboli et de ore peccato Adae" ("Many are the benefits of this day since it is on this day that Christ the Son of the living God arose after harrowing hell and after releasing the human race from the devil's maw and from the sin of Adam").[13] The same theme is celebrated in the eleventh-century homily for Easter from the Leabhar Breac manuscript, similarly headed and closely reliant on earlier exegetical materials:

> For many are its wonders and marvels ... in it Christ arose from the dead, after binding the devil in hell; in it the souls of the righteous of the five ages of the world came out of hell into paradise; in it will be the famous day, the great Day of Judgement.[14]

That the theme of the Harrowing might have suggested complex theological issues to Irish exegetes is implied by Boniface's complaints about the Irish Clement, who is said by Boniface to have held that Christ's Descent into Hell had freed all souls there, both righteous and unrighteous.[15] This is a preoccupation which persists in Irish treatments of the *EN* in the later Middle Ages.

---

interpretatio dates from before the middle of the seventh century; cf. Martin McNamara, "The Irish Affiliations of the *Catechesis Celtica*," *Celtica* 21 (1990): 291–334. This is perhaps an indication that the tradition of the Harrowing was not yet known to the Irish church in a fixed *EN* state.

[12] The *Catechesis Celtica* is dependent on a number of earlier Irish exegetical works and in particular on a seventh-century Irish compilation, the *Liber questionum in euangeliis.*

[13] McNamara, "The Irish Affiliations," 317.

[14] E. R. Atkinson, ed., *The Passions and Homilies from the Leabhar Breac*, Todd Lecture Series (Dublin: Royal Irish Academy, 1887), 390.

[15] Noted by Ó Cróinín in Michael Ryan, ed., *The Illustrated Archaeology of Ireland* (Dublin: Town House and Country House, 1991), 135. Cf. *EN* A 23.1, where Inferus rebukes Satan: "Et in quo nullam culpam cognouisti quare sine ratione iniuste eum crucifigere ausus fuisti et ad nostram regionem innocentem et iustum perduxisti, et totius mundi noxios, impios et iniustos perdidisti" ("Why did you venture without cause to crucify unjustly him against whom you found no blame, and to bring into our realm the innocent and righteous one, and to lose the guilty and the ungodly and unrighteous of the whole world?"). I owe this reference to Z. Izdorczyk.

1. The Book of Cerne

The first substantial piece of evidence for the knowledge of the *Evangelium Nicodemi* traditions in Ireland is the Harrowing of Hell text from the Book of Cerne, which Dumville has shown to be an eighth-century text of Irish provenance.[16] As Dumville has pointed out, the text does not provide evidence of direct knowledge of the *EN* and shows only occasional general congruence with the *Descensus Christi ad inferos*.[17] Besides the Psalter, to which all versions of the *DI* are ultimately indebted, the Cerne text is related to the pseudo-Augustinian "Sermo 160"[18] and, with additional material on Adam and Eve, to a lost Latin piece posited as a source of the Old English Blickling Homily 7.[19] Thus the Cerne composition attests to another variant of the apocryphon in circulation in Ireland and also, as Dumville suggests, to the liturgical amplification of the theme in a meta-dramaturgical form.[20] In this context, it may be significant that the two of the earliest complete texts of the *EN* from the ninth century seem to have insular connections, thus implying at the least a hospitable context for the tradition of the apocryphon.[21]

---

[16] The text, originally published by A. B. Kuypers, ed., *The Prayer Book of Aedeluald the Bishop, Commonly Called the Book of Cerne* (Cambridge: The University Press, 1902), 196–98, has been re-edited by David N. Dumville, "Liturgical Drama and Panegyric Responsory from the Eighth Century? A Re-examination of the Origin and Contents of the Ninth-Century Section of the Book of Cerne," *Journal of Theological Studies* 23 (1972): 376–77.

[17] Dumville, "Liturgical Drama," 377.

[18] Printed in PL 39:2059–61. For the relationship between paragraphs 2 to 4 of this pseudo-Augustinian sermon and *EN* 23–24.1, see pp. 49–50 above.

[19] R. Morris, ed., *The Blickling Homilies of the Tenth Century*, EETS OS, vol. 73 (London: N. Trübner, 1880), 86–89.

[20] Dumville, "Liturgical Drama," 388.

[21] Zbigniew Izydorczyk, *Manuscripts of the "Evangelium Nicodemi": A Census*, Subsidia Mediaevalia, vol. 21 (Toronto: Pontifical Institute of Mediaeval Studies, 1993), nos. 25 and 133. No. 25, Bern, Bürgerbibliothek MS. 582, a Sankt Gallen manuscript, contains a copy of Adamnán's *De locis sanctis* as well as the *EN*; no. 133, Laon, Bibliothèque municipale MS. 265, was used and annotated by Martin Hibernensis in the Cathedral library of Laon. A third manuscript, no. 334, Saint-Omer, Bibliothèque municipale MS. 202, from the monastery of Saint-Bertin, has some Old English glosses of the eleventh century, suggesting that the manuscript was in England. Nos. 133 and 334 also contain a collection of saints' lives and homiletic material; this is also the context in which the first Irish translation of the *EN* is found in Leabhar Breac. The whole question deserves further study.

2. Early Old Irish texts

Two Marian poems in Old Irish, dating from the early eighth century and attributed to one Blathmac, a poet historically identifiable from Irish annalistic and genealogical records, have also been seen by Dumville as influenced by the EN.[22] Such an impression may have been encouraged by the fact that these pieces occur in the same manuscript as and in proximity to an Irish poetic version of the apocryphal *Gospel of Thomas*, and, indeed were edited together by Carney.[23] The same opinion has since been repeated by Hughes in his recent edition of the later Irish versions of the EN.[24]

Since these two poems by Blathmac are of high literary merit and since their evidence has been considered as significant for the history of the early circulation of our apocryphon, it may be useful to examine them in some detail. In extracting the relevant material for discussion here, one is aware of how difficult it is to do justice to the devotional complexity and the rich cultural cross-fertilization achieved by Blathmac between Christian exegetical materials and the terminology of native Irish social praxis. Thus, for example, the legal relationship of Jesus and the Jewish people, which forms the basis for the treatment of the Passion events, is presented from the perspective of a native Irish system of social relations.[25]

The general purpose of apocryphal materials in the poems is to deepen and embellish the relationship between the literal and spiritual meanings of the canonical accounts of salvation history. Before turning to the Harrowing of Hell, the central motif of the EN, I shall briefly consider two other themes, also present in the pseudo-gospel. The first occurs in Poem 1, in the initial and simplest narrative account of the events of the Passion.[26] Here the soldier who pierced the side of Christ with a lance, fused with the Roman centurion who testified to Christ's divinity after Christ's death, is named Longinus and described as having been cured of his blindness:

---

[22] Dumville, "Biblical Apocrypha," 304–9.

[23] Blathmac Son of Cu Brettan, *The Poems of Blathmac Son of Cu Brettan*, ed. James Carney, Irish Texts Society, vol. 47 (Dublin: Educational Co. of Ireland, 1964).

[24] Ian Hughes, ed., *Stair Nicoméid: The Irish Gospel of Nicodemus*, Irish Texts Society, vol. 55 (London: Irish Text Society, 1991), xi.

[25] Irish scholars have noted these legal touches, but as yet no proper study has been made of the poems' total indebtedness to apocryphal materials or to Irish exegetical learning.

[26] Blathmac, *The Poems*, 16–23, qq. 44–64.

O du-ruidmiset am-ne
Ísu combu thorise
do-luid Longinus iar sin
dïa guin cosind láigin.

Ó fu-rócbath a chride,
mac ríg na secht noebnime,
do-rórtad fín fu roenu,
fuil Críst trïa geltoebu.

Toesca tobraith coimdeth dil
ro-baithais mullach nÁdaim,
dég ad-rumedair int éu
cruchae Crist ina béulu.

Dond fuil chétnai—ba cain n-am!—
is trait ron-icc in n-ógdall,
ossé díb dornnaib co glé
oc imbeirt inna láigne.

(When they thought that Jesus could be approached, Longinus
then came to wound him with the spear.

The king's son of the seven holy heavens, when his heart was
pierced, wine was spilled upon the pathways [i.e., the declivi-
ties of his body?], the blood of Christ (flowing) through his
gleaming sides.

The flowing blood from the side of the dear Lord baptized the
head of Adam, for the shaft of the cross of Christ had aimed
at his mouth.

By the same blood—it was a fair occasion!—he instantly cured
the fully blind man as he was openly with his two hands ply-
ing the lance.)[27]

In the numerous iconographical depictions of the Crucifixion in
Ireland from the eighth to the twelfth centuries, the centurion and the
sponge bearer are, as here, the standard figures flanking Christ.[28] As

---

[27] Ibid., 20–21, qq. 55–58. In this and in the quotations that follow, I have sil-
ently changed the editor's translation where I have felt it necessary.
[28] Cf. the relevant plates of Crucifixion scenes from metalwork and stone
crosses in Françoise Henry, *Irish Art in the Early Christian Period to 800 A. D.*
(London: Methuen, 1965); idem, *Irish Art during the Viking Invasions, 800–1020*
(London: Methuen, 1967); idem, *Irish Art in the Romanesque Period (1020–1170)*
(London: Methuen, 1970); and in Peter Harbison, *The High Crosses of Ireland*, vol.
3 (Bonn: R. Habelt, 1992), figs. 807–901.

Jennifer O'Reilly has noted, the frequent appearance of the lance-bearer
in Carolingian and Ottonian Crucifixion scenes in an attitude of acclamation and as the most significant witness to the divinity of the
wounded Christ is also paralleled by his role in Irish iconography.[29]
In the late seventh- or early eighth-century Durham Gospels' illustration of the Crucifixion, the lance-bearer is the only witness to be
labelled (cf. fol. 38v).[30] The early ninth-century St. Gall Codex 51 (p.
266) depicts the apocryphal story of his healing by Christ's blood.[31]
These Irish pictorial witnesses show the theme of Longinus contribut-
ing in a crucial way to a spiritual understanding of the Passion.

Blathmac's poem is, however, more complex. The quatrains quoted
above combine, in his mature yet impassioned expositional style, the
apocryphal theme of Longinus with that of Adam's baptism at Cal-
vary. They create an emotive link with the multi-faceted image of the
wounded Christ in majesty, who resumes in himself the whole of time
and the cosmos and who, by his Passion, initiates the sacramental acts
of the present age of salvation history. A link with the *EN* as a source
is unlikely because the set of exegetical and meditative relations active
here is much more complex than is suggested by the unremarkable
centurion material in the *EN*. I will return later to the absorption of
Longinian material in the Irish translations of the apocryphal gospel;
for the present, I should like to pose the question whether Blathmac's
understanding of the story of Longinus might not be governed by an
iconographic model; in numerous Irish depictions of the Crucifixion, as
in the poem, the lance-bearer grasps the spear firmly with both hands.[32]

---

[29] Jennifer O'Reilly, "Early Medieval Text and Image: The Wounded and
Exalted Christ," *Peritia* 6–7 (1987–88): 95.

[30] C. D. Verey, T. J. Browne, and E. Coatsworth, eds., *The Durham Gospels,*
Early English Manuscripts in Facsimiles, vol. 20 (Copenhagen: Rosenkilde and
Bagger, 1980), 61.

[31] J. J. G. Alexander, *Insular Manuscripts from the 6th to the 9th Century* (London: H. Miller, 1978), no. 44, pl. 203.

[32] Cf. the numerous Crucifixion plaques, from the early eighth-century
Athlone plaque (Michael Ryan, in *Trésors d'Irlande* [Paris: Association française
d'action artistique, 1983], 149) to the Clonmacnois plaque some four centuries
later (Raghnall Ó Floinn, "Irish Romanesque Crucifix Figures," in *Figures from the
Past: Studies in Figurative Art in Christian Ireland,* ed. Etienne Rynne [Dun Laog-
haire: Glendale, 1987], 168–88). Other details, such as the depiction of the rivulets
of blood on Christ's body, the adjective phrase "co glé," "clearly," and a possible
reading at q. 57cd of unemended MS. "at rumedhar" viz. past perfective form of
"ad-midithir," "to estimate" ("as they had estimated it [viz. envisaged it], the
shaft of the cross of Christ [was] in his mouth"), strengthen the visual aspects of
the scene. On the knowledge of Longinus in early Christian Ireland, see Pierre
David, "Une recueil de conférences monastiques irlandaises du VIII⁰ siècle. Notes
sur le manuscrit 43 de la bibliothèque du Chapitre de Cracovie," *Revue bénédictine*
49 (1937): 83, 86–87.

At the conclusion of the second poem, Blathmac refers to another apocryphal theme, the martyrdom of Enoch and Elijah at the hands of Antichrist at the end of the world.[33] This is an ancient tradition, reflected also in *EN* 25, which, as McNamara pointed out, has a long history in Ireland.[34] In view of the numerous references to the apocalyptic role of Enoch and Elijah scattered in early Irish texts, from the mid-seventh-century *De mirabilia sacrae scripturae* to the eleventh-century *Dá Brón Flatha Nimhe* ("The Two Sorrows of the Kingdom of Heaven"), Blathmac's citation should probably be considered as independent of the *EN*. The question of the circulation in Ireland of an apocryphal Book of Enoch is still a matter of scholarly debate.[35]

The most extended references to the Harrowing of Hell, the theme that prompted the association of Blathmac with the *EN*, occur in the second poem:

Is é ro-chés frisin croich,
buí adnacuil fo huarchloich,
ocus do-dechuid iar sin
du chuaird isnaib hifernaib.

Robu coscrach diä chur,
a gleten fri dïabul;
demun truag ro-decht a blat,
tucad airi a mórbrat.

Is do mac Ísu ro-lá
ima muin secht slabrada
ocus cotn-áraig—ní gó!—
i n-íchtur a thegdaiseo.

Táraill iarum a chorp leis
ó ru-llá de in móirgreis,
ocus as-réracht—scél nglé!—
diä Cásc iar tredensea.

A chorp crochtae ba buaid dó,
ro-cés testin fínfolo,
ní tánaic bréntu ná cruim
i n-aimsir a adnacuil.

---

[33] Blathmac, *The Poems*, 86–87, q. 258.
[34] McNamara, *The Apocrypha*, 24–27, no. 9; see further B. Ó Cuív, "Two Items from Irish Apocryphal Tradition," *Celtica* 10 (1973): 88.
[35] McNamara, *The Apocrypha*, 26–27.

Iarna chrocad frisind éo
do-cuaid i tír na mbithbéo;
ó ránaic rícheth cen mrath
ad-cotathae dagothrath.

Ce ro-chés galar n-endaig
is chath isnaib hifernaib
a chuimne la Críst ní mó
bith aibritiud cotulto.

Sirsan dot mac—dígrais dál!—
ron-ailt-siu a oenurán,
arbar sluaig, in méit di huaill,
dochum ríchid iar mórbuaid.

Céin-mair ro-chualae clais cóir
síl Adaim ima senóir
oca atlugud co glé
dia coimdith a tesaircne.

Deithbir döaib fáilte de
fri tórmach a muintire,
fri mac a flatho fíre,
fri loegán a slánsíde.

Tan ro-fer muinter nime
fáilte friä fírchride,
a Máire, do macán mass,
fiad a ngnúisib ro-ddérlas.

Ba gor, do macind amrae,
a Maire, in chondalbae;
ní tuinsea talmain ná nem
óclách badid n-amrathar.

Do Dia athair, ríg na ríg,
ó do-áirilb a chaíngním
do-ratad cumachtae nglan
i nnim ocus i talam.[36]

(It is he who suffered on the cross, who was buried beneath cold stone, and who went on a visit to hell.

He was victorious from fighting that, his battle with the Devil. Miserable Devil, his strength and a great prey were taken from him.

---

[36] Blathmac, *The Poems*, 58–65, qq. 174–86.

It is your son, Jesus, who cast seven chains about his neck and bound him—no falsehood!—in the depths of his dwelling.

Then he returned to his body when he cast off that great attack, and he arose—bright tidings!—on Easter day after three days.

His crucified body was as a victory to him; he suffered the shedding of winelike blood; no corruption or worm came to him at the time of his burial.

After he had been crucified on the cross, he went into the land of the ever-living; when he reached untreacherous heaven, he received good nursing.

Though he suffered both the grief of an innocent one and a battle in hell, Christ's memory of it was no more than if it had been a wink of sleep.

Happy for your only son whom you have reared—devoted union!—the fine host, the greatness of the rejoicing as they came towards Heaven after a great victory.

Happy he who has heard the harmonious choir of the race of Adam led by their ancestor, clearly thanking their Lord who had saved them.

It is fitting that they should welcome joyfully the increase to their household and the son of their true Lord, the darling of their safe other-world dwelling.

When the household of heaven welcomed their true darling, Mary, your beautiful son broke into tears in their presence.

Your fair and acclaimed son, Mary, was zealous in kin-love; there treads not the earth or heaven an equally renowned young warrior.

When he recounted his fair deed to God, the Father, king of kings, he was given full power in heaven and earth.)

It is this segment which led Dumville to conclude: "While speaking of Blathmac and the Harrowing of Hell, it must be recorded that there is no doubt that Blathmac was familiar with a version of the *Gospel of Nicodemus.*"[37] While the passage shows the author's ability to manipulate the various strands of the Harrowing of Hell theme (the levels of

---

[37] Dumville, "Biblical Apocrypha," 308.

hell, the binding of Satan in chains, the thanksgiving of the children of
Adam), there is no evidence that he was following a form of the apocryphon similar to that found in the extant *EN*. This narrative sequence
does not end with the Harrowing of Hell; rather, the poet continues
beyond the received boundaries of the Harrowing into an area of
greater interest to him, the heavenly glorification of Christ and his con-
stitution as Lord of the entire cosmos.

This sophisticated theological narrative is shaded in with native
Irish terminology that carries a rich and traditional social resonance.
Christ is the hero ("óclach," q. 185), the dutiful son ("mac gor," q. 185)
who receives his proper social due of sick-maintenance ("dagothrath,"
q. 179), his reward of rightful sovereignty ("fír flaith," q. 183),[38] and
the kingdom ("slánsíde," "tír na mbithbéo," qq. 179, 183)[39] after his
ordeal. Indeed, there are touches here not just of the mixed native/
Christian genre of the voyage narrative (*imramm*) but also of the native
Irish literary terminology of the *echtra*, the otherworld adventure genre,
in which sovereignty is earned after an otherworld ordeal or in which
the child of the otherworld offers himself up as an innocent sacrifice.[40] The insistence on the simultaneity of the otherworld and this-
world experience in quatrain 180 is theologically appropriate and not
unique in Irish devotional materials, paralleled as it is by similar insistence in native Irish *echtrae* tales.[41]

Dumville has also suggested that quatrain 187 ("Ní scél n-eris deit
in se, / is creiti a célmainde; / is iar n-eiséirgiu Críst gil / at-chuaid
dia apstalaib"; "This is no heretical account here for you; the prophetic
utterance is to be believed; it is after the Resurrection of the bright
Christ that he told it to his apostles") indicates a self-conscious defen-
siveness in Blathmac's use of an apocryphal source.[42] However, the
demonstrative "this" can hardly be read as a reference to the use of
apocryphal materials at this juncture; rather, it refers to the word "célmainde," which I translate as "prophetic utterance," a term used consistently by Blathmac to refer to his own composition.[43] The "it" of

---

[38] On the concept of the "truth" of the ruler as an Irish legal concept, see
Fergus Kelly, ed., *Audacht Moraind: The Testament of Morand*. (Dublin: Dublin Institute for Advanced Studies, 1974).

[39] On the cosmic and social meanings of "síd," see Tomás Ó Cathasaigh,
"The Semantics of 'Síd,' " *Eigse* 17–18 (1981): 137–55.

[40] Proinsias Mac Cana, "The Sinless Otherworld of *Immram Brain*," *Ériu* 27
(1976): 95–115; David N. Dumville, "*Echtrae* and *Immram*: Some Problems of Definition," *Ériu* 27 (1976): 73–94.

[41] Cf. John Carey, "Sequence and Causation in *Echtra Nerai*," *Ériu* 39 (1988):
67–74.

[42] Dumville, "Biblical Apocrypha," 308.

[43] See Blathmac, *The Poems*, 141, for Carney's discussion of this word.

the last clause is contextual and refers to the assumption of majesty by Christ as treated in the quatrains that follow. The "prophecy," or the inspired utterance, of Blathmac is fulfilled, and the words of the psalmist (q. 189), "The Lord said to my lord, sit at my right hand," have been realized in the words of the risen Christ himself (q. 186), "All power is given to me in heaven and on earth."

3. Late old and early Middle Irish texts

Beyond the poems of Blathmac, the next major literary work in the vernacular which combines the materials of Scripture and apocrypha is the late tenth-century biblical poem *Saltair na Rann*.[44] In the final sections of the poem (149 and 150), the events of the Passion are recounted, and the Harrowing of Hell is treated briefly (ll. 7769–80). Here again there is no indication that the scholar-poet had access to the *EN* as we know it. The traditions of Seth and the death of Adam which are incorporated into the *EN* appear in this text but derive from a demonstrably different source.[45] But there is, perhaps, some slight evidence that the linking of the theme of the Harrowing to the Fall of Adam and Eve is part of an Irish exegetical formula and becomes a standard topos of Irish vernacular devotional writing: Canto 8 of the *Saltair* concludes the account of the eating of the apple with an invocation to the King who "overthrew the host of cold hell, seizing them with a pitiful trembling, defeating in a difficult battle the envious armed outlaw."[46] Similarly, as we shall see, the poem on the Harrowing in the Book of Fermoy is constructed around this same modeling of the Fall and Redemption. Other linkages of the signs at Christ's death and the Harrowing with similar themes, such as the signs before Doomsday, occur in occasional saga texts. King Concobar mac Nessa's death, on Good Friday, is brought about by his fury at the druids' account of Christ's death. He thus becomes the first human to enter heaven with Christ after the Harrowing.[47] In the text on the death of Cú Cuchulainn, a segment of obscure rhetoric where the dead hero

---

[44] W. Stokes, ed., *Saltair na Rann*, Analecta Oxoniensia, Medieval and Modern Series, vol. 1, no. 3 (Oxford: Clarendon Press, 1883).

[45] D. Greene, F. Kelly, and B. O. Murdoch, *The Irish Adam and Eve Story from "Saltair na Rann"* (Dublin: Dublin Institute for Advanced Studies, 1976), 1:94–111 (text and translation), 2:136–46 (commentary).

[46] Greene and Kelly, *The Irish Adam and Eve Story*, 42–43.

[47] K. Meyer, ed., *Death Tales of the Ulster Heroes*, Todd Lecture Series, vol. 14 Royal Irish Academy (Dublin: 1906), 2–21.

speaks "siaburchobra" ("mystic utterance") is interrupted by a piece
marked *De adventu Christi*, in which the two victories of Christ seem to
be conflated; thus phrases such as the following are blended in with an
enumeration of the Doomsday signs: "... troethfaid Ísu iffern. imergib
áil Ádaim i flaith forbais foláim frris mbet formdig ingair fris failtniget
fris raidfet secht nime ... Ísu as uasliu. as isliu tria escartad iffirn"
("Christ will overcome hell through the forcible seizure of Adam from
a transient vain lordship, at which the impious will be envious, at
which the seven heavens will rejoice and proclaim ... Jesus is the
highest, he is the lowest by his Harrowing of Hell ...").[48]

The conclusion to be drawn from this examination of the relevant
pre-eleventh-century materials of Irish provenance seems to be that the
EN itself was not known in Ireland in this early period. Such evidence
as we have for the Irish use of Harrowing of Hell themes derives from
the period and/or area of textual influence in which the material represented by the *Descensus Christi ad inferos* was still in a fluid state and
the commonest Irish use of the material was in an exegetical anagogical context.

4. The Irish translations of the *Evangelium Nicodemi*

It is in the eleventh and twelfth centuries that actual translations of the
EN begin to appear in Ireland. The dating of these first—and, indeed,
principal—textual witnesses must be tentative, however, as the manuscripts that contain this translation work all date from the late fourteenth and early fifteenth centuries. Moreover, they occur in miscella-
ny-type manuscripts that contain a great amount of newly translated
religious material in the form of meditative texts on the Passion, lives
of continental saints, exempla, and sundry devotional and legendary
lore, although earlier devotional texts are often intercalated among
later items. In production as well as content, these new translations are
usually associated with the Gaelic political revival of the fourteenth
century and the later Observant friar reform movement in Ireland.[49]
Because of the mixed character of these manuscript collections and

---

[48] Richard Irvine Best et al., *The Book of Leinster*, vol. 2 (Dublin: Dublin Institute for Advanced Studies, 1961), lines 14199–215. I have interpreted MS. "imergib
áil" as "imb argabál," verbal noun of "ar.gaib," "carries off." A possible context
for this type of conflation may perhaps be found in the common use of the
phrase "in fine mundi" in Irish exegetical writing to describe the time of the
Incarnation and the Passion as well as the second coming of Christ. See Curran,
The Antiphonary, 53, 212, for appropriate references.
[49] Robin Flower, *The Irish Tradition* (Oxford: Clarendon Press, 1947).

because of the problems connected with dating on purely linguistic grounds, sorting out the chronology of any text's reception and transmission in later medieval Gaelic Ireland is always a difficult and precarious task.

As far as the Irish texts of the *EN* are concerned, M. McNamara was the first scholar to identify and describe all their variant forms.[50] For the purposes of organization, he divided the texts into their two ultimately constituent parts, *The Acts of Pilate* (no. 58) and various versions of *The Descent into Hell* (nos. 59–61). McNamara's very useful account stands as the best over-all guide to apocrypha in medieval Ireland in general. In the case of the *GN*, however, his listing is not complete, and his division of material gives a slightly distorted impression of the Irish reception of the *EN* as an integral text.

In Ian Hughes's recent edition,[51] the status of the complete text is restored, although the presentation of the first of the two Leabhar Breac versions (LB 1) does not address the question of its compositional integrity or of its significance as a witness to the transmission of the text. Otherwise, the editor presents the information on the manuscript versions clearly and makes some additions to the textual list. Thus we now know of six manuscripts containing an Irish *GN*, four of which—the versions in LB aside—represent complete and full versions of a fairly uniform text.[52] These four manuscripts include: the Yellow Book of Lecan (YBL; Hughes's base text), Leabhar Chlainne Suibhne (LCS), Liber Flavus Fergusiorum (LFF),[53] and Paris, BN MS. celt 1 (Par). They date from the late fourteenth (YBL) to the early sixteenth (LCS) centuries, the period of the Gaelic recovery in Ireland.[54] The translation of the *EN* which they contain is dated tentatively by the

---

[50] McNamara, *The Apocrypha*, 68–75, nos. 58–61.

[51] Hughes, *Stair Nicoméid*. Subsequent textual references will be to this edition. I also follow Hughes's abbreviated designations for the various versions, with the exception of the substitution of LFF, the more usual designation, for his LF1. An important review of Hughes's edition by Uáitéar Mac Gearailt, with much pertinent criticism, has appeared in *Cambridge Medieval Celtic Studies* 24 (1992): 105–8, in which the reviewer—correctly, in my view—re-asserts the importance and primacy of the LB 1 version and suggests from the evidence of some linguistic features that it might have been written in the eleventh century.

[52] Hughes, *Stair Nicoméid*, ix. A modernized version of LB 16, together with the accompanying homiletic materials, is found in Dublin, King's Inn Library MS. 10, fols. 43a–45c.

[53] The version from this manuscript has been recently translated by Máirie Herbert and M[artin] McNamara, *Irish Biblical Apocrypha: Selected Texts in Translation* (Edinburgh: T & T Clark, 1989), 60–88, 179.

[54] Both Atkinson, *The Passions,* and J. E. Caerwyn Williams, ed., "An Irish Harrowing of Hell," *Études celtiques* 9 (1960): 44–78, had expressed their intention of publishing the YBL text. It is perhaps fitting that the text was finally edited by Hughes, a pupil of Professor Williams.

editor as "slightly later" than the twelfth century.[55] All told, there is sufficient variation in all four manuscripts to indicate that these existing copies are versions at some remove from the presumed twelfth-century period of original translation. Hughes has noted correctly a general affinity of the Irish versions of the *EN* with the texts of Tischendorf's D[abc] group, although D[a] is of doubtful value here as a witness since it represents Fabricius's composite text.[56] Generous space is given in Hughes's editorial commentary to comparison between Latin and Irish versions.

The titles given as headings or colophons for these texts suggest that Irish vernacular tradition associated the apocryphon with the person of Nicodemus. They are as follows:

YBL "Páis in choimdead 7 scéla a chrochta annso sís" ("Herewith the Passion of the Lord and the account of his Crucifixion");

Par "Stair Nicoméid 7 Ioséph de Armathia" ("The account of Nicodemus and Joseph of Aramithea");

LFF "Gurub í Sdair Nicométt ara páis conuigi sin" (colophon; "And thus far it is the account of Nicodemus concerning his Passion");

LCS "Conad hí Sdair Nicoméid ar páis Chríst connice sin" (colophon; "And this is the account of Nicodemus concerning the Passion of Christ up to this point").

This titular agreement—YBL excepted—is also borne out, as we shall see, by LB 1 and is hardly surprising if we consider the apparent relationship of these texts to each other. Hughes suggests that LFF and LCS can be grouped together by certain textual affinities and derive, at one or more removes, from the same translation which gave rise to YBL, to Par, and—by a slightly divergent path—to LB 1a (*EN* 1–12.1).[57]

The complete texts of the *GN* represented by the above titles do not pose any particular problems of manuscript context. The case is more complicated, however, for the first of the two remaining versions, LB 1, only the second half of which is given by Hughes (LB 1b).[58] It may, therefore, be useful—as a supplement to Hughes—to discuss LB 1

---

[55] Hughes, *Stair Nicoméid*, xii.

[56] Zbigniew Izydorczyk, "The Unfamiliar *Evangelium Nicodemi*," *Manuscripta* 33 (1989): 172–74.

[57] Though the scribe of YBL does not mention Nicodemus in the heading, all the Irish texts wrongly include the name of Nicodemus in the list of those who indicted Christ in chap. 1.1. This suggests that the suppression of his name as the author in the prologue occurred in the first Irish translation or in the Latin exemplar.

[58] Hughes, *Stair Nicoméid*, 80–99. Most of the contents of LB, including the *GN*, have been edited by Atkinson, *The Passions*; for the *GN*, see pp. 113–24, 359–71; 143–51, 392–400.

in greater detail before discussing the extant texts as a group. The LB manuscript dates from the early fifteenth century and preserves the most important collection of Irish homiletic materials surviving. The linguistic dating of the texts and of the assemblage of the constituent contents is a complicated issue which Hughes does not discuss. Instead, he follows an older discussion of the dating of Middle and Modern Irish texts by Dottin and Ó Catháin and considers our text as compatible with a twelfth century date of composition.[59]

The first of the two texts in LB, LB 1, is divided into two non-sequential sections in the manuscript and is found in the context of homiletic materials of some antiquity, all relating to the Passion and Resurrection (pp. 157–72 of the manuscript). The first segment (*EN* 1–13.1) is preceded by a long digest of biblical history and a piece on the holy places in Jerusalem from Bede's summary of Adamnán's *De locis sanctis*. It is introduced as *Passio Domini Iesu Christi incipit*. The translation bears a general family resemblance to the other versions edited by Hughes and listed above, including the misplacement of Nicodemus's name in chapter 1. This first half of the apocryphon is followed by a section, divided into two parts, comprising the Passion narrative of Matthew with some additions and commentary. On two occasions, this commentary utilizes material which we find in the LB 1a version of the *GN* (e.g., the names of Pilate's wife and the Good Thief); it also identifies the borrowings with the phrase "as Nicodemus relates." This Matthean Passion and Resurrection material in LB has been studied by Mac Donncha, who dated it to the eleventh century.[60] It was also his opinion that the person who wrote and arranged our LB 1a (*EN* 1–13.1) and the Matthean material in sequence—the same sequence which eventually found its way into the early fifteenth-century LB manuscript—is the person who must be considered as the author of the Irish *GN*.[61] Mac Donncha did not, however, date this translation, which is assigned by Hughes to the twelfth century on vague linguistic grounds.[62] The Matthew account of the Resurrection, using a four-fold method of exegesis, follows these items; then come texts on the

---

[59] See Hughes, *Stair Nicoméid*, xii, for relevant references. For more recent dating work on LB materials, see F. Mac Donncha, "Seanmóireacht in Éirinn ó 1000 go 1200," in *An Léann Eaglasta in Éirinn 1000 go 1200*, ed. M. Mac Conmara (Dublin: Clóchomhar, 1982), 77–85; B. Ó Cuiv, "Some Versions of the Sixth Petition in the Pater Noster," *Studia Celtica* 14–15 (1979–80): 212–22; and Uáitéar Mac Gearailt, review of *Stair Nicoméid*, edited by Ian Hughes.
[60] F. Mac Donncha, "Páis agus Aiseiri Chriost in LB agus in Ls 10," *Éigse* 21 (1986): 181.
[61] Ibid., 177.
[62] Hughes, *Stair Nicoméid*, xxii–xxiii.

Day of Judgement and a bilingual homily on Good Friday, before we
return to a translation of the second part of the *EN*, with somewhat
abbreviated chapters 14–24 (LB 1b), the whole recast as a homily on
the Resurrection. This second part of the *GN* is introduced by a homiletic preface which uses a traditional Easter pericope "Ero mors tua, o
mors, et morsus tuus o inferne" (Hos. 13:14; "I will be your death, o
death, and your portion, o hell"),[63] and concludes at *EN* 24 with a traditional homiletic "run" on the joys of heaven. The introduction specifically contrasts Hosea's prophecy as the testimony of "consecrated
Scripture" with the *Descensus* narrative of the resurrected dead, "as
Nicodemus relates." The clear distinction shows a strong awareness of
the status of the *GN* as an apocryphal text; it also reveals, albeit indirectly, the inherited titular affiliations of LB 1b, suggesting strongly
that the ultimate source is a complete text of the *EN*. The translation
does not, however, seem to belong to the same family grouping as LB
1a and the others above. We are left, then, with the question of why
and when the present LB collection acquired this second layer of *GN*
material from another translation project[64] and how it relates to yet a
third, later in the manuscript.

One can see from this detailing of the textual context in LB that
these earliest surviving translations of the *EN* have been absorbed,
reshaped, and transmitted by their homiletic setting. Numerous incidental additions to the text of the *GN* as found in LB 1a alone can also
be traced to the same homiliarizing tendency and probably should not
be taken as representing a variant Latin source text. The LB 1 versions
of the pseudo-gospel thus assume a place within an older Irish exegetical tradition and provide a series of appropriate Easter readings for an
Irish community which during the eleventh and early twelfth centuries
may well have been undergoing a process of ecclesiastical reform.[65]
In the process, the community may have wished to recopy, upgrade,
and supplement their existing resources of monastic readings.

LB contains yet another Irish text of *EN* 11–27 (LB 2),[66] this time

---

[63] The same pericope occurs in the pseudo-Augustinian homily 161 (PL
39:2062) and is noted by Izydorczyk, "The Unfamiliar *Evangelium Nicodemi*," 186,
in PL 40:1194.

[64] Hughes is of the opinion that LB 1b derives from a condensed version.

[65] The whole collection of homiletic materials in LB and the fragments of
other collections scattered throughout Irish manuscripts are badly in need of re-
editing and further study. Apropos reform issues, Mac Donncha pointed out
("Páis agus," 177) that there is a marked drop in Latin translation aptitude between the Matthean material in LB and the translation of *GN* LB 1. This would
imply that these two texts are separated in time from each other or derive from
different ecclesiastical centers.

[66] Hughes, *Stair Nicoméid*, 102–21.

as part of a series of pieces on devotion to the cross, a general manuscript context shared also by the YBL, Par, LFF, and LCS versions. The LB 2 version contains numerous omissions and is even more condensed than LB 1b; it represents the furthest departure from the Latin A (Tischendorf's D) type of text which seems to underlie all the others. Of note in LB 2 are the novel Latin headings to introduce the speeches of the various characters and the retention of some Latin tags in the body of the text. It seems that by chapter 20, the scribe of LB 2 has become doubtful of the value of his material and uncertain how to understand and present it. From the beginning, he is particularly concerned with controlling the various dramatis personae of the narrative and is uncomfortable with the material on hell and its denizens. He designates speakers after the speeches of Joseph (17.1) and, more extensively, reminds readers that the words of Christ at 24.1, are reported by the sons of Simeon. Twice in chapter 20 he glosses the speeches of Hell and Satan with "Habitatores Inferni, is friu atberar Ifernd sund 7 is friu ro labair diabul 7 is fri diabul atberar Ifernd .i. na pecdaig" ("It is the inhabitants of hell who are here called Hell, and it is they whom the devil addressed, and it is the devil who is called Hell, that is, the sinners").[67]

The number and variety of *EN* translations contained in LB is thus striking. One might further note the several additions to the text in LB 1a (detailed below). In this instance, the glossing of the *GN* from an unknown source or sources may well reflect a tradition similar to that described above, where the Matthean LB material is itself glossed by recourse to the *GN*. Perhaps in this LB sequence of texts we are seeing a collection that reflects a continuum of learned tradition in a specific milieu, possibly at the monastery or ecclesiastical center which received and disseminated the *GN* in Ireland. Any of the monasteries in the Killaloe diocesan sphere of reform, for example, with its relative openness to continental influence from the tenth to the twelfth century and with its obvious connections to the cultural zone from which the scribes of LB later gleaned their material, might then be a candidate.[68] This must remain on the level of speculation, however, and specific questions remain concerning LB as a witness to the *GN*. Did a single and complete Latin text come into an Irish center of translation activity where it was exploited in three stages during this period? During the

---

[67] I suspect that the gloss existed in LB 2's exemplar and that the second "atberar" has been misread from "atbertatar," "they spoke to."

[68] Donnchadh Ó Corráin, "Foreign Connections and Domestic Politics: Killaloe and the Ui Briain in Twelfth-century Hagiography," in *Ireland and Medieval Europe*, ed. D. Whitelock et al. (Cambridge: Cambridge University Press, 1981), 213–31.

first two stages, it was utilized in the creation of a cycle of homiletic
discourses related to the liturgy of Holy Week; the third has no such
coherent liturgical anchor. Further, only the first of these translations,
LB 1a, represents the continuing line of Irish translation of the apocryphon. It seems that our understanding of the reception of the *EN* in
Ireland and the early stages of its transmission will not be possible
until all textual variants have been taken into account and a clearer
picture emerges of Irish translation activities in general in the later
Middle Ages.

5. The Irish *Gospel of Nicodemus*: textual features

I should now like to look at some specific features of these Irish texts
of the *GN* under the following headings:

a)   introductions, conclusions, and proper names;
b)   additions to the texts not found in the Latin versions; and
c)   variations among manuscripts which may be of help in under-
     standing textual transmission from Latin to Irish or the rela-
     tionships among the Irish versions.

a) *Introductions, conclusions, and proper names.* Like the Latin texts of *EN*
A, the Irish versions provide one prologue only. LB 1a makes a number of adjustments throughout the introductory section in order to
effect a smoother narrative flow. Thus the status of the prologue as
such is not recognized, and all the material contained therein is fused
with the main narrative. All the Irish versions agree that the date of
the trial of Jesus was the 20th of March; possibly the simple error of
dropping a single digit of the date ("XX" instead of "XXI") may have
been made at, or just before, the entry point of the text into Irish
circles. Herod's son is either not named (LFF, LCS) or given as Teod-
(b)air (LB 1, YBL). It is just possible that this is an attempt to incorporate the imperial name Theodosius from a D-type residual prologue,
such as that printed by Kim. The names of the consuls do not appear,
Pilate in the analogous role of secular authority being brought up at
this point. In all the versions, the list of Christ's accusers and the
names of the high priests show some confusion. Annas is consistently
misread as "Amias"/"Amyas"/"Amiass" and consistently appears
with "Caeifas." Among the accusers, the name represented by the
Latin variants "Somas"/"Somne"/"Sobna" is always rendered as
"Aibime." In chapter 10, the Irish names of the two thieves are Dismus
and Ie/asmus, in contrast to the Dismas and Gestas of the Latin. At
17.3, there is some confusion in YBL concerning the sons of Simeon.
Their names are given as "Fairius 7 Leuitus" ("Karius 7 Leuitius," LFF,

The Gospel of Nicodemus in Ireland 381

LCS; "Carinus 7 Leontius," LB 1; "Carinus 7 Leuitius," LB 2) and identified as "these we mentioned above" when, in fact, only the LB texts follow the Latin and introduce the names earlier. In this respect it may also be of interest to note that of the Irish versions only LB 2 specifies that Carinus and Leucius wrote separately (EN 17.3) and that they gave their writings separately to the accusing Jewish party and to Nicodemus and Joseph (EN 27.1). Perhaps it is a sensitivity to the residual traces in the EN of its original role as an important text in the early understanding of the Jewish dimension of evangelization that caused the author of LB 2 to see the possibility of redesigning the text as an exhortation to repentance of sin. Where the YBL-type texts emphasize the epistolary valediction of the Latin, "Pax vobis ..." at 27, LB 2 has an intensification of the hortatory phrase, "Paenitentiam agere et misereatur uestri": "'And you Jews,' said the sons of Simeon, 'make confession and repentance and praise the Lord, and remission of your sins and all the evil which you have done, shall be granted to you.'"[69]

b) *Additions to the texts.* On the whole, the Irish texts of the GN tend to omit material which might be judged repetitious; thus the dialogues in hell tend to be shortened somewhat in all versions and extremely so in the two LB texts. On the other hand, early modern Irish prose style is such that stylistic expansions and doublings are frequent, creating much small-scale variety among the various manuscript versions of a text. Thus Irish scribes tend to be more "editorial"—indeed "auctorial"—in their handling of texts than we might otherwise expect by comparison with scribal behavior in other medieval vernacular traditions. The process has been aptly termed "compatible readings" by Gillies in his edition of an Irish Harrowing of Hell piece from a slightly later period.[70] Thus, for example, at chapter 3.1, Pilate's speech, "Testem habeo solem quoniam nec unam culpam inueni in homine isto ..." appears in Irish as, "I take the sun [expanded to "sun and moon" in LFF, reflecting the common Irish literary topos of the oath to the elements] as a witness that I cannot find any earthly cause of death, nor blame, nor sin in that holy man." The most significant additions to the base EN text are to be found in LB 1, and I have

---

[69] Hughes, *Stair Nicoméid*, 46–47, 120–21. Cf. the address of Christ to the saints in LB 2, chap. 24.1: "behold the devil, fettered and damned by the tree of the cross, for he damned you by the tree of lust" (EN 24.1, "qui per lignum et diabolum et mortem damnati fuistis, modo videte per lignum damnatum diabolem et mortem"). The YBL-type texts show variants here also, which may indicate that the EN texts circulating in Ireland differed from Tischendorf's D[b].
[70] William Gillies, ed., "An Early Modern Irish *Harrowing of Hell*," *Celtica* 13 (1980): 33–34.

already alluded to the function of these glosses. They comprise: at 2.1,
the name of Pilate's wife and an additional note on the demonic origin
of her dream; at 5.1, a longish exegetical gloss on the temple and its
symbolic meaning; at 10, a description of the robe of Christ (purple,
magical, woven by Mary, and still in existence), with details drawn
from an unidentified legendary or apocryphal source. LB 1 also glosses
the account of the drink offered to Christ in chapter 10:

> tucsat do Ísu sin for barr shlati. Atberair is-in scriptúir, co n-id
> aire ro-s-cuindig Ísu in dig-sea is-in croich .i. co ro-piantá i n-a
> uile ballaib, ar ni boi ball de cen pian fo leith acht a thenga
> nama; 7 co-ropianta i-side o'n fhinaicet.

> (they gave it to him on the top of a rod. In the Scripture it is
> said that Jesus asked for this drink on the cross that He might
> be tortured in all his members, for there was not a limb of
> Him that had not been separately tortured, save His tongue
> alone, so that it, too, might be tortured by the vinegar.)[71]

At 12.1, LB 1 has an exegetical additional gloss on the significance of
women as first witnesses to the Resurrection.[72]

Like the Latin, LB 1 does not gloss the actions of Longinus in
chapter 10. In the other manuscripts, however, the miracle of his healing is added. The fullest version occurs in LFF and LCS:

> Is and sin da éirich ridire dona ridirib diarbo comainm Loingi-
> nus .i. dall 7 is amlaid do boi 7 aenchlaredain aigi gan shuil
> na cinn. 7 tuc da gai mor fa chomuir a slis Isu amail do sheo-
> ladh dho uair nir dhughraic neach da facaidh Isu a goin. 7 do
> reathastair fo chetoir da thuind asa slis .i. tond fola 7 tond
> usce 7 an fuil do sil ar fut an gadh do cumail Loinginus da
> edan hi 7 da fasadar da suil glana gormglasa na cinn 7 mar
> do-connairc dreach Isu do creid do (LCS do gach ni da nderna
> 7 da-cuala uadha) 7 do iar trocairi fair 7 fuair gan fuireach.
> (LFF)

> (Then a certain soldier called Loinginus [sic], that is "blind,"
> came forward and this is the way he was. His face was one
> flat surface and he had no eyes in his head. With a great spear
> he struck the side of Jesus, as he had been instructed, for no-
> one who could see Jesus wished to wound him. Immediately

---

[71] Atkinson, *The Passions*, 121, 368.

[72] This gloss may be drawn from a "Good Women"-type list, such as that
printed by Th. M. Chotzen, "La 'querelle des femmes' au Pays de Galles," *Revue
celtique* 48 (1931): 66.

there flowed two streams from Jesus' side, a stream of blood and a stream of water. And Loinginus rubbed on his forehead the blood which ran down his spear. Then two clear grey eyes appeared in his head, and when he saw thus the face of Jesus, he believed in him [in everything which he did and had heard of him, LCS], and asked his mercy.)

Other minor glosses may be noted here as it may be possible to match them with a specific Latin prototype or, as seems more likely, with an Irish glossing tradition:

1) At chapter 4.5, YBL et al.[73] add to the Jewish accusers' "It is for this that we have come that he may find death," the further "7 co scríbthar a ainm isin pobul," "and that his name be written down amongst the people." LB has "co scristar a ainm as in popul," "that his name be struck from the people."[74] On balance, LB's reading seems more plausible.

2) At 9.2, all versions gloss manna, "maind," as "arán na n-aingel," "bread of angels," and add faith and guidance to the list of benefits which God provided the Jewish people in the past. At this juncture, LB 1 also adds a comment on the water from the rock, "co mblas mela 7 mescai fhína," "with the taste of honey and the intoxication of wine."[75] Here one might also ask if there is not an imaginative development from the trace of a gloss in the rendering of the Latin "de petra" as "asin carcair cloiche," "out of the stone prison," by all the versions except YBL, which has an awkward doublet "charraic chloichi," "the rock of stone."

3) At 13.1, we may have a trace of a lost glossing of distinctly Irish provenance in LFF's addition to the description of the moment of the Resurrection. To the Latin "facta est terre motio"—deriving ultimately from the important variants in Matthew's account of the Resurrection (28:1–2)—LFF adds "tainich teimeal mor tar in grein," "a great gloom came over the sun." This detail may well go back to an Irish exegetical tradition which explained the "uespere" in Matthew's version of the Resurrection as a grammatical variant of "uesper," and drew on Vergilius Maro to define it: "uesper quidem dicitur quoties sol nubibus aut luna ferruginibus quacumque diei uel noctis hora contegitur" ("evening is said to be whenever the sun is covered with clouds or the moon with gloom, at whichever time of day or night").[76]

---

[73] By "YBL et al." I designate YBL and the other versions in agreement with it.
[74] Atkinson, *The Passions*, 118.
[75] Ibid., 120.
[76] McNamara, "The Irish Affiliations," 319.

4) Hughes has noted the possible significance of the gloss shared by LB 1 and Par. at 10.1—"In ni ro scribus ro scribus e," "what I have written I have written it"[77]—as an indication of transmission contact between the LB 1 and Par texts, though it should also be noted that LB 1a has a number of extra glosses clustered at this point which are not reflected in Par.

c) *Variations among manuscripts.* Frequently minor textual variations can be instructive. The several transmitters of the text found certain passages in the *EN* somewhat difficult of comprehension, and there is evidence they frequently struggled to make the best sense they could. The following examples with commentary may be helpful in demonstrating the ways in which the modern reader of the Irish texts might exploit the information provided in Hughes's edition or, on occasion, supplement it.

1) The various versions of the episode of the standard bearers (at chap. 1.6), with some confusion between voluntary and involuntary standard lowering, are laid out by Hughes in his introduction and may be compared there.[78]

2) At 2.5, there is a misunderstanding of the Latin which involves all versions in confusion. Pilate's "Adiuro vos per salutem Caesaris" ("I adjure you by the safety of Caesar") becomes

YBL   "Guidhim sib guru lughaidi(s) amurus Chesair"
LFF   "Guidhimsea sibhsi (gu tugthaidh bar luidhi reisin) guma lughaid amharus C."
LCS   "Guidim sib (go tugthai bar luighe ris sin) guru lughaide amharus Ch."
Par   "Guidim sib go luigthi fo laim C."
LB 1 "Guidimm sib co ro-luigthi i fhiadnaise C."[79]

Here the Irish versions flounder when faced with the unfamiliar concept of swearing "per salutem Caeseris," and each successive version moves further away from the original formulation. It is obvious that LB 1 and Par have the better readings, coming close to the sense with "that it may be sworn in the presence of C." and "that it may be sworn by C.'s hand," respectively. YBL is emended here by Hughes, who adds the extra phrase (in parentheses) from LFF and LCS to give a translation, "I beg of you (that you may take an oath), so that C.'s doubt may be the less"; but the YBL scribe's correction of "lughaidi"

---

[77] Atkinson, *The Passions*, 121.
[78] Hughes, *Stair Nicoméid*, xviii–xxii.
[79] Atkinson, *The Passions*, 116.

to "lughaidis," "that they may swear," seems to indicate that the scribe had an idea that the sense of the passage required him to keep this word within the range of the verb "lugaid," "swears." LFF and LCS attempt to control the sense by reworking the verb from "lugaid," "swears," to "do-beir luige," "makes an oath," and by recycling the simple verb form as the comparative adjective, "lugaide," "the less." The translation of Herbert and McNamara points to a possible solution of the crux; by taking LFF "amharus" as "an arus" and translating "that you may swear in the house of C.," a possible prototype, "guidim sib go ro-luighthi an arus C.," may be proposed, from which YBL, LFF, and LCS derive.

3) In the same section, confusion of verbal forms and possible loss of text in the Latin may have been the cause of a corresponding loss of cogency in the Irish version.

Lat "xii isti creduntur/credunt quoniam non est natus de fornicatione; et maleficus, et dixit se esse filium Dei et regem, et nos non credimur/credimus" ("those twelve are believed / believe that he was born of fornication; he [is] a conjurer, and he said he was the son of God and king, and we are not believed / do not believe").

LB 1 "Cretmit do'n da fer déc ut co ro-p mac mna pósta Ísu, 7 cid ed a ra-bba, is duine démnacdu he, uair ader sé fen, 'is mac Dé 7 is rig he,' 7 ní chretmit-ne do."[80]

YBL "Creidmaid-ne in dana fer déc ["don da fear dheg," LCS] úd corob mac mná pósta Hísu 7 gid ead ar aba, is duine deamnagda . . . 7 ní chretmaid-ne dó."

(LB and YBL: "We believe [in] those twelve men, that Jesus was the son of a married woman; nevertheless, he is a devilish person—he himself said that he was the son of God and a king—and we do not believe in him.")

Here, in all versions, the Irish text starts out on the wrong foot by misreading the person of the first verb—the error possibly beginning with a misreading of the original contracted ending "creit dno," "they indeed believe"—and has to provide the logical disclaimer, "gid ead ar aba," "nevertheless," in mid-sentence thereafter.

4) A similar problem returns in 13.2, in rendering the Latin statement:

Lat "Dixerunt eis Iudaei, 'Uiuit Dominus quia non credimus uobis . . .'" ("The Jews said to them, 'As the Lord lives, we do not believe you . . .'").

---

[80] Ibid.

YBL " 'Is beo ar tigernai ám,' ar siad, '7 is 'na fhiadnaisi adearmaid uair ní chredmit a beag daíb-si . . .' " (" 'Our lord indeed lives,' they said, 'and we say it in his presence for we believe nothing from you . . .' ").

LFF "is beo ar tigerna dar siad 7 ni adeirmid uair ni cretmid abairt dibsi . . ." (" 'our lord lives,' they said, 'and we do not say for we do not believe a word from you . . .' ").

LB 2 " 'Darin coimdid mbíi,' ol siat, 'ro cretsibar do Críst. . . .' "

Here the clumsy attempt of YBL and LFF to make some sense of the enigmatic Latin, results in greater awkwardness; the LB 2 version does better by entering into the irony of the Jewish response with a freer and heartily sarcastic "By the living God, you believe in Christ!"

5) A further example raises the problems of a straightforward scribal misreading and consequent reinterpretation of a passage which, in the Latin text, is imaginatively daring and which reflects an early speculation about Christ's activities between his Resurrection and Ascension. This time it remains unclear whether the misreadings were in the received Latin text or in the transmission of the Irish. At 15.6, the account of Joseph's dream, we have,

Lat "suspensa est domus a quattor angulis. Et uidi Iesum sicut fulgorem et pre timore cecidi in terram. Et tenens manum eleuauit me de terra <et> ros aque perfudit me" ("and the house was suspended by the four corners. And I saw Jesus like a flash of light and I fell down upon the earth for fear. But Jesus laying hold on my hand lifted me from the ground <and> dewy water was shed on me").

LB 1b "tuarcabad dímm a n-airde ó cethri hullib tegdais na carcrach i rabá 7 at-connarc Ísu ocus sé taitnemach amal gréin, 7 do rocharsa fri talum for mét mo omain. Tánic Ísu chucum iar sin, cor gab mo láim 7 rom tócaib ó lár 7 ro ráid frim . . ." ("the roof of the prison, where I was, was raised up by the four corners, and I saw Jesus, shining like the sun, and such was the extent of my fear that I threw myself to the ground. Then Jesus approached me, and he took my right hand in his and raised me up and said to me . . .").

YBL "ad-chonnarc aingeal i ngach cearnaich don taich 7 Hísu i mmór-mheadón ["an tighe," LFF] eaturru. Tuarascbáil a dealraid imorro ní fétaim-sea a tabairt acht do thoites-sa[81] ["suighis 7 da cuiris mo gnúis," LFF] mo gnúis ria lár re heagla. Ro gab-som

---

[81] Both "gnúis" and "thoites" are marked as emended in Hughes's text but without comment.

mo láim ndaeis ina láim 7 do thógaib mé do lár 7 do chraith róss
["rossa," LFF] tarum ..." ("I saw an angel in each corner of the
house and Jesus in the middle of the house between them. I am
unable to describe his appearance to you, except to say that I
threw myself face downwards in fear. He took my right hand in
his and raised me up and sprinkled rose-water over me ...").

Here, the simple confusion of "angulis"/"angelos" is sufficient to give
rise to the Irish variants. That the version with "angulis" lies behind
LB 1b is clear and one may presume that the mistake is made in one of
the other versions' prototypes. One might also note that both LB 1 and
LB 2 avoid representing the more unconventional aspects of the
scene.[82]

6) At 18.1, the Latin description of the first intimation of the Harrowing is rendered by YBL as follows:

Lat "Nos cum essemus cum omnibus patribus nostris positi in pro-
fundo in caligine tenebrarum, subito factus est aureus solis calor
purpureaque regalis lux inlustrans super nos" ("When we were,
with all our ancestors, seated in the deep, in obscurity of darkness, on a sudden there came a golden heat of the sun and a
purple and royal light shining upon us").

YBL "Mar do bámar 'maraen rer n-aithreachaib 7 rer máithreachaib
suidithi i fudomain a ndorchataig Hifrind, do thsoillsich co thin-
disnach in ruithean gréni órda 7 in corthair rígda aireagda
["oiredha" LFF] oraind gur shoilléir cách uaind dá chéle. Adaich
Domnaich do shundrud." ("When we were, along with our
fathers and mothers in the deep, in the darkness of hell, suddenly there shone a golden ray of the sun and a royal silver
["golden" LFF] pillar [from the presumed original "corcair,"
"purple"] on us so that each of us was visible to the other. It
was Saturday night.")

Here YBL expands "patribus" to the rather touching "fathers and
mothers" but a later reading "máitrech," "mothers," in chapter 27,[83]
is an obvious error for "mbraitrech[aib]," "brethern," and this probably lies behind the reading at 18 as well. YBL adds lively detail, "we
were all visible to each other," to the description of the light of Christ.

---

[82] The term "ros aquae" is itself an awkward one in Latin—the meaning
"dew" is present in the Greek version—and Hughes assumes (*Stair Nicoméid*, 26–
27) that "ross"/"rossa" of the Irish texts is to be translated as "rose water." The
LFF "rossa" might, however, be intended as a form of "frossa," "water drops,
dew."
[83] Hughes, *Stair Nicoméid*, 46.898.

Only YBL has the next phrase, one which may have begun as a gloss but which Hughes mistranslates, "It was a Sunday night to be precise." The phrase is meaningless in this context; "adaich Domnai ch" should properly be, and is normally understood in Irish as, "Saturday night." The passage continues with Adam's statement:

Lat   "Lux ista auctor luminis sempiterni est, qui nobis promisit transmittere coaeternum lumen suum . . ." ("That light is the author of everlasting light who promised to send to us his co-eternal light . . .").

LB 1   "In soillsi-so athair na sollsi marthanaigi do gell dún a shollsi fén is í tic cucaind anois" ("This light, the Father of eternal light that promised his own light to us, it is this which comes to us now").

LB 2   " 'Is fír, is hé so,' ol sé, 'auctor 7 magistir na sollsi suthaine 7 na fírsollsi diada. Ocus iss í so,' ol sé, 'in tshollsi ro gell Dia athar dúinne . . .' " (" 'It is true,' he said, 'he is the author and master of eternal light and of true divine light. And this,' he said, 'is the light which God the Father promised to us . . .' ").

YBL   "Is í in tshoillsi sea [om. LFF] ugdar na soillsi suthaine do neoch ["ineoch," LFF] do gell a comshoillsi suthain féin .i. in t-athair neamda, do chur chucaindi dár fóirigthin . . ." ("This light is the author of the eternal light of him who promised to send his own, i.e., the heavenly Father's, eternal co-light sent to us, for our aid . . .").

Here the Irish versions, in following the syntactically strained Latin word by word, either reproduce the awkwardness of the original (LB 1), simplify sensibly (LFF), or attempt to regain control by thorough recasting (LB 2) or by adding a gloss (YBL).

    7) At times, the evidence of the existing versions allows one to be quite precise about the changes introduced and the successive stages of copying which lie between the present versions and the original translation. For example, at 24, YBL et al. have, "do slánaich ó lamaib diabail sib a uasalthraig 7 a rignaeim" ("he has saved you, O noble patriarchs and kingly saints, from the hands of the devil"), for Latin "salvavit sibi dextera eius et brachium sanctum eius" ("his right hand and holy arm have won him victory"). The original Irish translation almost certainly had "do slanaich a lam des [MS. "dē"] 7 a rignaem sib," where the only slippage from the Latin is in the mistranslation of the possessive pronouns ("sibi" as "sib"). The next redactor misinterpreted "a lam des," "his right hand," as "a lam demuin [MS. "dē " ?]," "from the hand of the devil"; in the extant versions "rignaem," "holy arm," is understood as "rígnaem," "royal saints," and the extra balancing phrase "uasalathraig," "noble fathers," is added, possibly as an

explanatory gloss which is then incorporated, thus completely trans-
forming the statement.

8) On a small scale, one may notice how a particular version may
acquire divergent readings by mistaking the readings of its Irish exemplar. Two examples of single manuscript variants are drawn from LFF.
Chapters 4.2 and 4.3 offer two instances of a misunderstood Irish
abbreviation "⁊"; "Luigmit fo seach," "we swear in turn," derives
from a form "fo sea⁊," easily mistaken for "fo seaᵧ̄," "by Caesar," in
the exemplar; "mo thia⁊sa ⁊ meiseirghi," "my coming and my Resurrection," must be a mistaken reading, through an intermediary phrase
"mo theᵧ̄-sa," for "mo chesad-sa ⁊ mo aiseirghi," "my Crucifixion and
my Resurrection," of the other versions.

Yet another translation issue is raised by the following example. At
6.2, in the account of the healing of the blind man, "vidi statim" ("I
saw at once") creates problems for the Irish translator as the Irish verb
"ad-cí," "sees," is not used intransitively. Hence the variants: YBL,
"ad-chondarc hé fo chétóir," "he saw him immediately"; and LB 1,
"itconnarc ní focetoir," "he saw something immediately."[84] Here, the
LB version relies on an older Irish usage of the indefinite object pro-
noun "ní" with expressions of hearing and seeing to denote an other-
worldly phenomenon, and is in its own way, a quite intelligent reading
of the original.

Modern translators of the Irish *Gospel of Nicodemus* also face the
problems of interpretation. At 2.5, for example, the phrase "dáil ar
domun" is translated by Hughes and by Herbert and McNamara as
"worldly assembly." This fits the general context of the dissenting
Jews' non-juring stance but "ar domun" normally renders the Latin
"denique," "anywhere." In LB 2, chapter 26, "dorus dess Parrduis" is
translated as "the fair door of Paradise," when the Latin, "ad dexteram
Paradisi" indicates rather a correct reading of "dess," "right," thus
"the right door."

In general, the quality of Latin to Irish translation in the Irish *GN*
is respectable and reflects a fair standard of translation competence.
The method by which the translation has thrown up variants reflects
a process of intelligent reading, supplemented by glossing, of difficulties which are then incorporated into the text. Where the purpose of
the translator is to condense his received text, this is done intelligently.
One such condensed passage in LB 1b, at chapter 23, may be singled
out for special comment because of its literary qualities and because it
foreshadows the way in which a specifically Irish rhetorical device is
used in a later Irish adaptation of the *GN*. The Latin speech of Infernus

---

[84] Atkinson, *The Passions*, 119.

to Satan, itself one of the rhetorical highlights of the *Descensus*, begins
with four epithets and is organized as an address in four phases. The
Irish speech dispenses with four divisions and expands the list of initial curses in a series marked by alliteration and an attempt at abece-
darian organization:

> A oirchindig [leg. airchindig] na malarta [princeps perditio-
> nis], a thaísig in tairmtechtais [dux exterminationis?], a uctair
> [leg. auctair] in báis, / a bunad in díumais, / a cind na n-uli
> n-olc, a chotarsna, / a doeráin dúr-cride dicondircil, a dona
> deróil dobil díumsaig díscir daermitnig, a angbaid anfhéil
> imresnaig imchosaitig, a duine aimnertaig. . . .

> (O chief of mischief, leader of transgression, author of death,
> origin of pride, head of all evils, adversary, hard-hearted and
> merciless enslaver, wretched, insignificant, proud, shameless,
> contemptible, fierce, dishonorable, contentious, quarrelsome,
> listless person. . . .)

6. Hiberno-Latin elaborations of the *Evangelium Nicodemi*

It is clear that abbreviated and individual literary refashionings of the
EN, in particular of the *Descensus* section, circulated in Ireland from the
thirteenth century on. Lewis has recently edited one such Latin version
from an early fourteenth-century manuscript belonging to the Dominican convent in Limerick and containing other texts of distinctly Hiberno-
Norman interest.[85] As the editor notes, the account is typical of later
medieval reshapings of the *EN* in that the focus is on Joseph of Arimathea and the Harrowing of Hell. That it was composed and written in
Ireland is assumed by the editor, who notes that chapters 13 and 16 are
also omitted in LB 1.[86] Certainly the homiletic-type ending on the joys
of heaven is similar to a number of Irish homiletic runs in LB,[87] but
we simply do not know enough about the circulation of texts between
Gaelic and other religious houses in medieval Ireland to claim any
certain connection.

---

[85] David J. G. Lewis, "A Short Latin Gospel of Nicodemus Written in Ireland," *Peritia* 5 (1986): 263–75.

[86] Ibid., 266 n. 12.

[87] The homiletic recasting of the *Descensus* in LB (Atkinson, *The Passions*, 151,
400) has this form.

7. Two Irish texts on the Harrowing of Hell

There are also a number of rather free renderings of the *Descensus* material into Irish from late medieval Ireland, which in their several ways are indices of distinctive trends in the range of Irish religious writing in general in the period. Gillies has produced an edition of a *Harrowing of Hell* which survives in two manuscript versions.[88] He has summarized its content as follows:

> [It] gives only a brief resumé of events leading up to the Descent, a description of Christ's appearance as He approached Hell and of the innumerable torments endured by the captive souls, followed by two notes on the administrative hierarchy of Hell and on the duration of the captivity; and it then concludes rather abruptly with the breaking of the gates of Hell and the release of its inmates. On the other hand, this rhetorical framework is bulked out by the adoption of an extremely full rhetorical style, which dwells minutely on such points as Christ's wounds, the ferocity of his onset and, above all, on the description of Hell.[89]

This text is, then, an example, more striking than any we have hitherto encountered, of a native Irish literary development. As with many other Irish heroic or saga-type treatments of hagiographical subjects and religious themes, it also employs a mixed prose/verse format. The verses quoted in the text, however, are ascribed in general terms to "the author," "the heroic gospel," "the poet," "the latinist." None of the verses are quoted at length and none are older than the prose text itself. The editor has compared the description of hell to other Irish literary tours-de-force on the same subject and notes the particular contribution of this author to the topos.[90] To the Irish literary device of the alliterative prose "run" involving a series of adjectives, our author adds a further complicating abecederial arrangement. Here is some of the sequence running from 'g' to 'l':

> gormhsluagh [sic] gruamdha grancshūileach grāineamhail ['g]ā nguailghrīoschadh, 7 ilphiasda ingneacha āighthighi īchtair Ifrind ag imriosin 'mā n-iona<r>thra<igh>ibh, 7 ceith-

---

[88] Gillies, "An Early Modern Irish *Harrowing of Hell*"; signaled by McNamara, *The Apocrypha*, 71, no. 59A.

[89] Gillies, "An Early Modern Irish *Harrowing of Hell*," 32.

[90] For an account, with bibliography, of Irish descriptions of hell, see McNamara, *The Apocrypha*, 126–43, nos. 99–108.

earn chearrbhach chuirrcioch chretriabhach chosfhada ag ciorr-
bha[dh] na gclaon 7 na gcolach, 7 leōmhain loindmheara
lasamhla loinnerdha lasshūilecha līmhfhiaclacha leadurthacha
ac loitleadradh na laochanmann . . .

(a surly, mean-eyed, hateful dark host making them blaze on
coals, and the clawed, fearsome monsters of lowermost Hell
writhing around their entrails, and a hacking, crested, brindle-
chested, long-legged troop lacerating the wicked and the sinful, and eagerly-lively, blazing, brilliant, fiery-eyed, whet-
toothed, mangling lions savaging the gallant souls . . .)

In this type of rhetorical exuberance, Gillies sees the influence of
much older types of Irish Latin hymnodic forms. Certainly one senses
underneath the extravagant rhetoric a familiarity with an exegetical
context for devotional ideas on the Passion and Resurrection. Thus the
text begins with the familiar Irish exegetical practice of invoking time
and place, the latter—Jerusalem—being embroidered with an Irish
locational triad. Later, the analogy of Jonah is used competently, and
the dramatic description of the risen Christ still bearing his wounds is
theologically correct. Gillies notes also the resemblance between the
description of Christ rousing himself for battle and similar epic topoi
in Irish homiletic tradition. He also sees in some of the descriptive
terms used to refer to Christ's Harrowing of Hell other nativist tenden-
cies; for example, "orcuin," "destruction," is a formal tale category in
early Irish literature, and "derg-ruathar," "red onslaught," is a fairly
common term in early modern Irish saga titles. The editor considered
as premature any detailed analysis of the relationship of the piece to
the EN until such time as all Irish translations of the EN should be
available, but he suggested that the author drew on a general familiarity with elements of the apocryphal tradition and need not have de-
pended on a specific source. Despite the frequent references to "the
author," there is little to link the text directly with the EN. The description of Christ's breaking down the doors of hell is, perhaps, the closest
to the matter of the EN. Here one can venture to improve on Gillies's
understanding of the text. The statement "7 adbert ["+" in margin]
amhail tug a throighthi rē trēndorus treaphurdhaingean tromchomhla-
dhach tuaidhIfrinn tollite [emended by Gillies to "tollte"] gu tend
tulbhorb tolgdha trēbhriathrach" is read by Gillies as: "And . . . has
related how He put His feet to the secure, firm, heavy-valved strong
door of cavernous-hot northern Hell, firmly and full fiercely, forcefully
and imperiously." But it seems better, despite some awkwardness of
syntax, to give "tollite" its full *Descensus* resonance and translate:
"And he said—as he put his foot firmly to the secure, heavy-valved,
strong door of northern Hell—'Tollite,' firmly and full fiercely in a

threefold formulation." This text then, despite its nativist rhetoric, is more closely connected to a Latin model than Gillies allowed. A second short treatment of the Harrowing of Hell occurs in a manuscript (London, BL MS. Addit. 30512) from a prolific fifteenth-century scribe and translator, Uilliam Mac an Legha.[91] The text seems to consist of two distinct parts, and the second half is to be found circulating as an independent piece in two other manuscripts: in LCS mentioned above and in the early seventeenth-century BL MS. Egerton 137 as part of the Irish translation of the pseudo-Bonaventuran *Meditationes vitae Christi*, a textual pairing also found in English fifteenth-century manuscripts. Flower has summarized the contents of this piece as follows:

> ... a brief prologue relating the fall of man. The scene then changes to Hell, where Satan, fearing that Christ will come to harrow Hell, summons the Seven Deadly Sins in order to discover whether Christ has ever succumbed to their temptations. The Sins relate the story of Christ's resistance to their solicitations and His life on earth. Satan commits them to the depths of Hell once more, and Christ enters. There follows an altercation between Christ and Satan as to the right of possession since Adam's fall, at the conclusion of which Christ carries off the souls.[92]

Flower called attention to some general resemblances between this Irish treatment of the Harrowing and the late medieval English *Deuelis Perlament*[93] and concluded, as did the editor J. E. Caerwyn Williams, that the Irish texts must be related to an English source similar to the *Deuelis Perlament*. The introduction of the Deadly Sins is novel in the Irish piece though only three Sins actually speak. Both Flower and Williams assumed that the longer text in Addit. 30512 is a single unified narrative and that the other two derive from it, but McNamara has shown, by noting the contrast between the use of "Satan" in part 1 and "Diabul" in part 2, that Addit. 30512 is itself a composite text.[94] The

---

[91] Edited by J. E. Caerwyn Williams, "An Irish Harrowing of Hell," 44–78; McNamara *The Apocrypha*, 74–75, no. 61. For Mac an Legha, see Robin Flower, *Catalogue of Irish Manuscripts in the British Museum*, vol. 2 (London: Printed for the Trustees [W. Clowes], 1926), 473–74; idem, *The Irish Tradition*, 123–24, 132–33; and Andrew Breeze, "The Charter of Christ in Middle English, Welsh and Irish," *Celtica* 19 (1987): 118.

[92] Flower, *Catalogue*, 499.

[93] F. J. Furnivall, ed., *Hymns to the Virgin and Christ, "The Parliament of Devils" and Other Religious Poems* ... , EETS OS, vol. 24 (London: K. Paul, Trench, Trübner, 1867). See also above, pp. 245–47.

[94] McNamara, *The Apocrypha*, 75.

altercation between Christ and Satan in the second half, which is common to all three, is tacked on to a text resembling the *Deuelis Perlament*.
If one compares all three pieces, it is clear that the number of scribal
errors, changes, and omissions in the second part is such as to indicate
an indirect transmission relationship among them. Williams's suggestion that Mac an Legha himself may be the author of the piece in
Addit. 30512 must be modified; it cannot apply to the second part, and
the words cited as typical of Mac an Legha's usage elsewhere all occur
in the first half. Some auctorial control over the whole is, perhaps, evidenced by the fact that the change from "Satan" to "Diabul" is already
anticipated towards the end of the first part.[95] The suggestion that the
Deuelis Perlament-type text may derive from an English source points
to a comparatively new phenomenon in fifteenth-century Irish devotional writing. Indeed, Mac an Legha himself is the best example we
have of an Irish scribe extensively involved in translating works from
English for his Anglo-Irish patrons, the Butlers.

8. The Book of Fermoy

A poem in thirty-seven quatrains in the fifteenth-century Book of
Fermoy shows another way in which the *EN* material was incorporated
into Irish literary tradition.[96] Here the formal model is the eulogistic
praise poem, the acts of Christ being generally seen in religious bardic
verse as heroic in character. Hence the feat of the Harrowing can be
described in a way similar to the victorious "caithréim" or battle cam-
paign apotheosis of a native Irish lord. The narrative and dialogic
demands of the source Harrowing of Hell traditions are incorporated
into this. The relationship of the piece with the *EN* is only of the most
general kind, however. Precedents for the present poem's interest in
the seduction and Fall of Eve can be found in Irish vernacular literature: in the tenth-century *Saltair na Rann* and in the related and widely-
circulated prose biblical narratives.[97] By introducing the theme of the

---

[95] It would seem, from its incipit and length, that the unedited text in the
seventeenth-century Irish Manuscript, Brussels, Bibliothèque royale MS. 20978–9
(McNamara, *The Apocrypha*, 72, no. 59C) is another version of this text on the Harrowing. To this may now be added Maynooth Ls. G 1, fol. 81v. It is also possible
that the Life of Christ in the seventeenth-century paper part of Trinity College,
Dublin MS. H 2 17, p. 61, contains a *Descensus* segment, but the microfilm available to me of this manuscript is almost entirely illegible.
[96] O. Bergin, ed., "The *Harrowing of Hell* from the Book of Fermoy," *Ériu* 1
(1904): 112–19.
[97] McNamara, *The Apocrypha*, 14–19, nos. 1–1B, 7.

Fall and retaining the story of the quest of Seth, the poem succeeds in providing a new balance of interest between the two paradise micro-narratives as poles of reference. Smaller hellish details, such as the bellows and hammers of the tormenters, show the added influence of the description of hell topos, seen at work in the piece discussed above (sect. 7). That the theological problems of the Harrowing are still a lively subject of dispute in late medieval Ireland may be inferred from quatrains 34–35:[98]

> Atáit dáine ga rádh rind
> d'feruibh lóghmhura in léghinn.
> nach tuc as acht drong do dligh,
> in cass donn dona dáinib.

> Dáine ele rind gá rádh,
> ag nach fuil credemh comhlán,
> nach fuil duine, geal ná gorm,
> nochar ben uile a hiforn.

> (There are some among distinguished men of learning who tell us that the brown curly-haired One brought forth no men but those who merited it.

> Others, who have not perfect faith, tell us that there is no man white or black that He did not bring out forth, one and all, out of Hell.)

9. Bardic religious verse

Given the number of manuscript witnesses to the translation of the *EN* and the number of adaptations of the work in medieval Ireland, given also its compatibility with heroic themes in general, one might expect the Harrowing to be a favorite subject in the vast corpus of bardic religious verse which, in other respects, loves to dwell on the military aspects of Christ's saving acts. Surprisingly, however, the theme is little used.[99] It is briefly evident in the work of the thirteenth-century poets,

---

[98] Gillies, "An Early Modern Irish *Harrowing of Hell*," 54, has also noted a similar interest in this theological question in the interpolation on Judas in the F version of the text on the Harrowing discussed in sect. 7 above.

[99] Apart from the examples which I discuss, the theme is touched on in the following poems printed by Lambert McKenna in *Dioghluim Dána* (Dublin: Oifig an tSoláthair, 1938), nos. 38, qq. 5–8; 41, q. 41; 60, qq. 37–38, and in *Aithdioghluim Dána*, 2 vols., Irish Texts Society, vol. 37 (Dublin: Educational Co. of Ireland, 1939–40), nos. 55, q. 6; 56, q. 4; 58, q. 18; 60, qq. 12–13; 63, qq. 7–13, 18; 65, q. 32; 66, qq. 7, 9, 14, 25; 70, q. 21; 71, q. 13; 77, qq. 27, 38; 78, q. 4; 79, q. 18; 86, qq. 5–8, 23; 92, q. 19; 98, qq. 9, 15, 27, 29–31.

Donnchadh Mór Ó Dálaigh[100] and Giolla Brighde Mac Con Midhe,[101] and sporadically thereafter, but none of the great hymns to the holy cross—to take a relevant example—utilizes it to any extent. In Donnchadh Mór's poem on the Passion, the brief reference occurs in the context of the formula of the leaps of Christ, popular in insular circles:[102]

> Léim i nIfearnn uch do bhroid
> bith-shearbh do chruth is do chuid
> fuarais gliaidh is tóir 'mun troid
> gus an mbruid móir 'n-a dhiaidh dhuid.[103]

(The leap into hell—what a raid!, dread your appearance and your inheritance. You gained victory and a following from that fight, that great booty following behind you.)

In his famous poem, Giolla Brighde expresses the theme in the following manner:

> Maidin Domhnaigh Cásg don Choimdhidh
> ar gcreich ifirn 's a fhuil te;
> cosmhail bás do bharr na cruinne
> is crann lás a dhuille de.
>
> Fa phrímh do éirigh a hifiorn—
> nir fheidhm dó 's ní dhearna luas;
> Dia ar fhud na huamhadh re hothaigh,
> go rug sluaghadh sochraidh suas.
>
> . . . .
>
> Croich an rí do-rad a hiofurn
> —d'fhiora an bheatha ní bó dhíosg.[104]

(Sunday morning was the Lord's Easter when he harried hell with his blood still warm; similar was the death of the Lord of the universe to a tree that sheds its leaves.

---

[100] Lambert McKenna, ed., *Dán Dé: The Poems of Donnchadh Mór Ó Dálaigh and the Religious Poems in the Duanaire of the Yellow Book of Lecan* (Dublin: Educational Company of Ireland, 1922); for the poet, see introduction, viii.

[101] Giolla Brighde Mac Con Midhe, *The Poems of Giolla Brighde Mac Con Midhe*, ed. N. J. A. Williams, Irish Texts Society, vol. 51 (Dublin: Irish Text Society, 1980).

[102] Cf. Andrew Breeze, "The 'Leaps' That Christ Made. Varia VI," *Ériu* 40 (1989): 190–93, who, however, is not quite accurate in his interpretation of these quatrains.

[103] McKenna, *Dán Dé*, pp. 62, 137, no. 29, q. 22.

[104] Giolla Brighde, *The Poems*, pp. 236–40, no. 21, qq. 6–7, 13cd.

At prime he arose from hell—it was no effort to him and he
did not hurry; God was for a time through the caves [of hell]
until he brought up a hosting by way of inheritance.

. . . .

The king set up his cross in hell—to the men of the world it
was not a cow without milk.)

In the fifteenth century, the Harrowing of Hell motif resurfaces
briefly in the work of the prolific Tadhg Óg Ó hUiginn and his kinsmen Tuathal[105] and Pilip Bocht.[106] In Tuathal's poem 20, quatrain
18, there is reference to the two parties, accusers and defenders, at
Christ's trial, slight evidence that the *Gesta Pilati* section of the *EN* was
available to bardic poets. Here, as elsewhere, the motif of the healing
of Longinus is such a favorite of bardic verse as hardly to warrant
comment. Of this fifteenth-century material, the references in the
poems of friar Pilip Bocht Ó hUiginn may serve as exemplary for the
tradition as a whole. In the first example, a general plea for help and
forgiveness is encoded in a combination of various traditions about the
cross: the four constituent woods and the finding of the true cross.[107]
The first section of the poem concludes with a general summing up:

Tug dá shiol ó shin
nach bíodh is-tigh thuas
glóir nach tug ar tús
rug an chóir ó chruas
páis Dé is ann do fhás
nír bh'é an crann gan chnuas

Ag Ifearn mon-uar
ar mbithshealbh do bhíodh
rugadh an cheo ar gcúl
tugadh gá teo gníomh
t'oigheirbe ar an fhál
a romheirge an ríogh[108]

(To the children of that tree who had not yet gone to heaven
he gave a glory which had formerly been withheld. This was
no barren tree for on it grew God's Passion wresting justice
from severity.

---

[105] McKenna, *Dán Dé*, pp. 18, 86, no. 9, q. 30; and pp. 36–37, 103–5, no. 20, qq.
18, 28–29, 40–41, 45.
[106] *Pilip Bocht Ó hUiginn*, ed. Lambert McKenna (Dublin: Talbot Press, 1931),
pp. 11, 135, no. 3, qq. 19–20; pp. 22, 142, no. 5, sts. 28–31.
[107] McNamara, *The Apocrypha*, pp. 76–78, no. 63, and pp. 78–79, no. 65.
[108] No. 5, sts. 30–31.

Alas! Hell had retained our inheritance; but then the mist was dispelled and—no fiercer onslaught—the ramparts of hell were completely destroyed, o great royal standard.)

The second example from Pilip Bocht's work is unfortunately much mutilated in its manuscript so that we lack eight relevant quatrains. But the general play of metaphors is of interest here:

Bualadh a bhuille báire
don chruinne is sluagadh sídhe
ag cora ar gcean i n-úire
núidhe bhfola an cneadh chíghe.

. . . .

I n-asgaidh uile dhúinne
an macsain Muire móire
ní thug gá céim as cruaidhe
léim na huaidhe rug róinne

Dá ghaol fa gadhar tathfuinn
tamhan an dá chraobh gcomhchruinn
go rug léim ar leirg Ifrinn
mar dhrithlinn ndeirgréidh rothruim[109]

(His triumphant blow is as a hosting of fairy folk against the world; recalling our sins the breast wound bleeds afresh.

. . . .

Not without hope of return for us did the son of great Mary leap—was ever a step harder?—into the grave before us.

That tree-trunk composed of two co-equal stocks was like a hound chasing his folk; he leaped onto the massive ramparts of hell like an overpowering blazing red flame.)

Here we begin with an apocalyptic reference to the final destruction of the world, with an image from Irish secular saga—and still current folklore—of the destroying otherworld host. In folklore, as here, the theme shades into the motif of the fairy hurling game which requires that a hero from outside intervene in order that victory be achieved. Thus quatrain 19, with its image of Christ as the hound in the "game," carries an evocation of the great Ulster hero and savior of his people, Cú Chulainn ("the hound of Culann"), who, in the *Táin Bó Cuailnge*

---

[109] No. 3, qq. 4, 18–19.

saga, intervened with such irresistible force in the game at the court of the Ulster king.[110] Combined with this is the topos of the leaps of Christ. The theme of the hero who leaps across the ramparts recalls the specific saving gesture of Lugh, the divine savior of Tara in Irish mythological tradition.[111] Finally, the sequence of adjectives describing Christ as a flame recalls that specific Irish rhetorical drift in the Harrowing of Hell tradition which we have already seen in the piece edited by Gillies.

Such a figured and mannered condensation of traditional ideas is typical of religious bardic verse as a whole. Elision and tangential allusion are its methods of exposition and the mark of its refinement; in such a style, a long drawn-out narrative of Christ's adventures in hell would not be attractive to a poet. The striking phrase and the theological and exegetical underpinnings alone are utilized. Furthermore, an inherited totalizing apocalyptic focus becomes a theologically and devotionally *sine qua non* of religious bardic verse, in which the salvational emphasis generally falls on the relationship between Christ's Passion and his second coming at the Last Judgement, on the one hand, and sinful humanity's proper response, on the other. In such a focus, the Harrowing of Hell is squeezed out of the frame, so to speak, and appears only sporadically as a marginal flourish to a cluster of devotional ideas perceived to be already balanced and complete.

By the beginning of the seventeenth century, Ireland is in crisis and the native cultural milieu irretrievably in decline. Paradoxically, it is in these years that the final and agonizing urgencies of Gaelic culture *in extremis* find both a secular and religious voice of great power. A brilliant phase of literary productivity briefly ensues. But the period when an apocryphal gospel could be mined to devotional purpose for its doctrinal aptness and striking rhetorical figures is drawing to a close. Typical of the waning attraction of such material is its weak theological echo in a poem possibly by an Ó hUiginn archbishop of Tuam at the beginning of the seventeenth century:

Tig ar ar gceann — fa céim oirrdheirc —
oidhre Dé do nimh a-nall;
creach na Cásg gibé dar beanadh
is é an grásd dob fheadhan ann.[112]

---

[110] Cf. Cecile O'Rahilly, ed., *Táin Bó Cuailnge. Recension 1* (Dublin: Dublin Institute for Advanced Studies, 1976), 15–17, 36–37.

[111] Cf. the poem of Gofraidh Fionn Ó Dálaigh, edited by Bergin in *Essays and Studies Presented to William Ridgeway on His Sixtieth Birthday, 6 August 1913*, ed. E. C. Quiginn (Cambridge: University Press, 1913), 323–32.

[112] McKenna, *Aithdioghluim Dána*, pp. 294, 180, no. 77, q. 38.

(God's Son came down from heaven—glorious that coming!—
His grace was the troop which made the Easter-raid, whoever
they were who were taken.)

By this time the Counter-Reformation is well under way in Ireland and
a new standard of religious propriety in devotional writing is becom-
ing the norm. The themes of the *Gospel of Nicodemus* survive, however,
as do so many medieval religious themes of this kind in Ireland, in
popular songs and folklore. Angela Partridge has made a study of popular Passion laments in Ireland and notes the ample use therein of our
themes.[113] She also notes that the very popular theme of the cock
crowing from the cooking pot to announce the Resurrection, first found
in the Greek B-versions of the *Acts of Pilate*, made its way into late
medieval legends in the West.[114] Perhaps our survey may fittingly
conclude with the naive but no less appealing last lines of one of these
songs, "Toradh na Paíse" ("The Fruits [recte "hunt"] of the Passion"):

D'éirigh an t-éinín a bhí in iochtar na coille,
Do ghread a sciatháin agus do ghlaoidh ar Mhac Muire;
D'éirigh Mac Muire ó lic na péine,
Is do chuaidh sé go Limbó go dtí sna hAithreacha Naomhtha;
Do thug sé leis iad ag caitheamh an fhéasta
San áit nár ghádh dhóibh biadh ná éadach,
Cl mh ná pluidí chun codlata 'dhéanamh;
Solus geal Dé chugainn, agus suan síorraidhe na bhFlaitheas go
bhfaghaidh ár n-anam le chéile. . . .[115]

(The little bird rose from the bottom of the wood,
He shook his wings and called on the son of Mary;
The son of Mary rose from his bed of pain,
And he went to limbo, to the holy patriarchs;
He brought them out with him to consume the feast,
In the place where they lacked neither food nor clothing,
Feather-beds or quilts to be able to sleep soundly;

---

[113] Angela Partridge, *Caoineadh na dTrí Muire* (Dublin: An Clóchomhar Tta, 1983), 72–75.

[114] Ibid., 73.

[115] Ibid., 223. The text printed by Partridge is a composite Northern text, first collected and edited by my late kinsman Fr. L. Murray (*An tUltach*, Nollag, 1936, 11–13). The word "coille," "wood," in the first line quoted may be an error for "coire," "pot," thus a reference to the cock crowing motif above. Another version, from West Clare (Partridge, *Caoineadh na dTrí Muire*, 226), fills out line three above with, "D'iompair sé an Chroich go ndeachaidh go geatai Eifrinn, Gur réab sé na geataí óna chéile," "He carried his Cross to the gates of hell, and he tore the gates apart."

May the bright light of God come to us and may our souls
enjoy the eternal rest of heaven together. . . .)

However naive this may seem as a devotional statement, one can still
see the underlying frame of the source apocryphon, and no one can
doubt its adequacy or sincerity as a simple expression of faith. For an
impoverished peasantry, the belief that the joys of heaven are now
open to all believers because of the triumph of Christ over hell carries
all the connotations of a socially powerful wish-fulfilment, of a desire
for a world more equitable than this present dispensation. This popular song appropriates the essentials of the *EN*'s themes in a manner
that fully realizes their ancient emotional and imaginative attraction
and affords a living clue to the phenomenon of their longevity.

The *Gospel of Nicodemus* in the Literature of Medieval Wales

DAVID N. KLAUSNER

he poets of medieval Wales had a particular fondness for the apocryphal and legendary texts which formed an expansion of and commentary on the canonical Scriptures. The religious poetry of the *gogynfeirdd*, the "relatively early poets," who wrote under the patronage of the native Welsh princes of the twelfth and thirteenth centuries, abounds in apocryphal, frequently numerological, themes: the five ages of the world, the fifteen signs before Doomsday, the number of Christ's wounds.[1] Descriptions of hell are frequent and are often linked to a penitential mode. Such an atmosphere provided a rich and fertile soil for the *Evangelium Nicodemi*, and yet the mechanism by which the poets came into contact with this material requires some consideration.

The *gogynfeirdd* "for the most part must have been monoglot Welshmen"; moreover, there is no evidence prior to the fifteenth century of Welsh poets with clerical education.[2] Although the historical sources for bardic training are extremely thin, the norm seems to have been some form of apprenticeship. Whether this was generally an individual training based on the relationship between bard and student, or whether bardic schools existed, is a moot point. Several of the poets speak of themselves as teachers, but this instruction must have been

---

[1] The *gogynfeirdd*, or as they are also (and more precisely) known, the *Beirdd y Tywysogion*, "Poets of the Princes," wrote under the patronage of the native Welsh leaders between about 1100 and the loss of independence in 1282. Poems by thirty-five of them have survived, a total of about 12,500 lines, of which three-quarters is devoted to the praise of patrons. Their religious poetry is largely penitential. The themes of medieval Welsh religious poetry are discussed generally by D. Simon Evans, *Medieval Religious Literature* ([Cardiff:] University of Wales Press, 1986), 16–33, and Andrew Breeze, "The Number of Christ's Wounds," *Bulletin of the Board of Celtic Studies* 32 (1985): 84–91.

[2] J. E. Caerwyn Williams, "Medieval Welsh Religious Prose," in *Proceedings of the First Celtic Congress, 1963* (Cardiff: University of Wales Press, 1966), 66.

largely, perhaps entirely, oral.[3] By the early fourteenth century there seems to have developed some interest, in addition to the complex techniques of native Welsh poetry, in the art of grammar as it was understood in the schools of western Europe, and Welsh versions of the grammar of Donatus (known as "dwned" in Welsh) began to appear for the use of poets without Latin. The first of these which has survived dates from about 1322–1327, and is clearly a clerical production, associated with the name Einion Offeiriad ("Einion the Priest").

Despite the poets' interest in religious narrative and scriptural motifs, it seems unlikely that their knowledge of Scripture was extensive. Very little of the canonical Scriptures was translated into Welsh until the sixteenth century and, although the poets were familiar enough with the names and stories of the Bible, preaching, liturgy, and pictorial sources seem much more likely sources for this familiarity than knowledge of the scriptural texts themselves.[4] This mode of transmission is much more difficult to gauge in Welsh than in English because of the complete lack of surviving sermons. Glanmor Williams suggests that it is nonetheless possible to extrapolate the existence of a vernacular sermon tradition: "It can be argued that a people which set such store by the arts of rhetoric and declamation, and which could produce such outstanding preachers in Latin as Thomas Wallensis and John Wallensis, would hardly have been utterly indifferent to pulpit oratory."[5]

Considering the poets' interest in apocryphal themes, it is surprising that no Old Testament apocrypha were translated into Welsh, though some Old Testament midrash does survive in early versions.[6] A far greater range of New Testament apocrypha and pseudepigrapha appears in Welsh versions, including two apocryphal gospels, the *Pseudo-Matthaei evangelium*, and the *Evangelium Nicodemi (EN)*.[7] Other

---

[3] Ceri W. Lewis, "The Court Poets: Their Function, Status and Craft," in *A Guide to Welsh Literature*, ed. A. O. H. Jarman and Gwilym Rees Hughes (Swansea: C. Davies, 1976), 140.

[4] Among the passages from the canonical Scriptures which appear in Welsh translations are Jn. 1:1–14 and Matt. 27:1–28:7, as well as versions of the Ten Commandments and the Lord's Prayer. The late fourteenth-century text known as *Y Bibyl Ynghymraec* would suggest a Welsh version of the Bible, but it is largely an adaptation of the *Promptuarium Bibliae*. It does, however, contain Welsh translations of Gen. 1:1–2 and 2:21–23. See Thomas Jones, "Pre-Reformation Welsh Versions of the Scriptures," *The National Library of Wales Journal* 4 (1946): 97–114.

[5] Glanmor Williams, *The Welsh Church From Conquest to Reformation* (Cardiff: University of Wales Press, 1976), 510.

[6] John Jenkins, "Medieval Welsh Scriptures, Religious Legends, and Midrash," *Transactions of the Honourable Society of Cymmrodorion* (1919–20): 95–140.

[7] Mary Williams, "Llyma Vabinogi Iessu Grist," *Revue celtique* 33 (1912): 184–248; J. E. Caerwyn Williams, "Efengyl Nicodemus yn Gymraeg," *Bulletin of the*

apocryphal texts translated into Welsh include the *Transitus beatae Mariae* and the *Epistola Lentuli*.[8] A Welsh version of Pilate's letter to Claudius is appended to the *Gospel of Nicodemus* in several manuscripts,[9] and translations of the related texts *Historia Pilati* and *Vindicta Salvatoris* also survive.[10] These translations were certainly clerical in origin; centers of learning flourished at Cistercian monasteries such as Strata Florida and nearby Llanbadarn Fawr, both in Cardiganshire, and in more than one case there is clear evidence of aristocratic commissioning of the translation of a Latin text into Welsh.[11] The question of course arises why the translation of such apocryphal texts seems to have taken precedence over the translation of canonical Scriptures in medieval Wales. J. E. Caerwyn Williams suggests that "their primary appeal lay in their interest as narratives, and especially as narratives in which the marvellous and the miraculous had free rein."[12]

Although there is no question that the text of the *EN* was known in medieval Wales, the situation is somewhat complicated by a confusion over which text is properly designated by the title. As J. E. Caerwyn Williams notes in his edition of the Welsh *Efengyl Nicodemus*, none of the surviving medieval copies of the text uses that name.[13] When such a title does appear in manuscript sources, it is invariably given to the midrash text relating the story of Seth, the oil of mercy, and Adam's three grains. As Caerwyn Williams points out, this text is more appropriately designated in Welsh as *Ystorya Adaf*, a title which does appear in some manuscripts. The confusion has persisted, however, and the text edited by the Rev. Robert Williams in his *Selections from the Hengwrt MSS* under the title "Evengyl Nicodemus" is in fact the Seth-Adam story.[14]

Board of Celtic Studies 14 (1952): 108–12; idem, "Efengyl Nicodemus," *Bulletin of the Board of Celtic Studies* 14 (1952): 257–73.

[8] J. E. Caerwyn Williams, "Transitus Beatae Mariae a Thestunau Cyffelyb," *Bulletin of the Board of Celtic Studies* 18 (1959): 131–57; idem, "Epistola Lentuli," *Bulletin of the Board of Celtic Studies* 15 (1953): 280–81.

[9] J. E. Caerwyn Williams, "Medieval Welsh Religious Prose," 65–97; idem, "Efengyl Nicodemus," 272–73.

[10] Melville Richards, "Ystoria Bilatus," *Bulletin of the Board of Celtic Studies* 9 (1937): 42–49; J. E. Caerwyn Williams, "Ystorya Titus Aspassianus," *Bulletin of the Board of Celtic Studies* 9 (1937–39): 221–30.

[11] Gruffudd Bola, likely a monk of Strata Florida, translated the Athanasian Creed for Efa, daughter of Maredudd ab Owain, lord of Deheubarth and great grandson of the Lord Rhys, the major patron of Strata Florida in the late twelfth century; see J. E. Caerwyn Williams, "Medieval Welsh Religious Prose," 66–67.

[12] Ibid., 81.

[13] J. E. Caerwyn Williams, "Efengyl Nicodemus yn Gymraeg," 108; idem, "Efengyl Nicodemus."

[14] Rev. Robert Williams, *Selections from the Hengwrt MSS Preserved in the*

The "true" *Gospel of Nicodemus* survives in Welsh translation in a small number of closely related manuscripts, of which only three are older than the sixteenth century. J. E. Caerwyn Williams's study of the texts identified three different versions (A, B, and C). All three of the early texts are examples of version A; these Williams designated as texts I–III.[15] The text of version A belongs clearly to group usually called *Evangelium Nicodemi* A, and parallels closely the text of Einsiedeln, Stiftsbibliothek MS. 326. As in the Einsiedeln manuscript, the Welsh text begins with the dating prologue (though the years differ), and gives the full text of the *Gesta Pilati* and the *Descensus Christi ad inferos*, ending with Pilate's letter to Claudius. The earliest of the three manuscripts of version A is National Library of Wales MS. Peniarth 5 (The White Book of Rhydderch), fols. xxx–xxxvj[v], dating from the first quarter of the fourteenth century (text I).[16] Text II is preserved in National Library of Wales MS. Llanstephan 27, fols. 106v–25r, and dates from about 1400. It is closely related to text I, though Caerwyn Williams suggests it is more likely that the two are derived—directly or indirectly—from a single exemplar, than that one is a copy of the other.[17] Text III, from the last half of the fifteenth century, is found in National Library of Wales MS. Llanstephan 2, pp. 320–44. It shows many small differences from texts I and II, and although it is still generally similar to the other texts of version A, it could perhaps, as Williams points out, represent a different translation. It does not include the letter of Pilate to Claudius. Five other copies of version A survive in hands of the sixteenth and seventeenth centuries, three of them in identifiable hands of well-known scribes (Rhydderch Lewis ap Owen, David Parry, and John Jones, Gellilyfdy).

Version B was translated by Dafydd Fychan, a Glamorgan priest, in the fourteenth century. On a commission from Rhys ap Tomas ab Einion, Dafydd translated *Ffordd y Brawd Odrig* (*Beati Oderici perigrinatio*), and it is possible that the translation of the *EN* may also have been made at Rhys's request. Version C is based on Wynkyn de Worde's

Peniarth Library, vol. 2 (London: T. Richards, 1892), 243–50. Jenkins, "Medieval Welsh Scriptures," 121–31. The pamphlet printed several times during the eighteenth century under the title *Histori Nicodemus* is also the Old Testament midrash text. The pamphlets are listed by Eiluned Rees, *Libri Walliae: A Catalogue of Welsh Books and Books Printed in Wales, 1546–1820*, vol. 1 (Aberystwyth: National Library of Wales, 1987), nos. 3726–34.

[15] The manuscripts are listed and discussed by Caerwyn Williams, "Efengyl Nicodemus yn Gymraeg," 108–12. Of the ten manuscripts listed, two date from the sixteenth century, and five from the seventeenth or later.

[16] Edited by Caerwyn Williams, "Efengyl Nicodemus," 257–73.

[17] Caerwyn Williams, "Efengyl Nicodemus yn Gymraeg," 109.

English translation of 1509.[18] Versions B and C are found only in late manuscripts, and only one example of each is known: B in the hand of Benjamin Simon, copied around the middle of the eighteenth century, and C in the hand of Iolo Morganwg, copied sometime between 1775 and 1825.

Individual motifs from the apocryphon are common in the literature of Wales from the twelfth through the sixteenth century, especially in religious poetry. In particular, references to the Harrowing of Hell appear frequently enough to indicate widespread knowledge of the story, although it is not always clear from which immediate source they are derived. Cynddelw Brydydd Mawr ("the great poet"; fl. ca. 1155–1200), the best-known and most prolific of the *gogynfeirdd*, uses the theme in his "marwysgafn," or death-bed poem. Cynddelw explains the appropriateness of addressing his prayer for salvation to Christ on the basis of the Harrowing of Hell:[19]

> Dyfu Grist yng nghnawd, Priawd prifed,
> Dyfu ym mru Mair, Mab dymuned;
> Dyfu bumoed byd o boen galled,
> O dwyll, o dywyll trydwyll trefred,
> O anghyffred gadw, o gadarn alar,
> O garchar esgar pan ysgared.
> Ac Ef yw ein Llyw, ein llwyr nodded
> A farn wrth ein gwaith ar ein gweithred;
> Ac Ef, Arglwydd nef, tangnef tynged,
> A'n dug o gyfrgoll pan archolled;
> Ac Ef dwyre in, ac ef daered – Ei fudd,
> Ac Ef, Udd, ni'n lludd an llesäed.... (Vv. 46–57)[20]

(Christ incarnate came, possessor of supremacy, he came in Mary's womb, the longed-for Son, the world's five ages came out of terrible pain, from deceit, from the deceitful darkness of our sinful abode, from a grievous custody, from long sorrow, from the enemy's prison that they were freed. And he is our

---

[18] Glanmor Williams, *The Welsh Church*, 86, 100; Ceri W. Lewis, "The Literary Tradition of Morgannwg down the Middle of the Sixteenth Century," in *Glamorgan County History*, vol. 3, *The Middle Ages*, ed. T. B. Pugh (Cardiff: University of Wales Press, 1971), 549–50. See above, pp. 255–56.

[19] Cynddelw's surviving output constitutes more than 30 per cent of the *gogynfeirdd* repertoire. His use of the Harrowing of Hell theme in this poem is noted by Catherine A. McKenna, *The Medieval Welsh Religious Lyric: Poems of the Gogynfeirdd, 1137–1282* (Belmont, MA: Ford & Bailie, 1991), 89.

[20] *Gwaith Cynddelw Brydydd Mawr*, vol. 2, ed. N. A. Jones and A. P. Owen, Cyfres Beirdd y Tywysogion, vol. 4 (Cardiff: University of Wales Press, 1995), 336.

helm, our complete protection, who judges our deeds according to our acts, and he, the Lord of heaven, source of peace,
our destiny, brought us from damnation when he was pierced,
and he will rise for us and we will receive his bounty, and he,
the Lord, will not deny us our help. . . .)

Cynddelw makes use of the common link between the Harrowing
of Hell and the theme of the five ages of man, but does not use the latter to introduce a list of the prophets released from hell, as later poets
often did. The same linking is used more succinctly by Cynddelw's
contemporary, Llywelyn Vardd (fl. 1150–1175), who speaks of Christ,
"A warawd pym oes byd o geithiwed uffern" ("who rescued the five
ages of the world from the bonds of hell").[21]
Einion ap Gwalchmai (fl. ca. 1203–1223) uses both these themes in
one poem, but separates them. Einion's prayer for pardon and for help
in resisting sin includes the desire to be able to bear pain as Christ
once did on the cross. In this context, the five ages are used numero-
logically, related to Christ's five wounds:

Porthaist er pym oes gloes glas ferau
Pym weli, Celi celfyddodau (vv. 37–38)[22]

(You bore the blue nails' pain, the five wounds, for the sake of
the five ages, God of arts).

As an example of Christ's power of salvation, the Harrowing of Hell is
then briefly mentioned in a lyrical expansion on the events of the Passion and its aftermath:

Gwedi doeth Ef y'r diöddau
Dug anrhaith uffern yn Ei afflau (vv. 57–58)[23]

(After he came purposefully, he brought the spoils of hell in
his grasp).

One of the most elaborate uses of the Harrowing of Hell story is
found in a poem addressed both to God and to the prince Llywelyn ap
Iorwerth (b. 1173, d. 1240) by Dafydd Benfras (fl. 1230–1260). In the
poem "I Dduw ac i Lywelyn Fab Iorwerth," Dafydd claims that his
commitment to Llywelyn is exceeded only by his commitment to God:

[21] Henry Lewis, ed., *Hen Gerddi Crefyddol* (Cardiff: University of Wales Press,
1931), 83, v. 73.
[22] J. E. Caerwyn Williams and P. I. Lynch, eds., *Gwaith Meilyr Brydydd a'i
Ddisgynyddion*, Cyfres Beirdd y Tywysogion, vol. 1 (Cardiff: University of Wales
Press, 1994), 462.
[23] Ibid., 463.

Gvedy y gvr uchot uchaf llav diheu
ar eilgvr goreu meu ymadav
Llywelyn vrdyn urdas idav (vv. 55–57)[24]

(After the Man above of true supreme power, my pledge is to
the man next in goodness, the worthy Llywelyn, honor be to
him).

The parallel is extended by matching a description of Llywelyn's
success in fighting the English ("lu [y] loegyr," v. 68) with the narrative of Christ's victory over hell:

Didestyl oed en lle llu vrth syllyav
dyd y kymerth crist croc yn eidav
yggwaelavt uffern affleu vrav einyoes
yd oed bedeiroes yn ymdarav
A llu o bryfet yn eu briwav
A llit boethuan dan yn eu deifyav
a llys afreit gwrys na gwryssyav oe phleit
ae lliavs eneit yn direidyav
A llvyr dywyllvc drvc vrth drigyav
A llen[g] gythreuleit yny threulav
A llawer bvysti heb ystyryav ket
a llawer sychet trvydet trvyddav
A lluoed pobloed pavb ynathav
A lleot a rot yn eu rvydav
A lle yd oed druan drvy adav cain
y werin wirin y warandav
Pan dyuu y mab rat oed reit vrthav
yr porth yn damorth a davn arnav
y uffern bytwern heb adav ychweith
yn vn boregweith yv hanreithyav
Achaws pymoes byt y bu yndav
uchelvr mirein byrdrein drvydav
Vcheldat vab rat rac rvydav y havl
gwae nyvo deduavl y dyd adav
Mihangel pandel y daly drostav
yn erbyn kythreul kythrud seinyav (vv. 21–46)[25]

(The place of the host was in chaos as they watched the day
Christ took up the cross as his own, mortal grasping fear in

[24] Sister N. Bosco, "Dafydd Benfras and His *Red Book* Poems," *Studia Celtica* 22/23 (1987–88): 87–89.
[25] Ibid., 88.

the pit of hell, the four ages were making preparations, and a
host of worms rending them, and the wrath of the fire's heat
burning them, and a court, fighting on its behalf is useless,
and its various spirits causing harm. And there was a total
darkness of evil there and a multitude of demons laying it
waste, and great ferocity without the thought of help and
therefore a great thirst for freedom. And the host of people all
silent and the lions and the wheel holding them captive, and
where it was said through Cain's promise for the saintly ones
listening to him, when the Son of Grace came to hell, the
dangerous swamp without escape, one morning to harrow it,
he was needed to help in our confinement, and with blessings
for him. For the sake of the five ages of the world he was
there, the fair nobleman, with short thorns through him, the
Son of Grace of a glorious Father, to resist the perversion of
his right. Woe to him who is not just on the coming day when
Michael comes to take a stand for him against the Devil
sounding alarms!).

A poem attributed to Gruffudd ap yr Ynad Goch (fl. ca. 1280) presents the story in the context of an elaborate and horrific description of
the pains of hell:[26]

Ystyryent pum oes byt eu bot ym madeu,
Pan aeth un Mab Duw, y dyd goreu,
Y drws porth uffern gethern gaetheu.
Y wan heb annoc, a'e groc o'e greu,
Y sarff aflawen yn y eneu.
Yd oed yn berwi, ub o'r bareu,
Seith canmil peireit o eneideu;
A glaweir ac ot, a seirff a llewot,
A phawb heb annot yn y boenneu;
A'r kethri osclawc, a'r kythreul cornawc,
A'r kyrn llym sodlawc ar y sodleu.... (Vv. 31–41)[27]

(The five ages of the world are mindful of their pardon, when
the only Son of God went on the best day through hell's gate
to the captive host, to attack without urging, with his cross
and his blood, to pierce the fearsome serpent in the mouth.
There was boiling, oh! the tortures; seven hundred thousand

[26] On the attribution of this poem to Gruffudd, see Catherine A. McKenna,
"The Religious Poetry Attributed to Gruffudd ap yr Ynad Goch," *Bulletin of the
Board of Celtic Studies* 29 (1981): 277–81.
[27] Henry Lewis, *Hen Gerddi Crefyddol*, 99.

cauldrons of souls, and rain and snow, and serpents and lions, and each without respite from the pains, and sharp nails and horned devils with horrible sharp points on their heels. . . .)

The motif found elaborate expression in the poets of the fourteenth century writing in the new *cywydd* meter (the poets are generally known as the *cywyddwyr*). Iolo Goch (b. ca. 1320, d. 1398), for example, describes the Harrowing in terms of the release of the prophets traditionally associated with the five ages of man:

Ac yno daw ein gwiwner,
Adda a'i blant, nawcant nêr,
A llu Noe hen, angen oedd,
Yn fore, a'i niferoedd -
Llawenydd a fydd i'w fam,
Lliw wybrol - a llu Abram,
A llyw y rhain â llu rhydd,
Moesen yn llenwi'r meysydd,
A llu hardd Dafydd, yn llwyr,
Broffwyd, lleiswyd y llaswyr,
A Phawl ebostol y ffydd,
Iôr mwyn, a ddaw i'r mynydd,
Ef a'i nifer pêr parawd
A droes i'r ffydd, drysor ffawd;
A rhod yr haul, drawl dramawr,
A'r lloer a ddisgyn i'r llawr,
A'r saith wiw blaned a'r sêr
O'r nefoedd fry a'u nifer;
Ac o uffern, herwwern hir,
O garchar hwynt a gyrchir,
Llidiog blin daufiniog bla,
Llu Satan mewn lliw swta. (Vv. 61–82)[28]

(And then came our worthy lord, Adam and his child, lord of nine hundred; and the host of old Noah, it was needful, early, with his multitude—his mother will be joyful, an ethereal color—and Abraham's host and their leader, with a free host; Moses filling the meadows; and the beautiful host of David the prophet, all together, will put aside the psalms; and Paul the apostle of faith, the gentle lord, and he will come up, he and the sweet ready host, he who turned to the faith, the

---

[28] *Gwaith Iolo Goch*, ed. D. R. Johnston (Cardiff: University of Wales Press, 1988), 111–12.

treasure of fate, and the sun's orb, the huge combustion, and
the moon will fall to the ground, and the seven worthy plan-
ets and the stars from the heavens above and their multitude,
and from hell, the swamp of long exile, they are fetched from
prison, from the furious, angry, double-edged plague, the
ashen-colored host of Satan.)

Siôn Cent (fl. ca. 1400–1430/45—the dates have not been established with certainty) was a moralist, taking as his principal theme the
transience of earthly life and the urgency of repentance. His poetry
includes frequent descriptions of the pains of hell, in which the materials of the apocryphon are used in an orthodox fashion, enlivened by
the poet's unusual satirical tone:[29]

A'r trydydd dydd, ŵr tradoeth,
O garchar daear y doeth.
Ac yno'r aeth, bennaeth bern,
Barth affwys i borth uffern:
A thynnodd niferoedd Nêr
I nefoedd ei holl nifer.
Tynnodd Addaf a Dafydd
A Moesen, a phen y ffydd.
Tynnodd Abram lân a'i lu
A Noe hen wedi hynny. (Vv. 17–26)[30]

(And on the third day, a most wise man came from the prison
of the earth. And then he, chief of sorrow, went towards the
abyss to the gate of hell. And he pulled the hosts of the Lord
into the heavens, his entire host: he pulled Adam and David
and Moses, and the head of the faith. He pulled Abraham the
pure and his host, and old Noah after that.)

Siôn uses the theme more succinctly in his poem on avoiding God's
anger, "Rhag digio Duw":

Tynnodd yn ôl dioddef
Trwy dân poeth bobl noeth i nef. (Vv. 17–18)[31]

(After torment he pulled the naked people to heaven through
the hot fire.)

---

[29] Cf. Jean Rittmueller, "The Religious Poetry of Siôn Cent," *Proceedings of the
Harvard Celtic Colloquium* 3 (1983): 107–48.
[30] Henry Lewis, Thomas Roberts, and Ifor Williams, eds., *Cywyddau Iolo Goch
ac Eraill* (Cardiff: University of Wales Press, 1925), 258.
[31] Ibid., 275.

Materials related to the *Gospel of Nicodemus* continued to find a place in the poetry of the Welsh Catholic poets of the later fifteenth and early sixteenth centuries. Dafydd Trevor (d. ca. 1528), a cleric-poet from Anglesey, uses a reference to the Harrowing of Hell in a somewhat unusual manner in his *cywydd* "I Dduw Iesu" ("To the Lord Jesus"):

Deugeinawr, deg ogonedd,
Had Iesu fu yn y bedd.
Gwedi cyfodi o'n câr
I gyrchu pawb o'i garchar,
Ar ôl yr holl feistrolaeth,
I ne' fry ynof yr aeth. (Vv. 23–28)[32]

(Forty hours, a fine glory, Jesus' seed lay in the grave.[33] After our beloved one arose to fetch everyone from his prison, after the total victory, he went to heaven above in me.)

Perhaps the most elaborate use of the *Gospel of Nicodemus* is in the Welsh Passion Play from the late fifteenth or early sixteenth century, which includes a full treatment of the Harrowing of Hell similar to that found in most of the English biblical play cycles. As Gwenan Jones pointed out in her edition of the play,[34] the Welsh play as a whole shows both similarities and differences from contemporary English plays, though, like the English plays, it is unlikely to be based on a direct knowledge of the apocryphon. The large number of minor variations from either the Latin text or its Welsh translation would suggest that the material is derived from popular traditions, especially from sermons, though the lack of survival of sermon literature in Welsh makes it impossible to establish this with any certainty. In its retelling of the Harrowing of Hell, it is thoroughly orthodox in its material, though the sequence of events does not correspond to any of the surviving English cycles, and Gwenan Jones is likely right that the play is independent of the direct influence of the English plays.[35] As in all the English plays except that from Chester, the episode opens with an introductory speech of self-identification by the Soul of Christ. In the Welsh play, however, this leads immediately to the discussion between

---

[32] The poem has not been published, but was edited by Irene George, "Syr Dafydd Trefor—Ei Oes a'i Waith" (M.A. diss., University College of Wales, Aberystwyth, 1929), 216–17.

[33] The image is of Christ's burial as the planting of the seed of Redemption.

[34] Gwenan Jones, *A Study of Three Welsh Religious Plays* (Bala: R. Evans & Son, 1939), 82–86.

[35] Ibid., 86.

Satan and Lucifer, and to Christ's demand for the gates to be opened, omitting the sequence of prophetic statements by Adam, John the Baptist, and various other prophets, derived from the apocryphon. Christ's demand that the gates be opened contains the traditional echo of Psalm 24 (Vulgate 23):

> Agorwch ych drysse
> holl wassnaethwyr vffernlle
> ac yn ychel dyrchefwch.... (Vv. 793–95)[36]

(Open your gates all servants of hell, and lift them high....)

Satan and Lucifer confer over what to do about this invasion in terms which contain clear echoes of the apocryphal gospel, including reference to the prior raising of Lazarus:

Satan:	Y mae wrth ych gorchymyn vffern dan gloe kedyrn ac yn sikir gwedi kav a rhaffav kadwynav heyrn
Lissipher:	Ai vo ywr brenin gorychel a aeth a lassar heb ddim kel a oedd gennym ni yngharchar mewn heyrn bar diogel
Satan:	Je varglwydd yfo sydd yna j weithred yw dyfod yma an ysbeilio ni yw i fryd j gyd am ssilltydd adda
Lissipher:	Gorchymyn nid oferedd om kedernid am anrydedd ywch nas gatoch lle i bwyvi mae e yn ddifri yn i vowredd
	Pan oedd ef yn galw lasar ni veiddiwn i ddwyn i far na ffrwytho dim i ymladd val dyna radd anhygar (vv. 757–76)[37]

(Satan: "By your command hell is under strong locks and closed securely with heavy iron chains." Lucifer: "Is he the sublime king who took Lazarus openly, who was with us in

---

[36] Ibid., 218.
[37] Ibid., 216–18.

prison within secure iron bars?" Satan: "Yes, my lord, he is here, his task is to come here and to rob us is his delight, because of the descendants of Adam." Lucifer: "I order, not vainly, by my strength and honor, that you not let him come in the place where I am; he is terrible in his power. When he was calling Lazarus I did not dare to bear his anger, nor to succeed at all in battle; that was an unpleasant situation!").

The extensive conversation between Christ and Satan found in the York and Towneley plays is entirely missing in the Welsh play. Although the prophets are not given the opportunity to speak from behind hell's gates prior to Christ's appearance, two of them (Adam and David) are given speeches of praise as they are released from the bonds of hell:

Dafydd Broffwyd:
    Hael Jessu or gwraidd ganaid
    bv gan dy bobyl wiliaid
    padriairch a ffroffwidi
    maen yn dy henwi yn honaid (vv. 813–16)[38]

(Generous Jesus of bright stock, your people have been waiting for you, patriarchs and prophets, they name you with renown).

It should be noted that although the position of David's speech corresponds to the normal form of *EN* 14.2, its content only vaguely recalls the lines of the apocryphon, which constitute a tissue of references to the Psalms: "Cantate Domino canticum nouum quia mirabilia fecit Dominus. Saluauit sibi dextera eius et brachium sanctum eius. Notum fecit Dominus salutare suum, ante conspectum gentium reuelauit iustitiam suam" (Ps. 97:1–2; "Sing a new song to the Lord, for he has done marvellous things; his right hand has wrought salvation for him and his holy arm. The Lord has made known his salvation; before the face of all nations he revealed his righteousness").[39]

The Soul of Christ and the archangel Michael lead the procession to heaven as in the apocryphon, but the following speeches by Enoch and Elijah are omitted, as are the speeches of the Good Thief and the damned woman which are found in the Chester play.

Although the Passion Play contains by far the most extensive use of the *EN* in Welsh literature, it is unlikely to be based on an intimate

---

[38] Ibid., 220.

[39] H. C. Kim, ed., *The Gospel of Nicodemus: Gesta Salvatoris*, Toronto Medieval Latin Texts, vol. 2 (Toronto: Pontifical Institute of Mediaeval Studies, 1973), 45.

knowledge of the text of the apocryphon. It also shows no direct borrowing from the English Harrowing of Hell plays, though its author may well have been familiar with them. Like those plays, it is likely to be based on popular treatments of the Harrowing of Hell in sermon literature and such non-dramatic treatments as versified Passion narratives.

Other details from the apocryphon appear with less frequency in Welsh literature. The story of Longinus's blindness and its cure through the blood of Christ is included in the Welsh Passion Play, as are brief speeches by the two Thieves, who are identified as Dismas and Desmas, a variant of the names given in the *EN*, Dismas and Gestas. The names of the two thieves are also found with some frequency in the "rood poems," addressed to pilgrimage crosses, which became popular in the fifteenth century.[40] The poem on the rood of Brecon by Hywel Dafi (fl. 1450–1480), for example, agrees with the "Passion Play" in calling them Dismas and Desmas.[41]

The Welsh interest in apocryphal narrative provided a fertile ground for the thematic material of the *EN* to take root. Nevertheless, it is precisely the thematic, motivic use of the gospel's narrative that suggests that the individual motifs were far better known in Wales than the text of the apocryphon itself. Although Welsh poets were well acquainted with the stories, from the *gogynfeirdd* of the twelfth and thirteenth centuries, through the *cywyddwyr* of the fourteenth and fifteenth centuries, to the Catholic poets immediately preceding the Reformation in the sixteenth century, it seems from their use of isolated motifs in traditional manners that these were known principally from extra-textual sources, from preaching and from literary traditions.

[40] Glanmor Williams, *The Welsh Church*, 110–11, 478–80.
[41] Hartwell Jones, "Celtic Britain and the Pilgrim Movement," *Y Cymmrodor* 23 (1912): 303.

Appendix

The *Evangelium Nichodemi* in Medieval Cornish Literature

No translations of the apocryphon into early Cornish survive, and evidence of its influence is limited to the latter two of the three biblical plays which make up the *Ordinalia*, the Creation, the Passion, and the Resurrection. The Passion Play includes a short Longinus (here Longeus) scene, and the third play, the *Ordinale de Resurrexione Domini nostri Jhesu Christi*, though it concentrates on the appearances to Mary Magdalene and Thomas, includes a relatively brief account of the Harrowing of Hell.[42] The play's version of the narrative varies considerably from the apocryphon, and it is unlikely to be derived directly from it. As Janet Bakere notes in her study of the *Ordinalia*,[43] several of the variations in detail from the *EN* are paralleled by early French plays, notably the *Passion d'Arras* and Armand Greban's *Mystère de la Passion*, and the Cornish play may possibly share a common source with these. Thus in the *Ordinale* it is Pilate, not the Jews, who orders Joseph of Arimathea's imprisonment for the burial of Christ. Unusually, the Cornish play includes Nicodemus in the imprisonment and miraculous release. The Cornish character of Joseph's jailor is otherwise unknown except in Greban's *Passion*. As in the two French plays, it is Lucifer rather than Hell who replies to Christ's demand, "Atollite portas."

The list of prophets and ancestors who speak after the Harrowing of Hell is revised from the apocryphon and includes only Adam, Eve, Enoch, Elijah, and the thief Dismas. Bakere points out that the list appears to have been revised to include only those persons who have had a previous part in the trilogy.[44] The meetings with Enoch, Elijah, and Dismas are paralleled in the French plays, though the French scenes are far more elaborate than in the *Ordinale*.

The story of Seth's search for the oil of mercy, which appears briefly in his speech in the apocryphon, and in more fully developed form in the related *Vita Adae et Evae* texts (including the Welsh *Ystorya Adaf*), is told at some length in the *Ordinale de origine mundi*.[45] Seth does not appear in the *Ordinale de resurrexione*.

---

[42] Edwin Norris, ed., *The Ancient Cornish Drama* (Oxford: Oxford University Press, 1859) 2:10–25, vv. 97–306.

[43] Janet A. Bakere, *The Cornish Ordinalia: A Critical Study* (Cardiff: University of Wales Press, 1980), 94.

[44] Ibid., 95.

[45] Norris, *The Ancient Cornish Drama*, 1: 52–69, vv. 684–916.

The large number of variations from the *Evangelium* text would suggest that the playwright drew his knowledge of the Harrowing of Hell from texts other than the apocryphon itself, although as Bakere points out, "the number and complex relationships of the versions in which the apocryphal *Gospel of Nichodemus* circulated in the Middle Ages make it impossible to be certain about which tradition was directly influential on the *Ordinalia*."[46]

---

[46] Bakere, *The Cornish Ordinalia*, 97.

Thematic Bibliography of the *Acts of Pilate*[1]

RÉMI GOUNELLE

ZBIGNIEW IZYDORCZYK

℘he following bibliography consists of three thematically arranged parts, each with a distinct focus and scope: "Part 1: The *Acts of Pilate*" deals with the *Gospel of Nicodemus* (*GN*) itself, its editions, translations, transmission, and contents; "Part 2: Supplementary texts and studies" brings together items useful for the study of the apocryphon's cultural and textual backgrounds and legacies; and "Part 3: Iconography and the *Acts of Pilate*" is devoted to its impact on visual arts.

Part 1 was originally conceived as an independent project (cf. no. 32 below) and differs in perspective from the rest of this volume. While the preceding essays emphasize the fluidity and intertextuality of the *GN* in the later Middle Ages, this part of the bibliography concentrates on one specific, if multifaceted, work and its translations: the *Acts of Pilate* as defined and circumscribed by the *Bibliotheca hagio-*

---

[1] It is with much gratitude that we should like to acknowledge the help of the other members of the research team engaged in preparation of new editions of all linguistic versions of the *Acts of Pilate* (*AP*), under the auspices of the Association pour l'étude de la littérature apocryphe chrétienne, for the Corpus Christianorum, Series Apocryphorum: J.-D. Dubois (coordinator), C. Furrer (Greek A), B. Outtier (Armenian and Georgian), A. Frey (Syriac), R. Beylot (Ethiopic), and R. Roquet (Coptic). Collaborating with the editorial project are also B. Tambrun-Krasker (Greek A), T. A. Smith (Slavonic), and F. Vienne (Arabic). We owe special thanks to J. Gijsel, M. McNamara, C. Paupert, P.-H. Poirier, R. Stichel, and S. Voicu for their assistance in verifying numerous titles in the libraries to which they had access, to J.-C. Picard for many useful bibliographical suggestions, and to D. Addor and E. Steffek, students at the Faculté de théologie, Université de Lausanne, for the laborious task of proofreading, for which they generously volunteered.

graphica Graeca (no. 371 below) under items 779t, u, v, and w. Consequently, there is little in this section on other Pilate apocrypha, such as
Pilate's correspondence with Tiberius or Herod or the narrative of the
death of Joseph of Arimathea, even though they may be closely related
to the *AP*.[2] Similarly, there is little in it on works influenced by the
AP, and nothing on publications which, although ostensibly evoking
the *AP* in their titles, are not concerned with the apocryphon as defined above.[3] What this part of the bibliography does present, however, is a comprehensive listing of editions and translations of the *AP*
in both its Eastern and Western linguistic versions, as well as an extensive inventory of commentaries on textual, linguistic, literary, historical, and theological features of those versions.[4] It is intended as a non-

---

[2] For bibliographies on those works, one may consult M. Geerard's *Clavis
apocryphorum* and J. H. Charlesworth and J. R. Müller's *New Testament Apocrypha
and Pseudepigrapha: A Guide to Publications* (nos. 375 and 374 below); some of them
are also included in Part 2 of this bibliography.

[3] Such is, for instance, William Dennes Mahan's immensely popular fabrication
sometimes entitled *The Acts of Pilate* or *Report of Pilate* and based on an English
translation of a short story by Joseph Méry (1798–1867), *Ponce Pilate à Vienne* (William Dennes Mahan, *The Acta Pilati. Important Testimony of Pontius Pilate, Recently
Discovered, Being His Official Report to the Emperor Tiberius, Concerning the Crucifixion of Christ*, ed. George Slutter [Shelbyville, Ind.: M. B. Robbins, 1879]; it was
originally published in 1879 under the title *A Correct Transcript of Pilate's Court*).
On this forgery, see Edgar J. Goodspeed, *Strange New Gospels* (Chicago: University
of Chicago Press, 1931), 42–62, and Per Beskov, *Strange Tales about Jesus* (Philadelphia: Fortress Press, 1985), 51–56. Similarly, the Welsh pamphlet printed several
times under the title *Histori Nicodemus* contains an Old Testament midrash relating the story of Seth and Adam's three grains, not the *Gospel of Nicodemus* proper
(*Histori Nicodemus neu yn hytrach Ysgrifen Nicodemus, o herwydd na dderbyniodd yr
Eglwys, ond pediar Efengyl. . . . A osodwyd allan gan Dafydd Jones . . .* [Argraphwyd
yn y Mwythig ac ar werth yno gan Tho: Durston, ca. 1745; reprinted several times
in 1745 and in 1750, 1772, ca. 1800]; *Hanes Nicodemus; neu, yn hytrach, ysgrifen
Nicodemus, an na dderbyniodd yr Eglwys ond pediar Efengyl. . . . A osodwyd allan gan
Dafydd Jones . . .* [Caerfyrddin: Argraffwyd gan J. Evans, 1812]; R. Williams, ed.,
Selections from the Hengwrt MSS Preserved in the Peniarth Library, vol. 2 [London:
T. Richards, 1892]). Those publications which apply the title *Acts of Pilate* to other
Pilate apocrypha have been noted in Part 2 of the bibliography.

[4] We are aware that, despite our efforts, the list of editions and translations
of the *AP* is not exhaustive. For example, we have not been able to identify the
1742 German edition of the "pietistisch-separatistischen Burle(n)burger Bibel,"
whose eighth volume contains "Des Jüngers Nicodemi Evangelium von unsers
Meisters und Heylands Jesu Christi Leiden und Auferstehung" (cf. no. 335, which
bears the same title), according to K. L. Schmidt, *Kanonische und apokryphe
Evangelien und Apostelgeschichten* (Basel: H. Majer, 1944), 64 n. 54. Also, the
Swedish edition published in Stockholm in 1818 and mentioned by F. Münter,
"Probabilien zur Leidengeschichte aus dem Evangelium des Nicodemus," 319 n.
5 (no. 439), has so far elluded us, as has "Philippi Kegelii Anhang zum geistlichen
Weg-Weiser nach dem himmlischen Vatterland" (see no. 332), from which many
later German editions were derived.

discursive complement to the essays and as the first necessary step towards the writing of a history of research on the *AP*'s eminently complex tradition.

The first of the three sections into which Part 1 has been subdivided is devoted to editions/translations of and studies on various linguistic versions of the *AP*. Within the individual subsections dealing with Greek and Latin, Eastern, and medieval Western traditions, items are grouped under respective language headings,[5] first editions and translations, then studies on the texts and manuscripts.[6] The final subsection, also organized by languages, gathers modern, post-1600 translations of the *AP* from Greek, Latin, or earlier vernacular sources, but it omits—albeit with a few exceptions (e.g., no. 320)—contemporary translations of translations, such as, for example, the Polish rendering of Amiot's French version (no. 327).[7]

The second section of Part 1 signals references to the *AP* in a few polyglot bibliographical repertories and lists selected introductions to the apocryphon in dictionaries, encyclopedias, and general histories of early Christian literature. Here completeness was neither possible nor advisable, since almost every religious dictionary, encyclopedia, and lexicon evokes the apocryphon at some point. The items included in this section have been selected for either their typicality or their influence. This material may reveal to a careful reader the evolution of popular, "vulgate" notions about the apocryphon from the eighteenth to the late twentieth century.

Specific studies seeking to explore or elucidate the *AP* are presented in the third section. Those dealing with its origin (date, composition) and transmission are given first. They are followed by studies focused on chapters 1–16 (the trial, Crucifixion, Resurrection, and Ascension of Christ) and by those concerned with chapters 17–27 (the account of Christ's Descent into Hell). Although such a division of the *AP* into two parts (chaps. 1–16 and 17–27) is no longer generally accepted, having been replaced by a tripartite division (1–11, 12–16, 17–27, with some differences of opinion as to where the first section

---

[5] Part 1 includes only those languages in which versions of the *AP* are actually preserved. References to those linguistic traditions which may have known the *AP* but which now preserve only related Pilate apocrypha can be found in Part 2, sect. 3. Recensions of the *AP* in various Slavonic languages have been assembled together under a single heading, "Slavonic."

[6] Generally, catalogues of manuscript or incunabula collections have been excluded from this bibliography to avoid drowning the works dealing specifically with the *AP* in a flood of references easily identifiable through other bibliographical guides.

[7] Daniel-Rops and F. Amiot, eds., *Apokryfy Nowego Testamentu*, Polish translation by Z. Romanowiczowa (London: Veritas, 1955), pp. 111–21.

ends), the history of research on the apocryphon necessitated, in fact, the adoption of the traditional bipartite structure for this portion of the bibliography.

"Part 2: Supplementary texts and studies," presenting background and ancillary sources for the study of the *AP*'s heritage, both complements and enlarges upon the first part. It relaxes the original focus on the narrowly defined *AP* and broadens the scope to include a wider range of works, both literary and scholarly, whose engagement with the apocryphon is less pronounced or sustained yet still noteworthy. Such broadening of perspective aligns this part of the bibliography with the general perspective of the preceding essays but precludes any possibility of exhaustive coverage. In fact, the vernacular sections of Part 2 are heavily indebted to the bibliographic material provided by the contributors in the footnotes to their essays and reflect the contributors' (and our) judgements as to which bibliographic items are important or useful for the study of the apocryphon's legacy.

The opening section of the second part provides references to selected editions of those patristic texts which attest to the presence of the *AP* in the early Christian milieu. This is followed by a section devoted to the origin and content of the *AP* but, in contrast to the corresponding section of Part 1, the studies listed here explore not so much the apocryphon itself as the themes or topics related to it and cultural or religious trends with which it was connected.

The third section of Part 2 presents works which originated in or are indebted to the *AP*. Placed here are free adaptations and transformations of the apocryphon, such as, for example, its Greek and Latin poetic renditions or its abridgements by Jacobus a Voragine and Vincent of Beauvais. The section includes also a selection of other Pilate apocrypha, especially those in languages which do not preserve the *AP* itself (e.g., Arabic, Ethiopic) as well as those bound up with the vernacular traditions of the *GN*; vernacular compositions which either allude to or exploit the *EN* proper or one of its Latin derivatives; biographical studies on translators responsible for particular vernacular versions; and other similar materials. It excludes, however, works which upon closer investigation have turned out not to have been influenced by or otherwise related to the *EN*.[8]

---

[8] Such are, for example, editions of various Old English poems which allude to the Harrowing of Hell; W. Gillies, ed., "An Early Modern Irish Harrowing of Hell," *Celtica* 13 (1980): 32–55; W. Stokes, ed., *Saltair na Rann*, Analecta Oxoniensia, Medieval and Modern Series, vol. 1, no. 3 (Oxford: Clarendon Press, 1883); D. Greene, F. Kelly, and B. O. Murdoch, eds., *The Irish Adam and Eve Story from "Saltair na Rann,"* 2 vols. (Dublin: Dublin Institute for Advanced Studies, 1976); Blathmac Son of Cu Brettan, *The Poems of Blathmac Son of Cu Brettan*, ed. J. Carney,

Like its counterpart in the first part, this portion of Part 2 is organized according to linguistic traditions, beginning with Greek and Latin, followed by Eastern languages, and concluding with medieval Western vernaculars. Under each language heading, the items are again divided into editions and studies. A vast majority of the titles listed here are taken from the bibliographical footnotes to the preceding essays.

While the first two parts of this bibliography are concerned primarily with the *AP*'s textual traditions, the third and last part groups together studies on its iconographic posterity. "Part 3: Iconography and the *Acts of Pilate*" focuses almost exclusively on discursive studies of the *AP*'s influence on visual arts (i.e., on those studies which describe, expound, elucidate, or otherwise discuss this influence). Publications that merely reproduce images derived from or indebted to the apocryphon are too numerous to be inventoried in this bibliography.

*

As the following listing of printed editions and studies on the *AP* reveals, the apocryphon's popularity was not confined to the medieval period: the *AP* continued to appeal to popular tastes and to attract scholarly attention throughout the early modern and modern periods. In order to highlight this continuity and, especially, to chronicle the history of scholarship on the apocryphon, we have adopted a chronological basis for the arrangement of items. The following five editions of the *AP* marked the main stages in its publication history and opened new avenues of research on it:

- The Latin version published by J. B. Herold in 1555 (no. 20 below) and reissued by J. Grynaeus in 1569 (no. 21) provided the basis for most early modern commentaries on the apocryphon and for its subsequent re-editions.
- The most influential of those re-editions was that of J. A. Fabricius, who included the *EN* in his *Codex apocryphus Noui*

Irish Texts Society, vol. 47 (Dublin: Educational Co. of Ireland, 1964); W. H. Beuken, ed., *Van den levene ons Heren*, 2 pts., Zwolse drukken en herdrukken, vols. 60A and 60B (Zwolle: W. E. J. Tjeenk Willink, 1968); C. T. Carr, ed., *Von unsers herren liden: A Middle High German Poem, Edited from the British Museum Manuscript, Additional 24946*, Publications of the University of Manchester, Germanic Series, vol. 3 (Manchester: University Press, 1929); Otfrid von Weißenburg, *Otfrids Evangelienbuch*, ed. O. Erdmann, 6th ed. prepared by L. Wolff, Altdeutsche Textbibliothek, vol. 49 (Tübingen: Niemeyer, 1973); E. Schröder, ed., *Die Kaiserchronik eines Regensburger Geistlichen*, MGH, Dt. Chron., vol. 1, pt. 1 (1892; repr., Munich: Monumenta Germaniae Historica, 1984).

Testamenti, published in 1703 (no. 22). It remained the standard text for over a century.

- It was not until 1804 that the first modern edition of the Greek text of the *AP* appeared. It was prepared and published by A. Birch in his *Auctarium Codicis apocryphi N. T. Fabriciani* (no. 1).
- In 1832, J. C. Thilo (no. 2) reinvigorated research on the *AP* by publishing his edition of Greek and Latin texts, both with extensive and still useful commentaries. It is to this edition that studies between 1832 and 1853 generally refer.
- In 1853, C. de Tischendorf (no. 4) published a new edition of Greek and Latin texts; its revised version appeared in 1876. Tischendorf's edition immediately received considerable critical attention and remains a milestone in the history of research on the apocryphon. Even though it is now generally out of date, it has not yet been superseded by any later publication. The majority of studies postdating 1853 relied on this edition and its editorial assumptions. It is also this edition that first distinguished between two Latin forms of the *Descensus Christi ad inferos* (*EN* 17–27) and between two Greek recensions (A, covering chaps. 1–16, and B, covering chapters 1–27). Consequently, almost all studies on the textual forms of the Latin *DI* and the Greek *AP* 1–16 reported in this bibliography are indebted to Tischendorf.

*

Bibliographical items are arranged and presented in the following manner:

- *Arrangement of titles.* Under each heading, items are listed in ascending chronological order, from the oldest to the most recent. Titles published in the same year are classed in alphabetical order by author (or by title if by the same author or anonymous). Works published in a series (e.g., in Patrologia Graeca or Patrologia Latina) are placed under the date on which the edition of the series commenced. Items that are not dated are placed according to their surmised or most likely date of publication.
- *Numbering and internal references.* Each item is listed only once and is accorded a unique number. Re-edited and thematically related items are cross-referenced by means of the abbreviation "no(s)." followed by the relevant number(s).
- *Re-editions and reprintings.* Whenever they involve a significant change in title, re-editions of earlier publications are listed as

separate items. Similarly, collective editions of articles originally published as independent pieces also constitute separate entries. Simple reprints, however, are usually indicated in the same entry as the original edition.

- *Annotations.* Whenever the character of a publication has required or invited a comment, annotations are provided in square brackets. These brief notes give page references for the texts or discussions of the *AP* and identify the nature or focus of the relevant material.
- *Index.* The bibliography concludes with an alphabetical index of authors, editors, translators, titles (if publications are anonymous), and printers (for publications before 1600).

An asterisk (*) before an item indicates that we believe it is particularly useful, informative, or important in the history of research on the *AP*.

Part 1: The *Acts of Pilate*

1.1. Textual traditions: editions, translations, studies
1.1.1. Greek and Latin traditions
1.1.1.1. Editions

Dual (Greek and Latin)

1 Birch, A., ed. *Auctarium Codicis apocryphi N. T. Fabriciani. . . .* Vol. 1.
   Copenhagen: Arntzen et Hartier, 1804. [Pp. 1–154: Latin *EN* A
   from Einsiedeln, Stiftsbibliothek MS. 326 (cf. nos. 24, 27), and
   Rome, Biblioteca Corsiniana MS. 1146; and first edition of Greek
   AP.]
2 *Thilo, J. C., ed. *Codex apocryphus Novi Testamenti.* Vol. 1. Leipzig:
   F. C. G. Vogel, 1832. Only one volume published. [Pp. cxviii–clx,
   487–802. Includes extensive, still unsurpassed textual commentary.
   Reproduced or translated in nos. 3, 308, 325, 357a; cf. also no. 33.]
3 Giles, J. A., ed. *Codex apocryphus Novi Testamenti. The Uncanonical
   Gospels and Other Writings. . . .* Vol. 1. London: D. Nutt, 1852. [Pp.
   150–219: text reproduced from Thilo (no. 2), but without Thilo's
   commentary.]
4 *Tischendorf, C. de, ed. *Evangelia apocrypha, adhibitis plurimis
   codicibus Graecis et Latinis, maximam partem nunc primum consultis
   atque ineditorum copia insignibus.* 1853. 2d rev. ed., Leipzig:
   H. Mendelssohn, 1876. Reprint, Hildesheim: G. Olms, 1966. The
   first edition printed at Athens in 1853 has the title page in Greek.
   [Pp. liv–lxxvii, 210–434: still-standard edition, reproduced or translated in nos. 11, 13, 145, 293, 296, 299, 306–7, 310, 312, 314, 316, 320,
   323, 330, 344, 346–55, 357, 359; cf. also nos. 5, 428, 492, 494–95.]

Greek

5 Tischendorf, C. de, ed. *Apocalypses apocryphae Mosis, Esdrae, Pauli,
   Iohannis, item Mariae dormitio, additis evangeliorum et actuum apocry-
   phum supplementis.* Leipzig: H. Mendelssohn, 1866. [Pp. lxi–lxiv:
   "Ad Gesta Pilati Graece A: Dantur exempla scripturae e codice
   Monacensi nondum adhibito." Cf. no. 4.]
6 Huidekoper, F., ed. *Acts of Pilate, from a Transcript of the Codex Designated by Thilo as Paris D.* Cambridge: J. Wilson and Son, 1887.
   [Text based on Fr. Duebner's transcript, made in 1856, of Paris BN
   MS. gr. 808 (*olim Regius* 2342²), extending only to *AP* 14.3. The edition uses different font sizes, reflecting the assumed antiquity of
   individual sections of the narrative; it does not follow the traditional division into chapters. Cf. no. 308.]
7 Ἱστορία ἀκριβὴς περὶ τοῦ κατὰ τὴν σταύρωσιν καὶ ἀνάστασιν
   τοῦ Κυρίου καὶ Σωτῆρος ἡμῶν Ἰησοῦ Χριστοῦ τελεσθέντων,

συγγραφεῖσα τὸ πρῶτον ὑπὸ 'Ιουδαίου τινὸς Αἰνέα, συγχρόνου τοῦ Κυρίου, μεταφρασθεῖσα μὲν εἰς τὴν Λατινίδα γλῶσσαν ὑπὸ Νικοδήμου τοπάρχου τοῦ ἐκ 'Ρώμης μετενεχθεῖσα δ' εἰς τὴν 'Ελληνικὴν ὑπὸ μοναχοῦ ἀνωνύμου, σώζεται δὲ ἔν τινι χειρογράφῳ ἐν τῷ 'Αγίῳ "Ορει, καὶ ἐκδίδεται τὸ πρῶτον ἤδη εἰς φῶς.... Athens: n.p., 1889. [Recension B. Cf. nos. 8–9.]

8   'Ιστορία ἀκριβὴς περὶ τῶν τελεσθέντων κατὰ τὴν σταύρωσιν καὶ ἀνάστασιν τοῦ Κυρίου καὶ Σωτῆρος ἡμῶν 'Ιησοῦ Χριστοῦ, συγγραφεῖσα τὸ πρῶτον ὑπὸ 'Ιουδαίου τινὸς Αἰνέα, συγχρόνου τοῦ Κυρίου, μεταφρασθεῖσα μὲν εἰς τὴν Λατινίδα γλῶσσαν ὑπὸ Νικοδήμου τοπάρχου τοῦ ἐκ 'Ρώμης, μετενεχθεῖσα δὲ εἰς τὴν 'Ελληνικὴν ὑπὸ 'Αβερκίου ἱερονομάχου 'Αγιορείτου, σώζεται ἔν τινι χειρογράφῳ ἐν τῷ 'Αγίῳ "Ορει, ἐκδιδόντος νῦν ὑπὸ 'Ραφαὴλ Κοκορέλη, κελευστοῦ ξυλουργοῦ τοῦ πολεμικοῦ ναυτικοῦ. Athens: Σπυρίδων Κουσουλίνος, 1895. Reissued in Athens: Π. Α. Πετράκος, 1912, with a minor change in the title (P. Κοκορέλης became 'Υδραῖος, ἀπόστρατος σημαιοφόρος τοῦ Βασιλικοῦ Ναυτικοῦ). [Recension B. Cf. nos. 7, 9.]

9   'Ιστορία ἀκριβὴς περὶ τῶν κατὰ τὴν σταύρωσιν καὶ ἀνάστασιν τοῦ Κυρίου καὶ Σωτῆρος ἡμῶν 'Ιησοῦ Χριστοῦ τελεσθέντων, συγγραφεῖσα τὸ πρῶτον ὑπὸ 'Ιουδαίου τινὸς Αἰνέα, συγχρόνου τοῦ Κυρίου, μεταφρασθεῖσα μὲν εἰς τὴν Λατινίδα γλῶσσαν ὑπὸ Νικοδήμου τοπάρχου τοῦ ἐκ 'Ρώμης, μετενεχθεῖσα δ' εἰς τὴν 'Ελληνικὴν ὑπὸ 'Αβερκίου ἱερονομάχου 'Αγιορείτου, σώζεται δὲ ἔν τινι χειρογράφῳ ἐν τῷ 'Αγίῳ "Ορει, ἐκδιδόντος ὑπὸ Δ. Παπαγοπούλου. Athens, n.d. [Recension B. Cf. nos. 7–8.]

10   Lake, K., ed. "Texts from Mount Athos." Studia Biblica et Ecclesiastica 5, no. 2 (1902): 152–63. [AP A from Mount Athos MS. Laura Λ 117.]

11   Vannutelli, P., ed. "Actorum Pilati textus synoptici." Synoptica (1936–38). Reprinted as a separate volume in no. 12. [Synopsis of Greek AP A and B (chaps. 1–16), as published by Tischendorf (no. 4), with variants incorporated into edited text.]

12   *Vannutelli, P., ed. Actorum Pilati textus synoptici. Rome: Apud Auctorem, 1938. Reprint of no. 11.

13   Alvarez-Campos, S. Corpus Marianum patristicum. Vol. 4, pt. 2. Burgos: Aldecoa, 1979. [Pp. 531–33: chaps. 1.1, 2.3–6, and 16.2 of AP A reproduced from Tischendorf (no. 4).]

See also nos. 1–4, 34, 35, 371.

Latin

14 *Evangelium Nichodemi Incipit feliciter.* Augsburg: Günther Zainer, ca. 1473.

15 *Praefatio in gesta Domini nostri Jesu Christi secundum Nicodemum* [sig. on 1 recto]. *Passio Domini nostri Jesu Christi secundum Nicodemum* [sig. on 2 verso]. Milan: Printer for Boninus Mombritius, [1475?]. Reissued in Rome in [1490?].

16 *Evangelium Nicodemi domini nostri ihesu cristi discipuli. de eiusdem passione. In lege et prophetis fundatum ex antiquissimis libris extractum bene correctum et nouiter impressum.* Leipzig: Melchior Lotter, ca. 1499 and 1516. Reissued in Copenhagen: Paul Ræff, 1514 and 1516.

17 *Historia sive evangelium Nycodemi de gestis a principibus sacerdotum de passione et resurrectione domini. que inventa est litteris hebraicis a theodosio magno imperatore in iherusalem in pretorio pontij pylati in codicibus publicis.* Cologne: Cornelius von Zierikzee, ca. 1499–1500. [The edition attributed to Angelus Ugoletus, prepared at the same time, was probably also printed by Cornelius von Zierikzee.]

18 Fantis, A. de, ed. *Opera nuper in lucem prodeuntia. Liber Gratie spiritualis visionum et revelationum Beate Methildis. . . . Evangelium Beati Nichodemi de passione Christi. . . . Epistola Lentuli ad Romanos de persona et effigie et moribus Christi.* Venice: n.p., 1522.

19 *Gesta Saluatoris nostri Iesu Christi secundum Nicodemum, quę inuenit Theodozius magnus Imperator in Ierusalem, in praetorio Pontij Pilati, ex hebraica lingua in latinam translata, hactenus non excusa. Anno M. D. xxxviij. Mense Martio.* Antwerp: Guillelmus Montanus, 1538. Reissued in Paris by Vivantius Gaultherot in 1545.

20 Heroldus, B. J., ed. *Orthodoxographa theologicae sacrosanctae ac syncerioris fidei doctores numero LXXVI. . . .* Basel: [H. Petri], 1555. [Cf. nos. 21, 22.]

21 Grynaeus, J. J., ed. *Monumenta S. Patrum orthodoxographa, hoc est, Theologiae sacrosanctae ac syncerioris fidei Doctores, numero circiter LXXXV. . . .* Vol. 2. Basel: H. Petri, 1569. [Pp. 643–59: text reproduced from Heroldus (no. 20). Cf. nos. 22, 23, 303, 305.]

22 Fabricius, J. A., ed. *Codex apocryphus Noui Testamenti.* Vol. 1. 1703. 2d ed., Hamburg: Sumptu viduæ Benjam. Schiller et Joh. Christoph. Kisneri, 1719. [Pp. 204–301: corrects *EN* printed in *Orthodoxographa* (nos. 20, 21); surveys ancient and contemporary opinions concerning *EN*. Cf. nos. 23–25, 36, 266, 324, 339.]

23 Jones, J. *A New and Full Method of Settling the Canonical Authority of the New Testament. . . .* Vol. 2. 1726. 2d ed., Oxford: Clarendon Press, 1798. [Pp. 262–353: corrects Grynaeus (no. 21); adopts Fabricius's (no. 22) division into chapters; includes English translation. Cf. no. 303.]

24 Hess, J. J. *Bibliothek der heiligen Geschichte. Beiträge zur Beförderung des biblischen Geschichtstudiums, mit Hinsicht auf die Apologie des Christenthums.* Vol. 1. Zürich: Drell, Gesner, Füssli, 1791. [Pp. 235–83: compares Einsiedeln, Stiftsbibliothek MS. 326 (cf. nos. 1, 27), with Fabricius's edition (no. 22).]

25 Schmidius [Schmidt, C. C. L.], ed. *Corpus omnium veterum apocryphorum extra Biblia.* Vol. 1. Hadamariae: Sumptibus Almae Literariae, 1804. [Pp. 57–108: text reproduced from Fabricius (no. 22).]

26 Haydon, F. S., ed. *Eulogium (historiarum sive temporis): Chronicon ab orbe condito usque ad annum Domini M. CCC. LXVI. a monacho quodam Malmesburiensi exaratum.* Vol. 1. Rer. Brit. M. A. Script., vol. 9. London: Longman, Brown, Green, Longmans, and Roberts, 1858. [Pp. 92–141: *EN* A embedded in a chronicle. Edited from Cambridge, Trinity College MS. R. 7. 2; Dublin, Trinity College MS. 497; London, BL MS. Cotton Galba E. VII; London, Lincoln Inn Library MS. Hale 73.]

27 *Kim, H. C., ed. *The Gospel of Nicodemus: Gesta Salvatoris.* Toronto Medieval Latin Texts, vol. 2. Toronto: Pontifical Institute of Mediaeval Studies, 1973. [*EN* A from Ensiedeln, Stiftsbibliothek, MS. 326 (cf. nos. 1, 24), corrected against Oxford, Bodl. Lib. MS. Laud. Misc. 79.]

28 Smith Collett, K. A. "The Gospel of Nicodemus in Anglo-Saxon England." Ph.D. diss., University of Pennsylvania, 1981. [Survey of Latin MSS written or owned in Anglo-Saxon England; includes editions of *EN* B from Cambridge, Corpus Christi College MS. 288 (cf. no. 30), and *EN* A from Oxford, Bodl. Lib. MS. Fairfax 17.]

29 Lewis, D. J. G., ed. "A Short Latin *Gospel of Nicodemus* Written in Ireland." *Peritia* 5 (1986): 262–75. [Abridged version from London, BL MS. Royal 13 A. 14.]

30 Gounelle, R. "Recherches sur le manuscrit CCCC 288 des *Acta Pilati.*" Mémoire présenté pour l'obtention de la maîtrise ès lettres classiques, Université Paris X-Nanterre, 1989. [Includes edition and French translation of *EN* B. Cf. no. 28.]

31 Philippart, G., ed. "Les Fragments palimpsestes de l'Évangile de Nicodème dans le *Vindobonensis 563* (Ve s.?)." *Analecta Bollandiana* 107 (1989): 171–88. [Text from the oldest MS. of *EN.* Cf. nos. 39, 42.]

32 Gounelle, R. "Recherches sur les *Actes* apocryphes *de Pilate.* Les *Actes de Pilate* transmis par le ms. Bayerische Staatsbibliothek, Clm 28168. Introduction et édition accompagnées d'une bibliographie raisonnée des *Actes de Pilate.*" Mémoire de troisième cycle. Institut d'histoire de la réformation, Geneva, 1993. [Includes edition of Clm 28168.]

See also nos. 1–4, 76, 145, 211, 225, 266, 373, 428, 582.

1.1.1.2. Studies

Greek

33   Thilo, J. C. *Acta S. Thomae Apostoli ex codd. pariss. primum edidit et adnotationibus illustravit. . . . Praemissa est notitia uberior novae Codicis apocryphi Fabriciani editionis.* Leipzig: F. C. G. Vogel, 1823. [Pp. xxx–lii. Cf. no. 2.]

34   Gounelle, R. "Recherches sur les *Actes* apocryphes *de Pilate* grecs, recension B." Mémoire présenté pour l'obtention du Diplôme d'Études Approfondies. 2 vols. Université Paris X-Nanterre, 1991. [Vol. 2 includes editions of two passages (Prol.–1.6 and 11.3–12.2) in three recensions of *AP* B. Cf. no. 35.]

35   *Gounelle, R. "*Acta Pilati* grecs B (BHG 779u–w), traditions textuelles." *Recherches augustiniennes* 26 (1992): 273–94. [Includes editions of chaps. 11.3, 11.5, and 12.2 in three recensions of *AP* B. Cf. no. 34.]

See also no. 371.

Latin

36   Fabricius, J. A., ed. *Codicis apocryphi Novi Testamenti, pars tertia nunc primum edita.* 1719. 2d rev. ed., Hamburg: C. Herold, 1743. [Pp. 465–85: additional notes on *EN*. Cf. no. 22.]

37   Robinson, J. A. *Apocrypha anecdota.* Texts and Studies, vol. 2, pt. 3. Cambridge: Cambridge University Press, 1893. [Pp. 146–47: on *EN* in London, BL MS. Royal 5 E. XIII.]

38   Siegmund, A. *Die Überlieferung der griechischen christlichen Literatur in der lateinischen Kirche.* Abhandlungen der Bayerischen Benediktiner-Akademie, vol. 5. Munich-Pasing: Filser-Verlag, 1949. [Pp. 35–36: lists MSS. of *EN* antedating the twelfth century. Cf. nos. 43, 376.]

39   Philippart, G. "Fragments palimpsestes latins du Vindobonensis 563 (Ve siècle?). Évangile selon S. Matthieu. Évangile de l'enfance selon Thomas. Évangile de Nicodème." *Analecta Bollandiana* 90 (1972): 391–411. [Cf. nos. 31, 42.]

40   Backus, I. Review of *Apokryfy Nowego Testamentu*, vol. 1, *Ewangelie Apokryficzne*, edited by M. Starowieyski (no. 357). *Revue de théologie et de philosophie* 114, no. 1 (1982): 81–82. [Notes sixteenth-century editions.]

41   Landes, R. "A Libellus from St. Martial of Limoges Written in the Time of Ademar of Chabannes (998–1034)." *Scriptorium* 37 (1983): 178–204. [Pp. 190 n. 48, 206: on Ademar's copy of *EN*.]

42   Despineux, M. "Une Version latine palimpseste du Ve siècle de l'Évangile de Nicodème (*Vienne, ÖNB MS 563*)." *Scriptorium* 42 (1988): 176–83. [Cf. nos. 31, 39.]

43 *Izydorczyk, Z. "The Unfamiliar *Evangelium Nicodemi." Manu-scripta* 33 (1989): 169–91. [Surveys editions, manuscripts, and textual traditions. Cf. no. 376.]

See also nos. 28, 30, 32–33, 247, 373, 376, 380, 428, 949.

1.1.2. Eastern traditions
1.1.2.1. Armenian
Editions and translations
44 Conybeare, F. C., ed. "Acta Pilati." In *Studia biblica et ecclesiastica: Essays Chiefly in Biblical and Patristic Criticism*, 4:59–132. Oxford: Clarendon Press, 1896. [Texts from Paris, BN MSS. arm. 110 and arm. 178, retroverted into Greek and Latin, respectively; original Armenian texts not given.]
45 *Tayets'i, H. E. *T'angaran haykakan hin ew nor dprut'eants'*. Vol. 2, *Ankanon girk' nor ktakaranats'*. Venice: San Lazzaro, 1898. [Pp. 313–45: two conflated recensions.]

See also no. 370.

1.1.2.2. Coptic
Editions and translations
46 *Rossi, F., ed. *Trascrizione di un codice copto del Museo Egizio di Torino con illustrazione e note*. Memorie della Reale accademia delle scienze di Torino, 2d ser., vol. 35. Turin: Stamperia reale, 1883. Reprinted in no. 47. [Pp. 163–250: transcript of Turin Papyrus no. 1. Cf. nos. 51, 352.]
47 Rossi, F., ed. *I papiri copti del Museo Egizio di Torino*. 2 vols. Turin, 1887–92. Reprint of no. 46. [1:7–90, 2:237ff. Cf. nos. 51, 352.]
48 *Lacau, P., ed. "Acta Pilati." In *Fragments d'apocryphes coptes*, Mémoires publiés par les Membres de l'Institut français d'archéologie orientale du Caire, vol. 9, pp. 1–12. Cairo: Institut français d'archéologie orientale, 1904. [Fragments of *AP* in Paris, BN MSS. copt. 129^{17}, fol. 50, and copt. 129^{18}, fol. 140 (cf. nos. 49, 52); pp. 15–18: *Homilia de lamentis Mariae* (cf. nos. 533, 572, 580, 598, 603, 634, 646, 654, 657, 888).]
49 Révillout, E., ed. *Les Apocryphes coptes, II. Acta Pilati et supplément à l'Évangile des douze apôtres*. Patrologia Orientalis, vol. 9, no. 2. Paris: F. Didot, 1907. Reissued in 1957. [Pp. 57–132: text (including Lacau's fragments, no. 48), with French translation.]
50 Barns, J. W. B. "Bodleian Fragments of a Sa'îdic Version of the Acta Pilati." In *Coptic Studies in Honor of Walter Ewing Crum*, edited by M. Malinine, Bulletin of the Byzantine Institute of America, vol. 2, pp. 245–50. Boston, Mass.: Byzantine Institute, 1950.

51 Vandoni, M., and T. Orlandi, eds. *Vangelo di Nicodemo*. Pt. 1, *Testo copto dai papiri di Torino*. Pt. 2, *Traduzione dal copto e commentario*. Testi e documenti per lo studio dell'antichità, vols. 15 and 15a. Milan: Instituto Editoriale Cisalpino, 1966. [Cf. nos. 46–47, 352.]

See also no. 352.

Studies
52 Lemm, O. von. "Kleine koptische Studien XXVI–XLV." *Izvestiia Imperatorskoj Akademii Nauk* (St. Petersburg), 5th series, vol. 21, no. 3 (1904): 76–89 ("XLII. Eine neutestamentliche apokryphe Geschichte") and 151–61 ("XLIV. Eine neue Bartholomäus–Apokalypse"). Reprinted in no. 55. [Studies on no. 48.]
53 Baumstark, A. Review of *Les Évangiles des douze Apôtres et de saint Barthélémy*, by E. Révillout. *Revue biblique* 3 (1906): 253–59.
54 Haase, F. *Literarkritische Untersuchungen zur orientalisch-apokryphen Evangelienliteratur*. Leipzig: J. C. Hinrichs, 1913. [Pp. 11–22, 67–76.]
55 Lemm, O. von. "Kleine koptische Studien XXVI–XLV." In *Kleine koptische Studien I–LVIII*, Subsidia Byzantina, vol. 10. Leipzig: Zentralantiquariat der DDR, 1972. Reprint of no. 52.
56 Orlandi, T. "Gli apocrifi copti." *Augustinianum* 23 (1983): 57–71. [Pp. 66–67.]

1.1.2.3. Georgian
Editions
57 Khakhanov, A., ed. "Evangelie Nikodima." *Drevnosti vostochnyia: Trudy Vostochnoj kommissii Imperatorskogo moskovskogo arkheologicheskogo obshchestva* (Moscow), vol. 3, no. 1 (1907): 1–20. [Text from a sixteenth-century MS. (now lost), with Russian translation and commentary.]
58 Džavachišvili, I. A. *Sinis mt'is k'art'ul helnacert'a aǧceriloba*. Tbilisi: Academy of Sciences, 1947. [Text from Sinaï MS. Georg. 78.]
59 *K'urc'ikiže, C'., ed. *Nik'odimosis apok'rip'uli c'ignis k'art'uli versia*. Tbilisi: Mecniereba, 1985. [Based on all extant MSS.]

1.1.2.4. Palestinian Aramaic
Editions
60 Schulthess, F., ed. *Christlich-palästinische Fragmente aus der Omajjaden-Moschee zu Damascus*. Abhandlungen der königlichen Gesellschaft der Wissenschaften zu Göttingen, philologisch–historische Klasse, N.F., vol. 8, no. 3. Berlin: Weidmannsche Buchhandlung, 1905. [Pp. 24, 134–35: fragments 20 and 21 contain excerpts from *AP*.]

Studies
61   Brock, S. "A Fragment of the *Acta Pilati* in Christian Palestinian Aramaic." *Journal of Theological Studies*, n.s., 22 (1971): 157–59. [Identifies fragments edited by Schulthess (no. 60).]

1.1.2.5. Slavonic
Editions and translations
62   Hanka, V., ed. "Čtenie Nikodemovo: co še dálo při umučení Páně. Pavěst krásná o drevu Kříže Svatého...." *Abhandlungen der kön. böhmischen Gesellschaft der Wissenschaften*, vol. 5, no. 11, pp. 227–56. Prague, 1860. Reprinted in no. 63. [*GN* in Old Czech.]
63   Hanka, V., ed. *Čtenie Nikodemovo: co še dálo při umučení Páně. Pavěst krásná o drevu Kříže Svatého....* Prague: Komissi u Rivnace v Museum, 1861. Reprint of no. 62. [*GN* in Old Czech.]
64   Pypin, A. N., ed. *Lozhnyia i otrechennyia knigi russkoj stariny*. Pamiatniki starinnoj russkoj literatury izdavaemye grafom Grigoriem Kushelevym-Bezborodko, vol. 3, Slavistic Printings and Reprintings, vol. 97, no. 2. 1862. Reprint, The Hague: Mouton, 1970. [Pp. 91–108: "short version." Cf. nos. 65, 67–68, 71, 75, 79, 86.]
65   Daničić, G. "Dva apokrifna jevangjelja." *Starine* (Jugoslovenska Akademija Znanosti i Umiejetnosti, Zagreb) 4 (1872): 130–54. [Pp. 146–49: partial edition of "short version." Cf. nos. 64, 67–68, 71, 75, 79, 86.]
66   Stojanović, L., ed. "Nekoliko rukopisa iz bečke Carske Biblioteke." *Glasnik Srpskog učenog društva* (Belgrade) 63 (1885): 89–120. ["Long version." Cf. nos. 70, 76–78.]
67   Porfir'ev, I. Ia., ed. *Apokrificheskiia skazaniia o novozavetnykh litsakh i sobytiiakh, po rukopisiam Solovetskoj biblioteki*. Sbornik Otdeleniia russkogo iazyka i slovesnosti Imperatorskoj Akademii Nauk, vol. 52, no. 4. St. Petersburg: Tipografiia Imperatorskoj Akademii Nauk, 1890. [Pp. 21–36, 164–97: discussion and edition of "short version." Cf. nos. 64–65, 68, 71, 75, 79, 86.]
68   Speranskij, M. N., ed. "Slavianskiia apokrificheskiia evangeliia." In *Trudy vos'mogo arkheologicheskogo s'ezda v Moskve, 1890*. Moscow: Tovarishchestvo tip. A. I. Mamotova, 1895. [2:92–133, 144–55: "short version." Cf. nos. 64–65, 67, 71, 75, 79, 86.]
69   Brückner, A. "Z rękopisów petersburskich. III. Powieści." *Prace Filologiczne* 5 (1899). [Excerpts from *GN* in Old Polish. Cf. nos. 72–74, 89, 91, 94, 98, 366.]
70   Franko, I., ed. *Apokryfy i lehendy z ukraïns'kykh rukopysiv*. Pamiatnyky ukraïns'ko-rus'koï movy i literatury, edited by S. Komarevs'kyi, vol. 2. Lvov: Naukove Tovarystvo im. Shevchenka, 1899. [Pp. 252–72, 293–304: "long version." Cf. nos. 66, 76–78.]
71   Iagich, I. "Kriticheskia zametki k slavianskomu perevodu dvukh apokrificheskikh skazanij." *Izvestiia Otdeleniia russkogo iazyka i*

slovesnosti Imperatorskoj Akademii Nauk (St. Petersburg) 3, no. 3 (1898): 793–822. ["Short version." Cf. nos. 64–65, 67–68, 75, 79, 86.]
72 Brückner, A. *Literatura religijna w Polsce średniowiecznej.* Vol. 3, *Legendy i modlitewniki. Szkice literackie i obyczajowe.* Warsaw: Gebethner i Wolff, 1904. [Pp. 11–15: excerpts from and comments on *GN* in Old Polish. Cf. nos. 69, 73–74, 89, 91, 94, 98, 366.]
73 Vrtel-Wierczyński, S., ed. *Wybór tekstów staropolskich do roku 1543.* 1930. Warsaw: Państwowy Zakład Wydawnictw Szkolnych, 1950. [Includes *GN* in Old Polish. Cf. nos. 69, 72, 74, 89, 91, 94, 98, 366.]
74 Vrtel-Wierczyński, S., ed. *Sprawa chędoga o męce Pana Chrystusowej i Ewangelia Nikodema.* Poznań: Nakładem Poznańskiego Towarzystwa Przyjaciół Nauk, 1933. [*GN* in Old Polish. Cf. nos. 69, 72–73, 89, 91, 94, 98, 366.]
75 Aitzetmüller, R. *Mihanović Homiliar.* Graz: Akademische Druck- und Verlagsanstalt, 1957. [Facsimile of MS. containing "short version," translated in Bulgaria prior to the twelfth century. Cf. nos. 64–65, 67–68, 71, 79, 86.]
76 *Vaillant, A., ed. *L'Évangile de Nicodème: Texte slave et texte latin.* Centre de recherches d'histoire et de philologie de la IVème section de l'E. P. H. E, vol. 2, Hautes études orientales, vol. 1. Geneva: Droz, 1968. ["Long version," with Latin retroversion. Cf. nos. 66, 70, 77–78.]
77 Alban, J., trans. "Évangile de Nicodème." *Cahiers d'études cathares*, 2d ser., 71 (1976): 34–47; 77 (1976): 19–34. [French translation of Vaillant's Slavic text (no. 76). Cf. also nos. 66, 70, 78.]
78 Mareš, F. W., ed. *An Anthology of Church Slavonic Texts of Western (Czech) Origin.* Slavische Propyläen Texte in Neu- und Nachdrucken, vol. 127. Munich: Fink, 1979. [Pp. 31–40: excerpts from "long version." Cf. nos. 66, 70, 76–77.]
79 Petkanova, D., ed. *Stara bŭlgarska literatura.* Vol. 1, *Apocrifi.* Sofia: Bŭlgarski pisatel, 1981. [Pp. 148–66: *GN* in Old Bulgarian; pp. 375–77: notes. Cf. nos. 64–65, 67–68, 71, 75, 86.]

See also nos. 366, 369, 372.

Studies
80 Novaković, S. "Bugarski zbornik prošlog veka." *Starine* (Jugoslovenska Akademija Znanosti i Umijetnosti, Zagreb) 6 (1874): 29, 45–47.
81 Bulgakov, F. I. "Skazaniia o strastiakh gospodnikh." *Pamiatniki drevnej pis'mennosti i iskusstva* 1 (1878–79): 153–86.
82 Barsov, E. V. "O vozdejstvii apokrifov na obriad i ikonopis'." *Zhurnal Ministerstva narodnago prosveshcheniia* 242 (1885): 97–115. [Pp. 110–111.]

83   Sumtsov, C. F. "Ocherki istorii iuzhno-russkikh apokrificheskikh znanij i pesen." *Kievskaia starina* 19 (1887): 31–36.

84   Popov, A. N. "Bibliograficheskie materialy. . . ." *Chtenia v Imp. Obshchestve istorii i drevnostej rossijskikh pri Moskovskom Universitete* (1889): 11, 28, 44–46. [Cited after Charlesworth (no. 374).]

85   Polívka, G. "Evangelium Nicodemovo w literaturách slovanských." *Časopis Musea královstvi českého* 64 (1890): 255–75, 535–78; 65 (1891): 94–100, 440–60.

86   Nachov, N. A. "Tikveshki r''kopis ili sbornik ot apokrifni skazaniia, legendi, povesti. . . ." *Sbornik za narodni umotvoreniia: nauka i knizhnina* 8 (1892): 400–402. [On *GN* in Old Bulgarian. Cf. nos. 64–65, 67–68, 71, 75, 79.]

87   Polívka, G. "Descriptions and Excerpts" (in Russian). *Starine* (Jugoslovenska Akademija Znanosti i Umiejetnosti, Zagreb) 24 (1892): 115–18, 124–29. [Cited after Charlesworth (no. 374).]

88   Makarij, Metropolitan of Russia. *Velikiia Minei chetii.* St. Petersburg: Arkheograficheskaia Kommissia, 1899. [13–15 Nov.; cols. 1874–905.]

89   Brückner, A. "Apokryfy średniowieczne. Cz. II." *Rozprawy Akademii Umiejętności, Wydział Filologiczny* 40 (1905). [Pp. 281–87: on *GN* in Old Polish. Cf. nos. 69, 72–74, 91, 94, 98, 366.]

90   Sobolevskij, A. I. "Slovarnyj material izvlechennyj iz Nikodimova Evangelia po Sofijskomu spisku XIV veka." In *Materialy i issledovaniia v oblasti slavianskoj filologii i arkheologii,* Sbornik Otdeleniia russkogo iazyka i slovesnosti Imperstorskoj Akademii Nauk, vol. 88, pp. 81–91. St. Petersburg: Tipografiia Imperatorskoj Akademii Nauk, 1910.

91   Radliński, I. *Apokryfy judaistyczno-chrześcijańskie w polskich przeróbkach.* Warsaw, 1911. [On *GN* in Old Polish. Cf. nos. 69, 72–74, 89, 94, 98, 366.]

93   Sviatski, D. *Evangelie Nikodima pri tsvete zvezd. Istorico-astronomicheskii kommentarii.* St. Petersburg, 1914. [Cited after Starowieyski (no. 357).]

94   Bargieł, M. "O lokalizacji i różnicach językowych 'Sprawy chędogiej' i 'Ewangelii Nikodema.' " *Rozprawy Komisji Językow. Łódzkiego Towarzystwa Nauk* 7 (1959). [On language of *GN* in Old Polish. Cf. nos. 69, 72–74, 89, 91, 98, 366.]

95   Ivanov, A. I. *Literaturnoe nasledie Maksima Greka: Kharakteristika, atributsii, bibliografiia.* Leningrad: Izdatel'stvo "Nauka." [Pp. 87–88: on unpublished sixteenth-century Russian translation by Maksim the Greek.]

96   Štefanić, V., et al. *Hrvatska književnost.* Zagreb, 1969. [Pp. 146–48, 154–58.]

97 Grabar, B. "Über das Problem der längeren Fassung des Nikode-
    musevangeliums in der älteren slavischen Literatur." In *Byzance et*
    les Slaves: Études de civilisation. Mélanges Ivan Dujčev, 201–6. Paris:
    Association des amis des études archéologiques des mondes
    byzantino-slaves et du christianisme oriental, 1979. [On Glagolithic
    fragments of *GN*.]
98 Adamczyk, M. *Biblijno-apokryficzne narracje w literaturze staropolskiej*
    do końca XVI wieku. Uniwersytet Adama Mickiewicza w Poznaniu,
    Seria Filologia Polska, vol. 9. Poznań: Uniwersytet Adama Mickie-
    wicza, 1980. [Pp. 70–72: on *GN* in Old Polish. Cf. nos. 69, 72–74,
    89, 91, 94, 366.]

1.1.2.6. Syriac
Editions and translations
99 *Rahmani, I. E., ed. and trans. *Hypomnemata Domini nostri seu Acta*
    Pilati antiqua versio Syriaca. Studia Syriaca, vol. 2. Typis Patriarcha-
    libus in Seminario Scharfensi in Monte Libano, 1908. [*AP* and
    additional Pilate apocrypha from two acephalous MSS., with Latin
    translation. Cf. no. 100.]
100 Sedláček, J., trans. *Neue Pilatusakten*. Sitzungsberichte der köni-
    glichen böhmischen Gesellschaft der Wissenschaften, Klasse für
    Philosophie, Geschichte und Philologie, vol. 2. Prague, 1909 (1908).
    [Art. 9: German translation of Rahmani (no. 99).]
101 Mingana, A. *Catalogue of the Mingana Collection of Mss. Now in the*
    Possession of the Trustees of the Woodbrooke Settlement, Selly Oak,
    Birmingham. Vol. 3, *Additional Christian Arabic and Syriac Manu-*
    scripts. Cambridge: W. Heffer and Sons, 1939. [Pp. 79–85: text from
    MS. Mingana Syriac 639, with English translation, in parallel with
    James's translation of Greek *AP* A (no. 316; cf. also no. 317).]

Studies
102 Brock, S. "Notes on Some Texts in the Mingana Collection."
    Journal of Semitic Studies 14 (1969): 211–12.

See also no. 54.

1.1.3. Medieval Western traditions

See no. 231.

1.1.3.1. Castilian, Catalan, Occitan
Editions
103 *Al quest libre ha nom gamaliel en lo qual se comptator lo proces de la passio de iesu crist e es per la manera ques segueir.* Barcelona: Pere Miguel, 1493. [*Gamaliel* in Catalan. Cf. nos. 104–6, 111, 119–20, 184–86, 193, 200, 363, 679–80, 686, 776.]

104 *La passio de Jesu Christ segons que recita lo mestre Gamaliel.* . . . Barcelona: Carlos Amorós, ca. 1510. Reprinted ca. 1512. [*Gamaliel* in Catalan. Cf. nos. 103, 105–6, 111, 119–20, 184–86, 193, 200, 363, 679–80, 686, 776.]

105 Juan de Molina, ed. *La passio de Jesu Christ segons que recita lo mestre Gamaliel.* . . . Valencia: n.p., 1517. [*Gamaliel* in Catalan. Cf. nos. 103–4, 106, 111, 119–20, 184–86, 193, 200, 363, 679–80, 686, 776.]

106 Juan de Molina, ed. *Gamaliel, nuevamente traducido en lengua castellana, historiado y con mucha diligencia reconocido y enmendado.* Sevilla: Juan Cromberger, 1534. This edition is apparently a reprint of an earlier Castilian edition, now lost, of Valencia, 1522. [*Gamaliel* in Castilian. Cf. nos. 103–5, 111, 119–20, 184–86, 193, 200, 363, 679–80, 686, 776.]

107 Raynouard, F. J. M. *Lexique roman ou dictionnaire de la langue des troubadours.* . . . Vol. 1. Paris: Silvestre, 1838. [P. 577: excerpt on Christ's Descent into Hell, in Occitan; cf. Migne (no. 326), cols. 1099–1100.]

108 Amer, M. V., ed. *Compendi historial de la Biblia que ab lo títol de "Genesi de Scriptura" trelladá del provençal a la llengua catalana mossen Guillem Serra en l'any M. CCCC. LI.* Barcelona: Biblioteca Catalana, 1873. [*Lo Gènesi* from Paris, BN MS. esp. 541, in Catalan. Cf. nos. 109–10, 113–14, 117, 121.]

109 Lespy, V., and P. Raymond, eds. *Récits d'histoire sainte en béarnais.* 2 vols. Pau: Société des bibliophiles du Béarn, 1876–77. [*Lo Gènesi* from Paris, BN MS. n.a. 4131, in Occitan. Cf. nos. 108, 110, 113–14, 117, 121.]

110 *Suchier, H., ed. *Denkmäler provenzalischer Literatur und Sprache.* Vol. 1. Halle: Niemeyer, 1883. [Pp. 1–84, 481–95: *Sens e razos d'una escriptura,* in Occitan (cf. nos. 115–16); pp. 398–461, 495–96: *Lo Gènesi* in Catalan and Occitan; pp. 573–88, 497–98: *Lo Gènesi* in Italian. Cf. nos. 108–9, 113–14, 117, 121.]

111 Armengol Valenzuela, P., ed. *Obras de S. Pedro Pascual, Mártir, obispo de Jaen y religioso de la Merced.* Vol. 1, *Nueve leyendas o contemplaciones, el Libro de Gamaliel, la Destrucció de Jerusalem.* Rome: F. Cuggiani, 1905. [*Gamaliel* in Catalan. Cf. nos. 103–6, 119–20, 184–86, 193, 200, 363, 679–80, 686, 776.]

112 Moliné i Brasés, E., ed. "Passió, mort, resurrecció i aparicions de N. S. Jesucrist." *Estudis universitaris catalans* 3 (1909): 65–74, 155–59,

260–64, 349–51, 459–63, 542–46; 4 (1910): 99–109, 499–508. [A transcript of *E la mira car tot era ensems,* in Catalan. Cf. no. 118, 683, 687.]

See also no. 363.

Studies

113 Morel-Fatio, A. Review of *Compendi historial de la Biblia que ab lo títol de "Genesi de Scriptura" trelladá del provençal a la llengua catalana mossen Guillem Serra en l'any M. CCCC. LI,* by M. V. Amer (no. 108). *Romania* 4 (1875): 481. [On Amer's edition of *Lo Gènesi.* Cf. nos. 109–10, 114, 117, 121.]

114 Rohde, P. "Die Quellen der Romanischen Weltchronik." In *Denkmäler provenzalischen Literatur und Sprache,* edited by H. Suchier, 589–638. Halle: Niemeyer, 1883. [On sources of *Lo Gènesi.* Cf. nos. 108–10, 113, 117, 121.]

115 Suchier, H. "Zu den altfranzösischen Bibelübersetzungen." *Zeitschrift für romanische Philologie* 8 (1884): 413–29. [P. 429: on Turin, Biblioteca Nazionale MS. L. VI. 36a, now destroyed, containing *Sens e razos d'una escriptura* in French. Cf. nos. 110, 116.]

116 Meyer, P. "Légendes pieuses en provençal." In *Histoire littéraire de la France,* edited by P. Meyer, 32:78–108. Paris: Imprimerie nationale, 1898. [P. 104f.: on *Sens e razos d'una escriptura,* in Occitan. Cf. nos. 110, 115.]

117 Mas, J. "Notes documentals de llibres antichs a Barcelona." *Boletín de la Real Academia de Buenas Letras de Barcelona* 8 (1915): 155–67, 238–51, 330–45, 400–406, 444–63. [P. 240: *Lo Gènesi* mentioned in a medieval book list. Cf. nos. 108–10, 113–14, 121.]

118 Massó i Torrents, J. *Repertori de l'antiga literatura catalana.* Vol. 1. Barcelona: Alpha, 1932. [Pp. 43, 380–84: remarks on Moliné i Brasés's transcription of Catalan *E la mira car tot era ensems* (no. 112). Cf. nos. 683, 687.]

119 Brunel, C. F. "Notice du ms. 60 de la Bibliothèque de la Ville de Rodez." *Bibliothèque de l'École des chartes* 94 (1933): 1. [On MS. containing *Gamaliel* in Occitan. Cf. nos. 103–6, 111, 120, 184–86, 193, 200, 363, 679–80, 686, 776.]

120 Le Merrer, M. "D'une source narrative occitane de la Passion provençale et des mystères rouergats: L'*Évangile de Gamaliel.*" In *La Vie théâtrale dans les provinces du Midi, Actes du IIe colloque de Grasse, 1976,* 45–50. Tübingen: Y. Giraud, 1980. [Argues for Occitan origin of *Gamaliel.* Cf. nos. 103–6, 111, 119, 184–86, 193, 200, 363, 679–80, 686, 776.]

121 Mandigorra Llavata, L. "Leer en la Valencia del trescientos. El libro y la lectura en Valencia a través de la documentación notarial (1300–1410)." 2 vols. Ph.D. diss., Universitat de València, 1989. [2:

71–72: *Lo Gènesi* mentioned in a medieval book list. Cf. nos. 108–10, 113–14, 117.]

See also no. 231.

1.1.3.2. Dutch, Low German

Editions

122 Jan van Boendale. *Der leken spieghel, leerdicht van den jare 1330, toegekend aan Jan Deckers, klerk der stad Antwerpen.* Edited by M. de Vries. 4 pts. Leiden: D. du Mortier (en zoon), 1844–48. [Chap. 36: *GN* in Middle Dutch verse, with facsimiles. Cf. nos. 127, 704, 706.]

123 Jacobs, J., ed. "Een nieuw Mnl. handschrift van het Evangelie van Nicodemus." In *Verslagen en Mededelingen der Koninklijke Vlaamse Academie voor Taal- en Letterkunde*, 546–87. Gent: Erasmus, 1926. [Middle Dutch prose translation B. Cf. no. 124.]

124 Cumps, J., ed. "De Middelnederlandse prozavertalingen van het *Evangelium Nicodemi*." Licentiaatsverhandeling, Leuven, 1963. [Middle Dutch prose translations A (cf. no. 853) and B (cf. no. 123).]

125 Masser, A., ed. *Dat ewangelium Nicodemi van deme lidende vnses heren Ihesu Christi. Zwei mittelniederdeutsche Fassungen.* Texte des späten Mittelalters und der frühen Neuzeit, vol. 29. Berlin: E. Schmidt, 1978. [Low German prose version L (cf. nos. 128, 223, 853) and Low German adaptation of High German prose version E (cf. no. 225).]

See also nos. 361–62, 364.

Studies

126 Moll, W. "De boekerij van het St. Barbara-Klooster te Delft in de tweede helft der vijftiende eeuw. . . ." *Kerkhistorisch Archief* 4 (1866): 209–85. [*GN* mentioned in a medieval book catalogue.]

127 Mak, J. J. "Boendale-Studies, III. Boendale en *Pseudo-Petrus.*" *Tijdschrift voor Nederlandse Taal- en Letterkunde* 77 (1959): 65–111. [Discusses sources of *Der leken spieghel*, containing *GN* in Middle Dutch verse. Cf. nos. 122, 704, 706.]

128 Scheurkogel, L. "Dat ander Pasenael, de Noordnederlandse vertaling van de *Legenda aurea.*" Ph.D. diss, Groningen, 1990. [Pp. 34–50: description of The Hague, Koninklijke Bibliotheek MS. 133 E 6, containing Low German version L (cf. nos. 125, 223, 853). For *Legenda area*, see also nos. 600, 632, 640, 681, 684–85, 689, 697, 715, 801, 803, 828, 846.]

See also nos. 223, 853.

1.1.3.3. English
Editions and translations

129 *Here begynneth the treatys of Nycodemus gospell.* London: Julian Notary, 1507. [Cf. nos. 183, 368.]

130 *Nychodemus Gospell.* London: Wynkyn de Worde, 1509. Reissued in 1511, 1512, 1518, and 1532. [Cf. nos. 183, 368.]

131 *Here after foloweth a treatyse taken out of a boke whiche sometyme Theodosius the Emperour found in Iherusalem in the pretorye of Pylate of Ioseph of Armathy.* London: Wynkyn de Worde, [1510?]. [Cf. nos. 183, 368.]

132 *Nychodemus gospell.* London: John Skot, 1529. Reissued in [1537?]. [Cf. nos. 183, 368.]

133 Wheloc, A., ed. *Historiæ Ecclesiasticæ Gentis Anglorum Libri V. a Venerabili Beda Presbytero scripti . . . ab augustissimo veterum Anglo-Saxonum Rege Aluredo (sive Alfredo) examinati; ejúsque paraphrasi Saxonicâ eleganter explicati . . . cum annotationibus & analectis è publicis Veteris Ecclesiæ Anglicanæ Homiliis, aliiusque MSS. Saxonicis hinc indè excerptis. . . .* Cambridge: R. Daniel, 1643. Reissued in 1644. [Bk. 1, chap. 25, pp. 77–78: short excerpts in Old English (*GN* 24.1, 25.1) from CUL MS. Ii. 2. 11. Cf. nos. 134, 136–37, 139, 141–42, 145, 147, 153–55, 158, 160–61, 166, 173–74, 432.]

134 Thwaites, J., ed. *Heptateuchus, liber Job, et evangelium Nicodemi; anglo-saxonice. Historiae Judith fragmentum; dano-saxonice.* Oxford: Sheldonianus, 1698. [First edition of *GN* in Old English. Cf. nos. 133, 136–37, 139, 141–42, 145, 147, 153–55, 158, 160–61, 166, 173–74, 432.]

135 Morris, R., ed. *Cursor mundi (The Cursor of the World).* Pt. 3. EETS OS, vol. 62. London: K. Paul, Trench, Trübner, 1876. [Vv. 17289–18582 translate *EN* 17–28. Cf. nos. 149, 181.]

136 Hulme, W. H., ed. "The Old English Version of the Gospel Nicodemus." *PMLA* 13 (1898): 457–542. Reprinted in no. 139. [Texts from Cambridge, UL MS. Ii. 2. 11, and London, BL MS. Cotton Vitellius A. XV. Cf. nos. 133–34, 137, 139, 141–42, 145, 147, 153–55, 158, 160–61, 166, 173–74, 432.]

137 Hulme, W. H., ed. "The Old English Gospel of Nicodemus." *Modern Philology* 1 (1903–4): 579–614. [Text from London, BL MS. Cotton Vespasian D. XIV. Cf. nos. 133–34, 136, 139, 141–42, 145, 147, 153–55, 158, 160–61, 166, 173–74, 432.]

138 *Hulme, W. H., ed. *The Middle English Harrowing of Hell and Gospel of Nicodemus.* EETS ES, vol. 100. London: K. Paul, Trench, Trübner, 1908. [Cf. nos. 140, 152.]

139 Hulme, W. H., ed. *The Old English Version of the Gospel of Nicodemus.* Quarto Monographs V, vol. 27. University of Chicago Press,

n.d. Reprint of no. 136. [Cf. nos. 133–34, 136–37, 141–42, 145, 147, 153–55, 158, 160–61, 166, 173–74, 432.]

140 Klotz, F., ed. *Das mittelenglische strophische Evangelium Nicodemi, mit einer Einleitung kritisch.* . . . Königsberg i. Pr.: Karg und Manneck, 1913. [Cf. nos. 138, 152.]

141 Warner, R. N.-D., ed. *Early English Homilies from the Twelfth-Century MS Vesp. D XIV.* EETS OS, vol. 152. London: K. Paul, Trench, Trübner, 1917. [Pp. 77–88: Old English text from London, BL MS. Cotton Vespasian D. XIV. Cf. nos. 133–34, 136–37, 139, 142, 145, 147, 153–55, 158, 160–61, 166, 173–74, 432.]

142 Crawford, S. J., ed. *The Gospel of Nicodemus.* Anglo-Saxon Texts, vol. 1. Edinburgh: I. B. Hutchen, 1927. [Old English text from Cambridge, University Library MS. Ii. 2. 11, with some readings from London, BL MS. Cotton Vitellius A. XV. Cf. nos. 133–34, 136–37, 139, 141, 145, 147, 153–55, 158, 160–61, 166, 173–74, 432.]

143 Holden, A. W., ed. "The Gospel of Nicodemus in Middle English Prose from British Museum MS Egerton 2658, John Rylands English MS. 895, Bodleian Library MS. Bodley 207, Stonyhurst College MS. XLIII." Master's thesis, University of London, 1951.

144 Kim, H. C., ed. "The Gospel of Nicodemus Translated by John Trevisa." Ph.D. diss., University of Washington, 1963. [Cf. nos. 157, 159, 168, 176, 179, 733, 750.]

145 Allen, T. P., ed. "A Critical Edition of the Old English Gospel of Nicodemus." Ph.D. diss., Rice University, 1968. [Includes hypothetical Latin version culled from Tischendorf's edition (no. 4). Cf. nos. 133–34, 136–37, 139, 141–42, 147, 153–55, 158, 160–61, 166, 173–74, 432.]

146 Lindström, B., ed. *A Late Middle English Version of the Gospel of Nicodemus Edited from British Museum MS Harley 149.* Acta Universitatis Upsaliensis, Studia Anglistica Upsaliensia, vol. 18. Uppsala: Almqvist & Wiksell, 1974. [Includes two French translations from Paris, BN MS. f. fr. 1850 (text "C") and London, BL MS. Egerton 2710 (text "B"). Cf. no. 198.]

147 Swanton, M., ed. and trans. *Anglo-Saxon Prose.* London: Dent, 1975. [Pp. 139–57: modern English translation of Old English GN. Cf. nos. 133–34, 136–37, 139, 141–42, 145, 153–55, 158, 160–61, 166, 173–74, 432.]

148 Drennan, J. F., ed. "A Short Middle English Prose Translation of the *Gospel of Nicodemus.*" Ph.D. diss., University of Michigan, 1980. [Cf. nos. 151, 169–72, 180, 209.]

149 Horall, S. M., gen. ed. *The Southern Version of Cursor Mundi.* Vol. 4, edited by P. H. J. Mous. Ottawa Mediaeval Studies and Texts, vol. 14. Ottawa: University of Ottawa Press, 1986. [Vv. 17289–18638 translate *EN* 12–27 and Pilate's letter to Rome. Cf. nos. 135, 181.]

150 Hill, B., ed. "The Middle English Prose Version of the *Gospel of Nicodemus* from Washington, Library of Congress pre-Ac 4." *Notes and Queries* 232 (1987): 156–75. [Cf. nos. 163, 175, 178.]

151 *Marx, C. W., and J. F. Drennan, eds. *The Middle English Prose Complaint of Our Lady and Gospel of Nicodemus.* Middle English Texts, vol. 19. Heidelberg: C. Winter, 1987. [Includes source text in Anglo-Norman from London, BL MS. Royal 20 B. V. Cf. nos. 148, 169–72, 180, 209.]

See also nos. 368, 432.

Studies

152 Horstmann, C. "Gregorius auf dem Steine aus Ms. Cotton. Cleop. D IX, nebst Beiträgen zum Evangelium Nicodemi." *Archiv für das Studium der neueren Sprachen und Literaturen* 57 (1877): 59–73. [On GN in London, BL MS. Cotton Galba E. IX, and excerpts from London, BL MS. Harley 4196. Cf. nos. 138, 140.]

153 Hulme, W. H. "The Relation of the Old English Version of the Gospel of Nicodemus to the Latin Original." *Modern Language Notes* 13 (1898): 149. [Brief summary of a lecture. Cf. nos. 133–34, 136–37, 139, 141–42, 145, 147, 154–55, 158, 160–61, 166, 173–74, 432.]

154 Schmitt, A. *Die Sprache des altenglischen Bearbeitung des Evangeliums Nicodemi.* Munich diss. Weimar, 1905. [Cf. nos. 133–34, 136–37, 139, 141–42, 145, 147, 153, 155, 158, 160–61, 166, 173–74, 432.]

155 Straub, F. *Lautlehre der jungen Nicodemus-Version in Vespasian D.xiv.* Würzburg diss. Würzburg, 1908. [Cf. nos. 133–34, 136–37, 139, 141–42, 145, 147, 153–54, 158, 160–61, 166, 173–74, 432.]

156 Gerould, G. H. *Saints' Legends.* Boston: Houghton Mifflin, 1916. [See index, s.v. "Nicodemus, Gospel of," for brief discussions of various English versions.]

157 Perry, A. J., ed. *Dialogus inter Militem et Clericum, Richard Fitz-Ralph's Sermon: 'Defensio Curatorum' and Methodius: 'þe Bygynnyng of þe World and þe Ende of Worldes,' translated by John Trevisa.* EETS OS, vol. 167. London: Oxford University Press, 1925. [Pp. xci–xciv: on John Trevisa's translation of GN. Cf. nos. 144, 159, 168, 176, 179, 733, 750.]

158 Förster, M. "Der Inhalt der altenglischen Handschrift Vespasianus D. XIV." *Englishe Studien* 53 (1919–20): 46–68. [On MS. containing GN in Old English. Cf. nos. 133–34, 136–37, 139, 141–42, 145, 147, 153–55, 160–61, 166, 173–74, 432.]

159 Hammond, E. P., ed. "John Shirley: Two Versified Tables of Contents." In *English Verse between Chaucer and Surrey*, edited by E. P. Hammond, 194–96. Durham, N. C.: Duke University Press, 1927.

[On John Shirley's ascription of a translation of *GN* to John Trevisa. Cf. nos. 144, 157, 168, 176, 179, 733, 750.]

160 Förster, M. "The Donations of Leofric to Exeter." In *The Exeter Book of Old English Poetry*, introduced by R. W. Chambers, M. Förster, and R. Flower, 10–32. London: P. Lund, 1933. [On Cambridge, UL MS. Ii. 2. 11, containing *GN* in Old English. Cf. nos. 133–34, 136–37, 139, 141–42, 145, 147, 153–55, 158, 161, 166, 173–74, 432.]

161 Förster, M. "Zum altenglischen Nicodemus-Evangelium." *Archiv für das Studium der neueren Sprachen und Literaturen* 107 (1901): 311–21. [Cf. nos. 133–34, 136–37, 139, 141–42, 145, 147, 153–55, 158, 160, 166, 173–74, 432.]

162 Doyle, A. I. "An Unrecognized Piece of *Piers the Ploughman's Creed* and Other Work by Its Scribe." *Speculum* 34 (1959): 428–36. [Pp. 430–32: on Worcester Cathedral MS. F 172, containing *GN* in Middle English prose. Cf. no. 177.]

163 Hill, B. "A Newly-Identified Middle English Prose Version of the Gospel of Nicodemus." *Notes and Queries* 204 (1959): 243. [Library of Congress MS. 4. Cf. nos. 150, 175, 178.]

164 Foster, F. A. "Legends of Jesus and Mary." In *A Manual of the Writings in Middle English 1050–1500*, edited by J. Burke Severs, 2:447–57, 639–44. The Connecticut Academy of Arts and Sciences, 1970.

165 Shields, H. "Bishop Turpin and the Source of *Nycodemus gospell.*" *English Studies* 53 (1972): 497–502. [On a paleographical error in early printed editions.]

166 Handley, R. "British Museum MS. Cotton Vespasian D. XIV." *Notes and Queries* 219 (1974): 243–50. [On MS. containing *GN* in Old English. Cf. nos. 133–34, 136–37, 139, 141–42, 145, 147, 153–55, 158, 160–61, 173–74, 432.]

167 Hogg, J., ed. *The Speculum devotorum of an Anonymous Carthusian of Sheen.* Analecta Cartusiana, vol. 13. Salzburg: Institut für englische Sprache und Literatur, Universität Salzburg, 1974. [P. 312: on a late medieval rejection of *GN*.]

168 Power, K. H. "A Newly Identified Prose Version of the Trevisa Version of the Gospel of Nicodemus." *Notes and Queries* 223 (1978): 5–7. [Cf. nos. 144, 157, 159, 176, 179, 733, 750.]

169 Moe, P. "The Middle English Prose *Gospel of Nicodemus:* A Newly Identified Version." *Notes and Queries* 224: 3 (1979): 203–4. [Huntington Library MS. HM 144. Cf. nos. 148, 151, 170–72, 180, 209.]

170 Drennan, J. F. "The *Complaint of Our Lady* and *Gospel of Nicodemus* of MS Pepys 2498." *Manuscripta* 24 (1980): 164–70. [Cf. nos. 148, 151, 169, 171–72, 180, 209.]

171 Drennan, J. F. "The Middle English *Gospel of Nicodemus* in Huntington Library MS. HM. 144." *Notes and Queries* 205, no. 4 (1980): 297–98. [Cf. nos. 148, 151, 169–70, 172, 180, 209.]

172 Marx, C. W. "Beginnings and Endings: Narrative-linking in Five Manuscripts from the Fourteenth and Fifteenth Centuries and the Problem of Textual 'Integrity.' " In *Manuscripts and Readers in Fifteenth-Century England*, edited by D. Pearsall, 70–81. Cambridge: D. S. Brewer, 1983. [Argues that *Complaint of Our Lady* and *Gospel of Nicodemus* form a narrative sequence. Cf. nos. 148, 151, 169–71, 180, 209.]

173 Healey, A. di Paolo. "Anglo-Saxon Use of the Apocryphal Gospel." In *The Anglo-Saxons: Synthesis and Achievement*, edited by J. D. Woods and D. A. E. Pelteret, 93–104. Waterloo (Ontario): Wilfrid Laurier University Press, 1985. [On *GN* in Old English. Cf. nos. 133–34, 136–37, 139, 141–42, 145, 147, 153–55, 158, 160–61, 166, 174, 432.]

174 Greenfield, S. B., and D. G. Calder. *A New Critical History of Old English Literature*. New York: New York University Press, 1986. [P. 199: on *GN* in Old English. Cf. nos. 133–34, 136–37, 139, 141–42, 145, 147, 153–55, 158, 160–61, 166, 173, 432.]

175 Krochalis, J. "The Benedictine Rule for Nuns: Library of Congress MS 4*." *Manuscripta* 30 (1986): 21–34. [On MS. containing *GN* in Middle English prose. Cf. nos. 150, 163, 178.]

176 Fowler, D. C. "The Middle English Gospel of Nicodemus in Winchester MS 33." *Leeds Studies in English*, n.s., 19 (1988): 67–83. [On Trevisa's translation (cf. nos. 144, 157, 159, 168, 179, 733, 750). Prints excerpt from Gregory of Tours, *Libri historiarum X*, 1.21 (cf. no. 475), which precedes *EN* in some MSS.]

177 Christianson, C. P. "Evidence for the Study of London's Late Medieval Manuscript-Book Trade." In *Book Production and Publishing in Britain, 1375–1475*, edited by J. Griffiths and D. Pearsall, 87–108. Cambridge: Cambridge University Press, 1989. [P. 101 n. 43: on Worcester Cathedral MS. F 172, containing *GN* in Middle English prose. Cf. no. 162.]

178 Hill, B. "Some Problems in Washington, Library of Congress MS Faye-Bond 4." In *In Other Words: Transcultural Studies . . . Presented to H. H. Meier*, edited by J. L. MacKenzie and R. Todd, 35–44. Dordrecht: Foris, 1989. [On MS. containing *GN* in Middle English prose. Cf. nos. 150, 163, 175.]

179 Lyall, R. J. "Materials: the Paper Revolution." In *Book Production and Publishing in Britain, 1375–1475*, edited by J. Griffiths and D. Pearsall, 11–29. Cambridge: Cambridge University Press, 1989. [On dating John Shirley's MS. of Trevisa's *GN*. Cf. nos. 144, 157, 159, 168, 176, 733, 750.]

180 Pickering, O. S. "Brotherton Collection MS 501: A Middle English Anthology Reconsidered." *Leeds Studies in English*, n.s., 21 (1990): 141–65. [On MS. containing *Complaint of Our Lady* and *Gospel of Nicodemus*. Cf. nos. 148, 151, 169–72, 209.]

181 Thompson, J. "Textual Interpolations in the Cotton Manuscript of the *Cursor Mundi*." *Neuphilologische Mitteilungen* 92 (1991): 15–28. [On GN in *Cursor mundi*. Cf. nos. 135, 149.]

182 Taavitsainen, I., and C. W. Marx. "A Seventeenth-Century English Manuscript of *The Gospel of Nicodemus* in Royal Library of Stockholm, MS Huseby 71." *Notes and Queries* 239 (1994): 150–55.

183 Marx, C. W. "Julian Notary, Wynkyn de Worde, and the Earliest Printed Texts of the Middle English *Gospel of Nicodemus*." In *Neuphilologische Mitteilungen* 96 (1995): 389–98. [Cf. nos. 129–30, 132.]

See also nos. 28, 231, 275, 314, 737, 740, 744–45, 748.

1.1.3.4. French
Editions

184 *La Vie de Jesu Crist*. Robin Foucquet, 1485. Frequently reissued, including Lyon, 1488; Lyon: Jaques Arnoullet, 1495; Lyon: Claude Nourry, 1501. [Cf. nos. 103–6, 111, 119–20, 185–86, 193, 200, 363, 679–80, 686, 776.]

185 *Passion de N.-S.-Jésus-Christ, faicte et traitée par le bon maistre Gamaliel et Nicodemus son neveu, et le bon chevalier Joseph Dabrimatie translatée du latin en françois*. Paris: J. Trepperel, 1492. Reissued in 1497. [Incorporates "long version" attributed to Gamaliel. Cf. nos. 103–6, 111, 119–20, 184, 186, 193, 200, 363, 679–80, 686, 776.]

186 *La Vie de Jesu-Christ. – La Mort et passion de Iesucrist, laquelle fut composée par les bons et expers-maîtres, Nichodemus et Joseph d'Arimathie. – La Destruction de Hierusalem et vengeance de nostre Saulveur et Redempteur Jésus-Christ, faicte par Vespasien et Titus son fils*. Lyon: Jehan de Chandeney, 1510. Frequently reissued under various titles, including two editions in Lyon: la Veuve de Barnabé Chaussard, n. d. (the first was entitled *La Vie de Jesu-Christ . . .*, and the second, *Vita Christi. . .*); Lyon: Cl. Nourry, 1515 and 1527; Poitiers, 1524; Poitiers: Jehan de Marnef, 1535; Lyon: Le Prince, 1538; Lyon, 1544; Toulouse, 1544; Lyon: Jean Canterel, 1551 (*La Mort et passion de Jesuchrist*). [Incorporates "long version" attributed to Gamaliel. Cf. nos. 103–6, 111, 119–20, 184–85, 193, 200, 363, 679–80, 686, 776.]

187 *La Passion de notre sauveur Jésus-Christ et la resurrection*. Paris: Simon Calvarin, [between 1571 and 1593].

188 Paris, A. P. *Les Manuscrits françois de la bibliothèque du roi*. Vols. 2, 3, 4, 7. Paris, 1838–48. [See especially 2:82–85, 97–110; 3:5–9, 386–92; 4:12–14, 30–31; 7:220–22, 377–84.]

189 Reinsch, R., ed. "Maître André de Coutances, Le Roman de la résurrection de Jésus-Christ. Bearbeitung des Evangeliums Nicodemi, nach der einzigen Londoner Hs. des 13. Jahrunderts." *Archiv für das Studium der neueren Sprachen und Litteraturen* 64 (1880): 161–96. [Cf. nos. 190, 201.]

190 *Paris, G., and A. Bos, eds. *Trois Versions rimées de l'Évangile de Nicodème par Chrétien, André de Coutances et un anonyme.* Société des anciens textes français, vol. 22. 1885. Reprint, New York: Johnson Reprint Corp., 1968. [Cf. nos. 189, 192, 199, 201–202.]

191 Meyer, P. "Légendes hagiographiques en français." In *Histoire littéraire de la France,* edited by P. Meyer, 33:328–458. Paris: Imprimerie nationale, 1906.

192 Pfuhl, E., ed. *Die weitere Fassung der altfranzösischen Dichtung in achtsilbigen Reimpaaren über Christi Höllenfart und Auferstehung (Fortsetzung der eigentlichen Passion) nach fünf Hss. in Cambridge, Paris und Turin herausgegeben....* Greifswald: H. Adler, 1909. [Cf. no. 190.]

193 Le Merrer, M., ed. "Édition de la version en prose de l'Évangile de Nicodème d'après cinq manuscrits du XIVᵉ et XVᵉ siècles." Mémoire de maîtrise, Université de Caen, 1968. ["Long version," attributed to Gamaliel. Cf. nos. 103–6, 111, 119–20, 184–86, 200, 363, 679–80, 686, 776.]

194 *Ford, A. E., ed. "Old French Prose Versions of the *Gospel of Nicodemus.*" Ph.D. diss., University of Pennsylvania, 1971. [Cf. no. 195.]

195 *Ford, A. E., ed. *L'Évangile de Nicodème: Les Versions courtes en ancien français et en prose.* Publications romanes et françaises, vol. 125. Geneva: Droz, 1973. [Cf. nos. 194, 203, 205.]

196 Quinn, E. C., and M. Dufau, eds. *The Penitence of Adam: A Study of the Andrius MS.* Romance Monographs, vol. 36. University, Miss.: Romance Monographs, 1980. [Includes *GN* in French prose (beginning with Joseph of Arimathea), with English translation (pp. 92–103, 125–36).]

See also nos. 146, 151.

Studies

197 Champollion-Figeac, J. J. *Documents historiques inédits tirés des collections manuscrites de la Bibliothèque Nationale ou des bibliothèques des départements....* Vol. 4. Paris: F. Didot, 1848. [Pp. 421–23: on *GN* in MS. 7693 of Bibliothèque impériale in Paris. The author announces his intention to publish the text, but there is no evidence of such a publication.]

198 Meyer, P. "Notice du ms. Egerton 2710 du Musée Britannique." *Bulletin de la Société des anciens textes français* 15 (1889): 72–97. [On MS. of *GN* in French prose. Cf. no. 146.]

199 Meyer, P. "Note sur un nouveau manuscrit de la traduction en vers de l'Évangile de Nicodème par Chrétien." *Bulletin de la Société des anciens textes français* 24 (1898): 81–84. [Cf. nos. 190, 202.]

200 Roy, É. *Le Mystère de la passion en France du XIVe au XVIe siècle.* Revue Bourguignonne, vols. 13–14. 1903–4. Reprint, Geneva: Slatkine, 1974. [Pp. 325–45: on *Passion selon Gamaliel,* i.e., "long version" of *GN.* Cf. nos. 103–6, 111, 119–20, 184–86, 193, 363, 679–80, 686, 776.]

201 Owen, D. D. R. *The Vision of Hell: Infernal Journeys in Medieval French Literature.* New York: Barnes and Noble, 1970. [Pp. 99–101: on André de Coutances's poetic version of *GN.* Cf. nos. 189–90.]

202 Blaess, M. "Les Manuscrits français dans les monastères anglais au moyen âge." *Romania* 94 (1973): 321–58. [Items 98 and 931: two copies (now lost) of Chrétien's *GN.* Cf. nos. 190, 199.]

203 O'Gorman, R. Review of *L'Évangile de Nicodème: Les Versions courtes en ancien français et en prose,* edited by A. E. Ford (no. 195). *Cahiers de civilisation médiévale* 19 (1976): 59–61. [Cf. no. 205.]

204 Russell, D. W., ed. *La Vie de Saint Laurent: An Anglo-Norman Poem of the Twelfth Century.* Anglo-Norman Texts, vol. 34. London: Westfield College Press, 1976. [Pp. 1–4: on Paris, BN MS. f. fr. 19525, containing *GN* in Middle French prose.]

205 Sneddon, C. R. Review of *L'Évangile de Nicodème: Les Versions courtes en ancien français et en prose,* edited by A. E. Ford (no. 195). *French Studies* 31 (1977): 441–42. [Cf. no. 203.]

206 Hill, B. "British Library MS. Egerton 613." *Notes and Queries* 223 (1978): 394–409, 492–501. [On MS. containing *GN* in Middle French prose.]

207 Shields, H. "Légendes religieuses en ancien français (MS. 951 de la Bibliothèque de Trinity College à Dublin)." *Scriptorium* 34 (1980): 59–71. [Pp. 65–66: on unedited *GN* in Middle French prose. Cf. no. 211.]

208 Bozóky, E. "Les Apocryphes bibliques." In *Le Moyen âge et la Bible,* edited by P. Riché and G. Lobrichon, Bible de tous les temps, vol. 4, pp. 429–48. Paris: Beauchesne, 1984.

209 Marx, C. W. "A Newly Identified Fragment of the Anglo-Norman Prose *Complaint of Our Lady* and *Gospel of Nicodemus* in Cambridge University Library MS Dd. 4. 35." *Notes and Queries* 236 (1991): 157–58. [Cf. nos. 148, 151, 169–72, 180.]

210 Carozzi, C. *Le Voyage de l'âme dans l'au-delà d'après la littérature latine (Ve-XIIIe siècle).* Collection de l'École française de Rome, vol. 189. Palais Farnèse: École française de Rome, 1994. [Pp. 3, 421–22: on *EN* and its traditions in Reims region.]

211 Izydorczyk, Z. "The Latin Source of an Old French Gospel of Nicodemus." *Revue d'histoire des textes* 25 (1995): 265–79. [Includes excerpts from unedited Latin and French versions. Cf. no. 207.]

See also nos. 231, 740, 742, 744–45.

1.1.3.5. High German
Editions
212 *Evangelium Nicodemi uß dem Latein ins teudtsch bracht.* N.p., 1496.
[Listed by Budik (no. 230), but now lost.]
213 *Euangelium Nicodemi / auß dem Latein ins Teütsch gebracht / In welchem
vil hüpscher puncten / die die andern Euangelisten nit setzen / begriffen
werden (doch jnen nit wider) fast nützlich zulesen.* N.p., n.d. Frequently
reprinted in the early sixteenth century. [Cf. nos. 216, 218, 334.]
214 *Evangelischer Bericht von dem Leben Jesu Christi, welches Nichodemus ... beschrieben....* Eisenberg: n.p., n.d. Published also in Magde-
burg: J. Siegelers Wwe, n.d. [Cf. nos. 331–32, 336, 340, 342–43.]
215 *Dat Evangelium des heiligen Nicodemy / welcker ys gewesen ein Furst der
Juden / vnde ein vorborgen Junger des Heren.* Dantzick: Franciscus
Rhode, 1538.
216 *Evangelion Nicodemi / Auss dem Latein in die Teutsch sprach verandert.
In welchem vil hübscher puncten / die die andern evangelisten nit setzen /
begriffen werden / doch jnen nicht zuwider / fast nützlich zu lesen.* (Often
reprinted, sometimes without any indication of place or date.)
Marburg: Andreas Kolb, 1555, 1561, and 1605. Reissued also in 1579;
Cologne, 1591; Leipzig, 1616 and 1676; and Schmalkalden, 1687. [Cf.
nos. 213, 218, 334.]
217 *Evangelium Nicodemi / das ist: Die Historia vom Leiden / Sterben und
Aufferstehung Jhesu Christi.... Itzt von newem aus dem Latein in hoch
Deutsche spraach verdolmetscht.* Marburg: Andreas Kolb, 1568.
218 *Evangelion Nicodemi Deutsch Inn welchem viel schöner Puncten / so die
andern Euangelisten nicht setzen / begriffen werden / (doch inen nicht
Zuwider) fast nüsslich zu lesen.... Item / Copey und Abschrifft des Brieffs,
so der Edessenisch König Abagarus an Jesum geschrieben hat, dergleichen
die gnedige Gegenantwort, &c. Sampt beygesetztem Vrteil über Jhesum
Christum uncorn Herrn.* N.p., 1582. [Cf. nos. 213, 216, 334.]
219 Bachmann, A., and S. Singer, eds. *Deutsche Volksbücher. Aus einer
Zürcher Handschrift des fünfzehnten Jahrhunderts herausgegeben.* Bibliothek des Litterarischen Vereins in Stuttgart, vol. 185. 1889. Reprint,
Hildesheim: G. Olms, 1973. [Prose translation F. Cf. no. 225.]
220 Heinrich von Hesler. *Das Evangelium Nicodemi.* Edited by K. Helm.
Bibliothek des Litterarischen Vereins, vol. 224. 1902. Reprint, Hildesheim: G. Olms, 1976. [Verse translation. Cf. nos. 232, 234, 236, 238,
240, 244–45, 823, 843.]
221 Piontek, A., ed. *Die Mittelhochdeutsche Übersetzung des Nikodemus-
Evangeliums in der Augsburger Handschrift (Ms. 3) und in der Münchener Handschrift (Cgm. 5018).* Greiswald: H. Adler, 1909. [Prose translation A. Cf. nos. 223, 225.]
222 Gundacker von Judenburg. *Gundackers von Judenburg "Christi Hort"
aus der Wiener Handschrift.* Edited by J. Jaksche. Deutsche Texte des

Mittelalters, vol. 18. Berlin: Weidmannsche Buchhandlung, 1910. [Verse rendition of *GN*. Cf. nos. 235, 239, 837, 841.]

223 Vollmer, H. "Das Evangelium Nicodemi in deutscher Prosa." *Bibel und deutsche Kultur* 6 (1936): 200–29. [Prose translations A (High German; cf. nos. 221, 225) and L (Low German; cf. nos. 125, 128, 853).]

224 Jänecke, K. *Der spiegel des lidens cristi. Eine oberrheinische Handschrift aus dem Beginn des XV. Jahrhunderts in der Stadtbibliothek zu Colmar (Ms. 306).* Hannover: [Gebr. Jänecke], 1964. [Pp. 162–65: excerpts from prose translation E[7]. Cf. no. 225.]

225 *Masser, A., and M. Siller, eds. *Das Evangelium Nicodemi in spätmittelalterlicher deutscher Prosa. Texte.* Germanische Bibliothek, 4th ser., Texte und Kommentar. Heidelberg: C. Winter, 1987. [Includes versions A to H, Latin *editio princeps*, and first German printed edition. Cf. nos. 219, 221, 223–24, 248–49, 845, 854, 861.]

226 Konrad von Heimesfurt. *Unser vrouwen hinvart und Diu urstende.* Edited by K. Gärtner and W. J. Hoffmann. Altdeutsche Textbibliothek, vol. 99. Tübingen: Niemeyer, 1989. [*GN* in verse. Cf. nos. 228, 237, 247, 816, 820, 839, 842, 850.]

227 Hoffmann, W. J., ed. "Die ostmitteldeutsche Übersetzung des *Evangelium Nicodemi* in der Den Haager Handschrift 73 E 25 (Übersetzung K). Untersuchungen und Text." *Vestigia Bibliae* 9/10 (1987/88, published in 1991): 216–73. [Prose translation K. Cf. nos. 229.]

228 Konrad von Heimesfurt. *Diu urstende.* Edited by K. Gärtner and W. J. Hoffmann. Altdeutsche Textbibliothek, vol. 106. Tübingen: Niemeyer, 1991. [*GN* in verse; teaching edition. Cf. nos. 226, 237, 247, 816, 820, 839, 842, 850.]

Studies

229 Lorsbach, G. W. *Quaedam de vetusta Evangelii S. Nicodemi interpretatione germanica.* Herboner Schulprogram, 1802. [Includes excerpts from prose translation K. Cf. nos. 227.]

230 Budik, P. A. "Zur Kenntnis seltener Bücher." *Serapeum* 2 (1841). [P. 152: mentions German edition printed in 1496, now lost. Cf. no.212.]

231 *Wülcker, R. P. *Das Evangelium Nicodemi in der abendländischen Literatur. Nebst drei excursen....* Paderborn: F. Schöningh, 1872.

232 Amersbach, K. *Über die Identität des Verfassers des gereimten Evangeliums Nicodemi mit Heinrich Hesler.* 2 vols. Schulprogramm Gymnasium Konstanz. Konstanz: F. Stadler, 1883–84. [Cf. nos. 220, 234, 236, 238, 240, 244–45, 823, 843.]

233 Piper, P. H. E. *Die geistliche Dichtung der Mittelalter....* Berlin: W. Spemann, 1888–89.

234 Helm, K. *Untersuchungen über Heinrich Heslers Evangelium Nicodemi.* Habilitationsschrift. Halle a. S.: E. Karras, 1899. [Cf. nos. 220, 232, 236, 238, 240, 244–45, 823, 843.]

235 Stübiger, K. *Untersuchungen zu Gundacker von Judenburg.* Germanische Studien, vol. 15. 1922. Reprint, Nendeln, Liechtenstein: Kraus Reprint Corp., 1967. [Pp. 79–123: on *Christi Hort.* Cf. nos. 222, 239, 837, 841.]

236 Boor, H. de. "Stilbeobachtungen zu Heinrich von Hesler." In *Vom Werden des deutschen Geistes. Festgabe Gustav Ehrismann,* edited by P. Merker and W. Stammler, 124–48. Berlin: W. de Gruyter, 1925. Reprinted in no. 238. [On Heinrich von Hesler as author of the High German *Evangelium Nicodemi.* Cf. nos. 220, 232, 234, 240, 244–45, 823, 843.]

237 Klibansky, E. *Gerichtsszene und Prozeßform in den erzählenden deutschen Dichtungen des 12.–14. Jahrhunderts.* Germanische Studien, vol. 40. 1925. Reprint, Nendeln, Liechtenstein: Kraus Reprint Corp., 1967. [Pp. 9–16: on Konrad von Heimesfurt's references to contemporary judicial procedures in *Urstende.* Cf. nos. 226, 228, 247, 816, 820, 839, 842, 850.]

238 Boor, H. de. "Stilbeobachtungen zu H. von Hesler." In H. de Boor, *Kleine Schriften,* 1:1–20. Berlin, 1964. Reprint of no. 236. [Cf. nos. 220, 232, 234, 236, 240, 244–45, 823, 843.]

239 Geith, K.-E. "Eine Quelle zu Gundackers von Judenburg *Christi Hort.*" *Zeitschrift für deutsches Altertum* 97 (1968): 57–68. [Cf. nos. 222, 235, 837, 841.]

240 Masser, A. "Eine unbekannte Handschrift vom Evangelium Nicodemi Heinrichs von Hesler." *Zeitschrift für deutsche Philologie* 91 (1972): 321–36. [Cf. nos. 220, 232, 234, 236, 238, 244–45, 823, 843.]

241 Purkart, J., and A. Masser. "Einige Nachtrage zu den Fragmenten des 'Evangelium Nicodemi' aus Michaelbeuern." *Zeitschrift für deutsche Philologie* 93 (1974): 443–47.

242 *Steinhauser, M. "Die mittelalterlichen hoch deutschen Handschriften des Nikodemusevangeliums. Prolegomena zu einer Edition." Ph.D. diss., Innsbruck, 1975.

243 Masser, A. *Bibel- und Legendenepik des deutschen Mittelalters.* Grundlagen der Germanistik, vol. 19. Berlin: E. Schmidt, 1976. [Pp. 117–24: on verse renditions of *GN.*]

244 Wiedmer, P. *Sündenfall und Erlösung bei Heinrich von Hesler. Ein Beitrag zum Verständnis der deutschen Bibelepik des späten Mittelalters.* Basler Studien zur deutschen Sprache und Literatur, vol. 53. Bern: Francke, 1977. [Pp. 11–20: on theological thought in Heinrich's *Evangelium Nicodemi* (cf. nos. 220, 232, 234, 236, 238, 240, 245, 823, 843); pp. 25–83: on significance of digressions in that work.]

245 Gärtner, K. "Neue Fragmente von Heinrichs von Hesler Evangelium Nicodemi." *Zeitschrift für deutsches Altertum* 107 (1978): 206–15. [Cf. nos. 220, 232, 234, 236, 238, 240, 244, 823, 843.]

246 Schelb, A. V. "Evangelium Nicodemi." In *Die deutsche Literatur des Mittelalters. Verfasserlexikon,* 2d rev. ed., edited by K. Ruh, 2:659–63.

Berlin: W. de Gruyter, 1980.

247 Hoffmann, W. J. "Konrad von Heimesfurt. Untersuchungen zu Quellen, Überlieferung und Wirkung seiner beiden Werke *Unser vrouwen hinvart* und *Urstende.*" Ph.D. diss., Universität Trier, 1987. [Includes classification of MSS. of Latin *EN* B. Cf. nos. 226, 228, 237, 816, 820, 839, 842, 850.]

248 Kunze, K. Review of *Das Evangelium Nicodemi in spätmittelalterlicher deutscher Prosa. Texte,* edited by A. Masser and M. Siller (no. 225). *Anzeiger für deutsches Altertum* 99 (1988): 194–97. [Identifies additional MS. of version F. Cf. no. 249.]

249 Geith, K.-E. Review of *Das Evangelium Nicodemi in spätmittelalterlicher deutscher Prosa. Texte,* edited by A. Masser and M. Siller (no. 225). *Arbitrium* 7 (1989): 286–89. [Cf. no. 248.]

See also nos. 853–54.

1.1.3.6. Irish

Editions and translations

250 Atkinson, E. R., ed. *The Passions and Homilies from the Leabhar Breac.* Todd Lecture Series. Dublin: Royal Irish Academy, 1887. [Pp. 113–24, 359–71; 143–51, 392–400. Cf. nos. 254–55, 876.]

251 *Herbert, M., and M. McNamara, trans. *Irish Biblical Apocrypha: Selected Texts in Translation.* Edinburgh: T & T Clark, 1989. [Pp. 60–88, 179.]

252 *Hughes, I., ed. *Stair Nicoméid: The Irish Gospel of Nicodemus.* Irish Texts Society, vol. 55. London: Irish Text Society, 1991. [Cf. no. 256.]

See also no. 367.

Studies

253 Dumville, D. N. "Biblical Apocrypha and the Early Irish: A Preliminary Investigation." *Proceedings of the Royal Irish Academy* 73C (1973): 299–338.

254 Ó Cuív, B. "Some Versions of the Sixth Petition in the Pater Noster." *Studia Celtica* 14–15 (1979): 212–22. [On dating Leabhar Breac, which contains three versions of *GN.* Cf. nos. 250, 255, 876.]

255 Mac Donncha, F. "Seanmóireacht in Éirinn ó 1000 go 1200." In *An Léann Eaglasta in Éirinn 1000 go 1200,* edited by M. Mac Conmara, 77–85. Dublin: Clóchomhar, 1982. [On dating Leabhar Breac, which contains three versions of *GN.* Cf. nos. 250, 254, 876.]

256 Mac Gearailt, U. Review of *Stair Nicoméid: The Irish Gospel of Nicodemus,* edited by I. Hughes (no. 252). *Cambridge Medieval Celtic Studies* 24 (1992): 105–8.

See also no. 608.

1.1.3.7. Italian
Editions
257 Guasti, C., ed. *Il Passio o Vangelo di Nicodemo, volgarizzato nel buon secolo della lingua, e non mai fin qui stampato.* Scelta di curiosità litterarie inedite o rare dal secolo XIII al XIX, vol. 12. Bologna: Romagnoli, 1862.

See also no. 110.

Studies
258 Lami, G. *De eruditione Apostolorum liber singularis, in quo multa quae primitivorum christianorum litteras, doctrinas, scripta, placita, studia, conditionem, censum, mores et ritus attinent. . . .* Florence: B. Paperini, 1738. [P. 181: references to MSS. of *GN*.]
259 Iannucci, A. A. "The *Gospel of Nicodemus* in Medieval Italian Literature." *Quaderni d'italianistica* 14, no. 2 (1993): 191–220.

See also no. 231.

1.1.3.8. Norse
Editions
260 Klemming, G. E., ed. *Svenska medeltidens bibelarbeten.* Vol. 2. Samlingar utgifna af svenska fornskrift-sällskapet, vol. 9. Stockholm: Norstedt & söner, 1848–55. [Pp. 373–411: *GN* in Old Swedish prose. Cf. nos. 262, 269.]
261 Unger, C. R., ed. *Heilagra manna søgur: Fortællinger og legender om hellige mænd og kvinder.* Vol. 2. Oslo: Bentzen, 1877. [Pp. 1–20: Old Norse-Icelandic *Niðrstigningarsaga* from four MSS.; pp. 287–309: story of Pilate in *Stephanus saga*. Cf. nos. 264–65, 267–68, 270–73, 276, 279–84, 911–12, 930.]
262 *Klemming, G. E., ed. "Nicodemi Evangelium, efter Oxenstjernska Codex." In *Klosterläsning,* edited by G. E. Klemming, Samlinger utgifna af svenska fornskrift-sällskapet, vol. 15, pp. 377–419. Stockholm: Norstedt & söner, 1877–78. [*GN* in Old Swedish prose. Cf. nos. 260, 269.]
263 Collijn, I. "Nyfunna fragment af fornsvenska handskrifter bland räkenskapsomslagen i Kammararkivet." *Samlaren* 34 (1913): 275–93. [*GN* in Old Danish verse. Cf. nos. 266, 274.]
264 Finnur Jónsson, ed. *AM 623, 4°: Helgensagaer.* Samfund til udgivelse af gammel nordisk litteratur, vol. 52. Copenhagen: Jørgensen, 1927. [Pp. 1–9: Old Norse-Icelandic *Niðrstigningarsaga* from AM 623 4°. Cf. nos. 261, 265, 267–68, 270–73, 276, 279–84, 911–12, 930.]

265 Holtsmark, A., ed. *A Book of Miracles: MS No. 645 4to of the Arna-Magnæan Collection in the University Library of Copenhagen.* Corpus Codicum Islandicorum Medii Aevi, vol. 12. Copenhagen: Munksgaard, 1938. [Facsimile of MS. containing Old Norse-Icelandic *Niðrstigningarsaga.* Cf. nos. 261, 264, 267–68, 270–73, 276, 279–84, 911–12, 930.]

266 *Brøndum-Nielsen, J., ed. *Et gammeldansk Digt om Christi Opstandelse efter Fragment Stockh. A 115 (c. 1325).* Det Kongelige Danske Videnskabernes Selskab, Historisk-filologiske Meddelelser, vol. 35, pt. 1. Copenhagen: Munksgaard, 1955. [*GN* in Old Danish verse; pp. 74–78: Latin text of Fabricius (no. 22). Cf. nos. 263, 274.]

Studies

267 Larsson, L., ed. *Isländska handskriften No 645 4° i den Arnamagnæanske Samlingen på Universitetsbiblioteket i København i diplomatarisk aftryck utgifven: I. Handskriftens äldre del.* Lund: Malmström, 1885. [Pp. ii–iii: on the oldest MS. of Old Norse-Icelandic *Niðrstigningarsaga.* Cf. nos. 261, 264–65, 268, 270–73, 276, 279–84, 911–12, 930.]

268 Mogk, E. *Geschichte der norwegisch-isländischen Literatur.* 2d rev. ed. Strasbourg: Trübner, 1904. [P. 890: on Norwegian origin of *Niðrstigningarsaga.* Cf. nos. 261, 264–65, 267, 270–73, 276, 279–84, 911–12, 930.]

269 Gödel, V. *Sveriges medeltidslitteratur. Proveniens.* Stockholm: Nordiska bokhandeln, 1916. [P. 46: on MS. of *GN* in Old Swedish prose. Cf. nos. 260, 262.]

270 Turville-Petre, G. *Origins of Icelandic Literature.* Oxford: Clarendon Press, 1953. [Pp. 127–28: on Old Norse-Icelandic *Niðrstigningarsaga.* Cf. nos. 261, 264–65, 267–68, 271–73, 276, 279–84, 911–12, 930.]

271 Seip, D. A. *Nye studier i norsk språkhistorie.* Oslo: Aschehoug, 1954. [Pp. 84, 135: on Norwegian origin of *Niðrstigningarsaga.* Cf. nos. 261, 264–65, 267–68, 270, 272–73, 276, 279–84, 911–12, 930.]

272 Magnús Már Lárusson. "Um Niðurstigningarsögu." *Skírnir* 129 (1955): 159–68. [Cf. nos. 261, 264–65, 267–68, 270–71, 273, 276, 279–84, 911–12, 930.]

273 Paasche, F. *Norges og Islands litteratur inntil utgangen av middelalderen.* Revised edition by A. Holtsmark. In F. Bull et al., *Norsk Litteraturhistorie,* vol. 1. Oslo: Aschehoug, 1957. [P. 299: on vocabulary of Norse mythology in Old Norse-Icelandic *Niðrstigningarsaga.* Cf. nos. 261, 264–65, 267–68, 270–72, 276, 279–84, 911–12, 930.]

274 Gad, T. *Legenden i dansk middelalder.* Copenhagen: Dansk Videnskabs Forlag, 1961. [Pp. 253, 278: on *GN* in Old Danish verse. Cf. nos. 263, 266.]

275 Aho, G. L. "A Comparison of Old English and Old Norse Treatments of Christ's Harrowing of Hell." Ph.D. diss., University of Oregon, 1966.

276 Bekker-Nielsen, H. "Nikodemusevangeliet." In *Kulturhistorisk Leksikon for nordisk middelalder*, vol. 12, cols. 308–10. Copenhagen: Rosenkilde and Bagger, 1967. [On Norwegian origin of *Niðrstigningarsaga*. Cf. nos. 261, 264–65, 267–68, 270–73, 279–84, 911–12, 930.]

277 Gschwantler, O. "Christus, Thor und die Midgardschlange." In *Festschrift für Otto Höfler zum 65. Geburtstag*, edited by H. Birkhan and O. Gschwantler, 145–68. Vienna: Notring, 1968. [On several Norse versions of *GN*.]

278 Overgaard, M., ed. *The History of the Cross-Tree down to Christ's Passion: Icelandic Legend Versions*. Editiones Arnamagnæanæ, Series B, vol. 26. Copenhagen: Munksgaard, 1968. [Pp. cxx–cxxi, 79–82: on a lost Old Norse-Icelandic translation.]

279 Aho, G. L. "*Niðrstigningarsaga*: An Old Norse Version of Christ's Harrowing of Hell." *Scandinavian Studies* 41 (1969): 150–59. [Cf. nos. 261, 264–65, 267–68, 270–73, 276, 280–84, 911–12, 930.]

280 Marchand, J. W. "Leviathan and the Mousetrap in the *Niðrstigningarsaga*." *Scandinavian Studies* 47 (1975): 328–38. [Cf. nos. 261, 264–65, 267–68, 270–73, 276, 279, 281–84, 911–12, 930.]

281 Jónas Kristjánsson. "Learned Style or Saga Style?" In *Specvlvm norroenvm: Norse Studies in Memory of Gabriel Turville-Petre*, edited by U. Dronke et al., 260–92. Odense: Odense University Press, 1981. [On style in Old Norse-Icelandic *Niðrstigningarsaga*. Cf. nos. 261, 264–65, 267–68, 270–73, 276, 279–80, 282–84, 911–12, 930.]

282 Haugen, O. E. "The Evaluation of Stemmatic Evidence. Recension and Revision of *Niðrstigningar saga*." In *The Sixth International Saga Conference 28.7.–2.8.1985, Workshop Papers*, 1:423–50. Copenhagen: The Arnamagnaean Institute, 1985. [Cf. nos. 261, 264–65, 267–68, 270–73, 276, 279–81, 283–84, 911–12, 930.]

283 Kirby, I. J. *Bible Translation in Old Norse*. Université de Lausanne, Publications de la Faculté des lettres, vol. 27. Geneva: Droz, 1986. [P. 35: on dating Old Norse-Icelandic *Niðrstigningarsaga*. Cf. nos. 261, 264–65, 267–68, 270–73, 276, 279–82, 284, 911–12, 930.]

284 Haugen, O. E. "Stamtre og tekstlandskap: Studiar i resensjonsmetodikk med grunnlag i Niðrstigningar saga." Ph.D. diss., University of Bergen, 1992. [Cf. nos. 261, 264–65, 267–68, 270–73, 276, 279–83, 911–12, 930.]

285 Wolf, K. "Om en 'tabt' islandsk oversættelse af Nikodemusevangeliet." *Arkiv för nordisk filologi* 107 (1992): 167–79. [On post-medieval MSS. of two Old Norse-Icelandic translations.]

286 Wolf, K. "The Influence of the *Evangelium Nicodemi* on Norse Literature: A Survey." *Mediaeval Studies* 55 (1993): 219–42.

1.1.3.9. Portuguese
Studies
287 Martins, M. "O Evangelho de Nicodemos e las Cartas de Abgar e de Pilatos nos *Autos dos Apóstolos.*" *Itinerarium* 1 (1955): 846–53.

1.1.3.10. Welsh
Editions
288 Williams, J. E. Caerwyn, ed. "Efengyl Nicodemus." *Bulletin of the Board of Celtic Studies* 14 (1952): 257–73. [Version A from National Library of Wales MS. Peniath 5.]

Studies
289 Williams, J. E. Caerwyn. "Efengyl Nicodemus yn Gymraeg." *Bulletin of the Board of Celtic Studies* 14 (1952): 108–12.
290 Lewis, C. W. "The Literary Tradition of Morgannwg down the Middle of the Sixteenth Century." In *Glamorgan County History,* vol. 3, *The Middle Ages,* edited by T. B. Pugh. Cardiff: University of Wales Press, 1971. [Pp. 549–50: on versions B and C. Cf. no. 291.]
291 Williams, G. *The Welsh Church From Conquest to Reformation.* Cardiff: University of Wales Press, 1976. [Pp. 86, 100: on versions B and C. Cf. no. 290.]

1.1.4. Modern translations based on Greek and Latin (post-1600)

See also no. 30.

1.1.4.1. Africaans
292 Müller, J. J., ed. *Nuwe-Testamentiese Apokriewe.* 1959. Reprint, Pretoria: N. G. Kerk-Uitgewers, 1974. [Pp. 26–49.]

1.1.4.2. Catalan
293 Puig, A., gen. ed. *Apòcrifs del Nou Testament.* Clàssics del cristianisme, vol. 17. Barcelona: Facultat de teologia de Catalunya, Fundació enciclopèdia catalana, 1990. [Pp. 227–67: translation of Tischendorf's (no. 4) Greek *AP* A and *DI* from Greek *AP* B.]

1.1.4.3. Czech
294 Merell, J. *Starokřesťanské apokryfy.* Prague: Nakladatelství Vyšehrad, 1942. [Pp. 17–20: chap. 1 only.]

1.1.4.4. Danish
295 Gregersen, H. G., trans. *De apokryfiske evangelier til Ny Testamente eftersæt.* Odense: Milo'ske boghandel, 1886. [Pp. 136–222: translations of Greek *AP* A and B (chaps. 1–16), Latin *EN* A (chaps. 1–16), three forms of *DI,* and additional Pilate apocrypha.]

1.1.4.5. Dutch, Flemish

296 Cleeff, L. van, and C. P. H. de Groot, trans. *De Apokryfe Evangeliën. Naar de nieuwste uitgaven van C. Tischendorf vertaald.* Amsterdam: Brinkman, 1867. [Cf. no. 4.]

297 Bakels, H., ed. *Nieuwtestamentische Apocriefen.* Amsterdam: Maatschappij voor goede en goedkoope lectuur, 1922. [Pp. 354–405.]

298 Ruts, C., ed. *De Apocriefen uit het Nieuw Testament.* Vol. 1, *Evangeliën en kerkstemmen.* Brussels, 1927. [Pp. 141–70.]

299 Klijn, A. F. J., ed. *Apokriefen van het Nieuwe Testament.* Vol. 1. Kampen: J. H. Kok, 1984. [Pp. 56–91: translation of Tischendorf's (no. 4) Greek *AP* A and chaps. 17–27 from Greek *AP* B.]

1.1.4.6. English

300 [Warren, J.] *Nichodemus his gospel.* [Rouen]: J. Cousturier, [ca. 1635]. "To the reader" signed "Iohn Warrin priest." Reproduced in English Recusant Literature 1558–1640, vol. 271 (Ilkley: The Scholar Press, 1975). A revised edition appeared in London in 1646, with "To the reader" signed "J. W[arren]."

301 *The Gospel of Nicodemus. In thirteen chapters.* Newcastle, [1775?]. [Cited after British Museum, *General Catalogue of Printed Books* (London: Printed for the Trustees, 1963), 171:707.]

302 *Gospel of Nicodemus, Translated from the Original Hebrew.* Leeds: J. Binns, 1795.

303 Hone, W., ed. *The Apocryphal New Testament; Being all the Gospels, Epistles, and Other Pieces Now Extant; Attributed in the First Four Centuries to Jesus Christ, His Apostles, and Their Companions, and not Included in the New Testament by Its Compilers....* London: W. Hone, 1820. Reprinted, sometimes with minor changes in the title, at least fifty times. [Reproduces Jones's translation (no. 23) of Grynaeus (no. 21). Cf. no. 305.]

304 Henkle, M., of Clark County, Ohio, trans. *Gospel of Nicodemus, the Believing Jew: Translated from the German.* Columbus, Ohio: Lewis and Glover, 1826.

305 *The Apocryphal New Testament Comprising the Gospels and Epistles Now Extant, That in the First Four Centuries Were More or Less Accredited to the Apostles and Their Coadjutors ... with Notes and Emendations from the Writings of William Wake ... and Rev. Nathaniel Lardner....* London: Simpkin, Marshall, Hamilton, Kent. Reissued at Mokelumne Hill, California: Health Research, 1970. [According to a prefatory note, based on Grynaeus (no. 21); a version of Hone (no. 303).]

306 Cowper, B. H., ed. *The Apocryphal Gospels.* London: Williams and Norgate, 1867. Reprinted several times. [Pp. lxxxv–cii, 227–388: translation of Tischendorf's (no. 4) Greek *AP* A and B, Latin *EN* A

and *DI* B. Cf. nos. 313, 315, 318.]

307 *Walker, A., trans. "The Gospel of Nicodemus." In *Apocryphal Gospels, Acts and Revelations*, edited by A. Roberts and J. Donaldson, Ante-Nicene Christian Library, vol. 16, pp. xi–xii, 125–222. Edinburgh: T. & T. Clark, 1870. For an American edition, see no. 309. [Translation of Tischendorf's (no. 4, 1853 edition) Greek *AP* A and B, Latin *EN* A and *DI* B. Cf. nos. 310, 312–13, 317, 319.]

308 Huidekoper, F. *Indirect Testimony of History to the Genuineness of the Gospels*. New York: J. Miller, 1880. [Pp. 4–6, 105–42: parallel translation of Greek texts in Thilo's (no. 2) MSS. Paris A (*AP* A) and Paris D (*AP* B), chaps. 1–14.3. The edition uses different font sizes, reflecting the assumed antiquity of individual sections of the narrative; it does not follow the traditional division into chapters. Cf. no. 6.]

309 *Walker, A., trans. "The Gospel of Nicodemus." In *The Ante-Nicene Fathers*, edited by A. C. Coxe, 8:416–559. 1886. Reprint, Grand Rapids, Mich.: Wm B. Eerdmans, 1951. American edition of no. 307. [Cf. nos. 310, 312–13, 317, 319.]

310 Clough, W. O., ed. *Jesus before Pilate. A Monograph of the Crucifixion Including the Reports, Letters and Acts of Pontius Pilate Concerning the Trial and Crucifixion of Jesus of Nazareth*. Indianapolis: R. Douglass, 1891. [Pp. 37–134: Walker's (no. 307; cf. nos. 309, 312–13, 317, 319) translation of Tischendorf's (no. 4) Greek *AP* A and B (chaps. 1–16), Latin *EN* A (chaps. 1–16); Tischendorf's (no. 495) and Lardner's (no. 484) comments on *AP*; early Christian testimonies about *AP*; and additional Pilate apocrypha.]

311 Donehoo, J. De Q. *The Apocryphal and Legendary Life of Christ*. 1903. Reprinted, New York: Hodder & Stoughton, 1911. [Pp. 298–409: an account of the Passion incorporating much of EN.]

312 Orr, J., ed. *New Testament Apocryphal Writings*. 1903. 2d ed., London: J. M. Dent & Sons, 1923. [Pp. xii–xiii, 38–71: Walker's translation (no. 307; cf. nos. 309–10, 313, 317, 319) of Tischendorf's (no. 4) Greek *AP* A; pp. 126–30: notes.]

313 Pick, B., ed. *The Extracanonical Life of Christ, Being a Record of the Acts and Sayings of Jesus of Nazareth Drawn from Uninspired Sources*. New York: Funk & Wagnalls, 1903. [Pp. 140–204: chaps. 1–28 (rearranged), adapted from translations of Cowper (no. 306; cf. nos. 315, 318) and Walker (no. 307; cf. nos. 309–10, 312, 317, 319).]

314 Wescott, A., trans. *The Gospel of Nicodemus, and Kindred Documents. Translated with an Introduction. . . .* London: Heath and Cranton & Ouseley, 1914. [Pp. 61–119: translation of Tischendorf's (no. 4) Latin *EN* A; pp. 24–26: comments on *EN* in English literature.]

315 Cowper, B. H., ed. *The Great Rejected Books of the Biblical Apocrypha*. The Sacred Books and Early Literature of the East, vol. 14. Lon-

don: Heath, Cranton and Ouseley, 1917. [Pp. 325–402. Cf. nos. 306, 313, 318.]

316 *James, M. R., ed. *The Apocryphal New Testament.* 1924. Rev. ed., Oxford: Oxford University Press, 1953. [Pp. 94–146: translation of Tischendorf's (no. 4) entire Greek *AP* A, of excerpts from first sixteen chapters of Greek *AP* B, and of all versions of *DI* (Latin A and B, Greek B) in a synoptic format. Cf. nos. 101, 317.]

317 Lightfoot, J. B., M. R. James, H. B. Swete, et al. *Excluded Books of the New Testament.* London: E. Nash & Grayson, 1927. [Pp. 52–108: Walker's (no. 307; cf. nos. 309–10, 312–13, 319) translation of Greek *AP* A and James's (no. 316; cf. no. 101) of Latin *DI* A.]

318 Rappoport, A. S. *Mediaeval Legends of Christ.* London: I. Nicholson and Watson, 1934. [Pp. 208–9: short excerpt from Cowper's translation (no. 306; cf. nos. 313, 315) on John the Baptist's arrival in hell.]

319 Schonfield, H. J., ed. *Readings from the Apocryphal Gospels.* London: T. Nelson and Sons, 1940. [Pp. 109–64: Walker's translation (no. 307; cf. nos. 309–10, 312–13, 317).]

320 Hennecke, E., ed. *New Testament Apocrypha.* Vol. 1, *Gospels and Related Writings.* Revised by W. Schneemelcher, English translation edited by R. McL. Wilson. 1963. [Pp. 501–30, 533–36: Tischendorf's (no. 4) Greek *AP* A, chaps. 17–27 from Greek *AP* B, extracts from Latin *DI* A and B. Translated from German (no. 348)]. Rev. ed., Cambridge: J. Clarke, 1991. [Cf. nos. 321–22.]

321 Cameron, R., ed. *The Other Gospels: Non-canonical Gospel Texts.* Guildford (Surrey): Lutterworth Press, 1983. [Pp. 163–82, 191: Hennecke-Schneemelcher-Wilson translation (no. 320). Cf. nos. 322, 348.]

322 *Funk, R. W. *New Gospel Parallels....* Vol. 2, *John and the Other Gospels.* Foundations and Facets. Philadelphia: Fortress Press, 1985. [Pp. 288–346: Hennecke-Schneemelcher-Wilson translation of Greek *AP* A (no. 320; cf. nos. 321, 348), with parallels from canonical gospels and other apocrypha.]

323 *Elliott, J. K., trans. *The Apocryphal New Testament. A Collection of Apocryphal Christian Literature in an English Translation.* Oxford: Clarendon Press, 1993. [Pp. 164–204: translation of Tischendorf's (no. 4) Greek *AP* A and chaps. 17–27 from Greek *AP* B, and of Latin *DI* A and B.]

See also nos. 23, 196.

1.1.4.7. French

324 Abbé B**** [Nigon de Berty, S.], ed. *Collection d'anciens évangiles ou monumens du premier siècle du Christianisme, extraits de Fabricius, Grabius, & autres savans.* London: n.p., 1769. [Pp. 48–49, 164–235: Voltaire's (F.-M. Arouet's) translation of Fabricius (no. 22). Cf. nos.

379, 511.] Reproduced as part of multivolume publications in 1770, 1771, 1772, 1773, 1775, and 1784–89. For its modern critical edition, prepared by B. E. Schwarzbach, see *The Complete Works of Voltaire*, vol. 69 (Oxford: Voltaire Foundation, 1994), 39–43 (details of earlier editions), 100, 174–217 (text).

325 Brunet, G., trans. *Les Évangiles apocryphes: Suivis d'une notice sur les principaux livres apocryphes de l'Ancien Testament, traduits et annotés d'après l'édition de J. C. Thilo.* 1848. 2d ed., Paris: A. L. Herold, 1863. [Pp. 230–84: translation of Thilo's Latin text (no. 2); pp. 215–30: important bibliographic introduction. Cf. no. 326, 328–29.]

326 Migne, J.-P., ed. "Nicodème (Évangile de Nicodème)." In *Dictionnaire des apocryphes.* Vol. 1. Troisième et dernière encyclopédie théologique, vol. 23. Paris: J.-P. Migne, 1856. [Cols. 1087–1138: reproduces Brunet's translation (no. 325). Cf. nos. 328–29.]

327 Amiot, F., ed. *Évangiles apocryphes.* Paris: A. Fayard, 1952. [Pp. 145–56: paraphrase of chaps. 1–16 and partial translation of chaps. 17–27 from Latin *EN* A.]

328 Crépon, P., ed. *Les Évangiles apocryphes.* Paris: Retz, 1983. Reissued in 1989 in the collection of Retz-Poche. [Pp. 95–131: adaptation of Migne's text (no. 326). Cf. nos. 325, 329.]

329 Mopsik, Ch., ed. *Apocryphes du Nouveau Testament. Les Évangiles de l'ombre.* Paris: Éditions Lieu Commun, 1984. [Pp. 123–51: adaptation of Migne's text (no. 326; cf. nos. 325, 328).]

330 Quéré, F., ed. *Les Évangiles apocryphes.* Points inédits sagesse, vol. 34. Paris: Seuil, 1983. [Pp. 127–59: translation of Tischendorf's (no. 4) Greek *AP* A and chaps. 17–27 from Greek *AP* B (not Latin B, as erroneously stated on p. 125).]

See also nos. 48–49.

1.1.4.8. German

331 *Evangelischer Bericht von dem Leben Jesu Christi. Welches Nicodemus, ein Rabbi und Oberster der Jüden, beschrieben, wie er solches selbst gesehen und erfahren, weil er ein Nachfolger und heimlicher Jünger Jesu Christi gewesen; auch sind viel schöne Stücke und Geschichte dabey zu finden, welche die Evangelisten nicht beschrieben haben. Wie dann auch die erschrecklichen Straffen und Plagen der XII. jüdischen Stämme.* Chemnitz, 1703. [Not verified. Cf. nos. 214, 332, 336, 340, 342–43.]

332 *Evangelium Nicodemi, oder: Historischer Bericht von dem Leben Jesu Christi, welches. Nicodemus, ein Rabbi und Oberster der Jüden, beschrieben, wie er solches selbst gesehen und erfahren, weil er ein Nachfolger und heimlicher Jünger Jesu Christi gewesen; auch sind viel schöne Stücke und Geschichte dabey zu finden, welche die Evangelisten nicht beschrieben haben. Nebst einer Historie von einem Rabbi und Obersten der*

Jüden, welcher öffentlich bekannt: daß Christus Gottes Sohn sey. Aus des Hn. Philippi Kegelii Anhang zum geistlichen Weg-Weiser nach dem himmlischen Vatterland &c. genommen. Wie dann auch die erschrecklichen Straffen und Plagen der XII. jüdischen Stämme. Hamburg, 1713. Reprinted with minor orthographic changes at Lancaster, Pa.: J. Bailey, 1784 and 1791; Hägestaun (Hagerstown), Md.: J. Gruber, 1796; Harrisburg, Pa.: J. S. Wiestling, 1819; Reading, Pa.: C. A. Bruckman, 1819; Lancaster, Pa.: J. Bär, 1843; Reutlingen: Kurtz, 1861 and 1875. [Cf. nos. 214, 331, 336, 340, 342–43.]

333 *Evangelium Nicodemi, oder eigendliche Erzehlung einiger besonderen und merkwürdigen Umständen von der Passion, Auferstehung und Höllen-Fahrt Jesu Christi . . . Aus dem Hebräischen und Lateinischen ins Teutsche gebracht. . . .* 1740. [Cited after British Museum, *General Catalogue of Printed Books* (London: Printed for the Trustees, 1963), 171:708.]

334 *Die Beschreibung des Evangeliums Nicodemi. Von dem Leyden unsers Herren Jesu Christi, wie er von den Juden, als ein uebelthäter Zauberer, ect: vor Pilato fälschlich verklagt, und unschuldig zum Tod verurtheilt worden. Wie auch von seiner Begräbniß, Auferstehung u. Himmelfahrt ect: Welches beschrieben worden in dem dreysigsten Jahr des Kayserthums Tyberii.* Ephrata: Verlags M:M, 1748. Reprinted from Marburg 1561 edition (no. 216). [Cf. nos. 213, 218.]

335 *Des Jüngers Nicodemi Evangelium von unsers Meisters und Heylands Jesu Christi Leyden und Auferstehung.* Ephrata: [Die Brüderschaft], 1764.

336 Homan, J. G., ed. *Das Evangelium Nicodemus, oder, gewißer Bericht von dem Leben, Leiden und Sterben, unsers Heilands Jesu Christi, und von den zwölf Stämmen der Juden und sonst noch mehr schöne Stücke, wo das mehrste von den Evangelisten nicht beschrieben worden ist, beschrieben von Nicodemus, ein Priester und Oberster der Jüden und ein heimlicher Jünger und Nachfolger Jesu. . . . Aus Herrn Philippi Kegelii Anhang zum geistlichen Wegweiser nach dem himmlischen Vaterlande &c. genommen.* Reading, Pa.: C. A. Bruckman, 1819. [Cf nos. 214, 331–32, 340, 342–43.]

337 *Das apokryphische Neue Testament, eine Sammlung aller Evangelien, Episteln und anderer Schriften, welche in den ersten vier Jahrhunderten Jesu Christo, seinen Aposteln und deren Gefährten zugeschrieben wurden, und in dem eigentlichen Neuen Testament nicht enthalten sind. Aus den ursprünglichen Manuscripten übersetzt und in einen Band zusammen getragen.* Lancaster, Pa.: J. Bär, 1830.

338 Borberg, K. F., ed. *Bibliothek der neu-testamentlichen Apokryphen.* Vol. 1, *Die apokryphischen Evangelien und Apostelgeschichten. In's Deutsche übersetzt und mit Einleitungen und Anmerkungen geleitet.* Stuttgart: Literatur-Comptoir, 1841.

339 Lützelbelger, E. K. J., trans. *Das Protevangelium Jacobi, zwei Evangelien der Kindheit Jesu und die Acten des Pilatus oder das Evangelium Nicodemi, aus der Sammlung neutestamentlichen Apokryphen von Fabricius in Deutsche übersetzt.* Nuremberg: Bauer und Kaspe, 1842. [Cf. no. 22.]

340 Wolff, O. L. B., ed. *Höchst wichtige und erbauliche Geschichte vom dem Leben Jesu Christi, welches Nicodemus, ein Rabbiner und Oberster der Juden, beschrieben hat, wie er solches selbst gesehen und erfahren, weil er des Herrn Jesu Christi heimlicher Jünger und Nachfolger gewesen ist.* Volksbücher, vol. 48. Leipzig: W. Wigand, 1848. [Cf. nos. 214, 331–32, 336, 342–43.]

341 Clemens, R., ed. *Die geheimgehalten oder sogenannten apokryphischen Evangelien. . . .* Vol. 4, *Das Evangelium des Nikodemus und die Akten des Pilatus.* Stuttgart: J. Scheible, 1850. [Translation of Greek *AP*, chaps. 1–27.]

342 Westphalus, C. D., ed. *Evangelischer Bericht von dem Leben Jesu Christi, welches Nicodemus, ein Rabbi und Oberster der Juden, beschrieben &c. Sammt Bericht von einem Juden Ahasverus, welcher vorgiebt, er sei bei der Kreuzigung Christi gewesen.* Stuttgart: Kurtz, 1856. [Cf. nos. 214, 331–32, 336, 340, 343.]

343 *Glaubhafter Bericht von dem Leben Jesu Christi, welches Nicodemus, ein Rabbi und Oberster der Juden, beschrieben, wie er solches selbst gesehen und erfahren, weil er ein Nachfolger und heimlicher Jünger Jesu Christi gewesen. Nebst einem Anhange von verschiedenen Nachrichten, welche die Evangelisten nicht mitgetheilt haben.* Hamburg, [1881]. [Not verified. Cf. nos. 214, 331–32, 336, 340, 342.]

344 Michaelis, W., ed. *Die apokryphen Schriften zum Neuen Testament.* Sammlung Dieterich, vol. 129. Bremen: Schünemann, 1956. [Pp. 132–214: translation of Tischendorf's (no. 4) Greek *AP* A and chaps. 17–27 from Greek *AP* B, with copious notes.]

345 Vogler, W. *Judas Iskarioth. Untersuchungen zu Tradition und Redaktion von Texten des Neuen Testaments und ausserkanonischer Schriften.* Theologische Arbeiten, vol. 42. Berlin: Evangelische Verlagsanstalt, 1983. [P. 129: story of Judas's death transmitted by some MSS. of Greek *AP* B. Cf. nos. 347, 357, 514–15, 663, 709, 866, 874.]

346 Weidinger, E., ed. *Die Apokryphen. Verborgene Bücher der Bibel.* Aschaffenburg: P. Pattlock, 1985. Reprinted in no. 350. [Pp. 465–90: translation of Tischendorf's (no. 4) Greek *AP* A (without the prologues) and chaps. 17–27 from Greek *AP* B.]

347 Klauck, H.-J. *Judas – ein Jünger des Herrn.* Quaestiones disputatae, vol. 111. Freiburg i. Br.: Herder, 1987. [Pp. 131–32: story of Judas's death transmitted by some MSS. of Greek *AP* B. Cf. nos. 345, 357, 514–15, 663, 709, 866, 874.]

348 *Scheidweiler, F., trans. "Nikodemusevangelium. Pilatusakten und

Höllenfahrt Christi." In *Neutestamentliche Apokryphen in deutscher Übersetzung*, vol. 1, *Evangelien*, 5th ed., edited by W. Schneemelcher, 395–424. Tübingen: J. C. B. Mohr (Paul Siebeck), 1987. [Translation of Tischendorf's (no. 4) Greek *AP* A, chaps. 17–27 from Greek *AP* B, and extracts from Latin *DI* A and B. Cf. nos. 320–22.]

349 Schindler, A., ed. *Apokryphen zum Alten und Neuen Testament, hrsg., eingeleitet und erläutert von A. Schindler, mit 20 Handzeichnungen von Rembrandt*. Manesse Bibliothek der Weltliteratur. Zürich: Manesse Verlag, 1988. [Pp. 491–542: translation of Tischendorf's (no. 4) Greek *AP* A and chaps. 17–27 from Greek *AP* B.]

350 Weidinger, E., ed. *Apokryphe Bibel. Die verborgenen Bücher der Bibel*. [Aschaffenburg:] Pattloch Verlag, 1991. Reprint of no. 346. [Pp. 294–317.]

1.1.4.9. Italian

351 Craveri, M., ed. *I vangeli apocrifi*. Turin: G. Einaudi, 1969. [Pp. 299–377: translation of Tischendorf's (no. 4) Greek *AP* A, Greek *AP* B (excerpts from chaps. 1–16, complete chaps. 17–27), and parts of Latin *DI* A and B.]

352 *Moraldi, L., ed. *Apocrifi del Nuovo Testamento*. Classici delle religioni, sezione 5. Vol. 1. Turin: UTET, 1971. [Pp. 519–653: translation of Turin Papyrus (Coptic; cf. nos. 46–47, 51), Tischendorf's (no. 4) Greek *AP* A, Latin *EN* (chaps. 1–16), and all forms of *DI* (Greek B, Latin A and B).]

353 *Erbetta, M., ed. *Gli apocrifi del Nuovo Testamento*. Vol. 1, pt. 2, *Vangeli: Infanzia e passione di Cristo. Assunzione di Maria*. Turin: Marietti, 1981. [Pp. 231–87: translation of Tischendorf's (no. 4) Greek *AP* A; prologue and chaps. 1.1–4, 10, 11.2–5, and 16–17 from Greek *AP* B (the rest summarized); Latin *DI* A and B. Cf. no. 354.]

354 Gharib, G. *Testi mariani del primo millenio*. Vol. 1. Rome: Citta Nuova Editrice, 1989. [Pp. 863, 878–80: excerpts from Erbetta's (no. 353) translation of Tischendorf's (no. 4) Greek *AP* B (chaps. 10.1–4 and 11.4–5).]

1.1.4.10. Polish

355 Szefler, P. "Apokryfy o męce i zmartwychwstaniu Chrystusa Pana." *Roczniki Teologiczno-Kanoniczne* 9, no. 4 (1962): 75–105. [Translation of Tischendorf's (no. 4) Greek *AP* A.]

356 Starowieyski, M. "Wybór tekstów apokryficznych." *Znak* 29 (1977): 551–56. [Translation of Greek *DI*.]

357 *Starowieyski, M., ed. *Apokryfy Nowego Testamentu*. Vol. 1, *Ewangelie apokryficzne*. Pt. 2. Lublin: Towarzystwo Naukowe Katolickiego Uniwersytetu Lubelskiego, 1986. [Pp. 420–60: translation of Tischendorf's (no. 4) Greek *AP* A; account of Judas's death

(Tischendorf, pp. 289–91; cf. nos. 345, 347, 514–15, 663, 709, 866, 874), chap. 10.2 (Tischendorf's text plus variants from MS. C), chap. 10.4 (from MS. C), all from Greek *AP* B; *DI* in all its versions (Greek B, Latin A and B); and additional Pilate apocrypha. Cf. no. 40.]

1.1.4.11. Russian

357a Vega (Nikodim, bishop of Eniseisk and Krasnoiarsk), trans. *Apo-krificheskiia skazaniia o Khriste.* Vol. 1, *Kniga Nikodimova.* St. Peters-burg: Gosudarstvennaia Tipografiia, 1912. [Translates chaps. 1–29, apparently from Thilo (no. 2); the introduction includes numerous quotations from early modern editions.]

See also no. 57.

1.1.4.12. Spanish

358 González-Blanco, E., trans. *Los evangelios apócrifos.* Vol. 2. 1935. Bib-lioteca personal Jorge Luis Borges, vol. 30. Barcelona: Ediciones Orbis, 1987. [Pp. 279–317.]

359 *Santos Otero, A. de, ed. *Los evangelios apócrifos.* Biblioteca de autores cristianos, vol. 148. 1956. 6th ed., Madrid: Le Editorial Catolica, 1988. [Pp. 390–465: translation of Tischendorf's (no. 4) Greek *AP* A, chaps. 17–27 from Greek *AP* B, and Latin *DI* B.]

360 Bagatti, B., and F. García. *La Vida de Jesús en los apócrifos del Nuevo Testamento.* Cuardenos de Tierra Santa, vol. 10. Jerusalem: Francis-can Printing Press, 1978. [Pp. 65–71, 76: translation of chaps. 1–8.]

1.2. Bibliographic repertories and general introductions to the *Acts of Pilate*

1.2.1. Bibliographic repertories

361 Campbell, M.-F.-A.-G. *Annales de la typographie néerlandaise au XVe siècle.* The Hague: M. Nijhof, 1874. [Pp. 324–28, items 1153–68: edi-tions of *Dat Lyden ende die Passie Ons Heren Jhesu Christi,* incorpor-ating portions of Middle Dutch prose translation D, printed be-tween 1477 and ca. 1528. Cf. nos. 362, 364, 692–94, 696, 705, 853.]

362 Campbell, M.-F.-A.-G. *Annales de la typographie néerlandaise au XVe siècle. 2. supplément.* The Hague: M. Nijhoff, 1884. [P. 28: editions of *Dat Lyden ende die Passie Ons Heren Jhesu Christi,* incorporating por-tions of Middle Dutch prose translation D, printed between 1477 and ca. 1528. Cf. nos. 361, 364, 692–94, 696, 705, 853.]

363 Ribelles Comín, J. *Bibliografía de la lengua valenciana.* Madrid: Tipo-grafia de la "Revista de Archivos, Bibliotecas y Museos," 1915. [1:450–57: summary of *Gamaliel* and references to its early printed editions. Cf. nos. 103–6, 111, 119–20, 184–86, 193, 200, 679–80, 686, 776.]

364 Nijhoff, W., and M. E. Kronenberg. *Nederlandsche Bibliographie van*

1500 tot 1540. Vols. 2 and 3, pt. 2. The Hague: M. Nijhoff, 1923. [Vol. 2, p. 695, items 3678–80, and vol. 3, pt. 2, pp. 49–50, item 4381: early editions of *Dat Lyden ende die Passie Ons Heren Jhesu Christi.* Cf. nos. 361–62, 692–94, 696, 705, 853.]

365 Stegmüller, F. *Repertorium Biblicum medii aevi.* Vol. 1. Madrid: Consejo Superior de Investigaciones Científicos, Instituto Francisco Suárez, 1940 [corr. 1950]. [Pp. 148–53, item 179.]

366 Pollak, R. *Piśmiennictwo staropolskie.* Vol. 1. Bibliografia literatury polskiej "Nowy Korbut," vol. 2. Państwowy Instytut Wydawniczy, 1963. [P. 229: bibliography of *GN* in Old Polish. Cf. nos. 69, 72–74, 89, 91, 94, 98.]

367 *McNamara, M. *The Apocrypha in the Irish Church.* Dublin: Dublin Institute for Advanced Studies, 1975. [Pp. 68–75, items 58–61.]

368 Pollard, A. W., and G. R. Redgrave. *A Short-Title Catalogue of Books Printed in England, Scotland, and Ireland and of English Books Printed Abroad 1475–1640.* 2d ed. Revised and enlarged by W. A. Jackson, F. S. Ferguson, and K. F. Pantzer. 3 vols. London: The Bibliographical Society, 1976–91. [Items 18565–70a: earliest printed editions of *GN* in English. Cf. nos. 129–32.]

369 *Santos Otero, A. de. *Die handschriftliche Überlieferung der altslavischen Apokryphen.* Vol. 2. Berlin: W. de Gruyter, 1981. [Pp. 61–98. Supplemented and corrected by no. 372.]

370 Voicu, S. J. "Gli apocrifi armeni." *Augustinianum* 23 (1983): 161–80. [P. 179, item 54.]

371 *Halkin, F. *Nouum auctarium Bibliothecae hagiographicae Graecae.* Subsidia Hagiographica, vol. 65. Bruxelles: Société des Bollandistes, 1984. [Items 779 t–w.]

372 *Thomson, F. J. "Apocrypha Slavica: II." *The Slavonic and East European Review* 63, no. 1 (1985): 79–83. [Supplements and corrects no. 369.]

373 *Fros, H. *Bibliotheca hagiographica Latina antiquae et mediae aetatis. Novum supplementum.* Subsidia Hagiographica, vol. 70. Bruxelles: [Société des Bollandistes], 1986. [Items 4151 p–t.]

374 Charlesworth, J. H., and J. R. Müller. *The New Testament Apocrypha and Pseudepigrapha: A Guide to Publications, with Excursuses on Apocalypses.* ATLA Bibliography Series, vol. 17. Metuchen: The American Theological Library Association and the Scarecrow Press, 1987. [Pp. 271–77, 337–43. Although more extensive than Geerard's *Clavis* (no. 375), this repertory is more awkward to use because it lists the material, rather indiscriminately, under two separate headings.]

375 *Geerard, M. *Clavis apocryphorum Novi Testamenti.* Corpus Christianorum, Series Apocryphorum. Turnhout: Brepols, 1992. [Pp. 43–48, item 62.]

376 *Izydorczyk, Z. *Manuscripts of the "Evangelium Nicodemi": A Census.* Subsidia Mediaevalia, vol. 21. Toronto: Pontifical Institute of Mediaeval Studies, 1993. [Cf. no. 43.]

1.2.2. General introductions

377 Ittigius, L. T. *Bibliotheca patrum apostolicorum Græco-Latina.* Leipzig: J. H. Richter, 1699. [Pp. 25–31: notes on Latin and vernacular versions.]

378 Dupin, L. E. *Dissertation préliminaire ou prolégomènes sur la Bible pour servir de supplément à la bibliothèque des auteurs ecclésiastiques.* Vol. 2. Paris: A. Pralard, 1701. [P. 90.]

379 Voltaire [Arouet, F.-M.]. "Christianisme (recherches historiques sur le christianisme)." In *Dictionnaire philosophique.* 1765. For a modern critical edition of the *Dictionnaire,* prepared by C. Mervaud et al., see *The Complete Works of Voltaire,* vol. 35 (Oxford: Voltaire Foundation, 1994). [The note on GN was first added to the 1765 edition; it is found in pt. 1, pp. 563–64 of Mervaud's edition. Cf. nos. 324, 511.]

379a Kleuker, J. F. *Ueber die Apokryphen des Neuen Testaments.* Ausführliche Untersuchung der Gründe für die Aechtheit und Glaubwürdigkeit der schriftlichen Urkunden des Christentums, pt. 3, vol. 5. Hamburg: Fr. Perthes, 1798. [Pp. xii–xxii, 215–20.]

380 Paulus, H. E. G. *Theologisch-exegetisches Conservatorium oder Auswahl aufbewahrungswerther Aufsätze und zerstreuter Bemerkungen über die alt- und neutestamentlichen Religionsurkunden. . . .* Vol. 1, *Eine Reihenfolge von Erörterungen über den Ursprung der drei ersten kanonischen und mehrerer apokryphischen Evangelien.* Heidelberg: A. Oswald, 1822. [Pp. 181–91: on origins of EN; pp. 192–94: on Paris, BN MS. lat. 3338, containing Latin EN.]

381 Guénebault, L.-J. *Dictionnaire iconographique des figures, légendes et actes des saints, tant de l'ancienne que de la nouvelle loi, et répertoire alphabétique des attributs qui sont donnés le plus ordinairement aux saints par les artistes.* Petit-Montrouge: [J.-P. Migne], 1850. [Col. 917.]

382 Smith, W. S., ed. *A Dictionary of the Bible, Comprising Its Antiquities, Biography, Geography, and Natural History.* Boston: Little, Brown, 1863. [2: 875–76, s.v. "Pilate (Pontius)."]

383 Sabatier, A. "Apocryphes du Nouveau Testament." In *Encyclopédie des sciences religieuses,* edited by F. Lichtenberger, 1:415–23. Paris: Sandoz et Fischbacher, 1877. [P. 418.]

384 Harnack, A. *Geschichte der altchristliche Literatur bis Eusebius.* Leipzig: J. C. Hinrichs, 1893–97. [Vol. 1, pt. 1, pp. 21–24; vol. 1, pt. 2, pp. 865, 907, 922–23; vol. 2, pt. 1, pp. 603–12.]

385 Ehrhard, A. *Die altchristliche Literatur und ihre Erforschung seit 1880. Allgemeines Uebersicht und erster Literaturbericht (1880–1884).* Strass-

burger theologische Studien, vol. 1, nos. 4–5. Freiburg i. Br.: B. Herder, 1894. [Pp. 144–46.]

386 Krueger, G. *Geschichte der altchristlichen Literatur in den ersten drei Jahrhunderten.* Grundriss der theologischen Wissenschaften, vol. 2, no. 3. Freiburg: J. C. B. Mohr, 1895. [P. 36.]

387 Hofmann, R. "Apokryphen des Neuen Testaments." In *Realency-klopädie für protestantische Theologie und Kirche,* 3d ed., 1:653–70. Leipzig: J. C. Hinrichs, 1896. [Cols. 658–60.]

388 Batiffol, P. *Ancienne Littérature chrétienne.* Vol. 1, *La Littérature grecque.* Bibliothèque de l'enseignement supérieur de l'histoire ecclésiastique. 1897. 3d ed., Paris: V. Lecoffre, 1901. [Pp. 38–39.]

389 Bardenhewer, O. *Geschichte der altkirlichen Literatur.* Vol. 1. 1902. 2d ed., Freiburg i. Br.: Herder, 1913. [Pp. 543–47.] Reprint, Darmstadt: Wissenschaftliche Buchgesellschaft, 1962.

390 Hennecke, E. *Handbuch zu den neutestamentlichen Apokryphen....* Tübingen: J. C. B. Mohr, 1904. [Pp. 143–53.]

391 *Dobschütz, E. von. "Nicodemus, Gospel of." In *A Dictionary of the Bible,* edited by J. Hastings, 3:544–47. New York: C. Scribner's Sons, 1919. [Distinguishes among various Greek and Latin recensions.]

392 Purves, G. T. "Pilate." In *A Dictionary of the Bible,* edited by J. Hastings, 3:878–79. New York: C. Scribner's Sons, 1919.

393 Zhebelev, S. A. *Evangeliia kanonicheskie i apokrificheskie.* St. Petersburg: Ogni, 1919. [Pp. 94–103.]

394 Amman, E. "Apocryphes du Nouveau Testament." In *Dictionnaire de la Bible. Supplément,* 1:459–533. Paris: Letouzey et Ané, 1928. [Pp. 486–88.]

395 *Altaner, B., and A. Stuiber. *Patrologie. Leben, Schriften und Lehre der Kirchenväter.* 1938. 8th ed., Fribourg i. Br.: Herder, 1978. [Pp. 127–28, 574.]

396 Amman, E. "Évangiles apocryphes." In *Dictionnaire de théologie catholique,* vol. 5, pt. 2, cols. 1624–40. Paris: Letouzey et Ané, 1939. [See especially cols. 1639–40.]

397 Schmidt, K. L. *Kanonische und apokryphe Evangelien und Apostelgeschichten.* Abhandlungen zur Theologie des Alten und Neuen Testaments, vol. 5. Basel: H. Majer, 1944. [Pp. 62–65, 76–80.]

398 Vaganay, L. "Apocryphes du Nouveau Testament." In *Catholicisme. Hier. Aujourd'hui. Demain,* edited by G. Jacquemet, 1:699–704. Paris: Letouzey et Ané, 1948. [P. 701.]

399 Sinko, T. *Literatura grecka.* Vol. 3, pt. 1, *Literatura grecka za cesarstwa rzymskiego.* Cracow: Polska Akademia Umiejętności, 1951. [Pp. 103–5.]

400 Daniel-Rops [H. Petiot]. "Évangiles apocryphes." *Table ronde* 58 (1952): 94–99, 102–3.

401 Pasquero, F. "Apocrifi di Pilato." In *Enciclopedia cattolica,* 9:1473.

Vatican City: Ente per l'Enciclopedia cattolica e per il Libro cattolico, 1952.

402 Quasten, J. *Patrology*. Vol. 1. Utrecht: Spectrum Publ., 1953. [Pp. 115–18.]

403 Bonsirven, J., and C. Bigaré. "Apocryphes du Nouveau Testament." In *Introduction à la Bible* ..., edited by A. Feuillet and A. Robert, 2:755–56. Tournai: Desclée, 1959.

404 Michl, J. "Evangelien – II. Apokryphe Evangelien." In *Lexikon für Theologie und Kirche*, 3:1217–33. Freiburg i. Br.: Herder, 1959. [Col. 1226.]

405 Bauer, J. B. *Die neutestamentlichen Apokryphen*. Die Welt der Bibel, vol. 21. Düsseldorf: Patmos-Verlag, 1968. [Pp. 55–58.]

406 Barabas, S. "Nicodemus, Gospel of." In *The Zondervan Pictorial Encyclopedia of the Bible*, edited by M. C. Tenney and S. Barabas, 4:453. Grand Rapids: Zondervan Pub. House, 1975.

407 Wilson, R. McL. "Pilate, Acts of." In *The Zondervan Pictorial Encyclopedia of the Bible*, edited by M. C. Tenney and S. Barabas, 4:789ff. Grand Rapids: Zondervan Pub. House, 1975.

408 Wilson, R. McL. "Apokryphen des Neuen Testaments." In *Theologische Realenzyklopädie*, 3:316–62. Berlin: W. de Gruyter, 1978. [Pp. 337–38.]

409 Masser, A., et al. "Apokryphen." In *Lexikon des Mittelalters*, 1:759–70. Munich: Artemis Verlag, 1980.

410 Laepple, A. *Ausserbiblische Jesusgeschichten. Ein Plädoyer für die Apokryphen*. Munich: Don Bosco Verlag, 1983. [Pp. 105–16.]

411 Gero, S. "Apocryphal Gospels. A Survey of Textual and Literary Problems." In *Aufstieg und Niedergang der Römischen Welt. Geschichte und Kultur Roms im Spiegel der neueren Forschung*, pt. 2, *Principat*, vol. 25, pt. 5, *Religion (Vor-konstantinisches Christentum: Leben und Umwelt Jesu; Neues Testament [Kanonische Schriften und Apokryphen], Forts.)*, edited by W. Haase, 3967–96. Berlin: W. de Gruyter, 1988. [Pp. 3986–87.]

412 Gori, F. "Gli apocrifi e i padri." In *Complementi interdisciplinari di Patrologia*, edited by A. Quacquarelli, 223–72. Rome: Città Nuova Editrice, 1989. [Pp. 265–66.]

413 Elliott, J. K. "The Apocryphal Gospels." *Expository Times* 103 (1991): 8–15. [P. 12.]

414 Jefford, C. N. "Pilate, Acts of." In *The Anchor Bible Dictionary*, edited by D. N. Freedman et al., 5:371–72. New York: Doubleday, 1992.

415 Rebell, W. *Neutestamentliche Apokryphen und apostolische Väter*. München: Chr. Kaiser, 1992. [Pp. 103–5.]

416 Amphoux, C. B. *La Parole qui devint évangile. L'Évangile, ses rédacteurs, son auteur*. Paris: Seuil, 1993. [See index, s.v. "Actes de Pilate," "Évangile de Nicodème," and "Pilate."]

417 Bernt, C. "Nikodemusevangelium." In *Lexikon des Mittelalters,* 6:1163–64. Munich: Artemis & Winkler Verlag, 1993.

418 Focant, C. *Les Évangiles apocryphes.* Horizons de la foi, vol. 58. Brussels: Connaître la Bible, 1994. [Pp. 32–34.]

1.3. Studies on the *Acts of Pilate*
1.3.1. Date, composition, transmission

419 "Recueil de traités sur la chronologie en général, sur le jour de la mort de Jésus-Christ, sur le temps auquel J.-C. célébra la Pâque, sur les azymes, sur les images, sur le monothéisme, sur l'origine du monachisme, sur les écrits de S. Denis, sur les Actes de Pilate, sur la généalogie de J.-C., sur l'origine et la grandeur et souveraineté des papes, sur la donation de Constantin." Arras, Bibl. mun. MS. 162 (197), saec. XVII.

420 "Sur les actes de Pilate et sur le témoignage de Josèphe touchant la divinité de Jésus-Christ." Avignon, Bibl. mun. MS. 60, pp. 52–68, saec. XVII ex. [Cf. no. 421.]

421 "Dissertation neuvième: sur les actes de Pilate et le témoignage de Josèphe." In "Recueil V. Conrart," vol. 16, Paris, Bibl. de l'Arsenal MS. 5425, pp. 1183–90, saec. XVII. [Seeks to prove authenticity of *AP.* Cf. no. 420.]

422 Brunn, G. L. *Disquisitio historico-critica de indole, aetate et usu libri apocryphi, vulgo inscripti Evangelium Nicodemi.* Berlin: n.p., 1794.

423 Spoerlin, S. J. "De indole, scope et aetate evangelii apocryphi Nicodemi dissertatio." Strasbourg, Bibl. Nat. et univ. MS. 296 (latin 248), fol. 113. AD 1813.

424 Maury, L. F. A. "L'Évangile de Nicodème, de la date de cet ouvrage, et des circonstances auxquelles on peut en attribuer la rédaction." *Revue de philologie, de littérature et d'histoire ancienne* 2, no. 5 (1847): 428–49. Revised and expanded in nos. 425 and 426. [Devoted mostly to *DI* (*EN* 17–27).]

425 Maury, L. F. A. "Nouvelles Recherches sur l'époque à laquelle a été composé l'ouvrage connu sous le nom d'Évangile de Nicodème." *Mémoires de la Société des antiquaires de France* 20 (1850): 341–90. Revised and expanded version of no. 424; further revised in 426. [Devoted mostly to *DI* (*EN* 17–27).]

426 Maury, L. F. A. *Croyances et légendes de l'Antiquité. Essais de critique appliquée à quelques points d'histoire et de mythologie.* Paris: Didier, 1863. Revised and expanded version of nos. 424–25. [Pp. 290–332: "Histoire d'un évangile apocryphe: l'Évangile de Nicodème"; pp. 333–51: "Une légende des premiers temps du christianisme: La Véronique" (cf. nos. 524–25).]

427 *Lipsius, R. A. *Die Pilatus-Akten kritisch untersucht.* 1871. 2d ed., Kiel: Schwers'sche Buchhandlung, 1886.

428 Schönbach, A. Review of *Evangelia apocrypha*, edited by C. de Tischendorf (no. 4). *Anzeiger für deutsches Altertum und deutsche Litteratur* 2 (1876): 149–212. [Pp. 152–55: variants from Graz, Universitätsbibliothek MS. 793; pp. 173–80: *Cura sanitatis Tiberii* (cf. nos. 432, 590–91, 610).]

429 Harris, J. R. *The Homeric Centones and the Acts of Pilate*. London: C. J. Clay & Sons, 1898. [Cf. no. 430.]

430 Dobschütz, E. von. Review of *The Homeric Centones and the Acts of Pilate*, by J. R. Harris (no. 429). *Theologische Literaturzeitung* 11 (1899): 333–35.

431 Mommsen, T. "Die Pilatusakten." *Zeitschrift für die neutestamentliche Wissenschaft und die Kunde der älteren Kirche* 3 (1902): 198–205.

432 Darley, E. *Les Acta Salvatoris. Un Évangile de la passion & de la résurrection et une mission apostolique en Aquitaine.* Paris: A. Picard & Fils, 1913. [Includes translation of Old English *GN* (pp. 15–46; cf. nos. 133–34, 136–37, 139, 141–42, 145, 147, 153–55, 158, 160–61, 166, 173–74) and edition of Latin *Cura sanitatis Tiberii* (pp. 47–51; cf. nos. 428, 590–91, 610).]

433 Darley, E. *Les Actes du Sauveur, la lettre de Pilate, la Mission de Volusien, de Nathan, la Vindicte. Leurs origines et leurs transformations.* Paris: A. Picard, 1919. [Cf. nos. 619, 674, 713, 776, 791, 938.]

434 O'Ceallaigh, G. C. "Dating the Commentaries of Nicodemus." *Harvard Theological Review* 56 (1963): 21–58. [Frequently cited but largely superseded by later studies.]

435 Cazzaniga, I. "Osservazioni critiche al testo del 'prologo' del Vangelo di Nicodemo." *Instituto Lombardo – Academia di scienze e lettere, classe lettere* 102 (1968): 535–48.

436 Speyer, W. *Die literarische Fälschung im heidnischen und christlichen Altertum. Ein Versuch ihrer Deutung.* Munich: C. H. Beck, 1971. [Pp. 148, 242–46: on *AP* as forgery.]

437 *Dubois, J.-D. "Les *Actes de Pilate* au quatrième siècle." In *Apocrypha – Le Champ des apocryphes* 2, *La Fable apocryphe* 2 (1991): 85–98.

1.3.2. The *Acts of Pilate*, chapters 1–16 (trial of Jesus, his death, and his Resurrection)

438 Münter, F. *Sandsynlige Tillaeg til Christi lidelses Historie of Nikodemi Evangelium.* Wissenschaftliche Verhandlungen der seeländischen Conventes, vol. 2, no. 3. Copenhagen, 1816. Revised in no. 439.

439 Münter, F. "Probabilien zur Leidengeschichte aus dem Evangelium des Nicodemus." *Archiv für alte und neue Kirchengeschichte (Staudlin's Archiv)* 5 (1822): 317–45. Revised German version of no. 438.

440 Tischendorf, C. von. *Pilati circa Christum iudicio quid lucis afferatur ex Actis Pilati.* Leipzig: A. D. Winter, 1855.

441 Dobschütz, E. von. "Der Process Jesu nach den *Acta Pilati.*" *Zeitschrift für die neutestamentliche Wissenschaft und die Kunde der älteren Kirche* 3 (1902): 89–114.

442 Peter, H. "Pontius Pilatus, der Landpfleger in Judäia." *Neue Jahrbücher für das klassische Altertum, Geschichte und deutsche Literatur* 19 (1907): 1–40. [See especially pp. 22–36, passim.]

443 Krealing, C. H. "The Episode of the Roman Standards at Jerusalem." *Harvard Theological Review* 35 (1942): 263–89.

444 Jonge, M. de. *Nicodemus and Jesus: Some Observations on Misunderstanding and Understanding in the Fourth Gospel.* The Manson Memorial Lecture, 1971. [Pp. 335–59.]

445 Chabrol, C. "Remarques sur deux textes apocryphes (Actes de Pilate et Évangile de Pierre)." In *Le Récit évangélique,* edited by C. Chabrol and L. Marin, 66–73. Bibliothèque de sciences religieuses. Paris: Aubier, 1974.

446 Gatti, A. *Il processo di Gesu nei piu antichi apocrifi della Passione.* Jerusalem, 1975.

447 Lémonon, J.-P. *Pilate et le gouvernement de la Judée. Textes et monuments.* Études bibliques. Paris: J. Gabalda, 1981. [Pp. 258–65. Cf. no. 453.]

448 Lowe, M. "IOUDAIOI of the Apocrypha. A Fresh Approach to the Gospels of James, Pseudo-Thomas, Peter and Nicodemus." *Novum Testamentum* 23, no. 1 (1981): 56–90.

449 Bammel, E. "The Trial before Pilate." In *Jesus and the Politics of His Day,* edited by E. Bammel and C. F. D. Moule, 415–51. Cambridge: Cambridge University Press, 1984.

450 Lampe, G. W. H. "The Trial of Jesus in the *Acta Pilati.*" In *Jesus and the Politics of His Day,* edited by E. Bammel and C. F. D. Moule, 173–82. Cambridge: Cambridge University Press, 1984.

451 Dubois, J.-D. "L'Affaire des étendards de Pilate dans le premier chapitre des *Actes de Pilate.*" In *Papers Presented to the Tenth International Conference on Patristic Studies, Oxford 24–29 August 1987,* edited by E. A. Livingstone, Studia Patristica, vol. 19, pp. 351–58. Louvain: Peeters Press, 1989.

452 Dubois, J.-D. "La Représentation de la Passion dans la liturgie du Vendredi Saint: les *Actes de Pilate* et la liturgie ancienne de Jérusalem." In *Liturgie et anthropologie. Conférences St-Serge, XXVIe semaine d'études liturgiques,* edited by A. M. Triacca and A. Pistoia, 77–89. Rome: C. L. V.-Edizioni Liturgiche, 1990.

453 Lémonon, J.-P. "Ponce Pilate: Documents profanes, Nouveau Testament et traditions ecclésiales." In *Aufstieg und Niedergang der Römischen Welt. Geschichte und Kultur Roms im Spiegel der neueren Forschung,* pt. 2, *Principat,* vol. 26, pt. 1, *Religion (Vor-konstantinisches Christentum: Neues Testament [Sachthemen]),* edited by W.

Haase, 739–78. Berlin: W. de Gruyter 1992. [Especially pp. 772–75. Cf. no. 447.]

1.3.3. The *Acts of Pilate*, chapters 17–27 (Descent into Hell)

454 Beausobre, I. de. *Histoire de Manichée et du manichéisme.* Vol. 1. Amsterdam: J. F. Bernard, 1734. [Pp. 370–75.]

455 Saint-Marc-Girardin. "L'Épopée chrétienne depuis les premiers temps jusqu'à Klopstock. Seconde partie." *Revue des Deux-Mondes,* n.s., 15 août 1849: 631–38.

456 "De consensu huius orationis [Ps.-Eusebius of Alexandria, 'Sermo 15'] cum Euangelio Nicodemi." In PG 86:411–14. [Cf. nos. 564, 576, 613, 643, 650–51.]

457 Lipsius, R. A. *Die apokryphen Apostelgeschichten und Apostellegenden.* Vol. 2, pt. 1. Braunschweig: C. A. Schwetschke und Sohn, 1884. [Pp. 364–66: on relationship between *AP* and *Acta Pauli*.]

458 *Monnier, J. *La Descente aux enfers, étude de pensée religieuse, d'art et de littérature.* Paris: Fischbacher, 1904. [Pp. 91–107.]

459 Vitti, A. M. "Descensus Christi ad Inferos ex I Pet. III, 19–20; IV, 6 et iuxta Apocrypha." *Verbum Domini* 7 (1927): 111–18, 138–44, 171–81.

460 MacCulloch, J. A. *The Harrowing of Hell. A Comparative Study of an Early Christian Doctrine.* Edinburgh: T. & T. Clark, 1930. [See index, s.v. "Gospel of Nicodemus."]

461 *Kroll, J. *Gott und Hölle. Der Mythos vom Descensuskampfe.* Leipzig: B. G. Teubner, 1932. [See index, s.v. "Evangelium Nicodemi."]

462 Goguel, M. *La Foi à la résurrection de Jésus dans le christianisme primitif. Étude d'histoire et de psychologie religieuses.* Paris: E. Leroux, 1933. [Pp. 385–88.]

463 Piankoff, A. "La Descente aux enfers dans les textes égyptiens et dans les apocryphes coptes." *Bulletin de la Société d'archéologie copte* 7 (1941): 33–46.

464 Hoffman, R. J. "Confluence in Early Christian and Gnostic Literature. The *Descensus Christi ad Inferos* (*Acta Pilati* XVII–XXVII)." *Journal for the Study of the New Testament* 10 (1981): 42–60. [Cf. no. 558.]

465 Izydorczyk, Z. "The Inversion of Paschal Events in the Old English *Descent into Hell.*" *Neuphilologische Mitteilungen* 91 (1990): 439–47. [Pp. 441–42: on the Resurrection before the Descent in *EN*.]

466 Kaestli, J.-D. "À la découverte d'un évangile apocryphe: Les *Questions de Barthélémy.*" *Annuaire. École pratique des hautes études. V^e section: Sciences religieuses* 94 (1985–86): 459–64. [Suggests that the Descent in *Questiones* is older than that in *AP*. Cf. no. 467.]

467 Kaestli, J.-D., and P. Cherix. *L'Évangile de Barthélémy d'après deux récits apocryphes: "Questions de Barthélémy," "Livre de la Résurrection*

de Jésus-Christ par l'apôtre Barthélémy." Turnhout: Brepols, 1993. [See index, s.v. "Actes de Pilate" for parallels between these texts and *EN*, especially *DI*. Cf. no. 466.]

468 Gounelle, R. "Pourquoi, selon l'évangile de Nicodème, le Christ est-il descendu aux enfers?" In *Le Mystère apocryphe. Introduction à une littérature méconnue*, edited by J.-D. Kaestli and D. Marguerat, Essais bibliques, vol. 26. Geneva: Labor et Fides, 1995. [Pp. 67–84.]

See also nos. 424-26.

Part 2: Supplementary texts and studies

2.1. Patristic attestations of the *Acts of Pilate*
2.1.1. Greek

469 Justin Martyr. *Apologies. Texte grec, traduction française, introduction et index.* Edited by L. Pautigny. Paris: A. Picard, 1904. [References to some "Acts" of Pilate in chaps. 35.9, 48.3. Cf. nos. 483–84, 489, 493, 501, 504.]

470 Floëri, F., and P. Nautin, eds. *Homélies pascales.* Vol. 3. Sources chrétiennes, vol. 48. Paris: Cerf, 1957. [P. 127: *AP* mentioned in pseudo-Chrysostomian homily, dating from 387.]

471 Eusebius of Caesarea. *The Ecclesiastical History.* Translated by K. Lake. The Loeb Classical Library. 2 vols. Cambridge, Mass.: Harvard University Press, 1964–65. [References to Pilate's correspondence with Rome and to "hypomnēmata" of Pilate in chaps. 1.9.3 (1:74–75), 2.2.1–2 (1:110–11), 9.5.1 (2:338–39), 9.7.1 (2:340–43). Cf. nos. 474, 505.]

472 Epiphanius. *Panarion.* Edited by K. Holl, revised by J. Dummer. GCS, vol. 31. Berlin: Akademie Verlag, 1980. [References to Quartodecimans' use of *AP* in chaps. 50.1.5 and 50.1.8.]

2.1.2. Latin

473 Orosius, Paulus. *Pauli Orosii Historiarum adversum paganos libri VII.* Edited by C. Zangemeister. CSEL, vol. 5. Vienna: apud C. Geroldi Filium Bibliopolam Academiae, 1882. [Chap. 7.4 (p. 441): mentions Pilate's dispatches to Tiberius.]

474 Eusebius of Caesarea. *Die Kirchengeschichte. Die lateinische Übersetzung des Rufinus.* Edited by E. Schwarz and T. Mommsen. 3 pts. *Eusebius Werke*, vol. 2., GCS, vol. 9. Leipzig: J. C. Hinrichs, 1903–9. [Chaps. 1.9.3 (1:72), 1.11.9 (1:80), 2.2.1–2 (1:111), 9.5.1 (2:810), 9.6.3 (2:813), 9.7.1 (2:814): references to Pilate's correspondence and "Acta Pilati." Cf. nos. 471, 505.]

475 Gregory of Tours. *Gregorii episcopi Turonensis Libri historiarum X.* 2d ed. Edited by B. Krusch and W. Levison. MGH, Script. rer. Mer.,

vol. 1. pt. 1. 1951. Reprint, Hannover: Impensis Bibliopolii Hahniani, 1965. [Chaps. 1.21 and 1.24: references to Pilate's correspondence with Rome and to Joseph of Arimathea. Cf. no. 176.]
476 Tertullian. *Q. S. Fl. Tertulliani Apologeticum*. Edited by E. Dekkers. In *Quinti Septimi Florentis Tertulliani Opera*, pt. 1, *Opera catholica. Adversus Marcionem*, 77–171. CC SL, vol. 1. Turnhout: Brepols, 1954. [Chaps. 5.2–3, 21.24: references to Pilate's dispatches to Rome. Cf. no. 504.]

2.2. Diverse studies on the *Acts of Pilate*
2.2.1. Date, composition, transmission
477 Bibliander, Thomas. *Protoevangelium sive de natalibus Iesu Christi et ipsius matris Virginis Mariae sermo historicus diui Iacobi minoris....* Basel: apud Ioh. Oporinum, 1552. [P. 21: on apocryphal character of *EN*. Cf. nos. 500, 503, 508, 510.]
478 Carlile, Christopher. *A Discovrse, Concerning two diuine Positions, The first effectually concluding, that the soules of the faithfull fathers, deceased before Christ, went immediately to heauen. The Second sufficientlye setting forth vnto vs Christians, what we are to conceiue, touching the descension of our Sauiour Christ into hell: Publiquely disputed at a Commencement in Cambridge, Anno Domini 1552. Purposefuly written at the first by way of confutation, against a Booke of Richard Smith of Oxford, D. of Diuinity....* London: Roger Ward, 1582. [Fols. 52v–53r: Protestant ridicule of *DI*.]
479 Schneedorfer, L. A. *De libris apocryphis Noui Testamenti* and *De apocryphis Noui Testamenti*. České Budějovice, Státni vědecká knihovna MS. 1 VB 1331.
480 Le Nain De Tillemont, L. S. *Mémoires pour servir à l'histoire ecclésiastique des six premiers siècles justifiez par les citations des auteurs originaux*. 2 vols. 1693–94. 2d corr. ed., Venice: F. Pitteri, 1732.
481 Calmet, Dom A. "Dissertation sur les évangiles apocryphes." In *Commentaire littéral sur tous les livres de l'Ancien et du Nouveau Testament: L'Évangile de S. Matthieu*. Paris: Emery, 1725. [Pp. cix–cxxx.]
482 [Beausobre, I. de.] *De Novi Foederis libris apocryphis dissertatio*. Berlin, 1734.
483 Henke, H. P. C. *De Pontii Pilati actis in causa Domini nostri ad imperatorem Tiberivm missis probabilia*. Helmstadt: Literis Viduae P. D. Schnorrii Acad. Typogr., 1784. [On various attestations of *AP*. Cf. nos. 484, 489, 493, 501, 504.]
484 Lardner, N. *The Works of Nathaniel Lardner, D. D., with a Life by Dr. Kipps*. Vol. 6, *A Supplement to the Second Part of the Credibility of the Gospel History*. 1788. Reprint, London: Westley & Davis, 1834. [Pp. 605–22: on Tiberius's knowledge about Jesus Christ. Cf. nos. 310, 483, 489, 493, 501, 504.]

485 Kleuker, J.-F. *Ausführliche Untersuchung der Gründe für die Ächtheit und Glaubwürdigkeit der schriftlichen Urkunden des Christenthums.* Vol. 5, pt. 3, *Über die Apokryphen des Neuen Testaments.* Hamburg: F. Perthes, 1798. [Pp. 215–23.]

486 Pallard, J. *Dissertation sur les livres apocryphes du Nouveau Testament.* Geneva: G. Fick, 1828. [Pp. 5–6, 13–14, 22, 26, 28–29, 33–38, 42.]

487 Arens, F. J. *De evangeliorum apocryphorum in canonicis usu historico, critico, exegetico.* Göttingen: Dieterich, 1835. [Especially pp. 17–20 and 33–36.]

488 Weitzel, C. L. *Die christliche Passafeier der drei ersten Jahrhunderte. . . .* Pforzheim: Flammer und Hoffmann, 1848. [Pp. 248ff.]

489 Hilgenfeld, A. *Kritische Untersuchungen über die Evangelien Justins's, der clementinischen Homilien und Marcion's, ein Beitrag zur Geschichte der ältesten Evangelien-Literatur.* Halle: C. A. Schwetschke, 1850. [Pp. 173, 242ff. Cf. nos. 469, 483–84, 493, 501, 504.]

490 Pons, J. *Recherches sur les apocryphes du Nouveau Testament. Thèse historique et critique . . . pour obtenir le grade de bachelier en théologie, Faculté de théologie de Montauban.* Montauban: Imprimerie de Forestié neveu, 1850. [Pp. 25, 33, 38–39, 44–47].

491 Hofmann, R. *Das Leben Jesu nach den Apokryphen: im Zusammenhang aus den Quellen erzählt und wissenschaftlich untersucht.* Leipzig: F. Voigt, 1851. [Pp. 177ff., 334–471.]

492 Tischendorf, C. von. *Evangelia apocrypha siue de evangeliorum apocryphorum origine et usu disquisitio historico-critica.* Verhandelingen, uitgegeven door het Haagsche Genootschap tot verdediging van de Christelijke godsdienst, vol. 12. The Hague: Thierry et Mensing, 1851. [Cf. no. 4.]

493 Volkmar, G. *Über Justin den Märtyrer und sein Verhältniss zu unsern Evangelien. . . .* Zürich: E. Kiesling, 1853. [Pp. 40f.: on patristic attestations of *AP.* Cf. nos. 469, 483–84, 489, 501, 504.]

494 Hilgenfeld, W. "Constantin Tischendorf als Defensor Fidei." *Zeitschrift für wissenschaftliche Theologie* 1865: 340–43. [Cf. no. 4.]

495 Tischendorf, C. von. *Wann wurden unsere Evangelien verfasst.* 1865. 4th ed., Leipzig: J. C. Hinrichs, 1866. This work was translated into numerous languages. [Pp. 82–89. Cf. nos. 4, 310.]

496 Nicolas, M. *Études sur les évangiles apocryphes.* Paris: Michel Levy Frères, 1866. [Pp. 245–61, 283–317, 355–83, 403–14.]

497 Scholten, J. H. *De oudste getuigenissen angaande de Schriften des Nieuwen Testaments historisch onderzoot.* Leiden: P. Engels, 1866.

498 Variot, J. *Les Évangiles apocryphes. Histoire littéraire, forme primitive, transformations.* Paris: E. Thorin, 1878. [Pp. 93–138, 233–328.]

499 Waite, C. B. *History of the Christian Religion to the Year Two Hundred.* Chicago: C. V. Waite, 1881. [Pp. 177–212.]

500 Reusch, F. H., ed. *Die Indices librorum prohibitorum des sechzehnten*

Jahrhunderts. 1886. Reprint, Nieuwkoop: B. de Graaf, 1961. [Pp. 272, 287: *EN* among forbidden books. Cf. nos. 477, 503, 508, 510.]

501 Kattenbusch, F. *Das apostolische Symbol. Seine Entstehung, sein geschichtlicher Sinn, seine ursprüngliche Stellung im Kultus und in der Theologie der Kirche. Ein Beitrag zur Symbolik und Dogmengeschichte.* Vol. 2, *Verbereitung und Bedeutung des Taufsymbols.* Pt. 2. Leipzig: J. C. Hinrichs, 1900. [Pp. 631–37: on Justin's reference to "Acta Pilati." Cf. nos. 469, 483–84, 489, 493, 504.]

502 Bauer, W. *Das Leben Jesu im Zeitalter der neutestamentlichen Apokryphen.* Tübingen: J. C. B. Mohr (P. Siebeck), 1909. [See index, s.v. "Acta Pilati."]

503 Dobschütz, E. von, ed. *Das Decretum Gelasianum de libris recipiendis et non recipiendis.* Texte und Untersuchungen zur Geschichte der altchristlichen Literatur, vol. 38. Leipzig: J. C. Hinrichs, 1912. [P. 298. Cf. nos. 477, 500, 508, 510.]

504 Goguel, M. *Jésus de Nazareth. Mythe ou histoire?* Bibliothèque historique. Paris: Payot, 1925. [Pp. 50–55: on earliest attestations of *AP* (Justin, Tertullian). Cf. nos. 469, 476, 483–84, 489, 493, 501.]

505 Eisler, R. Ἰησοῦς βασιλεὺς οὐ βασιλεύσας: *Die messianische Unabhängigkeitsbewegung vom Auftreten Johannes des Täufers bis zum Untergang Jakobs des Gerechten.* . . . Religionswissenschaftliche Bibliothek, vol. 9. Heidelberg: C. Winter, 1929. [1:xxxii–xxxv: on "Acts of Pilate" published by Maximin Daïa. Cf. nos. 471, 474.]

506 Saintyves, P. [E. Nourry]. "De la nature des évangiles apocryphes et de leur valeur hagiographique." *Revue de l'histoire des religions* 106 (1932): 435–57.

507 Schmidt, K. L. *Kanonische und apokryphe Evangelien und Apostelgeschichten.* Abhandlungen zur Theologie des Alten und Neuen Testaments, vol. 5. Basel: H. Majoer, 1944. [Pp. 62–65, 76–80.]

508 MacDonald, J., and A. J. B. Higgins. "The Beginnings of Christianity according to the Samaritans." *New Testament Studies* 18 (1971): 54–80. [P. 67: *EN* in a list of apocrypha. Cf. nos. 477, 500, 503, 510.]

509 Hamman, A. G. "La Résurrection du Christ dans l'antiquité chrétienne." *Revue des sciences religieuses* 49 (1975): 305–9. Reprinted in no. 512.

510 Bujanda, J. M. de, ed. *Index de l'Université de Louvain 1546, 1550, 1558.* Sherbrooke, Québec: Centre d'études de la renaissance, 1986. [Pp. 339–40: *EN* among forbidden books. Cf. nos. 477, 500, 503, 508.]

511 Schwarzbach, B. E. "The Sacred Genealogy of a Voltairean Polemic: The Development of Critical Hypotheses Regarding the Composition of the Canonical and Apocryphal Gospels." In *Studies on Voltaire and the Eighteenth Century*, 245:338–42. Oxford: Voltaire Foundation, 1986. [On Voltaire's use of *EN*. Cf. nos. 324, 379.]

512 Hamman, A. G. "La Résurrection du Christ dans l'antiquité chré-

tienne." In *Études patristiques. Méthodologie – Liturgie – Histoire – Théologie*, Théologie historique, vol. 85, pp. 402–6. Paris: Beauchesne, 1991. Reprint of no. 509.

2.2.2. Trial of Jesus, his death, and his Resurrection
(*Acts of Pilate*, chaps. 1–16)

513 Paulus, H. E. G. *Exegetisches Handbuch über die drei ersten Evangelien.* Vol. 3, pt. 1. Heidelberg: C. F. Winter, 1832. [Pp. 640–43: on Procula. Cf. nos. 529, 531, 535, 543.]

514 Gaidoz, H. "Le pèlerinage de saint Jacques de Compostelle." *Mélusine* 6 (1892–93), 23–24 and plate 1. [On the cock crowing in a pot, prophesying Judas's suicide. Cf. nos. 345, 347, 357, 515, 663, 709, 866, 874.]

515 Gaidoz, H. "Le coq cuit qui chante." *Mélusine* 6 (1892–93), 25–27. [Cf. nos. 345, 347, 357, 514, 663, 709, 866, 874.]

516 Kunze, J. *Das neu aufgefundene Bruchstück des sog. Petrusevangeliums übersetzt und beurteilt.* Leipzig: Dörffling und Franke, 1893. Reprinted with corrections in no. 521. [Cf. nos. 517-20, 523, 526.]

517 Schubert, H. von. *Die Composition des pseudopetrinischen Evangelien-Fragments (mit einer synoptischen Tabelle als Ergänzungsheft).* Berlin: Reuther & Reichard, 1893. [Pp. 175–96. Cf. nos. 516, 518–21, 523, 526.]

518 Wabnitz, A. "Les Fragments de l'Évangile et de l'Apocalypse de Pierre (suite)." *Revue de théologie de Montauban* 2 (1893): 356–70. [Cf. nos. 516–17, 519–21, 523, 526.]

519 Zahn, Th. "Das Evangelium des Petrus." *Neue kirchliche Zeitschrift* 4 (1893): 143–80, 181–218. Reprinted in no. 520. [Cf. nos. 516–18, 521, 523, 526.]

520 Zahn, Th. *Das Evangelium des Petrus.* Erlangen: Deichert, 1893. Reprint of no. 519. [Cf. nos. 516–18, 521, 523, 526.]

521 Kunze, J. "Das Petrusevangelium." *Neue Jahrbücher für deutsche Theologie* 2 (1893): 583–604; 3 (1894): 58–104. Reprint, with corrections, of no. 516. [Cf. nos. 517–20, 523, 526.]

522 Resch, A. *Aussercanonische Paralleltexte.* Texte und Untersuchungen, vol. 10, nos. 1–5. Leipzig: J. C. Hinrichs, 1893–97.

523 Stanton, V. H. "The Gospel of Peter, Its Early History and Character Considered in Relation to the History of the Recognition in the Church of the Canonical Gospels." *Journal of Theological Studies* 2 (1900): 1–25. [Cf. nos. 516–21, 526.]

524 Darley, E. *Fragments d'anciennes chroniques d'Aquitaine.* Bordeaux: Feret et fils, 1906. [On Veronica. Cf. nos. 426, 525.]

525 Darley, E. *Sainte Véronique.* La Rochelle: Société des archives historiques de la Saintonge et de l'Aunis, 1907. [Cf. nos. 426, 524.]

526 Vaganay, L. *L'Évangile de Pierre.* Études bibliques. Paris: Gabalda, 1930. [See index, s.v. "Acta Pilati." Cf. nos. 516–21, 523.]

527 Schonfield, H. J. *According to the Hebrews. A New Translation of the Jewish Life of Jesus (the Toldoth Jeshu), with an Inquiry into the Nature of Its Sources.* ... London: Duckworth, 1937. [P. 130: on the Crucifixion in a garden. Cf. no. 534.]

528 Burdach, K. *Der Gral. Forschungen über seinen Ursprung und seinen Zusammenhang mit der Longinuslegende.* 1938. Reprint, Darmstadt: Wissenschaftliche Buchgesellschaft, 1974. [Pp. 224–32: on the name "Longinus." Cf. nos. 535, 544, 871, 878, 889, 893, 896.]

529 Fascher, E. "Das Weib des Pilatus (Mt. 27, 19). Eine Studie zu Mt 27, 19." *Theologische Literaturzeitung* 4 (1947): 201–4. [Cf. nos. 513, 531, 535, 543.]

530 Ehrhardt, A. "Pontius Pilatus in der frühchristlichen Mythologie." *Evangelische Theologie* 9 (1949–50): 433–47.

531 Fascher, E. "Das Weib des Pilatus (Mt. 27, 19)." In *Das Weib des Pilatus (Matthäus 27, 19) – Die Auferweckung der Heiligen (Matthäus 27, 51–53). Zwei Studien zur Geschichte der Schriftauslegung,* 5–31. Hallische Monographien, vol. 20. Halle (Saale): M. Niemeyer, 1951. [Cf. nos. 513, 529, 535, 543.]

532 Gaiffier, B. de. Review of *Gesammelte Aufsätze zur Kulturgeschichte Spaniens,* vols. 9 and 10 (Münster in Westfalen: Aschendorff, 1954 and 1955). *Analecta Bollandiana* 74 (1956): 273–4. [On the cult of St. Dismas in Spain. Cf. nos. 535, 943.]

533 Cothenet, E. "Marie dans les apocryphes." In *Maria. Études sur la sainte Vierge,* edited by H. Du Manoir, 6:106–13. Paris: Beauchesne, 1961. [Cf. nos. 48, 572, 580, 598, 603, 634, 646, 654, 657, 888.]

534 Bammel, E. "Excerpts from a New Gospel?" *Novum Testamentum* 10 (1968): 5–6. Reprinted in no. 537. [P. 130: on the Crucifixion in a garden. Cf. no. 527.]

535 Metzger, B. M. "Names for the Nameless in the New Testament: A Study in the Growth of Christian Tradition." In *New Testament Studies: Philological, Versional, and Patristic,* edited by B. M. Metzger, 23–43. New Testament Tools and Studies, vol. 10. Leiden: E. J. Brill, 1980. [Comments on onomastic traditions derived from *AP*. Cf. nos. 513, 528–29, 531–32, 543–44, 871, 878, 889, 893, 896, 943.]

536 Bammel, E. "Jesus as a Political Agent in a Version of the Josippon." In *Jesus and the Politics of His Day,* edited by E. Bammel and C. F. D. Moule. Cambridge: Cambridge University Press, 1984. Reprinted in no. 537. [P. 208: *AP* in the context of polemics between Judaism and Christianity.]

537 Bammel, E. *Judaïca: kleine Schriften.* Wissenschaftliche Untersuchungen zum Neuen Testament, vol. 37. Tübingen: J. C. B. Mohr and P. Siebeck, 1986. Reprint of nos. 534, 536. [Pp. 243, 300. Cf. no. 527.]

538 Corrington, G. P. *The "Divine Man." His Origin and Function in Hellenistic Popular Religion.* American University Studies, ser. 7, Theol-

ogy and Religion, vol. 17. New York: Peter Lang, 1986. [Pp. 283–86.]

539 La Potterie, I. de. *La Passion de Jésus selon l'Évangile de Jean. Texte et Esprit.* Lire la Bible, vol. 73. Paris: Cerf, 1986. [P. 99: à propos Jn. 18:36 and its parallel in *AP.*]

540 Geerard, M. "Marie-Madeleine, dénonciatrice de Pilate." *Sacris Erudiri* 31 (1989–90): 139–48.

541 Légasse, S. *Le Procès de Jésus.* Vol. 1, *L'Histoire.* Lectio Divina, vol. 156. Paris: Cerf, 1994. [Pp. 140–41: on the girdle of the crucified Jesus.]

542 Pietersma, A. *The Apocryphon of Jannes and Jambres the Magicians....* Religions in the Graeco-Roman World, vol. 119. Leiden: E. J. Brill, 1994. [See index, s.v. "Acts of Pilate."]

543 Kany, R. "Die Frau des Pilatus und ihr Name." Ein Kapitel aus der Geschichte neutestamentlicher Wissenschaft. *Zeitschrift für die neutestamentliche Wissenschaft* 86, nos. 1–2 (1995): 104–10. [Cf. nos. 513, 529, 531, 535.]

544 Beggiato, F. "Il perdono di Longino: Un' utilizzazione del Supporto intertestuale nella scelta tra varianti." In *L'intertestualità romanza.* Rome: Bagatto Libri, forthcoming. [On Longinus, cured from blindness by Christ's blood. Cf. nos. 528, 535, 871, 878, 889, 893, 896.]

2.2.3. Descent into Hell (*Acts of Pilate*, chaps. 17–27)

545 Messenger, R. E. "The Descent Theme in Medieval Latin Hymns." *Transactions and Proceedings of the American Philological Association* 67 (1936): 126–47. [Cf. nos. 611, 618, 875, 879.]

546 Cabaniss, A. "The Harrowing of Hell, Psalm 24, and Pliny the Younger: A Note." *Vigiliae Christianae* 7 (1953): 65–74. [Cf. nos. 549, 557.]

547 Simon, M. *Hercule et le Christianisme.* Publications de la Faculté des lettres de l'Université de Strasbourg. Paris: Belles Lettres, 1955. [Pp. 112–14: parallels between the pagan myth and *EN.*]

548 Quinn, E. C. *The Quest of Seth for the Oil of Life.* Chicago: University of Chicago Press, 1962. [On *EN* 19.1. Cf. nos. 552, 559–61, 586, 606.]

549 Rose, A. " 'Attolite portas, principes, vestras ...' Aperçus sur la lecture chrétienne du Ps. 24 (23) B." In *Miscellanea liturgica in onore di Sua Eminenza il cardinale Giacomo Lercaro, acivescovo di Bologna,* 1: 453–78. Rome: Desclée, 1966. [Cf. nos. 546, 557.]

550 Turner, R. V. " 'Descendit ad Inferos': Medieval Views on Christ's Descent into Hell and the Salvation of the Ancient Just." *Journal of the History of Ideas* 27 (1966): 173–94.

551 Bell, A. R. "The Harrowing of Hell: A Study of Its Reception and Artistic Interpretation in Early Medieval European Literature." Ph.D. diss., University of Maryland, 1971.

552 Nagel, M. "La Vie greque d'Adam et d'Ève. Apocalypse de Moïse." 2 vols. Thèse présentée devant l'Université de Strasbourg II. Univer-

sité de Lille III: Service de reproduction des thèses, 1974. [1:159–75: on Seth's trip to paradise and archangel's prophecy (*EN* 19.1). Cf. nos. 548, 559–61, 586, 606.]

552a Murray, C. *Symbols of Church and Kingdom*. London: Cambridge University Press, 1975. [See index, s.v. "Gospel of Nicodemus."]

553 Orbe, A. *Cristología Gnóstica. Introducción a la soteriología de los siglos II y III*. Vol. 2. Biblioteca de autores cristianos, vol. 385. Madrid: La Editorial Catolica, 1976. [See index of names for numerous references to *AP*.]

554 Sheerin, D. "St. John the Baptist in the Lower World." *Vigiliae Christianae* 30 (1976): 1–22. [Cf. nos. 566, 576, 650–51, 653, 671–72.]

555 Junod, E. "Actes apocryphes et hérésies: Le Jugement de Photius." In *Les Actes apocryphes des Apôtres. Christianisme et monde païen*, edited by F. Bovon et al., Publications de la Faculté de théologie de l'Université de Genève, vol. 4. Geneva: Labor et Fides, 1981. [Pp. 16–18: on Leucius.]

556 Le Goff, J. *Naissance du purgatoire*. Bibliothèque des histoires. Paris: Gallimard, 1981. [P. 68: on *EN*'s role in evolution of notions concerning purgatory.]

557 Cooper, A. "Ps 24: 7–10: Mythology and Exegesis." *Journal of Biblical Literature* 102 (1983): 37–60. [Cf. nos. 546, 549.]

558 Poirier, P.-H. "La *Protennoia trimorphe (NH* XIII, 1) et le vocabulaire du *Descensus ad Inferos*." *Le Muséon* 96 (1983): 193–204. [Cf. no. 464.]

559 Albert, J.-P. "Le Légendaire médiéval des aromates: Longévité et immortalité." In *Le Corps humain: Nature, culture, surnaturel. Congrès national des Sociétés savantes. Montpellier, 1985*, 37–48. Paris: CTHS, 1985. [On oil of mercy and Tree of Life (*EN* 19.1). Cf. nos. 548, 552, 560–61, 586, 606.]

560 Bertrand, D. A. *La Vie grecque d'Adam et Ève. Introduction, texte, traduction et commentaire. . . .* Recherches intertestamentaires, vol. 1. Paris: A. Maisonneuve, 1987. [Pp. 61–65: on genetic relationship between Seth episodes in *Vita Adae et Evae* and *EN* 19.1. Cf. nos. 548, 552, 559, 561, 586, 606.]

561 Forsyth, N. *The Old Enemy: Satan and the Combat Myth*. Princeton: University Press, 1987. [Pp. 228–32: on Seth's quest for oil of mercy (*EN* 19.1). Cf. nos. 548, 552, 559–60, 586, 606.]

562 Minois, G. *Histoire des enfers*. Paris: Fayard, 1991. [Pp. 90–91.]

2.3. Texts related or indebted to the *Acts of Pilate*
2.3.1. Greek and Latin traditions
2.3.1.1. Greek

Editions

563 Pseudo-Epiphanius. "Sancti Patris nostri Epiphanii episcopi Cypri oratio in divini corporis sepulturam Domini et Servatoris nostri Jesu Christi, et in Josephum qui fuit ab Arimathæa, et in Domini in infernum descensum, post salutarem passionem admirabiliter factum." In PG 43:439A–64D. [Possibly related to *DI.*]

564 Pseudo-Eusebius of Alexandria. "In diabolum et orcum." In PG 86: 383–404. [Possibly related to *DI.* Cf. nos. 456, 576, 613, 643, 650–51.]

565 Pseudo-Eusebius of Alexandria. "In sancta et magna parasceve, et in sanctam passionem Domini." In PG 62:721–24. [Possibly related to *DI.* Cf. nos. 576, 613, 643, 650–51.]

566 Pseudo-Eusebius of Alexandria. "Oratio de adventu et annuntiatione Joannis (Baptistæ) apud inferos." In PG 86:509–26. [Possibly related to *DI.* Cf. nos. 554, 576, 650–51, 653, 671–72.]

567 Smirnov, Ia. "Ob odnom otryvke iz apokrificheskago Evangeliia Nikodima." *Trudy Otdeleniia arkheologii drevne-klassicheskoj, vizantijskoj i zapadno-evropejskoj, Zapiski Imperatorskago russkago arkheologicheskago obshchestva,* n.s., 3 (1897): 422–25. [Commentary, indebted to *AP*, on divine liturgy of John Chrysostom, written by Germanus of Constantinopol. Cf. no. 577.]

568 Lambros, S. «Βυζαντινὴ σκηνοθετικὴ διάταξις τῶν Παθῶν τοῦ Χριστοῦ». Νέος Ἑλληνομνήμων 13 (1916): 381–406. [On religious play in Bibl. Apost. Vat. MS. Pal. gr. 367, inspired by *AP*. Cf. nos. 569–70, 581, 584.]

569 Vogt, A. "Études sur le théâtre byzantin I. Un Mystère de la Passion." *Byzantion* 6 (1931): 37–74. [Includes French translation. Cf. nos. 568, 570, 581, 584.]

570 Mahr, A. C. *The Cyprus Passion Cycle.* Publications in Mediaeval Studies, vol. 9. Notre Dame, Ind.: Notre Dame University Press, 1947. [Includes English translation. Cf. nos. 568–69, 581, 584.]

571 Tuilier, A. *Grégoire de Nazianze – Christus Patiens.* Sources Chrétiennes, vol. 149. Paris: Cerf, 1969. [Pp. 65, 163 n. 2, 169 n. 2, 181 n. 2, 183 n. 3–4, 197 n. 2, 309 n. 1: on possible parallels between *Christus Patiens* and *AP*. Cf. no. 585.]

572 Bouvier, B. *Le Mirologue de la Vierge. Chansons et poèmes grecs sur la Passion du Christ.* Vol. 1, *La Chanson populaire du Vendredi Saint, avec une étude musicale par S. Baud-Bovy.* Bibliotheca Helvetica Romana, vol. 16. Geneva: Institut Suisse de Rome, 1976. [Gives liturgical parallels to Greek *AP* B; announces (p. 5) that the second volume will be "une étude diachronique du thème de la Passion

du Christ vue à travers la sensibilité de sa Mère." Cf. nos. 48, 533,
580, 598, 603, 634, 646, 654, 657, 888.]
573 Aubineau, M. *Les Homélies festales d'Hésychius de Jérusalem.* 2 vols.
Subsidia Hagiographica Graeca, vol. 59. Brussels: Société des Bollandistes, 1978–80. [See index, s.v. "Acta Pilati," for numerous
parallels between these homilies and *AP.*]
574 Gronewald, M. "Kein durchtriebener Räufer (P. Lit. Lond. 245 =
Ps.-Eusebius, Sermo 17)." *Zeitschrift für Papyrologie und Epigraphik*
34 (1979): 22–25.

Studies
575 Allatius, L. *De libris ecclesiasticis Graecorum dissertationes duae.* Paris,
1645. [P. 235: on Pentecostary published in Venice in 1579, which
mentions Greek *AP* and the Descent.]
576 Augusti, J. C. G. *Eusebii Emeseni quae supersunt opuscula Graeca.*
Elberfeld: H. Buescher, 1829. [Pp. 163–68: on relationship between
ps.-Eusebius of Alexandria's sermons (nos. 564–66) and *AP.* Cf.
also nos. 456, 613, 643, 650–51, 653, 671–72.]
577 Dobschütz, E. von. "Coislinianus 296." *Byzantinische Zeitschrift* 12
(1903): 534–67. [P. 541: on Germanus of Constantinopol's commentary on the liturgy of John Chrysostom. Dobschütz announced his
intention to re-edit the text but apparently never carried it out. Cf.
no. 567.]
578 La Piana, G. "Le rappresentazioni sacre e la poesia ritmica drammatica nella letteratura bizantina dalle origini al seculo IX." *Roma
e l'Oriente* 3 (1911–12): 36–44, 105–18, 392–93. Revised and expanded in no. 579.
579 La Piana, G. *Le rappresentazioni sacre nella letteratura bizantina dalle
origini al seculo IX con rapporti al teatro sacro d'occidente.* 1912. Reprint, London: Variorum Reprints, 1971. Revised and expanded
no. 578. [See index, s.v. "Nicodemo (Vangelo di)."]
580 Alexiou, M. "The Lament of the Virgin in Byzantine Literature
and Modern Greek Folk-Songs." *Byzantine and Modern Greek
Studies* 1 (1975): 111–40. [Cf. nos. 48, 533, 572, 598, 603, 634, 646,
654, 657, 888.]
581 Baud-Bovy, S. "Le Théâtre religieux, Byzance et l'Occident."
Ἑλληνικά 28, no. 2 (1975): 328–49. [Cf. nos. 568–70, 584.]
582 Czerniatowicz, J. "Euangelium Nicodemi a Stanislao Marennio
carmine Graeco scriptum." *Eos. Commentarii Societatis Philologiae
Polonorum* (Wroclaw) 71: 2 (1983): 167–86. [Sixteenth-century rendition of Latin *EN* into Greek verse.]
583 Poirier, P.-H. "La *Descente aux enfers* dans le cycle pascal byzantin." In *Mélanges offerts au Cardinal Louis-Albert Vachon,* 354–69.
Université de Laval (Québec), 1989.

584 Gounelle, R. "À propos d'une refonte de la *Narratio Iosephi* jadis confondue avec les *Acta Pilati* et d'un drame religieux qu'elle a inspiré." *Apocrypha* 5 (1994): 165–88. [Cf. nos. 568–70, 581.]
585 Starowieyski, M. "Les Apocryphes dans la tragédie *Christus Patiens*." *Apocrypha* 5 (1994): 269–88. [Pp. 280–85: on relationship between *Christus Patiens* and *AP*. Cf. no. 571.]

2.3.1.2. Latin

Editions
586 Petrus de Natalibus. *Catalogus sanctorum et gestorum eorum ex diuersis voluminibus collectus.* Lyons: J. Sacon, 1519. [Fol. 35rb: Seth episode (*EN* 19.1; cf. nos. 548, 552, 559–61, 606); fol. 65rb: summary of *EN*, 26.]
587 Vincent of Beauvais. *Speculum historiale.* 1624. Reprint, Graz: Akademische Druck- u. Verlagsanstalt, 1965. [Frequent references to *EN* in chaps. 40, 41, 48; summary of *EN* 12–27 in chaps. 56–63. Cf. nos. 641, 688, 695, 778, 787, 799, 805, 860.]
588 Vincent of Beauvais. *Speculum naturale.* 1624. Reprint, Graz: Akademische Druck- u. Verlagsanstalt, 1964. [Col. 8: *EN* referred to as *Evangelium Nazaraeorum.* Cf. no. 633.]
589 Bruno Segniensis. "In die resurrectionis." In *Maxima bibliotheca veterum patrum*, 6:753–54. Lyon: Apud Anissonios, 1677. [Homily inspired by *DI*.]
590 Foggini, P. F. *De Romano Divi Petri itinere.* Florence: Typ. Manniano, 1741. [Pp. 37–46: *Cura sanitatis Tiberii*. Cf. nos. 428, 432, 591, 610.]
591 Mansi, J. D., ed. *Stephani Baluzii Tutelensis Miscellanea novo ordine digesta. . . .* Vol. 4. Lucca: V. Junctinius, 1764. [Pp. 55–60: *Cura sanitatis Tiberii*. Cf. nos. 428, 432, 590, 610.]
592 Durham Cathedral. *Catalogues of the Library of Durham Cathedral.* Publications of the Surtees Society, vol. 7. London: J. B. Nichols and Son, 1838. [P. 119: the earliest mention of the title *Evangelium Nicodemi*.]
593 Caesarius of Arles. "Homilia prima. De Paschate." In *PL* 67:1041–43. [Ps.-Augustinian "Sermo 160," textually related to *EN*. Cf. nos. 595–96, 600, 608, 611, 618, 626–28, 630a, 637, 711, 717, 812, 821–22, 830.]
594 Honorius Augustodunensis. "De paschali die." In *PL* 172:927–42. [Cols. 932D-33A: on Joseph of Arimathea.]
595 Martin of Laon. "Sermo vicesimo quintus. De resurrectione Domini." In *PL* 208:925–32. [Ps.-Augustinian "Sermo 160," textually related to *EN*. Cf. nos. 593, 596, 600, 608, 611, 618, 626–28, 630a, 637, 711, 717, 812, 821–22, 830.]

596 Pseudo-Augustine. "Sermo 160: De pascha II." In PL 39:2059–61. [Textually related to *EN*. Cf. nos. 593, 595, 600, 608, 611, 618, 626–28, 630a, 637, 711, 717, 812, 821–22, 830.]

597 Pseudo-Juvencus. "Triumphus Christi heroicus." In PL 19:385–88. [Reminiscent of *EN*.]

598 Pseudo-Anselmus. *Dialogus beatae Mariae et Anselmi*. In PL 159:271–90. [Frequently co-occurs with *EN* in MSS. Cf. nos. 48, 533, 572, 580, 603, 634, 646, 654, 657, 888.]

599 Werner of St. Blasius. "Sermo de resurrectione Domini." In PL 157:921B–29A. [Indebted to *EN*.]

600 Jacobus a Voragine. *Jacobi a Voragine Legenda aurea vulgo Historia Lombardica dicta*. Edited by Th. Graesse. 1846. 3d ed., 1890. Reprint, Osnabrück: O. Zeller, 1969. [Excerpts from and references to *EN* in chaps. 53, 54, 67, 68; summary of ps.-Augustinian "Sermo 160" (cf. nos. 593, 595–96, 608, 611, 618, 626–28, 630a, 637, 711, 717, 812, 821–22, 830) and *DI* in chap. 54. For *Legenda area*, see also nos. 128, 632, 640, 681, 684–85, 689, 697, 715, 801, 803, 828, 846.]

601 Massmann, H. F., ed. *Der keiser und der kunige buoch oder die sogenannte Kaiserchronik, Gedicht des zwölften Jahrhunderts*. Pt. 3. Quedlinburg: G. Basse, 1854. [Pp. 579–80, 605–6: *De Veronilla*, attached to *EN* in some MSS.]

602 Pseudo-Bonaventura. *Meditationes vitae Christi*. In *S. R. E. Cardinalis S. Bonaventurae Opera omnia* . . . , edited by A. C. Peltier, 12:509–630. Paris: L. Vivès, 1868. [Frequently evokes *EN* (cf. pp. 608, 613, 619, 623) and co-occurs with *EN* in MSS. Cf. no. 700.]

603 Schade, O., ed. *Interrogatio sancti Anshelmi de passione Domini*. Königsberg: Typis academicis Dalkowskianis, 1870. [Frequently co-occurs with *EN* in MSS. Cf. nos. 48, 533, 572, 580, 598, 634, 646, 654, 657, 888.]

604 Matthew of Paris. *Matthæi Parisiensis, monachi Sancti Albani, Chronica majora*. Vol. 1, *The Creation to A.D. 1066*. Edited by H. R. Luard. Rer. Brit. M. A. Script., vol. 57. London: Longman, 1872. [Pp. 95–96: *Epistola Pilati ad Claudium*, usually part of *EN*.]

605 Ludolph of Saxony. *Vita Jesu Christi*. Edited by L. M. Rigollet. Vol. 4. Paris: V. Palmé, 1878. [Many references to *EN* (cf. pp. 58, 84, 169–70, 205); co-occurs with *EN* in MSS.]

606 Meyer, W., ed. "Vita Adae et Evae." In *Abhandlungen der philosophisch-philologischen Classe der königlich bayerischen Akademie der Wissenschaften*, 14:178–250. Munich: Verlag der K. Akademie, in Commission bei G. Franz, 1878. [Includes Seth's trip to paradise and archangel's prophecy (*EN* 19.1). Cf. nos. 548, 552, 559–61, 586.]

607 Thompson, E. M. "Apocryphal Legends." *Journal of the British Archaeological Association* 37 (1881): 239–53. [*De arbore crucis Domini*, attached to *EN* in some MSS.]

608 Kuypers, A. B., ed. *The Prayer Book of Aedeluald the Bishop, Commonly Called the Book of Cerne.* Cambridge: The University Press, 1902. [Pp. 196–98: semi-dramatic text (edited also in no. 628) based on ps.-Augustinian "Sermo 160" (cf. nos. 593, 595–96, 600, 611, 618, 626–27, 637, 711, 717, 812, 821–22, 830).]

609 Vögtlin, A., ed. *Vita beate virginis Marie et Salvatoris rhythmica.* Bibliothek des Litterarischen Vereins, vol. 180. Tübingen: Gedruckt für den Litterarischen Verein in Stuttgart, 1888. [Many references to *EN,* passim, but the poem is not directly based on it. Cf. nos. 616, 802, 813, 819.]

610 Dobschütz, E. von. *Christusbilder. Untersuchungen zur christlichen Legende.* Texte und Untersuchungen zur Geschichte der altchristlichen Literatur, vol. 18, N.F., vol. 3. Leipzig: J. C. Hinrichs, 1899. [Pp. 209–14, 157**–203**: *Cura sanitatis Tiberii.* Cf. nos. 428, 432, 590–91.]

611 Dreves, G. M., ed. *Prosarium Lemovicense. Die Prosen der Abtei St. Martial zu Limoges aus Troparien des 10., 11. und 12. Jahrhunderts.* Leipzig: Fues's Verlag (R. Reisland), 1899. [P. 59: "Cantat omnis turba ..."; pp. 65–66: "O beata et venerabilis virgo Maria alma ..."; and pp. 67–68: "Clara gaudia, festa paschalia ..."; all three hymns are indebted to ps.-Augustinian "Sermo 160" (cf. nos. 593, 595–96, 600, 608, 618, 626–28, 630a, 637, 711, 717, 812, 821–22, 830). For other hymns, see nos. 545, 875, 879.]

612 Horstmann, C., ed. *Nova legenda Angliae: As Collected by John of Tynemouth, John Capgrave, and Others, and First Printed, with New Lives, by Wynkyn de Worde. . . .* Vol. 2. Oxford: Clarendon Press, 1901. [Pp. 78–80: John of Glastonbury's summary of *EN* 12–15 (on Joseph of Arimathea). Cf. nos. 631, 794.]

613 Rand, E. K., ed. "Sermo de confusione diaboli." *Modern Philology* 2 (1904): 261–78. [Latin version of sermons ascribed to Eusebius of Alexandria and possibly related to *DI.* Cf. nos. 456, 564–65, 576, 643, 650–51.]

614 Winterfeld, P. von, ed. *Poëtae Latini aevi Carolini.* Vol. 4, pt. 1. MGH. Berlin: apud Weidmannos, 1904. [Pp. 636–37: "Versum de contentione Zabuli cum Averno," based on *EN.* Cf. no. 639.]

615 Wyclif, John. *De veritate Sacrae Scripturae.* Edited by R. Buddensieg. Wyclif Society. Vol. 1. London: Trübner, 1905–7. [P. 237: a medieval commendation of *EN.*]

616 Päpke, M. *Das Marienleben des Schweizers Wernher. Mit Nachträgen zu Vögtlins Ausgabe der Vita Marie rhythmica.* Palaestra, vol. 81. Berlin: Mayer & Müller, 1913. [Prints glosses and source references missing from Vögtlin's edition (no. 609). Cf. nos. 802, 813, 819.]

617 Dobschütz, E. von. "A Collection of Old Latin Bible Quotations: *Somnium Neronis.*" *Journal of Theological Studies* 16 (1915): 1–27. [A

frequent appendix to *EN.* Cf. no. 630.]

618 Strecker, K., ed. *Poëtae Latini aevi Carolini.* Vol. 4, pt. 2. MGH. Berlin: apud Weidmannos, 1923. [Pp. 565–69: "Audite omnes canticum mirabile . . .," based on ps.-Augustinian "Sermo 160" (cf. nos. 593, 595–96, 600, 608, 611, 626–28, 630a, 637, 711, 717, 812, 821–22, 830). For other hymns, see nos. 545, 875, 879.]

619 Kölbing, E., and M. Day, eds. *The Siege of Jerusalem.* EETS OS, vol. 188. London: Oxford University Press, 1932. [Pp. 83–85: *Vindicta Salvatoris.* Cf. nos. 433, 674, 713, 776, 791, 938.]

620 Young, K. *The Drama of the Medieval Church.* 2 vols. 1933. Reprint, Oxford: Clarendon Press, 1967. [1:164–66, 172–75, 425: liturgical texts with potential links to *EN.* Cf. nos. 622, 624.]

621 Lefèvre, Y., ed. *L'Elucidarium et les lucidaires.* Paris: E. de Boccard, 1954. [P. 391: mentions *EN.*]

622 Andrieu, M., ed. *Les "Ordines Romani" du haut moyen âge.* Vol. 4, *Les textes (suite) ("Ordines" XXXV–XLIX).* Louvain: "Specilegium Sacrum Lovaniense," 1956. [Pp. 339–49: liturgical ceremony possibly related to *EN.* Cf. nos. 620, 624.]

623 Albert the Great. *De resurrectione.* Edited by W. Kübel. In *Sancti doctoris ecclesiae Alberti Magni . . . Opera omnia,* vol. 26. Münster in Westfalen: Aschendorff, 1958. [Pp. 262, 263, 270: references to *EN* in theological contexts.]

624 Alexander of Villa Dei. *Ecclesiale.* Edited by L. R. Lind. Lawrence: University of Kansas Press, 1958. [Vv. 603–22: liturgical ceremony with echoes of *EN.* Cf. nos. 620, 622.]

625 Paulus Crosnensis Ruthenus. *Pauli Crosnensis Rutheni Carmina.* Edited by M. Cytowska. Warsaw: Państwowe Wydawnictwo Naukowe, 1962. [Pp. 172–79: "Sapphicon de inferorum vestatione et triumpho Christi," reminiscent of *EN.*]

626 Thomas Aquinas. *Summa theologiae.* Vol. 54. Edited by R. T. A. Murphy. New York: Blackfriars in conjunction with McGraw-Hill Book Co., 1965. [P. 166: reference to ps.-Augustinian "Sermo 160." Cf. nos. 593, 595–96, 600, 608, 611, 618, 627–28, 630a, 637, 711, 717, 812, 821–22, 830.]

627 Eusebius "Gallicanus." *Collectio homiliarum, de qua critice disseruit Ioh. Leroy.* Edited by Fr. Glorie. 2 vols. CC SL, vols. 101 and 101A. Turnhout: Brepols, 1970. [1:141–43, 1:145–50, 2:881–86: portions of ps.-Augustinian "Sermo 160" in ps.-Eusebian homilies "De pascha I," "De pascha IA," and "De resurrectione domini." Cf. nos. 593, 595–96, 600, 608, 611, 618, 626, 628, 630a, 637, 711, 717, 812, 821–22, 830.]

628 Dumville, D. N. "Liturgical Drama and Panegyric Responsory from the Eighth Century? A Re-examination of the Origin and Contents of the Ninth-Century Section of the Book of Cerne." *Jour-*

nal of Theological Studies 23 (1972): 374–406. [Semi-dramatic text (edited also in no. 608) based on ps.-Augustinian "Sermo 160" (cf. nos. 593, 595–96, 600, 611, 618, 626–27, 630a, 637, 711, 717, 812, 821–22, 830).]

629 Erasmus, Desiderius. *Opera omnia Desiderii Erasmi Roterdami.* Vol. 1, pt. 3, *Colloquia.* Edited by L.-E. Halkin, F. Bierlaire, and R. Hoven. Amsterdam: North-Holland, 1972. [P. 418: Erasmus mentions a copy of *EN* displayed in the Cathedral Church in Canterbury.]

630 Speyer, W. "Neue Pilatus-Apokryphen." *Vigiliae Christianae* 32 (1978): 53–59. [*Somnium Neronis*, frequently attached to *EN*. Cf. no. 617.]

630a Ozimic, D., ed. *Der pseudo-augustinische Sermo CLX.* . . . Dissertationen der Universität Graz, no. 47. Graz, 1979. [Pseudo-Augustinian "Sermo 160." Cf. nos. 593, 595–96, 600, 608, 611, 618, 626–28, 637, 711, 717, 812, 821–22, 830.]

631 John of Glastonbury. *The Chronicle of Glastonbury Abbey: An Edition, Translation and Study of John of Glastonbury's "Cronica sive Antiquitates Glastoniensis Ecclesie."* Edited by J. P. Carley; translated by D. Townsend. Bury St. Edmunds, Suffolk: Boydell Press, 1985. [P. 46: summary of *EN* 12–15 (on Joseph of Arimathea). Cf. nos. 612, 794.]

632 Knape, J. "Die Historia apocrypha der Legenda aurea (dt.)." In J. Knape and K. Strobel, *Zur Deutung von Geschichte in Antike und Mittelalter,* Bamberger Hochschulschriften, vol. 11, pp. 113–72. Bamberg: Bayerische Verlagsanstalt, 1985. [*Historia apocrypha of the Legenda aurea*, Latin and German versions. For *Legenda area*, see also nos. 128, 600, 640, 681, 684–85, 689, 697, 715, 801, 803, 828, 846.]

633 Thomas of Chobham. *Summa de arte praedicandi.* Edited by F. Morenzoni. CC CM, vol. 82. Turnhout: Brepols, 1988. [P. 110: *EN* referred to as *Evangelium Nazaraeorum.* Cf. no. 588.]

634 Marx, C. W. "The *Quis dabit* of Oglerius of Tridino, Monk and Abbot of Locedio." *Journal of Medieval Latin* 4 (1994): 118–29. [Frequently co-occurs with *EN* in MSS. Cf. nos. 48, 533, 572, 580, 598, 603, 646, 654, 657, 888.]

Studies

635 Brückner, A. "Średniowieczna poezya łacińska w Polsce." *Rozprawy Akademii Umiejętności w Krakowie. Wydział Filologiczny* 16 (1892): 304–72. Continued in no. 636. [On MSS. of *Palestra*, verse rendition of *EN*. Cf. nos. 638, 642.]

636 Brückner, A. "Średniowieczna poezya łacińska w Polsce. Część druga." *Rozprawy Akademii Umiejętności w Krakowie. Wydział Filologiczny* 22 (1893): 1–62. Continuation of no. 635. [On MSS. of *Palestra*, verse rendition of *EN*. Cf. nos. 638, 642.]

637 Young, K. "The Harrowing of Hell in Liturgical Drama." *Transactions of the Wisconsin Academy of Sciences, Arts, and Letters* 16, no. 2 (1909): 889–947. [On liturgical use of ps.-Augustinian "Sermo 160" (cf. nos. 593, 595–96, 600, 608, 611, 618, 626–28, 630a, 711, 717, 812, 821–22, 830); raises doubts about *EN*'s influence on liturgical drama.]

638 Langosch, K. "Überlieferungsgeschichte der mittellateinischen Literatur." In *Geschichte der Textüberlieferung der antiken und mittelalterlichen Literatur*, edited by K. Langosch et al., 2:9–185. Zürich: Atlantis, 1964. [P. 80: on *Palestra*, verse rendition of *EN*. Cf. nos. 635–36, 642.]

639 Brunhölzl, F. *Geschichte der lateinischen Literatur des Mittelalters.* Vol. 1, *Von Cassiodor bis zum Ausklang der karolingischen Erneurung.* Munich: W. Fink, 1975. [On "Versum de contentione Zabuli cum Averno," based on *EN*. Cf. no. 614.]

640 Fleith, B. "Le Classement des quelque 1000 manuscrits de la *Legenda aurea* latine en vue de l'établissement d'une histoire de la tradition." In *Legenda aurea: Sept siècles de diffusion. Actes du colloque international sur la Legenda aurea: Texte latin et branches vernaculaires*, edited by B. Dunn-Lardeau, 19–24. Montréal: Éditions Bellarmin, 1986. [Cf. nos. 128, 600, 632, 681, 684–85, 689, 697, 715, 801, 803, 828, 846.]

641 Duchenne, M.-C., G. G. Guzman, and J. B. Voorbij. "Une Liste des manuscrits du *Speculum historiale* de Vincent de Beauvais." *Scriptorium* 41 (1987): 286–94. [Cf. nos. 587, 688, 695, 778, 787, 799, 805, 860.]

642 Beine, W. "Palestra." In *Die deutsche Literatur des Mittelalters: Verfasserlexikon*, 2d rev. ed., edited by K. Ruh, 7:275–77. Berlin: W. de Gruyter, 1989. [On verse adaptation of *EN*. Cf. nos. 635–36, 638.]

643 Izydorczyk, Z. "Two Newly Identified Manuscripts of the *Sermo de confusione diaboli*." *Scriptorium* 43 (1989): 253–55. [Cf. nos. 456, 564–65, 576, 613, 650–51.]

2.3.2. Eastern traditions
2.3.2.1. Arabic

Editions
644 Krachkovskij, I., ed. "Novozavetnyj apokrif v arabskoj rukopisi 885–886 goda po R. Khr." *Vizantijskij vremennik* 14 (1907): 246–75. [Ephraem Syrus's homily on catabasis. Cf. no. 647.]

645 Galtier, E., ed. "Le Martyre de Pilate." In *Mémoires et fragments inédits*, edited by E. Chassinat, 31–103. Cairo: Institut français d'archéologie orientale, 1912. [*Homilia de morte Pilati*. Cf. nos. 646, 657–60.]

646 Mingana, A., ed. "Timothy's Apology for Christianity, the Lament

of the Virgin, the Martyrdom of Pilate." In *Woodbrooke Studies: Christian Documents in Syriac, Arabic and Garshuni*, edited and translated by A. Mingana, 2:241–333. Cambridge: W. Heffer and Sons, 1928. [Editions and translations of *Homilia de morte Pilati* (cf. nos. 645, 657–60) and *Homilia de lamentis Mariae* (cf. nos. 48, 533, 572, 580, 598, 603, 634, 654, 657, 888).]

647 Garitte, G., ed. "Homélie d'Éphrem 'Sur la mort et le diable.' Version géorgienne et version arabe." *Le Muséon* 82 (1969): 123–63. [Cf. no. 644.]

Studies

648 Graf, G. *Geschichte der christlichen arabischen Literatur.* Vol. 1, *Die Übersetzungen.* Studi e testi, vol. 118. Vatican City: Biblioteca Apostolica Vaticana, 1944. [Pp. 238–40: on translations of Pilate apocrypha.]

2.3.2.2. Armenian
Editions

649 *On the Coming of Jesus to Jerusalem; Secondly, on the Passion He Suffered under Judge Pilate* (in Armenian). Constantinopol, 1710. [Uses first Armenian recension of *AP.* Cf. no. 652.]

650 Der Nersessian, S. "An Armenian Version of the Homilies on the Harrowing of Hell." *Dumbarton Oaks Papers* 8 (1954): 203–24. [Possibly related to *DI.* Cf. nos. 456, 554, 564–566, 576, 613, 643, 651, 653, 671–72.]

651 Der Nersessian, S. "A Homily on the Raising of Lazarus and the Harrowing of Hell." In *Biblical and Patristic Studies in Memory of Robert Pierce Casey*, edited by J. N. Birdsall and R. W. Thomson, 219–34. Freiburg i. Br.: Herder, 1963. [Possibly related to *EN.* Cf. nos. 456, 554, 564–66, 576, 613, 643, 650, 653, 671–72.]

652 Bogharian, N. *Great Catalogue of St. James Manuscripts* (in Armenian). Vol. 6. Jerusalem: Les Presses de Saint-Jacques, 1972. [Pp. 77–81: excerpts from Jerusalem, St. James Monastery MS. 1752, copied at Caesarea in 1675. Cf. no. 649.]

653 Lafontaine, G. "La Version arménienne du sermon d'Eusèbe d'Alexandrie 'Sur la venue de Jean aux Enfers.' " *Le Muséon* 91 (1978): 87–104. [Possibly related to *EN.* Cf. nos. 554, 566, 576, 671–72.]

2.3.2.3. Coptic
Editions

654 Révillout, E. *Les Apocryphes coptes, I.* Patrologia Orientalis, vol. 2, pt. 2. Paris: F. Didot, 1907. [Pp. 170–74: *Homilia de lamentis Mariae.* Cf. nos. 48, 533, 572, 580, 598, 603, 634, 646, 657, 888.]

655 Monneret de Villard, U. *Le leggende orientali sui magi evangelici.*
Studi e testi, vol. 163. Vatican: Biblioteca Apostolica Vaticana,
1952. [P. 192: attestation of liturgical use of *AP*.]

656 Coquin, R. G., and G. Godron. "Un encomion copte sur Marie-
Madeleine attribué à Cyrille de Jérusalem." *Bulletin de l'Institut
français d'archéologie orientale* 90 (1990): 169–212.

2.3.2.4. Ethiopic

Editions

657 Oudenrijn, M.-A. van den. *Gamaliel. Aethiopische Texte zur Pilatusliteratur.* Freiburg: Universitätsverlag, 1959. [Editions and German
translations of *Homilia de morte Pilati* (cf. nos. 645–46, 658–60) and
Homilia de lamentis Mariae (cf. nos. 48, 533, 572, 580, 598, 603, 634,
646, 654, 888); the author of the latter knew only Greek *AP* A.]

658 Cerulli, E. "L'Oriente Cristiano nell'unità delle sue tradizioni." In
*Atti del Convegno Internazionale sul tema: L'Oriente Cristiano nella
storia della civiltà (Roma 31 marzo–3 aprile 1963, Firenze 4 aprile 1963),*
Problemi attuali di scienza e di cultura, quaderno no. 62, 9–43.
Rome: Accademia Nazionale dei Lincei, 1964. Reprinted in no. 659.
[*Homilia de morte Pilati.* Cf. nos. 645–46, 657, 660.]

659 Cerulli, E. *La letteratura etiopica con un saggio sull'Oriente Cristiano.*
3d enl. ed. Florence: G. S. Sansoni, 1968. Reprint of no. 658. [Pp.
193–229. Cf. nos. 645–46, 657, 660.]

660 Beylot, R., ed. and trans. *Le Martyre de Pilate ethiopien.* Patrologia
Orientalis, vol. 45, fasc. 4, no. 204. Turnhout: Brepols, 1993.
[Includes French translation. Cf. nos. 645–46, 657–59.]

Studies

661 Cerulli, E. "Tiberius and Pontius Pilate in Ethiopian Tradition and
Poetry." *Proceedings of the British Academy* 59 (1973): 141–58.

662 Cerulli, E. "Un Hymne éthiopien à Pilate sanctifié." *Mélanges de
l'Université Saint-Joseph* 49 (1975–76): 591–94.

663 Cowley, R. W. "The So-called 'Ethiopic *Book of the Cock*' – Part of
an Apocryphal Passion Gospel, *The Homily and Teaching of our
Fathers the Holy Apostles.*" *Journal of the Royal Asiatic Society* 1
(1985): 16–22. [Cf. nos. 345, 347, 357, 514–15, 709, 866, 874.]

664 Beylot, R. "Bref Aperçu des principaux textes éthiopiens dérivés
des *Acta Pilati.*" *Langues orientales anciennes. Philologie et linguistique*
1 (1988): 181–95.

665 Piovanelli, P. "Les Aventures des apocryphes en Ethiopie." *Apocrypha* 4 (1993): 197–224. [Pp. 210–12.]

2.3.2.5. Georgian

Studies

666 Esbroeck, M. van. "L'Histoire de l'Église de Lydda dans deux textes géorgiens." *Bedi Kartlisa* 35 (1977): 108–31. [*Narratio Iosephi de Arimathaea.*]

667 Esbroeck, M. van. "Jean II de Jérusalem et les cultes de saint Étienne, de la Saint-Sion et de la Croix." *Analecta Bollandiana* 102 (1984): 101–5.

See also no. 647.

2.3.2.6. Slavonic

Editions

668 Karskij, E. F., ed. *Zapadnoruskij sbornik XV-go veka.* Sbornik Otdele-niia russkogo iazyka i slovesnosti Imperstorskoj Akademii Nauk, vol. 65, no. 8. St. Petersburg: Tipografia Imperatorskoj Akademii Nauk, 1897. [Pp. 9–12: a text on the Passion (*GN*?).]

669 Il'inskij, G., ed. "Apokrif 'Acta Pilati' v spiske Orbel'skoj Triodi XIII veka." *Russkij filologicheskij vestnik* 56 (1906): 213–17. [A text combining *Anaphora* and *Paradosis,* not *AP* proper. Cf. no. 676.]

670 Tupikov, N. M., ed. " 'Strasti Khristovy' v zapadnorusskom spiske XV veka." Pamiatniki drevnej pis'mennosti i iskusstva, vol. 140, pp. 1–85. St. Petersburg: Tipografiia Imperatorskoj Akademii Nauk, 1901. [A Passion text indebted to *EN* and related apocrypha.]

671 Iatsimirskij, A. I., ed. "K istorii apokrifov i legend v iuzhnoslavian-skoj pis'mennosti." *Izvestiia Otdelenija russkogo iazyka i slovesnoti Imperatorskoj Akademii Nauk* 14, no. 3 (1909): 103–59. [Pp. 103–7: a homily on John the Baptist's coming into hell, ascribed to Eusebius of Alexandria. Cf. nos. 554, 566, 576, 653, 672.]

672 Kniazevskaia, O. A., V. G. Dem'ianov, and M. V. Liapon, eds. *Uspenskij sbornik XII-XIII vv.* Moscow: Nauka, 1971. [Pp. 358–68: a homily on John the Baptist's coming into hell, ascribed to Eusebius of Alexandria. Cf. nos. 554, 566, 576, 653, 671.]

673 Hitchcock, D. R., ed. *The Appeal of Adam to Lazarus in Hell.* Slavistic Printings and Reprintings, vol. 302. The Hague: Mouton, 1979.

674 Hamm, J., ed. *Acta Pilati i Cvitje.* Stari Pisci Hrvatski, vol. 40. Zagreb: Jugoslavenska Akademija Znanosti i Umjetnosti, 1987. [A story of Pilate, related to *Vindicta Salvatoris,* not *AP.* On *Vindicta,* see also nos. 433, 619, 713, 776, 791, 938.]

Studies

675 Brückner, A. "Kleine Mittheilungen. VI. Passio Christi polnisch und russisch." *Archiv für slavische Philologie* 11 (1888): 620–22.

2.3.2.7. Syriac

Editions

676 Gibson, M. D., ed. *Apocrypha Sinaitica.* Studia Sinaitica, vol. 5. London: C. J. Clay and Sons, 1896. [*Anaphora Pilati* and *Paradosis Pilati,* from Mount Sinaï, St. Catherine Monastery MS. Syr. 82. Cf. no. 669.]

Studies

677 Zeegers-Vander Vorst, N. "Quatre pièces apocryphes néotestamentaires." In *IIIᵉ Symposium Syriacum 1980. Les Contacts du monde syriaque avec les autres cultures (Goslar, 7–11 septembre 1980),* edited by R. Lavenant, pp. 65–77, Orientalia Christiana Analecta, vol. 221. Rome: Institutum Studiorum Orientalium, 1983.

2.3.3. Medieval Western traditions

2.3.3.1. Catalan, Occitan

Editions

678 Isabel de Villena. *Vita Christi.* Edited by R. Miquel i Planas. 3 vols. Barcelona: Biblioteca Catalana, 1916. [Catalan elaboration of the Descent.]

679 Hernando i Delgado, J., ed. "La destrucció de Jerusalem. La venjança que féu de la mort de Jesuchrist Vespesià e Titus son fill." *Miscel·lània de textos medievals* 5 (1989): 1–116. [Possibly related to *Gamaliel.* Cf. nos. 103–6, 111, 119–20, 184–86, 193, 200, 363, 680, 686, 776.]

Studies

680 Chabaneau, C. "La Prise de Jérusalem ou la vengeance du sauveur." *Revue des langues romanes* 32 (1888): 581–608; 33 (1889): 31–46, 600–609. [On potential links between *Gamaliel* and *La destrucció de Jerusalem.* Cf. nos. 103–6, 111, 119–20, 184–86, 193, 200, 363, 679, 686, 776.]

681 Meyer, P. "Traduction provençale de la *Légende dorée.*" *Romania* 27 (1898): 93–137. [Cf. nos. 128, 600, 632, 640, 684–85, 689, 697, 715, 801, 803, 828, 846.]

682 Miquel y Planas, R. *Estudi històrich y crítich sobre la antiga novela catalana.* Barcelona: n.p., 1912. [Pp. 54–58: on a life of Jesus in Paris, BN MS. esp. 486, possibly indebted to Latin *DI* A.]

683 Coromines, J. "Les llegendes rimades de la Bíblia de Sevilla." In *Lleures i converses d'un filòleg,* 216–45. Barcelona: El pi de les tres branques, 1971. [On *Biblia rimada,* which reproduces portions of *E la mira car tot era ensems.* Cf. nos. 112, 118, 687.]

684 Brunel, G. "*Vida de sant Frances.* Versions en langue d'oc et en catalan de la *Legenda aurea:* Essai de classement des manuscrits."

Revue d'histoire des textes 6 (1976): 219–65. [On Catalan and Occitan translations of *Legenda aurea*. Cf. nos. 128, 600, 632, 640, 681, 685, 689, 697, 715, 801, 803, 828, 846.]

685 Coromines, J. Preface to *Vides de sants rosselloneses*, edited by Ch. S. Maneikis Kniazzeh and E. J. Neugaard, vol. 1. Barcelona: Fundació Salvador Vives Casajuana, 1977. [Pp. xvii–xxii: on Catalan translations of *Legenda aurea*. Cf. nos. 128, 600, 632, 640, 681, 684, 689, 697, 715, 801, 803, 828, 846.]

686 Hasenohr, G. "À propos de la *Vie de Nostre Benoit Saulveur Jhesus Crist.*" *Romania* 102 (1981): 352–91. [On *EN*'s influence on *Vie* (cf. no. 770); confirms Occitan origin of *Gamaliel* (cf. nos. 103–6, 111, 119–20, 184–86, 193, 200, 363, 679–80, 776).]

687 Ukas, C. "New Research on the *Bíblia rimada:* the Apocryphal Legends." In *Actes del tercer colloqui d'estudis catalans a Nord-Amèrica (Toronto, 1982): Estudis en honor de Josep Roca-Pons*, edited by P. Boehne, J. Massot i Muntaner, and N. B. Smith, 123–38. Barcelona: Publicacions de l'Abadia de Montserrat, 1982. [On *Biblia rimada*, which incorporates part of *E la mira car tot era ensems*. Cf. nos. 112, 118, 683.]

688 Badia, L. "Frontí i Vegeci, mestres de cavalleria en Català als segles XIV i XV." *Boletín de la Real Academia de Buenas Letras de Barcelona* 39 (1983–84): 191–215. [On Catalan translations of *Speculum historiale*. Cf. nos. 587, 641, 695, 778, 787, 799, 805, 860.]

689 Rubió i Balaguer, J. *Història de la literatura catalana.* Vol. 1. Barcelona: Publicacions de l'Abadia de Montserrat, 1984. [Pp. 136, 138, 281: on Catalan translations of *Legenda aurea*. Cf. nos. 128, 600, 632, 640, 681, 684–85, 697, 715, 801, 803, 828, 846.]

2.3.3.2. Cornish
Editions
690 Norris, E., ed. *The Ancient Cornish Drama.* 2 vols. Oxford: Oxford University Press, 1859. [2:10–25: vv. 97–306 indirectly influenced by *EN*.]

Studies
691 Bakere, J. A. *The Cornish Ordinalia: A Critical Study.* Cardiff: University of Wales Press, 1980. [On indirect influence of *EN*.]

See also no. 749.

2.3.3.3. Dutch, Low German
Editions
692 *Liden ende passie Ons Heren.* Gouda: [Gerard Leeu], 1477. Reissued by various printers in 1482, 1484, 1486–88, 1487, 1488, 1489, 1490,

1491, 1497, 1506?, 1510, and 1528? For details, see nos. 361–62, and 364 above. [*Lyden* 1, incorporating Nicodemean material from Middle Dutch prose translation D. Cf. nos. 693–94, 696, 705, 853.]

693 '*t Wonderlyk Euangelium van Nicodemus, verrijkt met bondige uitleggingen, begrijpende kortelijk den ouden en nieuwen toestand der H. Roomsche Kerck, door den eerwaerdigen Aquila Oreinus, bisschop tot Calorchos*. Antwerp: W. Aertsens, 1655. The second part of the volume is entitled '*t Wonderlyk Euangelium van Nicodemus. Gedrukt na de alderoudste copye Tot Leyden, by Pieter Janzoon, onder de toorn van Sinte Pancracius Kerck. Anno 1478.* [Cf. nos. 361–62, 364, 692, 694, 696, 705, 853.]

694 '*t Wonderlyck Euangelium van Nicodemus, gedruckt na de alder-oudtste copye tot Leyden, by Pieter Iansoon, onder den toorn van Sinte Pancracius kerck, anno 1418. En wederom in't licht gebracht door den eerwaerdigen Aquila Oreinus, bisschop tot Calorchos.* 1665. Reissued, Rotterdam: Hugo Rijck-hals, 1671. The second part of the volume is entitled '*t Wonderlyck Euangelium, verrijckt met beondighe uyt-leggingen, begrijpende kortelijck den ouden en nieuwen toestandt der H. Roomsche Kerck, door den hoogh-geleerden Arnoldus Montanius.* [*Lyden* 1, incorporating Nicodemean material from Middle Dutch prose translation D. Cf. nos. 361–62, 364, 692–93, 696, 705, 853.]

695 Jacob van Maerlant. *Jacob van Maerlant's Spiegel Historiael....* Edited by M. de Vries and E. Verwijs. Pt. 1. Leiden: Brill, 1863. [Chaps. 33 and 36–39. Cf. nos. 587, 641, 688, 778, 787, 799, 805, 860.]

696 Holder, A., ed. *Dat Lyden ende die Passie ons Heren Jhesu Christi.* Bibliotheek van Middelnederlandse Letterkunde, vol. 19. Groningen: J. B. Wolters, 1877. [Incorporates Nicodemean material from Middle Dutch prose translation D. Cf. nos. 361–62, 364, 692–94, 705, 853.]

697 Dirc van Delf, Meester. *Tafel van den Kersten Ghelove.* Pt. 3A, *Somerstuc.* Edited by L. M. Fr. Daniels. Tekstuitgaven van Ons Geestelijk Erf, vol. 6. Antwerp: Centrale boekhandel "Neerlandia," 1938. [Includes an account of the Descent, based on *Legenda aurea*; cf. no. 698. On *Legenda aurea*, see also nos. 128, 600, 632, 640, 681, 684–85, 689, 715, 801, 803, 828, 846.]

698 Dirc van Delf, Meester. *Tafel van den Kersten Ghelove.* Pt. 1, *Inleiding en registers.* Edited by L. M. Fr. Daniels. Tekstuitgaven van Ons Geestelijk Erf, vol. 4. Antwerp: Centrale boekhandel "Neerlandia," 1939. [Pp. 102–10: on *Tafelbloek* based on Dirc van Delf's *Tafel*. Cf. no. 697.]

699 Indestege, L., ed. *Die Passie Jhesu naar een zestiende-eeuws handschrift in het Provinciaal Museum te Hasselt.* Maaseik: H. van der Donck, 1948. [Includes details from *EN*; related to the tract edited by Schelb (no. 824; cf. no. 858).]

700 De Bruin, C. C., ed. *Tleven Ons Heren Ihesu Cristi. Het Pseudo-Bona-ventura-Ludolfiaanse Leven van Jesus.* Corpus Sacrae Scripturae Neerlandicae Medii Aevi, Miscellanea, vol. 2. Leiden: Brill, 1980. [Several references to *EN;* see, for example, chaps. 36, 51. Cf. no. 602.]

701 Jacob van Maerlant. *Historie van den Grale und Boek van Merline.* Edited by T. Sodman. Niederdeutsche Studien, vol. 26. Cologne: Böhlau, 1980. [Corrects Robert de Boron's *Roman du Saint-Graal* on the basis of *EN.* Cf. nos. 702, 762, 792–93.]

Studies

702 te Winkel, J. "De Boron's Joseph d'Arimathie en Merlin in Maerlant's vertaling." *Tijdschrift voor Nederlandsche Taal- en Letterkunde* 1 (1881): 305–63. [On Maerlant's use of *EN* to correct Robert de Boron. Cf. nos. 701, 762, 792–93.]

703 Lievens, R. *Jordanus van Quedlinburg in de Nederlanden. Een onderzoek van de handschriften.* Koninklijke Vlaamse Academie voor Taalen Letterkunde, ser. 6, vol. 82. Gent: Secretarie der Academie, 1958. [Pp. 13–19: on Jordanus van Quedlinburg's *Articuli LXV de passione Domini,* which cites *EN* several times.]

704 Mak, J. J. "Boendale en de Bijbel." *Nederlands Archief voor Kerkgeschiedenis,* n.s., 43 (1960): 221–49. [Cf. nos. 122, 127, 706.]

705 Grosheide, D. " 't Wonderlyk Euangelium van Nicodemus." *Het Boek,* Derde Reeks, 34 (1961): 133–41. [On editions of *Dat Lyden ende die Passie Ons Heren Jhesu Christi,* incorporating Nicodemean material from Middle Dutch prose translation D. Cf. nos. 361–62, 364, 692–94, 696, 853.]

706 Buuren, A. v., and H. van Dijk. "Boendale, Jan Van." In *Lexikon des Mittelalters,* 2:307–8. Munich: Artemis Verlag, 1983. [On author of *GN* in Middle Dutch verse. Cf. nos. 122, 127, 704.]

2.3.3.4. English

Editions

707 *Here begynneth the Life of Joseph of Armathia.* London: R. Pynson, 1520. [In verse; includes summary of *EN* 12–15.]

708 *Joseph of Arimathaea's Testimony, Concerning Divers Men Which Had Been Dead, Were Risen Again to Life, and Especially of Simeon's Two Sons, Garius and Levicius....* [1790?] [Paraphrase of part of *EN.* Cited after British Museum, *General Catalogue of Printed Books* (London: Printed by the Trustees, 1963), 119:187.]

709 Child, F. J. "St. Stephen and Herod." In *English and Scottish Populars Ballads.* Vol. 1. Boston, Mass., 1857. [Pp. 232–42: on the cock crowing in a pot; mentions also Faroese, Swedish, Norwegian, Danish, Dutch, French, Spanish, Italian, Breton, Wendish, Greek, and Coptic versions. Cf. nos. 345, 347, 357, 514–15, 663, 866, 874.]

710 Furnivall, F. J., ed. *Hymns to the Virgin and Christ, "The Parliament of Devils" and Other Religious Poems.* . . . EETS OS, vol. 24. London: K. Paul, Trench, Trübner, 1867. [*Devils' Parliament*, influenced by *EN*. Cf. no. 727.]

711 Morris, R., ed. *The Blickling Homilies of the Tenth Century.* EETS OS, vol. 73. London: N. Trübner, 1880. [The seventh homily is based on ps.-Augustinian "Sermo 160" (cf. nos. 593, 595–96, 600, 608, 611, 618, 626–28, 630a, 637, 717, 812, 821–22, 830).]

712 Langland, William. *The Vision of William Concerning Piers the Plowman.* Edited by W. W. Skeat. 2 vols. Oxford: Clarendon Press, 1886. [Passus B 18 (C 20) influenced by *EN*. Cf. nos. 719, 722, 751, 753–54.]

713 Assmann, B., ed. *Angelsächsische Homilien und Heiligenleben.* 1889. Reprint, with introduction by P. Clemoes. Darmstadt: Wissenschaftliche Buchgesellschaft, 1964. [Pp. 93–94, 181–92: *Vindicta Salvatoris* in Old English. Cf. nos. 433, 619, 674, 776, 791, 938.]

714 Pollard, A. W., ed. *English Miracle Plays Moralities and Interludes.* 1890. 8th ed., Oxford: Clarendon Press, 1927. [Pp. 166–72: *The Middle English Harrowing of Hell*. Cf. nos. 138, 716, 720, 734.]

715 Foster, F. A., ed. *A Stanzaic Life of Christ.* EETS OS, vol. 166. London: H. Milford, 1926. [Poetic rendition of *GN* (cf. nos. 718, 731, 752), drawn from *Legenda aurea* (cf. nos. 128, 600, 632, 640, 681, 684–85, 689, 697, 801, 803, 828, 846).]

716 Ker, N. R., introd. *Facsimile of British Museum MS. Harley 2253.* EETS OS, vol. 255. London: Oxford University Press, 1965. [*The Middle English Harrowing of Hell*. Cf. nos. 138, 714, 720, 734. On Harley 2253, see also nos. 740, 742, 744–45.]

717 Luiselli Fadda, A. M., ed. " 'De Descensu Christi ad Inferos': Una inedita omelia anglosassone." *Studi medievali* 13 (1972): 989–1011. [An Old English homily based on ps.-Augustinian "Sermo 160." On "Sermo," see also nos. 593, 595–96, 600, 608, 611, 618, 626–28, 630a, 637, 711, 812, 821–22, 830.]

718 Lumiansky, R. M., and D. Mills, eds. *The Chester Mystery Cycle.* 2 vols. EETS SS, vols. 3 and 9. Oxford University Press, 1974–86. [The Harrowing of Hell play (cf. no. 732) based on *Stanzaic Life of Christ* (cf. nos. 715, 731, 752) and *GN*.]

719 Langland, William. *Piers Plowman: The B Version.* Edited by G. Kane and E. T. Donaldson. London: The Athlone Press, 1975. [Passus 18 influenced by *EN*. Cf. nos. 712, 722, 751, 753–54.]

720 Pearsall, D., and I. C. Cunningham, intro. *The Auchinleck Manuscript, National Library of Scotland Advocates' MS. 19.2.1.* London: The Scolar Press in association with The National Library of Scotland, 1977. [A facsimile of MS. containing *The Middle English Harrowing of Hell*. Cf. nos. 138, 714, 716, 734.]

721 Sauer, W., ed. *The Metrical Life of Christ.* Middle English Texts, vol. 5. Heidelberg: C. Winter, 1977. [Vv. 3300–449, 4138–307: accounts of the Harrowing and Joseph of Arimathea indebted to *EN.*]

722 Langland, William. *Piers Plowman: An Edition of the C-Text.* Edited by D. Pearsall. York Medieval Texts, 2d ser. Berkeley: University of California Press, 1978. [Passus 20 influenced by *EN.* Cf. nos. 712, 719, 751, 753–54.]

723 Beadle, R., ed. *The York Plays.* York Medieval Texts, 2d ser. London: E. Arnold, 1982. [Plays 29, 30, 33, 36, 37, and 38 influenced by *GN.* Cf. nos. 728–30, 739.]

724 Meredith, P., ed. *The Passion Play from the N. Town Manuscript.* London: Longman, 1990. [Several portions of "Prologue," "Passion Play 1," and "Passion Play 2" ultimately based on *GN.* Cf. no. 725.]

725 Spector, S., ed. *The N-Town Play: Cotton MS Vespasian D. 8.* 2 vols. EETS SS, vol. 11. Oxford: Oxford University Press, 1991. [Several portions of "Prologue," "Passion Play 1," and "Passion Play 2" ultimately based on *GN.* Cf. no. 724.]

726 Love, Nicholas. *Nicholas Love's "Mirror of the Blessed Life of Jesus Christ."* Edited by M. G. Sargent. New York: Garland, 1992. [Cf. no. 736.]

727 Marx, C. W., ed. *The Devils' Parliament and the Harrowing of Hell and Destruction of Jerusalem.* Middle English Texts, vol. 25. Heidelberg: C. Winter, 1993. [Both poems influenced by *EN.* Cf. nos. 710, 735, 741.]

Studies

728 Craigie, W. A. "The *Gospel of Nicodemus* and the *York Mystery Plays.*" In *An English Miscellany Presented to Dr. Furnivall in Honour of His Seventy-fifth Birthday,* 52–61. Oxford: Clarendon Press, 1901. [Cf. nos. 723, 729–30, 739.]

729 Clark, E. G. "The York Plays and the *Gospel of Nichodemus.*" *PMLA* 43 (1928): 153–61. [Cf. nos. 723, 728, 730, 739.]

730 Frank, G. "On the Relation between the York and Towneley Plays." *PMLA* 44 (1929): 313–19. [On *GN*'s influence on York (cf. nos. 723, 728–29, 739) and Towneley plays.]

731 Wilson, R. H. "The *Stanzaic Life of Christ* and the Chester Plays." *Studies in Philology* 28 (1931): 413–32. [Cf. nos. 715, 718, 732, 752.]

732 Lumiansky, R. M. "Comedy and Theme in the Chester Harrowing of Hell." *Tulane Studies in English* 10 (1960): 5–12. [Cf. nos. 718, 731.]

733 Fowler, D. C. "New Light on John Trevisa." *Traditio* 18 (1962): 289–317. [Cf. nos. 144, 157, 159, 168, 176, 179, 750.]

734 Miller, B. D. H. "The Early History of Bodleian MS. Digby 86." *Annuale mediaevale* 4 (1963): 23–55. [On MS. containing *The Middle*

English Harrowing of Hell. Cf. nos. 138, 714, 716, 720.]

735 Pickering, O. S. "The Temporale Narratives of the South English Legendary." *Anglia* 91 (1973): 425–55. [On *Harrowing of Hell and Destruction of Jerusalem.* Cf. no. 727.]

736 Salter, E. *Nicholas Love's "Myrrour of the Blessed Lyf of Jesu Christ."* Analecta Cartusiana, vol. 10. Salzburg: Institut für englische Sprache und Literatur, Universität Salzburg, 1974. [Cf. no. 726.]

737 Tamburr, K. "The Harrowing of Hell in the English Mystery Cycles: Perspectives on the Corpus Christi Drama." Ph.D. diss., University of Virginia, 1974.

738 Wallace, D. D., Jr. "Puritan and Anglican: The Interpretation of Christ's Descent into Hell in Elizabethan Theology." *Archiv für Reformationsgeschichte* 69 (1978): 248–87.

739 Reiss, E. "The Tradition of Moses in the Underworld and the York Plays of the Transfiguration and Harrowing." *Mediaevalia* 5 (1979): 141–64. [Cf. nos. 723, 728–30.]

740 Revard, C. "Richard Hurd and MS Harley 2253." *Notes and Queries* 224 (1979): 199–202. [On MS. containing *GN* in Middle French prose and *The Middle English Harrowing of Hell.* Cf. nos. 138, 716, 742, 744–45.]

741 Marx, C. W. "The Devil's Rights and the Deception of the Devil: Theological Background and Presentations in Middle English Literature, with an Edition of the *Devils' Parliament.*" 2 vols. Ph.D. diss., University of York, 1981. [Cf. nos. 727, 757.]

742 Revard, C. "Three More Holographs in the Hand of the Scribe of MS Harley 2253 in Shrewsbury." *Notes and Queries* 226 (1981): 199–200. [On MS. containing *GN* in Middle French prose and *The Middle English Harrowing of Hell.* Cf. nos. 138, 716, 740, 744–45.]

743 Campbell, J. J. "To Hell and Back: Latin Tradition and Literary Use of the *Descensus ad Inferos* in Old English." *Viator* 13 (1982): 107–58. [Argues that there is little evidence of direct influence of *EN* on Old English literature.]

744 Revard, C. "*Gilote et Iohane:* An Interlude in B. L. MS Harley 2253." *Studies in Philology* 79 (1982): 122–46. [On MS. containing *GN* in Middle French prose and *The Middle English Harrowing of Hell.* Cf. nos. 138, 716, 740, 742, 745.]

745 Revard, C. "Scribe of MS Harley 2253." *Notes and Queries* 227 (1982): 62–63. [On MS. containing *GN* in Middle French prose and *The Middle English Harrowing of Hell.* Cf. nos. 138, 716, 740, 742, 744.]

746 Bell, L. M. "*Hel Our Queen:* An Old Norse Analogue to an Old English Female Hell." *The Harvard Theological Review* 76, no. 2 (1983): 263–68.

747 Finnegan, R. F. "The *Gospel of Nicodemus* and the *Dream of the Rood* 148b-156." *Neuphilologische Mitteilungen* 84, no. 3 (1983): 338–43.

748 Izydorczyk, Z. "The Legend of the Harrowing of Hell in Middle English Literature." Ph.D. diss., University of Toronto, 1985. [Discusses dissemination of *EN* in England.]

749 Marx, C. W. "The Problem of the Doctrine of the Redemption in the ME Mystery Plays and the *Cornish Ordinalia*." *Medium Ævum* 54 (1985): 20–32. [On doctrinal issues surrounding the Harrowing. Cf. nos. 690–91.]

750 Ball, R. M. "Thomas Cyrcetur, a Fifteenth-Century Theologian and Preacher." *Journal of Ecclesiastical History* 37 (1986): 205–39. [On an owner of MS. containing Trevisa's translation of *GN*. Cf. nos. 144, 157, 159, 168, 176, 179, 733.]

751 Waldron, R. A. "Langland's Originality: The Christ-Knight and the Harrowing of Hell." In *Medieval English Religious and Ethical Literature: Essays in Honour of G. H. Russell*, edited by G. Kratzmann and J. Simpson. Cambridge: D. S. Brewer, 1986. [On Passus B 18 (C 20) of *Piers Plowman*. Cf. nos. 712, 719, 722, 753–54.]

752 Johnson, I. "Prologue and Practice: Middle English Lives of Christ." In *The Medieval Translator: The Theory and Practice of Translation in the Middle Ages*, edited by R. Ellis, 69–85. Cambridge: D. S. Brewer, 1989. [On *Stanzaic Life of Christ*. Cf. nos. 715, 718, 731.]

753 Godden, M. *The Making of "Piers Plowman."* London: Oxford University Press, 1990. [Pp. 138–51: on *Piers Plowman* B 18. Cf. nos. 712, 719, 722, 751, 754.]

754 Simpson, J. *"Piers Plowman": An Introduction to the B-text.* London: Longman, 1990. [Pp. 208–16: on *Piers Plowman* B 18. Cf. nos. 712, 719, 722, 751, 753.]

755 Cutforth, S. "Delivering the Damned in Old English Homilies: An Additional Note." *Notes and Queries* 238 (1993): 435–37. [On a homily in Cambridge, Corpus Christi College MS. 303, influenced by *EN*.]

756 Marx, C. W. "British Library Harley MS. 1740 and Popular Devotion." In *England in the Fifteenth Century*, edited by N. Rogers, 207–22. Harlaxton Medieval Studies, vol. 4. Stamford: P. Watkins, 1994.

757 Marx, C. W. *The Devil's Rights and the Redemption in the Literature of Medieval England.* Cambridge: D. S. Brewer, 1995. [Doctrinal contexts for use of *GN*. Cf. no. 741.]

2.3.3.5. French
Editions

758 Greban, Arnoul. *Le Mystère de la Passion d'Arnoul Gréban.* Edited by G. Paris and G. Raynaud. Paris: F. Didot, 1878. [Many themes derived from *EN*. Cf. no. 782.]

759 Foster, F. A., ed. *The Northern Passion: Four Parallel Texts and the French Original.* 2 vols. EETS OS, vols. 145, 147. London: Oxford

University Press, 1913–16. [2:102–25: *Passion des jongleurs* from Cambridge, Trinity College MS. O. 2. 14. Cf. nos. 761, 764, 774.]

760 Sommer, H. O., ed. *The Vulgate Version of the Arthurian Romances.* Vol. 7. Washington: Carnegie Institution, 1916. [Includes *Livre d'Artus*, incorporating material derived from *GN* in French.]

761 Frank, G., ed. *La Passion du Palatinus.* Classiques français du moyen âge, vol. 30. Paris: Champion, 1922. [The Harrowing based on *Passion des jongleurs*. Cf. nos. 759, 764, 775.]

762 Robert de Boron. *Le Roman de l'estoire dou Graal.* Edited by W. A. Nitze. Classiques français du moyen âge, vol. 57. Paris: Champion, 1927. [Vv. 439–960: on Joseph of Arimathea and the Harrowing. Cf. nos. 701–2, 792–93.]

763 Nitze, W. A., and T. Atkinson, eds. *Le Haut Livre du Graal: Perlesvaus.* 2 vols. Chicago: University of Chicago Press, 1932–37. [On Joseph of Arimathea.]

764 Frank, G., ed. *La Passion d'Autun.* Paris: Société des anciens textes français, 1934. [The Harrowing based on *Passion des jongleurs*. Cf. nos. 759, 761, 774.]

765 Roach, W., ed. *The Continuations of the Old French "Perceval" of Chrétien de Troyes.* Vol. 3, pt. 1, *The First Continuation.* Philadelphia: American Philosophical Society, 1952. [Vv. 17561–778: on Joseph of Arimathea.]

766 Chrétien de Troyes. *Le Roman de Perceval ou le Conte du Graal.* Edited by W. Roach. 2d ed., Geneva: Droz, 1959. [Vv. 585–88: a reference to *EN.*]

767 Rutebeuf. *Œuvres complètes de Rutebeuf.* Edited by E. Faral and J. Bastin. 2 vols. Paris: Picard, 1959–60. [P. 238, vv. 76–82: a reference to *EN.*]

768 Ruelle, P., ed. *Huon de Bordeaux.* Université libre de Bruxelles: Travaux de la Faculté de philosophie et lettres, vol. 20. Brussels: Presses universitaires, 1960. [Vv. 2036–38: a reference to *EN.* Cf. no. 789.]

769 Runnalls, G. A., ed. *Le Mystère de la Passion Nostre Seigneur du manuscrit 1131 de la Bibliothèque Sainte-Geneviève.* Textes littéraires français, vol. 206. Geneva: Droz, 1974.

770 Meiss, M., and E. H. Beatson, eds. *La Vie de Nostre Benoit Sauveur Ihesucrist & La Saincte Vie de Nostre Dame.* New York: New York University Press, 1977. [Thematic influence of *EN.* Cf. no. 686.]

771 Guillaume de Lorris and Jean de Meun. *Le Roman de la Rose.* Edited by F. Lecoy. Vol. 3. Classiques français du moyen âge, vol. 98. Paris: Champion, 1979. [Vv. 18749–56: a reference to *EN.*]

772 Blangez, G., ed. *Ci nous dit: Recueil d'exemples moraux.* 2 vols. Société des anciens textes français. Paris: Picard, 1979–86. [Chaps. 83a, 109, 112: thematic influence of *EN.*]

773 Robert de Boron. *Merlin, roman du XIIIe siècle.* Edited by A. Micha. Textes littéraires français. Paris: Droz, 1980. [Vv. 1–16 influenced by *DI* A.]

774 Perry, A. J. A., ed. *La Passion des jongleurs.* Textes, dossiers, documents, vol. 4. Paris: Beauchesne, 1981. [Cf. nos. 759, 761, 764.]

775 Roach, W., ed. *The Continuations of the Old French "Perceval" of Chrétien de Troyes.* Vol. 5, *The Third Continuation By Manessier.* Philadelphia: American Philosophical Society, 1983. [Vv. 32689–770: on Joseph of Arimathea.]

776 Ford, A. E., ed. *La Vengeance de Nostre-Seigneur. The Old and Middle French Prose Versions: the Version of Japheth.* Studies and Texts, vol. 63. Toronto: Pontifical Institute of Mediaeval Studies, 1984. [Translation of *Vindicta Salvatoris* (cf. nos. 433, 619, 674, 713, 791, 938); possibly related to *Gamaliel* (cf. nos. 103–6, 111, 119–20, 184–86, 193, 200, 363, 679–80, 686).]

777 DuBruck, E. E., ed. *La Passion Isabeau: Une Édition du manuscrit Fr. 966 de la Bibliothèque Nationale de Paris.* New York: Peter Lang, 1990. [Cf. no. 798.]

778 O'Gorman, R., ed. "The Text of the Middle French *Évangile de Nicodème* from Paris, Bibliothèque Nationale, f. fr. 15219." *Medium Ævum* 61 (1992): 298–302. [Translation of Vincent of Beauvais's adaptation of *DI*. Cf. nos. 587, 641, 688, 695, 787, 799, 805, 860.]

Studies

779 Berger, S. *La Bible française au moyen âge.* Paris: Imprimerie nationale, 1884. [Pp. 157–99: on *Bible historiale*, incorporating portions of *GN*. Cf. nos. 780, 790, 797.]

780 Bonnard, J. *Les Traductions de la Bible en vers français au moyen âge.* 1884. Reprint, Geneva: Slatkine, 1967. [Pp. 3–8: on *Bible historiale*, incorporating portions of *GN*. Cf. nos. 779, 790, 797.]

781 Becker, W. "Die Sage von der Höllenfahrt Christi in der altfranzösischen Literatur." *Romanische Forschungen* 32 (1913): 897–972.

782 Champion, P. *Histoire poétique du quinzième siècle.* 2 vols. Bibliothèque du XVe siècle. Paris: Champion, 1923. [2:133–88: on the work of Arnoul Greban. Cf. no. 758.]

783 Cohen, G. *Histoire de la mise en scène dans le théâtre religieux français du moyen âge.* Paris: Champion, 1926. [Pp. 92–99: on staging of the Harrowing of Hell.]

784 Wright, J. G. *A Study of the Themes of the Resurrection in the Medieval French Drama.* Bryn Mawr, Pa., 1935. [Extensive comments on *EN*'s influence.]

785 Lods, J. *Le Roman de Perceforest.* Société de publications romanes et françaises, vol. 32. Geneva: Droz, 1951. [Pp. 33–34: on *GN* incorporated into this romance.]

786 Frank, G. *The Medieval French Drama.* Oxford: Clarendon Press, 1954. [Numerous comments on *EN*'s influence.]

787 Knowles, C. "Jean de Vignay, un traducteur de XIVe siècle." *Romania* 75 (1954): 353–83. [On Jean de Vignay's translation of *Speculum historiale.* Cf. nos. 587, 641, 688, 695, 778, 799, 805, 860.]

788 Loomis, R. S. *The Grail: From Celtic Myth to Christian Symbol.* Cardiff: University of Wales Press, 1963. [On Joseph of Arimathea, passim.]

789 O'Gorman, R. "The Legend of Joseph of Arimathea and the Old French Epic *Huon De Bordeaux.*" *Zeitschrift für romanische Philologie* 80 (1964): 35–42. [Cf. no. 768.]

790 Jauss, H. R., ed. *La Littérature didactique, allégorique, et satirique.* Grundriss der romanischen Literaturen des Mittelalters, vol. 6, pt. 1. Heidelberg: C. Winter, 1968. [Pp. 29–30: on *Bible historiale*, incorporating portions of *GN.* Cf. nos. 779–80, 797.]

791 Micha, A. "Une Rédaction de la *Vengeance de Notre Seigneur.*" In *Mélanges offerts à Rita Lejeune*, 2:1291–98. Gembloux: J. Duculot, 1969. [Lists MSS. of *Selon la sentence du philozophe Aristote*, which absorbs much of *EN* material. On *Vengeance*, see nos. 433, 619, 674, 713, 776, 938.]

792 O'Gorman, R. "The Prose Version of Robert de Boron's *Joseph d'Arimathie.*" *Romance Philology* 23 (1970): 449–61. [Cf. nos. 701–2, 762, 793.]

793 O'Gorman, R. "La Tradition manuscrite du *Joseph d'Arimathie* en prose de Robert de Boron." *Revue d'histoire des textes* 1 (1971): 145–81. [Cf. nos. 701–2, 762, 792.]

794 Lagorio, V. M. "The Evolving Legend of St Joseph of Glastonbury." *Speculum* 46 (1971): 209–31. [Associates *EN*'s popularity in England with the cult of Joseph of Arimathea. Cf. nos. 612, 631, 795.]

795 Lagorio, V. M. "Joseph of Arimathea: The *Vita* of a Grail Saint." *Zeitschrift für romanische Philologie* 91 (1975): 54–68. [Associates *EN*'s popularity in England with the cult of Joseph of Arimathea. Cf. 794.]

796 Le Merrer, M. "Figure de Joseph d'Arimathie: sa chasteté, sa proximité de Dieu." *Senefiance Aix-en-Provence* 11 (1982): 229–52.

797 McGeer, R. P. "Guyart Desmoulins, the Vernacular Master of Histories and His *Bible Historiale.*" *Viator* 14 (1983): 211–44. [Cf. nos. 779–80, 790.]

798 DuBruck, E. E. "The *Passion Isabeau* (1398) and Its Relationship to Fifteenth-Century *Mystères de la Passion.*" *Romania* 107 (1986): 77–91. [Cf. no. 777.]

799 Paulmier-Foucart, M., and S. Lusignan. "Vincent de Beauvais et l'histoire du *Speculum Maius.*" *Journal des savants* (1990): 97–124.

[Pp. 120–21: on Jean de Vignay's translation of *Speculum historiale*. Cf. nos. 587, 641, 688, 695, 778, 787, 805, 860.]

2.3.3.6. High German
Editions

800 Mone, F. J., ed. "Altteutsche Predigten." *Anzeiger für Kunde der teutschen Vorzeit* 8 (1839): 409–33, 509–30. [Pp. 525–27: a sermon on the Descent. Cf. nos. 801, 806, 831, 851, 859.]

801 Grieshaber, F. K. *Deutsche Predigten des XIII. Jahrhunderts.* 1844. Reprint, Hildesheim: G. Olms, 1978. [Pp. 137–50: "Schwarzwälder Prediger's" summary of *DI* in *Legenda aurea* (cf. nos. 128, 600, 632, 640, 681, 684–85, 689, 697, 715, 803, 828, 846). On vernacular sermons, see also nos. 800, 806, 831, 851, 859.]

802 Philipp, Bruder. *Bruder Philipps des Carthäusers Marienleben.* Edited by H. Rückert. Bibliothek der gesamten deutschen National-Literatur, vol. 34. 1853. Reprint, Amsterdam: Rodopi, 1966. [Translation of *Vita beate virginis Marie et Salvatoris rhythmica*, containing references and allusions to *EN*. Cf. nos. 609, 616, 813, 819.]

803 Hahn, K. A., ed. *Das Alte Passional.* Frankfurt a. M.: H. L. Brönner, 1857. [Based on ps.-Nicodemean material from *Legenda aurea* (cf. nos. 128, 600, 632, 640, 681, 684–85, 689, 697, 715, 801, 828, 846).]

804 Birlinger, A. "Ein Spiel von der Urstend Christi." *Archiv für das Studium der neueren Sprachen und Literaturen* 39 (1866): 367–400. [*Münchner Osterspiel*, influenced by *EN*. This edition has been superseded by no. 827.]

805 Twinger, Jacob, von Königshofen. *Straßburger Weltchronik.* In *Die Chroniken der oberrheinischen Städte. Straßburg*, vol. 2, Die Chroniken der deutschen Städte vom 14. bis ins 16. Jahrhundert, vol. 9. 1871. Reprint, Göttingen: Vandenhoeck & Ruprecht, 1961. [Incorporates Nicodemean material from *Speculum historiale*. Cf. nos. 587, 641, 688, 695, 778, 787, 799, 860.]

806 Jeitteles, A., ed. *Altdeutsche Predigten aus dem Benedictinerstifte St. Paul in Kärnten.* Altdeutsche Handschriften aus Oesterreich, vol. 1. Innsbruck: Wagner'sche Universitäts-Buchhandlung, 1878. [Pp. 75–78: a homily on the Descent. Cf. nos. 800, 801, 831, 851, 859.]

807 Hartmann, A., ed. *Das Oberammergauer Passionsspiel in seiner ältesten Gestalt.* 1880. Reprint, Schaan, Liechtenstein: Sändig, 1982. [Pp. 1–100: *Augsburger Passionsspiel*, influenced by *EN*; see especially vv. 2371–402, 2419–28.]

808 Milchsack, G., ed. *Heidelberger Passionsspiel.* Bibliothek des Litterarischen Vereins, vol. 150. Tübingen: Litt. Verein, 1880. [Trial before Pilate indebted to *EN*.]

809 Froning, R., ed. *Das Drama des Mittelalters.* 3 vols. Deutsche National-Litteratur, vol. 14. 1891–92. Reprint, Darmstadt: Wissen-

schaftliche Buchgesellschaft, 1964. [See 2:340–74: *Frankfurter Dirigierrolle;* 2:375–534: *Frankfurter Passionsspiel;* 2:547–864: *Alsfelder Passionsspiel* (cf. no. 847).]

810 Wackernell, J. E., ed. *Altdeutsche Passionsspiele aus Tirol mit Abhandlungen über ihre Entwicklung.* . . . 1897. Reprint, Walluf bei Wiesbaden: Sändig, 1972. [Pp. 201–17: *Tiroler Passion,* indebted to *EN.* Cf. nos. 826, 829, 849.]

811 Schröder, E. "Fragmente aus Gundacker von Judenburg und Heinrich von Hesler. Mitgeteilt von Ferdinand Menčik." *Zeitschrift für deutsches Altertum* 50 (1908): 386–91. [Fragment of a compilation of three verse translations of *EN* (cf. nos. 220, 222, 226), which lies behind Heinrich von München's *Weltchronik* (cf. nos. 814–15, 818, 844, 855).]

812 Waag, A., ed. *Kleinere deutsche Gedichte des XI. und XII. Jahrhunderts.* 2d ed. Altdeutsche Textbibliothek, vol. 10. Halle a. S.: Niemeyer, 1916. [Pp. 87–123: vv. 985–1050 of *Die Hochzeit* indebted to ps.-Augustinian "Sermo 160" (cf. nos. 593, 595–96, 600, 608, 611, 618, 626–28, 630a, 637, 711, 717, 821–22, 830).]

813 Päpke, M., ed. *Das Marienleben des Schweizers Wernher aus der Heidelberger Handschrift.* Deutsche Texte des Mittelalters, vol. 27. Berlin: Weidmannsche Buchhandlung, 1920. [Translation of *Vita beate virginis Marie et Salvatoris rhythmica.* Cf. nos. 609, 616, 802, 819.]

814 Kleinmayr, H. von. "Handschriftliches zur Pilatuslegende." *Zeitschrift für deutsches Altertum* 62 (1925): 241–50. [Fragment of a compilation of three verse translations of *EN* (cf. nos. 220, 222, 226), which lies behind Heinrich von München's *Weltchronik* (cf. nos. 811, 815, 818, 844, 855).]

815 Vollmer, H., ed. *Die Neue Ee, eine neutestamentliche Historienbibel.* Materialien zur Bibelgeschichte und religiösen Volkskunde des Mittelalters, vol. 4. Berlin: Weidmannsche Buchhandlung, 1929. [Prose rendition of *GN* material from Heinrich von München's *Weltchronik.* Cf. nos. 811, 814, 818, 844, 855.]

816 Havich der Kellner. *Havich der Kellner, Sankt Stephans Leben. Aus der Berliner Handschrift.* Edited by R. J. McClean. Deutsche Texte des Mittelalters, vol. 35. Berlin: Weidmannsche Buchhandlung, 1930. [Havich der Kellner draws on Konrad von Heimesfurt's *Urstende.* Cf. nos. 226, 228, 237, 247, 820, 839, 842, 850.]

817 Maurer, F., ed. *Die Erlösung: Eine geistliche Dichtung des 14. Jahrhunderts.* Deutsche Literatur, Reihe geistliche Dichtung des Mittelalters, vol. 6. 1934. Reprint, Darmstadt: Wissenschaftliche Buchgesellschaft, 1964. [Vv. 5375–586 show strong affinity to *EN.* Cf. nos. 836, 840.]

818 Gichtel, P., ed. *Die Weltchronik Heinrichs von München in der Runkelsteiner Handschrift des Heinz Sentlinger.* Schriftenreihe zur baye-

rischen Landesgeschichte, vol. 28. Munich: Beck, 1937. [Pp. 164–68: text compiling three verse redactions of *GN* (cf. nos. 220, 222, 226). Cf. also nos. 811, 814–15, 844, 855.]

819 Walther von Rheinau. *Das Marienleben Walthers von Rheinau.* Edited by E. Perjus. 2d rev. ed. Acta Academiae Aboenensis, Humaniora, vol. 17, no. 1. Åbo: Åbo Akademi, 1949. [Translation of *Vita beate virginis Marie et Salvatoris rhythmica.* Cf. nos. 609, 616, 802, 813.]

820 Zatočil, L. "Befreiung der Altväter." *Sborník Prací Filosofické Fakulty Brněnské University, Řada Literárně Vědná* 14, no. D 12 (1965): 75–93. [Influenced by Konrad von Heimesfurt's *Urstende.* Cf. nos. 226, 228, 237, 247, 816, 839, 842, 850.]

821 Ava, Frau. *Die Dichtungen der Frau Ava.* Edited by F. Maurer. Altdeutsche Textbibliothek, vol. 66. Tübingen: Niemeyer, 1966. [Vv. 1732–83 of *Leben Jesu* based on ps.-Augustinian "Sermo 160" (cf. nos. 593, 595–96, 600, 608, 611, 618, 626–28, 630a, 637, 711, 717, 812, 822, 830).]

822 Neuschäfer, D., ed. *Das Anegenge: Textkritische Studien. Diplomatischer Abdruck. Kritische Ausgabe. Anmerkungen zum Text.* Medium Ævum, Philologische Studien, vol. 8. Munich: Fink, 1966. [Vv. 3157–260 based on ps.-Augustinian "Sermon 160" (cf. nos. 593, 595–96, 600, 608, 611, 618, 626–28, 630a, 637, 711, 717, 812, 821, 830).]

823 Krämer, S. *Die sogenannte Weihenstephaner Chronik. Text und Untersuchung.* Münchener Beiträge zur Mediävistik und Renaissance-Forschung, vol. 9. Munich: Arbeo-Gesellschaft, 1972. [Pp. 90–96, 260–62: text influenced by Heinrich von Hesler's *Evangelium Nicodemi.* Cf. nos. 220, 232, 234, 236, 238, 240, 244–45, 843.]

824 Schelb, A. V. "Die Handschriftengruppe *Do der minnenklich got.* Ein Beitrag zur spätmittelalterlichen Passionsliteratur." Ph.D. diss., Freiburg, 1972. [Pp. 434–38: adaptation of *EN.* Cf. nos. 699, 858.]

825 Schottmann, B., ed. and trans. *Das Redentiner Osterspiel. Mittelniederdeutsch und Neuhochdeutsch.* Reclams Universal-Bibliothek, vol. 9744–47. Stuttgart: Philipp Reclam jun., 1975. [Vv. 261–754 strongly influenced by *EN.*]

826 Knorr, A. *Villinger Passion. Literarhistorische Einordnung und erstmalige Herausgabe des Urtextes und der Überarbeitungen.* Göppinger Arbeiten zur Germanistik, vol. 187. Göppingen: A. Kümmerle, 1976. [On influence of *Tiroler Passion.* Cf. nos. 810, 829, 849.]

827 Thoran, B., ed. *Das Münchner Osterspiel (Cgm 147 der Bayerischen Staatsbibliothek München).* Litterae, vol. 43. Göppingen: A. Kümmerle, 1977. [Vv. 36–467: the Harrowing of Hell closely based on *EN.* Cf. no. 804.]

828 Williams, U., and W. Williams-Krapp, eds. *Die Elsässische Legenda aurea.* Vol. 1, *Das Normalcorpus.* Texte und Textgeschichte, vol. 3.

Tübingen: Niemeyer, 1980. [Pp. 268–69: on Joseph of Arimathea; pp. 269–72: on the Descent. On *Legenda aurea*, see nos. 128, 600, 632, 640, 681, 684–85, 689, 697, 715, 801, 803, 846.]

829 Williams-Krapp, W. *Überlieferung und Gattung. Zur Gattung "Spiel" im Mittelalter. Mit einer Edition von "Sündenfall und Erlösung" aus der Berliner Handschrift mgq 496.* Untersuchungen zur deutschen Literaturgeschichte, vol. 28. Tübingen: Niemeyer, 1980. [Poetic text influenced by *Tiroler Passion.* Cf. nos. 810, 826, 849.]

Studies

830 Schröder, E. *Das Anegenge. Eine litterarhistorische Untersuchung.* Quellen und Forschungen zur Sprach- und Culturgeschichte der germanischen Völker, vol. 44. Straßburg: K. J. Trübner, 1881. [Pp. 54–55: on ps.-Augustinian "Sermo 160" (cf. nos. 593, 595–96, 600, 608, 611, 618, 626–28, 630a, 637, 711, 717, 812, 821–22) as source of poems on the Harrowing.]

831 Kraus, C. v. *"Vom Rechte" und "die Hochzeit." Eine literar-historische Untersuchung.* Sitzungsberichte der Kaiserlichen Akademie der Wissenschaften in Wien, Phil.-hist. Kl., vol. 123, no. 4, 1891. [P. 125: on the Descent in Easter sermons. Cf. nos. 800, 801, 806, 851, 859.]

832 Duriez, G. *Les Apocryphes dans le drame religieux en Allemagne au moyen âge.* Mémoires et travaux publiés par des professeurs des Facultés catholiques de Lille, vol. 10. Lille: R. Giard, 1914. [Pp. 44–68: on sources of the Descent episode in German plays.]

833 *Schmidt, K. W. Ch. *Die Darstellung von Christi Höllenfahrt in den deutschen und den ihnen verwandten Spielen des Mittelalters.* Marburg: H. Bauer, 1915. [Pp. 16–66.]

834 Oliger, L. "Die deutsche Passion des Johannes von Zazenhausen O.F.M. Weihbischofs von Trier († c. 1380)." *Franziskanische Studien* 15 (1928): 245–51. [Text influenced by *EN.* Cf. no. 848.]

835 Ruh, K. "Der Passionstraktat des Heinrich von St. Gallen." 2 vols. Ph.D. diss., Zürich, 1940. [1:xcv–xcviii: on excerpts from *EN* incorporated into Heinrich's tract; 2:27–29, on Claus Schulmeister's Passion tract, also indebted to *EN.*]

836 Bergmann, R. *Studien zu Entstehung und Geschichte der deutschen Passionsspiele des 13. und 14. Jahrhunderts.* Münstersche Mittelalter-Schriften, vol. 14. Munich: Fink, 1972. [On Hessian group of plays influenced by *Erlösung.* Cf. nos. 817, 840, 849.]

837 Fechter, W. "Gundacker von Judenburg und *Mai und Beaflor."* *Amsterdamer Beiträge zur älteren Germanistik* 7 (1974): 187–208. [On author of verse rendition of *EN.* Cf. nos. 222, 235, 239, 841.]

838 Thoran, B. *Studien zu den österlichen Spielen des deutschen Mittelalters (Ein Beitrag zur Klärung ihrer Abhängigkeit voneinander).* 2d ed. Göppinger Arbeiten zur Germanistik, vol. 199. Göppingen: A. Küm-

merle, 1976. [Investigates sources of Harrowing of Hell plays.]

839 Williams-Krapp, W. "Befreiung der Altväter." In *Die deutsche Literatur des Mittelalters. Verfasserlexikon,* 2d rev. ed., edited by K. Ruh, 1:667. Berlin: W. de Gruyter, 1978. [Influenced by Konrad von Heimesfurt's *Urstende.* Cf. nos. 226, 228, 237, 247, 816, 820, 842, 850.]

840 Hennig, U. "Erlösung." In *Die deutsche Literatur des Mittelalters. Verfasserlexikon,* 2d rev. ed., edited by K. Ruh, 2:599–602. Berlin: W. de Gruyter, 1980. [On *Erlösung's* indebtedness to *EN* and its influence on drama. Cf. nos. 817, 836.]

841 Fechter, W. "Gundacker von Judenburg." In *Die deutsche Literatur des Mittelalters. Verfasserlexikon,* 2d rev. ed., edited by K. Ruh, 3:303–6. Berlin: W. de Gruyter, 1981. [On author of verse rendition of *EN.* Cf. nos. 222, 235, 239, 837.]

842 Geith, K.-E. "Hawich der Kellner." In *Die deutsche Literatur des Mittelalters. Verfasserlexikon,* 2d rev. ed., edited by K. Ruh, 3:561–63. Berlin: W. de Gruyter, 1981. [On author of *Stephanslegende,* indebted to Konrad von Heimesfurt's *Urstende.* Cf. nos. 226, 228, 237, 247, 816, 820, 839, 850.]

843 Masser, A. "Heinrich von Hesler." In *Die deutsche Literatur des Mittelalters. Verfasserlexikon,* 2d rev. ed., edited by K. Ruh, 3:749–55. Berlin: W. de Gruyter, 1981. [On author of the High German *Evangelium Nicodemi.* Cf. nos. 220, 232, 234, 236, 238, 240, 244–45, 823.]

844 Gärtner, K. "Die Reimvorlage der *Neuen Ee.* Zur Vorgeschichte der neutestamentlichen deutschen Historienbibel." *Vestigia Bibliae* 4 (1982): 12–22. [On prose rendition of Heinrich von München's *Weltchronik* (cf. nos. 811, 814–15, 818, 855), incorporating portions of three verse translations of *EN* (cf. nos. 220, 222, 226).]

845 Gärtner, K. "Klosterneuburger Evangelienwerk." In *Die deutsche Literatur des Mittelalters. Verfasserlexikon,* 2d rev. ed., edited by K. Ruh, 4:1248–58. Berlin: W. de Gruyter, 1983. [On a composite text incorporating prose translation H. Cf. nos. 224, 854, 861.]

846 Kunze, K. "Jacobus a Voragine." In *Die deutsche Literatur des Mittelalters. Verfasserlexikon,* 2d rev. ed., edited by K. Ruh, 4:448–66. Berlin: W. de Gruyter, 1983. [On German translations of *Legenda aurea.* Cf. nos. 128, 600, 632, 640, 681, 684–85, 689, 697, 715, 801, 803, 828.]

847 Linke, H. "Hültscher, Henrich." In *Die deutsche Literatur des Mittelalters. Verfasserlexikon,* 2d rev. ed., edited by K. Ruh, 4:293–94. Berlin: W. de Gruyter, 1983. [On author of two scenes in *Alsfelder Passionsspiel,* both based on *EN.* Cf. no. 809.]

848 Ruh, K. "Johannes von Zazenhausen." In *Die deutsche Literatur des Mittelalters. Verfasserlexikon,* 2d rev. ed., edited by K. Ruh, 4:827–30. Berlin: W. de Gruyter, 1983. [Johannes mentions *EN* in his tract on the passion, *Erit vita quasi pendens ante te.* Cf. no. 834.]

849 Bergmann, R. "Spiele, Mittelalterliche geistliche." In *Reallexikon der deutschen Literaturgeschichte,* edited by P. Merker and W. Stammler, 4:64–100. Berlin: W. de Gruyter, 1984. [Pp. 80–81: on Hessian group of plays, influenced by *EN* (cf. no. 836); pp. 82–83: on *Tiroler Passion* (cf. nos. 810, 826, 829).]

850 Fechter, W. "Konrad von Heimesfurt." In *Die deutsche Literatur des Mittelalters. Verfasserlexikon,* 2d rev. ed., edited by K. Ruh, 5:198–202. Berlin: W. de Gruyter, 1985. [On author of *Diu urstende* (*GN* in verse). Cf. nos. 226, 228, 237, 247, 816, 820, 839, 842.]

851 Ladisch-Grube, D. "Kuppitsch'sche Predigtsammlung." In *Die deutsche Literatur des Mittelalters. Verfasserlexikon,* 2d rev. ed., edited by K. Ruh, 5:452–54. Berlin: W. de Gruyter, 1985. [Cf. nos. 800, 801, 806, 831, 859.]

852 Ruh, K. "Leben Jesu *Induimini dominum.*" In *Die deutsche Literatur des Mittelalters. Verfasserlexikon,* 2d rev. ed., edited by K. Ruh, 5:635–36. Berlin: W. de Gruyter, 1985. [Influenced by *EN.*]

853 Williams-Krapp, W. *Die deutschen und niederländischen Legendare des Mittelalters. Studien zu ihrer Überlieferungs-, Text- und Wirkungsgeschichte.* Texte und Textgeschichte, vol. 20. Tübingen: Niemeyer, 1986. [Pp. 40–41, 46, 220: descriptions of MSS. that contain High German prose translations of *EN;* p. 74: MSS. of Low German translation (cf. nos. 125, 128, 223); p. 77: MSS. of Middle Dutch translation A (cf. no. 124); pp. 76, 92–100, 128: MSS. of *Lyden* 3 (cf. nos. 361–62, 364, 692–94, 696, 705).]

854 Gärtner, K., and B. Schnell. "Die Neisser Handschrift des *Klosterneuburger Evangelienwerks.*" *Vestigia Bibliae* 9/10 (1987/88, published in 1991): 155–67. [On MS. of composite work incorporating prose translation H. Cf. nos. 225, 845, 861.]

855 Kornrumpf, G. "Die Weltchronik Heinrichs von München. Zu Überlieferung und Wirkung." In *Festschrift für Ingo Reiffenstein zum 60. Geburtstag,* edited by P. K. Stein, A. Weiss, and G. Hayer, 493–509. Göppinger Arbeiten zur Germanistik, vol. 478. Göppingen: A. Kümmerle, 1988. [A detailed study of Heinrich's chronicle (cf. nos. 811, 814–15, 818, 844), incorporating portions of three verse translations of *EN* (cf. nos. 220, 222, 226).]

856 Masser, A. "Das Evangelium Nicodemi und das mittelalterliche Spiel." *Zeitschrift für deutsche Philologie* 107, no. 1 (1988): 48–66.

857 Knape, J. "Pilatus." In *Die deutsche Literatur des Mittelalters. Verfasserlexikon,* 2d rev. ed., edited by K. Ruh, 7:669–82. Berlin: W. de Gruyter, 1989.

858 Schelb, A. V. "Passionstraktat *Do der minnenklich got.*" In *Die deutsche Literatur des Mittelalters. Verfasserlexikon,* 2d rev. ed., edited by K. Ruh, 7:353–55. Berlin: W. de Gruyter, 1989. [Influenced by *EN.* Cf. nos. 699, 824.]

859 Whisnant, N. E. "St. Pauler Predigten." In *Die deutsche Literatur des Mittelalters. Verfasserlexikon,* 2d rev. ed., edited by K. Ruh, 7:366–69. Berlin: W. de Gruyter, 1989. [On sermons evoking the Descent. Cf. nos. 800, 801, 806, 831, 851.]

860 Weigand, R. "Elements of the *Speculum historiale* in German Universal Chronicles of the Late Middle Ages." In *Vincent de Beauvais: Intentions et réceptions d'une œuvre encyclopédique au moyen âge,* edited by M. Paulmier-Foucart, S. Lusignan, and A. Nadeau, 391–411. Saint-Laurent, Quebec: Bellarmin, 1990. [Cf. nos. 587, 641, 688, 695, 778, 787, 799, 805.]

861 Kornrumpf, G. "Das *Klosterneuburger Evangelienwerk* des österreichischen Anonymus. Datierung, neue Überlieferung, Originalfassung." *Vestigia Bibliae* 9/10 (1987/88, published in 1991): 115–31. [Cf. nos. 225, 845, 854.]

2.3.3.7. Irish

Editions

862 Warren, F. E., ed. *The Antiphonary of Bangor.* 2 vols. Henry Bradshaw Society, vols. 4 and 10. London: Harrison and Sons, 1893. [Cf. nos. 875, 879.]

863 Bergin, O., ed. "The Harrowing of Hell from the Book of Fermoy." *Ériu* 4 (1904): 112–19. [Distantly resembles *EN.*]

864 McKenna, L., ed. *Dán Dé: The Poems of Donnchadhu Mór Ó Dálaigh and the Religious Poems in the Duanaire of the Yellow Book of Lecan.* Dublin: Educational Company of Ireland, 1922. [Poems 9, 20, and 29 contain references to the Harrowing.]

865 Pilip Bocht Ó hUiginn. *Pilip Bocht Ó hUiginn.* Edited by L. McKenna. Dublin: Talbot Press, 1931. [Poems 3 and 5 contain references to the Harrowing.]

866 Murray, Fr. L., ed. "Toradh na Paíse." In *An tUltach* Nollag (1936): 11–13. [A popular Passion lament, evoking the cock crowing from a cooking pot. Cf. nos. 345, 347, 357, 514–15, 663, 709, 874.]

867 McKenna, L., ed. *Diogluim Dána.* Dublin: Oifig an tSolátair, 1938. [Poems 38, 41, and 60 contain references to the Harrowing.]

868 McKenna, L., ed. *Aithdiogluim Dána.* 2 vols. Irish Texts Society, vol. 37. Dublin: Educational Co. of Ireland, 1939. [Numerous poems with references to the Harrowing.]

869 Williams, J. E. Caerwyn, ed. "An Irish Harrowing of Hell." *Études celtiques* 9 (1960): 44–78. [Translated (?) by Uilliam Mac an Legha. Cf. nos. 872, 877.]

870 Giolla Brighde Mac Con Midhe. *The Poems of Giolla Brighde Mac Con Midhe.* Edited by N. J. A. Williams. Irish Texts Society, vol. 51. Dublin: Irish Text Society, 1980. [Pp. 236–40: a poetic text evoking the Harrowing.]

Studies

871 David, P. "Une recueil de conférences monastiques irlandaises du VIIIe siècle. Notes sur le manuscrit 43 de la bibliothèque du Chapitre de Cracovie." *Revue bénédictine* 49 (1937): 62–89. [On knowledge of Longinus in early Christian Ireland. Cf. nos. 528, 535, 544, 878, 889, 893, 896.]

872 Flower, R. *The Irish Tradition.* Oxford: Clarendon Press, 1947. [On Uilliam Mac an Legha, translator (?) of *Harrowing of Hell.* Cf. nos. 869, 877.]

873 Bischoff, B. "Wendepunkte in der Geschichte der lateinischen Exegese in Frühmittelalter." *Sacris Erudiri* 6 (1954): 189–281. [On use of apocrypha in Irish exegetical writings.]

874 Partridge, A. *Caoineadh na dTrí Muire.* Dublin: An Clóchomhar Tta, 1983. [Pp. 72–75, 223, 226: on a popular Passion lament, evoking the cock crowing from a cooking pot. Cf. no. 345, 347, 357, 514–15, 663, 709, 866.]

875 Curran, M., ed. *The Antiphonary of Bangor and the Early Irish Monastic Liturgy.* Blackrock, Co. Dublin: Irish Academic Press, 1984. [Pp. 54–58, 214–15: text of and comments on hymn "Precamur Patrem," incorporating the Descent theme (cf. nos. 862, 879; on other liturgical hymns, see nos. 545, 611, 618).]

876 Mac Donncha, F. "Páis agus Aiseiri Chriost in LB agus in Ls 10." *Éigse* 21 (1986): 170–93. [On Matthean Passion and Resurrection material in Leabhar Breac, incorporating details from *EN.* Cf. nos. 250, 254–55.]

877 Breeze, A. "The Charter of Christ in Middle English, Welsh and Irish." *Celtica* 19 (1987): 111–20. [P. 118: on Uilliam Mac an Legha, translator (?) of *Harrowing of Hell.* Cf. nos. 869, 872.]

878 O'Reilly, J. "Early Medieval Text and Image: The Wounded and Exalted Christ." *Peritia* 6–7 (1987–88): 72–118. [P. 95: on Longinus. Cf. nos. 528, 535, 544, 871, 889, 893, 896.]

879 Howlett, D. "The Earliest Writers at Home and Abroad." *Peritia* 8 (1994): 1–17. [On "Precamur Patrem," a hymn incorporating the Descent theme (cf. nos 862, 875); on other liturgical hymns, see nos. 545, 611, 618.]

2.3.3.8. Italian

Editions

880 Sacchetti, F. *I sermoni evangelici.* Edited by O. Gigli. Florence: Le Monnier, 1857. [Item 46: sermon on the Descent.]

881 Roediger, F., ed. *Contrasti antichi: Cristo e Satana.* Florence: Alla Libreria Dante, 1887. [A Florentine play ultimately derived from *EN.*]

882 Galli, G., ed. *Laudi inedite dei Disciplinati umbri scelte di sui codici più antichi.* Bergamo: Istituto Italiano d'Arti Grafiche, 1910. [Pp. 60–71,

105–7: the Harrowing in Perugian *laude*. Cf. nos. 884, 886–87, 894.]

883 Tenneroni, A., ed. *Sacre rappresentazioni per le fraternite d'Orvieto nel Codice Vittorio Emmanuele 528*. Rome: Tipografia del Senato di Giovanni Bardi, 1914. [Pp. 57–60: the Harrowing of Hell *lauda* from Orvieto.]

884 Toschi, P., ed. *L'antico dramma sacro italiano*. 2 vols. Florence: Libreria Editrice Fiorentina, 1926. [1:181–200: the Harrowing of Hell *lauda* from Perugia (cf. nos. 882, 886–87, 894); 2:315–67: Good Friday *devozione* evoking the Harrowing (cf. nos. 897–98).]

885 De Bartholomaeis, V., ed. *Il teatro abruzzese del medio evo*. Bologna: Zanichelli, 1924. [Pp. 32–40: the Harrowing of Hell *lauda* from L'Aquila.]

886 Bonfantini, M., ed. *Le sacre rappresentazioni italiane*. Milan: Bompiani, 1942. [Pp. 69–87: the Harrowing of Hell *lauda* from Perugia. Cf. nos. 882, 884, 887, 894.]

887 De Bartholomaeis, V., ed. *Laude drammatiche e rappresentazioni sacre*. 3 vols. Florence: Le Monnier, 1943. [See especially 1:53–55, for *devozioni* evoking the Harrowing; 1:242–58, for the Harrowing of Hell *lauda* from Perugia (Cf. nos. 882, 884, 886, 894); 2:183–96, for the Harrowing in Roman Resurrection Play; 2:297–302, for *Festum resurrectionis*, with a short sequence on the Harrowing.]

888 Ugolini, F. A., ed. *Testi volgari abruzzesi del Duecento*. Turin: Rosenberg and Sellier, 1959. [Pp. 8–50: *Lamentatio beatae Mariae de filio*, indebted to Latin *DI* B. Cf. nos. 48, 533, 572, 580, 598, 603, 634, 646, 654, 657.]

889 Contini, G., ed. *Poeti del Duecento*. Vol. 1. Milan: Ricciardi, 1960. [Pp. 389–92, 402–6, 597–624: poems evoking Longinus. Cf. nos. 528, 535, 544, 871, 878, 893, 896.]

890 Banfi, L., ed. *Sacre rappresentazioni del Quattrocento*. Turin: UTET, 1963. [Pp. 373–422: Florentine Resurrection Play.]

891 Cicerchia, N. "*La Passione* and *La Risurrezione*." In *Cantari religiosi senesi del Trecento*, edited by G. Varanini. Bari: Laterza, 1965. [Pp. 307–447, 542–51: "La Risurrezione," indebted to *EN*.]

892 Dante Alighieri. *La Commedia secondo l'antica vulgata*. 4 vols. Edited by G. Petrocchi. Milan: Mondadori, 1966–67. [Echoes of *EN* in *Inferno*. Cf. nos. 900–902.]

893 Varanini, G., ed. *Laude dugentesche*. Padua: Antenore, 1972. [Pp. 107–20: references to Longinus. Cf. nos. 528, 535, 544, 871, 878, 889, 896.]

894 Faccioli, E., ed. *Il teatro italiano. Dalle origini al Quattrocento*. Vol. 1. Turin: Einaudi, 1975. [Pp. 90–112: the Harrowing of Hell *lauda* from Perugia. Cf. nos. 882, 884, 886–87.]

895 Cornagliotti, A., ed. *La passione di Revello*. Turin: Centro Studi Piemontesi, 1976. [Influenced by *DI* A.]

896 Varanini, G., L. Banfi, and A. Ceruti Burgio, eds. *Laude cortonesi dal secolo XIII al XV*. 4 vols. Firenze: Olschki, 1981–85. [Texts no. 31 and 32: references to Longinus. Cf. nos. 528, 535, 544, 871, 878, 889, 893.]

Studies

897 D'Ancona, A. "Le devozioni del giovedì e del venerdì santo." *Rivista di filologia romanza* 2 (1875): 1–24. [On Good Friday devozione, evoking the Harrowing. Cf. nos. 884, 898.]

898 D'Ancona, A. *Origini del teatro italiano*. 2 vols. Turin: Loescher, 1891. [Mentions a lost play of the Harrowing of Hell (1:289); discusses Good Friday *devozione*, evoking the Harrowing (1:184–207; cf. nos. 884, 897).]

899 De Bartholomaeis, V. *Origini della poesia drammatica italiana*. 2d ed., Turin: Società Editrice Internazionale, 1952. [Many references to *laude* containing the Harrowing.]

900 Iannucci, A. A. "Beatrice in Limbo: A Metaphoric Harrowing of Hell." *Dante Studies* 97 (1979): 23–45. [Cf. nos. 892, 901–2.]

901 Iannucci, A. A. "Limbo: The Emptiness of Time." *Studi danteschi* 52 (1979–80): 69–128. [Cf. nos. 892, 900, 902.]

902 Iannucci, A. A. "Dottrina e allegoria in *Inferno* VIII, 67 – IX, 105." In *Dante e le forme dell'allegoresi*, edited by M. Picone, 99–124. Ravenna: Longo, 1987. [Cf. nos. 892, 900–901.]

2.3.3.9. *Norse*

Editions

903 *En kort Beskriffvelse Om Pilati Fodsel: Herkomst, lefnet oc Endeligt. Disligest om Jesus Christi U-skylige Dold oc Pijne: Oc om hans Opstandelse oc Himmelfart: Oc meget mere som denne Historie indeholder*. Copenhagen, 1663. Reprinted in *Danske folkeboger*, vol. 1 (Copenhagen, 1975), 127–78. [Cf. nos. 907–8, 916, 918–21, 931–33.]

904 Keyser, R., and P. A. Munch, eds. *Norges gamle love indtil 1387*. 5 vols. Oslo: Det Kgl. Norske Videnskabers Selskab, 1846–95. [2:306: a reference to the Harrowing in a legal context.]

905 Jón Sigurðsson and Guðbrandr Vigfússon, eds. *Biskupa sögur*. 2 vols. Copenhagen: Möller, 1858–78. [2:546–57: *Niðurstigningsvísur*, in verse, paraphrasing much of *EN*. Cf. nos. 913, 915, 922, 924–25, 929.]

906 Jensen, R. "Ljómur." *Aarbøger for nordisk oldkyndighed og historie* (1869): 311–88. [Mentions the Harrowing. Cf. no. 914.]

907 Unger, C. R., ed. *Postola sögur: Legendariske fortællinger om apostlernes liv deres kamp for Kristendommens udbredelse samt deres martyrdød*. Oslo: Bentzen, 1874. [Pp. 151–53, 154–59: a story of Pilate. Cf. nos. 903, 908, 916, 918–21, 931–33.]

908 Brandr Jónsson. *Gyðinga saga: En bearbejdelse fra midten af det 13.*

årh. ved Brandr Jónsson. Edited by Guðmundur Þorláksson. Samfund til udgivelse af gammel nordisk litteratur, vol. 6. Copenhagen: Møller, 1881. [Pp. 88–90, 93–100: a story of Pilate. Cf. nos. 903, 907, 916, 918–21, 931–33.]

909 Björn Magnússon Ólsen, ed. *Den Tredje og Fjærde Grammatiske Afhandling i Snorres Edda tilligemed de Grammatiske Afhandlingers Prolog og To Andre Tillæg.* Samfund til udgivelse af gammel nordisk litteratur, vol. 12. Copenhagen: Knudtzon, 1884. [P. 144: a reference to the Harrowing in a grammatical treatise.]

910 Geete, R., ed. *Svenska böner från medeltiden.* Samlingar utgifna af svenska fornskrift-sällskapet, vols. 131, 133, 135. Stockholm: Norstedt & söner, 1907–9. [Swedish prayers alluding to *EN*. Cf. nos. 917, 928.]

911 Finnur Jónsson, ed. *Den norsk-islandske skjaldedigtning.* A1–2 (tekst efter håndskrifterne) and B1–2 (rettet tekst). 1908–15. Reprint, Copenhagen: Gyldendal, 1967 [A] and 1973 [B]. [B2:406: a potential echo of *Niðrstigningarsaga* in *Lilja* (cf. nos. 261, 264–65, 267–68, 270–73, 276, 279–84, 912, 930); B1:427, B1:630, B2:166: poetic references to the Harrowing.]

912 Paasche, F. *Lilja. Et kvad til Guds moder.* Oslo: Aschehoug, 1915. [A potential echo of *Niðrstigningarsaga*. Cf. nos. 261, 264–65, 267–68, 270–73, 276, 279–84, 911, 930.]

913 Jón Arason of Hólar. *Jón Arasons religiøse digte.* Edited by Finnur Jónsson. Det Kongelige Danske Videnskabernes Selskab, Historisk-filologiske Meddelelser, vol. 2, pt. 2. Copenhagen: Høst & Søn, 1918. [Pp. 58–69: *Niðurstigningsvísur*, in verse, paraphrasing much of *EN* (cf. nos. 905, 915, 922, 924–25, 929); pp. 20, 23: references to the Harrowing.]

914 Jón Helgason, ed. "Færøiske studier: I. Den eldste optegnelse av færøiske kvad. – II. Ljómur på Færøiene." *Maal og minne* (1924): 29–48. [A reference to the Harrowing in the Faroese version of *Ljómur*. Cf. no. 906.]

915 Jón Helgason, ed. *Íslenzk miðaldakvæði: Islandske digte fra senmiddelalderen.* Vol. 1, pt. 2. Copenhagen: Munksgaard, 1936. [Pp. 221–38: *Niðurstigningsvísur*, in verse, paraphrasing *EN* material (cf. nos. 905, 913, 922, 924–25, 929); several poems with references to the Harrowing.]

916 Nielsen, N., ed. *Sjælens Trøst ("Siæla trøst").* Universitets-jubilæets Danske Samfund. Copenhagen: Schultz, 1937–52. [Pp. 28–30: a legend of Pilate. Cf. nos. 903, 907–8, 918–21, 931–33.]

917 Nielsen, K. M., ed. *Middelalderens danske bønnebøger.* 4 vols. Copenhagen: Gyldendal, 1945–63. [Danish prayers alluding to the Harrowing. Cf. nos. 910, 928.]

918 Henning, S., ed. *Siælinna thrøst. Første delin aff the bokinne som kallas*

Siælinna thrøst. Samlingar utgifna af svenska fornskrift-sällskapet, vol. 59. Uppsala: Almquist & Wiksell, 1954. [Pp. 265–72: a legend of Pilate. Cf. nos. 903, 907–8, 916, 919–21, 931–33.]

919 Loth, A., ed. *Reykjahólabók: Islandske helgenlegender.* 2 vols. Editiones Arnamagnæanæ, Series A, vols. 15–16. Copenhagen: Reitzel, 1969–70. [1:213–45: *Stephaus saga* (cf. nos. 926–27), incorporating Pilate's legend. On stories of Pilate in Old Norse, see also nos. 903, 907–8, 916, 918, 920–21, 931–33.]

920 Martin, H., ed. "The Legend of Pontius Pilate in Icelandic and Middle Low German: An Edition of Two Manuscripts." Ph.D. diss., University of Wisconsin-Madison, 1971. [Cf. nos. 903, 907–8, 916, 918–19, 921, 931–33.]

921 Wolf, K. "An Extract of *Gyðinga saga* in Lbs. 714 8vo." In *Opuscula*, vol. 9, Bibliotheca Arnamagnæana, vol. 39, pp. 189–202. Copenhagen: Reitzel, 1991. [A story of Pilate. Cf. nos. 903, 907–8, 916, 918–20, 931–33.]

Studies

922 Jón Þorkelsson. *Om digtningen på Island i det 15. og 16. Århundrede.* Copenhagen: Høst, 1888. [P. 328: ascribes *Niðurstigningsvísur* to Jón Arason of Holar. Cf. nos. 905, 913, 915, 924–25, 929.]

923 Paasche, F. *Kristendom og kvad. En studie i norrøn middelalder.* Oslo: Aschehoug, 1914. [Pp. 105, 128: on references to the Harrowing in two Icelandic poems.]

924 Páll Eggert Ólason. *Menn og menntir siðskiptaaldarinnar á Íslandi.* Vol. 1. Reykjavik: Bókaverzlun Guðm. Gamalíelssonar, 1919. [P. 419: ascribes *Niðurstigningsvísur* to Jón Arason of Holar (cf. nos. 905, 913, 915, 922, 925, 929); p. 417: on the Harrowing in Icelandic literature.]

925 Finnur Jónsson. *Den oldnorske og oldislandske Litteraturs Historie.* 3 vols. Copenhagen: Gad, 1920–24. [3:129: ascribes *Niðurstigningsvísur* to Jón Arason of Holar. Cf. nos. 905, 913, 915, 922, 924, 929.]

926 Widding, O., and H. Bekker-Nielsen. "En senmiddelalderlig legendesamling." *Maal og minne* (1960): 105–28. [On sources of *Stephanus saga.* Cf. nos. 919, 927.]

927 Widding, O., and H. Bekker-Nielsen. "Low German Influence on Late Icelandic Hagiography." *The Germanic Review* 37 (1962): 237–62. [On sources of *Stephanus saga.* Cf. nos. 919, 926.]

928 Gad, T. "Kristus." *Kulturhistorisk Leksikon for nordisk middelalder,* 9:365–77. Copenhagen: Rosenkilde and Bagger, 1964. [P. 376: references to the Harrowing in Swedish and Danish prayers. Cf. nos. 910, 917.]

929 Jakob Benediktsson. "Kristdigte." In *Kulturhistorisk Leksikon for nordisk middelalder,* vol. 9, cols. 292–94. Copenhagen: Rosenkilde and

Bagger, 1964. [Ascribes *Niðurstigningsvísur* to Jón Arason of Holar. Cf. nos. 905, 913, 915, 922, 924–25.]

930 Hill, T. D. "Number and Pattern in *Lilja.*" *Journal of English and Germanic Philology* 69 (1970): 561–67. [P. 563: on a possible echo of *Niðrstigningarsaga* in *Lilja.* Cf. nos. 261, 264–65, 267–68, 270–73, 276, 279–84, 911–12.]

931 Martin, H. "The Legend of Pontius Pilate." *Amsterdamer Beiträge zur älteren Germanistik* 5 (1973): 95–188. [Cf. nos. 903, 907–8, 916, 918–21, 932–33.]

932 Jón Helgason. "Gyðinga saga i Trondheim." In *Opuscula,* vol. 5, Bibliotheca Arnamagnæana, vol. 31, pp. 343–76. Copenhagen: Munksgaard, 1975. [On Pilate's legend. Cf. nos. 903, 907–8, 916, 918–21, 931, 933.]

933 Wolf, K. " 'Lífssaga Pilati' in Lbs. 4270 4to." *Proceedings of the PMR Conference* 12/13 (1987–88): 239–62. [Cf. nos. 903, 907–8, 916, 918–21, 931–32.]

2.3.3.10. Welsh

Editions

934 Lewis, H., T. Roberts, and I. Williams, eds. *Cywyddau Iolo Goch ac Eraill.* Cardiff: University of Wales Press, 1925. [P. 258, vv. 17–26: a poetic reference to the Harrowing. Cf. no. 941.]

935 George, I. "Syr Dafydd Trefor—Ei Oes a'i Waith." M.A. diss., University College of Wales, Aberystwyth, 1929. [Pp. 216–17, vv. 23–28: a poetic reference to the Harrowing.]

936 Lewis, H., ed. *Hen Gerddi Crefyddol.* Cardiff: University of Wales Press, 1931. [P. 99, vv. 31–41: a reference to the Harrowing in a poem attributed to Gruffud ap yr Ynad Goch.]

937 Richards, M. "Ystoria Bilatus." *Bulletin of the Board of Celtic Studies* 9 (1937): 42–49. [On Pilate.]

938 Williams, J. E. Caerwyn. "Ystorya Titus Aspassianus." *Bulletin of the Board of Celtic Studies* 9 (1937–39): 221–30. [Translation of *Vindicta Salvatoris.* Cf. nos. 433, 619, 674, 713, 776, 791.]

939 Jones, G., ed. *A Study of Three Welsh Religious Plays.* Bala: R. Evans & Son, 1939. [The Welsh "Passion Play," indebted to *EN* (pp. 216–18, vv. 757–76).]

940 Bosco, Sister N. "Dafydd Benfras and His *Red Book* Poems." *Studia Celtica* 22/23 (1987–88): 49–117. [P. 88, vv. 21–46: elaborate use of the Harrowing.]

941 Iolo Goch. *Gwaith Iolo Goch.* Edited by D. R. Johnston. Cardiff: University of Wales Press, 1988. [Pp. 112–13, vv. 61–82: a reference to the Harrowing. Cf. no. 934.]

942 Cynddelw Brydydd Mawr. *Gwaith Cynddelw Brydydd Mawr.* Vol. 2.

Edited by N. A. Jones and A. P. Owen. Cyfres Beirdd y Tywysogion, vol. 4. Cardiff: University of Wales Press, 1995. [Poem 18, vv.
46–57: a reference to the Harrowing. Cf. no. 946.]

Studies

943 Jones, H. "Celtic Britain and the Pilgrim Movement." *Y Cymmrodor*
23 (1912). [P. 303: on the names "Dismas" and "Desmas." Cf. nos.
532, 535.]

944 Williams, J. E. Caerwyn. "Medieval Welsh Religious Prose." In
Proceedings of the First Celtic Congress, 1963. Cardiff: University of
Wales Press, 1966. [Pp. 65–97: Pilate's letter to Claudius.]

945 Rittmueller, J. "The Religious Poetry of Siôn Cent." *Proceedings of
the Harvard Celtic Colloquium* 3 (1983): 107–48. [On poetic references
to the Harrowing.]

946 McKenna, C. A. *The Medieval Welsh Religious Lyric: Poems of the
Gogynfeirdd, 1137–1282.* Belmont, MA: Ford & Bailie, 1991. [P. 89:
on Cynddelw Brydydd Mawr's use of the Harrowing. Cf. no. 942.]

Part 3: Iconography and the *Acts of Pilate*

947 Usov, S. A. "Miniatiury k grecheskomu kodeksu evangeliia VI
veka, otkrytomu v Rossano." In *Drevnosti. Trudy Imperatorskogo Mos-
kovskago arkheologicheskago obshchestva* 9 (1881): 37–78. [Claims the
illustrations in *Codex Rossanensis* are influenced by *AP*. Cf. no. 950.]

948 Millet, G. "Mosaïques de Daphni." *Monuments Piot* 2 (1895): 204–14.

949 Erbach-Fuersternau, A. von. "L'Evangelo di Nicodemo." *Archivio
storico dell'arte* 2, no. 3 (1896): 225–37. [A study of an illuminated
MS. of *EN*, Madrid, Bibl. Nat. MS. Vitr. 23–8.]

950 Haseloff, A. *Codex Purpureus Rossanensis. Die Miniaturen der griechischen Evangelien-Handschrift in Rossano nach photographischen Auf-
nahmen.* Berlin and Leipzig: Giesecke & Devrient, 1898. [Pp. 9–10:
disagrees with Usov (no. 947).]

951 Mâle, É. *L'Art religieux du XIIIe siècle en France.* 1898. 8th ed., Paris:
A. Colin, 1948.

952 Rushforth, G. McN. "The *Descent into Hell* in Byzantine Art." In
Papers of the British School at Rome, 1:114–19. London: R. Clay and
Sons, 1902.

953 Leclercq, H. "Apocryphes." In *Dictionnaire d'archéologie chrétienne
et de liturgie,* 1:2574–76. Paris: Letouzey et Ané, 1924.

954 Bauer, M. "Die Ikonographie der Höllenfahrt Christi von ihren
Anfängen bis zum 16. Jahrhundert." Masch. Diss., Göttingen, 1948.

955 Villette, J. *La Résurrection du Christ dans l'art chrétien du IIe au VIIe
siècle.* Bibliothèque d'érudition artistique. Paris: H. Laurens, 1957.
[Pp. 89–106.]

956 Schulz, H. J. "Die 'Höllenfahrt' als 'Anastasis.' Eine Untersuchung über Eigenart und dogmengeschichtliche Voraussetzungen byzantinischer Osterfrömmigkeit." *Zeitschrift für katholische Theologie* 81 (1959): 1–66.

957 Lucchesi Palli, E. "Höllenfahrt Christi." In *Lexikon der christlichen Ikonographie*, edited by E. Kirschbaum, 2:322–32. Rome: Herder, 1970.

958 Weitzmann, K. "The Selection of Texts for Cyclic Illustration in Byzantine Manuscripts." In *Byzantine Books and Bookmen*, 69–109. Washington, D. C.: Dumbarton Oaks, Center for Byzantine Studies, 1975.

959 Davis-Weyer, C. "Die ältesten Darstellungen der Hadesfahrt Christi, des Evangelium Nikodemi und ein Mosaik der Zeno-Kapelle." In *Roma e l'età carolingia. Atti delle giornate di studio 3–8 maggio 1976 a cura dello Instituto di storia dell'arte dell'Universita di Roma*, 183–94. Rome: Multigrafica Editrice, 1976.

960 Bagatti, B. "L'iconografia della Discesa agli Inferi del Signore." *La Terra Santa* 52 (1977): 155–61.

961 Worthen, T. F. "The Harrowing of Hell in the Art of the Italian Renaissance." 2 vols. Ph.D. diss., University of Iowa, 1981.

962 *Bagatti, B. "L'iconografia dell'Anastasis o Discesa agli inferi." *Liber Annuus* 32 (1982): 239–72. [Discusses typical representations of the Descent since the fourth century.]

963 *Kartsonis, A. D. *ANASTASIS. The Making of an Image*. Princeton: University Press, 1986. [See index, s.v. "Apocryphon"; minimizes *AP*'s importance for emergence of iconography of the Descent.]

964 Vantini, G. "The Faras Golgotha and the Apocrypha." *Nubica* 1–2 (1987–88): 653–89.

965 Hudry, M. "Les Apocryphes dans l'iconographie des églises et chapelles savoyardes." *Apocrypha – Le Champ des apocryphes* 2, *La Fable apocryphe* 2 (1991): 255–56.

966 Thierry, N. "L'Illustration des apocryphes dans les églises de Cappadoce." *Apocrypha – Le Champ des apocryphes* 2, *La Fable apocryphe* 2 (1991): 226–28.

967 Davidson, C. and Th. H. Seiler, eds. *The Iconography of Hell*. Kalamazoo: Publications of the Medieval Institute of Western Michigan University, 1992.

968 Thierry, N. "Le Thème de la descente du Christ aux enfers en Cappadoce." Δελτίον τῆς χριστιανικῆς 'αρχαιολογικῆς ἑταιρείας 4 (1993–94): 59–66.

See also nos. 381, 458, 551.

Index of Authors

This index lists all authors, editors, printers (before 1600), translators, and titles of works published anonymously. Italicized references preceded by the abbreviation "*no(s)*." are to items in the Thematic Bibliography; references in Roman typeface preceded by the abbreviation "p." are to page numbers of the introduction to the Bibliography.

Index of Manuscripts

This index covers all the essays, including the Thematic Bibliography. All references in Roman typeface are to pages; italicized references preceded by the abbreviation "*no(s)*." are to items in the Thematic Bibliography.

Index of Names, Subjects, and Texts

This index covers the names of medieval persons, titles of medieval works, and a wide range of subjects discussed in the foregoing essays. It does not extend to the Thematic Bibliography because the Bibliography is internally cross-referenced. Anonymous works are cited by title; all others are indexed under the author, with cross-references under the title. All references are to page numbers. Two abbreviations are used: *EN* for *Evangelium Nicodemi* and *GN* for *Gospel of Nicodemus*.

* * *

Gospel of Nicodemus

Landslǫg of King Magnús Hákonarson lagabœtir, 278, 286
Langland, William, *Piers Plowman*,
244–45, 247
Last Judgement, 14, 99, 134–36,
141–44, 146n, 310n, 319, 339,
399, 410. *See also*: Antichrist;
Doomsday, fifteen signs of;
eschatology; Michael (Archangel)
laude: origin of, 175; types of,
175–76. *See also*: Cortona, *laude*
from; *Disciplinati*; L'Aquila,
laude from; *Lamentatio beate
Marie de filio*; Orvieto, *laude*
from; Perugia, *laude* from;
Pianto delle Marie, Il; Venetian
Good Friday *devozione*
Leabhar Breac, 13, 364, 365n; Irish
GN in, 375–89
Leeu, Gheraert, 356
Legend of the Cross before Christ,
252
Legenda aurea. See Jacobus a Vora-
gine, *Legenda aurea*
Legendae. See Hrotsvitha of Gan-
dersheim, *Legendae*
legendaries, 345; High German,
327–28. *See also*: *Gospel of Nico-
demus*, manuscript contexts;
Heiligen Leben, Der; Jacobus a
Voragine, *Legenda aurea*; *Old
Swedish Legendary*; *South Eng-
lish Legendary*; *Tractatus de
legenda sanctorum*
Legrand, Jacques, *Livre de Bonne
moeurs*, 253
Leiðarvísan, 277
Leken spieghel, Der. See Jan van
Boendale, *Der leken spieghel*
Leofric (bishop), 208
letter from heaven, 92
Leucius (supposed author), 76
Leucius and Carinus, 5–6, 51, 76,
104, 112, 117–18, 149, 162, 234,
244, 265, 273, 276, 281, 320,
332, 381; as characters on

stage, 332; in Greek *DI*, 169;
named Alexander and Rufus,
159, 169–70, 185–88. *See also*:
Gospel of Nicodemus; Simon of
Cyrene
Liber Angeli, 362n
*Liber de gestis ac trina beatissimorum
trium regum translatione. See*
Johannes de Hildesheim, *Liber
de gestis ac trina beatissimorum
trium regum translatione*
Liber questionum in euangeliis, 364n
Library. See Photius, *Library*
Libre dels àngels. See Eiximenis,
Francesc, *Libre dels àngels*
Libro, Il. See Uguccione da Lodi, *Il
Libro*
Life of Adam and Eve (in Greek), 49
Líknrbraut, 277
Lilja. See Eysteinn Ásgrímsson,
Lilja
limbo, 84, 173, 177–79, 181, 183,
185–90, 192, 194–97, 200, 204–5,
217, 323, 357, 400; as "nobile
castello," 201–3; in *La passione
del Colosseo*, 194. *See also*: hell
liturgy
apocrypha in, 92
catabasis in, 93
dedication of the church, 94
Easter Matins at Prüfening, 98
echoes of, in *EN*, 93–94
Elevatio crucis, 94, 178, 328
of Holy Saturday, 363
of Holy Week, 380
GN in, 93–94
influence of, 178, 292
of Jerusalem 26, 40
legitimizing *EN*, 94
of mass, 93
of Palm Sunday, 94
and performance of *laude*, 176
pseudo–Augustinian "Sermo
160" in, 98
veneration of saints, 94–95
See also: *Antiphonary of Bangor*;
antiphons; Book of Cerne;

Werner of St. Blasius, "Sermo de resurrectione Domini," 86n
Wilhelm Durandus, *Rationale divinorum officiorum*, 339
Woitsdorf, Franciscus, *Sermones de tempore*, 99
Wyclif, John, *De veritate Sacrae Scripturae*, 249
Wynkyn de Worde, 255, 406

Y Bibyl Ynghymraec, 404
York mystery cycle, 241–42; Harrowing of Hell in, 241–42, 245, 247, 415
Ystorya Adaf, 405, 417

Zainer, Günter, 59

Contributors

Ann Dooley, Department of Celtic Studies, University of Toronto

Jean-Daniel Dubois, École pratique des hautes études, Sciences religieuses, Paris

Rémi Gounelle, Faculté de théologie, Université de Lausanne

Werner J. Hoffmann, Sprach- und Literaturwissenschaftliche Fakultät, Katholische Universität Eichstätt

Amilcare A. Iannucci, Department of Italian Studies, University of Toronto

Josep Izquierdo, Department of Filologia Catalana, Universitat de València

Zbigniew Izydorczyk, Department of English, University of Winnipeg

David N. Klausner, Department of English and Centre for Medieval Studies, University of Toronto

C. W. Marx, Department of English, University of Wales, Lampeter

Richard O'Gorman, Department of French and Italian, University of Iowa; published posthumously

Kirsten Wolf, Department of Icelandic, University of Manitoba

The apocryphal *Gospel of Nicodemus* was perhaps the most popular Passion-Resurrection narrative of late medieval Europe. Translated from Latin into most European vernaculars, it survives in a profusion of linguistic forms and versions. This series of studies, written by noted scholars specializing in different linguistic and literary traditions, examines the presence of the pseudo-gospel in Western literature of the Middle Ages. The studies cover a vast territory, both thematically and linguistically: they discuss networks of translations, adaptations, thematic borrowings, and allusions in Romance (Latin, French, Catalan, Occitan, and Italian), Germanic (English, High German, Dutch, Low German, and Norse), and Celtic (Irish, Welsh, and Cornish) vernaculars.

The book concludes with the first comprehensive bibliography of publications on the *Gospel of Nicodemus*. Its scope is larger than the collective scope of the essays, for it is intended as a guide to research on the apocryphon in all its linguistic versions, including those in ancient Eastern languages. The bibliography is arranged thematically, with brief annotations, cross-references, and an author/editor index that helps to locate bibliographic items easily and efficiently.

Zbigniew Izydorczyk is an associate professor in the Department of English at the University of Winnipeg, Canada.

MRTS

MEDIEVAL & RENAISSANCE TEXTS & STUDIES
is the major publishing program of the
Arizona Center for Medieval and Renaissance Studies
at Arizona State University, Tempe, Arizona.

MRTS emphasizes books that are needed —
texts, translations, and major research tools.

MRTS aims to publish the highest quality scholarship
in attractive and durable format at modest cost.